Principles of Microeconomics

Karl E. Case • Ray C. Fair • Sharon M. Oster

Principles of Microeconomics

Second Custom Edition for the University of Texas

Taken from:
Principles of Microeconomics, Twelfth Edition
by Karl E. Case, Ray C. Fair, Sharon M. Oster

Cover Art: Courtesy of EyeWire/Getty Images.

Taken from:

Principles of Microeconomics, Twelfth Edition
by Karl E. Case, Ray C. Fair, Sharon M. Oster
Copyright © 2017, 2014, 2012 by Pearson Education, Inc.
New York, NY 10013

This special edition published in cooperation with Pearson Education, Inc.

Pearson Education, Inc., 330 Hudson Street, New York, New York 10013
A Pearson Education Company
www.pearsoned.com

Printed in the United States of America

1   16

000200010272043574

EJ

ISBN 10: 1-323-44292-8
ISBN 13: 978-1-323-44292-0

About the Authors

Karl E. Case is Professor of Economics Emeritus at Wellesley College where he has taught for 34 years and served several tours of duty as Department Chair. He is a Senior Fellow at the Joint Center for Housing Studies at Harvard University and a founding partner in the real estate research firm of Fiserv Case Shiller Weiss, which produces the S&P Case-Shiller Index of home prices. He serves as a member of the Index Advisory Committee of Standard and Poor's, and along with Ray Fair he serves on the Academic Advisory Board of the Federal Reserve Bank of Boston.

Before coming to Wellesley, he served as Head Tutor in Economics (director of undergraduate studies) at Harvard, where he won the Allyn Young Teaching Prize. He was Associate Editor of the *Journal of Economic Perspectives* and the *Journal of Economic Education*, and he was a member of the AEA's Committee on Economic Education.

Professor Case received his B.A. from Miami University in 1968; spent three years on active duty in the Army, and received his Ph.D. in Economics from Harvard University in 1976.

Professor Case's research has been in the areas of real estate, housing, and public finance. He is author or coauthor of five books, including *Principles of Economics, Economics and Tax Policy*, and *Property Taxation: The Need for Reform*, and he has published numerous articles in professional journals.

For the last 25 years, his research has focused on real estate markets and prices. He has authored numerous professional articles, many of which attempt to isolate the causes and consequences of boom and bust cycles and their relationship to regional and national economic performance.

Ray C. Fair is Professor of Economics at Yale University. He is a member of the Cowles Foundation at Yale and a Fellow of the Econometric Society. He received a B.A. in Economics from Fresno State College in 1964 and a Ph.D. in Economics from MIT in 1968. He taught at Princeton University from 1968 to 1974 and has been at Yale since 1974.

Professor Fair's research has primarily been in the areas of macroeconomics and econometrics, with particular emphasis on macroeconometric model building. He also has done work in the areas of finance, voting behavior, and aging in sports. His publications include *Specification, Estimation, and Analysis of Macroeconometric Models* (Harvard Press, 1984); *Testing Macroeconometric Models* (Harvard Press, 1994); *Estimating How the Macroeconomy Works* (Harvard Press, 2004), and *Predicting Presidential Elections and Other Things* (Stanford University Press, 2012).

Professor Fair has taught introductory and intermediate macroeconomics at Yale. He has also taught graduate courses in macroeconomic theory and macroeconometrics.

Professor Fair's U.S. and multicountry models are available for use on the Internet free of charge. The address is http://fairmodel.econ.yale.edu. Many teachers have found that having students work with the U.S. model on the Internet is a useful complement to an introductory macroeconomics course.

Sharon M. Oster is the Frederic Wolfe Professor of Economics and Management and former Dean of the Yale School of Management. Professor Oster joined Case and Fair as a coauthor in the ninth edition of this book. Professor Oster has a B.A. in Economics from Hofstra University and a Ph.D. in Economics from Harvard University.

Professor Oster's research is in the area of industrial organization. She has worked on problems of diffusion of innovation in a number of different industries, on the effect of regulations on business, and on competitive strategy. She has published a number of articles in these areas and is the author of several books, including *Modern Competitive Analysis* and *The Strategic Management of Nonprofits*.

Prior to joining the School of Management at Yale, Professor Oster taught for a number of years in Yale's Department of Economics. In the department, Professor Oster taught introductory and intermediate microeconomics to undergraduates as well as several graduate courses in industrial organization. Since 1982, Professor Oster has taught primarily in the Management School, where she teaches the core microeconomics class for MBA students and a course in the area of competitive strategy. Professor Oster also consults widely for businesses and nonprofit organizations and has served on the boards of several publicly traded companies and nonprofit organizations.

Brief Contents

Contents

Preface

Our goal in the 12th edition, as it was in the first edition, is to instill in students a fascination with both the functioning of the economy and the power and breadth of economics. The first line of every edition of our book has been "The study of economics should begin with a sense of wonder." We hope that readers come away from our book with a basic understanding of how market economies function, an appreciation for the things they do well, and a sense of the things they do poorly. We also hope that readers begin to learn the art and science of economic thinking and begin to look at some policy and even personal decisions in a different way.

What's New in This Edition?

- The 12th edition has continued the changes in the *Economics in Practice* boxes that we began several editions ago. In these boxes, we try to bring economic thinking to the concerns of the typical student. In many cases, we do this by spotlighting recent research, much of it by young scholars. Some of the many new boxes include:
  - Chapter 3 uses behavioral economics to ask whether having unusually sunny weather increases consumer purchasess of convertible cars.
  - Chapter 6 looks at data from Indian reservations to trace out the incidence of excise taxes.
  - In Chapter 7 we describe recent work on how Uber drivers differ from regular cab drivers.
  - Many people currently buy clothes and shoes on line. Chapter 15 describes a recent paper that asks how much value does increased variety in shoe selection produce for consumers?
  - In Chapter 21 we describe work that uses children's height in India to examine hunger and gender inequality.
  - Chapter 22, our new chapter, contains three boxes, examining the Moving to Opportunity program, birth weight and infant mortality, and the effects of the minimum wage.

In other cases we use recent events or common situations to show the power and breadth of economic models:
  - In Chapter 8 we use the example of a Taylor Swift concert to explain fixed versus variable costs.
  - In Chapter 9 we explore economies to scale with the example of Google's advantages in the search market.
  - In Chapter 13 we describe "net neutrality" and use it to explore the structure of the telecommunications market.
  - In Chapter 16 we look at how firms use carbon prices to motivate managers to be more conscious in the investment decisions about the environment.

It is our hope that students will come to see both how broad the tools of economics are and how exciting is much of the new research in the field. For each box, we have also added questions to take students back from the box to the analytics of the textbook to reinforce the underlying economic principles of the illustrations.

- As in the previous edition, we have reworked some of the chapters to streamline them and to improve readability. In this edition, Chapter 16 has been considerably reworked to include a more comprehensive and up-to-date analysis of environmental issues. This chapter now focuses on externalities, public goods, and common resources. Social choice has been moved to the chapter covering public finance. Chapter 18 has also been substantially reworked to reflect the increased worldwide concern with issues of inequality. Finally, Chapter 21 has been revised to include more of the modern approach to economic development, including discussion of the millennium challenge.

- We have added a new chapter, Chapter 22, "Critical Thinking About Research," which we are quite excited about. It may be the first time a chapter like this has been included in an introductory economics text. This chapter covers the research methodology of economics. We highlight some of the key concerns of empirical economics: selection issues, causality, statistical significance, and regression analysis. Methodology is a key part of economics these days, and we have tried to give the introductory student a sense of what this methodology is.

- Many new questions and problems at the end of the chapters have been added.

The Foundation

The themes of *Principles of Microeconomics*, 12th edition, are the same themes of the first eleven editions. The purposes of this book are to introduce the discipline of economics and to provide a basic understanding of how economies function. This requires a blend of economic theory, institutional material, and real-world applications. We have maintained a balance between these ingredients in every chapter. The hallmark features of our book are as follows:

1. Three-tiered explanations of key concepts (*stories-graphs-equations*)
2. Intuitive and accessible structure
3. International coverage

Three-Tiered Explanations: Stories-Graphs-Equations

Professors who teach principles of economics are faced with a classroom of students with different abilities, backgrounds, and learning styles. For some students, analytical material is difficult no matter how it is presented; for others, graphs and equations seem to come naturally. The problem facing instructors and textbook authors is how to convey the core principles of the discipline to as many students as possible without selling the better students short. Our approach to this problem is to present most core concepts in the following three ways.

First, we present each concept in the context of a simple intuitive **story** or example in words often followed by a table. Second, we use a **graph** in most cases to illustrate the story or example. And finally, in many cases where appropriate, we use an **equation** to present the concept with a mathematical formula.

Microeconomic Structure

The organization of the microeconomic chapters continues to reflect our belief that the best way to understand how market economies operate—and the best way to understand basic economic theory—is to work through the perfectly competitive model first, including discussions of output markets (goods and services) and input markets (land, labor, and capital), and the connections between them before turning to noncompetitive market structures such as monopoly and oligopoly. When students understand how a simple, perfectly competitive system works, they can start thinking about how the pieces of the economy "fit together." We think this is a better approach to teaching economics than some of the more traditional approaches, which encourage students to think of economics as a series of disconnected alternative market models.

Learning perfect competition first also enables students to see the power of the market system. It is impossible for students to discuss the efficiency of markets as well as the problems that arise from markets until they have seen how a simple, perfectly competitive market system produces and distributes goods and services. This is our purpose in Chapters 6 through 11.

Chapter 12, "General Equilibrium and the Efficiency of Perfect Competition," is a pivotal chapter that links simple, perfectly competitive markets with a discussion of market

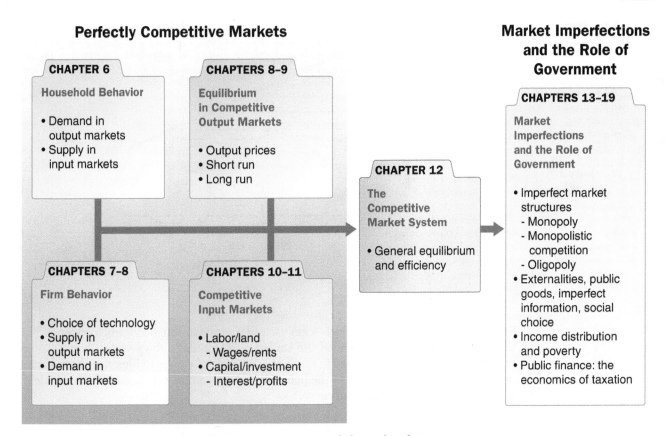

▲ FIGURE II.2 **Understanding the Microeconomy and the Role of Government**

imperfections and the role of government. Chapters 13 through 15 cover three noncompetitive market structures—monopoly, monopolistic competition, and oligopoly. Chapter 16 covers externalities, public goods, and social choice. Chapter 17, which is new to this edition, covers uncertainty and asymmetric information. Chapters 18 and 19 cover income distribution as well as taxation and government finance. The visual at the top of this page (Figure II.2 from page 110), gives you an overview of our structure.

International Coverage

As in previous editions, we continue to integrate international examples and applications throughout the text. This probably goes without saying: The days in which an introductory economics text could be written with a closed economy in mind have long since gone.

Tools for Learning

As authors and teachers, we understand the challenges of the principles of economics course. Our pedagogical features are designed to illustrate and reinforce key economic concepts through real-world examples and applications.

Economics in Practice

As described earlier, the *Economics in Practice* feature focuses on recent research or events that support a key concept in the chapter and help students think about the broad and exciting applications of economics to their lives and the world around them. Each box contains a question or two to further connect the material they are learning with their lives.

▶ **FIGURE 3.9 Excess Demand, or Shortage**
At a price of $1.75 per bushel, quantity demanded exceeds quantity supplied. When excess *demand* exists, there is a tendency for price to rise. When quantity demanded equals quantity supplied, excess demand is eliminated and the market is in equilibrium. Here the equilibrium price is $2.00 and the equilibrium quantity is 40,000 bushels.

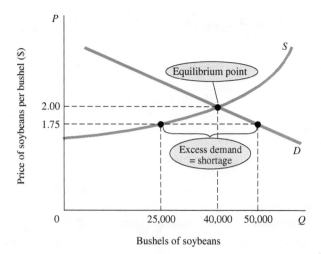

Graphs

Reading and interpreting graphs is a key part of understanding economic concepts. The Chapter 1 Appendix, "How to Read and Understand Graphs," shows readers how to interpret the 200-plus graphs featured in this book. We use red curves to illustrate the behavior of firms and blue curves to show the behavior of households. We use a different shade of red and blue to signify a shift in a curve.

Problems and Solutions

Each chapter and appendix ends with a problem set that asks students to think about and apply what they've learned in the chapter. These problems are not simple memorization questions. Rather, they ask students to perform graphical analysis or to apply economics to a real-world situation or policy decision. More challenging problems are indicated by an asterisk. Many problems have been updated. The solutions to all of the problems are available in the *Instructor's Manuals*. Instructors can provide the solutions to their students so they can check their understanding and progress.

Digital features located in MyEconLab

MyEconLab is a unique online course management, testing, and tutorial resource. It is included with the eText version of the book or as a supplement to the print book. Students and instructors will find the following online resources to accompany the twelfth edition:

• **Concept Checks:** Each section of each learning objective concludes with an online Concept Check that contains one or two multiple choice, true/false, or fill-in questions. These checks act as "speed bumps" that encourage students to stop and check their understanding of fundamental terms and concepts before moving on to the next section. The goal of this digital resource is to help students assess their progress on a section-by-section basis, so they can be better prepared for homework, quizzes, and exams.

• **Animations:** Graphs are the backbone of introductory economics, but many students struggle to understand and work with them. Select numbered figures in the text have a supporting animated version online. The goal of this digital resource is to help students understand shifts in curves, movements along curves, and changes in equilibrium values. Having an animated version of a graph helps students who have difficulty interpreting the static version in the printed text. Graded practice exercises are included with the animations. Our experience is that many students benefit from this type of online learning.

- **Learning Catalytics:** Learning Catalytics is a "bring your own device" Web-based student engagement, assessment, and classroom intelligence system. This system generates classroom discussion, guides lectures, and promotes peer-to-peer learning with real-time analytics. Students can use any device to interact in the classroom, engage with content, and even draw and share graphs.

  To learn more, ask your local Pearson representative or visit www.learningcatalytics.com.

- **Digital Interactives:** Focused on a single core topic and organized in progressive levels, each interactive immerses students in an assignable and auto-graded activity. Digital Interactives are also engaging lecture tools for traditional, online, and hybrid courses, many incorporating real-time data, data displays, and analysis tools for rich classroom discussions.

- **Dynamic Study Modules:** With a focus on key topics, these modules work by continuously assessing student performance and activity in real time and using data and analytics, provide personalized content to reinforce concepts that target each student's particular strengths and weaknesses.

- **NEW: Math Review Exercises:** MyEconLab now offers a rich array of assignable and auto-graded exercises covering fundamental math concepts geared specifically to principles and intermediate economics students. Aimed at increasing student confidence and success, our new math skills review Chapter R is accessible from the assignment manager and contains over 150 graphing, algebra, and calculus exercises for homework, quiz, and test use. Offering economics students warm-up math assignments, math remediation, or math exercises as part of any content assignment has never been easier!

- **Graphs Updated with Real-Time Data from FRED:** Approximately 25 graphs are continuously updated online with the latest available data from FRED (Federal Reserve Economic Data), which is a comprehensive, up-to-date data set maintained by the Federal Reserve Bank of St. Louis. Students can display a pop-up graph that shows new data plotted in the graph. The goal of this digital feature is to help students understand how to work with data and understand how including new data affects graphs.

- **Interactive Problems and Exercises Updated with Real-Time Data from FRED:** The end-of-chapter problems in select chapters include real-time data exercises that use the latest data from FRED.

MyEconLab for the Instructor

Instructors can choose how much or how little time to spend setting up and using MyEconLab. Here is a snapshot of what instructors are saying about MyEconLab:

> MyEconLab offers [students] a way to practice every week. They receive immediate feedback and a feeling of personal attention. As a result, my teaching has become more targeted and efficient.—Kelly Blanchard, Purdue University
> Students tell me that offering them MyEconLab is almost like offering them individual tutors.—Jefferson Edwards, Cypress Fairbanks College
> MyEconLab's eText is great—particularly in that it helps offset the skyrocketing cost of textbooks. Naturally, students love that.—Doug Gehrke, Moraine Valley Community College

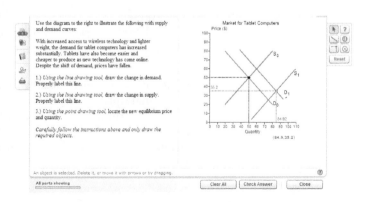

Each chapter contains two preloaded homework exercise sets that can be used to build an individualized study plan for each student. These study plan exercises contain tutorial resources, including instant feedback, links to the appropriate learning objective in the eText, pop-up definitions from the text, and step-by-step guided solutions, where appropriate. After the initial setup of the course by the instructor, student use of these materials requires no further instructor setup. The online grade book records each student's performance and time spent on the tests and study plan and generates reports by student or chapter.

Alternatively, instructors can fully customize MyEconLab to match their course exactly, including reading assignments, homework assignments, video assignments, current news assignments, and quizzes and tests. Assignable resources include:

- Preloaded exercise assignments sets for each chapter that include the student tutorial resources mentioned earlier
- Preloaded quizzes for each chapter that are unique to the text and not repeated in the study plan or homework exercise sets
- Study plan problems that are similar to the end-of-chapter problems and numbered exactly like the book to make assigning homework easier
- *Real-Time-Data Analysis Exercises*, marked with ⊕, allow students and instructors to use the very latest data from FRED. By completing the exercises, students become familiar with a key data source, learn how to locate data, and develop skills in interpreting data.
- In the eText available in MyEconLab, select figures labeled MyEconLab Real-time data ⊕ allow students to display a pop-up graph updated with real-time data from FRED.
- *Current News Exercises*, provide a turnkey way to assign gradable news-based exercises in MyEconLab. Each week, Pearson scours the news, finds a current microeconomics and macroeconomics article, creates exercises around these news articles, and then automatically adds them to MyEconLab. Assigning and grading current news-based exercises that deal with the latest micro and macro events and policy issues has never been more convenient.
- *Experiments in MyEconLab* are a fun and engaging way to promote active learning and mastery of important economic concepts. Pearson's Experiments program is flexible, easy-to-assign, auto-graded, and available in single- and multiplayer versions.
  - Single-player experiments allow your students to play against virtual players from anywhere at any time so long as they have an Internet connection.
  - Multiplayer experiments allow you to assign and manage a real-time experiment with your class.
  - Pre- and post-questions for each experiment are available for assignment in MyEconLab.
  - For a complete list of available experiments, visit **www.myeconlab.com**.
- Test Item File questions that allow you to assign quizzes or homework that will look just like your exams
- Econ Exercise Builder, which allows you to build customized exercises

Exercises include multiple-choice, graph drawing, and free-response items, many of which are generated algorithmically so that each time a student works them, a different variation is presented.

MyEconLab grades every problem type except essays, even problems with graphs. When working homework exercises, students receive immediate feedback, with links to additional learning tools.

Customization and Communication MyEconLab in MyLab/Mastering provides additional optional customization and communication tools. Instructors who teach distance-learning courses or very large lecture sections find the MyLab/Mastering format useful because they can upload course documents and assignments, customize the order of chapters, and use communication features such as Document Sharing, Chat, ClassLive, and Discussion Board.

MyEconLab for the Student

MyEconLab puts students in control of their learning through a collection of testing, practice, and study tools tied to the online, interactive version of the textbook and other media resources. Here is a snapshot of what students are saying about MyEconLab:

- It was very useful because it had EVERYTHING, from practice exams to exercises to reading. Very helpful.—student, Northern Illinois University
- I would recommend taking the quizzes on MyEconLab because it gives you a true account of whether or not you understand the material.—student, Montana Tech
- It made me look through the book to find answers, so I did more reading.—student, Northern Illinois University

Students can study on their own or can complete assignments created by their instructor. In MyEconLab's structured environment, students practice what they learn, test their understanding, and pursue a personalized study plan generated from their performance on sample tests and from quizzes created by their instructors. In Homework or Study Plan mode, students have access to a wealth of tutorial features, including:

- Instant feedback on exercises that helps students understand and apply the concepts
- Links to the eText to promote reading of the text just when the student needs to revisit a concept or an explanation
- Step-by-step guided solutions that force students to break down a problem in much the same way an instructor would do during office hours
- Pop-up key term definitions from the eText to help students master the vocabulary of economics
- A graphing tool that is integrated into the various exercises to enable students to build and manipulate graphs to better understand how concepts, numbers, and graphs connect

Additional MyEconLab Tools   MyEconLab includes the following additional features:

- **Enhanced eText**—Students actively read and learn, and with more engagement than ever before, through embedded and auto-graded practice, real-time data-graph updates, animations, and more.
- **Print upgrade**—For students who wish to complete assignments in MyEconLab but read in print, Pearson offers registered MyEconLab users a loose-leaf version of the print text at a significant discount.
- **Glossary flashcards**—Every key term is available as a flashcard, allowing students to quiz themselves on vocabulary from one or more chapters at a time.

MyEconLab content has been created through the efforts of Chris Annala, State University of New York–Geneseo; Charles Baum, Middle Tennessee State University; Peggy Dalton, Frostburg State University; Carol Dole, Jacksonville University; David Foti, Lone Star College; Sarah Ghosh, University of Scranton; Satyajit Ghosh, Universtity of Scranton; Woo Jung, University of Colorado; Chris Kauffman, University of Tennessee–Knoxville; Russell

Kellogg, University of Colorado–Denver; Katherine McCann, University of Delaware; Daniel Mizak, Frostburg State University; Christine Polek, University of Massachusetts–Boston; Mark Scanlan, Stephen F. Austin State University; Leonie L. Stone, State University of New York–Geneseo; and Bert G. Wheeler, Cedarville University.

Other Resources for the Instructor

The following supplements are designed to make teaching and testing flexible and easy and are available for *Micro, Macro,* and *Economics* volumes.

Instructor's Manuals

Two *Instructor's Manuals*, one for *Principles of Microeconomics* and one for *Principles of Macroeconomics*, were prepared by Tony Lima of California State University, East Bay (Hayward, California). The *Instructor's Manuals* are designed to provide the utmost teaching support for instructors. They include the following content:

- Detailed *Chapter Outlines* include key terminology, teaching notes, and lecture suggestions.
- *Topics for Class Discussion* provide topics and real-world situations that help ensure that economic concepts resonate with students.
- Unique *Economics in Practice* features that are not in the main text provide extra real-world examples to present and discuss in class.
- *Teaching Tips* provide tips for alternative ways to cover the material and brief reminders on additional help to provide students. These tips include suggestions for exercises and experiments to complete in class.
- *Extended Applications* include exercises, activities, and experiments to help make economics relevant to students.
- *Excel Workbooks*, available for many chapters, make it easy to customize numerical examples and produce graphs.
- *Solutions* are provided for all problems in the book.

Four Test Item Files

We have tailored the Test Item Files to help instructors easily and efficiently assess student understanding of economic concepts and analyses. Test questions are annotated with the following information:

- **Difficulty:** 1 for straight recall, 2 for some analysis, 3 for complex analysis
- **Type:** Multiple-choice, true/false, short-answer, essay
- **Topic:** The term or concept the question supports
- **Skill:** Fact, definition, analytical, conceptual
- **AACSB:** See description in the next section.

The Test Item Files include questions with tables that students must analyze to solve for numerical answers. The Test Item Files also contain questions based on the graphs that appear in the book. The questions ask students to interpret the information presented in the graph. Many questions require students to sketch a graph on their own and interpret curve movements.

Microeconomics Test Item File, by Randy Methenitis of Richland College: The Microeconomics Test Item File includes over 2,700 questions. All questions are machine gradable and are either multiple-choice or true/false. This Test Item File is for use with the 12th edition of *Principles of Microeconomics* in the first year of publication. It is available in a computerized format using TestGen EQ test-generating software and is included in MyEconLab.

Microeconomics Test Item File Discussion and Short Answer, by Richard Gosselin of Houston Community College: This second Test Item File includes 1,000 conceptual problems, essay questions, and short-answer questions. Application-type problems ask students to draw graphs and analyze tables. The Word files are available on the Instructor's Resource Center (www.pearsonhighered.com/educator).

Macroeconomics Test Item File by Randy Methenitis of Richland College: The Macroeconomics Test Item File includes over 2,900 questions. All questions are machine gradable and are either multiple-choice or true/false. This Test Item File is for use with the 12th edition of *Principles of Macroeconomics* in the first year of publication. This Test Item File is available in a computerized format using TestGen EQ test-generating software and included in MyEconLab.

Macroeconomics Test Item File: Discussion and Short Answer, by Richard Gosselin of Houston Community College: This second Test Item File includes 1,000 conceptual problems, essay questions, and short-answer questions. Application-type problems ask students to draw graphs and analyze tables. The Word files are available on the Instructor's Resource Center (www.pearsonhighered.com/educator).

The Test Item Files were checked for accuracy by the following professors:

Leon J. Battista, Bronx Community College; Margaret Brooks, Bridgewater State College; Mike Casey, University of Central Arkansas; Mike Cohick, Collin County Community College; Dennis Debrecht, Carroll College; Amrik Dua, California State Polytechnic University, Pomona; Mitchell Dudley, The College of William & Mary; Ann Eike, University of Kentucky; Connel Fullencamp, Duke University; Craig Gallet, California State University, Sacramento; Michael Goode, Central Piedmont Community College; Steve Hamilton, California State Polytechnic University; James R. Irwin, Central Michigan University; Aaron Jackson, Bentley College; Rus Janis, University of Massachusetts, Amherst; Jonatan Jelen, The City College of New York; Kathy A. Kelly, University of Texas, Arlington; Kate Krause, University of New Mexico; Gary F. Langer, Roosevelt University; Leonard Lardaro, University of Rhode Island; Ross LaRoe, Denison University; Melissa Lind, University of Texas, Arlington; Solina Lindahl, California State Polytechnic University; Pete Mavrokordatos, Tarrant County College; Roberto Mazzoleni, Hofstra University; Kimberly Mencken, Baylor University; Ida Mirzaie, Ohio State University; Shahruz Mohtadi, Suffolk University; Mary Pranzo, California State University, Fresno; Ed Price, Oklahoma State University; Robert Shoffner, Central Piedmont Community College; James Swofford, University of South Alabama; Helen Tauchen, University of North Carolina, Chapel Hill; Eric Taylor, Central Piedmont Community College; Henry Terrell, University of Maryland; John Tommasi, Bentley College; Mukti Upadhyay, Eastern Illinois University; Robert Whaples, Wake Forest University; and Timothy Wunder, University of Texas, Arlington.

The Association to Advance Collegiate Schools of Business (AACSB) The authors of the Test Item File have connected select Test Item File questions to the general knowledge and skill guidelines found in the AACSB assurance of learning standards.

What Is the AACSB? AACSB is a not-for-profit corporation of educational institutions, corporations, and other organizations devoted to the promotion and improvement of higher education in business administration and accounting. A collegiate institution offering degrees in business administration or accounting may volunteer for AACSB accreditation review. The AACSB makes initial accreditation decisions and conducts periodic reviews to promote continuous quality improvement in management education. Pearson Education is a proud member of the AACSB and is pleased to provide advice to help you apply AACSB Assurance of Learning Standards.

What Are AACSB Assurance of Learning Standards? One of the criteria for AACSB accreditation is quality of the curricula. Although no specific courses are required, the AACSB expects a curriculum to include learning experiences in areas such as the following:

- Written and Oral Communication
- Ethical Understanding and Reasoning

- Analytic Thinking Skills
- Information Technology
- Diverse and Multicultural Work
- Reflective Thinking
- Application of Knowledge

Questions that test skills relevant to these guidelines are tagged with the appropriate standard. For example, a question testing the moral questions associated with externalities would receive the Ethical Understanding and Reasoning tag.

How Can Instructors Use the AACSB Tags?   Tagged questions help you measure whether students are grasping the course content that aligns with the AACSB guidelines noted earlier. This in turn may suggest enrichment activities or other educational experiences to help students achieve these skills.

TestGen

The computerized TestGen package allows instructors to customize, save, and generate classroom tests. The test program permits instructors to edit, add, or delete questions from the Test Item Files; analyze test results; and organize a database of tests and student results. This software allows for extensive flexibility and ease of use. It provides many options for organizing and displaying tests, along with search and sort features. The software and the Test Item Files can be downloaded from the Instructor's Resource Center (www.pearsonhighered .com/educator).

PowerPoint® Lecture Presentations

PowerPoint slides for *Principles of Microeconomics* and *Principles of Macroeconomics*, prepared by Jim Lee of Dickinson State University, are available:

- A comprehensive set of PowerPoint slides can be used by instructors for class presentations or by students for lecture preview or review. These slides include all the figures, photos, tables, key terms, and equations in the textbook. Instructors may download these PowerPoint presentations from the Instructor's Resource Center (www.pearsonhighered.com/educator).
- A student version of the PowerPoint slides are available as .pdf files. This version allows students to print the slides and bring them to class for note taking. Instructors can download these PowerPoint presentations from the Instructor's Resource Center. (www.pearsonhighered.com/educator).

Acknowledgments

We are grateful to the many people who helped us prepare the 12th edition. We thank David Alexander, our editor, and Lindsey Sloan, our program manager, for their help and enthusiasm.

Roberta Sherman, project manager, and Jeffrey Holcomb, our Team Lead of Project Management, ensured that the production process of the book went smoothly. In addition, we also want to thank Stephanie Raga of Integra Software Services, Inc., who kept us on schedule, and Jenell Forschler, who managed the research of the many photographs that appear in the book.

We want to give special thanks to Patsy Balin, Murielle Dawdy, and Tracy Waldman for their research assistance.

We also owe a debt of gratitude to those who reviewed and checked the 12th edition for accuracy. They provided us with valuable insight as we prepared this edition and its supplement package.

Reviewers of the 12th Edition

Bahram Adrangi, University of Portland
Anthony Andrews, Governors State
University
J Jeffrey Blais, Rhode Island College
Paula M. Cole, University of Denver
Karen Fitzner, DePaul University
James Frederick, UNC at Pembroke
Richard Gearhart, California State
University, Bakersfield
Wayne Hickenbottom, University of
Texas at Austin
Janet Koscianski, Shippensburg
University
Tim Kwock, University of Hawaii West
Oahu
Sangjoon Lee, Alfred University
David Lehmkuhl, Lakeland College
Benjamin Liebman, St. Joseph's University
Basel Mansour, New Jersey City University
Chris Phillips, Somerset Community
College
Sarah Quintanar, University of Arkansas
at Little Rock
Daniel Sichel, Wellesley College
John Solow, University of Iowa
Jadrian Wooten, Penn State University
Linus Yamane, Pitzer College

Reviewers of Previous Editions

The following individuals were of
immense help in reviewing all or part of
previous editions of this book and the
teaching/learning package in various
stages of development:

Cynthia Abadie, Southwest Tennessee
Community College
Shawn Abbott, College of the Siskiyous
Fatma Abdel-Raouf, Goldey-Beacom
College
Lew Abernathy, University of North
Texas
Rebecca Abraham, Nova Southeastern
University
Basil Adams, Notre Dame de Namur
University
Jack Adams, University of Maryland
Douglas K. Adie, Ohio University
Douglas Agbetsiafa, Indiana University,
South Bend
Sheri Aggarwal, University of Virginia
Carlos Aguilar, El Paso Community
College
Ehsan Ahmed, James Madison University
Ferhat Akbas, Texas A&M University
Sam Alapati, Rutgers University

Terence Alexander, Iowa State
University
John W. Allen, Texas A&M University
Polly Allen, University of Connecticut
Stuart Allen, University of North
Carolina at Greensboro
Hassan Aly, Ohio State University
Alex Anas, University at Buffalo, The
State University of New York
David Anderson, Centre College
Joan Anderssen, Arapahoe Community
College
Jim Angresano, Hampton-Sydney
College
Kenneth S. Arakelian, University of
Rhode Island
Harvey Arnold, Indian River Community
College
Nick Apergis, Fordham University
Bevin Ashenmiller, Occidental College
Richard Ashley, Virginia Technical
University
Birjees Ashraf, Houston Community
College Southwest
Kidane Asmeron, Pennsylvania State
University
Musa Ayar, University of Texas, Austin
James Aylesworth, Lakeland Community
College
Moshen Bahmani, University of
Wisconsin—Milwaukee
Asatar Bair, City College of San Francisco
Diana Bajrami, College of Alameda
Mohammad Bajwa, Northampton
Community College
Rita Balaban, University of North
Carolina, Chapel Hill
A. Paul Ballantyne, University of
Colorado, Colorado Springs
Richard J. Ballman, Jr., Augustana
College
King Banaian, St. Cloud State University
Nick Barcia, Baruch College
Henry Barker, Tiffin University
Robin Bartlett, Denison University
Laurie Bates, Bryant University
Kari Battaglia, University of North Texas
Leon Battista, Bronx Community College
Amanda Bayer, Swarthmore College
Klaus Becker, Texas Tech University
Richard Beil, Auburn University
Clive Belfield, Queens College
Willie J. Belton, Jr., Georgia Institute of
Technology
Daniel K. Benjamin, Clemson University
Charles A. Bennett, Gannon University
Emil Berendt, Siena Heights University
Daniel Berkowitz, University of Pittsburgh
Kurt Beron, University of Texas, Dallas
Derek Berry, Calhoun Community
College

Tibor Besedes, Georgia Institute of
Technology
Thomas Beveridge, Durham Technical
Community College
Anoop Bhargava, Finger Lakes CC
Eugenie Bietry, Pace University
Kelly Blanchard, Purdue University
Mannie Bloemen, Houston Community
College
Mark Bock, Loyola College in Maryland
Howard Bodenhorn, Lafayette College
Bruce Bolnick, Northeastern
University
Frank Bonello, University of Notre Dame
Jeffrey Bookwalter, University of
Montana
Antonio Bos, Tusculum College
Maristella Botticini, Boston University
George Bowling, St. Charles Community
College
G. E. Breger, University of South Carolina
Charles Callahan, III, State University of
New York at Brockport
Dennis Brennan, William Rainey Harper
Junior College
Anne E. Bresnock, California State
Polytechnic University, Pomona,
and the University of California, Los
Angeles
Barry Brown, Murray State University
Bruce Brown, California State
Polytechnic University, Pomona
Jennifer Brown, Eastern Connecticut
State University
David Brownstone, University of
California, Irvine
Don Brunner, Spokane Falls Community
College
Jeff Bruns, Bacone College
David Bunting, Eastern Washington
University
Barbara Burnell, College of Wooster
Alison Butler, Willamette University
Fred Campano, Fordham University
Douglas Campbell, University of
Memphis
Beth Cantrell, Central Baptist College
Kevin Carlson, University of
Massachusetts, Boston
Leonard Carlson, Emory University
Arthur Schiller Casimir, Western New
England College
Lindsay Caulkins, John Carroll University
Atreya Chakraborty, Boston College
Suparna Chakraborty, Baruch College of
the City University of New York
Winston W. Chang, University at Buffalo,
The State University of New York
Janie Chermak, University of New Mexico
David Ching, University of Hawaii
– Honolulu

Harold Christensen, Centenary College
Daniel Christiansen, Albion College
Susan Christoffersen, Philadelphia University
Samuel Kim-Liang Chuah, Walla Walla College
Dmitriy Chulkov, Indiana University, Kokomo
David Colander, Middlebury College
Daniel Condon, University of Illinois at Chicago; Moraine Valley Community College
Karen Conway, University of New Hampshire
Cesar Corredor, Texas A&M University
David Cowen, University of Texas, Austin
Tyler Cowen, George Mason University
Amy Cramer, Pima Community College, West Campus
Peggy Crane, Southwestern College
Barbara Craig, Oberlin College
Jerry Crawford, Arkansas State University
James Cunningham, Chapman University
Scott Cunningham, Baylor University
Elisabeth Curtis, Dartmouth
James D'Angelo, University of Cincinnati
David Dahl, University of St. Thomas
Sheryll Dahlke, Lees-McRae College
Joseph Dahms, Hood College
Sonia Dalmia, Grand Valley State University
Rosa Lea Danielson, College of DuPage
David Danning, University of Massachusetts, Boston
Minh Quang Dao, Eastern Illinois University
Amlan Datta, Cisco Junior College
David Davenport, McLennan Community College
Stephen Davis, Southwest Minnesota State University
Dale DeBoer, Colorado University, Colorado Springs
Dennis Debrecht, Carroll College
Juan J. DelaCruz, Fashion Institute of Technology and Lehman College
Greg Delemeester, Marietta College
Yanan Di, State University of New York, Stony Brook
Amy Diduch, Mary Baldwin College
Timothy Diette, Washington and Lee University
Vernon J. Dixon, Haverford College
Alan Dobrowolksi, Manchester Community College
Eric Dodge, Hanover College
Carol Dole, Jacksonville University

Michael Donihue, Colby College
Leslie Doss, University of Texas San Antonio
Shahpour Dowlatshahi, Fayetteville Technical Community College
Joanne M. Doyle, James Madison University
Robert Driskill, Ohio State University
James Dulgeroff, San Bernardino Valley College
Kevin Duncan, Colorado State University
Yvonne Durham, Western Washington University
Debra Sabatini Dwyer, State University of New York, Stony Brook
Gary Dymski, University of Southern California
David Eaton, Murray State University
Jay Egger, Towson State University
Erwin Ehrhardt, University of Cincinnati
Ann Eike, University of Kentucky
Eugene Elander, Plymouth State University
Ronald D. Elkins, Central Washington University
Tisha Emerson, Baylor University
Michael Enz, Western New England College
Erwin Erhardt III, University of Cincinnati
William Even, Miami University
Ali Faegh, Houston Community College
Noel J. J. Farley, Bryn Mawr College
Mosin Farminesh, Temple University
Dan Feaster, Miami University of Ohio
Susan Feiner, Virginia Commonwealth University
Getachew Felleke, Albright College
Lois Fenske, South Puget Sound Community College
William Field, DePauw University
Deborah Figart, Richard Stockton College
Barbara Fischer, Cardinal Stritch University
Mary Flannery, Santa Clara University
Bill Foeller, State University of New York, Fredonia
Fred Foldvary, Santa Clara University
Roger Nils Folsom, San Jose State University
Mathew Forstater, University of Missouri-Kansas City
Kevin Foster, The City College of New York
Richard Fowles, University of Utah
Sean Fraley, College of Mount Saint Joseph
Johanna Francis, Fordham University
Roger Frantz, San Diego State University
Mark Frascatore, Clarkson University

Amanda Freeman, Kansas State University
Morris Frommer, Owens Community College
Brandon Fuller, University of Montana
David Fuller, University of Iowa
Mark Funk, University of Arkansas, Little Rock
Alejandro Gallegos, Winona State University
Craig Gallet, California State University, Sacramento
N. Galloro, Chabot College
Bill Galose, Drake University
William Ganley, Buffalo State, SUNY
Martin A. Garrett, Jr., College of William and Mary
Tom Gausman, Northern Illinois University
Shirley J. Gedeon, University of Vermont
Jeff Gerlach, Sungkyunkwan Graduate School of Business
Lisa Giddings, University of Wisconsin, La Crosse
Gary Gigliotti, Rutgers University
Lynn Gillette, Spalding University
Donna Ginther, University of Kansas
James N. Giordano, Villanova University
Amy Glass, Texas A&M University
Sarah L. Glavin, Boston College
Roy Gobin, Loyola University, Chicago
Bill Godair, Landmark College
Bill Goffe, University of Mississippi
Devra Golbe, Hunter College
Roger Goldberg, Ohio Northern University
Joshua Goodman, New York University
Ophelia Goma, DePauw University
John Gonzales, University of San Francisco
David Gordon, Illinois Valley College
Richard Gosselin, Houston Community College
Eugene Gotwalt, Sweet Briar College
John W. Graham, Rutgers University
Douglas Greenley, Morehead State University
Thomas A. Gresik, University of Notre Dame
Lisa M. Grobar, California State University, Long Beach
Wayne A. Grove, Le Moyne College
Daryl Gruver, Mount Vernon Nazarene University
Osman Gulseven, North Carolina State University
Mike Gumpper, Millersville University
Benjamin Gutierrez, Indiana University, Bloomington
A. R. Gutowsky, California State University, Sacramento

Anthony Gyapong, Penn State University, Abington

David R. Hakes, University of Missouri, St. Louis

Bradley Hansen, University of Mary Washington

Stephen Happel, Arizona State University

Mehdi Haririan, Bloomsburg University of Pennsylvania

David Harris, Benedictine College

David Harris, San Diego State University

James Hartley, Mount Holyoke College

Bruce Hartman, California Maritime Academy of California State University

Mitchell Harwitz, University at Buffalo, The State University of New York

Dewey Heinsma, Mt. San Jacinto College

Sara Helms, University of Alabama, Birmingham

Brian Hill, Salisbury University

David Hoaas, Centenary College

Arleen Hoag, Owens Community College

Carol Hogan, University of Michigan, Dearborn

Harry Holzer, Michigan State University

Ward Hooker, Orangeburg-Calhoun Technical College

Bobbie Horn, University of Tulsa

John Horowitz, Ball State University

Ali Faegh, Houston Community College

Daniel Horton, Cleveland State University

Ying Huang, Manhattan College

Janet Hunt, University of Georgia

E. Bruce Hutchinson, University of Tennessee, Chattanooga

Creed Hyatt, Lehigh Carbon Community College

Ana Ichim, Louisiana State University

Aaron Iffland, Rocky Mountain College

Fred Inaba, Washington State University

Richard Inman, Boston College

Aaron Jackson, Bentley College

Brian Jacobsen, Wisconsin Lutheran College

Rus Janis, University of Massachusetts

Jonatan Jelen, The City College of New York

Eric Jensen, The College of William & Mary

Aaron Johnson, Missouri State University

Donn Johnson, Quinnipiac University

Paul Johnson, University of Alaska, Anchorage

Shirley Johnson, Vassar College

Farhoud Kafi, Babson College

R. Kallen, Roosevelt University

Arthur E. Kartman, San Diego State University

Hirshel Kasper, Oberlin College

Brett Katzman, Kennesaw State University

Bruce Kaufman, Georgia State University

Dennis Kaufman, University of Wisconsin, Parkside

Pavel Kapinos, Carleton College

Russell Kashian, University of Wisconsin, Whitewater

Amoz Kats, Virginia Technical University

David Kaun, University of California, Santa Cruz

Brett Katzman, Kennesaw State University

Fred Keast, Portland State University

Stephanie Kelton, University of Missouri, Kansas City

Deborah Kelly, Palomar College

Erasmus Kersting, Texas A&M University

Randall Kesselring, Arkansas State University

Alan Kessler, Providence College

Dominique Khactu, The University of North Dakota

Gary Kikuchi, University of Hawaii, Manoa

Hwagyun Kim, State University of New York, Buffalo

Keon-Ho Kim, University of Utah

Kil-Joong Kim, Austin Peay State University

Sang W. Kim, Hood College

Phillip King, San Francisco State University

Barbara Kneeshaw, Wayne County Community College

Inderjit Kohli, Santa Clara University

Heather Kohls, Marquette University

Janet Koscianski, Shippensburg University

Vani Kotcherlakota, University of Nebraska, Kearney

Barry Kotlove, Edmonds Community College

Kate Krause, University of New Mexico

David Kraybill, University of Georgia

David Kroeker, Tabor College

Stephan Kroll, California State University, Sacramento

Joseph Kubec, Park University

Jacob Kurien, Helzberg School of Management

Rosung Kwak, University of Texas at Austin

Sally Kwak, University of Hawaii-Manoa

Steven Kyle, Cornell University

Anil K. Lal, Pittsburg State University

Melissa Lam, Wellesley College

David Lang, California State University, Sacramento

Gary Langer, Roosevelt University

Anthony Laramie, Merrimack College

Leonard Lardaro, University of Rhode Island

Ross LaRoe, Denison University

Michael Lawlor, Wake Forest University

Pareena Lawrence, University of Minnesota, Morris

Daniel Lawson, Drew University

Mary Rose Leacy, Wagner College

Margaret D. Ledyard, University of Texas, Austin

Jim Lee, Fort Hays State University

Judy Lee, Leeward Community College

Sang H. Lee, Southeastern Louisiana University

Don Leet, California State University, Fresno

Robert J. Lemke, Lake Forest College

Gary Lemon, DePauw University

Alan Leonard, Wilson Technical Community College

Mary Lesser, Iona College

Ding Li, Northern State University

Zhe Li, Stony Brook University

Larry Lichtenstein, Canisius College

Benjamin Liebman, Saint Joseph's University

Jesse Liebman, Kennesaw State University

George Lieu, Tuskegee University

Stephen E. Lile, Western Kentucky University

Jane Lillydahl, University of Colorado at Boulder

Tony Lima, California State University, East Bay

Melissa Lind, University of Texas, Arlington

Al Link, University of North Carolina Greensboro

Charles R. Link, University of Delaware

Robert Litro, U.S. Air Force Academy

Samuel Liu, West Valley College

Jeffrey Livingston, Bentley College

Ming Chien Lo, St. Cloud State University

Burl F. Long, University of Florida

Alina Luca, Drexel University

Adrienne Lucas, Wellesley College

Nancy Lutz, Virginia Technical University

Kristina Lybecker, Colorado College

Gerald Lynch, Purdue University

Karla Lynch, University of North Texas

Ann E. Lyon, University of Alaska, Anchorage

Bruce Madariaga, Montgomery College

Michael Magura, University of Toledo

Marvin S. Margolis, Millersville University of Pennsylvania

Tim Mason, Eastern Illinois University

Don Mathews, Coastal Georgia Community College

Don Maxwell, Central State University

Nan Maxwell, California State University at Hayward

Roberto Mazzoleni, Hofstra University

Cynthia S. McCarty, Jacksonville State University

J. Harold McClure, Jr., Villanova University

Patrick McEwan, Wellesley College

Ronnie McGinness, University of Mississippi

Todd McFall, Wake Forest University

Rick McIntyre, University of Rhode Island

James J. McLain, University of New Orleans

Dawn McLaren, Mesa Community College

B. Starr McMullen, Oregon State University

K. Mehtaboin, College of St. Rose

Martin Melkonian, Hofstra University

Alice Melkumian, Western Illinois University

William Mertens, University of Colorado, Boulder

Randy Methenitis, Richland College

Art Meyer, Lincoln Land Community College

Carrie Meyer, George Mason University

Meghan Millea, Mississippi State University

Jenny Minier, University of Miami

Ida Mirzaie, The Ohio State University

David Mitchell, Missouri State University

Bijan Moeinian, Osceola Campus

Robert Mohr, University of New Hampshire

Shahruz Mohtadi, Suffolk University

Amyaz Moledina, College of Wooster

Gary Mongiovi, St. John's University

Terry D. Monson, Michigan Technological University

Barbara A. Moore, University of Central Florida

Joe L. Moore, Arkansas Technical University

Myra Moore, University of Georgia

Robert Moore, Occidental College

Norma C. Morgan, Curry College

W. Douglas Morgan, University of California, Santa Barbara

David Murphy, Boston College

John Murphy, North Shore Community College, Massachusetts

Ellen Mutari, Richard Stockton College of New Jersey

Steven C. Myers, University of Akron

Veena Nayak, University at Buffalo, The State University of New York

Ron Necoechea, Robert Wesleyan College

Doug Nelson, Spokane Community College

Randy Nelson, Colby College

David Nickerson, University of British Columbia

Sung No, Southern University and A&M College

Rachel Nugent, Pacific Lutheran University

Akorlie A. Nyatepe-Coo, University of Wisconsin LaCrosse

Norman P. Obst, Michigan State University

William C. O'Connor, Western Montana College

Constantin Ogloblin, Georgia Southern University

David O'Hara, Metropolitan State University

Albert Okunade, University of Memphis

Ronald Olive, University of Massachusetts, Lowell

Martha L. Olney, University of California, Berkeley

Kent Olson, Oklahoma State University

Jaime Ortiz, Florida Atlantic University

Theresa Osborne, Hunter College

Donald J. Oswald, California State University, Bakersfield

Mete Ozcan, Brooklyn College

Alexandre Padilla, Metropolitan State College of Denver

Aaron Pankratz, Fresno City College

Niki Papadopoulou, University of Cyprus

Walter Park, American University

Carl Parker, Fort Hays State University

Spiro Patton, Rasmussen College

Andrew Pearlman, Bard College

Charlie Pearson, Southern Maine Community College

Richard Peck, University of Illinois at Chicago

Don Peppard, Connecticut College

Elizabeth Perry, Randolph College

Nathan Perry, University of Utah

Joe Petry, University of Illinois-Urbana-Champaign

Joseph A. Petry, University of Illinois

Mary Ann Pevas, Winona State University

Chris Phillips, Somerset Community College

Jeff Phillips, Morrisville Community College

Frankie Pircher, University of Missouri, Kansas City

Tony Pizelo, Spokane Community College

Dennis Placone, Clemson University

Mike Pogodzinski, San Jose State University

Linnea Polgreen, University of Iowa

Elizabeth Porter, University of North Florida

Bob Potter, University of Central Florida

Ed Price, Oklahoma State University

Abe Qastin, Lakeland College

Kevin Quinn, St. Norbert College

Ramkishen S. Rajan, George Mason University

James Rakowski, University of Notre Dame

Amy Ramirez-Gay, Eastern Michigan University

Paul Rappoport, Temple University

Artatrana Ratha, St. Cloud State University

Michael Rendich, Westchester Community College

Lynn Rittenoure, University of Tulsa

Travis Roach, Texas Tech University

Brian Roberson, Miami University

Michael Robinson, Mount Holyoke College

Juliette Roddy, University of Michigan, Dearborn

Michael Rolleigh, University of Minnesota

Belinda Roman, Palo Alto College

S. Scanlon Romer, Delta College

Brian Rosario, University of California, Davis

Paul Roscelli, Canada College

David C. Rose, University of Missouri-St. Louis

Greg Rose, Sacramento City College

Richard Rosenberg, Pennsylvania State University

Robert Rosenman, Washington State University

Robert Rosenthal, Stonehill College

Howard Ross, Baruch College

Paul Rothstein, Washington University

Charles Roussel, Louisiana State University

Jeff Rubin, Rutgers University

Mark Rush, University of Florida

Dereka Rushbrook, Ripon College

Jerard Russo, University of Hawaii

Luz A. Saavedra, University of St. Thomas

William Samuelson, Boston University School of Management

Allen Sanderson, University of Chicago

David Saner, Springfield College – Benedictine University

Ahmad Saranjam, Bridgewater State College

David L. Schaffer, Haverford College

Eric Schansberg, Indiana University – Southeast

Robert Schenk, Saint Joseph's College

Ramon Schreffler, Houston Community College System (retired)

Adina Schwartz, Lakeland College

Jerry Schwartz, Broward Community College

Amy Scott, DeSales University

Gary Sellers, University of Akron

Atindra Sen, Miami University

Chad Settle, University of Tulsa

Jean Shackleford, Bucknell University

Ronald Shadbegian, University of Massachusetts, Dartmouth

Linda Shaffer, California State University, Fresno

Dennis Shannon, Southwestern Illinois College

Stephen L. Shapiro, University of North Florida

Paul Shea, University of Oregon

Geoff Shepherd, University of Massachusetts Amherst

Bih-Hay Sheu, University of Texas at Austin

David Shideler, Murray State University

Alden Shiers, California Polytechnic State University

Gerald Shilling, Eastfield College

Dongsoo Shin, Santa Clara University

Elias Shukralla, St. Louis Community College, Meramec

Anne Shugars, Harford Community College

Richard Sicotte, University of Vermont

William Simeone, Providence College

Scott Simkins, North Carolina Agricultural and Technical State University

Larry Singell, University of Oregon

Priyanka Singh, University of Texas, Dallas

Sue Skeath, Wellesley College

Edward Skelton, Southern Methodist University

Ken Slaysman, York College

John Smith, New York University

Paula Smith, Central State University, Oklahoma

Donald Snyder, Utah State University

Marcia Snyder, College of Charleston

David Sobiechowski, Wayne State University

John Solow, University of Iowa

Angela Sparkman, Itawamba Community College

Martin Spechler, Indiana University

David Spigelman, University of Miami

Arun Srinivasa, Indiana University, Southeast

David J. St. Clair, California State University at Hayward

Sarah Stafford, College of William & Mary

Richard Stahl, Louisiana State University

Rebecca Stein, University of Pennsylvania

Mary Stevenson, University of Massachusetts, Boston

Susan Stojanovic, Washington University, St. Louis

Courtenay Stone, Ball State University

Ernst W. Stromsdorfer, Washington State University

Edward Stuart, Northeastern Illinois University

Chris Stufflebean, Southwestern Oklahoma State University

Chuck Stull, Kalamazoo College

Kenneth Slaysman, York College of Pennsylvania

Della Sue, Marist College

Abdulhamid Sukar, Cameron University

Christopher Surfield, Saginaw Valley State University

Rodney B. Swanson, University of California, Los Angeles

James Swofford, University of Alabama

Bernica Tackett, Pulaski Technical College

Michael Taussig, Rutgers University

Samia Tavares, Rochester Institute of Technology

Timothy Taylor, Stanford University

William Taylor, New Mexico Highlands University

Sister Beth Anne Tercek, SND, Notre Dame College of Ohio

Henry Terrell, University of Maryland

Jennifer Thacher, University of New Mexico

Donna Thompson, Brookdale Community College

Robert Tokle, Idaho State University

David Tolman, Boise State University

Susanne Toney, Hampton University

Karen M. Travis, Pacific Lutheran University

Jack Trierweler, Northern State University

Brian M. Trinque, University of Texas at Austin

HuiKuan Tseng, University of North Carolina at Charlotte

Boone Turchi, University of North Carolina

Kristin Van Gaasbeck, California State University, Sacramento

Amy Vander Laan, Hastings College

Ann Velenchik, Wellesley College

Lawrence Waldman, University of New Mexico

Chris Waller, Indiana University, Bloomington

William Walsh, University of St. Thomas

Chunbei Wang, University of St. Thomas

John Watkins, Westminster

Janice Weaver, Drake University

Bruce Webb, Gordon College

Ross Weiner, The City College of New York

Elaine Wendt, Milwaukee Area Technical College

Walter Wessels, North Carolina State University

Christopher Westley, Jacksonville State University

Joan Whalen-Ayyappan, DeVry Institute of Technology

Robert Whaples, Wake Forest University

Leonard A. White, University of Arkansas

Alex Wilson, Rhode Island College

Wayne Winegarden, Marymount University

Jennifer Wissink, Cornell University

Arthur Woolf, University of Vermont

Paula Worthington, Northwestern University

Bill Yang, Georgia Southern University

Ben Young, University of Missouri, Kansas City

Darrel Young, University of Texas

Michael Youngblood, Rock Valley College

Jay Zagorsky, Boston University

Alexander Zampieron, Bentley College

Sourushe Zandvakili, University of Cincinnati

Walter J. Zeiler, University of Michigan

Abera Zeyege, Ball State University

James Ziliak, Indiana University, Bloomington

Jason Zimmerman, South Dakota State University

We welcome comments about the 12th edition. Please write to us care of David Alexander, Executive Editor, Pearson Economics, 501 Boylston Street, Boston, MA 02116.

Karl E. Case

Ray C. Fair

Sharon M. Oster

Save a Tree!

Many of the components of the teaching and learning package are available online. Online supplements conserve paper and allow you to select and print only the material you plan to use. For more information, please contact your Pearson sales representative.

Principles of
Microeconomics

The Scope and Method of Economics

1

The study of economics should begin with a sense of wonder. Pause for a moment and consider a typical day in your life. It might start with a bagel made in a local bakery with flour produced in Minnesota from wheat grown in Kansas. After class you drive with a friend on an interstate highway that is part of a system that took 20 years and billions of dollars to build. You stop for gasoline refined in Louisiana from Saudi Arabian crude oil. Later, you log onto the Web with a laptop assembled in Indonesia from parts made in China and Skype with your brother in Mexico City. You use or consume tens of thousands of things. Somebody organized men and women and materials to produce and distribute them. Thousands of decisions went into their completion, and somehow they got to you.

In the United States, about 150 million people—almost half the total population—work at hundreds of thousands of different jobs producing nearly $18 trillion worth of goods and services every year. Some cannot find work; some choose not to work. The United States imports more than $300 billion worth of automobiles and parts and more than $350 billion worth of petroleum and petroleum products each year; it exports around $140 billion worth of agricultural products, including food. In the modern economy, consumers' choices include products made all over the globe.

Economics is the study of how individuals and societies choose to use the scarce resources that nature and previous generations have provided. The key word in this definition is *choose*. Economics is a behavioral, or social, science. In large measure, it is the study of how people make choices. The choices that people make, when added up, translate into societal choices.

economics The study of how individuals and societies choose to use the scarce resources that nature and previous generations have provided.

Identify three key reasons to study economics. Think of an example from your life in which understanding opportunity costs or the principle of efficient markets could make a difference in your decision making.

opportunity cost The best alternative that we forgo, or give up, when we make a choice or a decision.

scarce Limited.

marginalism The process of analyzing the additional or incremental costs or benefits arising from a choice or decision.

The purpose of this chapter and the next is to elaborate on this definition and to introduce the subject matter of economics. What is produced? How is it produced? Who gets it? Why? Is the result good or bad? Can it be improved?

Why Study Economics?

There are three main reasons to study economics: to learn a way of thinking, to understand society, and to be an informed citizen.

To Learn a Way of Thinking

Probably the most important reason for studying economics is to learn a way of thinking. Economics has three fundamental concepts that, once absorbed, can change the way you look at everyday choices: opportunity cost, marginalism, and the working of efficient markets.

Opportunity Cost What happens in an economy is the outcome of thousands of individual decisions. People must decide how to divide their incomes among all the goods and services available in the marketplace. They must decide whether to work, whether to go to school, and how much to save. Businesses must decide what to produce, how much to produce, how much to charge, and where to locate. Economic analysis provides a structured way of thinking about these types of decisions.

Nearly all decisions involve trade-offs. A key concept that recurs in analyzing the decision-making process is the notion of *opportunity cost*. The full "cost" of making a specific choice includes what we give up by not making the best alternative choice. The best alternative that we forgo, or give up, when we make a choice or a decision is called the **opportunity cost** of that decision.

When asked how much a movie costs, most people cite the ticket price. For an economist, this is only part of the answer: to see a movie takes not only a ticket but also time. The opportunity cost of going to a movie is the value of the other things you could have done with the same money and time. If you decide to take time off from work, the opportunity cost of your leisure is the pay that you would have earned had you worked. Part of the cost of a college education is the income you could have earned by working full-time instead of going to school.

Opportunity costs arise because resources are scarce. **Scarce** simply means limited. Consider one of our most important resources—time. There are only 24 hours in a day, and we must live our lives under this constraint. A farmer in rural Brazil must decide whether it is better to continue to farm or to go to the city and look for a job. A hockey player at the University of Vermont must decide whether to play on the varsity team or spend more time studying.

Marginalism A second key concept used in analyzing choices is the notion of **marginalism**. In weighing the costs and benefits of a decision, it is important to weigh only the costs and benefits that arise from the decision. Suppose, for example, that you live in New Orleans and that you are weighing the costs and benefits of visiting your mother in Iowa. If business required that you travel to Kansas City anyway, the cost of visiting Mom would be only the additional, or *marginal*, time and money cost of getting to Iowa from Kansas City.

There are numerous examples in which the concept of marginal cost is useful. For an airplane that is about to take off with empty seats, the marginal cost of an extra passenger is essentially zero; the total cost of the trip is roughly unchanged by the addition of an extra passenger. Thus, setting aside a few seats to be sold at big discounts through www.priceline.com or other Web sites can be profitable even if the fare for those seats is far below the average cost per seat of making the trip. As long as the airline succeeds in filling seats that would otherwise have been empty, doing so is profitable.

Efficient Markets—No Free Lunch Suppose you are ready to check out of a busy grocery store on the day before a storm and seven checkout registers are open with several people in each line. Which line should you choose? Clearly you should go to the shortest line! But if everyone thinks this way—as is likely—all the lines will be equally long as people move around. Economists often loosely refer to "good deals" or risk-free ventures as *profit opportunities*. Using the term loosely, a profit opportunity exists at the checkout lines when one line is shorter than the others. In general, such profit opportunities are rare. At any time, many people are searching for them; as a consequence, few exist. Markets like this, where any profit opportunities are eliminated almost instantaneously, are said to be **efficient markets**. (We discuss *markets*, the institutions through which buyers and sellers interact and engage in exchange, in detail in Chapter 2.)

> **efficient market** A market in which profit opportunities are eliminated almost instantaneously.

The common way of expressing the efficient markets concept is "there's no such thing as a free lunch." How should you react when a stockbroker calls with a hot tip on the stock market? With skepticism. Thousands of individuals each day are looking for hot tips in the market. If a particular tip about a stock is valid, there will be an immediate rush to buy the stock, which will quickly drive up its price. This view that very few profit opportunities exist can, of course, be carried too far. There is a story about two people walking along, one an economist and one not. The non-economist sees a $20 bill on the sidewalk and says, "There's a $20 bill on the sidewalk." The economist replies, "That is not possible. If there were, somebody would already have picked it up."

There are clearly times when profit opportunities exist. Someone has to be first to get the news, and some people have quicker insights than others. Nevertheless, news travels fast, and there are thousands of people with quick insights. The general view that large profit opportunities are rare is close to the mark and is powerful in helping to guide decision making.

> The study of economics teaches us a way of thinking and helps us make decisions.

To Understand Society

Another reason for studying economics is to understand society better. Past and present economic decisions have an enormous influence on the character of life in a society. The current state of the physical environment, the level of material well-being, and the nature and number of jobs are all products of the economic system.

At no time has the impact of economic change on a society been more evident than in England during the late eighteenth and early nineteenth centuries, a period that we now call the **Industrial Revolution**. Increases in the productivity of agriculture, new manufacturing technologies, and development of more efficient forms of transportation led to a massive movement of the British population from the countryside to the city. At the beginning of the eighteenth century, approximately 2 out of 3 people in Great Britain worked in agriculture. By 1812, only 1 in 3 remained in agriculture; by 1900, the figure was fewer than 1 in 10. People jammed into overcrowded cities and worked long hours in factories. England had changed completely in two centuries—a period that in the run of history was nothing more than the blink of an eye.

> **Industrial Revolution** The period in England during the late eighteenth and early nineteenth centuries in which new manufacturing technologies and improved transportation gave rise to the modern factory system and a massive movement of the population from the countryside to the cities.

The discipline of economics began to take shape during this period. Social critics and philosophers looked around and knew that their philosophies must expand to accommodate the changes. Adam Smith's *Wealth of Nations* appeared in 1776. It was followed by the writings of David Ricardo, Karl Marx, Thomas Malthus, and others. Each tried to make sense out of what was happening. Who was building the factories? Why? What determined the level of wages paid to workers or the price of food? What would happen in the future, and what *should* happen? The people who asked these questions were the first economists.

Societal changes are often driven by economics. Consider the developments in the early years of the World Wide Web. Changes in the ways people communicate with one another and with the rest of the world, largely created by private enterprise seeking profits, have affected almost every aspect of our lives, from the way we interact with friends and family to the jobs that we have and the way cities and governments are organized.

> The study of economics is an essential part of the study of society.

To Be an Informed Citizen

A knowledge of economics is essential to being an informed citizen. Between 2008 and 2013 much of the world struggled with a major recession and slow recovery, leaving millions of people around the world out of work. Understanding what happens in a recession and what the government can and cannot do to help in a recovery is an essential part of being an informed citizen.

Economics is also essential in understanding a range of other everyday government decisions at the local and federal levels. Why do governments pay for public schools and roads, but not cell phones? The federal government under President Barack Obama moved toward universal health care for U.S. citizens. What are the pros and cons of this policy? In some states, scalping tickets to a ball game is illegal. Is this a good policy or not? Every day, across the globe, people engage in political decision making around questions like these, questions that depend on an understanding of economics.

> To be an informed citizen requires a basic understanding of economics.

1.2 LEARNING OBJECTIVE

Describe microeconomics, macroeconomics, and the diverse fields of economics.

The Scope of Economics

Most students taking economics for the first time are surprised by the breadth of what they study. Some think that economics will teach them about the stock market or what to do with their money. Others think that economics deals exclusively with problems such as inflation and unemployment. In fact, it deals with all those subjects, but they are pieces of a much larger puzzle. Economists use their tools to study a wide range of topics.

The easiest way to get a feel for the breadth and depth of what you will be studying is to explore briefly the way economics is organized. First of all, there are two major divisions of economics: microeconomics and macroeconomics.

Microeconomics and Macroeconomics

microeconomics The branch of economics that examines the functioning of individual industries and the behavior of individual decision-making units—that is, firms and households.

Microeconomics deals with the functioning of individual industries and the behavior of individual economic decision-making units: firms and households. Firms' choices about what to produce and how much to charge and households' choices about what and how much to buy help to explain why the economy produces the goods and services it does.

Another big question addressed by microeconomics is who gets the goods and services that are produced? Understanding the forces that determine the distribution of output is the province of microeconomics. Microeconomics helps us to understand how resources are distributed among households. What determines who is rich and who is poor?

macroeconomics The branch of economics that examines the economic behavior of aggregates—income, employment, output, and so on—on a national scale.

Macroeconomics looks at the economy as a whole. Instead of trying to understand what determines the output of a single firm or industry or what the consumption patterns are of a single household or group of households, macroeconomics examines the factors that determine national output, or national product. Microeconomics is concerned with *household* income; macroeconomics deals with *national income*.

Whereas microeconomics focuses on individual product prices and relative prices, macroeconomics looks at the overall price level and how quickly (or slowly) it is rising (or falling). Microeconomics questions how many people will be hired (or fired) this year in a particular industry or in a certain geographic area and focuses on the factors that determine how much labor a firm or an industry will hire. Macroeconomics deals with *aggregate* employment and unemployment: how many jobs exist in the economy as a whole and how many people who are willing to work are not able to find work.

ECONOMICS IN PRACTICE

iPod and the World

It is impossible to understand the workings of an economy without first understanding the ways in which economies are connected across borders. The United States was importing goods and services at a rate of more than $2.8 trillion per year in 2014 and was exporting at a rate of more than $2.3 trillion per year.

For literally hundreds of years, the virtues of free trade have been the subject of heated debate. Opponents have argued that buying foreign-produced goods costs Americans jobs and hurts U.S. producers. Proponents argue that there are gains from trade—that all countries can gain from specializing in the production of the goods and services they produce best.

In the modern world, it is not always easy to track where products are made. A sticker that says "Made in China" can often be misleading. Recent studies of two iconic U.S. products, the iPod and the Barbie doll, make this complexity clear.

The Barbie doll is one of Mattel's best and longest selling products. The Barbie was designed in the United States. It is made of plastic fashioned in Taiwan, which came originally from the Mideast in the form of petroleum. Barbie's hair comes from Japan, while the cloth for her clothes mostly comes from China. Most of the assembly of the Barbie is also done in China, using, as we see, pieces from across the globe. A doll that sells for $10 in the United States carries an export value when leaving Hong Kong of $2, of which only 35 cents is for Chinese labor, with most of the rest covering transportation and raw materials. Because the Barbie comes to the United States from assembly in China and transport from Hong Kong, some would count it as being produced in China. Yet, for this Barbie, $8 of its retail value of $10 is captured by the United States![1]

The iPod is similar. A recent study by three economists, Greg Linden, Kenneth Kraemer, and Jason Dedrick, found that once one includes Apple's payment for its intellectual property, distribution costs, and production costs for some components, almost 80 percent of the retail price of the iPod is captured by the United States.[2] Moreover, for some of the

other parts of the iPod, it is not easy to tell exactly where they are produced. The hard drive, a relatively expensive component, was produced in Japan by Toshiba, but some of the components of that hard drive were actually produced elsewhere in Asia. Indeed, for the iPod, which is composed of many small parts, it is almost impossible to accurately tell exactly where each piece was produced without pulling it apart.

So, next time you see a label saying "Made in China" keep in mind that from an economics point of view, one often has to dig a little deeper to see what is really going on.

THINKING PRACTICALLY

1. What do you think accounts for *where* components of the iPod and Barbie are made?

[1] For a discussion of the Barbie see Robert Feenstra, "Integration of Trade and Disintegration of Production in the Global Economy," *Journal of Economic Perspectives,* Fall 1998: 31–50.

[2] Greg Linden, Kenneth Kraemer, and Jason Dedrick, "Who Profits from Innovation in Global Value Chains?" *Industrial and Corporate Change,* 2010: 81–116.

To summarize:

> Microeconomics looks at the individual unit—the household, the firm, the industry. It sees and examines the "trees." Macroeconomics looks at the whole, the aggregate. It sees and analyzes the "forest."

Table 1.1 summarizes these divisions of economics and some of the subjects with which they are concerned.

The Diverse Fields of Economics

Individual economists focus their research and study in many different areas. The subfields of economics are listed in Table 1.2 along with a sample research or policy question that an economist in this subfield might study.

TABLE 1.1   Examples of Microeconomic and Macroeconomic Concerns

Division of Economics	Production	Prices	Income	Employment
Microeconomics	*Production/output in individual industries and businesses* How much steel How much office space How many cars	*Prices of individual goods and services* Price of medical care Price of gasoline Food prices Apartment rents	*Distribution of income and wealth* Wages in the auto industry Minimum wage Executive salaries Poverty	*Employment by individual businesses and industries* Jobs in the steel industry Number of employees in a firm Number of accountants
Macroeconomics	*National production/output* Total industrial output Gross domestic product Growth of output	*Aggregate price level* Consumer prices Producer prices Rate of inflation	*National income* Total wages and salaries Total corporate profits	*Employment and unemployment in the economy* Total number of jobs Unemployment rate

TABLE 1.2   The Fields of Economics

Behavioral economics	Do aggregate household savings increase when we automatically enroll people in savings programs and let them opt out as opposed to requiring them to sign up?
Comparative economic systems	How does the resource allocation process differ in market versus command and control systems?
Econometrics	What inferences can we make based on conditional moment inequalities?
Economic development	Does increasing employment opportunities for girls in developing nations increase their educational achievement?
Economic history	How did the growth of railroads and improvement in transportation more generally change the U.S. banking systems in the nineteenth century?
Environmental economics	What effect would a tax on carbon have on emissions? Is a tax better or worse than rules?
Finance	Is high frequency trading socially beneficial?
Health economics	Do co-pays by patients change the choice and use of medicines by insured patients?
The history of economic thought	How did Aristotle think about just prices?
Industrial organization	How do we explain price wars in the airline industry?
International economics	What are the benefits and costs of free trade? Does concern about the environment change our views of free trade?
Labor economics	Will increasing the minimum wage decrease employment opportunities?
Law and economics	Does the current U.S. patent law increase or decrease the rate of innovation?
Public economics	Why is corruption more widespread in some countries than in others?
Urban and regional economics	Do enterprise zones improve employment opportunities in central cities?

The Method of Economics

1.3 LEARNING OBJECTIVE
Think about an example of bad causal inference leading to erroneous decision making. Identify the four main goals of economic policy.

Economics asks and attempts to answer two kinds of questions: positive and normative. **Positive economics** attempts to understand behavior and the operation of economic systems *without making judgments* about whether the outcomes are good or bad. It strives to describe what exists and how it works. What determines the wage rate for unskilled workers? What would happen if we abolished the corporate income tax? The answers to such questions are the subject of positive economics.

In contrast, **normative economics** looks at the outcomes of economic behavior and asks whether they are good or bad and whether they can be made better. Normative economics involves judgments and prescriptions for courses of action. Should the government subsidize or regulate the cost of higher education? Should the United States allow importers to sell foreign-produced goods that compete with U.S.-made products? Should we reduce or eliminate inheritance taxes? Normative economics is often called *policy economics*.

Of course, most normative questions involve positive questions. To know whether the government *should* take a particular action, we must know first if it *can* and second what the consequences are likely to be.

positive economics   An approach to economics that seeks to understand behavior and the operation of systems without making judgments. It describes what exists and how it works.

normative economics   An approach to economics that analyzes outcomes of economic behavior, evaluates them as good or bad, and may prescribe courses of action. Also called *policy economics*.

Theories and Models

In many disciplines, including physics, chemistry, meteorology, political science, and economics, theorists build formal models of behavior. A **model** is a formal statement of a theory. It is usually a mathematical statement of a presumed relationship between two or more variables.

A **variable** is a measure that can change from time to time or from observation to observation. Income is a variable—it has different values for different people and different values for the same person at different times. The price of a quart of milk is a variable; it has different values at different stores and at different times. There are countless other examples.

Because all models simplify reality by stripping part of it away, they are abstractions. Critics of economics often point to abstraction as a weakness. Most economists, however, see abstraction as a real strength.

The easiest way to see how abstraction can be helpful is to think of a map. A map is a representation of reality that is simplified and abstract. A city or state appears on a piece of paper as a series of lines and colors. The amount of reality that the mapmaker can strip away before the map loses something essential depends on what the map will be used for. If you want to drive from St. Louis to Phoenix, you need to know only the major interstate highways and roads. However, to travel around Phoenix, you may need to see every street and alley.

Like maps, economic models are abstractions that strip away detail to expose only those aspects of behavior that are important to the question being asked. The principle that irrelevant detail should be cut away is called the principle of **Ockham's razor** after the fourteenth-century philosopher William of Ockham.

Be careful—although abstraction is a powerful tool for exposing and analyzing specific aspects of behavior, it is possible to oversimplify. Economic models often strip away a good deal of social and political reality to get at underlying concepts. When an economic theory is used to help formulate actual government or institutional policy, political and social reality must often be reintroduced if the policy is to have a chance of working.

The appropriate amount of simplification and abstraction depends on the use to which the model will be put. To return to the map example: You do not want to walk around San Francisco with a map made for drivers—there are too many very steep hills.

model   A formal statement of a theory, usually a mathematical statement of a presumed relationship between two or more variables.

variable   A measure that can change from time to time or from observation to observation.

Ockham's razor   The principle that irrelevant detail should be cut away.

All Else Equal   It is usually true that whatever you want to explain with a model depends on more than one factor. Suppose, for example, that you want to explain the total number of miles driven by automobile owners in the United States. Many things might affect total miles driven. More or fewer people may be driving. This number, in turn, can be affected by changes in the driving age, by population growth, or by changes in state laws. Other factors might include the price of gasoline, the household's income, the number and age of children in the household, the distance from home to work, the location of shopping facilities, and the availability and quality of public transport. When any of these variables change, the members of the household may drive more or less. If changes in any of these variables affect large numbers of households across the country, the total number of miles driven will change.

Very often we need to isolate or separate these effects. For example, suppose we want to know the impact on driving of a higher tax on gasoline. This increased tax would raise the price of gasoline at the pump, and this could reduce driving.

To isolate the impact of one single factor, we use the device of *ceteris paribus*, **or all else equal**. We ask, "What is the impact of a change in gasoline price on driving behavior, ceteris paribus, or assuming that nothing else changes?" If gasoline prices rise by 10 percent, how much less driving will there be, assuming no simultaneous change in anything else—that is, assuming that income, number of children, population, laws, and so on, all remain constant? Using the device of ceteris paribus is one part of the process of abstraction. In formulating economic theory, the concept helps us simplify reality to focus on the relationships that interest us.

Expressing Models in Words, Graphs, and Equations Consider the following statements: Lower airline ticket prices cause people to fly more frequently. Higher gasoline prices cause people to drive less and to buy more fuel-efficient cars. By themselves, these observations are of some interest. But for a firm, government, or an individual to make good decisions, oftentimes they need to know more. How much does driving fall when prices rise? Quantitative analysis is an important part of economics as well. Throughout this book, we will use both graphs and equations to capture the quantitative side of our economic observations and predictions. The appendix to this chapter reviews some graphing techniques.

Cautions and Pitfalls In formulating theories and models, it is especially important to seperate causation from correlation.

What Is Really Causal? In much of economics, we are interested in cause and effect. But cause and effect are often difficult to figure out. Recently, many people in the United States have begun to worry about consumption of soda and obesity. Some areas have begun taxing soda, trying to raise the price so that people will drink less of it. Is this working? Answering this question turns out to be hard. Suppose we see that one city raises the tax and at more or less the same time, soda consumption falls. Did the increased tax and price really *cause* all or most of the change in behavior? Or perhaps the city that voted the soda tax increase is more health conscious than its neighbors and it is that health consciousness that accounts for both the town's decision to raise taxes *and* its reduction in soda purchases. In this case, raising taxes in the neighboring towns will not necessarily reduce soda consumption. Sorting out causality from correlation is not always easy, particularly when one wants a quantitative answer to a question.

In our everyday lives, we often confuse causality. When two events occur in a sequence, it seems natural to think A caused B. I walked under a ladder and subsequently stubbed my toe. Did the ladder cause my bad luck? Most of us would laugh at this. But everyday we hear stock market analysts make a similar causal jump. "Today the Dow Jones industrial average rose 100 points on heavy trading due to progress in talks between Israel and Syria." How do they know this? Investors respond to many news events on any given day. Figuring out which one, if any, causes the stock market to rise is not easy. The error of inferring causality from two events happening one after the other is called the ***post hoc, ergo propter hoc*** fallacy ("after this, therefore because of this"). The *Economics in Practice* box describes a causality confusion in looking at peer effects.

Testing Theories and Models: Empirical Economics In science, a theory is rejected when it fails to explain what is observed or when another theory better explains what is observed. The collection and use of data to test economic theories is called **empirical economics**.

Numerous large data sets are available to facilitate economic research. For example, economists studying the labor market can now test behavioral theories against the actual working experiences of thousands of randomly selected people who have been surveyed continuously since the 1960s. Macroeconomists continuously monitoring and studying the behavior of the national economy at the National Bureau of Economic Research (NBER), analyze thousands of items of data, collected by both government agencies and private companies, over the Internet. Firms like Google, Uber, and Amazon have an enormous amount of data about individual consumers that they analyze with the help of PhD economists to understand consumers' buying

---

ceteris paribus, or all else equal A device used to analyze the relationship between two variables while the values of other variables are held unchanged.

post hoc, ergo propter hoc Literally, "after this (in time), therefore because of this." A common error made in thinking about causation: If Event A happens before Event B, it is not necessarily true that A caused B.

empirical economics The collection and use of data to test economic theories.

ECONOMICS IN PRACTICE

Does Your Roommate Matter for Your Grades?

Most parents are concerned about their children's friends. Often they worry that if one of their children has a misbehaving friend, their own child will be led astray. And, in fact, in many areas of life, there are strong indications that *peer effects* matter. The likelihood that a child will be obese, have difficulties in school, or engage in criminal activity all seem to be higher if their friends also have these issues. And yet, in looking at peer effects, it is not hard to see the problem of causality we described in the text. At least to some extent, children choose their own friends. The father worried about the bad influence of his son's friends on his own son should perhaps be equally worried about what his son's choice of friends says about that son's inclinations. Did the friends cause the misbehavior or did an inclination toward mischief cause the son's choice of friends?

Sorting out causality in peer effects, given that peer groups are oftentimes partially a matter of choice, is difficult. But several recent economics studies of the effect of roommates on college grades do a nice job of sorting out the causality puzzle. Dartmouth college, in common with many other schools, randomly assigns roommates to freshmen. In this case, part of a student's peer group—his or her roommate—is not a matter of choice, but a matter of chance. Bruce Sacerdote, a professor at Dartmouth, used data on freshmen academic and social performance, combined with their background data, to test the peer effects from different types of roommates.[1] Sacerdote found that after taking into account many background characteristics, there were strong roommate effects both on grade point average, effort in school, and fraternity membership.

Of course, a roommate is only part of one's peer group. At the U.S. Air Force Academy, students are assigned to 30-person squadrons with whom they eat, study, live, and do intramural sports. Again, these groups were randomly assigned, so one did not have the problem of similarly inclined people choosing one another. Scott Carrell, Richard Fullerton, and James West found that for this intense peer group, there were strong peer effects on academic effort and performance.[2] The bottom line: Choose your friends wisely!

THINKING PRACTICALLY

1. Would you expect college seniors who choose their own roommates to have more or less similar grades than college freshmen who are assigned as roommates? Why or why not?

[1] Bruce Sacerdote, "Peer Effects with Random Assignment: Results for Dartmouth Roommates," *Quarterly Journal of Economics*, 2001: 681–704.
[2] Scott E. Carrell, Richard L. Fullerton, and James E. West, "Does Your Cohort Matter? Measuring Peer Effects in College Achievement," *Journal of Labor Economics*, 2009: 439–464.

behavior and improve the profitability of their businesses. In doing this analysis, economicsts have learned to be especially careful about causality issues.

In the natural sciences, controlled experiments, typically done in the lab, are a standard way of testing theories. In recent years, economics has seen an increase in the use of experiments, both in the field and in the lab, as a tool to test its theories. One economist, John List of Chicago, tested the effect on prices of changing the way auctions for rare baseball cards were run by sports memorabilia dealers in trade shows. (The experiment used a standard Cal Ripkin Jr. card.) Another economist, Keith Chen of UCLA, has used experiments with monkeys to investigate the deeper biological roots of human decision making.

Economic Policy

Economic theory helps us understand how the world works, but the formulation of *economic policy* requires a second step. We must have objectives. What do we want to change? Why? What is good and what is bad about the way the system is operating? Can we make it better?

Such questions force us to be specific about the grounds for judging one outcome superior to another. What does it mean to be better? Four criteria are frequently applied in judging economic outcomes:

1. Efficiency
2. Equity
3. Growth
4. Stability

Efficiency In physics, "efficiency" refers to the ratio of useful energy delivered by a system to the energy supplied to it. An efficient automobile engine, for example, is one that uses a small amount of fuel per mile for a given level of power.

In economics, **efficiency** means *allocative efficiency*. An efficient economy is one that produces what people want at the least possible cost. If the system allocates resources to the production of goods and services that nobody wants, it is inefficient. If all members of a particular society were vegetarians and somehow half of all that society's resources were used to produce meat, the result would be inefficient.

The clearest example of an efficient change is a voluntary exchange. If you and I each want something that the other has and we agree to exchange, we are both better off and no one loses. When a company reorganizes its production or adopts a new technology that enables it to produce more of its product with fewer resources, without sacrificing quality, it has made an efficient change. At least potentially, the resources saved could be used to produce more of something else.

Inefficiencies can arise in numerous ways. Sometimes they are caused by government regulations or tax laws that distort otherwise sound economic decisions. Suppose that land in Ohio is best suited for corn production and that land in Kansas is best suited for wheat production. A law that requires Kansas to produce only corn and Ohio to produce only wheat would be inefficient. If firms that cause environmental damage are not held accountable for their actions, the incentive to minimize those damages is lost and the result is inefficient.

Equity While efficiency has a fairly precise definition that can be applied with some degree of rigor, **equity** (fairness) lies in the eye of the beholder. To many, fairness implies a more equal distribution of income and wealth. For others, fairness involves giving people what they earn. In 2013, French economist Thomas Piketty's popular new book *Capital in the Twenty-First Century*, brought new historical data to our attention on the extent of inequality across the Western world.

Growth As the result of technological change, the building of machinery, and the acquisition of knowledge, societies learn to produce new goods and services and to produce old ones better. In the early days of the U.S. economy, it took nearly half the population to produce the required food supply. Today less than 2 percent of the country's population works in agriculture.

When we devise new and better ways of producing the goods and services we use now and when we develop new goods and services, the total amount of production in the economy increases. **Economic growth** is an increase in the total output of an economy. If output grows faster than the population, output per person rises and standards of living increase. Rural and agrarian societies become modern industrial societies as a result of economic growth and rising per capita output.

Some policies discourage economic growth, and others encourage it. Tax laws, for example, can be designed to encourage the development and application of new production techniques. Research and development in some societies are subsidized by the government. Building roads, highways, bridges, and transport systems in developing countries may speed up the process of economic growth. If businesses and wealthy people invest their wealth outside their country rather than in their country's industries, growth in their home country may be slowed.

Stability Economic **stability** refers to the condition in which national output is growing steadily, with low inflation and full employment of resources. During the 1950s and 1960s, the U.S. economy experienced a long period of relatively steady growth, stable prices, and low unemployment. The decades of the 1970s and 1980s, however, were not as stable. The United States experienced two periods of rapid price inflation (more than 10 percent) and two periods

efficiency In economics, "efficiency" means "allocative efficiency." An efficient economy is one that produces what people want at the least possible cost.

equity Fairness.

economic growth An increase in the total output of an economy.

stability A condition in which national output is growing steadily, with low inflation and full employment of resources.

of severe unemployment. In 1982, for example, 12 million people (10.8 percent of the work-force) were looking for work. The beginning of the 1990s was another period of instability, with a recession occurring in 1990–1991. In 2008–2009, much of the world, including the United States, experienced a large contraction in output and rise in unemployment, the effects of which lasted until 2013. This was clearly an unstable period.

The causes of instability and the ways in which governments have attempted to stabilize the economy are the subject matter of macroeconomics.

An Invitation

This chapter has prepared you for your study of economics. The first part of the chapter invited you into an exciting discipline that deals with important issues and questions. You cannot begin to understand how a society functions without knowing something about its economic history and its economic system.

The second part of the chapter introduced the method of reasoning that economics requires and some of the tools that economics uses. We believe that learning to think in this powerful way will help you better understand the world.

As you proceed, it is important that you keep track of what you have learned in previous chapters. This book has a plan; it proceeds step-by-step, each section building on the last. It would be a good idea to read each chapter's table of contents at the start of each chapter and scan each chapter before you read it to make sure you understand where it fits in the big picture.

——————— SUMMARY ———————

1. *Economics* is the study of how individuals and societies choose to use the scarce resources that nature and previous generations have provided.

1.1 WHY STUDY ECONOMICS? *p. 2*

2. There are many reasons to study economics, including (a) to learn a way of thinking, (b) to understand society, and (c) to be an informed citizen.

3. The best alternative that we forgo when we make a choice or a decision is the *opportunity cost* of that decision.

1.2 THE SCOPE OF ECONOMICS *p. 4*

4. *Microeconomics* deals with the functioning of individual markets and industries and with the behavior of individual decision-making units: business firms and households.

5. *Macroeconomics* looks at the economy as a whole. It deals with the economic behavior of aggregates—national output, national income, the overall price level, and the general rate of inflation.

6. Economics is a broad and diverse discipline with many special fields of inquiry. These include economic history, international economics, and urban economics.

1.3 THE METHOD OF ECONOMICS *p. 7*

7. Economics asks and attempts to answer two kinds of questions: positive and normative. *Positive economics* attempts to understand behavior and the operation of economies without making judgments about whether the outcomes are good or bad. *Normative economics* looks at the results of economic behavior and asks whether they are good or bad and whether they can be improved.

8. An economic *model* is a formal statement of an economic theory. Models simplify and abstract from reality.

9. It is often useful to isolate the effects of one variable on another while holding "all else constant." This is the device of *ceteris paribus*.

10. Models and theories can be expressed in many ways. The most common ways are in words, in graphs, and in equations.

11. Figuring out causality is often difficult in economics. Because one event happens before another, the second event does not necessarily happen as a result of the first. To assume that "after" implies "because" is to commit the fallacy of *post hoc, ergo propter hoc*.

12. *Empirical economics* involves the collection and use of data to test economic theories. In principle, the best model is the one that yields the most accurate predictions.

13. To make policy, one must be careful to specify criteria for making judgments. Four specific criteria are used most often in economics: *efficiency, equity, growth, and stability*.

REVIEW TERMS AND CONCEPTS

ceteris paribus, or all else equal, p. 8

economic growth, *p. 10*

economics, *p. 1*

efficiency, *p. 10*

efficient market, *p. 3*

empirical economics, *p. 8*

equity, *p. 10*

Industrial Revolution, *p. 3*

macroeconomics, *p. 4*

marginalism, *p. 2*

microeconomics, *p. 4*

model, *p. 7*

normative economics, *p. 7*

Ockham's razor, *p. 7*

opportunity cost, *p. 2*

positive economics, *p. 7*

post hoc, ergo propter hoc, p. 8

scarce, *p. 2*

stability, *p. 10*

variable, *p. 7*

PROBLEMS

All problems are available on MyEconLab.

1.1 WHY STUDY ECONOMICS

LEARNING OBJECTIVE: Identify three key reasons to study economics. Think of an example from your life in which understanding opportunity costs or the principle of efficient markets could make a difference in your decision making.

1.1 One of the scarce resources that constrain our behavior is time. Each of us has only 24 hours in a day. How do you go about allocating your time in a given day among competing alternatives? How do you go about weighing the alternatives? Once you choose a most important use of time, why do you not spend all your time on it? Use the notion of opportunity cost in your answer.

1.2 Every Friday night, Gustavo pays $39.99 to eat nothing but crab legs at the all-you-can-eat seafood buffet at the M Resort in Las Vegas. On average, he consumes 28 crab legs each Friday. What is the average cost of each crab leg to Gustavo? What is the marginal cost of an additional crab leg?

1.3 For each of the following situations, identify the full cost (opportunity cost) involved:
   a. Monique quits her $50,000 per-year job as an accountant to become a full-time volunteer at a women's shelter.
   b. The Agrizone Corporation invests $12 million in a new inventory tracking system.
   c. Taylor receives $500 from his grandmother for his birthday and uses it all to buy shares of stock in Harley-Davidson, Inc.
   d. Hector decides to spend the summer backpacking across Europe after he graduates from Tulane University.
   e. After receiving her master's degree, Molly chooses to enter the doctoral program in Behavioral Science at the University of Texas.
   f. Sanjay chooses to use his vacation time to paint the exterior of his house.
   g. After a night of karaoke, Tiffany forgets to set her alarm and sleeps through her Calculus final exam.

1.4 On the *Forbes* 2015 list of the World's Billionaires, Bill Gates ranks at the top with a net worth of $79.2 billion.

Does this "richest man in the world" face scarcity, or does scarcity only affect those with more limited incomes and lower net worth?

Source: "The World's Billionaires," Forbes, March 2, 2015.

1.2 THE SCOPE OF ECONOMICS

LEARNING OBJECTIVE: Describe microeconomics, macroeconomics, and the diverse fields of economics.

2.1 **[Related to the *Economics in Practice* on p. 5]** Log onto www.census.gov/foreign-trade/statistics/state/. In the State Trade by Commodity and Country section, click on "Exports and Imports", then click on "Exports" for your state. There you will find a list of the top 25 commodities produced in your state which are exported around the world. In looking over that list, are you surprised by anything? Do you know any of the firms that produce these items? Search the Internet to find a company that does. Do some research and write a paragraph about this company: what it produces, how many people it employs, and whatever else you can learn about the firm. You might even call the company to obtain the information.

2.2 Explain whether each of the following is an example of a macroeconomic concern or a microeconomic concern.
   a. The Federal Aviation Administration (FAA) is considering increasing the number of takeoff and landing slots available at Ronald Reagan Washington National Airport.
   b. The president has proposed increasing the marginal tax rate for people whose annual earnings exceed $275,000 and lowering the marginal tax rate for those who earn less than $275,000.
   c. Walmart announced that it will increase its starting wage for employees to $10 per hour by February 2016.
   d. Congress extends the maximum duration for the collection of unemployment benefits from 26 weeks to 52 weeks.

1.3 THE METHOD OF ECONOMICS

LEARNING OBJECTIVE: Think about an example of bad causal inference leading to erroneous decision making. Identify the four main goals of economic policy.

3.1 In the summer of 2007, the housing market and the mortgage market were both in decline. Housing prices in most U.S. cities began to decline in mid-2006. With prices falling and the inventory of unsold houses rising, the production of new homes fell to around 1.5 million in 2007 from 2.3 million in 2005. With new construction falling dramatically, it was expected that construction *employment* would fall and that this would have the potential of slowing the national economy and increasing the general unemployment rate. Go to www.bls.gov and check out the recent data on total employment and construction employment. Have they gone up or down from their levels in August 2007? What has happened to the unemployment rate? Go to www.fhfa.gov and look at the housing price index. Have home prices risen or fallen since August 2007? Finally, look at the latest GDP release at www.bea.gov. Look at residential and nonresidential investment (Table 1.1.5) during the last 2 years. Do you see a pattern? Does it explain the employment numbers? Explain your answer

3.2 Which of the following statements are examples of positive economic analysis? Which are examples of normative analysis?
   a. A devaluation of the U.S. dollar would increase exports from the United States.
   b. Increasing the federal tax on gasoline would cause shipping costs in the United States to increase.
   c. Florida should devote all revenues from its state lottery to improving public education.
   d. Eliminating the trade embargo with Cuba would increase the number of Cuban cigars available in the United States.
   e. As a public safety measure, the state of Texas should not pass legislation that allows people with concealed handgun permits to carry concealed weapons on college campuses.

3.3 In 2012, Colorado and Washington became the first states to legalize marijuana for recreational use, and have since been joined by Oregon, Alaska and Washington, D.C. In 2014, Colorado is reported to have received more than $50 million in tax revenue from the sale of recreational marijuana, much of which was slated to be used for school construction. The potential for increased tax revenues and the benefits these revenues can provide has a number of other states contemplating the possible legalization of recreational-use marijuana.
   a. Recall that efficiency means producing what people want at the least cost. Can you make an efficiency argument in favor of states allowing the recreational use of marijuana?
   b. What nonmonetary costs might be associated with legalizing marijuana use? Would these costs have an impact on the efficiency argument you presented in part a?
   c. Using the concept of equity, argue for or against the legalization of recreational-use marijuana.
   d. What do you think would happen to the flow of tax revenue to state governments if all 50 states legalized marijuana?

3.4 [**Related to the *Economics in Practice* on p. 9**] Most college students either currently have, or at one time have had, roommates or housemates. Think about a time when you have shared your living space with one or more students, and describe the effect this person (or people) had on your college experience, such as your study habits, the classes you took, your grade point average, and the way you spent time away from the classroom. Now describe the effect you think you had on your roommate(s). Were these roommates or housemates people you chose to live with, or were they assigned randomly? Explain if you think this made a difference in your or their behavior?

3.5 Explain the pitfalls in the following statements.
   a. People who eat kale on a regular basis are more likely to exercise every day than people who do not eat kale. Therefore, exercising daily causes people to eat kale.
   b. Whenever the Chicago Cubs are down by 2 runs in the eighth inning, they usually come back to win whenever self-proclaimed Cubs fanatic Cassandra decides to watch the game with her pet ferret Bobo. Last night with the Cubs down by 2 runs in the eighth, Cassandra rushed to grab Bobo and as she expected, the Cubs won the game. Obviously, the Cubs won because Cassandra watched the game with Bobo by her side.
   c. The manager of a large retail furniture store found that sending his least productive salespeople to a week-long motivational training workshop resulted in a 15 percent increase in sales for those employees. Based on this success, the manager decided to spend the money to send all of his other salespeople to this workshop so sales would increase for everyone.

CHAPTER 1 APPENDIX: How to Read and Understand Graphs

LEARNING OBJECTIVE

Understand how data can be graphically represented.

graph A two-dimensional representation of a set of numbers or data.

time series graph A graph illustrating how a variable changes over time.

Economics is the most quantitative of the social sciences. If you flip through the pages of this or any other economics text, you will see countless tables and graphs. These serve a number of purposes. First, they illustrate important economic relationships. Second, they make difficult problems easier to understand and analyze. Finally, they can show patterns and regularities that may not be discernible in simple lists of numbers.

A **graph** is a two-dimensional representation of a set of numbers, or data. There are many ways that numbers can be illustrated by a graph.

Time Series Graphs

It is often useful to see how a single measure or variable changes over time. One way to present this information is to plot the values of the variable on a graph, with each value corresponding to a different time period. A graph of this kind is called a **time series graph**. On a time series graph, time is measured along the horizontal scale and the variable being graphed is measured along the vertical scale. Figure 1A.1 is a time series graph that presents the total disposable personal income in the U.S. economy for each year between 1975 and 2014.[1] This graph is based on

▶ FIGURE 1A.1 **Total Disposable Personal Income in the United States: 1975–2014 (in billions of dollars)**

Source: See Table 1A.1.

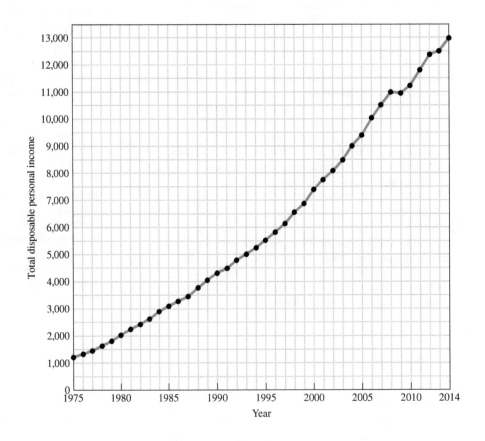

<hr>

[1] The measure of income presented in Table 1A.1 and in Figure 1A.1 is disposable personal income in billions of dollars. It is the total personal income received by all households in the United States minus the taxes that they pay.

	Total Disposable Personal Income		Total Disposable Personal Income
Year		**Year**	
1975	1,219	1995	5,533
1976	1,326	1996	5,830
1977	1,457	1997	6,149
1978	1,630	1998	6,561
1979	1,809	1999	6,876
1980	2,018	2000	7,401
1981	2,251	2001	7,752
1982	2,425	2002	8,099
1983	2,617	2003	8,486
1984	2,904	2004	9,002
1985	3,099	2005	9,401
1986	3,288	2006	10,037
1987	3,466	2007	10,507
1988	3,770	2008	10,994
1989	4,052	2009	10,943
1990	4,312	2010	11,238
1991	4,485	2011	11,801
1992	4,800	2012	12,384
1993	5,000	2013	12,505
1994	5,244	2014	12,981

TABLE 1A.1 Total Disposable Personal Income in the United States, 1975–2014 (in billions of dollars)

Source: U.S. Department of Commerce, Bureau of Economic Analysis.

the data found in Table 1A.1. By displaying these data graphically, we can see that total disposable income has increased every year between 1975 and 2014 except for a small dip in 2009.

Graphing Two Variables

More important than simple graphs of one variable are graphs that contain information on two variables at the same time. The most common method of graphing two variables is a graph constructed by drawing two perpendicular lines: a horizontal line, or **X-axis**, and a vertical line, or **Y-axis**. The axes contain measurement scales that intersect at 0 (zero). This point is called the **origin**. On the vertical scale, positive numbers lie above the horizontal axis (that is, above the origin) and negative numbers lie below it. On the horizontal scale, positive numbers lie to the right of the vertical axis (to the right of the origin) and negative numbers lie to the left of it. The point at which the graph intersects the Y-axis is called the **Y-intercept**. The point at which the graph intersects the X-axis is called the **X-intercept**. When two variables are plotted on a single graph, each point represents a pair of numbers. The first number is measured on the X-axis, and the second number is measured on the Y-axis.

Plotting Income and Consumption Data for Households

Table 1A.2 presents data from the Bureau of Labor Statistics (BLS) for 2012. This table shows average income and average spending for households ranked by income. For example, the average income for the top fifth (20 percent) of the households was $167,010 in 2012. The average spending for the top 20 percent was $99,368.

Figure 1A.2 presents the numbers from Table 1A.2 graphically. Along the horizontal scale, the X-axis, we measure average income. Along the vertical scale, the Y-axis, we measure average consumption spending. Each of the five pairs of numbers from the table is represented by a

X-axis The horizontal line against which a variable is plotted.

Y-axis The vertical line against which a variable is plotted.

origin The point at which the horizontal and vertical axes intersect.

Y-intercept The point at which a graph intersects the Y-axis.

X-intercept The point at which a graph intersects the X-axis.

▶ **FIGURE 1A.2**

Household Consumption and Income

A graph is a simple two-dimensional geometric representation of data. This graph displays the data from Table 1A.2. Along the horizontal scale (*X*-axis), we measure household income. Along the vertical scale (*Y*-axis), we measure household consumption.

Note: At point *A*, consumption equals $22,154 and income equals $9,988. At point *B*, consumption equals $32,632 and income equals $27,585.

Source: See Table 1A.2.

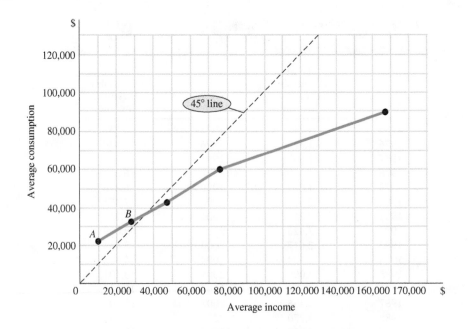

TABLE 1A.2	Consumption Expenditures and Income, 2012	
	Average Income Before Taxes	Average Consumption Expenditures
Bottom fifth	$ 9,988	$ 22,154
2nd fifth	27,585	32,632
3rd fifth	47,265	43,004
4th fifth	75,952	59,980
Top fifth	167,010	99,368

Source: Consumer Expenditures in 2012, U.S. Bureau of Labor Statistics.

positive relationship
A relationship between two variables, *X* and *Y*, in which a decrease in *X* is associated with a decrease in *Y*, and an increase in *X* is associated with an increase in *Y*.

negative relationship
A relationship between two variables, *X* and *Y*, in which a decrease in *X* is associated with an increase in *Y* and an increase in *X* is associated with a decrease in *Y*.

slope A measurement that indicates whether the relationship between variables is positive or negative and how much of a response there is in *Y* (the variable on the vertical axis) when *X* (the variable on the horizontal axis) changes.

point on the graph. Because all numbers are positive numbers, we need to show only the upper right quadrant of the coordinate system.

To help you read this graph, we have drawn a dotted line connecting all the points where consumption and income would be equal. *This 45-degree line does not represent any data.* Instead, it represents the line along which all variables on the *X*-axis correspond exactly to the variables on the *Y*-axis, for example, (10,000, 10,000), (20,000, 20,000), and (37,000, 37,000). The heavy blue line traces the data; the purpose of the dotted line is to help you read the graph.

There are several things to look for when reading a graph. The first thing you should notice is whether the line slopes upward or downward as you move from left to right. The blue line in Figure 1A.2 slopes upward, indicating that there seems to be a **positive relationship** between income and spending: The higher a household's income, the more a household tends to consume. If we had graphed the percentage of each group receiving welfare payments along the *Y*-axis, the line would presumably slope downward, indicating that welfare payments are lower at higher income levels. The income level/welfare payment relationship is thus a **negative relationship**.

Slope

The **slope** of a line or curve is a measure that indicates whether the relationship between the variables is positive or negative and how much of a response there is in *Y* (the variable on the vertical axis) when *X* (the variable on the horizontal axis) changes. The slope of a line between two points is

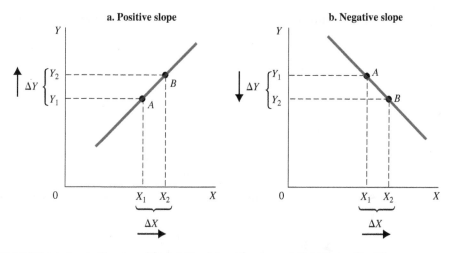

▲ **FIGURE 1A.3   A Curve with (a) Positive Slope and (b) Negative Slope**
A *positive* slope indicates that increases in *X* are associated with increases in *Y* and that decreases in *X* are associated with decreases in *Y*. A *negative* slope indicates the opposite—when *X* increases, *Y* decreases; and when *X* decreases, *Y* increases.

the change in the quantity measured on the *Y*-axis divided by the change in the quantity measured on the *X*-axis. We will normally use Δ (the Greek letter *delta*) to refer to a change in a variable. In Figure 1A.3, the slope of the line between points *A* and *B* is ΔY divided by ΔX. Sometimes it is easy to remember slope as "the rise over the run," indicating the vertical change over the horizontal change.

To be precise, ΔX between two points on a graph is simply X_2 minus X_1, where X_2 is the *X* value for the second point and X_1 is the *X* value for the first point. Similarly, ΔY is defined as Y_2 minus Y_1, where Y_2 is the *Y* value for the second point and Y_1 is the *Y* value for the first point. Slope is equal to

$$\frac{\Delta Y}{\Delta X} = \frac{Y_2 - Y_1}{X_2 - X_1}$$

As we move from *A* to *B* in Figure 1A.3(a), both *X* and *Y* increase; the slope is thus a positive number. However, as we move from *A* to *B* in Figure 1A.3(b), *X* increases [$(X_2 - X_1)$ is a positive number], but *Y* decreases [$(Y_2 - Y_1)$ is a negative number]. The slope in Figure 1A.3(b) is thus a negative number because a negative number divided by a positive number results in a negative quotient.

To calculate the numerical value of the slope between points *A* and *B* in Figure 1A.2, we need to calculate ΔY and ΔX. Because consumption is measured on the *Y*-axis, ΔY is 10,478 [$(Y_2 - Y_1) = (32,632 - 22,154)$]. Because income is measured along the *X*-axis, ΔX is 17,597 [$(X_2 - X_1) = (27,585 - 9,988)$]. The slope between *A* and *B* is

$$\frac{\Delta Y}{\Delta X} = \frac{10,478}{17,597} = +0.60.$$

Another interesting thing to note about the data graphed in Figure 1A.2 is that all the points lie roughly along a straight line. (If you look very closely, however, you can see that the slope declines as you move from left to right; the line becomes slightly less steep.) A straight line has a constant slope. That is, if you pick any two points along it and calculate the slope, you will always get the same number. A horizontal line has a zero slope (ΔY is zero); a vertical line has an "infinite" slope because ΔY is too big to be measured.

Unlike the slope of a straight line, the slope of a *curve* is continually changing. Consider, for example, the curves in Figure 1A.4. Figure 1A.4(a) shows a curve with a positive slope that decreases as you move from left to right. The easiest way to think about the concept of increasing

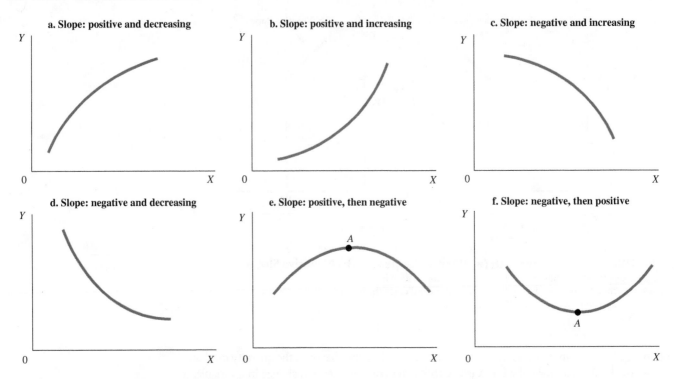

a. Slope: positive and decreasing

b. Slope: positive and increasing

c. Slope: negative and increasing

d. Slope: negative and decreasing

e. Slope: positive, then negative

f. Slope: negative, then positive

▲ FIGURE 1A.4 **Changing Slopes Along Curves**

or decreasing slope is to imagine what it is like walking up a hill from left to right. If the hill is steep, as it is in the first part of Figure 1A.4(a), you are moving more in the Y direction for each step you take in the X direction. If the hill is less steep, as it is further along in Figure 1A.4(a), you are moving less in the Y direction for every step you take in the X direction. Thus, when the hill is steep, slope ($\Delta Y/\Delta X$) is a larger number than it is when the hill is flatter. The curve in Figure 1A.4(b) has a positive slope, but its slope *increases* as you move from left to right.

The same analogy holds for curves that have a negative slope. Figure 1A.4(c) shows a curve with a negative slope that increases (in absolute value) as you move from left to right. This time think about skiing down a hill. At first, the descent in Figure 1A.4(c) is gradual (low slope), but as you proceed down the hill (to the right), you descend more quickly (high slope). Figure 1A.4(d) shows a curve with a negative slope that *decreases* (in absolute value) as you move from left to right.

In Figure 1A.4(e), the slope goes from positive to negative as X increases. In Figure 1A.4(f), the slope goes from negative to positive. At point A in both, the slope is zero. (Remember, slope is defined as $\Delta Y/\Delta X$. At point A, Y is not changing ($\Delta Y = 0$). Therefore, the slope at point A is zero.)

Some Precautions

When you read a graph, it is important to think carefully about what the points in the space defined by the axes represent. Table 1A.3 and Figure 1A.5 present a graph of consumption and income that is different from the one in Table 1A.2 and Figure 1A.2. First, each point in Figure 1A.5 represents a different year; in Figure 1A.2, each point represented a different group of households at the *same* point in time (2012). Second, the points in Figure 1A.5 represent *aggregate* consumption and income for the whole nation measured in *billions* of dollars; in Figure 1A.2, the points represented average *household* income and consumption measured in dollars.

It is interesting to compare these two graphs. All points on the aggregate consumption curve in Figure 1A.5 lie below the 45-degree line, which means that aggregate consumption is always less than aggregate income. However, the graph of average household income and consumption in Figure 1A.2 crosses the 45-degree line, implying that for some households, consumption is larger than income.

TABLE 1A.3 Aggregate Disposable Personal Income and Consumption for the United States, 1930–2014 (in billions of dollars)		
	Aggregate Disposable Personal Income	Aggregate Consumption
1930	75	70
1940	78	71
1950	215	192
1960	377	332
1970	762	648
1980	2,018	1,755
1990	4,312	3,826
2000	7,401	6,792
2010	11,238	10,202
2011	11,801	10,689
2012	12,384	11,083
2013	12,505	11,484
2014	12,981	11,928

Source: U.S. Department of Commerce, Bureau of Economic Analysis.

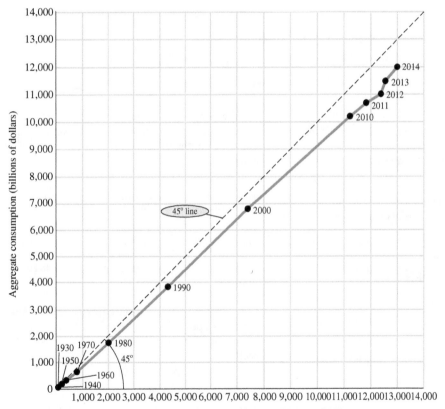

▲ **FIGURE 1A.5** **Disposable Personal Income and Consumption**

It is important to think carefully about what is represented by points in the space defined by the axes of a graph. In this graph, we have graphed income with consumption, as in Figure 1A.2, but here each observation point is national income and aggregate consumption in *different years*, measured in billions of dollars.

Source: See Table 1A.3.

APPENDIX SUMMARY

1. A *graph* is a two-dimensional representation of a set of numbers, or data. A *time series graph* illustrates how a single variable changes over time.

2. A graph of two variables includes an X (horizontal)-*axis* and a Y (vertical)-*axis*. The points at which the two axes intersect is called the *origin*. The point at which a graph intersects the Y-axis is called the *Y-intercept*. The point at which a graph intersects the X-axis is called the *X-intercept*.

3. The *slope* of a line or curve indicates whether the relationship between the two variables graphed is positive or negative and how much of a response there is in Y (the variable on the vertical axis) when X (the variable on the horizontal axis) changes. The slope of a line between two points is the change in the quantity measured on the Y-axis divided by the change in the quantity measured on the X-axis.

APPENDIX REVIEW TERMS AND CONCEPTS

graph, *p. 14*

negative relationship, *p. 16*

origin, *p. 15*

positive relationship, *p. 16*

slope, *p. 16*

time series graph, *p. 14*

X-axis, *p. 15*

X-intercept, *p. 15*

Y-axis, *p. 15*

Y-intercept, *p. 15*

APPENDIX PROBLEMS

All problems are available on MyEconLab.

CHAPTER 1 APPENDIX: HOW TO READ AND UNDERSTAND GRAPHS

LEARNING OBJECTIVE: Understand how data can be graphically represented.

1A.1 Graph each of the following sets of numbers. Draw a line through the points and calculate the slope of each line.

1		2		3		4		5		6	
X	Y	X	Y	X	Y	X	Y	X	Y	X	Y
1	5	1	25	0	0	0	40	0	0	0.1	100
2	10	2	20	10	10	10	30	10	10	0.2	75
3	15	3	15	20	20	20	20	20	20	0.3	50
4	20	4	10	30	30	30	10	30	10	0.4	25
5	25	5	5	40	40	40	0	40	0	0.5	0

1A.2 Plot the income and consumption data in the following table on a graph, with income on the X-axis. Does the data indicate a positive or negative relationship between income and consumption?

Households by Percentage	Average Income Before Taxes	Average Consumption Expenditures
Bottom fifth	$ 5,500	$ 16,000
2nd fifth	12,000	22,500
3rd fifth	37,800	35,000
4th fifth	59,000	46,800
Top fifth	95,000	72,500

1A.3 For each of the graphs in Figure 1, determine whether the curve has a positive or negative slope. Give an intuitive explanation for what is happening with the slope of each curve.

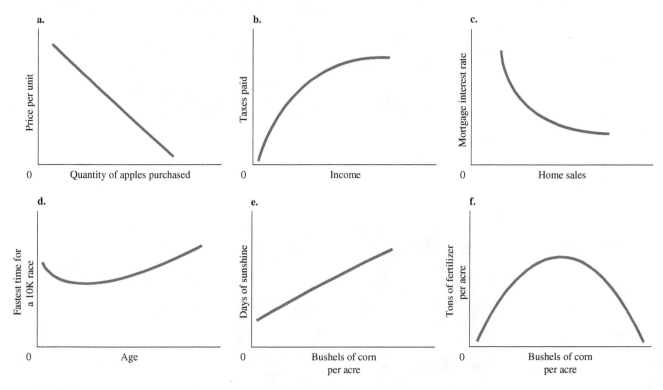

▲ FIGURE 1

1A.4 The following table shows the relationship between the price of organic turkeys and the number of turkeys sold by Godfrey's Free-Range Gobblers.
  a. Is the relationship between the price of turkeys and the number of turkeys sold by Godfrey's Free-Range Gobblers a positive relationship or a negative relationship? Explain.
  b. Plot the data from the table on a graph, draw a line through the points, and calculate the slope of the line.

Price per Turkey	Quantity of Turkeys	Month
$ 16	70	September
20	80	October
52	160	November
36	120	December
8	50	January

1A.5 Calculate the slope of the demand curve at point A and at point B in the following figure.

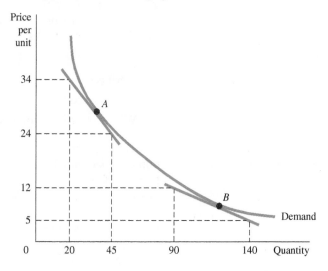

2

The Economic Problem: Scarcity and Choice

In the last chapter we provided you with some sense of the questions asked by economists and the broad methods that they use. As you read that chapter, some of you may have been surprised by the range of topics covered by economics. A look at the work done by the economists teaching at your own university will likely reveal a similarly broad range of interests. Some of your faculty will study how Apple and Samsung compete in smartphones. Others will look at discrimination in labor markets. Still others may be exploring the effects of microfinance in India. On the surface, these issues seem quite different from one another. But fundamental to each of these inquiries is the concern with choice in a world of scarcity. Economics explores how individuals make choices in a world of scarce resources and how those individual's choices come together to determine three key features of their society:

- What gets produced?
- How is it produced?
- Who gets what is produced?

This chapter explores these questions in detail. In a sense, this entire chapter *is* the definition of economics. It lays out the central problems addressed by the discipline and presents a framework that will guide you through the rest of the book. The starting point is the presumption that *human wants are unlimited but resources are not*. Limited or scarce resources force individuals and societies to choose among competing uses of resources—alternative combinations of produced goods and services—and among alternative final distributions of what is produced among households.

These questions are *positive or descriptive*. Understanding how a system functions is important before we can ask the normative questions of whether the system produces good or bad outcomes and how we might make improvements.

Economists study choices in a world of scarce resources. What do we mean by resources? If you look at Figure 2.1, you will see that resources are broadly defined. They include products of nature like minerals and timber, but also the products of past generations like buildings and factories. Perhaps most importantly, resources include the time and talents of the human population.

Things that are produced and then used in the production of other goods and services are called capital resources, or simply **capital**. Buildings, equipment, desks, chairs, software, roads, bridges, and highways are a part of the nation's stock of capital.

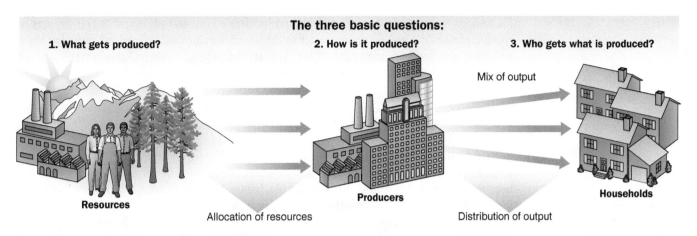

The three basic questions:

1. What gets produced?   **2. How is it produced?**   **3. Who gets what is produced?**

Mix of output

Resources   Producers   **Households**

Allocation of resources   Distribution of output

▲ **FIGURE 2.1   The Three Basic Questions**

Every society has some system or process that transforms its scarce resources into useful goods and services. In doing so, it must decide what gets produced, how it is produced, and to whom it is distributed. The primary resources that must be allocated are land, labor, and capital.

The basic resources available to a society are often referred to as **factors of production,** *or* **simply factors**. The three key factors of production are land, labor, and capital. The process that transforms scarce resources into useful goods and services is called **production**. In many societies, most of the production of goods and services is done by private firms. Private airlines in the United States use land (runways), labor (pilots and mechanics), and capital (airplanes) to produce transportation services. But in all societies, some production is done by the public sector, or government. Examples of government-produced or government-provided goods and services include national defense, public education, police protection, and fire protection.

Resources or factors of production are the **inputs** into the process of production; goods and services of value to households are the **outputs** of the process of production.

capital   Things that are produced and then used in the production of other goods and services.

factors of production (*or* **factors**)   The inputs into the process of production. Another term for resources.

production   The process that transforms scarce resources into useful goods and services.

Scarcity, Choice, and Opportunity Cost

In the second half of this chapter we discuss the global economic landscape. Before you can understand the different types of economic systems, it is important to master the basic economic concepts of scarcity, choice, and opportunity cost.

Understand why even in a society in which one person is better than a second at all tasks, it is still beneficial for the two to specialize and trade.

inputs *or* resources   Anything provided by nature or previous generations that can be used directly or indirectly to satisfy human wants.

outputs   Goods and services of value to households.

Scarcity and Choice in a One-Person Economy

The simplest economy is one in which a single person lives alone on an island. Consider Bill, the survivor of a plane crash, who finds himself cast ashore in such a place. Here individual and society are one; there is no distinction between social and private. *Nonetheless, nearly all the same basic decisions that characterize complex economies must also be made in a simple economy.* That is, although Bill will get whatever he produces, he still must decide how to allocate the island's resources, what to produce, and how and when to produce it.

First, Bill must decide *what* he wants to produce. Notice that the word *needs* does not appear here. Needs are absolute requirements; but beyond just enough water, basic nutrition, and shelter to survive, needs are very difficult to define. In any case, Bill must put his wants in some order of priority and make some choices.

Next, he must look at the *possibilities*. What can he do to satisfy his wants given the limits of the island? In every society, no matter how simple or complex, people are constrained in what they can do. In this society of one, Bill is constrained by time, his physical condition, his knowledge, his skills, and the resources and climate of the island.

Given that resources are limited, Bill must decide *how* to best use them to satisfy his hierarchy of wants. Food would probably come close to the top of his list. Should he spend his time gathering fruits and berries? Should he clear a field and plant seeds? The answers to those questions depend on the character of the island, its climate, its flora and fauna (*are* there any fruits and berries?), the extent of his skills and knowledge (does he know anything about farming?), and his preferences (he may be a vegetarian).

Opportunity Cost   The concepts of *constrained choice* and *scarcity* are central to the discipline of economics. They can be applied when discussing the behavior of individuals such as Bill and when analyzing the behavior of large groups of people in complex societies.

Given the scarcity of time and resources, if Bill decides to hunt, he will have less time to gather fruits and berries. He faces a trade-off between meat and fruit. There is a trade-off between food and shelter, too. As we noted in Chapter 1, the best alternative that we give up, or forgo, when we make a choice is the **opportunity cost** of that choice.

Bill may occasionally decide to rest, to lie on the beach, and to enjoy the sun. In one sense, that benefit is free—he does not have to buy a ticket to lie on the beach. In reality, however, relaxing does have an opportunity cost. The true cost of that leisure is the value of the other things Bill could have otherwise produced, but did not, during the time he spent on the beach.

The trade-offs that are made in this kind of society are vividly and often comically portrayed in the reality television shows that show groups of strangers competing on some deserted island, all trying to choose whether it is better to fish, hunt for berries, build a hut, or build an alliance. Making one of these choices involves giving up an opportunity to do another, and in many episodes we can see the consequences of those choices.

opportunity cost   The best alternative that we give up, or forgo, when we make a choice or decision.

Scarcity and Choice in an Economy of Two or More

Now suppose that another survivor of the crash, Colleen, appears on the island. Now that Bill is not alone, things are more complex and some new decisions must be made. Bill's and Colleen's preferences about what things to produce are likely to be different. They will probably not have the same knowledge or skills. Perhaps Colleen is good at tracking animals and Bill has a knack for building things. How should they split the work that needs to be done? Once things are produced, the two castaways must decide how to divide them. How should their products be distributed?

The mechanism for answering these fundamental questions is clear when Bill is alone on the island. The "central plan" is his; he simply decides what he wants and what to do about it. The minute someone else appears, however, a number of decision-making arrangements immediately become possible. One or the other may take charge, in which case that person will decide for both of them. The two may agree to cooperate, with each having an equal say, and come up with a joint plan; or they may agree to split the planning as well as the production duties. Finally, they may go off to live alone at opposite ends of the island. Even if they live apart, however, they may take advantage of each other's presence by specializing and trading.

Modern industrial societies must answer the same questions that Colleen and Bill must answer, but the mechanics of larger economies are more complex. Instead of two people living together, the United States has more than 300 million people. Still, decisions must be made about what to produce, how to produce it, and who gets it.

Specialization, Exchange, and Comparative Advantage   The idea that members of society benefit by specializing in what they do best has a long history and is one of the most important and powerful ideas in all of economics. David Ricardo, a major nineteenth-century British economist, formalized the point precisely. According to Ricardo's **theory of comparative advantage**, specialization and free trade will benefit all trading parties, even when some are "absolutely" more efficient producers than others. Ricardo's basic point applies just as much to Colleen and Bill as it does to different nations.

To keep things simple, suppose that Colleen and Bill have only two tasks to accomplish each week: gathering food to eat and cutting logs to burn. If Colleen could cut more logs than Bill in one day and Bill could gather more nuts and berries than Colleen could, specialization would clearly lead to more total production. Both would benefit if Colleen only cuts logs and Bill only gathers nuts and berries, as long as they can trade.

theory of comparative advantage   Ricardo's theory that specialization and free trade will benefit all trading parties, even those that may be "absolutely" more efficient producers.

ECONOMICS IN PRACTICE

Frozen Foods and Opportunity Costs

In 2012, $44 billion of frozen foods were sold in U.S. grocery stores, one quarter of it in the form of frozen dinners and entrées. In the mid-1950s, sales of frozen foods amounted to only $1 billion, a tiny fraction of the overall grocery store sales. One industry observer attributes this growth to the fact that frozen food tastes much better than it did in the past. Can you think of anything else that might be occurring?

The growth of the frozen dinner entrée market in the last 50 years is a good example of the role of opportunity costs in our lives. One of the most significant social changes in the U.S. economy in this period has been the increased participation of women in the labor force. In 1950, only 24 percent of married women worked; by 2013, that fraction had risen to 58 percent. Producing a meal takes two basic ingredients: food and time. When both husbands and wives work, the opportunity cost of time for housework—including making meals—goes up. This tells us that making a home-cooked meal became more expensive in the last 50 years. A natural result is to shift people toward labor-saving ways to make meals. Frozen foods are an obvious solution to the problem of increased opportunity costs.

Another, somewhat more subtle, opportunity cost story is at work encouraging the consumption of frozen foods. In 1960, the first microwave oven was introduced. The spread of this device into America's kitchens was rapid. The microwave turned out to be a quick way to defrost and cook those frozen entrées. So this technology lowered the opportunity cost of making frozen dinners, reinforcing the advantage these meals had over home-cooked meals. Microwaves made cooking with frozen foods cheaper once opportunity cost was considered while home-cooked meals were becoming more expensive.

The entrepreneurs among you also might recognize that the rise we described in the opportunity cost of the home-cooked meal *contributed* in part to the spread of the microwave, creating a reinforcing cycle. In fact, many entrepreneurs find that the simple tools of economics—like the

idea of opportunity costs—help them anticipate what products will be profitable for them to produce in the future. The growth of the two-worker family has stimulated many entrepreneurs to search for labor-saving solutions to family tasks.

The public policy students among you might be interested to know that some researchers attribute part of the growth in obesity in the United States to the lower opportunity costs of making meals associated with the growth of the markets for frozen foods and the microwave. (See David M. Cutler, Edward L. Glaeser, and Jesse M. Shapiro, "Why Have Americans Become More Obese?" *Journal of Economic Perspectives*, Summer 2003: 93–118.)

THINKING PRACTICALLY

1. Many people think that soda consumption also leads to increased obesity. Many schools have banned the sale of soda in vending machines. Use the idea of opportunity costs to explain why some people think these bans will reduce consumption. Do you agree?

Suppose instead that Colleen is better than Bill both at cutting logs *and* gathering food. In particular, whereas Colleen can gather 10 bushels of food per day, Bill can gather only 8 bushels. Further, while Colleen can cut 10 logs per day, Bill can cut only 4 per day. In this sense, we would say Colleen has an **absolute advantage** over Bill in both activities.

Thinking about this situation and focusing just on the productivity levels, you might conclude that it would benefit Colleen to move to the other side of the island and be by herself. Since she is more productive both in cutting logs and gathering food, would she not be better off on her own? How could she benefit by hanging out with Bill and sharing what they produce? One of Ricardo's lasting contributions to economics has been his analysis of exactly this situation. His analysis, which is illustrated in Figure 2.2, shows both how Colleen and Bill should divide the work of the island and how much they will gain from specializing and exchanging even if, as in this example, one party is absolutely better at everything than the other party.

absolute advantage

A producer has an absolute advantage over another in the production of a good or service if he or she can produce that product using fewer resources (a lower absolute cost per unit).

comparative advantage
A producer has a comparative advantage over another in the production of a good or service if he or she can produce that product at a lower *opportunity cost.*

The key to this question is remembering that Colleen's time is limited: this limit creates an opportunity cost. Though Bill is less able at all tasks than Colleen, having him spend time producing something frees up Colleen's time and this has value. The value from Bill's time depends on his comparative advantage. A producer has a **comparative advantage** over another in the production of a good or service if he or she can produce the good or service at a lower opportunity cost. First, think about Bill. He can produce 8 bushels of food per day, or he can cut 4 logs. To get 8 additional bushels of food, he must give up cutting 4 logs. Thus, *for Bill, the opportunity cost of 8 bushels of food is 4 logs.* Think next about Colleen. She can produce 10 bushels of food per day, or she can cut 10 logs. She thus gives up 1 log for each additional bushel; so *for Colleen, the opportunity cost of 8 bushels of food is 8 logs.* Bill has a comparative advantage over Colleen in the production of food because he gives up only 4 logs for an additional 8 bushels, whereas Colleen gives up 8 logs.

Think now about what Colleen must give up in terms of food to get 10 logs. To produce 10 logs she must work a whole day. If she spends a day cutting 10 logs, she gives up a day of gathering 10 bushels of food. Thus, *for Colleen, the opportunity cost of 10 logs is 10 bushels of food.* What must Bill give up to get 10 logs? To produce 4 logs, he must work 1 day. For each day he cuts logs, he gives up 8 bushels of food. He thus gives up 2 bushels of food for each log; so *for Bill, the opportunity cost of 10 logs is 20 bushels of food.* Colleen has a comparative advantage over Bill in the production of logs because she gives up only 10 bushels of food for an additional 10 logs, whereas Bill gives up 20 bushels.

Ricardo argued that two parties can benefit from specialization and trade even if one party has an absolute advantage in the production of both goods if each party takes advantage of his or her comparative advantage. Let us see how this works in the current example.

Suppose Colleen and Bill both want equal numbers of logs and bushels of food. If Colleen goes off on her own and splits her time equally, in one day she can produce 5 logs and 5 bushels of food. Bill, to produce equal amounts of logs and food, will have to spend more time on the wood than the food, given his talents. By spending one third of his day producing food and two thirds chopping wood, he can produce $2\frac{2}{3}$ units of each. In sum, when acting alone $7\frac{2}{3}$ logs and bushels of food are produced by our pair of castaways, most of them by Colleen. Clearly Colleen is a better producer than Bill. Why should she ever want to join forces with clumsy, slow Bill?

The answer lies in the gains from specialization, as we can see in Figure 2.2. In block a, we show the results of having Bill and Colleen each working alone chopping logs and gathering food: $7\frac{2}{3}$ logs and an equal number of food bushels. Now, recalling our calculations indicating that Colleen has a comparative advantage in wood chopping, let's see what happens if we assign Colleen to the wood task and have Bill spend all day gathering food. This system is described in block b of Figure 2.2. At the end of the day, the two end up with 10 logs, all gathered by Colleen and 8 bushels of food, all produced by Bill. By joining forces and specializing, the two have increased their production of both goods. This increased production provides an incentive for Colleen and Bill to work together. United, each can receive a bonus over what he or she could produce separately. This bonus—here $2\frac{1}{3}$ extra logs and $\frac{1}{3}$ bushel of food—represent the gains from specialization. Of course if both Bill and Colleen really favor equal amounts of the two goods, they could adjust their work time to get to this outcome; the main point here is that the total production increases with some specialization.

The simple example of Bill and Colleen should begin to give you some insight into why most economists see value in free trade. Even if one country is absolutely better than another country at producing everything, our example has shown that there are gains to specializing and trading.

A Graphical Presentation of the Production Possibilities and Gains from Specialization   Graphs can also be used to illustrate the production possibilities open to Colleen and Bill and the gains they could achieve from specialization and trade.

Figure 2.3(a) shows all of the possible combinations of food and wood Colleen can produce given her skills and the conditions on the island, acting alone. Panel (b) does the same for Bill. If Colleen spends all of her time producing wood, the best she can do is 10 logs, which we show where the line crosses the vertical axis. Similarly, the line crosses the horizontal axis at 10 bushels of food, because that is what Colleen could produce spending full time producing food. We

a. Daily production with no specialization, assuming Colleen and Bill each want to consume an equal number of logs and food

	Wood (logs)	Food (bushels)
Colleen	5	5
Bill	$2\frac{2}{3}$	$2\frac{2}{3}$
Total	$7\frac{2}{3}$	$7\frac{2}{3}$

↓

b. Daily Production with Specialization

	Wood (logs)	Food (bushels)
Colleen	10	0
Bill	0	8
Total	10	8

◀ FIGURE 2.2

Comparative Advantage and the Gains from Trade

Panel (a) shows the best Colleen and Bill can do each day, given their talents and assuming they each wish to consume an equal amount of food and wood. Notice Colleen produces by splitting her time equally during the day, while Bill must devote two thirds of his time to wood production if he wishes to equalize his amount produced of the two goods. Panel (b) shows what happens when both parties specialize. Notice more units are produced of each good.

have also marked on the graph possibility C, where she divides her time equally, generating 5 bushels of food and 5 logs of wood.

Bill in panel (b) can get as many as 4 logs of wood or 8 bushels of food by devoting himself full time to either wood or food production. Again, we have marked on his graph a point F, where he produces $2\frac{2}{3}$ bushels of food and $2\frac{2}{3}$ logs of wood. Notice that Bill's production line is lower down than is Colleen's. The further to the right is the production line, the more productive is the individual; that is, the more he or she can produce of the two goods. Also notice that the slope of the two lines is not the same. Colleen trades off one bushel of food for one log of wood, while Bill gives up 2 bushels of food for one log of wood. These differing slopes show

a. Colleen's production possibilities

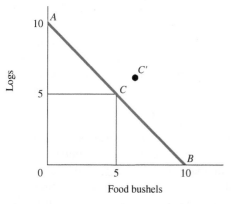

b. Bill's production possibilities

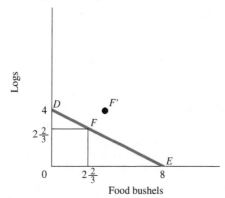

▲ FIGURE 2.3 **Production Possibilities with and without Trade**

This figure shows the combinations of food and wood that Colleen and Bill can each generate in one day of labor, working by themselves. Colleen can achieve independently any point along line ACB, whereas Bill can generate any combination of food and wood along line DFE. Specialization and trade would allow both Bill and Colleen to move to the right of their original lines, to points like C′ and F′. In other words, specialization and trade allow both people to be better off than they were acting alone.

the differing opportunity costs faced by Colleen and Bill. They also open up the possibility of gains from specialization. Try working through an example in which the slopes are the same to convince yourself of the importance of differing slopes.

What happens when the possibility of working together and specializing in either wood or food comes up? In Figure 2.2 we have already seen that specialization would allow the pair to go from production of $7\frac{2}{3}$ units of food and wood to 10 logs and 8 bushels of food. Colleen and Bill can split the $2\frac{1}{3}$ extra logs and the $\frac{1}{3}$ extra bushel of food to move to points like C' and F' in Figure 2.3, which were unachievable without cooperation. In this analysis we do not know how Bill and Colleen will divide the surplus food and wood they have created. But because there is a surplus means that both of them can do better than either would alone.

Weighing Present and Expected Future Costs and Benefits Very often we find ourselves weighing benefits available today against benefits available tomorrow. Here, too, the notion of opportunity cost is helpful.

While alone on the island, Bill had to choose between cultivating a field and just gathering wild nuts and berries. Gathering nuts and berries provides food now; gathering seeds and clearing a field for planting will yield food tomorrow if all goes well. Using today's time to farm may well be worth the effort if doing so will yield more food than Bill would otherwise have in the future. By planting, Bill is trading present value for future value.

The simplest example of trading present for future benefits is the act of saving. When you put income aside today for use in the future, you give up some things that you could have had today in exchange for something tomorrow. Because nothing is certain, some judgment about future events and expected values must be made. What will your income be in 10 years? How long are you likely to live?

We trade off present and future benefits in small ways all the time. If you decide to study instead of going to the dorm party, you are trading present fun for the expected future benefits of higher grades. If you decide to go outside on a very cold day and run 5 miles, you are trading discomfort in the present for being in better shape later.

Capital Goods and Consumer Goods A society trades present for expected future benefits when it devotes a portion of its resources to research and development or to investment in capital. As we said previously in this chapter, *capital* in its broadest definition is anything that has already been produced that will be used to produce other valuable goods or services over time.

Building capital means trading present benefits for future ones. Bill and Colleen might trade gathering berries or lying in the sun for cutting logs to build a nicer house in the future. In a modern society, resources used to produce capital goods could have been used to produce **consumer goods**—that is, goods for present consumption. Heavy industrial machinery does not directly satisfy the wants of anyone, but producing it requires resources that could instead have gone into producing things that do satisfy wants directly—for example, food, clothing, toys, or golf clubs.

consumer goods Goods produced for present consumption.

Capital is everywhere. A road is capital. Once a road is built, we can drive on it or transport goods and services over it for many years to come. A house is also capital. Before a new manufacturing firm can start up, it must put some capital in place. The buildings, equipment, and inventories that it uses comprise its capital. As it contributes to the production process, this capital yields valuable services over time.

Capital does not need to be tangible. When you spend time and resources developing skills or getting an education, you are investing in human capital—your own human capital. This capital will continue to exist and yield benefits to you for years to come. A computer program produced by a software company and available online may cost nothing to distribute, but its true intangible value comes from the ideas embodied in the program itself. It too is capital.

investment The process of using resources to produce new capital.

The process of using resources to produce new capital is called **investment**. (In everyday language, the term *investment* often refers to the act of buying a share of stock or a bond, as in "I invested in some Treasury bonds." In economics, however, investment *always* refers to the creation of capital: the purchase or putting in place of buildings, equipment, roads, houses, and the like.) A wise investment in capital is one that yields future benefits that are more valuable than the present cost. When you spend money for a house, for example, presumably you value its future benefits. That is, you expect to gain more in shelter services than you would from the things you could buy today with the same money. Because resources are scarce, the opportunity cost of every investment in capital is forgone present consumption.

The Production Possibility Frontier

A simple graphic device called the **production possibility frontier (ppf)** illustrates the principles of constrained choice, opportunity cost, and scarcity. The ppf is a graph that shows all the combinations of goods and services that can be produced if all of a society's resources are used efficiently. Figure 2.4 shows a ppf for a hypothetical economy. We have already seen a simplified version of a ppf in looking at the choices of Colleen and Bill in Figure 2.3. Here we will look more generally at the ppf.

On the Y-axis, we measure the quantity of capital goods produced. On the X-axis, we measure the quantity of consumer goods. All points below and to the left of the curve (the shaded area) represent combinations of capital and consumer goods that are possible for the society given the resources available and existing technology. Points above and to the right of the curve, such as point G, represent combinations that cannot currently be realized. You will recall in our example of Colleen and Bill that new trade and specialization possibilities allowed them to expand their collective production possibilities and move to a point like G. If an economy were to end up at point A on the graph, it would be producing no consumer goods at all; all resources would be used for the production of capital. If an economy were to end up at point B, it would be devoting all its resources to the production of consumer goods and none of its resources to the formation of capital.

While all economies produce some of each kind of good, different economies emphasize different things. About 13 percent of gross output in the United States in 2012 was new capital. In Japan, capital has historically accounted for a much higher percent of gross output, while in the Congo, the figure is about 7 percent. Japan is closer to point A on its ppf, the Congo is closer to B, and the United States is somewhere in between.

Points that are actually on the ppf are points of both full resource employment and production efficiency. (Recall from Chapter 1 that an efficient economy is one that produces the things that people want at the least cost. *Production efficiency* is a state in which a given mix of outputs is produced at the least cost.) Resources are not going unused, and there is no waste. Points that lie within the shaded area but that are not on the frontier represent either unemployment of resources or production inefficiency. An economy producing at point D in Figure 2.4 can produce more capital goods and more consumer goods, for example, by moving to point E. This is possible because resources are not fully employed at point D or are not being used efficiently.

production possibility frontier (ppf) A graph that shows all the combinations of goods and services that can be produced if all of society's resources are used efficiently.

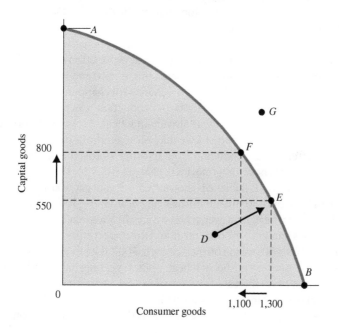

◀ **FIGURE 2.4**
Production Possibility Frontier
The ppf illustrates a number of economic concepts. One of the most important is *opportunity cost*. The opportunity cost of producing more capital goods is fewer consumer goods. Moving from E to F, the number of capital goods increases from 550 to 800, but the number of consumer goods decreases from 1,300 to 1,100.

Negative Slope and Opportunity Cost Just as we saw with Colleen and Bill, the slope of the ppf is negative. Because a society's choices are constrained by available resources and existing technology, when those resources are fully and efficiently employed, it can produce more capital goods only by reducing production of consumer goods. The opportunity cost of the additional capital is the forgone production of consumer goods.

The fact that scarcity exists is illustrated by the negative slope of the ppf. (If you need a review of slope, see the Appendix to Chapter 1.) In moving from point E to point F in Figure 2.4, capital production *increases* by 800 − 550 = 250 units (a positive change), but that increase in capital can be achieved only by shifting resources out of the production of consumer goods. Thus, in moving from point E to point F in Figure 2.4, consumer goods production *decreases* by 1,300 − 1,100 = 200 units (a negative change). The slope of the curve, the ratio of the change in capital goods to the change in consumer goods, is negative.

The value of the slope of a society's ppf is called the **marginal rate of transformation (MRT)**. In Figure 2.4, the MRT between points E and F is simply the ratio of the change in capital goods (a positive number) to the change in consumer goods (a negative number). It tells us how much society has to give up of one output to get a unit of a second.

marginal rate of transformation (MRT) The slope of the production possibility frontier (ppf).

The Law of Increasing Opportunity Cost The negative slope of the ppf indicates the trade-off that a society faces between two goods. In the example of Colleen and Bill, we showed the ppf as a straight line. What does it mean that the ppf here is bowed out?

In our simple example, Bill gave up two bushels of food for every one log of wood he produced. Bill's per-hour ability to harvest wood or produce food didn't depend on how many hours he spent on that activity. Similarly Colleen faced the same trade off of food for wood regardless of how much of either she was producing. In the language we have just introduced, the marginal rate of transformation was constant for Bill and Colleen; hence the straight line ppf. But that is not always true. Perhaps the first bushel of food is easy to produce, low-hanging fruit for example. Perhaps it is harder to get the second log than the first because the trees are farther away. The bowed out ppf tells us that the more society tries to increase production of one good rather than another, the harder it is. In the example in Figure 2.4, the opportunity cost of using society's resources to make capital goods rather than consumer goods increases as we devote more and more resources to capital goods. Why might that be? A common explanation is that when society tries to produce only a small amount of a product, it can use resources—people, land and so on—most well-suited to those goods. As a society spends a larger portion of its resources on one good versus all others, getting more production of that good often becomes increasingly hard.

Let's look at the trade-off between corn and wheat production in Ohio and Kansas as an example. In a recent year, Ohio and Kansas together produced 510 million bushels of corn and 380 million bushels of wheat. Table 2.1 presents these two numbers, plus some hypothetical combinations of corn and wheat production that might exist for Ohio and Kansas together. Figure 2.5 graphs the data from Table 2.1.

Suppose that society's demand for corn dramatically increases. If this happens, farmers would probably shift some of their acreage from wheat production to corn production. Such a shift is represented by a move from point C (where corn = 510 and wheat = 380) up and to the left along the ppf toward points A and B in Figure 2.5. As this happens, it becomes more difficult to produce additional corn. The best land for corn production was presumably already in corn, and the best land for wheat production was already in wheat. As we try to produce more corn, the land is less well-suited to that crop. As we take more land out of wheat production, we are taking increasingly better wheat-producing land. In other words, the opportunity cost of more corn, measured in terms of wheat foregone, increases.

Moving from point E to D, Table 2.1 shows that we can get 100 million bushels of corn (400 − 300) by sacrificing only 50 million bushels of wheat (550 − 500)—that is, we get 2 bushels of corn for every bushel of wheat. However, when we are already stretching the ability of the land to produce corn, it becomes harder to produce more and the opportunity cost increases. Moving from point B to A, we can get only 50 million bushels of corn (700 − 650) by sacrificing 100 million bushels of wheat (200 − 100). For every bushel of wheat, we now get only half a bushel of corn. However, if the demand for *wheat* were to increase substantially and we were to move down and to the right along the ppf, it would become increasingly difficult to produce wheat and the opportunity cost of wheat, in terms of corn foregone, would increase. This is the *law of increasing opportunity cost.*

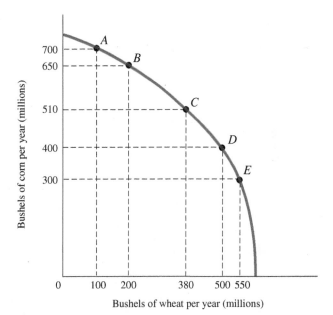

▲ **FIGURE 2.5 Corn and Wheat Production in Ohio and Kansas**
The ppf illustrates that the opportunity cost of corn production increases as we shift resources from wheat production to corn production. Moving from point E to D, we get an additional 100 million bushels of corn at a cost of 50 million bushels of wheat. Moving from point B to A, we get only 50 million bushels of corn at a cost of 100 million bushels of wheat. The *cost per bushel* of corn—measured in lost wheat—has increased.

TABLE 2.1	Production Possibility Schedule for Total Corn and Wheat Production in Ohio and Kansas	
Point on ppf	Total Corn Production (Millions of Bushels per Year)	Total Wheat Production (Millions of Bushels per Year)
A	700	100
B	650	200
C	510	380
D	400	500
E	300	550

Unemployment   During the Great Depression of the 1930s, the U.S. economy experienced prolonged unemployment. Millions of workers found themselves without jobs. In 1933, 25 percent of the civilian labor force was unemployed. This figure stayed above 14 percent until 1940. More recently, between the end of 2007 and 2010, the United States lost more than 8 million payroll jobs and unemployment rose to higher than 15 million.

In addition to the hardship that falls on the unemployed, unemployment of labor means unemployment of capital. During economic downturns or recessions, industrial plants run at less than their total capacity. When there is unemployment of labor and capital, we are not producing all that we can.

Periods of unemployment correspond to points inside the ppf, points such as D in Figure 2.4. Moving onto the frontier from a point such as D means achieving full employment of resources.

Inefficiency   Although an economy may be operating with full employment of its land, labor, and capital resources, it may still be operating inside its ppf (at a point such as D in Figure 2.4). It could be using those resources *inefficiently*.

Waste and mismanagement are the results of a firm operating below its potential. If you are the owner of a bakery and you forget to order flour, your workers and ovens stand idle while you figure out what to do.

Sometimes inefficiency results from mismanagement of the economy instead of mismanagement of individual private firms. Suppose, for example, that the land and climate in Ohio are

▶ FIGURE 2.6

Inefficiency from Misallocation of Land in Farming

Inefficiency always results in a combination of production shown by a point inside the ppf, like point *A*. Increasing efficiency will move production possibilities toward a point on the ppf, such as point *B*.

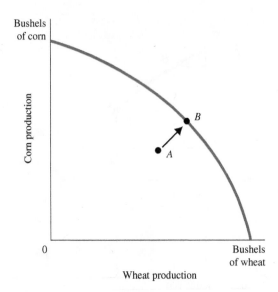

best-suited for corn production and that the land and climate in Kansas are best-suited for wheat production. If Congress passes a law forcing Ohio farmers to plant 50 percent of their acreage with wheat and Kansas farmers to plant 50 percent with corn, neither corn nor wheat production will be up to potential. The economy will be at a point such as *A* in Figure 2.6—inside the ppf. Allowing each state to specialize in producing the crop that it produces best increases the production of both crops and moves the economy to a point such as *B* in Figure 2.6.

The Efficient Mix of Output To be efficient, an economy must produce what people want. This means that in addition to operating *on* the ppf, the economy must be operating at the *right point* on the ppf. This is referred to as *output efficiency*, in contrast to production efficiency. Suppose that an economy devotes 100 percent of its resources to beef production and that the beef industry runs efficiently using the most modern techniques. If everyone in the society were a vegetarian and there were no trade, resources spent on producing beef would be wasted.

It is important to remember that the ppf represents choices available within the constraints imposed by the current state of agricultural technology. In the long run, technology may improve, and when that happens, we have *growth*.

economic growth An increase in the total output of an economy. Growth occurs when a society acquires new resources or when it learns to produce more using existing resources.

Economic Growth **Economic growth** is characterized by an increase in the total output of an economy. It occurs when a society acquires new resources or learns to produce more with existing resources. New resources may mean a larger labor force or an increased capital stock. The production and use of new machinery and equipment (capital) increase workers' productivity. (Give a man a shovel, and he can dig a bigger hole; give him a steam shovel, and wow!) Improved productivity also comes from technological change and *innovation*, the discovery and application of new, more efficient production techniques.

In the past few decades, the productivity of U.S. agriculture has increased dramatically. Based on data compiled by the Department of Agriculture, Table 2.2 shows that yield per acre in corn production has increased sixfold since the late 1930s, and the labor required to produce it has dropped significantly. Productivity in wheat production has also increased, at only a slightly less remarkable rate: Output per acre has more than tripled, whereas labor requirements are down nearly 90 percent. These increases are the result of more efficient farming techniques, more and better capital (tractors, combines, and other equipment), and advances in scientific knowledge and technological change (hybrid seeds, fertilizers, and so on). As you can see in Figure 2.7, changes such as these shift the ppf up and to the right.

Sources of Growth and the Dilemma of Poor Countries Economic growth arises from many sources. The two most important over the years have been the accumulation of capital and technological advances. For poor countries, capital is essential; they must build

TABLE 2.2 Increasing Productivity in Corn and Wheat Production in the United States, 1935–2009

	Corn		Wheat	
	Yield per Acre (Bushels)	Labor Hours per 100 Bushels	Yield per Acre (Bushels)	Labor Hours per 100 Bushels
1935–1939	26.1	108	13.2	67
1945–1949	36.1	53	16.9	34
1955–1959	48.7	20	22.3	17
1965–1969	78.5	7	27.5	11
1975–1979	95.3	4	31.3	9
1981–1985	107.2	3	36.9	7
1985–1990	112.8	NA[a]	38.0	NA[a]
1990–1995	120.6	NA[a]	38.1	NA[a]
1998	134.4	NA[a]	43.2	NA[a]
2001	138.2	NA[a]	43.5	NA[a]
2006	145.6	NA[a]	42.3	NA[a]
2007	152.8	NA[a]	40.6	NA[a]
2008	153.9	NA[a]	44.9	NA[a]
2009	164.9	NA[a]	44.3	NA[a]

[a] Data not available.

Source: U.S. Department of Agriculture, Economic Research Service, Agricultural Statistics, Crop Summary.

the communication networks and transportation systems necessary to develop industries that function efficiently. They also need capital goods to develop their agricultural sectors.

Recall that capital goods are produced only at a sacrifice of consumer goods. The same can be said for technological advances. Technological advances come from research and development that use resources; thus, they too must be paid for. The resources used to produce capital

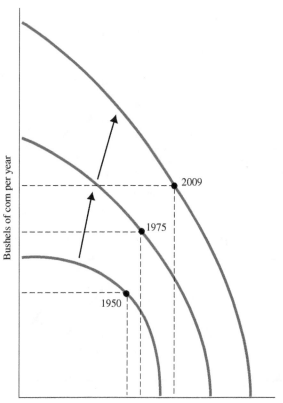

◀ FIGURE 2.7 **Economic Growth Shifts the PPF Up and to the Right**
Productivity increases have enhanced the ability of the United States to produce both corn and wheat. As Table 2.2 shows, productivity increases were more dramatic for corn than for wheat. Thus, the shifts in the ppf were not parallel.

goods—to build a road, a tractor, or a manufacturing plant—*and* to develop new technologies could have been used to produce consumer goods.

When a large part of a country's population is poor, taking resources out of the production of consumer goods (such as food and clothing) is difficult. In addition, in some countries, people wealthy enough to invest in domestic industries choose instead to invest abroad because of political turmoil at home. As a result, it often falls to the governments of poor countries to generate revenues for capital production and research out of tax collections.

All these factors have contributed to the growing gap between some poor and rich nations. Figure 2.8 shows the result using ppfs. On the bottom left, the rich country devotes a larger portion of its production to capital, whereas the poor country on the top left produces mostly consumer goods. On the right, you see the results: The ppf of the rich country shifts up and out further and faster.

The importance of capital goods and technological developments to the position of workers in less-developed countries is well-illustrated by Robert Jensen's study of South India's industry. Conventional telephones require huge investments in wires and towers and, as a result, many less developed areas are without landlines. Mobile phones, on the other hand, require a lower investment; thus, in many areas, people upgraded from no phones directly to cell phones. Jensen found that in small fishing villages, the advent of cell phones allowed fishermen to determine on any given day where to take their catch to sell, resulting in a large decrease in fish wasted and an increase in fishing profits. The ability of newer communication technology to aid development is one of the exciting features of our times. (See Robert Jensen, "The Digital Provide: Information Technology, Market Performance, and Welfare in the South Indian Fisheries Sector," *Quarterly Journal of Economics*, 2007: 879–924.)

Although it exists only as an abstraction, the ppf illustrates a number of important concepts that we will use throughout the rest of this book: scarcity, unemployment, inefficiency, opportunity cost, the law of increasing opportunity cost, economic growth, and the gains from trade.

▶ **FIGURE 2.8** **Capital Goods and Growth in Poor and Rich Countries**
Rich countries find it easier than poor countries to devote resources to the production of capital, and the more resources that flow into capital production, the faster the rate of economic growth. Thus, the gap between poor and rich countries has grown over time.

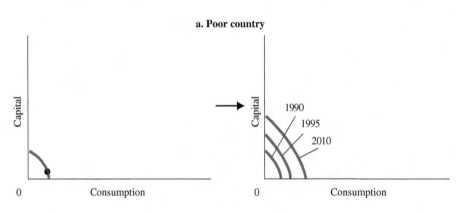

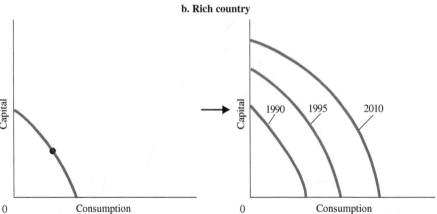

ECONOMICS IN PRACTICE

Trade-Offs among the Rich and Poor

In all societies, for all people, resources are limited relative to people's demands. There are, however, quite large differences in the kinds of trade-offs individuals face in rich versus poor countries.

In 1990, the World Bank defined the extremely poor people of the world as those earning less than $1 a day. Among development economists and policy makers, this figure continues to be used as a rough rule of thumb. In a recent survey, Abhijit Banerjee and Esther Duflo, two MIT economists, surveyed individuals living at this level in 13 countries across the world.[1] What did they learn about the consumption trade-offs faced by these individuals versus consumers in the United States?

It should not surprise you to learn that for the extremely poor, food is a much larger component of the budget. On average over the 13 countries, between 56 percent and 78 percent of consumption was spent on food. In the United States, just under 10 percent of the average budget goes to food. Even for the poorest consumers, however, biological need is not all determining. The Banerjee and Duflo study finds that in Udaipur, India, almost 10 percent of the typical food budget goes to sugar and processed foods rather than more nutritionally valuable grains. So even at these low levels of income, some choice remains. Perhaps more interestingly, almost 10 percent of the budget of those surveyed goes to weddings, funerals, and other festivals. In societies with very few entertainment outlets, Banerjee and Duflo suggest we

may see more demand for festivals, indicating that even in extremely poor societies, household choice plays a role.

THINKING PRACTICALLY

1. Why might we see a greater demand for festivals in poor countries than in rich ones? How might this be affected by choices available?

[1] Abhijit Banerjee and Esther Duflo, "The Economic Lives of the Poor," *Journal of Economic Perspective*, Winter 2007: 141–167.

The Economic Problem

Recall the three basic questions facing all economic systems: (1) What gets produced? (2) How is it produced? and (3) Who gets it?

When Bill was alone on the island, the mechanism for answering those questions was simple: He thought about his own wants and preferences, looked at the constraints imposed by the resources of the island and his own skills and time, and made his decisions. As Bill set about his work, he allocated available resources quite simply, more or less by dividing up his available time. Distribution of the output was irrelevant. Because Bill was the society, he got it all.

Introducing even one more person into the economy—in this case, Colleen—changed all that. Cooperation and coordination may give rise to gains that would otherwise not be possible. When a society consists of millions of people, coordination and cooperation become more challenging, but the potential for gain also grows. In large, complex economies, specialization can grow dramatically. The range of products available in a modern industrial society is beyond anything that could have been imagined a hundred years ago, and so is the range of jobs. Specialization plays a role in this.

The amount of coordination and cooperation in a modern industrial society is almost impossible to imagine. Yet something seems to drive economic systems, if sometimes clumsily and inefficiently, toward producing the goods and services that people want. Given scarce resources, how do large, complex societies go about answering the three basic economic questions? This is the economic problem, which is what this text is about.

Understand the central difference in the way command economies and market economies decide what is produced.

Economic Systems and the Role of Government

Thus far we have described the questions that the economic system must answer. Now we turn to the mechanics of the system. What is the role played by government in deciding what and how things are produced? There are many circumstances in which the government may be able to improve the functioning of the market.

Command Economies

command economy An economy in which a central government either directly or indirectly sets output targets, incomes, and prices.

In a pure **command economy**, like the system in place in the Soviet Union or China some years ago, the basic economic questions are answered by a central government. Through a combination of government ownership of state enterprises and central planning, the government, either directly or indirectly, sets output targets, incomes, and prices.

At present, for most countries in the world, private enterprise plays at least some role in production decisions. The debate today is instead about the extent and the character of government's role in the economy. Government involvement, in theory, may improve the efficiency and fairness of the allocation of a nation's resources. At the same time, a poorly functioning government can destroy incentives, lead to corruption, and result in the waste of a society's resources.

Laissez-Faire Economies: The Free Market

laissez-faire economy
Literally from the French: "allow [them] to do." An economy in which individual people and firms pursue their own self-interest without any government direction or regulation.

market The institution through which buyers and sellers interact and engage in exchange.

At the opposite end of the spectrum from the command economy is the **laissez-faire economy**. The term *laissez-faire*, which translated literally from French means "allow [them] to do," implies a complete lack of government involvement in the economy. In this type of economy, individuals and firms pursue their own self-interest without any central direction or regulation; the sum total of millions of individual decisions ultimately determines all basic economic outcomes. The central institution through which a laissez-faire system answers the basic questions is the **market**, a term that is used in economics to mean an institution through which buyers and sellers interact and engage in exchange.

In short:

> Some markets are simple and others are complex, but they all involve buyers and sellers engaging in exchange. The behavior of buyers and sellers in a laissez-faire economy determines what gets produced, how it is produced, and who gets it.

The following chapters explore market systems in great depth. A quick preview is worthwhile here, however.

Consumer Sovereignty In a free, unregulated market, goods and services are produced and sold only if the supplier can make a profit. In simple terms, making a *profit* means selling goods or services for more than it costs to produce them. You cannot make a profit unless someone wants the product that you are selling. This logic leads to the notion of **consumer sovereignty**: The mix of output found in any free market system is dictated ultimately by the tastes and preferences of consumers who "vote" by buying or not buying. Businesses rise and fall in response to consumer demands. No central directive or plan is necessary.

consumer sovereignty The idea that consumers ultimately dictate what will be produced (or not produced) by choosing what to purchase (and what not to purchase).

Individual Production Decisions: Free Enterprise Under a free market system, individual producers must also determine how to organize and coordinate the actual production of their products or services. In a free market economy, producers may be small or large. One person who is good with computers may start a business designing Web sites. On a larger scale, a group of furniture designers may put together a large portfolio of sketches, raise several million dollars, and start a bigger business. At the extreme are huge corporations such as Microsoft, Mitsubishi, Apple, and Intel, each of which sells tens of billions of dollars' worth of products every year. Whether the firms are large or small, however, production decisions in a market economy are made by separate private organizations acting in what they perceive to be their own interests.

Proponents of free market systems argue that the use of markets leads to more efficient production and better response to diverse and changing consumer preferences. If a producer is inefficient, competitors will come along, fight for the business, and eventually take it away. Thus, in a free market economy, competition forces producers to use efficient techniques of production and to produce goods that consumers want.

Distribution of Output   In a free market system, the distribution of output—who gets what—is also determined in a decentralized way. To the extent that income comes from working for a wage, it is at least in part determined by individual choice. You will work for the wages available in the market only if these wages (and the products and services they can buy) are sufficient to compensate you for what you give up by working. You may discover that you can increase your income by getting more education or training.

Price Theory   The basic coordinating mechanism in a free market system is price. A price is the amount that a product sells for per unit, and it reflects what society is willing to pay. Prices of inputs—labor, land, and capital—determine how much it costs to produce a product. Prices of various kinds of labor, or *wage rates*, determine the rewards for working in different jobs and professions. Many of the independent decisions made in a market economy involve the weighing of prices and costs, so it is not surprising that much of economic theory focuses on the factors that influence and determine prices. This is why microeconomic theory is often simply called *price theory*.

In sum:

> In a free market system, the basic economic questions are answered without the help of a central government plan or directives. This is what the "free" in free market means—the system is left to operate on its own with no outside interference. Individuals pursuing their own self-interest will go into business and produce the products and services that people want. Other individuals will decide whether to acquire skills; whether to work; and whether to buy, sell, invest, or save the income that they earn. The basic coordinating mechanism is price.

Mixed Systems, Markets, and Governments

The differences between command economies and laissez-faire economies in their pure forms are enormous. In fact, these pure forms do not exist in the world; all real systems are in some sense "mixed." That is, individual enterprise exists and independent choice is exercised even in economies in which the government plays a major role.

Conversely, no market economies exist without government involvement and government regulation. The United States has basically a free market economy, but government purchases accounted for slightly more than 18 percent of the country's total production in 2014 Governments in the United States (local, state, and federal) directly employ about 14 percent of all workers (15 percent including active duty military). They also redistribute income by means of taxation and social welfare expenditures, and they regulate many economic activities.

One of the major themes in this book, and indeed in economics, is the tension between the advantages of free, unregulated markets and the desire for government involvement. Identifying what the market does well, and where it potentially fails, and exploring the role of government in dealing with market failure is a key topic in policy economics. We return to this debate many times throughout this text.

Looking Ahead

This chapter described the economic problem in broad terms. We outlined the questions that all economic systems must answer. We also discussed broadly the two kinds of economic systems. In the next chapter, we analyze the way market systems work.

─────────────── **SUMMARY** ───────────────

1. Every society has some system or process for transforming into useful form what nature and previous generations have provided. Economics is the study of that process and its outcomes.

2. *Producers* are those who take resources and transform them into usable products, or *outputs*. Private firms, households, and governments all produce something.

2.1 SCARCITY, CHOICE, AND OPPORTUNITY COST *p. 23*

3. All societies must answer *three basic questions*: What gets produced? How is it produced? Who gets what is produced? These three questions make up the *economic problem*.

4. One person alone on an island must make the same basic decisions that complex societies make. When a society consists of more than one person, questions of distribution, cooperation, and specialization arise.

5. Because resources are scarce relative to human wants in all societies, using resources to produce one good or service implies *not* using them to produce something else. This concept of *opportunity cost* is central to understanding economics.

6. Using resources to produce *capital* that will in turn produce benefits in the future implies *not* using those resources to produce consumer goods in the present.

7. Even if one individual or nation is absolutely more efficient at producing goods than another, all parties will gain if they specialize in producing goods in which they have a *comparative advantage*.

8. A *production possibility frontier* (ppf) is a graph that shows all the combinations of goods and services that can be produced if all of society's resources are used efficiently. The ppf illustrates a number of important economic concepts: scarcity, unemployment, inefficiency, increasing opportunity cost, and economic growth.

9. *Economic growth* occurs when society produces more, either by acquiring more resources or by learning to produce more with existing resources. Improved productivity may come from additional capital or from the discovery and application of new, more efficient techniques of production.

2.2 ECONOMIC SYSTEMS AND THE ROLE OF GOVERNMENT *p. 36*

10. In some modern societies, government plays a big role in answering the three basic questions. In pure *command economies*, a central authority directly or indirectly sets output targets, incomes, and prices.

11. A *laissez-faire economy* is one in which individuals independently pursue their own self-interest, without any central direction or regulation, and ultimately determine all basic economic outcomes.

12. A *market* is an institution through which buyers and sellers interact and engage in exchange. Some markets involve simple face-to-face exchange; others involve a complex series of transactions, often over great distances or through electronic means.

13. There are no purely planned economies and no pure laissez-faire economies; all economies are mixed. Individual enterprise, independent choice, and relatively free markets exist in centrally planned economies; there is significant government involvement in market economies such as that of the United States.

14. One of the great debates in economics revolves around the tension between the advantages of free, unregulated markets and the desire for government involvement in the economy. Free markets produce what people want, and competition forces firms to adopt efficient production techniques. The need for government intervention arises because free markets are characterized by inefficiencies and an unequal distribution of income and experience regular periods of inflation and unemployment.

─────────── **REVIEW TERMS AND CONCEPTS** ───────────

absolute advantage, *p. 25*

capital, *p. 22*

command economy, *p. 36*

comparative advantage, *p. 26*

consumer goods, *p. 28*

consumer sovereignty, *p. 36*

economic growth, *p. 32*

factors of production (or factors), *p. 23*

inputs *or* resources, *p. 23*

investment, *p. 28*

laissez-faire economy, *p. 36*

marginal rate of transformation (MRT), *p. 30*

market, *p. 36*

opportunity cost, *p. 24*

outputs, *p. 23*

production, *p. 23*

production possibility frontier (ppf), *p. 29*

theory of comparative advantage, *p. 24*

PROBLEMS

All problems are available on MyEconLab.

2.1 SCARCITY, CHOICE, AND OPPORTUNITY COST

LEARNING OBJECTIVE: Understand why even in a society in which one person is better than a second at all tasks, it is still beneficial for the two to specialize and trade.

1.1 For each of the following, describe some of the potential opportunity costs:
  a. Going home for Thanksgiving vacation
  b. Riding your bicycle 20 miles every day
  c. The federal government using tax revenue to purchase 10,000 acres in Florida for use as a bird sanctuary
  d. A foreign government subsidizes its national airline to keep airfares down
  e. Upgrading to a balcony suite for your cruise around the Mediterranean Sea
  f. Staying up all night to watch season 5 of *Game of Thrones*

1.2 "As long as all resources are fully employed and every firm in the economy is producing its output using the best available technology, the result will be efficient." Do you agree or disagree with this statement? Explain your answer.

1.3 You are an intern to the editor of a small-town newspaper in Mallsburg, Pennsylvania. Your boss, the editor, asks you to write the first draft of an editorial for this week's paper. Your assignment is to describe the costs and the benefits of building a new bridge across the railroad tracks in the center of town. Currently, most people who live in this town must drive 2 miles through thickly congested traffic to the existing bridge to get to the main shopping and employment center. The bridge will cost the citizens of Mallsburg $25 million, which will be paid for with a tax on their incomes over the next 20 years. What are the opportunity costs of building this bridge? What are the benefits that citizens will likely receive if the bridge is built? What other factors might you consider in writing this editorial?

1.4 Alexi and Tony own a food truck that serves only two items, street tacos and Cuban sandwiches. As shown in the table, Alexi can make 80 street tacos per hour but only 20 Cuban sandwiches. Tony is a bit faster and can make 100 street tacos or 30 Cuban sandwiches in an hour. Alexi and Tony can sell all the street tacos and Cuban sandwiches that they are able to produce.

Output Per Hour

	Street Tacos	Cuban Sandwiches
Alexi	80	20
Tony	100	30

  a. For Alexi and for Tony, what is the opportunity cost of a street taco? Who has a comparative advantage in the production of street tacos? Explain your answer.
  b. Who has a comparative advantage in the production of Cuban sandwiches? Explain your answer.

  c. Assume that Alexi works 20 hours per week in the business. Assuming Alexi is in business on his own, graph the possible combinations of street tacos and Cuban sandwiches that he could produce in a week. Do the same for Tony.
  d. If Alexi devoted half of his time (10 out of 20 hours) to making street tacos and half of his time to making Cuban sandwiches, how many of each would he produce in a week? If Tony did the same, how many of each would he produce? How many street tacos and Cuban sandwiches would be produced in total?
  e. Suppose that Alexi spent all 20 hours of his time on street tacos and Tony spent 17 hours on Cuban Sandwiches and 3 hours on street tacos. How many of each item would be produced?
  f. Suppose that Alexi and Tony can sell all their street tacos for $2 each and all their Cuban Sandwiches for $7.25 each. If each of them worked 20 hours per week, how should they split their time between the production of street tacos and Cuban sandwiches? What is their maximum joint revenue?

1.5 Briefly describe the trade-offs involved in each of the following decisions. Specifically, list some of the opportunity costs associated with each decision, paying particular attention to the trade-offs between present and future consumption.
  a. After a stressful senior year in high school, Sherice decides to take the summer off instead of working before going to college.
  b. Frank is overweight and decides to work out every day and to go on a diet.
  c. Mei is diligent about taking her car in for routine maintenance even though it takes 2 hours of her time and costs $100 four times each year.
  d. Jim is in a hurry. He runs a red light on the way to work.

*1.6 The countries of Orion and Scorpius are small mountainous nations. Both produce granite and blueberries. Each nation has a labor force of 800. The following table gives production per month for each worker in each country. Assume productivity is constant and identical for each worker in each country.

	Tons of Granite	Bushels of Blueberries
Orion workers	6	18
Scorpius workers	3	12

Productivity of one worker for one month

  a. Which country has an absolute advantage in the production of granite? Which country has an absolute advantage in the production of blueberries?
  b. Which country has a comparative advantage in the production of granite? of blueberries?
  c. Sketch the ppf's for both countries.

d. Assuming no trading between the two, if both countries wanted to have equal numbers of tons of granite and bushels of blueberries, how would they allocate workers to the two sectors?

e. Show that specialization and trade can move both countries beyond their ppf's.

*1.7 Match each diagram in Figure 1 with its description here. Assume that the economy is producing or attempting to produce at point *A* and that most members of society like meat and not fish. Some descriptions apply to more than one diagram, and some diagrams have more than one description.

a. Inefficient production of meat and fish
b. Productive efficiency
c. An inefficient mix of output
d. Technological advances in the production of meat and fish
e. The law of increasing opportunity cost
f. An impossible combination of meat and fish

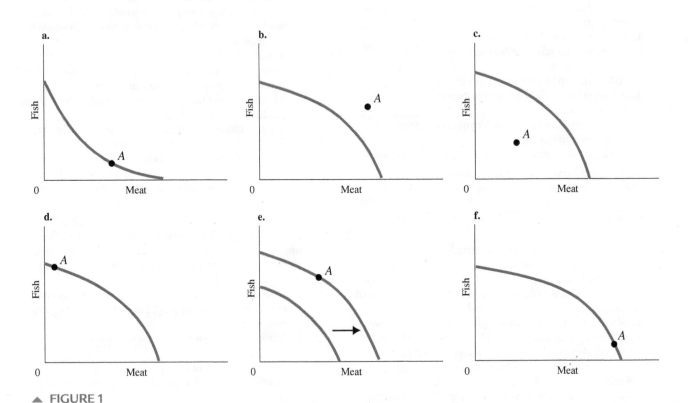

▲ **FIGURE 1**

1.8 A nation with fixed quantities of resources is able to produce any of the following combinations of carpet and carpet looms:

Yards of carpet (Millions)	Carpet looms (Thousands)
0	45
12	42
24	36
36	27
48	15
60	0

These figures assume that a certain number of previously produced looms are available in the current period for producing carpet.

a. Using the data in the table, graph the ppf (with carpet on the vertical axis).

b. Does the principle of "increasing opportunity cost" hold in this nation? Explain briefly. (*Hint:* What happens to the opportunity cost of carpet—measured in number of looms—as carpet production increases?)

c. If this country chooses to produce both carpet and looms, what will happen to the ppf over time? Why?

Now suppose that a new technology is discovered that allows an additional 50 percent of yards of carpet to be produced by each existing loom.

d. Illustrate (on your original graph) the effect of this new technology on the ppf.

e. Suppose that before the new technology is introduced, the nation produces 15 thousand looms. After the new technology is introduced, the nation produces 27 thousand looms. What is the effect of the new technology on the production of carpet? (Give the number of yards before and after the change.)

*Note: Problems with an asterisk are more challenging.

1.9 [**Related to the *Economics in Practice* on p. 25**] An analysis of a large-scale survey of consumer food purchases by Mark Aguiar and Erik Hurst indicates that retired people spend less for the same market basket of food than working people do. Use the concept of opportunity cost to explain this fact.

*1.10 Betty Lou has a car washing and detailing business. She charges $20 to wash a car, a process that takes her 20 minutes and requires no help or materials. For car detailing, a process requiring 1 hour, she charges $50 net of materials. Again, no help is required. Is anything puzzling about Betty Lou's pricing pattern? Explain your answer.

1.11 At the end of the 2014 NFL regular season, the Louisiana Lottery allowed customers to enter their non-winning New Orleans Saints scratch-off lottery game tickets in a final second-chance drawing, with a chance to win the 2015 Saints Season Prize Package Experience. This package includes 4 Plaza Sideline tickets and field passes to every 2015 Saints home game, a season parking pass, and overnight accommodations for each home game. Suppose you entered this second-chance drawing and won this Season Prize Package Experience for the Saints' 2015 season. Would there be a cost to you to attend the Saints' games during the 2015 season?

1.12 High school football is arguably more popular in West Texas than in any other region of the country. During football season, small towns seem to shut down on Friday nights as local high school teams take to the field, and for the following week the results of the games are the talk of each town. Taking into consideration that many of these towns are one hundred or more miles away from any medium-sized or large cities, what might be an economic explanation for the extreme popularity of high school football in these small West Texas towns?

1.13 The nation of Billabong is able to produce surfboards and kayaks in combinations represented by the data in the following table. Each number represents thousands of units. Plot this data on a production possibilities graph and explain why the data shows that Billabong experiences increasing opportunity costs.

	A	B	C	D	E
Surfboards	0	20	40	60	80
Kayaks	28	24	18	10	0

1.14 Explain how each of the following situations would affect a nation's production possibilities curve.
   a. A law is passed which makes community college tuition-free for all U.S. citizens.
   b. An unexpectedly mild spring results in a bumper crop of citrus fruit in both Florida and California.
   c. A change in immigration laws significantly increases the number of immigrant workers entering the country.
   d. The amount of time that unemployed workers can collect unemployment insurance is increased from 26 weeks to 96 weeks during a recession, resulting in workers remaining unemployed for a longer period of time.
   e. An innovation in desalinization technology allows for the more efficient conversion of salt water to fresh water.
   f. A radiation leak at a nuclear power plant results in the long-term evacuation of a 10,000 square-mile area, which significantly reduces the nation's productive capacity.

2.2 ECONOMIC SYSTEMS AND THE ROLE OF GOVERNMENT

LEARNING OBJECTIVE: Understand the central difference in the way command economies and market economies decide what is produced.

2.1 Describe a command economy and a laissez-faire economy. Do any economic systems in the world reflect the purest forms of command or laissez-faire economies? Explain.

2.2 Suppose that a simple society has an economy with only one resource, labor. Labor can be used to produce only two commodities—X, a necessity good (food), and Y, a luxury good (music and merriment). Suppose that the labor force consists of 100 workers. One laborer can produce either 5 units of necessity per month (by hunting and gathering) or 10 units of luxury per month (by writing songs, playing the guitar, dancing, and so on).
   a. On a graph, draw the economy's ppf. Where does the ppf intersect the Y-axis? Where does it intersect the X-axis? What meaning do those points have?
   b. Suppose the economy produced at a point *inside* the ppf. Give at least two reasons why this could occur. What could be done to move the economy to a point *on* the ppf?
   c. Suppose you succeeded in lifting your economy to a point on its ppf. What point would you choose? How might your small society decide the point at which it wanted to be?
   d. Once you have chosen a point on the ppf, you still need to decide how your society's production will be divided. If you were a dictator, how would you decide? What would happen if you left product distribution to the free market?

3

Demand, Supply, and Market Equilibrium

Chapters 1 and 2 introduced the discipline, methodology, and subject matter of economics. We now begin the task of analyzing how a market economy actually works. This chapter and the next present an overview of the way individual markets work, introducing concepts used in both microeconomics and macroeconomics.

In the simple island society discussed in Chapter 2, Bill and Colleen solved the economic problem directly. They allocated their time and used the island's resources to satisfy their wants. Exchange occurred in a relatively simple way. In larger societies, with people typically operating at some distance from one another, exchange can be more complex. *Markets* are the institutions through which exchange typically takes place.

This chapter begins to explore the basic forces at work in market systems. The purpose of our discussion is to explain how the individual decisions of households and firms together, without any central planning or direction, answer the three basic questions: What gets produced? How is it produced? Who gets what is produced? We begin with some definitions.

Firms and Households: The Basic Decision-Making Units

3.1 LEARNING OBJECTIVE

Understand the roles of firms, entrepreneurs, and households in the market.

Throughout this book, we discuss and analyze the behavior of two fundamental decision-making units: *firms*—the primary producing units in an economy—and *households*—the consuming units in an economy. Both are made up of people performing different functions and playing different roles. Economics is concerned with how those people behave, and the interaction among them.

A **firm** exists when a person or a group of people decides to produce a product or products by transforming *inputs*—that is, resources in the broadest sense—*into outputs*, the products that are sold in the market. Some firms produce goods; others produce services. Some are large, many are small, and some are in between. All firms exist to transform resources into goods and services that people want. The Colorado Symphony Orchestra takes labor, land, a building, musically talented people, instruments, and other inputs and combines them to produce concerts. The production process can be extremely complicated. For example, the first flautist in the orchestra combines training, talent, previous performance experience, score, instrument, conductor's interpretation, and personal feelings about the music to produce just one contribution to an overall performance.

firm An organization that transforms resources (inputs) into products (outputs). Firms are the primary producing units in a market economy.

Most firms exist to make a profit for their owners, but some do not. Columbia University, for example, fits the description of a firm: It takes inputs in the form of labor, land, skills, books, and buildings and produces a service that we call *education*. Although the university sells that service for a price, it does not exist to make a profit; instead, it exists to provide education and research of the highest quality possible.

Still, most firms exist to make a profit. They engage in production because they can sell their product for more than it costs to produce it. The analysis of a firm's behavior that follows rests on the assumption that *firms make decisions to maximize profits*. Sometimes firms suffer losses instead of earning profits. When firms suffer losses, we will assume that they act to minimize those losses.

An **entrepreneur** is someone who organizes, manages, and assumes the risks of a firm. When a new firm is created, someone must organize the new firm, arrange financing, hire employees, and take risks. That person is an entrepreneur. Sometimes existing firms introduce new products, and sometimes new firms develop or improve on an old idea, but at the root of it all is entrepreneurship.

entrepreneur A person who organizes, manages, and assumes the risks of a firm, taking a new idea or a new product and turning it into a successful business.

The consuming units in an economy are **households**. A household may consist of any number of people: a single person living alone, a married couple with four children, or 15 unrelated people sharing a house. Household decisions are based on individual tastes and preferences. The household buys what it wants and can afford. In a large, heterogeneous, and open society such as the United States, wildly different tastes find expression in the marketplace. A six-block walk in any direction on any street in Manhattan or a drive from the Chicago Loop south into rural Illinois should be enough to convince anyone that it is difficult to generalize about what people do and do not like.

households The consuming units in an economy.

Even though households have wide-ranging preferences, they also have some things in common. All—even the very rich—have ultimately limited incomes, and all must pay in some way for the goods and services they consume. Although households may have some control over their incomes—they can work more hours or fewer hours—they are also constrained by the availability of jobs, current wages, their own abilities, and their accumulated and inherited wealth (or lack thereof).

Input Markets and Output Markets: The Circular Flow

3.2 LEARNING OBJECTIVE

Understand the role of households as both suppliers to firms and buyers of what firms produce.

Households and firms interact in two basic kinds of markets: product (or output) markets and input (or factor) markets. Goods and services that are intended for use by households are

product *or* output markets
The markets in which goods and services are exchanged.

input *or* factor markets
The markets in which the resources used to produce goods and services are exchanged.

labor market The input/factor market in which households supply work for wages to firms that demand labor.

capital market The input/factor market in which households supply their savings, for interest or for claims to future profits, to firms that demand funds to buy capital goods.

land market The input/factor market in which households supply land or other real property in exchange for rent.

factors of production
The inputs into the production process. Land, labor, and capital are the three key factors of production.

exchanged in **product *or* output markets**. In output markets, firms *supply* and households *demand*.

To produce goods and services, firms must buy resources in **input *or* factor markets**. Firms buy inputs from households, which supply these inputs. When a firm decides how much to produce (supply) in output markets, it must simultaneously decide how much of each input it needs to produce the desired level of output. To produce smart phones Samsung and Apple need many inputs, including hardware and software and a variety of types of labor, both skilled and unskilled.

Figure 3.1 shows the *circular flow* of economic activity through a simple market economy. Note that the flow reflects the direction in which goods and services flow through input and output markets. For example, real goods and services flow from firms to households through output—or product—markets. Labor services flow from households to firms through input markets. Payment (most often in money form) for goods and services flows in the opposite direction.

In input markets, households *supply* resources. Most households earn their incomes by working—they supply their labor in the **labor market** to firms that demand labor and pay workers for their time and skills. Households may also loan their accumulated or inherited savings to firms for interest or exchange those savings for claims to future profits, as when a household buys shares of stock in a corporation. In the **capital market**, households supply the funds that firms use to buy capital goods. Households may also supply land or other real property in exchange for rent in the **land market**.

Inputs into the production process are also called **factors of production**. Land, labor, and capital are the three key factors of production. Throughout this text, we use the terms *input* and *factor of production* interchangeably. Thus, input markets and factor markets mean the same thing.

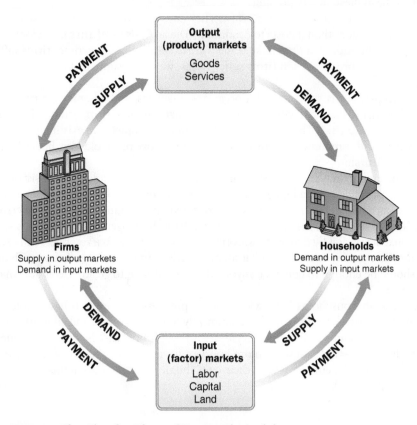

▲ **FIGURE 3.1** **The Circular Flow of Economic Activity**
Diagrams like this one show the circular flow of economic activity, hence the name *circular flow diagram*. Here goods and services flow clockwise: Labor services supplied by households flow to firms, and goods and services produced by firms flow to households. Payment (usually money) flows in the opposite (counterclockwise) direction: Payment for goods and services flows from households to firms, and payment for labor services flows from firms to households.

Note: Color Guide–In Figure 3.1 households are depicted in *blue* and firms are depicted in *red*. From now on all diagrams relating to the behavior of households will be blue or shades of blue and all diagrams relating to the behavior of firms will be red or shades of red. The green color indicates a monetary flow.

The supply of inputs and their prices ultimately determine household income. Thus, the amount of income a household earns depends on the decisions it makes concerning what types of inputs it chooses to supply. Whether to stay in school, how much and what kind of training to get, whether to start a business, how many hours to work, whether to work at all, and how to invest savings are all household decisions that affect income.

As you can see:

> Input and output markets are connected through the behavior of both firms and households. Firms determine the quantities and character of outputs produced and the types and quantities of inputs demanded. Households determine the types and quantities of products demanded and the quantities and types of inputs supplied.[1]

In 2015 a 12-pack of 12 oz. soda costs about $5, and many of you likely have one somewhere in your dormitory room. What determines the price of that soda? How can I explain how much soda you will buy in a given month or year? By the end of this chapter you will see the way in which prices in the market are determined by the interaction of buyers like you and suppliers like soda manufacturers. The model of supply and demand covered in this chapter is the most powerful tool of economics. By the time you finish this chapter we hope you will look at shopping in a different way.

Demand in Product/Output Markets

3.3 LEARNING OBJECTIVE

Understand what determines the position and shape of the demand curve and what factors move you along a demand curve and what factors shift the demand curve.

Every week you make hundreds of decisions about what to buy. Your choices likely look different from those of your friends or your parents. For all of you, however, the decision about what to buy and how much of it to buy ultimately depends on six factors:

- The *price of the product* in question.
- The *income available* to the household.
- The household's *amount of accumulated wealth*.
- The *prices of other products* available to the household.
- The household's *tastes and preferences*.
- The household's *expectations* about future income, wealth, and prices.

Quantity demanded is the amount (number of units) of a product that a household would buy in a given period *if it could buy all it wanted at the current market price*. Of course, the amount of a product that households finally purchase depends on the amount of product actually available in the market. The expression *if it could buy all it wanted* is critical to the definition of quantity demanded because it allows for the possibility that quantity supplied and quantity demanded are unequal.

quantity demanded The amount (number of units) of a product that a household would buy in a given period if it could buy all it wanted at the current market price.

Changes in Quantity Demanded versus Changes in Demand

In our list of what determines how much you buy of a product the price of that product comes first. This is no accident. The most important relationship in individual markets is between market price and quantity demanded. So that is where we will start our work. In fact, we begin by looking

---

[1] Our description of markets begins with the behavior of firms and households. Modern orthodox economic theory essentially combines two distinct but closely related theories of behavior. The "theory of household behavior," or "consumer behavior," has its roots in the works of nineteenth-century utilitarians such as Jeremy Bentham, William Jevons, Carl Menger, Leon Walras, Vilfredo Parcto, and F. Y. Edgeworth. The "theory of the firm" developed out of the earlier classical political economy of Adam Smith, David Ricardo, and Thomas Malthus. In 1890, Alfred Marshall published the first of many editions of his *Principles of Economics.* That volume pulled together the main themes of both the classical economists and the utilitarians into what is now called *neoclassical economics.* Although there have been many changes over the years, the basic structure of the model that we build can be found in Marshall's work.

at what happens to the quantity a typical individual demands of a product when all that changes is its price. Economists refer to this device as *ceteris paribus*, or "all else equal." We will be looking at the relationship between quantity demanded of a good by an individual or household when its price changes, holding income, wealth, other prices, tastes, and expectations constant. If the price of that 12-pack of soda were cut in half, how many more cases would you buy in a given week?

In thinking about this question it is important to focus on the price change alone and to maintain the all else equal assumption. If next week you suddenly found yourself with more money than you expected (perhaps a windfall from an aunt), you might well find yourself buying an extra 12-pack of soda even if the price did not change at all. To be sure that we distinguish clearly between changes in price and other changes that affect demand, throughout the rest of the text we will be precise about terminology. Specifically:

> Changes in the price of a product affect the *quantity demanded* per period. Changes in any other factor, such as income or preferences, affect *demand*. Thus, we say that an increase in the price of Coca-Cola is likely to cause a decrease in the *quantity of Coca-Cola demanded*. However, we say that an increase in income is likely to cause an increase in the *demand* for most goods.

Price and Quantity Demanded: The Law of Demand

demand schedule   Shows how much of a given product a household would be willing to buy at different prices for a given time period.

A **demand schedule** shows how much of a product a person or household is willing to purchase per time period (each week or each month) at different prices. Clearly that decision is based on numerous interacting factors. Consider Alex who just graduated from college with an entry-level job at a local bank. During her senior year, Alex got a car loan and bought a used Mini Cooper. The Mini gets 25 miles per gallon of gasoline. Alex lives with several friends in a house 10 miles from her workplace and enjoys visiting her parents 50 miles away.

How often Alex will decide to drive herself to work and parties, visit her family, or even go joy riding depends on many things, including her income and whether she likes to drive. But the price of gasoline also plays an important role, and it is this relationship between price and quantity demanded that we focus on in the law of demand. With a gasoline price of $3.00 a gallon, Alex might decide to drive herself to work every day, visit her parents once a week, and drive another 50 miles a week for other activities. This driving pattern would add up to 250 miles a week, which would use 10 gallons of gasoline in her Mini. The demand schedule in Table 3.1 thus shows that at a price of $3.00 per gallon, Alex is willing to buy 10 gallons of gasoline. We can see that this demand schedule reflects a lot of information about Alex including where she lives and works and what she likes to do in her spare time.

Now suppose an international crisis in the Middle East causes the price of gasoline at the pump to rise to $5.00 per gallon. How does this affect Alex's demand for gasoline, assuming that everything else remains the same? Driving is now more expensive, and we would not be surprised if Alex decided to take the bus some mornings or share a ride with friends. She might visit her parents less frequently as well. On the demand schedule given in Table 3.1, Alex cuts her desired consumption of gasoline by half to 5 gallons when the price goes to $5.00. If,

TABLE 3.1 Alex's Demand Schedule for Gasoline	
Price (per Gallon)	Quantity Demanded (Gallons per Week)
$ 8.00	0
7.00	2
6.00	3
5.00	5
4.00	7
3.00	10
2.00	14
1.00	20
0.00	26

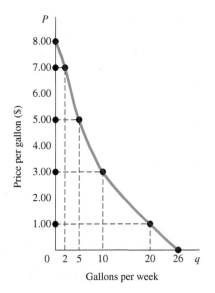

◀ **FIGURE 3.2 Alex's Demand Curve**

The relationship between price (*P*) and quantity demanded (*q*) presented graphically is called a demand curve. Demand curves have a negative slope, indicating that lower prices cause quantity demanded to increase. Note that Alex's demand curve is blue; demand in product markets is determined by household choice.

instead, the price of gasoline fell substantially, Alex might spend more time driving, and that is in fact the pattern we see in the table. This same information presented graphically is called a **demand curve**. Alex's demand curve is presented in Figure 3.2. You will note in Figure 3.2 that *quantity* (*q*) is measured along the horizontal axis and *price* (*P*) is measured along the vertical axis. This is the convention we follow throughout this book.

demand curve   A graph illustrating how much of a given product a household would be willing to buy at different prices.

Demand Curves Slope Downward

The data in Table 3.1 show that at lower prices, Alex buys more gasoline; at higher prices, she buys less. Thus, there is a *negative, or inverse, relationship between quantity demanded and price.* When price rises, quantity demanded falls, and when price falls, quantity demanded rises. Thus, demand curves always slope downward. This negative relationship between price and quantity demanded is often referred to as the **law of demand**, a term first used by economist Alfred Marshall in his 1890 textbook.

Some people are put off by the abstraction of demand curves. Of course, we do not actually draw our own demand curves for products. When we want to make a purchase, we usually face only a single price and how much we would buy at other prices is irrelevant. However, demand curves help analysts understand the kind of behavior that households are *likely* to exhibit if they are actually faced with a higher or lower price. We know, for example, that if the price of a good rises enough, the quantity demanded must ultimately drop to zero. The demand curve is thus a tool that helps us explain economic behavior and predict reactions to possible price changes.

Marshall's definition of a social "law" captures the idea:

law of demand   The negative relationship between price and quantity demanded: *Ceteris paribus*, as price rises, quantity demanded decreases; as price falls, quantity demanded increases during a given period of time, all other things remaining constant.

> The term "law" means nothing more than a general proposition or statement of tendencies, more or less certain, more or less definite…a *social law* is a statement of social tendencies; that is, that a certain course of action may be expected from the members of a social group under certain conditions.[2]

It seems reasonable to expect that consumers will demand more of a product at a lower price and less of it at a higher price. Households must divide their incomes over a wide range of goods and services. At $3.00 per gallon and 25 miles to a gallon, driving the 20 miles round trip to work costs Alex $2.40. It may look like a good deal relative to taking a bus. At $5.00 per gallon, the trip now costs $4.00. With the higher prices, Alex may have to give up her morning latte if she drives, and that may turn out to be too big a sacrifice for her. Now the bus may look better. As the price of gasoline rises, the opportunity cost of driving in terms of other types of consumption also rises and that is why Alex ends up driving less as the price of gasoline rises. Goods compete with one another for our spending.

[2] Alfred Marshall, *Principles of Economics*, 8th ed. (New York: Macmillan, 1948), p. 33. (The first edition was published in 1890.)

Economists use the concept of *utility* to explain the slope of the demand curve. We consume goods and services because they give us utility or satisfaction. As we consume more of a product within a given period of time, it is likely that each additional unit consumed will yield successively less satisfaction. The utility you gain from a second ice cream cone is likely to be less than the utility you gained from the first, the third is worth even less, and so on. This *law of diminishing marginal utility* is an important concept in economics. If each successive unit of a good is worth less to you, you are not going to be willing to pay as much for it. Thus, it is reasonable to expect a downward slope in the demand curve for that good.

Thinking about the ways that people are affected by price changes also helps us see what is behind the law of demand. Consider this example: Luis lives and works in Mexico City. His elderly mother lives in Santiago, Chile. Last year the airlines servicing South America got into a price war, and the price of flying between Mexico City and Santiago dropped from 20,000 pesos to 10,000 pesos. How might Luis's behavior change?

First, he is better off. Last year he flew home to Chile three times at a total cost of 60,000 pesos. This year he can fly to Chile the same number of times, buy exactly the same combination of other goods and services that he bought last year, and have 30,000 pesos left over. Because he is better off—his income can buy more—he may fly home more frequently. Second, the opportunity cost of flying home has changed. Before the price war, Luis had to sacrifice 20,000 pesos worth of other goods and services each time he flew to Chile. After the price war, he must sacrifice only 10,000 pesos worth of other goods and services for each trip. The trade-off has changed. Both of these effects are likely to lead to a higher quantity demanded in response to the lower price.

In sum:

> It is reasonable to expect quantity demanded to fall when price rises, ceteris paribus, and to expect quantity demanded to rise when price falls, ceteris paribus. Demand curves have a negative slope.

Other Properties of Demand Curves   Two additional things are notable about Alex's demand curve. First, it intersects the Y, or price, axis. This means that there is a price above which she buys no gasoline. In this case, Alex simply stops driving when the price reaches $8 per gallon. As long as households have limited incomes and wealth, all demand curves will intersect the price axis. For any commodity, there is always a price above which a household will not or cannot pay. Even if the good or service is important, all households are ultimately constrained, or limited, by income and wealth.

Second, Alex's demand curve intersects the X, or quantity, axis. Even at a zero price, there is a limit to how much she will drive. If gasoline were free, she would use 26 gallons, but not more. That demand curves intersect the quantity axis is a matter of common sense. Demand in a given period of time is limited, if only by time, even at a zero price.

To summarize what we know about the shape of demand curves:

1. They have a negative slope. An increase in price is likely to lead to a decrease in quantity demanded, and a decrease in price is likely to lead to an increase in quantity demanded.
2. They intersect the quantity (X) axis, a result of time limitations and diminishing marginal utility.
3. They intersect the price (Y) axis, a result of limited income and wealth.

That is all we can say; it is not possible to generalize further. The actual shape of an individual household demand curve—whether it is steep or flat, whether it is bowed in or bowed out—depends on the unique tastes and preferences of the household and other factors. Some households may be sensitive to price changes; other households may respond little to a change in price. In some cases, plentiful substitutes are available; in other cases, they are not. Thus, to fully understand the shape and position of demand curves, we must turn to the other determinants of household demand.

Other Determinants of Household Demand

Of the many factors likely to influence a household's demand for a specific product, we have considered only the price of the product. But household income and wealth, the prices of other goods and services, tastes and preferences, and expectations also matter to demand.

Income and Wealth   Before we proceed, we need to define two terms that are often confused, *income* and *wealth*. A household's **income** is the sum of all the wages, salaries, profits, interest payments, rents, and other forms of earnings received by the household *in a given period of time.* Income is thus a *flow* measure: We must specify a time period for it—income *per month* or *per year.* You can spend or consume more or less than your income in any given period. If you consume less than your income, you save. To consume more than your income in a period, you must either borrow or draw on savings accumulated from previous periods.

income   The sum of all a household's wages, salaries, profits, interest payments, rents, and other forms of earnings in a given period of time. It is a flow measure.

Wealth is the total value of what a household owns minus what it owes. Another word for wealth is **net worth**—the amount a household would have left if it sold all of its possessions and paid all of its debts. Wealth is a *stock* measure: It is measured at a given point in time. If, in a given period, you spend less than your income, you save; the amount that you save is added to your wealth. Saving is the flow that affects the stock of wealth. When you spend more than your income, you *dissave*—you reduce your wealth.

wealth *or* net worth   The total value of what a household owns minus what it owes. It is a stock measure.

Households with higher incomes and higher accumulated savings or inherited wealth can afford to buy more goods and services. In general, we would expect higher demand at higher levels of income/wealth and lower demand at lower levels of income/wealth. Goods for which demand goes up when income is higher and for which demand goes down when income is lower are called **normal goods**. Movie tickets, restaurant meals, and shirts are all normal goods.

normal goods   Goods for which demand goes up when income is higher and for which demand goes down when income is lower.

However, generalization in economics can be hazardous. Sometimes demand for a good falls when household income rises. When a household's income rises, it is likely to buy higher-quality meats—its demand for filet mignon is likely to rise—but its demand for lower-quality meats—chuck steak, for example—is likely to fall. At higher incomes, people can afford to fly. People who can afford to fly are less likely to take the bus long distances. Thus, higher income may *reduce* the number of times someone takes a bus. Goods for which demand tends to fall when income rises are called **inferior goods.**

inferior goods   Goods for which demand tends to fall when income rises.

Prices of Other Goods and Services   No consumer decides in isolation on the amount of any one commodity to buy. Instead, each decision is part of a larger set of decisions that are made simultaneously. Households must apportion their incomes over many different goods and services. As a result, the price of any one good can and does affect the demand for other goods. This is most obviously the case when goods are substitutes for one another. For Alex the bus is an alternative that she uses when gasoline gets expensive.

When an *increase* in the price of one good causes demand for another good to *increase* (a positive relationship), we say that the goods are **substitutes**. A *fall* in the price of a good causes a *decline* in demand for its substitutes. Substitutes are goods that can serve as replacements for one another.

substitutes   Goods that can serve as replacements for one another; when the price of one increases, demand for the other increases.

To be substitutes, two products do not need to be identical. Identical products are called **perfect substitutes.** Japanese cars are not identical to American cars. Nonetheless, all have four wheels, are capable of carrying people, and use fuel. Thus, significant changes in the price of one country's cars can be expected to influence demand for the other country's cars. Restaurant meals are substitutes for meals eaten at home, and flying from New York to Washington, D.C., is a substitute for taking the train. The *Economics in Practice* box describes substitution in the textbook market.

perfect substitutes   Identical products.

Often two products "go together"—that is, they complement each other. Bacon and eggs are **complementary goods**, as are cars and gasoline. When two goods are **complements**, a *decrease* in the price of one results in an *increase* in demand for the other and vice versa. For iPads and Kindles, for example, the availability of content at low prices stimulates demand for the devices.

complements, complementary goods   Goods that "go together"; a decrease in the price of one results in an increase in demand for the other and vice versa.

Tastes and Preferences   Income, wealth, and prices of goods available are the three factors that determine the combinations of goods and services that a household is *able* to buy. You know that you cannot afford to rent an apartment at $1,200 per month if your monthly income is only

Have You Bought This Textbook?

As all of you know full well, college textbooks are expensive. And, at first, it may seem as though there are few substitutes available for the cash-strapped undergraduate. After *all*, if your professor assigns Smith's *Principles of Biology* to you, you cannot go out and see if Jones' *Principles of Chemistry* is perhaps cheaper and buy it instead. As it turns out, as some recent work by Judy Chevalier and Austan Goolsbee[1] discovered, even when instructors require particular texts, when prices are high students have found substitutes. Even in the textbook market student demand does slope down!

Chevalier and Goolsbee collected data on textbooks from more than 1600 colleges for the years 1997–2001 to do their research. For that period, the lion's share of both new and used college textbooks was sold in college bookstores. Next, they looked at class enrollments for each college in the large majors, economics, biology, and psychology. In each of those classes they were able to learn which textbook had been assigned. At first, one might think that the total number of textbooks, used plus new, should match the class enrollment. After all, the text is required! In fact, what they found was the higher the textbook price, the more text sales fell below class enrollments.

So what substitutes did students find for the required text? While the paper has no hard evidence on this, students themselves gave them lots of suggestions. Many decide to share books with roommates. Others use the library more. These solutions are not perfect, but when the price is high enough, students find it worth their while to walk to the library!

THINKING PRACTICALLY

1. If you were to construct a demand curve for a required text in a course, where would that demand curve intersect the horizontal axis?
2. And this much harder question: In the year before a new edition of a text is published, many college bookstores will not buy the older edition. Given this *fact*, what do you think happens to the gap between enrollments and new plus used book sales in the year before a new edition of a text is expected?

[1] Judith Chevalier and Austan Goolsbee, "Are Durable Goods Consumers Forward Looking? Evidence From College Textbooks," *Quarterly Journal of Economics*, 2009: 1853–1884.

$400, but within these constraints, you are more or less free to choose what to buy. Your final choice depends on your individual tastes and preferences.

Changes in preferences can and do manifest themselves in market behavior. Thirty years ago the major big-city marathons drew only a few hundred runners. Now tens of thousands enter and run. The demand for running shoes, running suits, stopwatches, and other running items has greatly increased.

Within the constraints of prices and incomes, preference shapes the demand curve, but it is difficult to generalize about tastes and preferences. First, they are volatile: Five years ago more people smoked cigarettes and fewer people had smartphones. Second, tastes are idiosyncratic: Some people like to text, whereas others still prefer to use e-mail; some people prefer dogs, whereas others are crazy about cats. The diversity of individual demands is almost infinite.

One of the interesting questions in economics is why, in some markets, diverse consumer tastes give rise to a variety of styles, whereas in other markets, despite a seeming diversity in tastes, we find only one or two varieties. All sidewalks in the United States are a similar gray color, yet houses are painted a rainbow of colors. Yet it is not obvious on the face of it that people would not prefer as much variety in their sidewalks as in their houses. To answer this type of question, we need to move beyond the demand curve. We will revisit this question in a later chapter.

ECONOMICS IN PRACTICE

On Sunny Days People Buy Convertibles!

Cars are a durable good. Most people who buy new cars expect to keep them for a number of years. Cars also have many different features, including size, power, and styling. These features in turn influence consumer demand for one type of car or another. As economists we might well expect people to choose the type of car they buy thinking about which features of those cars they will enjoy over the next few years. A four-wheel-drive car is likely to be more attractive if I expect a lot of snow in the next months or years. A convertible would be fun if it is likely to be clear and sunny on average in my region of the country.

On the other hand, given that cars are durable, we would be surprised if the weather *on a particular day* influenced car purchases. If a potential car buyer wakes up to an unseasonably warm and sunny day in November, we might be surprised if he or she all of a sudden decides to buy a convertible. A sunny day is a good reason to take a hike, but not a good reason to buy a durable good like a convertible that depends for its enjoyment on a string of sunny days. And, yet, in recent work, Meghan Busse, an economist at Northwestern, and her co-authors found after examining more than 40 million car transactions that car purchasers were heavily influenced in their choice of cars by temporary weather fluctuations at the time of purchase.[1] A snow storm increased the likelihood of buying a four-wheel drive vehicle within the next week by 6 percent, holding constant the average snow in that area of the country. An increase of 10-degrees on a fall or spring day over the norm increased purchase of convertibles by almost 3 percent.

Behavioral economists looking at this case would argue that the snow or sun makes one feature of a car—its four-wheel drive feature or soft top—more **salient** or important to the consumer's decision to purchase.

THINKING PRACTICALLY

1. Economists predict that my interest in purchasing a convertible also depends on how much I think other people like convertibles. How is this prediction related to the durability of cars?

[1] Meghan Busse, Devon Pope, Jaron Pope, and Jorge Silva-Russo, "The Psychological Effect of Weather on Car Purchases," *Quarterly Journal of Economics,* February, 2015.

Expectations   What you decide to buy today certainly depends on today's prices and your current income and wealth. You also have expectations about what your position will be in the future. You may have expectations about future changes in prices too, and these may affect your decisions today.

There are many examples of the ways expectations affect demand. When people buy a house or a car, they often must borrow part of the purchase price and repay it over a number of years. In deciding what kind of house or car to buy, they presumably must think about their income today, as well as what their income is likely to be in the future.

As another example, consider a student in the final year of medical school living on a scholarship of $25,000. Compare that student with another person earning $12 an hour at a full-time job, with no expectation of a significant change in income in the future. The two have virtually identical incomes. But even if they have the same tastes, the medical student is likely to demand different goods and services, simply because of the expectation of a major increase in income later on.

Increasingly, economic theory has come to recognize the importance of expectations. We will devote a good deal of time to discussing how expectations affect more than just demand. For the time being, however, it is important to understand that demand depends on more than just *current* incomes, prices, and tastes.

TABLE 3.2	Shift of Alex's Demand Schedule Resulting from an Increase in Income	
	Schedule D_0	Schedule D_1
Price (per Gallon)	Quantity Demanded (Gallons per Week at an Income of $500 per Week)	Quantity Demanded (Gallons per Week at an Income of $700 per Week)
$ 8.00	0	3
7.00	2	5
6.00	3	7
5.00	5	10
4.00	7	12
3.00	10	15
2.00	14	19
1.00	20	24
0.00	26	30

Shift of Demand versus Movement along a Demand Curve

Recall that a demand curve shows the relationship between quantity demanded and the price of a good. Demand curves are constructed while holding income, tastes, and other prices constant. If income, tastes, or other prices change, we would have to derive an entirely new relationship between price and quantity.

Let us return once again to Alex. (See Table 3.1 and Figure 3.2 on pp. 46 and 47.) Suppose that when we derived the demand curve in Figure 3.2 Alex was receiving a salary of $500 per week after taxes. If Alex faces a price of $3.00 per gallon and chooses to drive 250 miles per week, her total weekly expenditure works out to be $3.00 per gallon times 10 gallons or $30 per week. That amounts to 6.0 percent of her income.

Suppose now she were to receive a raise to $700 per week after taxes. Alex's higher income may well raise the amount of gasoline being used by Alex *regardless* of what she was using before. The new situation is listed in Table 3.2 and graphed in Figure 3.3. Notice in Figure 3.3 that Alex's entire curve has shifted to the right—at $3.00 a gallon the curve shows an increase in the quantity demanded from 10 to 15 gallons. At $5.00, the quantity demanded by Alex increases from 5 gallons to 10 gallons.

The fact that demand *increased* when income increased implies that gasoline is a *normal good* to Alex.

▶ **FIGURE 3.3** **Shift of a Demand Curve Following a Rise in Income**

When the price of a good changes, we move *along* the demand curve for that good. When any other factor that influences demand changes (income, tastes, and so on), the demand curve shifts, in this case from D_0 to D_1. Gasoline is a normal good so an income increase shifts the curve to the right.

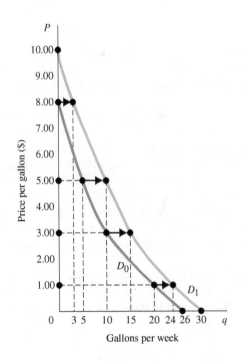

Gallons per week

The conditions under which we drew Alex's original demand curve have now changed. One of the factors affecting Alex's demand for gasoline (in this case, her income) has changed, creating a new relationship between price and quantity demanded. This is referred to as a **shift of a demand curve**.

It is important to distinguish between a change in quantity demanded—that is, some movement *along* a demand curve—and a shift of demand. Demand schedules and demand curves show the relationship between the price of a good or service and the quantity demanded per period, ceteris paribus. If price changes, quantity demanded will change—this is a **movement along a demand curve**. When any of the *other* factors that influence demand change, however, a new relationship between price and quantity demanded is established—this is a *shift of a demand curve*. The result, then, is a *new demand curve*. Changes in income, preferences, or prices of other goods cause a demand curve to shift:

Change in price of a good or service leads to
└──────▶ change in *quantity demanded* (**movement along a demand curve**).
Change in income, preferences, or prices of other goods or services leads to
└──────▶ change in *demand* (**shift of a demand curve**).

Figure 3.4 illustrates the differences between movement along a demand curve and shifting demand curves. In Figure 3.4(a), an increase in household income causes demand for hamburger (an inferior good) to decline, or shift to the left from D_0 to D_1. (Because quantity is measured on the horizontal axis, a decrease means a *shift to the left*.) In contrast, demand for steak (a normal good) increases, or *shifts to the right*, when income rises.

In Figure 3.4(b), an increase in the price of hamburger from $1.49 to $3.09 a pound causes a household to buy less hamburger each month. In other words, the higher price causes the *quantity demanded* to decline from 10 pounds to 5 pounds per month. This change represents a movement *along* the demand curve for hamburger. In place of hamburger, the household buys more chicken. The household's demand for chicken (a substitute for hamburger) rises—the demand curve shifts to the right. At the same time, the demand for ketchup (a good that complements hamburger) declines—its demand curve shifts to the left.

From Household Demand to Market Demand

So far we have been talking about what determines an individual's demand for a product. We ask the question: How many 12-packs of soda are you willing to buy per week when the price of that 12-pack is $5. This is a question you answer often in your life, whenever you go to the local store. We see the answer depends on how much money you have, how much you like soda, and what else is available to you at what price. Next time you go to the store and see a price change, we hope you think a bit more about your buying reaction.

Individual reactions to price changes are interesting, especially to the individual. But for us to be able to say something more general about prices in the market, we need to know about market demand.

Market demand is simply the sum of all the quantities of a good or service demanded per period by all the households buying in the market for that good or service. Figure 3.5 shows the derivation of a market demand curve from three individual demand curves. (Although this market demand curve is derived from the behavior of only three people, most markets have thousands, or even millions of demanders.) As the table in Figure 3.5 shows, when the price of a pound of coffee is $3.50, both household A and household C would purchase 4 pounds per month, while household B would buy none. At that price, presumably, B drinks tea. Market demand at $3.50 would thus be a total of 4 + 4, or 8 pounds. At a price of $1.50 per pound, however, A would purchase 8 pounds per month; B, 3 pounds; and C, 9 pounds. Thus, at $1.50 per pound, market demand would be 8 + 3 + 9, or 20 pounds of coffee per month.

The total quantity demanded in the marketplace at a given price is the sum of all the quantities demanded by all the individual households shopping in the market *at that price*. A market demand curve shows the total amount of a product that would be sold at each price if

shift of a demand curve The change that takes place in a demand curve corresponding to a new relationship between quantity demanded of a good and price of that good. The shift is brought about by a change in the original conditions.

movement along a demand curve The change in quantity demanded brought about by a change in price.

market demand The sum of all the quantities of a good or service demanded per period by all the households buying in the market for that good or service.

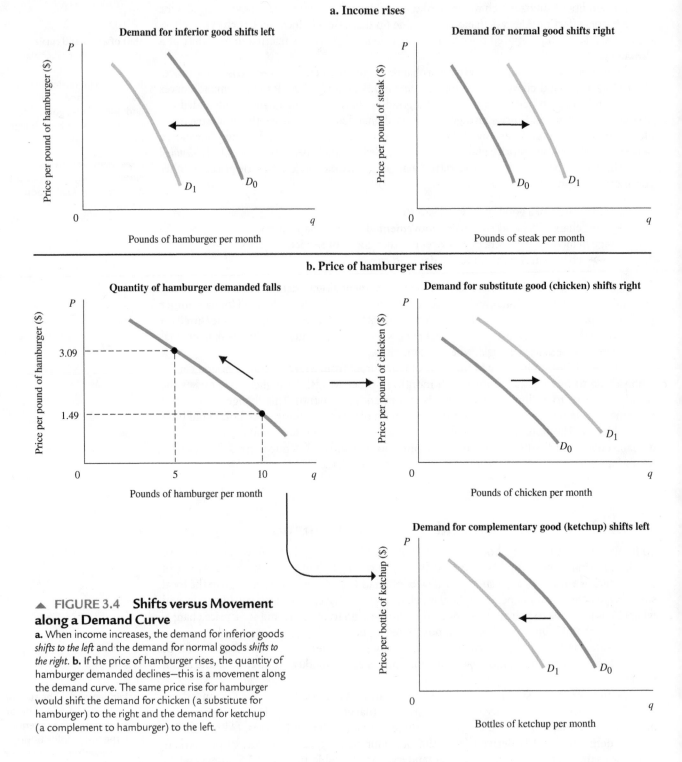

▲ FIGURE 3.4 **Shifts versus Movement along a Demand Curve**
a. When income increases, the demand for inferior goods *shifts to the left* and the demand for normal goods *shifts to the right*. **b.** If the price of hamburger rises, the quantity of hamburger demanded declines—this is a movement along the demand curve. The same price rise for hamburger would shift the demand for chicken (a substitute for hamburger) to the right and the demand for ketchup (a complement to hamburger) to the left.

households could buy all they wanted at that price. As Figure 3.5 shows, the market demand curve is the sum of all the individual demand curves—that is, the sum of all the individual quantities demanded at each price. Thus, the market demand curve takes its shape and position from the shapes, positions, and number of individual demand curves. If more people are in a market, more demand curves must be added and the market demand curve will shift to the right. Market demand curves may also shift as a result of preference changes, income changes, or changes in the price of substitutes or complements.

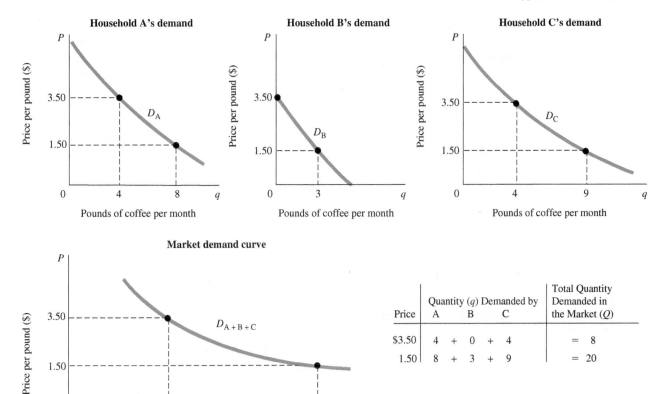

▲ **FIGURE 3.5 Deriving Market Demand from Individual Demand Curves**
Total demand in the marketplace is simply the sum of the demands of all the households shopping in a particular market. It is the sum of all the individual demand curves—that is, the sum of all the individual quantities demanded at each price.

As a general rule throughout this book, capital letters refer to the entire market and lowercase letters refer to individual households or firms. Thus, in Figure 3.5, Q refers to total quantity demanded in the market, while q refers to the quantity demanded by individual households.

An interesting feature of the demand curve in Figure 3.5 is that at different prices, the *type* of people demanding the product may change. When Apple halved the price of its iPhone in fall 2007, it announced that it wanted to make the iPhone available to a broader group of people. When prices fall, people like those in household B in Figure 3.5 move into markets that are otherwise out of their reach. When Apple introduced a new, improved, but much more expensive iPhone in the fall of 2014, its first sales were likely made to people who both had more resources and were more tech-savvy than the average old model iPhone user. Early adopters of products often look different from later users.

Supply in Product/Output Markets

Be able to distinguish between forces that shift a supply curve and changes that cause a movement along a supply curve.

We began our exploration of supply and demand some pages back with a simple question: Why is the average price of a 12-pack of soda $5 in 2015? So far we have seen one side of the answer: Given the tastes, incomes, and substitute products available in the United States, there are a lot of people willing to pay at least $5 for a 12-pack of soda! Now we turn to the other half of the market: How can we understand the behavior of the many firms selling that soda? What determines their willingness to sell soda? We refer to this as the supply side of the market.

Firms build factories, hire workers, and buy raw materials because they believe they can sell the products they make for more than it costs to produce them. In other words, firms supply goods and services like soda because they believe it will be profitable to do so. Supply decisions thus depend on profit potential. Because **profit** is the difference between revenues and costs, supply is likely to react to changes in revenues and changes in production costs. If the prices of soda are high, each 12-pack produces more revenue for suppliers because revenue is simply price per unit times units sold. So, just as in the case of buyers, the price will be important in explaining the behavior of suppliers in a market. It also typically costs suppliers something to produce whatever product they are bringing to market. They have to hire workers, build factories, and buy inputs. So the supply behavior of firms will also depend on costs of production.

In later chapters, we will focus on how firms decide *how* to produce their goods and services and explore the cost side of the picture more formally. For now, we will begin our examination of firm behavior by focusing on the output supply decision and the relationship between quantity supplied and output price, *ceteris paribus*.

profit The difference between revenues and costs.

Price and Quantity Supplied: The Law of Supply

Quantity supplied is the amount of a particular product that firms would be willing and able to offer for sale at a particular price during a given time period. A **supply schedule** shows how much of a product firms will sell at alternative prices.

Let us look at an agricultural market as an example. Table 3.3 itemizes the quantities of soybeans that an individual representative farmer such as Clarence Brown might sell at various prices. If the market paid $1.50 or less for a bushel for soybeans, Brown would not supply any soybeans: When Farmer Brown looks at the costs of growing soybeans, including the opportunity cost of his time and land, $1.50 per bushel will not compensate him for those costs. At $1.75 per bushel, however, at least some soybean production takes place on Brown's farm, and a price increase from $1.75 to $2.25 per bushel causes the quantity supplied by Brown to increase from 10,000 to 20,000 bushels per year. The higher price may justify shifting land from wheat to soybean production or putting previously fallow land into soybeans, or it may lead to more intensive farming of land already in soybeans, using expensive fertilizer or equipment that was not cost-justified at the lower price.

Generalizing from Farmer Brown's experience, we can reasonably expect an increase in market price, ceteris paribus, to lead to an increase in quantity supplied for Brown and farmers like him. In other words, there is a positive relationship between the quantity of a good supplied and price. This statement sums up the **law of supply**: An increase in market price will lead to an increase in quantity supplied, and a decrease in market price will lead to a decrease in quantity supplied.

The information in a supply schedule may be presented graphically in a **supply curve**. Supply curves slope upward. The upward, or positive, slope of Brown's curve in Figure 3.6 reflects this positive relationship between price and quantity supplied.

Note in Brown's supply schedule, however, that when price rises from $4 to $5, quantity supplied no longer increases. Often an individual firm's ability to respond to an increase in price is constrained by its existing scale of operations, or capacity, in the short run. For example, Brown's ability to produce more soybeans depends on the size of his farm, the fertility of his soil, and the types of equipment he has. The fact that output stays constant at 45,000 bushels per year suggests that he is running up against the limits imposed by the size of his farm, the quality of his soil, and his existing technology.

quantity supplied The amount of a particular product that a firm would be willing and able to offer for sale at a particular price during a given time period.

supply schedule Shows how much of a product firms will sell at alternative prices.

law of supply The positive relationship between price and quantity of a good supplied: An increase in market price, ceteris paribus, will lead to an increase in quantity supplied, and a decrease in market price will lead to a decrease in quantity supplied.

supply curve A graph illustrating how much of a product a firm will sell at different prices.

TABLE 3.3	Clarence Brown's Supply Schedule for Soybeans
Price (per Bushel)	Quantity Supplied (Bushels per Year)
$ 1.50	0
1.75	10,000
2.25	20,000
3.00	30,000
4.00	45,000
5.00	45,000

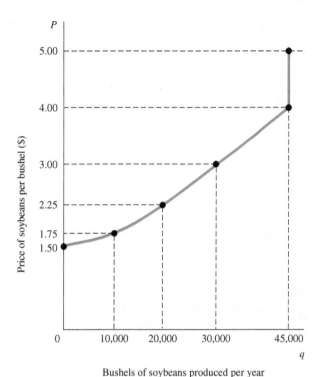

Bushels of soybeans produced per year

◀ FIGURE 3.6 **Clarence Brown's Individual Supply Curve**
A producer will supply more when the price of output is higher. The slope of a supply curve is positive. Note that the supply curve is red: Supply is determined by choices made by firms.

In the longer run, however, Brown may acquire more land or technology may change, allowing for more soybean production. The terms *short run and long run* have precise meanings in economics; we will discuss them in detail later. Here it is important only to understand that time plays a critical role in supply decisions. When prices change, firms' immediate response may be different from what they are able to do after a month or a year. Short-run and long-run supply curves are often different.

Other Determinants of Supply

Of the factors we have listed that are likely to affect the quantity of output supplied by a given firm, we have thus far discussed only the price of output. Other factors that affect supply include the cost of producing the product and the prices of related products.

The Cost of Production   For a firm to make a profit, its revenue must exceed its costs. As an individual producer, like Farmer Brown, thinks about how much to supply at a particular price, the producer will be looking at his or her costs. Brown's supply decision is likely to change in response to changes in the cost of production. Cost of production depends on a number of factors, including the available technologies and the prices and quantities of the inputs needed by the firm (labor, land, capital, energy, and so on).

Technological change can have an enormous impact on the cost of production over time. The introduction of fertilizers, the development of complex farm machinery, and the use of bioengineering to increase the yield of individual crops have all powerfully affected the cost of producing agricultural products. Technology has similarly decreased the costs of producing flat screen televisions. When a technological advance lowers the cost of production, output is likely to increase. When yield per acre increases, individual farmers can and do produce more. The production of electronic calculators, and later personal computers and smartphones, boomed with the development of inexpensive techniques to produce microprocessors.

Cost of production is also directly affected by the price of the factors of production. In the spring of 2008, the world price of oil rose to more than $100 per barrel from below $20 in 2002. As a result, cab drivers faced higher gasoline prices, airlines faced higher fuel costs, and manufacturing firms faced higher heating bills. The result: Cab drivers probably spent less time driving around looking for customers, airlines cut a few low-profit routes, and some manufacturing plants stopped running extra shifts. The moral of this story: Increases in input prices raise costs of production and are likely to reduce supply. The reverse occurred in 2009–2010 when oil prices fell back to $75 per barrel and more recently in 2014-2015 when oil prices again fell.

The Prices of Related Products Firms often react to changes in the prices of related products. For example, if land can be used for either corn or soybean production, an increase in soybean prices may cause individual farmers to shift acreage out of corn production into soybeans. Thus, an increase in soybean prices actually affects the amount of corn supplied.

Similarly, if beef prices rise, producers may respond by raising more cattle. However, leather comes from cowhide. Thus, an increase in beef prices may actually increase the supply of leather.

To summarize:

> Assuming that its objective is to maximize profits, a firm's decision about what quantity of output, or product, to supply depends on:
>
> 1. The price of the good or service.
> 2. The cost of producing the product, which in turn depends on:
>   - the price of required inputs (labor, capital, and land), and
>   - the technologies that can be used to produce the product.
> 3. The prices of related products.

Shift of Supply versus Movement along a Supply Curve

movement along a supply curve The change in quantity supplied brought about by a change in price.

shift of a supply curve The change that takes place in a supply curve corresponding to a new relationship between quantity supplied of a good and the price of that good. The shift is brought about by a change in the original conditions.

A supply curve shows the relationship between the quantity of a good or service supplied by a firm and the price that good or service brings in the market. Higher prices are likely to lead to an increase in quantity supplied, ceteris paribus. Remember: The supply curve is derived holding everything constant except price. When the price of a product changes ceteris paribus, a change in the quantity supplied follows—that is, a **movement along a supply curve** takes place. As you have seen, supply decisions are also influenced by factors other than price. New relationships between price and quantity supplied come about when factors other than price change, and the result is a **shift of a supply curve**. When factors other than price cause supply curves to shift, we say that there has been a *change in supply*.

Recall that the cost of production depends on the price of inputs and the technologies of production available. Now suppose that a major breakthrough in the production of soybeans has occurred: Genetic engineering has produced a superstrain of disease- and pest-resistant seed. Such a technological change would enable individual farmers to supply more soybeans at *any* market price. Table 3.4 and Figure 3.7 describe this change. At $3 a bushel, farmers would have produced 30,000 bushels from the old seed (schedule S_0 in Table 3.4); with the lower cost of production and higher yield resulting from the new seed, they produce 40,000 bushels (schedule S_1 in Table 3.4). At $1.75 per bushel, they would have produced 10,000 bushels from the old seed; but with the lower costs and higher yields, output rises to 23,000 bushels.

TABLE 3.4	Shift of Supply Schedule for Soybeans following Development of a New Disease-Resistant Seed Strain	
	Schedule S_0	Schedule S_1
Price (per Bushel)	Quantity Supplied (Bushels per Year Using Old Seed)	Quantity Supplied (Bushels per Year Using New Seed)
$ 1.50	0	5,000
1.75	10,000	23,000
2.25	20,000	33,000
3.00	30,000	40,000
4.00	45,000	54,000
5.00	45,000	54,000

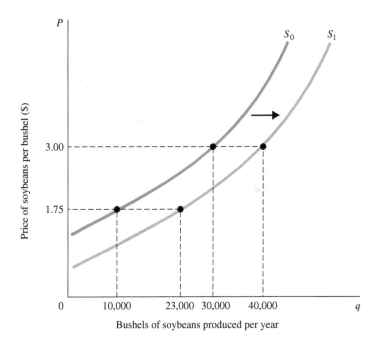

◀ **FIGURE 3.7** **Shift of the Supply Curve for Soybeans Following Development of a New Seed Strain**
When the price of a product changes, we move *along* the supply curve for that product; the quantity supplied rises or falls. When any other factor affecting supply changes, the supply curve *shifts*.

Increases in input prices may also cause supply curves to shift. If Farmer Brown faces higher fuel costs, for example, his supply curve will shift to the left—that is, he will produce less at any given market price. As Brown's soybean supply curve shifts to the left, it intersects the price axis at a higher point, meaning that it would take a higher market price to induce Brown to produce any soybeans at all.

As with demand, it is important to distinguish between *movements along* supply curves (changes in quantity supplied) and *shifts in* supply curves (changes in supply):

Change in price of a good or service leads to
    ⟶ change in *quantity supplied* (**movement along a supply curve**).
Change in costs, input prices, technology, or prices of related goods and services leads to
    ⟶ change in *supply* (**shift of a supply curve**).

From Individual Supply to Market Supply

So far we have focused on the supply behavior of a single producer. For most markets many, many suppliers bring product to the consumer, and it is the behavior of all of those producers together that determines supply.

Market supply is determined in the same fashion as market demand. It is simply the sum of all that is supplied each period by all producers of a single product. Figure 3.8 derives a market supply curve from the supply curves of three individual firms. (In a market with more firms, total market supply would be the sum of the amounts produced by each of the firms in that market.) As the table in Figure 3.8 shows, at a price of $3, farm A supplies 30,000 bushels of soybeans, farm B supplies 10,000 bushels, and farm C supplies 25,000 bushels. At this price, the total amount supplied in the market is 30,000 + 10,000 + 25,000, or 65,000 bushels. At a price of $1.75, however, the total amount supplied is only 25,000 bushels (10,000 + 5,000 + 10,000). Thus, the market supply curve is the simple addition of the individual supply curves of all the firms in a particular market—that is, the sum of all the individual quantities supplied at each price.

The position and shape of the market supply curve depends on the positions and shapes of the individual firms' supply curves from which it is derived. The market supply curve also depends on the number of firms that produce in that market. If firms that produce for a particular market are earning high profits, other firms may be tempted to go into that line of business. The popularity and profitability of professional football has, three times, led to the formation of new leagues. When new firms enter an industry, the supply curve shifts to the right. When firms go out of business, or "exit" the market, the supply curve shifts to the left.

market supply The sum of all that is supplied each period by all producers of a single product.

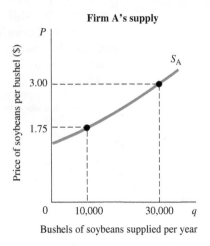

Firm A's supply

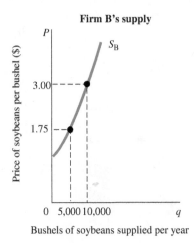

Firm B's supply

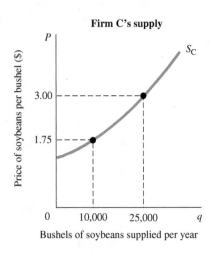

Firm C's supply

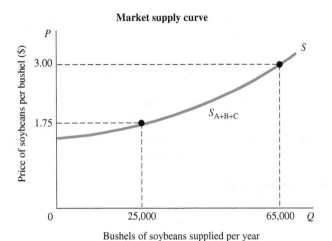

Market supply curve

Price	Quantity (q) Supplied by			Total Quantity Supplied in the Market (Q)
	A	B	C	
$3.00	30,000 +	10,000 +	25,000	= 65,000
1.75	10,000 +	5,000 +	10,000	= 25,000

▲ **FIGURE 3.8** **Deriving Market Supply from Individual Firm Supply Curves**
Total supply in the marketplace is the sum of all the amounts supplied by all the firms selling in the market. It is the sum of all the individual quantities supplied at each price.

Be able to explain how a market that is not in equilibrium responds to restore an equilibrium.

Market Equilibrium

So far, we have identified a number of factors that influence the amount that households demand and the amount that firms supply in product (output) markets. The discussion has emphasized the role of market price as a determinant of both quantity demanded and quantity supplied. We are now ready to see how supply and demand in the market interact to determine the final market price.

In our discussions, we have separated household decisions about how much to demand from firm decisions about how much to supply. The operation of the market, however, clearly depends on the interaction between suppliers and demanders. At any moment, one of three conditions prevails in every market: (1) The quantity demanded exceeds the quantity supplied at the current price, a situation called *excess demand*; (2) the quantity supplied exceeds the quantity demanded at the current price, a situation called *excess supply*; or (3) the quantity supplied equals the quantity demanded at the current price, a situation called **equilibrium**. At equilibrium, no tendency for price to change exists.

equilibrium The condition that exists when quantity supplied and quantity demanded are equal. At equilibrium, there is no tendency for price to change.

excess demand or shortage The condition that exists when quantity demanded exceeds quantity supplied at the current price.

Excess Demand

Excess demand, or a shortage, exists when quantity demanded is greater than quantity supplied at the current price. Figure 3.9, which plots both a supply curve and a demand curve on the same graph, illustrates such a situation. As you can see, market demand at

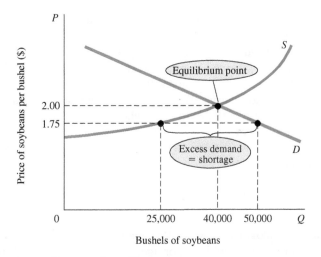

▲ FIGURE 3.9   **Excess Demand, or Shortage**

At a price of $1.75 per bushel, quantity demanded exceeds quantity supplied. When *excess demand* exists, there is a tendency for price to rise. When quantity demanded equals quantity supplied, excess demand is eliminated and the market is in equilibrium. Here the equilibrium price is $2.00 and the equilibrium quantity is 40,000 bushels.

$1.75 per bushel (50,000 bushels) exceeds the amount that farmers are currently supplying (25,000 bushels).

When excess demand occurs in an unregulated market, there is a tendency for price to rise as demanders compete against each other for the limited supply. The adjustment mechanisms may differ, but the outcome is always the same. For example, consider the mechanism of an auction. In an auction, items are sold directly to the highest bidder. When the auctioneer starts the bidding at a low price, many people bid for the item. At first, there is a shortage: Quantity demanded exceeds quantity supplied. As would-be buyers offer higher and higher prices, bidders drop out until the one who offers the most ends up with the item being auctioned. Price rises until quantity demanded and quantity supplied are equal.

At a price of $1.75 (see Figure 3.9 again), farmers produce soybeans at a rate of 25,000 bushels per year, but at that price, the demand is for 50,000 bushels. Most farm products are sold to local dealers who in turn sell large quantities in major market centers, where bidding would push prices up if quantity demanded exceeded quantity supplied. As price rises above $1.75, two things happen: (1) The quantity demanded falls as buyers drop out of the market and perhaps choose a substitute, and (2) the quantity supplied increases as farmers find themselves receiving a higher price for their product and shift additional acres into soybean production.[4]

This process continues until the shortage is eliminated. In Figure 3.9, this occurs at $2.00, where quantity demanded has fallen from 50,000 to 40,000 bushels per year and quantity supplied has increased from 25,000 to 40,000 bushels per year. When quantity demanded and quantity supplied are equal and there is no further bidding, the process has achieved an equilibrium, a situation in which *there is no natural tendency for further adjustment.* Graphically, the point of equilibrium is the point at which the supply curve and the demand curve intersect.

Increasingly, items are auctioned over the Internet. Companies such as eBay connect buyers and sellers of everything from automobiles to wine and from computers to airline tickets. Auctions are occurring simultaneously with participants located across the globe. The principles

---

[4] Once farmers have produced in any given season, they cannot change their minds and produce more, of course. When we derived Clarence Brown's supply schedule in Table 3.3, we imagined him reacting to prices that existed at the time he decided how much land to plant in soybeans. In Figure 3.9, the upward slope shows that higher prices justify shifting land from other crops. Final price may not be determined until final production figures are in. For our purposes here, however, we have ignored this timing problem. The best way to think about it is that demand and supply are *flows*, or *rates*, of production—that is, we are talking about the number of bushels produced *per production period*. Adjustments in the rate of production may take place over a number of production periods.

through which prices are determined in these auctions are the same: When excess demand exists, prices rise.

When quantity demanded exceeds quantity supplied, price tends to rise. When the price in a market rises, quantity demanded falls and quantity supplied rises until an equilibrium is reached at which quantity demanded and quantity supplied are equal.

This process is called *price rationing*. When the market operates without interference, price increases will distribute what is available to those who are willing and able to pay the most. As long as there is a way for buyers and sellers to interact, those who are willing to pay more will make that fact known somehow. (We discuss the nature of the price system as a rationing device in detail in Chapter 4.)

Excess Supply

excess supply *or* surplus
The condition that exists when quantity supplied exceeds quantity demanded at the current price.

Excess supply, *or* a surplus, exists when the quantity supplied exceeds the quantity demanded at the current price. As with a shortage, the mechanics of price adjustment in the face of a surplus can differ from market to market. For example, if automobile dealers find themselves with unsold cars in the fall when the new models are coming in, you can expect to see price cuts. Sometimes dealers offer discounts to encourage buyers; sometimes buyers themselves simply offer less than the price initially asked. After Christmas, most stores have big sales during which they lower the prices of overstocked items. Quantities supplied exceeded quantities demanded at the current prices, so stores cut prices. Many Web sites exist that do little more than sell at a discount clothing and other goods that failed to sell at full price during the past season.

Figure 3.10 illustrates another excess supply/surplus situation. At a price of $3 per bushel, suppose farmers are supplying soybeans at a rate of 65,000 bushels per year, but buyers are demanding only 25,000. With 40,000 bushels of soybeans going unsold, the market price falls. As price falls from $3.00 to $2.00, quantity supplied decreases from 65,000 bushels per year to 40,000. The lower price causes quantity demanded to rise from 25,000 to 40,000. At $2.00, quantity demanded and quantity supplied are equal. For the data shown here, $2.00 and 40,000 bushels are the equilibrium price and quantity, respectively.

Although the mechanism by which price is adjusted differs across markets, the outcome is the same:

When quantity supplied exceeds quantity demanded at the current price, the price tends to fall. When price falls, quantity supplied is likely to decrease and quantity demanded is likely to increase until an equilibrium price is reached where quantity supplied and quantity demanded are equal.

▶ **FIGURE 3.10 Excess Supply or Surplus**
At a price of $3.00, quantity supplied exceeds quantity demanded by 40,000 bushels. This excess supply will cause the price to fall.

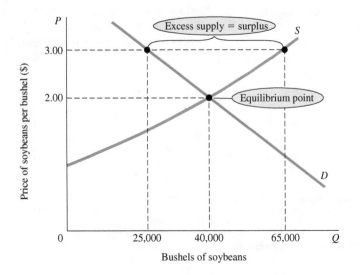

Changes in Equilibrium

When supply and demand curves shift, the equilibrium price and quantity change. The following example will help to illustrate this point and show us how equilibrium is restored in markets in which either demand or supply changes.

South America is a major producer of coffee beans. In the mid-1990s, a major freeze hit Brazil and Colombia and drove up the price of coffee on world markets to a record $2.40 per pound. Bad weather in Colombia in 2005 and more recently in 2012 caused similar shifts in supply.

Figure 3.11 illustrates how the freezes pushed up coffee prices. Initially, the market was in equilibrium at a price of $1.20. At that price, the quantity demanded was equal to quantity supplied (13.2 billion pounds). At a price of $1.20 and a quantity of 13.2 billion pounds, the demand curve (labeled D) intersected the initial supply curve (labeled S_0). (Remember that equilibrium exists when quantity demanded equals quantity supplied—the point at which the supply and demand curves intersect.)

The freeze caused a decrease in the supply of coffee beans. That is, the freeze caused the supply curve to shift to the left. In Figure 3.11, the new supply curve (the supply curve that shows the relationship between price and quantity supplied after the freeze) is labeled S_1.

At the initial equilibrium price, $1.20, there is now a shortage of coffee. If the price were to remain at $1.20, quantity demanded would not change; it would remain at 13.2 billion pounds. However, at that price, quantity supplied would drop to 6.6 billion pounds. At a price of $1.20, quantity demanded is greater than quantity supplied.

When excess demand exists in a market, price can be expected to rise, and rise it did. As the figure shows, price rose to a new equilibrium at $2.40. At $2.40, quantity demanded is again equal to quantity supplied, this time at 9.9 billion pounds—the point at which the new supply curve (S_1) intersects the demand curve.

Notice that as the price of coffee rose from $1.20 to $2.40, two things happened. First, the quantity demanded declined (a movement along the demand curve) as people shifted to substitutes such as tea and hot cocoa. Second, the quantity supplied began to rise, but within the limits imposed by the damage from the freeze. (It might also be that some countries or areas with high costs of production, previously unprofitable, came into production and shipped to

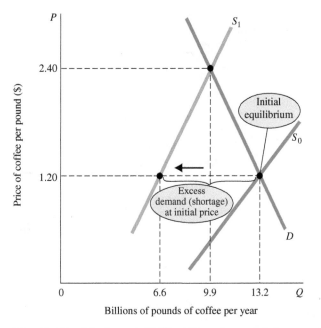

▲ **FIGURE 3.11   The Coffee Market: A Shift of Supply and Subsequent Price Adjustment**
Before the freeze, the coffee market was in equilibrium at a price of $1.20 per pound. At that price, quantity demanded equaled quantity supplied. The freeze shifted the supply curve to the left (from S_0 to S_1), increasing the equilibrium price to $2.40.

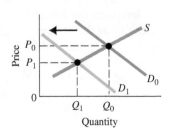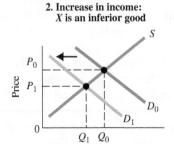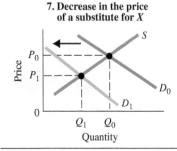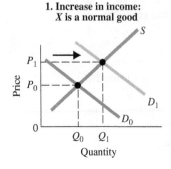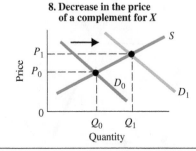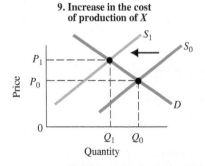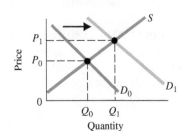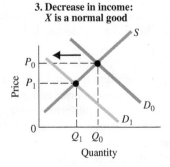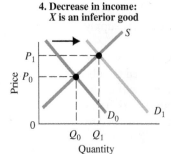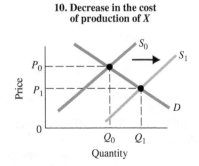

the world market at the higher price.) That is, the quantity supplied increased in response to the higher price *along* the new supply curve, which lies to the left of the old supply curve. The final result was a higher price ($2.40), a smaller quantity finally exchanged in the market (9.9 billion pounds), and coffee bought only by those willing to pay $2.40 per pound.

Figure 3.12 summarizes the possible supply and demand shifts that have been discussed and the resulting changes in equilibrium price and quantity. Study the graphs carefully to ensure that you understand them.

a. Demand shifts

b. Supply shifts

▲ FIGURE 3.12   **Examples of Supply and Demand Shifts for Product X**

ECONOMICS IN PRACTICE

Quinoa

Those of you who follow a vegetarian diet, or even those of you who are foodies, likely have had quinoa sometime within the last few months. Once eaten mostly by people in Peru and Bolivia, and a reputed favorite of the Incas, quinoa, a high-protein grain, has found a large market among food aficionados. Growth in vegetarianism effectively shifted the demand curve for quinoa to the right.

With an upward sloping supply curve, this shift in demand resulted in increased prices. Farmers grew richer, whereas some local consumers found themselves facing higher prices for a staple product. Over time, these higher prices encouraged more farmers to enter the quinoa market. This shifted the supply curve to the right, helping to moderate the price increases. But quinoa growing turns out to be a tricky affair. Quinoa grows best in high altitudes with cold climates. It thrives on soil fertilized by the dung of herds of llama and sheep. Thus, while supply clearly shifted with new farmer entry, the particular nature of the production process limited that shift and in the end, despite the supply response, prices increased.

THINKING PRACTICALLY

1. Use a graph to show the movement in prices and quantities described in the quinoa market.

Demand and Supply in Product Markets: A Review

As you continue your study of economics, you will discover that it is a discipline full of controversy and debate. There is, however, little disagreement about the basic way that the forces of supply and demand operate in free markets. If you hear that a freeze in Florida has destroyed a good portion of the citrus crop, you can bet that the price of oranges will rise. If you read that the weather in the Midwest has been good and a record corn crop is expected, you can bet that corn prices will fall. When fishermen in Massachusetts go on strike and stop bringing in the daily catch, you can bet that the price of local fish will go up.

Here are some important points to remember about the mechanics of supply and demand in product markets:

1. A demand curve shows how much of a product a household would buy if it could buy all it wanted at the given price. A supply curve shows how much of a product a firm would supply if it could sell all it wanted at the given price.
2. Quantity demanded and quantity supplied are always per time period—that is, per day, per month, or per year.
3. The demand for a good is determined by price, household income and wealth, prices of other goods and services, tastes and preferences, and expectations.
4. The supply of a good is determined by price, costs of production, and prices of related products. Costs of production are determined by available technologies of production and input prices.
5. Be careful to distinguish between movements along supply and demand curves and shifts of these curves. When the price of a good changes, the quantity of that good demanded or supplied changes—that is, a movement occurs along the curve. When any other factor that affects supply or demand changes, the curve shifts, or changes position.
6. Market equilibrium exists only when quantity supplied equals quantity demanded at the current price.

ECONOMICS IN PRACTICE

Why Do the Prices of Newspapers Rise?

In 2006, the average price for a daily edition of a Baltimore newspaper was $0.50. In 2007, the average price had risen to $0.75. Three different analysts have three different explanations for the higher equilibrium price.

Analyst 1: The higher price for Baltimore newspapers is good news because it means the population is better informed about public issues. These data clearly show that the citizens of Baltimore have a new, increased regard for newspapers.

Analyst 2: The higher price for Baltimore newspapers is bad news for the citizens of Baltimore. The higher cost of paper, ink, and distribution reflected in these higher prices will further diminish the population's awareness of public issues.

Analyst 3: The higher price for Baltimore newspapers is an unfortunate result of newspapers trying to make money as many consumers have turned to the Internet to access news coverage for free.

As economists, we are faced with two tasks in looking at these explanations: Do they make sense based on what we know about economic principles? And if they do make sense, can we figure out which explanation applies to the case of rising newspaper prices in Baltimore?

What is Analyst 1 saying? Her observation about consumers' new increased regard for newspapers tells us something about the demand curve. Analyst 1 seems to be arguing that tastes have changed in favor of newspapers, which would mean a shift in the demand curve to the right. With upward-sloping supply, such a shift would produce a price increase. So Analyst 1's story is plausible.

Analyst 2 refers to an increased cost of newsprint. This would cause production costs of newspapers to rise, shifting the supply curve to the left. A downward-sloping demand curve also results in increased prices. So Analyst 2 also has a plausible story.

Since Analyst 1 and Analyst 2 have plausible stories based on economic principles, we can look at evidence to see who is in fact right. If you go back to the graphs in Figure 3.12 on p. 64, you will find a clue. When demand shifts to the right (as in Analyst 1's story) the price rises, but so does the quantity as shown in Figure (a). When supply shifts to the left (as in Analyst 2's story) the price rises, but the quantity falls as shown in Figure (b). So we would look at what happened to newspaper circulation during this period to see whether the price increase is from the demand side or the supply side. In fact, in most markets, including Baltimore, quantities of newspapers bought have been falling, so Analyst 2 is most likely correct.

But be careful. Both analysts may be correct. If demand shifts to the right and supply shifts to the left by a greater amount, the price will rise and the quantity sold will fall.

What about Analyst 3? Analyst 3 clearly never had an economics course! Free Internet access to news is a substitute for print media. A decrease in the price of this substitute should shift the demand for newspapers to the left. The result should be a lower price, not a price increase. The fact that the newspaper publishers are "trying to make money" faced with this new competition does not change the laws of supply and demand.

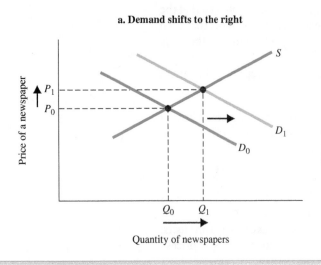

a. Demand shifts to the right

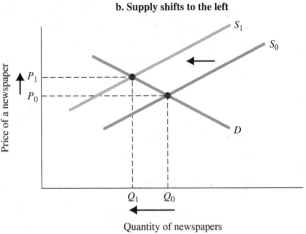

b. Supply shifts to the left

Looking Ahead: Markets and the Allocation of Resources

You can already begin to see how markets answer the basic economic questions of what is produced, how it is produced, and who gets what is produced. A firm will produce what is profitable to produce. If the firm can sell a product at a price that is sufficient to ensure a profit after production costs are paid, it will in all likelihood produce that product. Resources will flow in the direction of profit opportunities.

- Demand curves reflect what people are willing and able to pay for products; demand curves are influenced by incomes, wealth, preferences, prices of other goods, and expectations. Because product prices are determined by the interaction of supply and demand, prices reflect what people are willing to pay. If people's preferences or incomes change, resources will be allocated differently. Consider, for example, an increase in demand—a shift in the market demand curve. Beginning at an equilibrium, households simply begin buying more. At the equilibrium price, quantity demanded becomes greater than quantity supplied. When there is excess demand, prices will rise, and higher prices mean higher profits for firms in the industry. Higher profits, in turn, provide existing firms with an incentive to expand and new firms with an incentive to enter the industry. Thus, the decisions of independent private firms responding to prices and profit opportunities determine *what* will be *produced*. No central direction is necessary.

    Adam Smith saw this self-regulating feature of markets more than 200 years ago:

    > Every individual…by pursuing his own interest…promotes that of society. He is led…by an invisible hand to promote an end which was no part of his intention.[5]

    The term Smith coined, the *invisible hand*, has passed into common parlance and is still used by economists to refer to the self-regulation of markets.

- Firms in business to make a profit have a good reason to choose the best available technology—lower costs mean higher profits. Thus, individual firms determine *how* to produce their products, again with no central direction.

- So far, we have barely touched on the question of distribution—*who* gets what is produced? You can see part of the answer in the simple supply and demand diagrams. When a good is in short supply, price rises. As they do, those who are willing and able to continue buying do so; others stop buying.

    The next chapter begins with a more detailed discussion of these topics. How, exactly, is the final allocation of resources (the mix of output and the distribution of output) determined in a market system?

---

[5] Adam Smith, *The Wealth of Nations*, Modern Library Edition (New York: Random House, 1937), p. 456 (1st ed., 1776).

——— SUMMARY ———

1. In societies with many people, production must satisfy wide-ranging tastes and preferences, and producers must therefore specialize.

3.1 FIRMS AND HOUSEHOLDS: THE BASIC DECISION-MAKING UNITS *p. 43*

2. A *firm* exists when a person or a group of people decides to produce a product or products by transforming resources, or *inputs*, into *outputs*—the products that are sold in the market. Firms are the primary producing units in a market economy. We assume that firms make decisions to try to maximize profits.

3. *Households* are the primary consuming units in an economy. All households' incomes are subject to constraints.

3.2 INPUT MARKETS AND OUTPUT MARKETS: THE CIRCULAR FLOW *p. 43*

4. Households and firms interact in two basic kinds of markets: *product or output markets* and *input or factor markets*. Goods and services intended for use by households are exchanged in output markets. In output markets, competing firms supply and competing households demand. In input markets, competing firms demand and competing households supply.

5. Ultimately, firms choose the quantities and character of outputs produced, the types and quantities of inputs demanded, and the technologies used in production. Households choose the types and quantities of products demanded and the types and quantities of inputs supplied.

3.3 DEMAND IN PRODUCT/OUTPUT MARKETS *p. 45*

6. The quantity demanded of an individual product by an individual household depends on (1) price, (2) income, (3) wealth, (4) prices of other products, (5) tastes and preferences, and (6) expectations about the future.

7. *Quantity demanded* is the amount of a product that an individual household would buy in a given period if it could buy all that it wanted at the current price.

8. A *demand schedule* shows the quantities of a product that a household would buy at different prices. The same information can be presented graphically in a *demand curve*.

9. The *law of demand* states that there is a negative relationship between price and quantity demanded *ceteris paribus*: As price rises, quantity demanded decreases and vice versa. Demand curves slope downward.

10. All demand curves eventually intersect the price axis because there is always a price above which a household cannot or will not pay. Also, all demand curves eventually intersect the quantity axis because demand for most goods is limited, if only by time, even at a zero price.

11. When an increase in income causes demand for a good to rise, that good is a *normal good*. When an increase in income causes demand for a good to fall, that good is an *inferior good*.

12. If a rise in the price of good X causes demand for good Y to increase, the goods are *substitutes*. If a rise in the price of X causes demand for Y to fall, the goods are *complements*.

13. *Market demand* is simply the sum of all the quantities of a good or service demanded per period by all the households

buying in the market for that good or service. It is the sum of all the individual quantities demanded at each price.

3.4 SUPPLY IN PRODUCT/OUTPUT MARKETS *p. 55*

14. *Quantity supplied* by a firm depends on (1) the price of the good or service; (2) the cost of producing the product, which includes the prices of required inputs and the technologies that can be used to produce the product; and (3) the prices of related products.

15. *Market supply* is the sum of all that is supplied in each period by all producers of a single product. It is the sum of all the individual quantities supplied at each price.

16. It is important to distinguish between *movements* along demand and supply curves and *shifts* of demand and supply curves. The demand curve shows the relationship between price and quantity demanded. The supply curve shows the relationship between price and quantity supplied. A change in price is a movement along the curve. Changes in tastes, income, wealth, expectations, or prices of other goods and services cause demand curves to shift; changes in costs, input prices, technology, or prices of related goods and services cause supply curves to shift.

3.5 MARKET EQUILIBRIUM *p. 60*

17. When quantity demanded exceeds quantity supplied at the current price, *excess demand* (or a *shortage*) exists and the price tends to rise. When prices in a market rise, quantity demanded falls and quantity supplied rises until an equilibrium is reached at which quantity supplied and quantity demanded are equal. At *equilibrium*, there is no further tendency for price to change.

18. When quantity supplied exceeds quantity demanded at the current price, *excess supply* (or a *surplus*) exists and the price tends to fall. When price falls, quantity supplied decreases and quantity demanded increases until an equilibrium price is reached where quantity supplied and quantity demanded are equal.

——————— REVIEW TERMS AND CONCEPTS ———————

capital market, *p. 44*

complements, complementary goods, *p. 49*

demand curve, *p. 47*

demand schedule, *p. 46*

entrepreneur, *p. 43*

equilibrium, *p. 60*

excess demand *or* shortage, *p. 60*

excess supply *or* surplus, *p. 62*

factors of production, *p. 44*

firm, *p. 43*

households, *p. 43*

income, *p. 49*

inferior goods, *p. 49*

input *or* factor markets, *p. 44*

labor market, *p. 44*

land market, *p. 44*

law of demand, *p. 47*

law of supply, *p. 56*

market demand, *p. 53*

market supply, *p. 59*

movement along a demand curve, *p. 53*

movement along a supply curve, *p. 58*

normal goods, *p. 49*

perfect substitutes, *p. 49*

product *or* output markets, *p. 44*

profit, *p. 56*

quantity demanded, *p. 45*

quantity supplied, *p. 56*

shift of a demand curve, *p. 53*

shift of a supply curve, *p. 58*

substitutes, *p. 49*

supply curve, *p. 56*

supply schedule, *p. 56*

wealth *or* net worth, *p. 49*

PROBLEMS

All problems are available on MyEconLab.

3.1 FIRMS AND HOUSEHOLDS: THE BASIC DECISION-MAKING UNITS

LEARNING OBJECTIVE: Understand the roles of firms, entrepreneurs, and households in the market.

1.1 List three examples of entrepreneurs in the tech industry and the firms they created. Explain how these people fit the definition of entrepreneur.

3.2 INPUT MARKETS AND OUTPUT MARKETS: THE CIRCULAR FLOW

LEARNING OBJECTIVE: Understand the role of households as both suppliers to firms and buyers of what firms produce.

2.1 Identify whether each of the following transactions will take place in an input market or in an output market, and whether firms or households are demanding the good or service or supplying the good or service.
  a. Anderson works 37 hours each week as a clerk at the county courthouse.
  b. Mei Lin purchases a 3-week Mediterranean cruise vacation for her parents.
  c. Caterpillar doubles employment at its Huntsville, Alabama factory.
  d. The Greyson family sells their 250-acre ranch to Marriott so it can build a new resort and golf course.

3.3 DEMAND IN PRODUCT/ OUTPUT MARKETS

LEARNING OBJECTIVE: Understand what determines the position and shape of the demand curve and what factors move you along a demand curve and what factors shift the demand curve.

3.1 [Related to the *Economics in Practice* on p. 50] Merchandise sales for professional sports leagues is a multibillion dollar business, and leagues such as the NBA, NFL, and MLB have strict licensing rules for official league merchandise. Suppose you are a huge NBA fan and wish to purchase an authentic NBA jersey in large. Go to the NBA Store's Website at store.nba.com and click on "Jerseys." Select a team and then click on "Authentic" and find the price of the jerseys. Do the same for two other teams. Would the jerseys you found be considered perfect substitutes or just substitutes? Why? Do you think there are other products available that would be considered substitute products for the authentic jerseys you looked up? Briefly explain.

3.2 Explain whether each of the following statements describes a change in demand or a change in quantity demanded, and specify whether each change represents an increase or a decrease.
  a. Julio believes the price of tires will rise next month, so he purchases a set of 4 for his pickup truck today.
  b. After an article is published asserting that eating kale causes hair loss, sales of kale drop by 75 percent.
  c. The Oink-N-Chew company experiences a significant decline in sales when it doubles the price of its bacon-flavored bubblegum.
  d. An increase in the federal minimum wage results in a decline in sales of fast food.
  e. An unexpected decrease in the price of peanut butter results in an increase in banana sales.

3.3 For each of the five statements (a–e) in the previous question, draw a demand graph representing the appropriate change in quantity demanded or change in demand.

3.4 [Related to the *Economics in Practice* on p. 51] In the town of Hurley, Wisconsin, an unseasonably warm summer saw temperatures rising into the mid-90s for a weeklong stretch in July. This was almost 20 degrees above the average high temperature of 77 degrees for this hottest month of the year. This unexpected heat wave resulted in a significant increase in household purchases of central air conditioning systems, which are uncommon in this part of the country. Which determinant or determinants of demand were most likely factors in the households' decisions to purchase these air conditioning systems, and how would these purchases affect the demand curve for central air conditioning systems?

3.4 SUPPLY IN PRODUCT/OUTPUT MARKETS

LEARNING OBJECTIVE: Be able to distinguish between forces that shift a supply curve and changes that cause a movement along a supply curve.

4.1 The market for fitness trackers is made up of five firms, and the data in the following table represents each firm's quantity supplied at various prices. Fill in the column for the quantity supplied in the market, and draw a supply graph showing the market data.

	Quantity supplied by:					
PRICE	FIRM A	FIRM B	FIRM C	FIRM D	FIRM E	MARKET
$25	5	3	2	0	5	
50	7	5	5	3	6	
75	9	7	8	6	7	
100	11	10	11	9	8	

4.2 The following sets of statements contain common errors. Identify and explain each error:
  a. Supply decreases, causing prices to rise. Higher prices cause supply to increase. Therefore, prices fall back to their original levels.

b. The supply of pineapples in Hawaii increases, causing pineapple prices to fall. Lower prices mean that the demand for pineapples in Hawaiian households will increase, which will reduce the supply of pineapples and increase their price.

3.5 MARKET EQUILIBRIUM

LEARNING OBJECTIVE: Be able to explain how a market that is not in equilibrium responds to restore an equilibrium.

5.1 Illustrate the following with supply and demand curves:

a. With increased access to wireless technology and lighter weight, the demand for tablet computers has increased substantially. Tablets have also become easier and cheaper to produce as new technology has come online. Despite the shift of demand, prices have fallen.

b. Cranberry production in Massachusetts totaled 1.85 million barrels in 2013, a 15 percent decrease from the 2.12 million barrels produced in 2012. Demand decreased by even more than supply, dropping 2013 prices to $32.30 per barrel from $47.90 in 2012.

c. During the high-tech boom in the late 1990s, San Jose office space was in high demand and rents were high. With the national recession that began in March 2001, however, the market for office space in San Jose (Silicon Valley) was hit hard, with rents per square foot falling. In 2005, the employment numbers from San Jose were rising slowly and rents began to rise again. Assume for simplicity that no new office space was built during the period.

d. Before economic reforms were implemented in the countries of Eastern Europe, regulation held the price of bread substantially below equilibrium. When reforms were implemented, prices were deregulated and the price of bread rose dramatically. As a result, the quantity of bread demanded fell and the quantity of bread supplied rose sharply.

e. The steel industry has been lobbying for high taxes on imported steel. Russia, Brazil, and Japan have been producing and selling steel on world markets at $610 per metric ton, well below what equilibrium would be in the United States with no imports. If no imported steel was permitted into the country, the equilibrium price would be $970 per metric ton. Show supply and demand curves for the United States, assuming no imports; then show what the graph would look like if U.S. buyers could purchase all the steel that they wanted from world markets at $610 per metric ton; label the portion of the graph that represents the quantity of imported steel.

5.2 On Saturday, September 13, the Los Angeles Dodgers and the San Francisco Giants played baseball at AT&T Park in San Francisco. Both teams were in pursuit of league championships. Tickets to the game were sold out, and many more fans would have attended if additional tickets had been available. On that same day, the Miami Marlins and the Philadelphia Phillies played each other and sold tickets to only 26,163 people in Philadelphia.

The Phillies stadium, Citizens Bank Park, holds 43,651. AT&T Park in San Francisco holds 41,915. Assume for simplicity that tickets to all regular-season games are priced at $40.

a. Draw supply and demand curves for the tickets to each of the two games. (*Hint:* Supply is fixed. It does not change with price.) Draw one graph for each game.

b. Is there a pricing policy that would have filled the ballpark for the Phillies game?

c. The price system was not allowed to work to ration the San Francisco tickets when they were initially sold to the public. How do you know? How do you suppose the tickets were rationed?

5.3 Do you agree or disagree with each of the following statements? Briefly explain your answers and illustrate each with supply and demand curves.

a. The price of a good rises, causing the demand for another good to fall. Therefore, the two goods are substitutes.

b. A shift in supply causes the price of a good to fall. The shift must have been an increase in supply.

c. During 2009, incomes fell sharply for many Americans. This change would likely lead to a decrease in the prices of both normal and inferior goods.

d. Two normal goods cannot be substitutes for each other.

e. If demand increases and supply increases at the same time, price will clearly rise.

f. The price of good A falls. This causes an increase in the price of good B. Therefore, goods A and B are complements.

5.4 Through October 2014, the U.S. government administered two programs that affected the market for cigarettes. Media campaigns and labeling requirements, which are still in place, aim at making the public aware of the health dangers of cigarettes, and until 2014 the Department of Agriculture also maintained price supports for tobacco. Under this program, the supported price was above the market equilibrium price and the government limited the amount of land that could be devoted to tobacco production. Were these two programs at odds with the goal of reducing cigarette consumption? As part of your answer, illustrate graphically the effects of both policies on the market for cigarettes.

5.5 During the period 2006 through 2010, housing production in the United States fell from a rate of more than 2.27 million housing starts per year to a rate of less than 500,000, a decrease of greater than 80 percent. At the same time, the number of new households slowed to a trickle. Students without a job moved in with their parents, fewer immigrants came to the United States, and more of those already here went home. If there are fewer households, it is a decline in demand. If fewer new units are built, it is a decline in supply.

a. Draw a standard supply and demand diagram, which shows the demand for new housing units that are purchased each month, and the supply of new units built and put on the market each month. Assume that the quantity supplied and quantity demanded are equal at 45,000 units and at a price of $200,000.

b. On the same diagram show a decline in demand. What would happen if this market behaved like most markets?

c. Now suppose that prices did not change immediately. Sellers decided not to adjust price even though demand is below supply. What would happen to the number of homes for sale (the inventory of unsold new homes) if prices stayed the same following the drop in demand?

d. Now suppose that the supply of new homes put on the market dropped, but price still stayed the same at $200,000. Can you tell a story that brings the market back to equilibrium without a drop in price?

e. Go to www.census.gov/newhomesales. Look at the current press release, which contains data for the most recent month and the past year. What trends can you observe?

5.6 For each of the following statements, draw a diagram that illustrates the likely effect on the market for eggs. Indicate in each case the impact on equilibrium price and equilibrium quantity.

a. The surgeon general warns that high-cholesterol foods cause heart attacks.

b. The price of bacon, a complementary product, decreases.

c. The price of chicken feed increases.

d. Caesar salads become trendy at dinner parties. (The dressing is made with raw eggs.)

e. A technological innovation reduces egg breakage during packing.

*5.7 Suppose the demand and supply curves for eggs in the United States are given by the following equations:

$$Q_d = 100 - 20P$$
$$Q_s = 10 + 40P$$

where Q_d = millions of dozens of eggs Americans would like to buy each year; Q_s = millions of dozens of eggs U.S. farms would like to sell each year; and P = price per dozen eggs.

a. Fill in the following table:

Price (Per Dozen)	Quantity Demanded (Q_d)	Quantity Supplied (Q_s)
$ .50	____	____
$ 1.00	____	____
$ 1.50	____	____
$ 2.00	____	____
$ 2.50	____	____

b. Use the information in the table to find the equilibrium price and quantity.

c. Graph the demand and supply curves and identify the equilibrium price and quantity.

5.8 Housing policy analysts debate the best way to increase the number of housing units available to low-income households. One strategy—the demand-side strategy—is to provide people with housing vouchers, paid for by the government, that can be used to rent housing supplied by the private market. Another—a supply-side strategy—is to have the government subsidize housing suppliers or to build public housing.

a. Illustrate these supply- and demand-side strategies using supply and demand curves. Which results in higher rents?

b. Critics of housing vouchers (the demand-side strategy) argue that because the supply of housing to low-income households is limited and does not respond to higher rents, demand vouchers will serve only to drive up rents

and make landlords better off. Illustrate their point with supply and demand curves.

*5.9 Suppose the market demand for pizza is given by

$$Q_d = 300 - 20P$$ and the market supply for pizza is given by
$$Q_s = 20P - 100, \text{ where } P = \text{price (per pizza).}$$

a. Graph the supply and demand schedules for pizza using $5 through $15 as the value of P.

b. In equilibrium, how many pizzas would be sold and at what price?

c. What would happen if suppliers set the price of pizza at $15? Explain the market adjustment process.

d. Suppose the price of hamburgers, a substitute for pizza, doubles. This leads to a doubling of the demand for pizza. (At each price, consumers demand twice as much pizza as before.) Write the equation for the new market demand for pizza.

e. Find the new equilibrium price and quantity of pizza.

5.10 [**Related to the *Economics in Practice* on p. 65**] The growing popularity of quinoa has had an impact on the market for brown rice. With its higher fiber, protein, and iron content, quinoa is replacing brown rice as a staple food for many health-conscious individuals. Draw a supply and demand graph that shows how this increase in demand for quinoa has affected the market for brown rice. Describe what has happened to the equilibrium price and quantity of brown rice. What could brown rice producers do to return the price or quantity to the initial equilibrium price or quantity? Briefly explain if it is possible for brown rice producers to return both the price and quantity to the initial equilibriums without a change in consumer behavior.

5.11 The following table represents the market for solar wireless keyboards. Plot this data on a supply and demand graph and identify the equilibrium price and quantity. Explain what would happen if the market price is set at $60, and show this on the graph. Explain what would happen if the market price is set at $30, and show this on the graph.

Price	Quantity Demanded	Quantity Supplied
$ 10.00	28	0
20.00	24	3
30.00	20	6
40.00	16	9
50.00	12	12
60.00	8	15
70.00	4	18

5.12 [**Related to the *Economics in Practice* on p. 66**] Analyst 1 suggested that the demand curve for newspapers in Baltimore might have shifted to the right because people were becoming more literate. Think of two other plausible stories that would result in this demand curve shifting to the right.

*Note: Problems with an asterisk are more challenging.

4 Demand and Supply Applications

Every society has a system of institutions that determines what is produced, how it is produced, and who gets what is produced. In some societies, these decisions are made centrally, through planning agencies or by government directive. However, in every society, many decisions are made in a *decentralized* way, through the operation of markets.

Markets exist in all societies, and Chapter 3 provided a bare-bones description of how markets operate. In this chapter, we continue our examination of demand, supply, and the price system.

The Price System: Rationing and Allocating Resources

The market system, also called the *price system*, performs two important and closely related functions. First, it provides an automatic mechanism for distributing scarce goods and services. That is, it serves as a **price rationing** device for allocating goods and services to consumers when the quantity demanded exceeds the quantity supplied. Second, the price system ultimately determines both the allocation of resources among producers and the final mix of outputs.

4.1 LEARNING OBJECTIVE
Understand how price floors and price ceilings work in the market place.

price rationing   The process by which the market system allocates goods and services to consumers when quantity demanded exceeds quantity supplied.

Price Rationing

Consider the simple process by which the price system eliminates a shortage. Figure 4.1 shows hypothetical supply and demand curves for wheat. Wheat is produced around the world, with large supplies coming from Russia and from the United States. Wheat is sold in a world market and used to produce a range of food products, from cereals and breads to processed foods, which line the kitchens of the average consumer. Wheat is thus demanded by large food companies as they produce breads, cereals, and cake for households.

As Figure 4.1 shows, the equilibrium price of wheat was $160 per metric ton in the spring of 2010. At this price, farmers from around the world were expected to bring 61.7 million metric tons to market. Supply and demand were equal. Market equilibrium existed at a price of $160 per metric ton because at that price, quantity demanded was equal to quantity supplied. (Remember that equilibrium occurs at the point where the supply and demand curves intersect. In Figure 4.1, this occurs at point C.)

In the summer of 2010, Russia experienced its warmest summer on record. Fires swept through Russia, destroying a substantial portion of the Russian wheat crop. With almost a third of the world wheat normally produced in Russia, the effect of this environmental disaster on world wheat supply was substantial. In the figure, the supply curve for wheat, which had been drawn in expectation of harvesting all the wheat planted in Russia along with the rest of the world, now shifted to the left, from $S_{\text{spring 2010}}$ to $S_{\text{fall 2010}}$. This shift in the supply curve created a situation of excess demand at the old price of $160. At that price, the quantity demanded is 61.7 million metric tons, but the burning of much of the Russia supply left the world with only 35 millions of metric tons expected to be supplied. Quantity demanded exceeded quantity supplied at the original price by 26.7 million metric tons.

The reduced supply caused the price of wheat to rise sharply. As the price rises, the available supply is "rationed." Those who are willing and able to pay the most get it. You can see the market's rationing function clearly in Figure 4.1. As the price rises from $160, the quantity

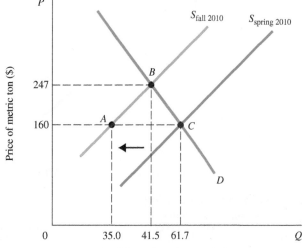

◀ **FIGURE 4.1**   **The Market for Wheat**
Fires in Russia in the summer of 2010 caused a shift in the world's supply of wheat to the left, causing the price to increase from $160 per metric ton to $247. The equilibrium moved from C to B.

demanded declines along the demand curve, moving from point C (61.7 million tons) toward point B (41.5 million tons). The higher prices mean that prices for products like Pepperidge Farm bread and Shredded Wheat cereal, which use wheat as an essential ingredient, also rise. People bake fewer cakes and begin to eat more rye bread and switch from Shredded Wheat to Corn Flakes in response to the price changes.

As prices rise, wheat farmers also change their behavior, though supply responsiveness is limited in the short term. Farmers outside of Russia, seeing the price rise, harvest their crops more carefully, getting more precious grains from each stalk. Perhaps some wheat is taken out of storage and brought to market. Quantity supplied increases from 35 million metric tons (point A) to 41.5 million tons (point B). The price increase has encouraged farmers who can to make up for part of the Russia wheat loss.

A new equilibrium is established at a price of $247 per metric ton, with 41.5 million tons transacted. The market has determined who gets the wheat: *The lower total supply is rationed to those who are willing and able to pay the higher price.*

This idea of "willingness to pay" is central to the distribution of available supply, and willingness depends on both desire (preferences) and income/wealth. Willingness to pay does not necessarily mean that only the rich will continue to buy wheat when the price increases. For anyone to continue to buy wheat at a higher price, his or her enjoyment comes at a higher cost in terms of other goods and services.

In sum:

> The adjustment of price is the rationing mechanism in free markets. Price rationing means that whenever there is a need to ration a good—that is, when a shortage exists—in a free market, the price of the good will rise until quantity supplied equals quantity demanded—that is, until the market clears.

There is some price that will clear any market you can think of. Consider the market for a famous painting such as Jackson Pollock's *No. 5, 1948*, illustrated in Figure 4.2. At a low price, there would be an enormous excess demand for such an important painting. The price would be bid up until there was only one remaining demander. Presumably, that price would be very high. In fact, the Pollock painting sold for a record $140 million in 2006. If the product is in strictly scarce supply, as a single painting is, its price is said to be *demand-determined*. That is, its price is determined solely and exclusively by the amount that the highest bidder or highest bidders are willing to pay.

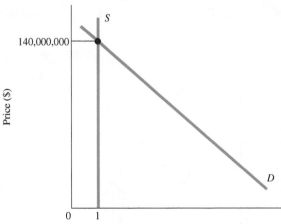

Quantity of Jackson Pollock's *"No. 5, 1948"*

▲ FIGURE 4.2   **Market for a Rare Painting**
There is some price that will clear any market, even if supply is strictly limited. In an auction for a unique painting, the price (bid) will rise to eliminate excess demand until there is only one bidder willing to purchase the single available painting. Some estimate that the *Mona Lisa* would sell for $600 million if auctioned.

One might interpret the statement that "there is some price that will clear any market" to mean "everything has its price," but that is not exactly what it means. Suppose you own a small silver bracelet that has been in your family for generations. It is quite possible that you would not sell it for *any* amount of money. Does this mean that the market is not working, or that quantity supplied and quantity demanded are not equal? Not at all. It simply means that *you* are the highest bidder. By turning down all bids, you must be willing to forgo what anybody offers for it.

Constraints on the Market and Alternative Rationing Mechanisms

On occasion, both governments and private firms decide to use some mechanism other than the market system to ration an item for which there is excess demand at the current price. Policies designed to stop price rationing are commonly justified in a number of ways.

The rationale most often used is fairness. It is not "fair" to let landlords charge high rents, not fair for oil companies to run up the price of gasoline, not fair for insurance companies to charge enormous premiums, and so on. After all, the argument goes, we have no choice but to pay—housing and insurance are necessary, and one needs gasoline to get to work. The Economics in Practice box on page 76 describes complaints against price increases following Hurricane Sandy in 2012. Regardless of the rationale for controlling prices, the following examples will make it clear that trying to bypass the pricing system is often more difficult and more costly than it at first appears.

Oil, Gasoline, and OPEC One of the most important prices in the world is the price of crude oil. Millions of barrels of oil are traded every day. It is a major input into virtually every product produced. It heats our homes, and it is used to produce the gasoline that runs our cars. Its production has led to massive environmental disasters as well as wars. Its price has fluctuated wildly, leading to major macroeconomic problems. But oil is like other commodities in that its price is determined by the basic forces of supply and demand. Oil provides a good example of how markets work and how markets sometimes fail.

The Organization of the Petroleum Exporting Countries (OPEC) is an organization of twelve countries (Algeria, Angola, Ecuador, Iran, Iraq, Kuwait, Libya, Nigeria, Qatar, Saudi Arabia, the United Arab Emirates, and Venezuela) that together had about one-third of the global market share of oil sales in 2015, although the supply of oil produced in the United States has been growing as a result of new developments in hydraulic fracturing (fracking). In 1973 and 1974, OPEC imposed an embargo on shipments of crude oil to the United States. What followed was a drastic reduction in the quantity of gasoline available at local gas pumps, given the large market share of OPEC at the time.

Had the market system been allowed to operate, refined gasoline prices would have increased dramatically until quantity supplied was equal to quantity demanded. However, the government decided that rationing gasoline only to those who were willing and able to pay the most was unfair, and Congress imposed a **price ceiling**, or maximum price, of $0.57 per gallon of leaded regular gasoline. That price ceiling was intended to keep gasoline "affordable," but it also perpetuated the shortage. At the restricted price, quantity demanded remained greater than quantity supplied, and the available gasoline had to be divided up somehow among all potential demanders.

You can see the effects of the price ceiling by looking carefully at Figure 4.3. If the price had been set by the interaction of supply and demand, it would have increased to approximately $1.50 per gallon. Instead, Congress made it illegal to sell gasoline for more than $0.57 per gallon. At that price, quantity demanded exceeded quantity supplied and a shortage existed. Because the price system was not allowed to function, an alternative rationing system had to be found to distribute the available supply of gasoline.

Several devices were tried. The most common of all nonprice rationing systems is **queuing**, a term that means waiting in line. During 1974, long lines formed daily at gas stations, starting

price ceiling A maximum price that sellers may charge for a good, usually set by government.

queuing Waiting in line as a means of distributing goods and services: a nonprice rationing mechanism.

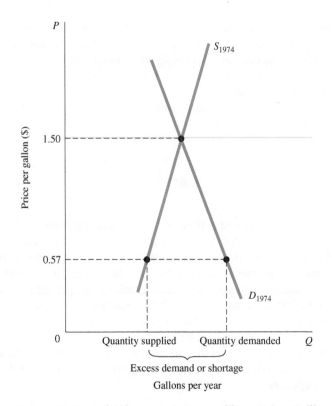

▲ FIGURE 4.3 **Excess Demand (Shortage) Created by a Price Ceiling**
In 1974, a ceiling price of $0.57 cents per gallon of leaded regular gasoline was imposed. If the price had been set by the interaction of supply and demand instead, it would have increased to approximately $1.50 per gallon. At $0.57 per gallon, the quantity demanded exceeded the quantity supplied. Because the price system was not allowed to function, an alternative rationing system had to be found to distribute the available supply of gasoline.

as early as 5 AM. Under this system, gasoline went to those people who were willing to pay the most, but the sacrifice was measured in hours and aggravation instead of dollars.[1]

favored customers Those who receive special treatment from dealers during situations of excess demand.

A second nonprice rationing device used during the gasoline crisis was that of **favored customers.** Many gas station owners decided not to sell gasoline to the general public, but to reserve their scarce supplies for friends and favored customers. Not surprisingly, many customers tried to become "favored" by offering side payments to gas station owners. Owners also charged high prices for service. By doing so, they increased the actual price of gasoline but hid it in service overcharges to get around the ceiling.

ration coupons Tickets or coupons that entitle individuals to purchase a certain amount of a given product per month.

Yet another method of dividing up available supply is the use of **ration coupons**. It was suggested in both 1974 and 1979 that families be given ration tickets or coupons that would entitle them to purchase a certain number of gallons of gasoline each month. That way, everyone would get the same amount regardless of income. Such a system had been employed in the United States during the 1940s when wartime price ceilings on meat, sugar, butter, tires, nylon stockings, and many other items were imposed.

When ration coupons are used with no prohibition against trading them, however, the result is almost identical to a system of price rationing. Those who are willing and able to pay the most buy up the coupons and use them to purchase gasoline, chocolate, fresh eggs, or anything else that

---

[1] You can also show formally that the result is inefficient—that there is a resulting net loss of total value to society. First, there is the cost of waiting in line. Time has a value. With price rationing, no one has to wait in line and the value of that time is saved. Second, there may be additional lost value if the gasoline ends up in the hands of someone who places a lower value on it than someone else who gets no gas. Suppose, for example, that the market price of gasoline if unconstrained would rise to $2 but that the government has it fixed at $1. There will be long lines to get gas. Imagine that to motorist A, 10 gallons of gas is worth $35 but that she fails to get gas because her time is too valuable to wait in line. To motorist B, 10 gallons is worth only $15, but his time is worth much less, so he gets the gas. In the end, A could pay B for the gas and both would be better off. If A pays B $30 for the gas, A is $5 better off and B is $15 better off. In addition, A does not have to wait in line. Thus, the allocation that results from nonprice rationing involves a net loss of value. Such losses are called *deadweight losses*. See p. 84 of this chapter.

ECONOMICS IN PRACTICE

Why Is My Hotel Room So Expensive? A Tale of Hurricane Sandy

In October 2012 Hurricane Sandy hit the northeastern United States. In New York, New Jersey, and Connecticut flooding in particular caused disruption. In the aftermath of the storm, as individuals and public workers began to clean up, prices for a number of items began to rise. At this point, you should be able to predict which prices likely rose the most.

Before Sandy struck we would expect that most of the markets in these states, as in other areas, were more or less in equilibrium. The only merchants who actually *could* raise prices after the storm are ones who face either a large shift to the right of the demand curve facing them or a shift to the left of the supply curve in their market. Otherwise, if merchants post Sandy raised prices, they would simply end up with surplus goods on the shelf. So if we want to predict which prices rose after Sandy, all we need to do is to look at those businesses facing large shifts in either their demand or supply curves after the storm. With many people forced out of their homes, hotel rooms became scarce. With power out, generators became more valuable. With trees down, tree removal services heard from many more customers. In other words, all of these businesses saw a large shift out of demand curves in their markets and none would find it easy to quickly increase their output levels. One can't really build a Holiday Inn overnight! Higher prices were now possible.

As it turned out, gas prices at the pump also rose. Yet one might well have thought that following Sandy, people would drive less, given the conditions of roads and business closings. Here, the more likely problem was a shift in the supply curve, as delivery trucks found it hard to restock gas stations. A shift in the supply curve made higher prices possible, particularly given the fact that those people who did need to go to work really needed that gas!

As we suggest in the text, in some cases government policy controls how much prices *are allowed* to rise after an emergency. In the case of Hurricane Sandy, all three states lodged

complaints of price gouging against numerous businesses, virtually all in the hotel, tree removal, gas station, or generator sales business. In New Jersey, a law against gouging prohibits price increases of more than 10 percent in an emergency situation. Connecticut and New York are more graphic in their definitions, but less precise. In these states, price gouging involves price increases in emergencies which are "unconscionably excessive." Economics will not be much help in translating that definition into a number. But at this point we hope you can see that economics can very much help us predict what kinds of businesses are likely to be charged with the offense.

THINKING PRACTICALLY

1. Gas prices rose after Sandy as supply shifted to the left, or inward, given transport problems. Transport problems likely also affected the delivery of Cheerios. Do you expect the price of Cheerios to also rise substantially? Why or why not?

is sold at a restricted price.[2] This means that the price of the restricted good will effectively rise to the market-clearing price. For instance, suppose that you decide not to sell your ration coupon. You are then forgoing what you would have received by selling the coupon. Thus, the "effective" price of the good you purchase will be higher (if only in opportunity cost) than the restricted price. Even when trading coupons is declared illegal, it is virtually impossible to stop black markets from developing. In a **black market**, illegal trading takes place at market-determined prices.

black market A market in which illegal trading takes place at market-determined prices.

Rationing Mechanisms for Concert and Sports Tickets   Tickets for sporting events such as the World Series, the Super Bowl, and the World Cup command huge prices in the open market. In many cases, the prices are substantially above the original issue price. One of the

---

[2] Of course, if you are assigned a number of tickets and you sell them, you are better off than you would be with price rationing. Ration coupons thus serve as a way of redistributing income.

hottest basketball tickets ever was one to the Boston Celtics and Los Angeles Lakers' NBA final series in 2010 that LA won in seven games. The online price for a courtside seat to one of the games in Los Angeles was $19,000.

You might ask why a profit-maximizing enterprise would not charge the highest price it could? The answer depends on the event. If the Chicago Cubs got into the World Series, the people of Chicago would buy all the tickets available for thousands of dollars each. But if the Cubs actually *charged* $2,000 a ticket, the hard-working fans would be furious: "Greedy Cubs Gouge Fans" the headlines would scream. Ordinary loyal fans earning reasonable salaries would not be able to afford those prices. Next season, perhaps some of those irate fans would change loyalties, supporting the White Sox over the Cubs. In part to keep from alienating loyal fans, prices for championship games are held down. It is interesting to look at this case to see how charging a ticket price lower than market plays out.

Let's consider a concert at the Staples Center, which has 20,000 seats. The supply of tickets is thus fixed at 20,000. Of course, there are good seats and bad seats, but to keep things simple, let's assume that all seats are the same and that the promoters charge $50 per ticket for all tickets. This is illustrated in Figure 4.4. Supply is represented by a vertical line at 20,000. Changing the price does not change the supply of seats. In the figure the quantity demanded at the price of $50 is 38,000, so at this price there is excess demand of 18,000.

Who would get to buy the $50 tickets? As in the case of gasoline, a variety of rationing mechanisms might be used. The most common is queuing, waiting in line. The tickets would go on sale at a particular time, and people would show up and wait. Now ticket sellers have virtual waiting rooms online. Tickets for the World Series go on sale at a particular time in September, and the people who log on to team Web sites at the right moment get into an electronic queue and can buy tickets. Often tickets are sold out in a matter of minutes.

There are also, of course, favored customers. Those who get tickets without queuing are local politicians, sponsors, and friends of the artist or friends of the players.

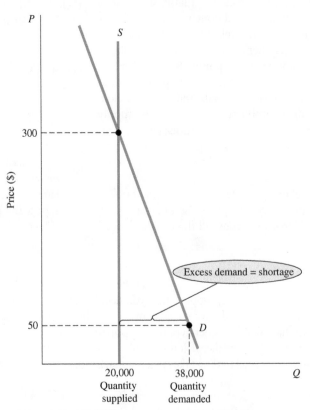

Tickets to a concert at the Staples Center

▲ **FIGURE 4.4** **Supply of and Demand for a Concert at the Staples Center**
At the face-value price of $50, there is excess demand for seats to the concert. At $50 the quantity demanded is greater than the quantity supplied, which is fixed at 20,000 seats. The diagram shows that the quantity demanded would equal the quantity supplied at a price of $300 per ticket.

But "once the dust settles," the power of technology and the concept of *opportunity cost* take over. Even if you get the ticket for the (relatively) low price of $50, that is not the true cost. The true cost is what you give up to sit in the seat. If people on eBay, StubHub, or Ticketmaster are willing to pay $300 for your ticket, that's what you must pay, or sacrifice, to go to the concert. Many people—even strong fans—will choose to sell that ticket. Once again, it is difficult to stop the market from rationing the tickets to those people who are willing and able to pay the most.

> No matter how good the intentions of private organizations and governments, it is difficult to prevent the price system from operating and to stop people's willingness to pay from asserting itself. Every time an alternative is tried, the price system seems to sneak in the back door. With favored customers and black markets, the final distribution may be even more unfair than what would result from simple price rationing.

Prices and the Allocation of Resources

Thinking of the market system as a mechanism for allocating scarce goods and services among competing demanders is revealing, but the market determines more than just the distribution of final outputs. It also determines what gets produced and how resources are allocated among competing uses.

Consider a change in consumer preferences that leads to an increase in demand for a specific good or service. During the 1980s, for example, people began going to restaurants more frequently than before. Researchers think that this trend, which continues today, is partially the result of social changes (such as a dramatic rise in the number of two-earner families) and partially the result of rising incomes. The market responded to this change in demand by shifting resources, both capital and labor, into more and better restaurants.

With the increase in demand for restaurant meals, the price of eating out rose and the restaurant business became more profitable. The higher profits attracted new businesses and provided old restaurants with an incentive to expand. As new capital, seeking profits, flowed into the restaurant business, so did labor. New restaurants need chefs. Chefs need training, and the higher wages that came with increased demand provided an incentive for them to get it. In response to the increase in demand for training, new cooking schools opened and existing schools began to offer courses in the culinary arts. This story could go on and on, but the point is clear:

> Price changes resulting from shifts of demand in output markets cause profits to rise or fall. Profits attract capital; losses lead to disinvestment. Higher wages attract labor and encourage workers to acquire skills. At the core of the system, supply, demand, and prices in input and output markets determine the allocation of resources and the ultimate combinations of goods and services produced.

Price Floor

As we have seen, price ceilings, often imposed because price rationing is viewed as unfair, result in alternative rationing mechanisms that are inefficient and may be equally unfair. Some of the same arguments can be made for price floors. A **price floor** is a minimum price below which exchange is not permitted. If a price floor is set above the equilibrium price, the result will be excess supply; quantity supplied will be greater than quantity demanded.

The most common example of a price floor is the **minimum wage**, which is a floor set for the price of labor. Employers (who demand labor) are not permitted under federal law to pay a wage less than $7.25 per hour (in 2015) to workers (who supply labor). Many states have much higher minimum wages; Washington, for example, had a minimum wage in 2015 of $9.47 per hour. Critics of the minimum wage argue that since it is above equilibrium, it may result in less labor hired.

price floor A minimum price below which exchange is not permitted.

minimum wage A price floor set for the price of labor.

Analyze the economic impact of an oil import tax.

Supply and Demand Analysis: An Oil Import Fee

The basic logic of supply and demand is a powerful tool of analysis. As an extended example of the power of this logic, we will consider a proposal to impose a tax on imported oil. The idea of taxing imported oil is hotly debated, and the tools we have learned thus far will show us the effects of such a tax.

In 2012 the United States imported 45 percent of its oil. Of the imports, 22 percent come from the Persian Gulf States. Given the political volatility of that area of the world, many politicians have advocated trying to reduce our dependence on foreign oil. One tool often suggested by both politicians and economists to accomplish this goal has been an import oil tax or tariff.

Supply and demand analysis makes the arguments of the import tax proponents easier to understand. Figure 4.5(a) shows the U.S. market for oil as of late 2012. The world price of oil is at slightly more than $80, and the United States is assumed to be able to buy *all the oil that it wants* at this price. This means that domestic producers cannot charge any more than $80 per barrel. The curve labeled *Supply* US shows the amount that domestic suppliers will produce at each price level. At a price of $80, domestic production is 7 million barrels per day. U.S. producers will produce at point A on the supply curve. The total quantity of oil demanded in the United States in 2012 was approximately 13 million barrels per day. At a price of $80, the quantity demanded in the United States is point B on the demand curve.

The difference between the total quantity demanded (13 million barrels per day) and domestic production (7 million barrels per day) is total imports (6 million barrels per day).

▶ **FIGURE 4.5 The U.S. Market for Crude Oil, 2012**

In 2012 the world market price for crude oil was approximately $80 per barrel. Domestic production in the United States that year averaged about 7 million barrels per day, whereas crude oil demand averaged just under 13 million barrels per day. The difference between production and consumption were made up of net imports of approximately 6 million barrels per day, as we see in panel (a).

If the government imposed a tax in this market of 33..33 percent, or $26.64, that would increase the world price to $106.64. That higher price causes quantity demanded to fall below its original level of 13 million barrels, while the price increase causes domestic production to rise above the original level. As we see in panel b, the effect is a reduction in import levels.

a. U.S. market, 2012

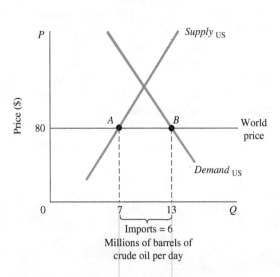

b. Effects of an oil import fee in the United States

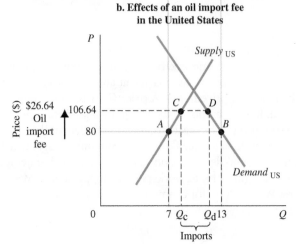

ECONOMICS IN PRACTICE

The Price Mechanism at Work for Shakespeare

Every summer, New York City puts on free performances of Shakespeare in the Park. Tickets are distributed on a first-come-first-serve basis at the Delacorte Theatre in the park beginning at 1 PM on the day of the show. People usually begin lining up at 6 AM when the park opens; by 10 AM the line has typically reached a length sufficient to give away all available tickets.

When you examine the people standing in line for these tickets, most of them seem to be fairly young. Many carry book bags identifying them as students in one of New York's many colleges. Of course, all college students may be fervent Shakespeare fans, but can you think of another reason for the composition of the line? Further, when you attend one of the plays and look around, the audience appears much older and much sleeker than the people who were standing in line. What is going on?

Although the tickets are "free" in terms of financial costs, their true price includes the value of the time spent standing in line. Thus, the tickets are cheaper for people (for example, students) whose time value is lower than they are for high-wage earners, like an investment banker from Goldman Sachs. The true cost of a ticket is $0 plus the opportunity cost of the time spent in line. If the average person spends 4 hours in line, as is done in the Central Park case, for someone with a high wage, the true cost of the ticket might be very high. For example, a lawyer who earns $300 an hour would be giving up $1,200 to wait in line. It should not surprise you to see more people waiting in line for whom the tickets are inexpensive.

What about the people who are at the performance? Think about our discussion of the power of entrepreneurs. In this case, the students who stand in line as consumers of the tickets also can play a role as producers. In fact, the students can produce tickets relatively cheaply by waiting in line. They

can then turn around and sell those tickets to the high-wage Shakespeare lovers. These days eBay is a great source of tickets to free events, sold by individuals with low opportunity costs of their time who queued up. Craigslist even provides listings for people who are willing to wait in line for you.

Of course, now and again we do encounter a busy business-person in one of the Central Park lines. Recently, one of the authors encountered one and asked him why he was waiting in line rather than using eBay, and he replied that it reminded him of when he was young, waiting in line for rock concerts.

THINKING PRACTICALLY

1. Many museums offer free admission one day a week, on a weekday. On that day we observe that museum-goers are more likely to be senior citizens than on a typical Saturday. Why?

Now suppose that the government levies a tax of $33\frac{1}{3}$ percent on imported oil. Because the import price is $80, this tax rate translates into a tax of $26.64, which increases the price per barrel paid by U.S. importers to $106.64 ($80 + $26.64). This new, higher price means that U.S. producers can also charge up to $106.64 for a barrel of crude. Note, however, that the tax is paid only on imported oil. Thus, the entire 106.64 paid for domestic crude goes to domestic producers.

Figure 4.5(b) shows the result of the tax. First, because of a higher price, the quantity demanded drops. This is a movement *along* the demand curve from point B to point D. At the same time, the quantity supplied by domestic producers increases. This is a movement *along* the supply curve from point A to point C. With an increase in domestic quantity supplied and a decrease in domestic quantity demanded, imports decrease, as we can see clearly as Q_d-Q_c is smaller than the original 6 billions barrels per day.

The tax also generates revenues for the federal government. The total tax revenue collected is equal to the tax per barrel ($26.64) times the number of imported barrels (Q_d-Q_c).

What does all of this mean? In the final analysis, an oil import fee would increase domestic production and reduce overall consumption. To the extent that one believes that Americans are consuming too much oil, the reduced consumption may be a good thing. We also see that the tax increases the price of oil in the United States.

Supply and Demand and Market Efficiency

Clearly, supply and demand curves help explain the way that markets and market prices work to allocate scarce resources. Recall that when we try to understand "how the system works," we are doing "positive economics."

Supply and demand curves can also be used to illustrate the idea of market efficiency, an important aspect of "normative economics." To understand the ideas, you first must understand the concepts of consumer and producer surplus.

Consumer Surplus

If we think hard about the lessons of supply and demand, we can see that the market forces us to reveal a great deal about our personal preferences. If you are free to choose within the constraints imposed by prices and your income and you decide to buy a hamburger for $2.50, you have "revealed" that a hamburger is worth at least $2.50 to you. Consumers reveal who they are by what they choose to buy and do.

This idea of purchases as preference revelation underlies a lot of the valuation economists do. Look at the demand curve in Figure 4.6(a). At the current market price of $2.50, consumers will purchase 7 million hamburgers per month. In this market, consumers who value a hamburger at $2.50 or more will buy it, and those who have lower values will do without.

As the figure shows, however, some people value hamburgers at more than $2.50. At a price of $5.00, for example, consumers would still buy 1 million hamburgers. These million hamburgers have a value to their buyers of $5.00 each. If consumers can buy these burgers for only $2.50, they would earn a **consumer surplus** of $2.50 per burger. Consumer surplus is the difference between the maximum amount a person is willing to pay for a good and its current market price. The consumer surplus earned by the people willing to pay $5.00 for a hamburger is approximately equal to the shaded area between point A and the price, $2.50.

The second million hamburgers in Figure 4.6(a) are valued at more than the market price as well, although the consumer surplus gained is slightly less. Point B on the market demand curve shows the maximum amount that consumers would be willing to pay for the second million hamburgers. The consumer surplus earned by these people is equal to the shaded area between

consumer surplus The difference between the maximum amount a person is willing to pay for a good and its current market price.

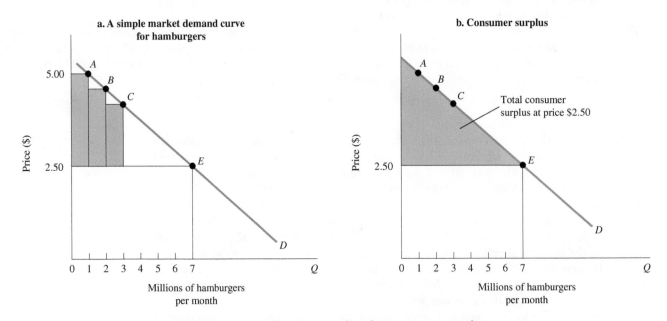

▲ **FIGURE 4.6** **Market Demand and Consumer Surplus**
As illustrated in Figure 4.6(a), some consumers (see point A) are willing to pay as much as $5.00 each for hamburgers. Since the market price is just $2.50, they receive a consumer surplus of $2.50 for each hamburger that they consume. Others (see point B) are willing to pay something less than $5.00 and receive a slightly smaller surplus. Because the market price of hamburgers is just $2.50, the area of the shaded triangle in Figure 4.6(b) is equal to total consumer surplus.

B and the price, $2.50. Similarly, for the third million hamburgers, maximum willingness to pay is given by point *C*; consumer surplus is a bit lower than it is at points *A* and *B*, but it is still significant.

The total value of the consumer surplus suggested by the data in Figure 4.6(a) is roughly equal to the area of the shaded triangle in Figure 4.6(b). To understand why this is so, think about offering hamburgers to consumers at successively lower prices. If the good were actually sold for $2.50, those near point *A* on the demand curve would get a large surplus; those at point *B* would get a smaller surplus. Those at point *E* would get no surplus.

Producer Surplus

Similarly, the supply curve in a market shows the amount that firms willingly produce and supply to the market at various prices. Presumably it is because the price is sufficient to cover the costs or the opportunity costs of production and give producers enough profit to keep them in business. When speaking of cost of production, we include everything that a producer must give up to produce a good.

A simple market supply curve like the one in Figure 4.7(a) illustrates this point quite clearly. At the current market price of $2.50, producers will produce and sell 7 million hamburgers. There is only one price in the market, and the supply curve tells us the quantity supplied at each price.

Notice, however, that if the price were just $0.75 (75 cents), although production would be much lower—most producers would be out of business at that price—a few producers would actually be supplying burgers. In fact, producers would supply about 1 million burgers to the market. These firms must have lower costs: They are more efficient or they have access to raw beef at a lower price or perhaps they can hire low-wage labor.

If these efficient, low-cost producers are able to charge $2.50 for each hamburger, they are earning what is called a **producer surplus**. Producer surplus is the difference between the current market price and the cost of production for the firm. The first million hamburgers would generate a producer surplus of $2.50 minus $0.75, or $1.75 per hamburger: a total of $1.75 million. The second million hamburgers would also generate a producer surplus because the price of $2.50 exceeds the producers' total cost of producing these hamburgers, which is above $0.75 but much less than $2.50.

The total value of the producer surplus received by producers of hamburgers at a price of $2.50 per burger is roughly equal to the shaded triangle in Figure 4.7(b). Those producers just able to make a profit producing burgers will be near point *E* on the supply curve and will earn very little in the way of surplus.

producer surplus The difference between the current market price and the cost of production for the firm.

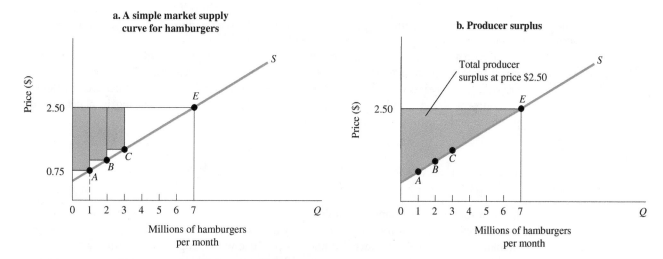

▲ **FIGURE 4.7   Market Supply and Producer Surplus**
As illustrated in Figure 4.7(a), some producers are willing to produce hamburgers for a price of $0.75 each. Because they are paid $2.50, they earn a producer surplus equal to $1.75. Other producers are willing to supply hamburgers at prices less than $2.50, and they also earn producers surplus. Because the market price of hamburgers is $2.50, the area of the shaded triangle in Figure 4.7(b) is equal to total producer surplus.

▶ FIGURE 4.8 **Total Producer and Consumer Surplus**
Total producer and consumer surplus is greatest where supply and demand curves intersect at equilibrium.

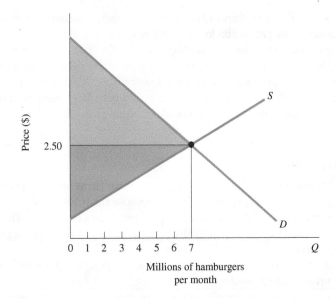

Competitive Markets Maximize the Sum of Producer and Consumer Surplus

In the preceding example, the quantity of hamburgers supplied and the quantity of hamburgers demanded are equal at $2.50. Figure 4.8 shows the total net benefits to consumers and producers resulting from the production of 7 million hamburgers. Consumers receive benefits in excess of the price they pay and equal to the blue shaded area between the demand curve and the price line at $2.50; the area is equal to the amount of consumer surplus being earned. Producers receive compensation in excess of costs and equal to the red-shaded area between the supply curve and the price line at $2.50; the area is equal to the amount of producer surplus being earned.

Now consider the result to consumers and producers if production were to be reduced to 4 million burgers. Look carefully at Figure 4.9(a). At 4 million burgers, consumers are willing to pay $3.75 for hamburgers and there are firms whose costs make it worthwhile to supply at a price as low as $1.50, yet something is stopping production at 4 million. The result is a loss of both consumer and producer surplus. You can see in Figure 4.9(a) that if production were expanded from 4 million to 7 million, the market would yield more consumer surplus and more producer surplus. The total loss of producer and consumer surplus from *underproduction* and, as we will see shortly, from overproduction is referred to as a **deadweight loss**. In Figure 4.9(a) the deadweight loss is equal to the area of triangle *ABC* shaded in yellow.

Figure 4.9(b) illustrates how a deadweight loss of both producer and consumer surplus can result from *overproduction* as well. For every hamburger produced above 7 million, consumers are willing to pay less than the cost of production. The cost of the resources needed to produce hamburgers above 7 million exceeds the benefits to consumers, resulting in a net loss of producer and consumer surplus equal to the yellow shaded area *ABC*.

deadweight loss   The total loss of producer and consumer surplus from underproduction or overproduction.

Potential Causes of Deadweight Loss From Under- and Overproduction

Most of the next few chapters will discuss perfectly competitive markets in which prices are determined by the free interaction of supply and demand. As you will see, when supply and demand interact freely, competitive markets produce what people want at the least cost, that is, they are efficient. Beginning in Chapter 13, however, we will begin to relax assumptions and will discover a number of naturally occurring sources of market failure. Monopoly power gives firms the incentive to underproduce and overprice, taxes and subsidies may distort consumer choices, external costs such as pollution and congestion may lead to over- or underproduction of some goods, and artificial price floors and price ceilings may have the same effects.

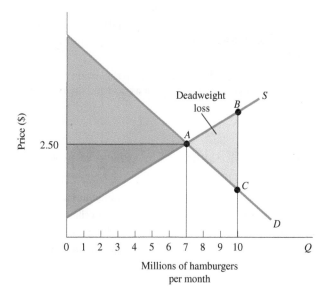

a. Deadweight loss from underproduction

b. Deadweight loss from overproduction

▲ **FIGURE 4.9   Deadweight Loss**

Figure 4.9(a) shows the consequences of producing 4 million hamburgers per month instead of 7 million hamburgers per month. Total producer and consumer surplus is reduced by the area of triangle *ABC* shaded in yellow. This is called the deadweight loss from underproduction. Figure 4.9(b) shows the consequences of producing 10 million hamburgers per month instead of 7 million hamburgers per month. As production increases from 7 million to 10 million hamburgers, the full cost of production rises above consumers' willingness to pay, resulting in a deadweight loss equal to the area of triangle *ABC*.

Looking Ahead

We have now examined the basic forces of supply and demand and discussed the market/price system. These fundamental concepts will serve as building blocks for what comes next. Whether you are studying microeconomics or macroeconomics, you will be studying the functions of markets and the behavior of market participants in more detail in the following chapters.

Because the concepts presented in the first four chapters are so important to your understanding of what is to come, this might be a good time for you to review this material.

──────── SUMMARY ────────

4.1 THE PRICE SYSTEM: RATIONING AND ALLOCATING RESOURCES *p. 73*

1. In a market economy, the market system (or price system) serves two functions. It determines the allocation of resources among producers and the final mix of outputs. It also distributes goods and services on the basis of willingness and ability to pay. In this sense, it serves as a *price rationing* device.

2. Governments as well as private firms sometimes decide not to use the market system to ration an item for which there is excess demand. Examples of nonprice rationing systems include *queuing, favored customers, and ration coupons.* The most common rationale for such policies is "fairness."

3. Attempts to bypass the market and use alternative nonprice rationing devices are more difficult and costly than

it would seem at first glance. Schemes that open up opportunities for favored customers, black markets, and side payments often end up less "fair" than the free market. A supply curve shows the relationship between the quantity producers are willing to supply to the market and the price of a good.

4.2 SUPPLY AND DEMAND ANALYSIS: AN OIL IMPORT FEE *p. 80*

4. The basic logic of supply and demand is a powerful tool for analysis. For example, supply and demand analysis shows that an oil import tax will reduce quantity of oil demanded, increase domestic production, and generate revenues for the government.

4.3 SUPPLY AND DEMAND AND MARKET EFFICIENCY *p. 82*

5. Supply and demand curves can also be used to illustrate the idea of market efficiency, an important aspect of normative economics.

6. *Consumer surplus* is the difference between the maximum amount a person is willing to pay for a good and the current market price.

7. *Producer surplus* is the difference between the current market price and the cost of production for the firm.

8. At free market equilibrium with competitive markets, the sum of consumer surplus and producer surplus is maximized.

9. The total loss of producer and consumer surplus from underproduction or overproduction is referred to as a *deadweight loss*.

REVIEW TERMS AND CONCEPTS

black market, *p. 77*
consumer surplus, *p. 82*
deadweight loss, *p. 84*
favored customers, *p. 76*

minimum wage, *p. 79*
price ceiling, *p. 75*
price floor, *p. 79*
price rationing, *p. 73*

producer surplus, *p. 83*
queuing, *p. 75*
ration coupons, *p. 76*

PROBLEMS

All problems are available on MyEconLab.

4.1 THE PRICE SYSTEM: RATIONING AND ALLOCATING RESOURCES

LEARNING OBJECTIVE: Understand how price floors and price ceilings work in the market place.

1.1 Illustrate the following with supply and demand curves:
   a. In November 2014, Andy Warhol's silkscreen artwork *Triple Elvis [Ferus Type]* was sold at Christie's Auction House in New York for $81.9 million.
   b. In March 2015, hogs in the United States were selling for 62 cents per pound, down from 98 cents per pound a year before. This was due primarily to the fact that supply had increased during the period.
   c. In 2015, the demand for organic produce continued to rise, and represented 11 percent of all produce purchased in U.S. supermarkets. At the same time, the number of farmers growing organic crops had increased by 119 percent since 2007. The overall result was a drop in the average price of organic produce and an increase in the quantity of organic produce sold.

1.2 Every demand curve must eventually hit the quantity axis because with limited incomes, there is always a price so high that there is no demand for the good. Do you agree or disagree? Why?

1.3 When excess demand exists for tickets to a major sporting event or a concert, profit opportunities exist for scalpers. Explain briefly using supply and demand curves to illustrate. Some argue that scalpers work to the advantage of everyone and are "efficient." Do you agree or disagree? Explain briefly.

1.4 In an effort to "support" the price of some agricultural goods, the Department of Agriculture pays farmers a subsidy in cash for every acre that they leave *unplanted*. The Agriculture Department argues that the subsidy increases the "cost" of planting and that it will reduce supply and increase the price of competitively produced agricultural goods. Critics argue that because the subsidy is a payment to farmers, it will reduce costs and lead to lower prices. Which argument is correct? Explain.

1.5 The rent for 2-bedroom apartments in Detroit has fallen from an average of $796 in September 2014 to $717 in March 2015. Demand for 2-bedroom apartments in Detroit was falling during this period as well. This is hard to explain because the law of demand says that lower prices should lead to higher demand. Do you agree or disagree? Explain your answer.

1.6 Illustrate the following with supply or demand curves:
   a. In Joseph Heller's iconic novel, *Catch 22*, one of the characters was paid by the government to not grow alfalfa. According to the story's narrator, "The more alfalfa he did not grow, the more money the government gave him, and he spent every penny he didn't earn on new land to increase the amount of alfalfa he did not produce."
   b. In 2015, Chipotle suspended the sale of pork at one-third of its restaurants due to animal welfare concerns, and this had a significant impact on the amount of chicken entrees it sold to customers.
   c. From 2007 to 2014, median income in the United States fell by 8 percent, shifting the demand for gasoline. During that same time period, crude oil prices fell 35 percent, shifting the supply of gasoline. At the new equilibrium, the quantity of gasoline sold is less than it was before. (Crude oil is used to produce gasoline.)

1.7 Illustrate the following with supply or demand curves:
   a. A situation of excess labor demand caused by a salary cap in the National Basketball Association (NBA).

b. The effect of a sharp decrease in gasoline prices on the demand for electric vehicles.

1.8 [**Related to the *Economics in Practice* on p. 77**] The feature states that in New Jersey, a law against price gouging prohibits price increases of more than 10 percent in an emergency situation. Assume that prior to Sandy the equilibrium price for portable generators was $100 and the equilibrium quantity was 200 units per month. After Sandy, demand increased to 500 units per month and generator sellers raised prices to the maximum amount allowed by law. Do you think that the new higher price will be high enough to meet the increased demand? Use a supply and demand graph to explain your answer.

1.9 In April 2015, the U.S. Energy Information Administration projected that the average retail price for regular-grade gasoline would be $2.45 per gallon for the remainder of the year. Do some research on the price of gasoline. Has this projection been accurate? What is the price of regular-grade gasoline today in your city or town? If it is below $2.45 per gallon, what are the reasons? Similarly, if it is higher than $2.45, what has happened to drive up the price? Illustrate with supply and demand curves.

1.10 Many cruise lines offer 5-day trips. A disproportionate number of these trips leave port on Thursday and return late Monday. Why might this be true?

1.11 [**Related to the *Economics in Practice* on p. 81**] Lines for free tickets to see free Shakespeare in Central Park are often long. A local politician has suggested that it would be a great service if the park provided music to entertain those who are waiting in line. What do you think of this suggestion?

1.12 The following graph represents the market for wheat. The equilibrium price is $20 per bushel and the equilibrium quantity is 14 million bushels.

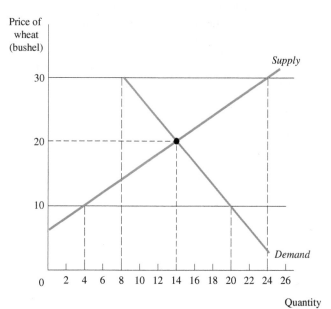

a. Explain what will happen if the government establishes a price ceiling of $10 per bushel of wheat in this market. What if the price ceiling was set at $30?

b. Explain what will happen if the government establishes a price floor of $30 per bushel of wheat in this market. What if the price floor was set at $10?

4.2 SUPPLY AND DEMAND ANALYSIS: AN OIL IMPORT FEE

LEARNING OBJECTIVE: Analyze the economic impact of an oil import tax.

2.1 Suppose that the world price of oil is $60 per barrel and that the United States can buy all the oil it wants at this price. Suppose also that the demand and supply schedules for oil in the United States are as follows:

Price ($ Per Barrel)	U.S. Quantity Demanded	U.S. Quantity Supplied
55	26	14
60	24	16
65	22	18
70	20	20
75	18	22

a. On graph paper, draw the supply and demand curves for the United States.

b. With free trade in oil, what price will Americans pay for their oil? What quantity will Americans buy? How much of this will be supplied by American producers? How much will be imported? Illustrate total imports on your graph of the U.S. oil market.

c. Suppose the United States imposes a tax of $5 per barrel on imported oil. What quantity would Americans buy? How much of this would be supplied by American producers? How much would be imported? How much tax would the government collect?

d. Briefly summarize the impact of an oil import tax by explaining who is helped and who is hurt among the following groups: domestic oil consumers, domestic oil producers, foreign oil producers, and the U.S. government.

2.2 Use the data in the preceding problem to answer the following questions. Now suppose that the United States allows no oil imports.

a. What are the equilibrium price and quantity for oil in the United States?

b. If the United States imposed a price ceiling of $65 per barrel on the oil market and prohibited imports, would there be an excess supply or an excess demand for oil? If so, how much?

c. Under the price ceiling, quantity supplied and quantity demanded differ. Which of the two will determine how much oil is purchased? Briefly explain why.

4.3 SUPPLY AND DEMAND AND MARKET EFFICIENCY

LEARNING OBJECTIVE: Explain how consumer and producer surplus are generated.

3.1 Use the following diagram to calculate total consumer surplus at a price of $12 and production of 500 thousand flu vaccinations per day. For the same equilibrium, calculate total producer surplus. Assuming price remained at $12 but production was cut to 200 thousand vaccinations per day, calculate producer surplus and consumer surplus. Calculate the deadweight loss from underproduction.

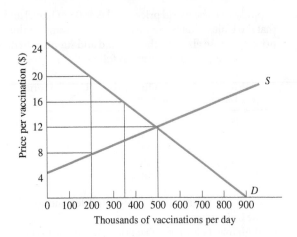

3.2 Suppose the market demand for a cup of cappuccino is given by $Q_D = 24 - 4P$ and the market supply for a cup of cappuccino is given by $Q_S = 8P - 12$, where P = price (per cup).
   a. Graph the supply and demand schedules for cappuccino.
   b. What is the equilibrium price and equilibrium quantity?
   c. Calculate consumer surplus and producer surplus, and identify these on the graph.

3.3 On April 20, 2010, an oil-drilling platform owned by British Petroleum exploded in the Gulf of Mexico, causing oil to leak into the gulf at estimates of 1.5 to 2.5 million gallons per day for well more than 2 months. As a result

of the oil spill, the government closed more than 25 percent of federal waters, which devastated the commercial fishing industry in the area. Explain how the reduction in supply from the reduced fishing waters either increased or decreased consumer surplus and producer surplus, and show these changes graphically.

3.4 The following graph represents the market for DVDs.

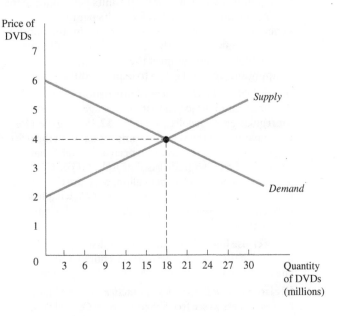

   a. Find the values of consumer surplus and producer surplus when the market is in equilibrium, and identify these areas on the graph.
   b. If underproduction occurs in this market, and only 9 million DVDs are produced, what happens to the amounts of consumer surplus and producer surplus? What is the value of the deadweight loss? Identify these areas on the graph.
   c. If overproduction occurs in this market, and 27 million DVDs are produced, what happens to the amounts of consumer surplus and producer surplus? Is there a deadweight loss with overproduction? If so, what is its value? Identify these areas on the graph.

Elasticity

5

The model of supply and demand we have just introduced tells us a good deal about how a change in the price of a good affects behavior. When McDonalds lowers the price of its hamburgers, you should understand why the volume they sell increases. Many universities want to fill up their football stadiums. You should see why low ticket prices for football games might help them to do this. If the government wants to cut the smoking rate in a country, you should see why raising prices through taxation might be advantageous.

But in many situations, including the examples just given, knowing the direction of a change is not enough. What we really need to know to help us make the right decisions is how big market reactions are. How *many* more fans would come to a football game if the price were lowered? Would the university get more fans by charging students more but giving them free hot dogs at the game? For profit-making firms, knowing the quantity that would be sold at a lowered price is key to their ability to increase profits. Should McDonald's lower the price of its Big Mac? For McDonald's, the answer depends on how many more hamburgers will be sold at the lower prices if and whether the new sales come at the expense of the sandwiches sold at Subway or McDonald's own Chicken McNuggets. How many potential new smokers will be deterred from smoking by higher cigarette prices the government has induced? Questions such as these lie at the core of economics. To answer these questions, we need to know the magnitude of market responses.

The importance of actual measurement cannot be overstated. Much of the research being done in economics today involves the collection and analysis of quantitative data that measure behavior. In business and in government, the ability to analyze large data sets (often called Big Data) is key to improved decision making.

Economists commonly measure market responsiveness using the concept of **elasticity**. Elasticity quantifies how sensitive one variable is to a change in a second. We often consider responsiveness or elasticity by looking at prices: How does demand for a product respond when its price changes? This is known as the *price elasticity of demand*. How does supply respond when prices change? This is the *price elasticity of supply*. As in the McDonald's example, sometimes it is important to know how the price of one good—for example, the Big Mac—affects the demand for another good—Chicken McNuggets. This is called the *cross-price elasticity of demand*.

elasticity A general concept used to quantify the response in one variable when another variable changes.

But the concept of elasticity goes well beyond responsiveness to price changes. As we will see, we can look at elasticities as a way to understand responses to changes in income and almost any other major determinant of supply and demand in a market. We begin with a discussion of price elasticity of demand.

5.1 LEARNING OBJECTIVE

Understand why elasticity is preferable as a measure of responsiveness to slope and how to measure it.

Price Elasticity of Demand

You have already seen the law of demand at work. All else equal, when prices rise, quantity demanded can be expected to decline. When prices fall, quantity demanded can be expected to rise. The normal negative relationship between price and quantity demanded is reflected in the downward slope of demand curves.

Slope and Elasticity

The slope of a demand curve may in a rough way reveal the responsiveness of the quantity demanded to price changes, but slope can be quite misleading. Consider the two demand curves in Figure 5.1 representing *exactly* the same data. The only difference between the two is that quantity demanded is measured in pounds in the graph on the left and in ounces in the graph on the right. When we calculate the numerical value of each slope, however, we get different answers. The curve on the left has a slope of $-\frac{1}{5}$, and the curve on the right has a slope of $-\frac{1}{80}$; yet the two curves represent the *exact same behavior*. If we had changed dollars to cents on the *y*-axis, the two slopes would be -20 and -1.25, respectively. (Review the Appendix to Chapter 1 if you do not understand how these numbers are calculated.)

The numerical value of slope depends on the units used to measure the variables on the axes. To correct this problem, we convert the changes in price and quantity to *percentages*. By looking at by how much the *percent* quantity demanded changes for a given *percent* price change, we have a measure of responsiveness that does not change with the unit of measurement. The price increase in Figure 5.1 leads to a decline of 5 pounds, or 80 ounces, in the quantity of steak demanded—a decline of 50 percent from the initial 10 pounds, or 160 ounces, whether we measure the steak in pounds or ounces.

In general, elasticity is defined as the ratio of the percentage change in one variable to the percentage change in a second. So, **price elasticity of demand** is simply the ratio of the percentage change in quantity demanded to the percentage change in price.

price elasticity of demand The ratio of the percentage change in quantity demanded to the percentage change in price; measures the responsiveness of quantity demanded to changes in price.

▶ FIGURE 5.1 **Slope Is Not a Useful Measure of Responsiveness**
Changing the unit of measure from pounds to ounces changes the numerical value of the demand slope dramatically, but the behavior of buyers in the two diagrams is identical.

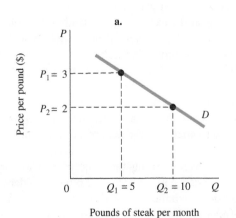

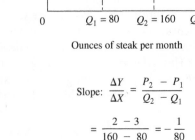

$$\text{price elasticity of demand} = \frac{\%\text{ change in quantity demanded}}{\%\text{ change in price}}$$

Percentage changes should always carry the sign (plus or minus) of the change. Positive changes, or increases, take a (+). Negative changes, or decreases, take a (−). The law of demand implies that price elasticity of demand is nearly always a negative number: Price increases (+) will lead to decreases in quantity demanded (−), and vice versa. Thus, the numerator and denominator should have opposite signs, resulting in a negative ratio.

Types of Elasticity

The elasticity of demand can vary between 0 and minus infinity. An elasticity of 0 indicates that the quantity demanded does not respond *at all* to a price change. A demand curve with an elasticity of 0 is called **perfectly inelastic** and is illustrated in Figure 5.2(a). A demand curve in which even the smallest price increase reduces quantity demanded to zero is known as a **perfectly elastic demand** curve and is illustrated in Figure 5.2(b). A good way to remember the difference between the two perfect elasticities is

perfectly inelastic demand
Demand in which quantity demanded does not respond at all to a change in price.

perfectly elastic demand
Demand in which quantity drops to zero at the slightest increase in price.

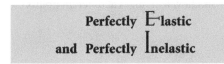

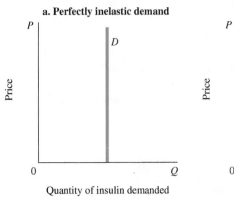

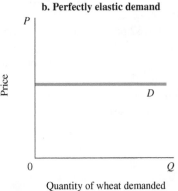

▲ **FIGURE 5.2   Perfectly Inelastic and Perfectly Elastic Demand Curves**
Figure 5.2(a) shows a perfectly inelastic demand curve for insulin. Price elasticity of demand is zero. Quantity demanded is fixed; it does not change at all when price changes. Figure 5.2(b) shows a perfectly elastic demand curve facing a wheat farmer. A tiny price increase drives the quantity demanded to zero. In essence, perfectly elastic demand implies that individual producers can sell all they want at the going market price but cannot charge a higher price.

What type of good might have a perfectly elastic demand curve? Suppose there are two identical vendors selling Good Humor bars on a beach. If one vendor increased the price, all buyers would flock to the second vendor. In this case, a small price increase costs the first vendor all its business; the demand is perfectly elastic. Products with perfectly inelastic demand are harder to find, but some life-saving medical products like insulin may be close, in that high price increases may elicit very little response in terms of quantity demanded.

Of course, most products have elasticities between the two extremes. When an elasticity is over 1.0 in absolute value,[1] we refer to the demand as **elastic**. In this case, the percentage change in quantity is larger in absolute value than the percentage change in price. Here consumers are responding a lot to a price change. When an elasticity is less than 1 in absolute value, it is referred to as **inelastic**. In these markets, consumers respond much less to price changes. The demand for oil is inelastic, for example, because even with a price increase, it is hard to substitute other products for oil. The demand for a Nestlé Crunch bar is much more elastic, in part because there are so many more substitutes.

elastic demand   A demand relationship in which the percentage change in quantity demanded is larger than the percentage change in price in absolute value (a demand elasticity with an absolute value greater than 1).

inelastic demand   Demand that responds somewhat, but not a great deal, to changes in price. Inelastic demand always has a numerical value between zero and 1.

---

[1] *Absolute value* or *absolute size* means ignoring the sign. The absolute value of −4 is 4.

unitary elasticity A demand relationship in which the percentage change in quantity of a product demanded is the same as the percentage change in price in absolute value (a demand elasticity with an absolute value of 1).

A special case is one in which the elasticity of demand is minus one. Here, we say demand has **unitary elasticity**. In this case, the percentage change in price is exactly equal to the percentage change in quantity demanded, in absolute value terms. As you will see when we look at the relationship between revenue and elasticities later in this chapter, unitary elastic demand curves have some interesting properties.

A warning: You must be careful about signs. Because it is generally understood that demand elasticities are negative (demand curves have a negative slope), they are often reported and discussed without the negative sign. For example, a technical paper might report that the demand for housing "appears to be inelastic with respect to price, or less than 1 (0.6)." What the writer means is that the estimated elasticity is −0.6, which is between zero and −1. Its absolute value is less than 1.

Calculate elasticities using several different methods and understand the economic relationship between revenues and elasticity.

Calculating Elasticities

In many areas, knowing the demand or supply elasticity will be key to knowing whether a government economic policy is wise or a business move will improve profits. It is important to know how we calculate an elasticity and how it changes at different points on a demand or supply curve.

Calculating Percentage Changes

We will use the data introduced in Figure 5.1(a) to do our elasticity calculations. In the figure we see that the quantity of steak demanded increases from 5 pounds (Q_1) to 10 pounds (Q_2) when price drops from \$3 to \$2 per pound. Thus, the change in quantity demanded is equal to $Q_2 - Q_1$, or 5 pounds. To convert this change into a percentage change, we must decide on a *base* against which to calculate the percentage. It is often convenient to use the initial value of quantity demanded (Q_1) as the base.

To calculate percentage change in quantity demanded using the initial value as the base, the following formula is used:

$$\% \text{ change in quantity demanded} = \frac{\text{change in quantity demanded}}{Q_1} \times 100\%$$

$$= \frac{Q_2 - Q_1}{Q_1} \times 100\%$$

In Figure 5.1(a), $Q_2 = 10$ and $Q_1 = 5$. Thus,

$$\% \text{ change in quantity demanded} = \frac{10 - 5}{5} \times 100\% = \frac{5}{5} \times 100\% = 100\%$$

Expressing this equation verbally, we can say that an increase in quantity demanded from 5 pounds to 10 pounds is a 100 percent increase from 5 pounds. Note that you arrive at exactly the same result if you use the diagram in Figure 5.1(b), in which quantity demanded is measured in ounces. An increase from Q_1 (80 ounces) to Q_2 (160 ounces) is a 100 percent increase.

We can calculate the percentage change in price in a similar way. Once again, let us use the initial value of *P*—that is, P_1—as the base for calculating the percentage. By using P_1 as the base, the formula for calculating the percentage change in *P* is

$$\% \text{ change in price} = \frac{\text{change in price}}{P_1} \times 100\%$$

$$= \frac{P_2 - P_1}{P_1} \times 100\%$$

In Figure 5.1(a), P_2 equals 2 and P_1 equals 3. Thus, the change in P, or ΔP, is a negative number: $P_2 - P_1 = 2 - 3 = -1$. Plugging the values of P_1 and P_2 into the preceding equation, we get

$$\% \text{ change in price} = \frac{2 - 3}{3} \times 100\% = \frac{-1}{3} \times 100\% = -33.3\%$$

In other words, decreasing the price from \$3 to \$2 is a 33.3 percent decline.

Elasticity Is a Ratio of Percentages

Once the changes in quantity demanded and price have been converted to percentages, calculating elasticity is a matter of simple division. Recall the formal definition of elasticity:

$$\text{price elasticity of demand} = \frac{\% \text{ change in quantity demanded}}{\% \text{ change in price}}$$

If demand is elastic, the ratio of percentage change in quantity demanded to percentage change in price will have an absolute value greater than 1. If demand is inelastic, the ratio will have an absolute value between 0 and 1. If the two percentages are equal, so that a given percentage change in price causes an equal percentage change in quantity demanded, elasticity is equal to an absolute value of 1.0; this is unitary elasticity.

Substituting the preceding percentages, we see that a 33.3 percent decrease in price leads to a 100 percent increase in quantity demanded; thus,

$$\text{price elasticity of demand} = \frac{+100\%}{-33.3\%} = -3.0$$

According to these calculations, the demand for steak is elastic when we look at the range between \$2 and \$3. A small price decrease in this range will result in a large increase in the quantity of steak demanded.

The Midpoint Formula

Although simple, the use of the initial values of P and Q as the bases for calculating percentage changes can be misleading. Let us return to the example of demand for steak in Figure 5.1(a), where we have a change in quantity demanded of 5 pounds. Using the initial value Q_1 as the base, we calculated that this change represents a 100 percent increase over the base. Now suppose that the price of steak rises to \$3 again, causing the quantity demanded to drop back to 5 pounds. How much of a percentage decrease in quantity demanded is this? We now have $Q_1 = 10$ and $Q_2 = 5$. With the same formula we used previously, we get

$$\% \text{ change in quantity demanded} = \frac{\text{change in quantity demanded}}{Q_1} \times 100\%$$

$$= \frac{Q_2 - Q_1}{Q_1} \times 100\%$$

$$= \frac{5 - 10}{10} \times 100\% = -50\%$$

Thus, an increase from 5 pounds to 10 pounds is a 100 percent increase (because the initial value used for the base is 5), but a decrease from 10 pounds to 5 pounds is only a 50 percent decrease (because the initial value used for the base is 10). This does not make much sense because in both cases, we are calculating elasticity on the same interval on the demand curve. Changing the "direction" of the calculation should not change the elasticity.

To solve the problem of choosing a base, a simple convention has been adopted. Instead of using the initial values of Q and P as the bases for calculating percentages, we use the *midpoints* or average of these variables as the bases. That is, we use the value halfway between P_1 and P_2 for the base in calculating the percentage change in price and the value halfway between Q_1 and Q_2 as the base for calculating percentage change in quantity demanded. This is called the **midpoint formula**. We'll see many examples throughout this chapter.

midpoint formula   A more precise way of calculating percentages using the value halfway between P_1 and P_2 for the base in calculating the percentage change in price and the value halfway between Q_1 and Q_2 as the base for calculating the percentage change in quantity demanded.

point elasticity   A measure of elasticity that uses the slope measurement.

Point Elasticity   One final method of calculating elasticities makes more direct use of slopes, and is called **point elasticity**.

We have defined elasticity as the percentage change in quantity demanded divided by the percentage change in price. We can write this as

$$\frac{\dfrac{\Delta Q}{Q_1}}{\dfrac{\Delta P}{P_1}}$$

where Δ denotes a small change and Q_1 and P_1 refer to the original price and quantity demanded. This can be rearranged and written as

$$\frac{\Delta Q}{\Delta P} \cdot \frac{P_1}{Q_1}$$

Notice that $\frac{\Delta Q}{\Delta P}$ is the reciprocal of the slope.

So another way to calculate the elasticity of the demand curve as we make small changes in price around the P_1, Q_1 point is to multiply the inverse of the slope by $\frac{P_1}{Q_1}$. In our example, we see in Figure 5.1(a) that the slope is $-\frac{1}{5}$, so the inverse slope is -5. With P_1 at 3 and Q_1 at 5, we calculate an elasticity at this point of $(-5)(3/5) = -3$, exactly as we did in the calculation on the previous page.

Using the point method of calculating an elasticity avoids our previous problem by calculating elasticity at a *point* on the demand curve rather than over a segment of the curve. This is important because as we have already seen and will now further explore, elasticities change as we move along a linear demand curve.

Elasticity Changes along a Straight-Line Demand Curve

Every point on a linear demand curve has the same slope. That is what makes it a straight line. By contrast, elasticity changes as we move along a linear demand curve.

Before we go through the calculations to show how elasticity changes along a demand curve, it is useful to think *why* elasticity might change as we vary price. Consider again McDonald's decision to reduce the price of a Big Mac. Suppose McDonald's found that at the current price of $3, a small price cut would generate a large number of new customers who wanted burgers. Demand, in short, was relatively elastic. What happens as McDonald's continues to cut its price? At the original price of $3, McDonald's had relatively few customers. It was easy to generate a big percentage increase in sales because sales were so low. As the price moves from $2.50 to $2.00, and the existing customer base grows, growing by 10 or 20 percent will be much harder. Increasing the number of customers by 10 people matters a lot less when your base is 100 than it did when the base was 10. It should come as no surprise that as we move down a typical straight-line demand curve, price elasticity falls. Demand becomes less elastic as price is reduced and quantity demanded increases. This lesson has important implications for price-setting strategies of firms.

Consider the demand schedule shown in Table 5.1 and the demand curve in Figure 5.3, describing Herb's choices about how many of his work day lunches to have in the office dining room. If lunch in the dining room were $10, Herb would eat there only twice a month. If the price of lunch fell to $9, he would eat there 4 times a month. If lunch were only a dollar, he would eat there 20 times a month.

TABLE 5.1	Demand Schedule for Office Dining Room Lunches
Price (per Lunch)	**Quantity Demanded (Lunches per Month)**
$ 11	0
10	2
9	4
8	6
7	8
6	10
5	12
4	14
3	16
2	18
1	20
0	22

We can calculate price elasticity of demand between points *A* and *B* on the demand curve in Figure 5.3. Moving from *A* to *B*, the price of a lunch drops from $10 to $9 (a decrease of $1) and the number of dining room lunches that Herb eats per month increases from two to four (an increase of two).

Using the midpoint formula, and substituting in the numbers in Table 5.1 we calculate the percentage change in quantity demanded as :

$$\% \text{ change in quantity demanded} = \frac{4 - 2}{(2 + 4)/2} \times 100\% = \frac{2}{3} \times 100\% = 66.7\%$$

Similarly for the percentage change in price we get:

$$\% \text{ change in price} = \frac{9 - 10}{(10 + 9)/2} \times 100\% = \frac{-1}{9.5} \times 100\% = -10.5\%$$

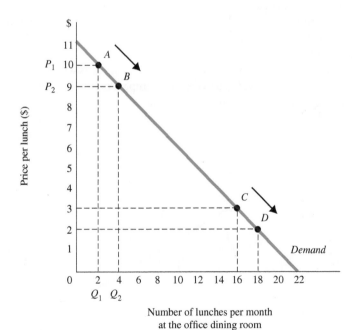

▲ **FIGURE 5.3 Demand Curve for Lunch at the Office Dining Room**
Between points *A* and *B*, demand is quite elastic at −6.33. Between points *C* and *D*, demand is quite inelastic at −.294.

Finally, we calculate elasticity by dividing.

$$\text{elasticity of demand} = \frac{\% \text{ change in quantity demanded}}{\% \text{ change in price}}$$

$$= \frac{66.7\%}{-10.5\%} = -6.33$$

The percentage change in quantity demanded is 6.33 times larger than the percentage change in price. In other words, Herb's demand between points *A* and *B* is quite responsive; his demand between points *A* and *B* is elastic.

Now consider moving along the *same* demand curve in Figure 5.3 between points *C* and *D*. At a price of $3, Herb eats in the office dining room 16 times per month. If the price drops to $2, he will eat there 18 times per month. Just as in the movement from *A* to *B*, when price falls $1 quantity demanded increases by two meals. Expressed in *percentage* terms, however, these changes are different.

By using the midpoints as the base, the $1 price decline is only a 10.5 percent reduction when price is around $9.50, between points *A* and *B*. The same $1 price decline is a 40 percent reduction when price is around $2.50, between points *C* and *D*. The two-meal increase in quantity demanded is a 66.7 percent increase when Herb averages only 3 meals per month, but it is only an 11.76 percent increase when he averages 17 meals per month. The elasticity of demand between points *C* and *D* is thus 11.76 percent divided by −40 percent, or −0.294. (Work these numbers out for yourself using the midpoint formula.)

The percentage changes between *A* and *B* are different from those between *C* and *D*, and so are the elasticities. Herb's demand is quite elastic (−6.4) between points *A* and *B*; a 10.5 percent reduction in price caused a 66.7 percent increase in quantity demanded. However, his demand is inelastic (−0.294) between points *C* and *D*; a 40 percent decrease in price caused only an 11.76 percent increase in quantity demanded.

We see in this example that Herb's demand becomes less elastic as we move down his demand curve. This will always be true for a linear demand curve, and the arithmetic is easily seen if we look back at the point elasticity formula. Elasticity was defined as $\frac{\Delta Q}{\Delta P} \cdot \frac{P}{Q}$. Although $\frac{\Delta Q}{\Delta P}$, which is the reciprocal of the slope, remains constant along the demand curve, $\frac{P}{Q}$ falls as we move down the demand curve. Thus, elasticity also falls.

Figure 5.4 shows the way in which elasticity changes along a linear demand curve. At the midpoint of the demand curve, elasticity is unitary (equal to −1). At higher prices, demand is elastic, and at lower prices, demand is inelastic.

Again, it is useful to keep in mind the underlying economics as well as the mathematics. At high prices and low quantities, it is easy to make a big impact on the level of sales. At low prices, appreciably increasing restaurant volumes is much harder. For businesses, this is an important point to keep in mind.

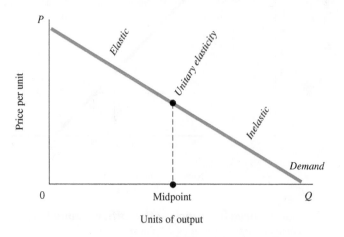

▲ **FIGURE 5.4**   **Point Elasticity Changes along a Demand Curve**

Elasticity and Total Revenue

As we saw in Chapter 4, the oil-producing countries have had some success keeping oil prices high by controlling supply. Reducing supply and driving up prices has increased the total oil revenues to the producing countries. We would not, however, expect this strategy to work for everyone. If an organization of banana-exporting countries (OBEC) had done the same thing, the strategy would not have worked.

Why? The key factor distinguishing the oil market from the banana market is the responsiveness of customers in the two markets to price changes. There are many reasonable substitutes for bananas. As the price of bananas rises, people simply eat fewer bananas as they switch to eating more pineapples or oranges. Many people are simply not willing to pay a higher price for bananas. If the banana cartel were to raise prices, it would see a large volume decline in its sales and its revenues would decrease.

Why is the oil market different? The answer lies in the demand elasticity. The quantity of oil demanded is not as responsive to a change in price as is the quantity of bananas demanded. In other words, the demand for oil is more inelastic than is the demand for bananas. In the oil industry consumers do not reduce consumption much in response to a price increase. As a result, these price increases can lead to revenue increases. One of the useful features of elasticity is that knowing the value of price elasticity allows us to quickly see what happens to a firm's revenue as it raises and cuts its prices. When demand is inelastic, raising prices will raise revenues; when (as in the banana case) demand is elastic, price increases reduce revenues.

We can now use the more formal definition of elasticity to make more precise our argument of why oil producers would succeed and banana producers would fail as they raise prices. In any market, $P \times Q$ is total revenue (TR) received by producers:

$$TR = P \times Q$$
$$\text{total revenue} = \text{price} \times \text{quantity}$$

The oil producers' total revenue is the price per barrel of oil (P) times the number of barrels its participant countries sell (Q). To banana producers, total revenue is the price per bunch times the number of bunches sold.

When price increases in a market, quantity demanded declines. As we have seen, when price (P) declines, quantity demanded (Q_D) increases. This is true in all markets. The two factors, P and Q_D, move in opposite directions:

effects of price changes on quantity demanded:
$$P \uparrow \ \rightarrow \ Q_D \downarrow$$
and
$$P \downarrow \ \rightarrow \ Q_D \uparrow$$

Because total revenue is the product of P and Q, whether TR rises or falls in response to a price increase depends on which is bigger: the percentage increase in price or the percentage decrease in quantity demanded. If the percentage decrease in quantity demanded is smaller than the percentage increase in price, total revenue will rise. This occurs when demand is *inelastic*. In this case, the percentage price rise simply outweighs the percentage quantity decline and $P \times Q = (TR)$ rises:

effect of price increase on a product with inelastic demand:
$$\uparrow P \times Q_D \downarrow \ = TR \uparrow$$

If, however, the percentage decline in quantity demanded following a price increase is larger than the percentage increase in price, total revenue will fall. This occurs when demand is *elastic*. The percentage price increase is outweighed by the percentage quantity decline:

effect of price increase on a product with elastic demand:	$\uparrow P \times Q_D \downarrow = TR \downarrow$

The opposite is true for a price cut. When demand is elastic, a cut in price increases total revenue:

effect of price cut on a product with elastic demand:	$\downarrow P \times Q_D \uparrow = TR \uparrow$

When demand is inelastic, a cut in price reduces total revenue:

effect of price cut on a product with inelastic demand:	$\downarrow P \times Q_D \uparrow = TR \downarrow$

Review the logic of these equations to make sure you thoroughly understand the reasoning. Having a responsive (or elastic) market is good when we are lowering prices because it means that we are dramatically increasing our units sold. But that same responsiveness is unattractive as we contemplate raising prices because now it means that we are losing customers. And, of course, the reverse logic works in the inelastic market. Note that if there is unitary elasticity, total revenue is unchanged if the price changes.

Facing inelastic demand, oil producers see a revenue increase with a price increase. In contrast, a banana cartel, facing elastic demand, loses so much business with a price cut that its revenue falls.

5.3 LEARNING OBJECTIVE

Identify the determinants of demand elasticity.

The Determinants of Demand Elasticity

We have begun to see how important elasticity is to decision making. But what determines elasticity? Why do we think the demand for oil is inelastic and the demand for bananas elastic?

Availability of Substitutes

The most important factor affecting demand elasticity is the availability of substitutes. Consider a number of farm stands lined up along a country road. If every stand sells fresh corn of roughly the same quality, Mom's Green Thumb will find it difficult to charge a price much higher than the competition charges because a nearly perfect substitute is available just down the road. The demand for Mom's corn is thus likely to be elastic: An increase in price will lead to a rapid decline in the quantity demanded of Mom's corn.

In the oil versus banana example, the demand for oil is inelastic in large measure because of the lack of substitutes. Most automobiles, millions of homes, and most industry use petroleum products. The current debate on climate control takes as a starting point the lack of substitutes for carbon-emitting oil products as it describes the difficulty of reducing emissions. The inelasticity of demand for oil has ramifications well beyond the oil market itself.

The Importance of Being Unimportant

When an item represents a relatively small part of our total budget, we tend to pay little attention to its price. For example, if you pick up a pack of mints once in a while, you might not notice an increase in price from 25 cents to 35 cents. Yet this is a 40 percent increase in price

ECONOMICS IN PRACTICE

Elasticities at a Delicatessen in the Short Run and Long Run

Frank runs a corner delicatessen and decides one Monday morning to raise the prices of his sandwiches by 10 percent. Because Frank knows a little economics, he expects that this price increase will cause him to lose some business because demand curves slope down, but he decides to try it anyway. At the end of the day, Frank discovers that his revenue has, in fact, gone up in the sandwich department. Feeling pleased with himself, Frank hires someone to create signs showing the new prices for the sandwich department. At the end of the month, however, he discovers that sandwich revenue is way down. What is going on?

The first thing to notice about this situation is that it poses a puzzle about what happens to revenue following a price increase. Seeing a linkage between price increases (or cuts) and revenue immediately leads an economist to think about *elasticity*. We remember from previously in the chapter that *when demand is elastic,* (that is, an *absolute value* greater than 1), *price increases reduce revenue* because a small price increase will bring a large quantity decrease, thus depressing revenue. Conversely, when demand is inelastic (that is, an absolute value less than 1), price increases do little to curb demand and revenues rise. In this case, Monday's price increase brings increases in revenue; therefore, this pattern tells us that the demand from Frank's customers appears to be inelastic. In the longer term, however, demand appears to be more elastic (revenue is down after a month). Another way to pose this puzzle is to ask why the monthly demand curve might have a different elasticity than the daily demand.

To answer that question, you need to think about what determines elasticity. The most fundamental determinant of demand elasticity is the availability of substitutes. In this case, the product we are looking at is sandwiches. At first, you might think that the substitutes for Monday's sandwich would be the same as the substitutes for the sandwiches for the rest of the month. But this is not correct. Once you are in Frank's store, planning to buy a sandwich, your demand tends to be relatively inelastic because your ability to substitute by going elsewhere or choosing a different lunch item

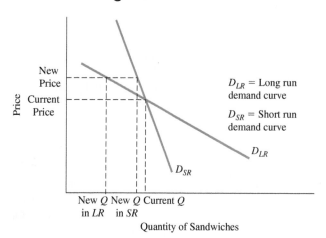

is relatively limited. You have already come to the part of town where Frank's Delicatessen is located, and you may already have chosen chips and a beverage to go along with your sandwich. Once you know that Frank's sandwiches are expensive, you can make different plans, and this broadening of your substitute choices increases your elasticity. In general, longer-term demand curves tend to be more elastic than shorter-term curves because customers have more time to contemplate the availability of substitutes.

The graph above shows the expected relationship between long-run and short-run demand for Frank's sandwiches. Notice if you raise prices above the current level, the expected quantity change read off the short-run curve is less than that from the long-run curve.

THINKING PRACTICALLY

1. Provide an example of a purchasing situation in which you think your own short- and long-run elasticities differ a lot and a second in which they are similar. What drives those differences?

(33.3 percent using the midpoint formula). In cases such as these, we are not likely to respond much to changes in price, and demand is likely to be inelastic.

Luxuries versus Necessities

Luxury goods, like yachts or Armani suits, tend to have relatively elastic demand, while necessities, like food, have inelastic demand. It is easy to give up owning a yacht (at least for most people) when the price rises, but few of us can give up food. In many ways, this distinction between luxuries and necessities really takes us back to the question of substitutes. Although there may be no product that is exactly like a yacht, there are many things that give us pleasures that act as substitutes for that yacht. Our need for food cannot be satisfied by anything other than food. You should also note that while our demand for food as a broad category is inelastic, our demand for any particular type of food—like bananas—is typically quite elastic. Again, the principle of substitution goes a long way in helping us to predict elasticity.

The Time Dimension

When the oil-producing nations first cut output and succeeded in pushing up the price of crude oil, few substitutes were immediately available. Demand was relatively inelastic, and prices rose substantially. During the last 30 years, however, there has been some adjustment to higher oil prices. Automobiles manufactured today get on average more miles per gallon, and some drivers have cut down on their driving. Millions of home owners have insulated their homes, most people have turned down their thermostats, and some people have explored alternative energy sources.

If your college decided to increase the price of dormitories or food service mid-year, it would be hard for you to move right away. In the short term, your demand for dorm space or a meal plan is relatively inelastic. But by the next semester many of you would likely have found alternative housing! Of course, the inelasticity of demand in the short run is one reason renters—including college dorm residents—insist on contracts that guarantee rents for a period of time with notice before changes are made!

All of this illustrates an important point: The elasticity of demand in the short run may be different from the elasticity of demand in the long run. In the longer run, demand is likely to become more elastic, or responsive, simply because households make adjustments over time and producers develop substitute goods. The *Economics in Practice* box on page 99 provides another look at the time dimension of elasticity.

5.4 LEARNING OBJECTIVE

Define and give examples of income elasticity, cross-price elasticity, and supply elasticity.

Other Important Elasticities

So far, we have been discussing price elasticity of demand, which measures the responsiveness of quantity demanded to changes in price. However, as we noted previously, elasticity is a general concept. Let us look briefly at three other important types of elasticity.

Income Elasticity of Demand

income elasticity of demand
A measure of the responsiveness of quantity demanded to changes in income.

Income elasticity of demand, which measures the responsiveness of quantity demanded to changes in income, is defined as

$$\text{income elasticity of demand} = \frac{\% \text{ change in quantity demanded}}{\% \text{ change in income}}$$

Measuring income elasticity is important for many reasons. In the last decade, there has been enormous growth in China, giving rise to increases in household income. What new goods are being demanded by those newly affluent consumers? As it turns out, one of the goods that has a high income elasticity is clean air. As people in China grow richer, they are increasingly demanding cleaner air. One way we see this is in the growth in demand for privately produced air filters. Another place we see the high income elasticity of demand for clean air is in demands made of the government in public protests and in other ways. Both governments and firms are interested in income elasticity as they think about what the future demands of people will look like.

Income elasticities can be positive or negative. During periods of rising income, people increase their spending on some goods (positive income elasticity) but reduce their spending on other goods (negative income elasticity). The income elasticity of demand for jewelry is positive, whereas the income elasticity of demand for cigarettes is negative. As incomes rise in many low-income countries, the birth rate falls, implying a negative income elasticity of demand for children. Also, as incomes rise in most countries, the demand for education and health care rises, a positive income elasticity.

Cross-Price Elasticity of Demand

Cross-price elasticity of demand, which measures the response of quantity of one good demanded to a change in the price of another good, is defined as

$$\text{cross-price elasticity of demand} = \frac{\% \text{ change in quantity of } Y \text{ demanded}}{\% \text{ change in price of } X}$$

cross-price elasticity of demand A measure of the response of the quantity of one good demanded to a change in the price of another good.

Like income elasticity, cross-price elasticity can be either positive or negative. A *positive* cross-price elasticity indicates that an increase in the price of *X* causes the demand for *Y* to rise. This implies that the goods are substitutes. For McDonald's, Big Macs and Chicken McNuggets are substitutes with a positive cross-price elasticity. In our previous example, as McDonald's lowered the price of Big Macs, it saw a decline in the quantity of McNuggets sold as consumers substituted between the two meals. If cross-price elasticity turns out to be *negative*, an increase in the price of *X* causes a decrease in the demand for *Y*. This implies that the goods are complements. Hot dogs and football games are complements with a negative cross-price elasticity.

As we have already seen, knowing the cross-price elasticity can be an important part of a company's business strategy. The cross-price elasticity between video games and game consoles is high and positive: the better and cheaper the video games, the more people want to buy consoles. Companies that make these game systems, like Microsoft and Sony, spend a lot of effort trying to ensure that exciting games are made for their platforms.

Elasticity of Supply

So far, we have focused on the consumer part of the market. But elasticity also matters on the producer's side.

Elasticity of supply, which measures the response of quantity of a good supplied to a change in price of that good, is defined as

$$\text{elasticity of supply} = \frac{\% \text{ change in quantity supplied}}{\% \text{ change in price}}$$

elasticity of supply A measure of the response of quantity of a good supplied to a change in price of that good. Likely to be positive in output markets.

In output markets, the elasticity of supply is likely to be a positive number—that is, a higher price leads to an increase in the quantity supplied, *ceteris paribus*. (Recall our discussion of upward-sloping supply curves in the preceding two chapters.)

The elasticity of supply is a measure of how easily producers can adapt to a price increase and bring increased quantities to market. In some industries, it is relatively easy for firms to increase their output. Ballpoint pens fall into this category, as does most software that has already been developed. For these products, the elasticity of supply is high. In the oil industry, supply is inelastic, much like demand.

In input markets, however, some interesting problems arise in looking at elasticity. Perhaps the most studied elasticity of all is the **elasticity of labor supply**, which measures the response of labor supplied to a change in the price of labor (the wage rate). Economists have examined household labor supply responses to government programs such as welfare, Social Security, the income tax system, need-based student aid, and unemployment insurance. The *Economics in Practice* box on page 102 explores labor elasticity.

elasticity of labor supply A measure of the response of labor supplied to a change in the price of labor.

In simple terms, the elasticity of labor supply is defined as

$$\text{elasticity of labor supply} = \frac{\% \text{ change in quantity of labor supplied}}{\% \text{ change in the wage rate}}$$

ECONOMICS IN PRACTICE

Tax Rates and Migration in Europe

With the formation of the European Union (EU), mobility of labor across Europe became quite easy. This is especially true for highly educated Europeans, who often have skills that are useful in many different areas and who may be multi-lingual. Despite sharing many policies centrally, countries in the EU are free to set their own income tax rates. As a result, there has been considerable debate on whether countries are using tax rates to lure highly skilled, highly productive people from other countries. Having read this chapter, you should see that the key economic question involves elasticity: how elastic (responsive) are highly skilled workers to changes in tax rates on their income?

This is exactly the question asked by a group of economists from London, Paris, Copenhagen, and Berkeley using data from Denmark.[2] Denmark, like much of Europe, has relatively high taxes on high wage earners. In 2009, for example, the average individual earning 100,000 euros a year in Denmark would pay 55 percent of those earnings in taxes. Seeking to bring highly skilled workers to the country, Denmark enacted a tax relief law aimed at these foreigners. For a 3-year period after coming to Denmark, foreigners earning more than 100,000 euros would face a flat 30 percent tax rate, rather than the graduated, but higher tax rate normally faced. The key question asked in the paper is how workers responded: what is the elasticity of labor migration in response to this change?

The researchers found a large response: an elasticity of migration of almost 2. A 10 percent reduction in the tax rate induced a 20 percent increase in migration. After a few years

of the policy, the fraction of foreigners in the top 0.5 percent of the income earners in Denmark increased from 4.0 percent to 7.5 percent. The authors concluded that for this group of workers, labor supply seems to be quite elastic across Europe.

THINKING PRACTICALLY

1. What features of the EU do you think increase the labor elasticity?

[2] Henrik Kleven, Camille Landais, Emmanuel Saez , Esben Schultz, "Migration and Wage effects of Taxing Top Earners: Evidence from the Foreigners' Tax Scheme in Denmark," *Quarterly Journal of Economics*, 1 (2014): 333-378.

It seems reasonable at first glance to assume that an increase in wages increases the quantity of labor supplied. That would imply an upward-sloping supply curve and a positive labor supply elasticity, but this is not necessarily so. An increase in wages makes workers better off: They can work the same number of hours and have higher incomes. One of the things workers might like to "buy" with that higher income is more leisure time. "Buying" leisure simply means working fewer hours, and the "price" of leisure is the lost wages. Thus, it is quite possible that to some groups, an increase in wages above some level will lead to a reduction in the quantity of labor supplied.

5.5 LEARNING OBJECTIVE

Understand the way excise taxes can be shifted to consumers.

What Happens When We Raise Taxes: Using Elasticity

Imagine you are the new mayor of a city with budget problems. One day you go grocery shopping and notice that a lot of people are buying avocados. Most of the buyers look affluent. Later that day you do a little homework and learn that in your city 1,000 avocados are sold per day. This might appear to be a golden opportunity for you to solve your budget problems. A quick calculation might lead you to think that a tax of $1.00 per avocado would bring in to the city

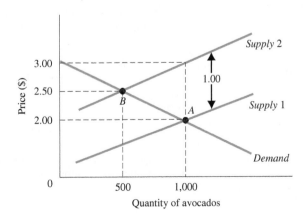

$365,000 per year in taxes, given that the city residents buy 1,000 avocados per day. Economists refer to per-unit taxes of this sort as **excise taxes**. In the United States we have excise taxes on gasoline and cigarettes among other products.

Excise tax   A per unit tax on a specific good.

Suppose you impose this tax, telling all the stores carrying avocados that for every avocado they sell, they have to pay the city $1.00. At the end of the year, your tax department discovers that the avocado tax has in fact only raised $182,500, half of what you expected. What do you think went wrong in your calculation?

The answer to the missing taxes lies in what we have learned about elasticities and can be seen using two diagrams. Before the tax was imposed, 1,000 avocados were sold per day across the city. Let us suppose the original price per unit was $2.00 at this quantity. We represent this in Figure 5.5.

From this figure we see there is an equilibrium in which supply equals demand at point A. Reading off the supply curve, we see that store owners are willing to sell 1,000 avocados at the $2.00 price. At this price, the store owners can pay farmers for the avocados and cover their own costs. We also see that consumers are willing to buy 1,000 avocados at this $2.00 price.

After the mayor imposes his tax, store owners essentially have a new cost. In addition to paying the farmers for their avocados, they also have to pay the mayor! The cost to the store is increased by $1.00 per unit because of the tax. If store owners were originally willing to supply 1,000 avocados at $2.00, it will take $3.00 to generate that same supply. If they get $3.00 per avocado and then pay the mayor his $1.00, they will be back to where they were before the tax, providing 1,000 avocados to the market.

In fact, the same logic applies to the whole supply curve. Everywhere it shifts up by $1.00 to represent the tax. In Chapter 3 we showed this same shift in supply curves resulting from an increase in costs. Here the cost is a tax. Figure 5.6 shows us what happens in this market when the tax is imposed and the supply curve shifts up by $1.00. *Supply* 2 represents the supply of the store owners after the $1.00 tax is imposed. There is a new equilibrium where supply equals demand at point B. At this new equilibrium, 500 avocados are sold and the price has risen to $2.50. Notice, however, that the full $2.50 does not in the end go to the storeowner. Of this $2.50, the government receives its $1.00 and the store owner receives $1.50. There is a wedge, or gap, between the price paid by the customer (here $2.50) and the price received by the store owner(here $1.50). The wedge represents the government tax.

There are several things to note here. First, the reason the mayor raised only half the taxes he expected was that the number of avocados sold fell by half after the tax was imposed. Why did this happen? Storeowners reacted to the cost increase created by the tax. To sell the original 1,000 units, they ask $3.00 per avocado. But consumers of avocados reacted to that attempt to increase prices! The downward slope of the demand curve tells us that people want fewer avocados when the price starts to rise. This is exactly the process we saw happening in the *Economics in Practice* box on Frank's delicatessen. In fact, the demand curve for avocados is relatively elastic in this region: we see a 50 percent decrease in quantity demand when prices rise by 25 percent. This should not surprise you: there are a lot of substitutes for avocados!

You should also note that likely no one is happy with the new tax. Consumers who continue to buy avocados have seen the price they pay go up by $0.50. Many other consumers stop buying avocados at all because they are too expensive. Storeowners are selling fewer avocados and are earning less on what they sell, since they receive $2.50 per avocado but have to pay the mayor $1.00, netting only $1.50. The mayor is earning less tax revenue than he had expected.

The culprit? The demand elasticity. The increased cost from the tax causes customers to shift away from their original purchase. The more elastic the curve, the more adjustment we would see. If consumers were completely inelastic, the storeowners could have raised prices by the full $1.00 and customers would have paid the $3.00 price for the original 1,000 avocados. The mayor would have received the $365,000 tax, and the only group hurt would have been the consumers, who now would pay a higher price. The mayor should find a less elastic product to tax!

Analyzing what happens when a tax is imposed is an exciting area of economics and clearly of central importance to policy making. We return to this topic later in the book in Chapter 19 when we cover public finance.

Looking Ahead

The purpose of this chapter was to convince you that measurement is important. If all we can say is that a change in one economic factor causes another to change, we cannot say whether the change is important or whether a particular policy is likely to work. The most commonly used tool of measurement is elasticity, and the term will recur as we explore economics in more depth.

We now return to the study of basic economics by looking in detail at household behavior. Recall that households *demand* goods and services in product markets but *supply* labor and savings in input or factor markets.

——— SUMMARY ———

1. *Elasticity* is a general measure of responsiveness that can be used to quantify many different relationships. If one variable A changes in response to changes in another variable B, the elasticity of A with respect to B is equal to the percentage change in A divided by the percentage change in B.

2. The slope of a demand curve is an inadequate measure of responsiveness because its value depends on the units of measurement used. For this reason, elasticities are calculated using percentages.

5.1 PRICE ELASTICITY OF DEMAND *p. 90*

3. *Price elasticity of demand* is the ratio of the percentage change in quantity demanded of a good to the percentage change in price of that good.

4. *Perfectly inelastic* demand is demand whose quantity demanded does not respond at all to changes in price; its numerical value is zero.

5. *Inelastic* demand is demand whose quantity demanded responds somewhat, but not a great deal, to changes in price; its numerical value is between zero and -1.

6. *Elastic* demand is demand in which the percentage change in quantity demanded is larger in absolute value than the percentage change in price. Its numerical value is less than -1.

7. *Unitary elasticity* of demand describes a relationship in which the percentage change in the quantity of a product demanded is the same as the percentage change in price; unitary elasticity has a numerical value of -1.

8. *Perfectly elastic* demand describes a relationship in which a small increase in the price of a product causes the quantity demanded for that product to drop to zero.

5.2 CALCULATING ELASTICITIES *p. 92*

9. There are a number of ways to calculate elasticity. The most common methods are the *midpoint formula*, which uses midpoint values for prices and quantities to calculate elasticity between two points on a demand curve, and the *point elasticity*, which calculates elasticity at a point by using the slope and the price and quantity values at that point.

10. If demand is elastic, a price increase will reduce the quantity demanded by a larger percentage than the percentage increase in price and total revenue $(P \times Q)$ will fall. If demand is inelastic, a price increase will increase total revenue.

11. If demand is elastic, a price cut will cause quantity demanded to increase by a greater percentage than the percentage decrease in price and total revenue will rise. If demand is inelastic, a price cut will cause quantity demanded to increase by a smaller percentage than the percentage decrease in price and total revenue will fall.

5.3 THE DETERMINANTS OF DEMAND ELASTICITY *p. 98*

12. The elasticity of demand depends on (1) the availability of substitutes, (2) whether a product is a luxury or necessity, and (3) the time frame in question.

   An inelastic demand exists for a product with few suitable substitutes, is considered a necessity, and there is a short time frame under consideration.

5.4 OTHER IMPORTANT ELASTICITIES *p. 100*

13. There are several other important elasticities. *Income elasticity of demand* measures the responsiveness of the quantity demanded with respect to changes in income. *Cross-price elasticity of demand* measures the response of the quantity of one good demanded to a change in the price of another good. *Elasticity of supply* measures the response of the quantity of a good supplied to a change in the price of that good. The *elasticity of labor supply measures* the response of the quantity of labor supplied to a change in the price of labor.

5.5 WHAT HAPPENS WHEN WE RAISE TAXES: USING ELASTICITY *p. 102*

14. The elasticity of demand determines in part how the imposition of an excise tax will affect consumers, suppliers, and the final revenue raised from the tax.

REVIEW TERMS AND CONCEPTS

PROBLEMS

All problems are available on MyEconLab.

5.1 PRICE ELASTICITY OF DEMAND

LEARNING OBJECTIVE: Understand why elasticity is preferable as a measure of responsiveness to slope and how to measure it.

1.1 The demand for hamburgers is shown in the following figures, with hamburgers priced in dollars in Figure *a* and pennies in Figure *b*. Calculate the slope of each demand curve and use your answers to explain why slope is not a useful measure of responsiveness of the quantity demanded to price changes. How can you use the information presented in these figures to obtain a more useful measure of responsiveness of the quantity demanded to price changes?

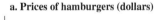

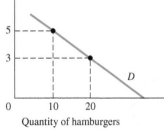

a. Prices of hamburgers (dollars)

Quantity of hamburgers

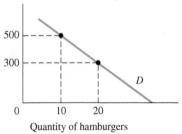

b. Prices of hamburgers (pennies)

Quantity of hamburgers

MyEconLab Visit **www.myeconlab.com** to complete these exercises online and get instant feedback. Exercises that update with real-time data are marked with art 🌐.

5.2   CALCULATING ELASTICITIES

LEARNING OBJECTIVE: Calculate elasticities using several different methods and understand the economic relationship between revenues and elasticity.

2.1 Fill in the missing amounts in the following table:

	% Change In Price	% Change In Quantity	Elasticity
Demand for the Apple iWatch	**a.**	− 25%	− 1.0
Demand for roses on Valentine's Day	+ 50%	**b.**	− 0.2
Demand for electronic cigarettes	− 10%	+ 38%	**c.**

2.2 Use the table in the preceding problem to defend your answers to the following questions:
 a. Would you recommend that Apple raise or lower its price for the iWatch to increase revenue?
 b. Would you recommend that florists raise their prices for roses on Valentine's Day if their only goal is to increase revenues?
 c. Would you recommend that electronic cigarette vendors cut prices to increase revenues?

2.3 Using the midpoint formula, calculate elasticity for each of the following changes in demand.

	P₁	P₂	Q₁	Q₂
Demand for:				
a. Cashews	$7.50 per pound	$6.00 per pound	800 pounds per month	1,000 pounds per month
b. Portable hard drive (1 terabyte)	$80	$120	75 per year	65 per year
c. 12-gauge copper wire	0.60 per lineal foot	0.45 per lineal foot	2,500 lineal feet per week	5,000 lineal feet per week
d. Toothpaste	$2.00 per tube	$2.40 per tube	10 tubes per month	9 tubes per month

2.4 A sporting goods store has estimated the demand curve for a popular brand of running shoes as a function of price. Use the diagram to answer the questions that follow.

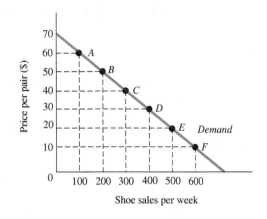

 a. Calculate demand elasticity using the midpoint formula between points A and B, between points C and D, and between points E and F.
 b. If the store currently charges a price of $50, then increases that price to $60, what happens to total revenue from shoe sales (calculate P × Q before and after the price change)? Repeat the exercise for initial prices being decreased to $40 and $20, respectively.
 c. Explain why the answers to a. can be used to predict the answers to b.

2.5 For each of the following scenarios, decide whether you agree or disagree and explain your answer.
 a. If the elasticity of demand for cocaine is −0.20 and the Drug Enforcement Administration succeeds in reducing supply substantially, causing the street price of the drug to rise by 50 percent, buyers will spend less on cocaine.
 b. Every year Christmas tree vendors bring tens of thousands of trees from the forests of New England to New York City and Boston. During the last 2 years, the market has been competitive; as a result, price has fallen by 10 percent. If the price elasticity of demand was −1.3, vendors would lose revenues altogether as a result of the price decline.
 c. If the demand for a good has unitary elasticity, or elasticity is −1, it is always true that an increase in its price will lead to more revenues for sellers taken as a whole.

2.6 For the following statements, decide whether you agree or disagree and explain your answer.
 a. The demand curve in Figure a is elastic.
 b. The demand curve in Figure b is inelastic.

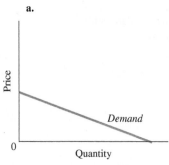

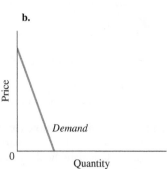

2.7 Taxicab fares in most cities are regulated. Several years ago, taxicab drivers in Boston obtained permission to raise their fares 10 percent, and they anticipated that revenues would increase by about 10 percent as a result. They were disappointed, however. When the commissioner granted the 10

percent increase, revenues increased by only about 5 percent. What can you infer about the elasticity of demand for taxicab rides? What were taxicab drivers assuming about the elasticity of demand?

*2.8 Studies have fixed the short-run price elasticity of demand for gasoline at the pump at −0.20. Suppose that international hostilities lead to a sudden cutoff of crude oil supplies. As a result, U.S. supplies of refined gasoline drop 10 percent.

   a. If gasoline were selling for $2.30 per gallon before the cut-off, how much of a price increase would you expect to see in the coming months?

   b. Suppose that the government imposes a price ceiling on gas at $2.30 per gallon. How would the relationship between consumers and gas station owners change?

2.9 Describe what will happen to total revenue in the following situations.

   a. Price decreases and demand is elastic.
   b. Price decreases and demand is inelastic.
   c. Price increases and demand is elastic.
   d. Price increases and demand is inelastic.
   e. Price increases and demand is unitary elastic.
   f. Price decreases and demand is perfectly inelastic.
   g. Price increases and demand is perfectly elastic.

2.10 Using the midpoint formula and the following graph, calculate the price elasticity of demand when the price changes from $3 to $8 and when the price changes from $8 to $14.

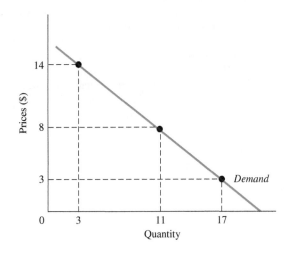

2.11 Use the following total revenue graph to identify which sections of the total revenue curve reflect elastic demand, inelastic demand, and unitary elastic demand. Explain your answers.

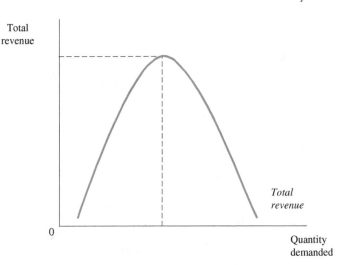

5.3 THE DETERMINANTS OF DEMAND ELASTICITY

LEARNING OBJECTIVE: Identify the determinants of demand elasticity.

3.1 **[Related to the *Economics in Practice* on p. 99]**
At Frank's Delicatessen, Frank noticed that the elasticity of customers differed in the short and longer term. Frank also noticed that his increase in the price of sandwiches had other effects on his store. In particular, the number of sodas sold declined while the number of yogurts sold went up. How might you explain this pattern?

3.2 For each of the following products, explain whether demand is likely to be elastic or inelastic.

   a. Tap water
   b. Orange juice
   c. Big Macs
   d. Insulin
   e. Samsung LED televisions
   f. Automobile tires

5.4 OTHER IMPORTANT ELASTICITIES

LEARNING OBJECTIVE: Define and give examples of income elasticity, cross-price elasticity, and supply elasticity.

4.1 Prior to 2005, it seemed like house prices always rose and never fell. When the demand for housing increases, prices in the housing market rise but not always by much. For prices to rise substantially, the supply of housing must be relatively inelastic. That is, if the quantity supplied increases rapidly whenever house prices rise, price increases will

*Note: Problems marked with an asterisk are more challenging.

remain small. Many have suggested government policies to increase the elasticity of supply. What specific policies might hold prices down when demand increases? Explain.

4.2 For each of the following statements, state the relevant elasticity and state what its value should be (negative, positive, greater than one, zero, and so on).
   a. The supply of labor is inelastic but slightly backward-bending.
   b. The demand for European vacations increases during times of rising incomes.
   c. The demand for hot dog buns rises when hot dog prices fall.
   d. The demand for Apple iPad Minis falls when the price of Samsung Galaxy Tabs falls.
   e. Pablo Picasso's most famous painting, *Guernica*, is housed in the Reina Sofia Museum in Madrid, and is not for sale at any price.
   f. The demand for mac-and-cheese rises during a time of severe recession and falling income.

4.3 The cross-price elasticity values for three sets of products are listed in the table below. What can you conclude about the relationships between each of these sets of products?

	Products A and B	Products C and D	Products E and F
Cross-price elasticity	−8.7	+5.5	0.0

4.4 Income elasticity of demand measures the responsiveness of demand to changes in income. Explain what is happening to demand and what kind of good is being represented in the following situations.
   a. Income is rising, and income elasticity of demand is positive.
   b. Income is rising, and income elasticity of demand is negative.
   c. Income is falling, and income elasticity of demand is positive.
   d. Income is falling, and income elasticity of demand is negative.

5.5 WHAT HAPPENS WHEN WE RAISE TAXES: USING ELASTICITY

LEARNING OBJECTIVE: Understand the way excise taxes can be shifted to consumers.

5.1 World famous Burpee Beer is brewed in the small town of West Burpee. Currently, the town of West Burpee levies a $2 per-case tax on all Burpee Beer, and the brewery sells 20,000 cases a year at a total price of $20 per case. The mayor of West Burpee has decided to erect a statue of himself in the town square at a cost of $20,000, and wants to raise the money from additional tax revenue from sales of Burpee Beer. He has asked each of the three town council members to come up with a plan to raise the additional $20,000, and their plans are as follows: Council member Simpson advises increasing the per-case tax by $1, Council member Milhouse advises raising the tax by $2 per case, and council member Flanders advises reducing the current tax by $0.50 per case. For each of the three council member's plans, determine the following:
   a. How many total cases of beer would need to be produced to increase tax revenue by exactly $20,000?
   b. What is the price elasticity of demand for Burpee Beer if the tax revenue increases by exactly $20,000?
   c. How much total revenue will Burpee Beer receive if the tax revenue increases by exactly $20,000?

5.2 [**Related to the *Economics in Practice* on p. 102**] In 2014, the Spanish government passed a law to change a regulation, known as the "Beckham law," on foreign athletes. This new law will require foreign professional athletes to pay the standard Spanish tax rate of 52 percent on earnings of more than 300,000 euros, up from the 24 percent rate they had been paying since 2005. For top-quality players, the elasticity of migration under the Beckham law was estimated to be 1.87 based on the average annual tax rate. Using this estimate of elasticity, what impact will this increased tax rate have on the migration of top-quality players in Spain?

PARToanstPART II

The Market System
Choices Made by Households and Firms

Now that we have discussed the basic forces of supply and demand, we can explore the underlying behavior of the two fundamental decision-making units in the economy: households and firms.

Figure II.1 presents a diagram of a simple competitive economy. The figure is an expanded version of the circular flow diagram first presented in Figure 3.1 on p. 44. It is designed to guide you through Part II (Chapters 6 through 12) of this book.

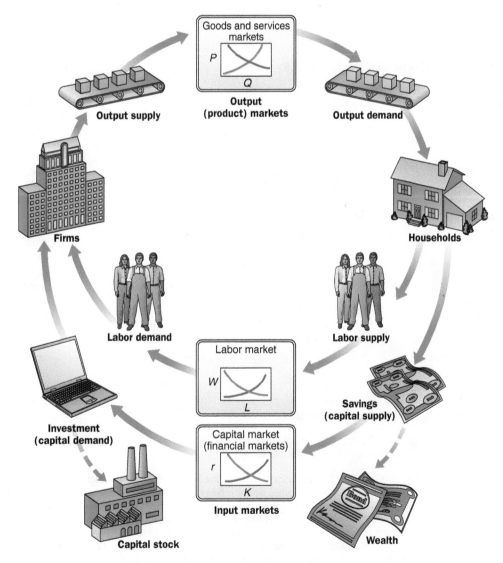

▲ FIGURE II.1 **Firm and Household Decisions**
Households demand in output markets and supply labor and capital in input markets. To simplify our analysis, we have not included the government and international sectors in this circular flow diagram. These topics will be discussed in detail later.

Households and firms interact in two kinds of markets: output (product) markets, shown at the top of Figure II.1, and input (factor) markets, shown at the bottom. Households *demand* outputs and *supply* inputs. In contrast, firms *supply* outputs and *demand* inputs. Chapter 6 explores the behavior of households, focusing first on household demand for outputs and then on household supply in labor and capital markets.

The remaining chapters in Part II focus on firms and the interaction between firms and households. Chapters 7 through 9 analyze the behavior of firms in output markets in both the short run and the long run. Chapter 10 focuses on the behavior of firms in input markets in general, especially the labor and land markets. Chapter 11 discusses the capital market in more detail. Chapter 12 puts all the pieces together and analyzes the functioning of a complete market system. Following Chapter 12, Part III of the book analyzes market imperfections as well as the potential for and pitfalls of government involvement in the economy. The plan for Chapters 6 through 19 is outlined in Figure II.2.

Recall that throughout this book, all diagrams that describe the behavior of households are drawn or highlighted in *blue*. All diagrams that describe the behavior of firms are drawn or highlighted in *red*. Look carefully at the supply and demand diagrams in Figure II.1; notice that in both the labor and capital markets, the supply curves are blue. The reason is that labor and capital are supplied by households. The demand curves for labor and capital are red because firms demand these inputs for production.

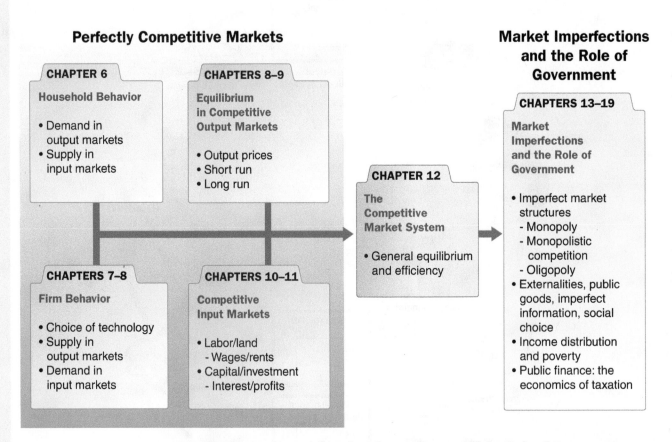

▲ FIGURE II.2 **Understanding the Microeconomy and the Role of Government**
To understand how the economy works, it helps to build from the ground up. We start in Chapters 6–8 with an overview of **household** and **firm** decision making in simple, perfectly competitive markets. In Chapters 9–11, we see how firms and households interact in **output markets** (product markets) and **input markets** (labor/ land and capital) to determine prices, wages, and profits. Once we have a picture of how a simple, perfectly competitive economy works, we begin to relax assumptions. Chapter 12 is a pivotal chapter that links perfectly competitive markets with a discussion of market imperfections and the role of government. In Chapters 13–19, we cover the three noncompetitive market structures (monopoly, monopolistic competition, and oligopoly), externalities, public goods, uncertainty and asymmetric information, and income distribution as well as taxation and government finance.

In Figure II.1, much of the detail of the real world is stripped away just as it is on a highway map. Figure II.1 is intended to serve as a map to help you understand basic market forces before we add more complicated market structures and government.

Before we proceed with our discussion of household choice, we need to make a few basic assumptions. These assumptions pertain to Chapters 6 through 12.

We first assume that households and firms possess all the information they need to make market choices. Specifically, we assume that households possess knowledge of the qualities and prices of everything available in the market. Firms know all that there is to know about wage rates, capital costs, technology, and output prices. This assumption is often called the assumption of **perfect knowledge**.

The next assumption is **perfect competition**. Perfect competition is a precisely defined form of industry structure. (The word *perfect* here does not refer to virtue. It simply means "total" or "complete.") In a perfectly competitive industry, no single firm has control over prices. That is, no single firm is large enough to affect the market price of its product or the prices of the inputs that it buys. This follows from two characteristics of competitive industries. First, a competitive industry is composed of many firms, each one small relative to the size of the industry. Second, every firm in a perfectly competitive industry produces exactly the same product; the output of one firm cannot be distinguished from the output of the others. Products in a perfectly competitive industry are said to be **homogeneous**.

These characteristics limit the decisions open to competitive firms and simplify the analysis of competitive behavior. Because all firms in a perfectly competitive industry produce virtually identical products and because each firm is small relative to the market, perfectly competitive firms have no control over the prices at which they sell their output. By taking prices as a given, each firm can decide only how much output to produce and how to produce it.

Agriculture is the classic example of a perfectly competitive industry. A wheat farmer in South Dakota has no control over the price of wheat. Prices are determined not by the individual farmers, but by the interaction of many suppliers and many demanders. The only decisions left to the wheat farmer are how much wheat to plant and when and how to produce the crop.

We also assume that each household is small relative to the size of the market. Households face a set of product prices that they individually cannot control. Prices are set by the interaction of many suppliers and many demanders.

By the end of Chapter 12, we will have a complete picture of an economy, but it will be based on this set of fairly restrictive assumptions. At first, this may seem unrealistic to you, but the lessons of these chapters turn out to apply to more complex, more realistic markets. Simplifying the picture allows us to better tell the economics story.

perfect knowledge The assumption that households possess a knowledge of the qualities and prices of everything available in the market and that firms have all available information concerning wage rates, capital costs, technology, and output prices.

perfect competition An industry structure in which there are many firms, each being small relative to the industry and producing virtually identical products, and in which no firm is large enough to have any control over prices.

homogeneous products Undifferentiated outputs; products that are identical to or indistinguishable from one another.

6

Household Behavior and Consumer Choice

Every day people in a market economy make decisions. Some of those decisions involve the products they plan to buy: Should you buy a Coke for lunch, a bottle of tea, or just drink water? Should you purchase a laptop computer or stick with your old desktop? Some decisions are about the labor market: Should you continue your schooling or go to work instead? Many decisions involve a time element. If you decide to buy a laptop, you may have to use your savings or borrow money. That will leave you with fewer choices about what you can buy in the future.

To many people, the decisions listed in the previous paragraph seem different from one another. As you will see in this chapter, however, from an economics perspective, these decisions have a great deal in common. In this chapter, we will develop a set of principles that can be used to understand decisions in the product market and the labor market—decisions for today and for the future.

As you read this chapter, you might want to think about some of the following questions, questions that you will be able to answer by chapter's end. Baseball, even when it was more popular than it is today, was never played year-round. Indeed, no professional sport has a year-round season. Is this break necessary to give the athletes a rest, or is there something about household choice that helps explain this pattern? When the price of gasoline rises, people drive less, but one study suggests that they also switch from brand name products to generics or store brands.[1] Why might this be? Studying household choice will help you understand many decisions that underpin our market economy.

---

[1] Dora Gicheva, Justine Hastings, and Sofia Villas-Boas, "Investigating Income Effects in Scanner Data: Do Gasoline Prices Affect Grocery Purchases?" *American Economic Review*, May 2010: 480–484.

A theme that will run through the analysis is the idea of *constrained choice*. We make decisions under constraints that exist in the marketplace. Household consumption choices are constrained by income, wealth, and existing prices. Household decisions about labor supply and job choice are clearly constrained by the availability of jobs and the existing structure of market wages.

Household Choice in Output Markets

6.1 LEARNING OBJECTIVE

Explain where the budget constraint comes from and the role it plays in household demand.

Every household must make three basic decisions:

1. How much of each product, or output, to demand
2. How much labor to supply
3. How much to spend today and how much to save for the future

As we begin our look at demand in output markets, you must keep in mind that the choices underlying the demand curve are only part of the larger household choice problem. Closely related decisions about how much to work and how much to save are equally important and must be made simultaneously with output–demand decisions.

The Determinants of Household Demand

As we saw in Chapter 3, several factors influence the quantity of a given good or service demanded by a single household:

- The price of the product
- The income available to the household
- The household's amount of accumulated wealth
- The prices of other products available to the household
- The household's tastes and preferences
- The household's expectations about future income, wealth, and prices

As we know, demand schedules and demand curves express the relationship between quantity demanded and price, *ceteris paribus*. A change in price leads to a movement along a demand curve. Changes in income, in other prices, or in preferences shift demand curves to the left or right. We can now dig in a little deeper to see the underpinnings of these demand curves. Doing so will help us use the lessons of supply and demand more effectively.

The Budget Constraint

A first step in understanding the household choice process is to figure out what choices are *possible* for households. If you look carefully at the list of items that influence household demand, you will see that the first four actually define the set of options available. Information on household income and wealth, together with information on product prices, tells us those combinations of goods and services that are affordable and those that are not.[2] Income, wealth, and prices define what we call household **budget constraint.**

budget constraint The limits imposed on household choices by income, wealth, and product prices.

The income, wealth, and price constraints that surround choice are best illustrated with an example. Consider Barbara, a recent graduate of a midwestern university who takes a job as an account manager at a public relations firm. Let us assume that she receives a salary of $1,000 per month (after taxes) and that she has no wealth and no credit. Barbara's monthly expenditures are limited to her flow of income. Table 6.1 summarizes some of the choices open to her.

---

[2] Remember that we drew the distinction between income and wealth in Chapter 3. *Income* is the sum of household earnings within a given period; it is a flow variable. In contrast, *wealth* is a stock variable; it is what a household owns minus what it owes at a given point in time.

TABLE 6.1	Possible Budget Choices of a Person Earning $1,000 per Month after Taxes				
Option	Monthly Rent	Food	Other Expenses	Total	Available?
A	$ 400	$ 250	$ 350	$ 1,000	Yes
B	600	200	200	1,000	Yes
C	700	150	150	1,000	Yes
D	1,000	100	100	1,200	No

A careful search of the housing market reveals four vacant apartments. The least expensive is a one-room studio with a small kitchenette that rents for $400 per month, including utilities (option A). If she lived there, Barbara could afford to spend $250 per month on food and still have $350 left over for other things.

About four blocks away is a one-bedroom apartment with wall-to-wall carpeting and a larger kitchen. It has more space, but the rent is $600, including utilities. If Barbara took this apartment, she might cut her food expenditures by $50 per month and have only $200 per month left for everything else.

In the same building as the one-bedroom apartment is an identical unit on the top floor of the building with a balcony facing west toward the sunset. The balcony and view add $100 to the monthly rent. To live there, Barbara would be left with only $300 to split between food and other expenses.

Just because she was curious, Barbara looked at a town house in the suburbs that was renting for $1,000 per month. Obviously, unless she could get along without eating or doing anything else that cost money, she could not afford it. The combination of the town house and any amount of food is outside her budget constraint.

Notice that we have used the information that we have on income and prices to identify different combinations of housing, food, and other items that are available to a single-person household with an income of $1,000 per month. We have said nothing about the process of choosing. Instead, we have carved out what is called a **choice set or opportunity set**, the set of options that is defined and limited by Barbara's budget constraint.

choice set or opportunity set The set of options that is defined and limited by a budget constraint.

Preferences, Tastes, Trade-Offs, and Opportunity Cost   So far, we have identified only the combinations of goods and services that are and are not available to Barbara. Within the constraints imposed by limited incomes and fixed prices, however, households are free to choose what they will and will not buy. Their ultimate choices are governed by their individual preferences and tastes.

It will help you to think of the household choice process as a way of allocating income over a large number of available goods and services. A change in the price of a single good changes the constraints within which households choose, and this may change the entire allocation of income. Demand for some goods and services may rise while demand for others falls. If the price of a plane ticket from Nashville to Miami decreases to $100, you may decide to take that trip. But doing so will also mean that you have $100 less to spend on other things, things you routinely buy. A complicated set of trade-offs lies behind the shape and position of a household demand curve for a single good. Whenever a household makes a choice, it is weighing the good or service that it chooses against all the other things that the same money could buy.

Consider again our young account manager and her options listed in Table 6.1. If she hates to cook, likes to eat at restaurants, and goes out three nights a week, she will probably trade off some housing for dinners out and money to spend on clothes and other things. She will probably rent the studio for $400. She may, however, love to spend long evenings at home reading, listening to classical music, and sipping tea while watching the sunset. In that case, she will probably trade off some restaurant meals, evenings out, and travel expenses for the added comfort of the larger apartment with the balcony and the view. As long as a household faces a limited budget—and all households ultimately do—the real cost of any good or service is the value of the other goods and services that could have been purchased with the same amount of money. The real cost of a good or service is its opportunity cost, and opportunity cost is determined by relative prices.

The Budget Constraint More Formally   Ann and Tom are struggling graduate students in economics at the University of Virginia. Their tuition is paid by graduate fellowships. They live as resident advisers in a first-year dormitory, in return for which they receive an apartment and meals. Their fellowships also give them $200 each month to cover all their other expenses. To simplify things, let us assume that Ann and Tom spend their money on only two things: meals at a local Thai restaurant and nights at a local jazz club, The Hungry Ear. Thai meals go for a fixed price of $20 per couple. Two tickets to the jazz club, including espresso, are $10.

As Figure 6.1 shows, we can graphically depict the choices that are available to our dynamic duo. The axes measure the *quantities* of the two goods that Ann and Tom buy. The horizontal axis measures the number of Thai meals consumed per month, and the vertical axis measures the number of trips to The Hungry Ear. (Note that price is not on the vertical axis here; we are not drawing a demand curve but a budget constraint.) Every point in the space between the axes represents some combination of Thai meals and nights at the jazz club. Which of these points can Ann and Tom purchase with a fixed budget of $200 per month? Which points are in the opportunity set and which are not?

Suppose the students in the dorm are driving Ann and Tom crazy and they want to avoid the dining hall at all costs. How many meals can Ann and Tom afford if that is all they spend their money on? The answer is simple: When income is $200 and the price of Thai meals is $20, they can afford $200 ÷ $20 = 10 meals. This decision is represented by point A on the budget constrain in Figure 6.1. It is *on* the horizontal axis because all the points on that axis are points at which Ann and Tom make no jazz club visits. Another possibility is that general exams are coming up and Ann and Tom decide to relax at The Hungry Ear to relieve stress. Suppose they choose to spend all their money on jazz and none of it on Thai food. How many jazz club visits can they afford? Again, the answer is simple: With an income of $200 and with the price of jazz/espresso at $10, they can go to The Hungry Ear $200 ÷ $10 = 20 times. This is the point labeled B in Figure 6.1. A and B represent "pure" purchase decisions, consuming either all jazz or all restaurant meals. But Ann and Tom can also choose to mix their spending. The line connecting points A and B shows us all the combinations of the two goods that Ann and Tom can afford to buy. Starting from point B, suppose Ann and Tom give up trips to the jazz club to buy more Thai meals. Each additional Thai meal "costs" two trips to The Hungry Ear. The opportunity cost of a Thai meal is two jazz club trips.

Point C on the budget constraint represents a compromise. Here Ann and Tom go to the club 10 times and eat at the Thai restaurant 5 times. To verify that point C is on the budget constraint, price it out: 10 jazz club trips cost a total of $10 × 10 = $100, and 5 Thai meals cost a total of $20 × 5 = $100. The total is $100 + $100 = $200.

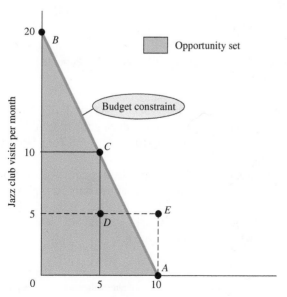

◀ FIGURE 6.1 **Budget Constraint and Opportunity Set for Ann and Tom**
A budget constraint separates those combinations of goods and services that are available, given limited income, from those that are not. The available combinations make up the opportunity set.

real income The set of opportunities to purchase real goods and services available to a household as determined by prices and money income.

The budget constraint divides all the points between the axes into two groups: those that can be purchased for $200 or less (the opportunity set) and those that are unavailable. Point *D* on the diagram costs less than $200; point *E* costs more than $200. The opportunity set is the shaded area in Figure 6.1.

Clearly, both prices and incomes affect the size of a household's opportunity set. If income rises, or if a price or a set of prices falls but income stays the same, the opportunity set gets bigger and the household is better off. If we define **real income** as the set of opportunities to purchase real goods and services, "real income" will have gone up in this case even if the household's money income has not. A U.S. dollar "feels" like much more money eating out in a rural restaurant in Mexico than it feels in midtown Manhattan because the prices are lower. A consumer's opportunity set expands as the result of a price decrease. On the other hand, when prices go up, we say that the household's "real income" has fallen.

The concept of real income is also very important in macroeconomics, which is concerned with measuring real output and the price level.

The Equation of the Budget Constraint

In addition to using graphs, we can use equations to describe the consumer's budget constraint. In the previous example, total expenditure on Thai meals plus total expenditure on jazz club visits must be less than or equal to Ann and Tom's income. Total expenditure on Thai meals is equal to the *price* of Thai meals times the number, or *quantity*, of meals consumed. Total expenditure on jazz club visits is equal to the *price* of a visit times the number, or *quantity*, of visits. That is,

$$\$20 \times \text{Thai meals} + \$10 \times \text{jazz visits} \leq \$200$$

If we let *X* represent the number of Thai meals and we let *Y* represent the number of jazz club visits and we assume that Ann and Tom spend their entire income on either *X* or *Y*, this can be written as follows:

$$20X + 10Y = \$200$$

This is the equation of the budget constraint—the line connecting points *A* and *B* in Figure 6.1. Notice that when Ann and Tom spend nothing at the jazz club, $Y = 0$. When you plug $Y = 0$ into the equation of the budget constraint, $20X = 200$ and $X = 10$. Since *X* is the number of Thai meals, Ann and Tom eat Thai food 10 times. Similarly, when $X = 0$, you can solve for *Y*, which equals 20. When Ann and Tom eat no Thai food, they can go to the jazz club 20 times.

In general, the budget constraint can be written

$$P_X X + P_Y Y = I,$$

where P_X = the price of *X*, *X* = the quantity of *X* consumed, P_Y = the price of *Y*, *Y* = the quantity of *Y* consumed, and *I* = household income.[3]

Budget Constraints Change When Prices Rise or Fall Now suppose the Thai restaurant is offering two-for-one certificates good during the month of November. In effect, this means that the price of Thai meals drops to $10 for Ann and Tom. How would the budget constraint in Figure 6.1 change?

First, point *B* would not change. If Ann and Tom spend all their money on jazz, the price of Thai meals is irrelevant. Ann and Tom can still afford only 20 trips to the jazz club. What has changed is point *A*, which moves to point *A′* in Figure 6.2. At the new lower price of $10, if Ann and Tom spent all their money on Thai meals, they could buy twice as many, $200 ÷ $10 = 20. The budget constraint *swivels*, as shown in Figure 6.2.

---

[3] You can calculate the slope of the budget constraint as $-P_X/P_Y$, the ratio of the price of *X* to the price of *Y*. This gives the trade-off that consumers face. In the example, $-P_X/P_Y = -2$, meaning to get another Thai meal, Ann and Tom must give up two trips to the jazz club.

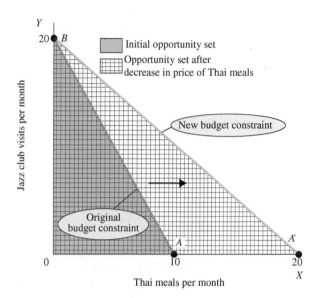

◀ FIGURE 6.2 **The Effect of a Decrease in Price on Ann and Tom's Budget Constraint**
When the price of a good decreases, the budget constraint swivels to the right, increasing the opportunities available and expanding choice.

The new, flatter budget constraint reflects the new trade-off between Thai meals and Hungry Ear visits. After the price of Thai meals drops to $10, the opportunity cost of a Thai meal is only one jazz club visit. The opportunity set has expanded because at the lower price, more combinations of Thai meals and jazz are available.

Figure 6.2 thus illustrates a very important point. When the price of a single good changes, more than just the quantity demanded of that good may be affected. The household now faces an entirely different problem with regard to choice—the opportunity set has expanded. At the same income of $200, the new lower price means that Ann and Tom might choose more Thai meals, more jazz club visits, or more of both. They are clearly better off. Notice that when the price of meals falls to $10, the equation of the budget constraint changes to $10X + 10Y = 200$, which is the equation of the line connecting points A' and B in Figure 6.2.

The Basis of Choice: Utility

6.2 LEARNING OBJECTIVE

Understand how the utility maximizing rule works in household choice of products.

utility The satisfaction a product yields.

The budget constraint shows us the combinations of products we can afford. But what determines which specific combination people choose? Here preferences come into play.

During the nineteenth century, the weighing of values was formalized into a concept called utility. Whether one item is preferable to another depends on how much **utility**, or satisfaction, it yields relative to its alternatives. How do we decide on the relative worth of a new puppy or a hedgehog?? A trip to the mountains or a weekend in New York City? As we make our choices, we are effectively weighing the utilities we would receive from all the possible available goods.

Although it is impossible to measure utility directly, the idea of utility as a measure of our tastes and preferences helps us better understand the process of choice. As we will see, even if we cannot measure utility, we can say a good deal about it.

Diminishing Marginal Utility

law of diminishing marginal utility The more of any one good consumed in a given period, the less satisfaction (utility) generated by consuming each additional (marginal) unit of the same good.

Suppose you live next to a store that sells homemade ice cream that you are crazy about. Even though you get a great deal of pleasure (utility) from eating ice cream, you do not spend your entire income on it. The first cone of the day tastes heavenly. The second is merely delicious. The third is still good, but it is clear that the glow is fading. Why? The answer is that the more of any one good we consume in a given period, the less satisfaction, or utility, we get from each *additional*, or marginal, unit.

In 1890, Alfred Marshall called this "familiar and fundamental tendency of human nature" the **law of diminishing marginal utility**. This so-called law has turned out to be helpful in

TABLE 6.2	Total Utility and Marginal Utility of Trips to the Club Per Week	
Trips to Club	Total Utility	Marginal Utility
1	12	12
2	22	10
3	28	6
4	32	4
5	34	2
6	34	0

understanding the behavior of people in a wide range of markets, from product markets and financial markets to labor markets.

Consider this numerical example. Frank loves country music, and a country band plays seven nights a week at a club near his house. Table 6.2 shows how the utility he derives from the band might change as he goes to the club more frequently. The first visit generates 12 "utils," or units of utility. When Frank goes back another night, he enjoys it, but not quite as much as the first night. The second night by itself yields 10 additional utils. **Marginal utility** is 10, while the **Total utility** derived from two nights at the club is 22. Three nights per week at the club provide 28 total utils; the marginal utility of the third night is 6 because total utility rose from 22 to 28. Figure 6.3 graphs total and marginal utility using the data in Table 6.2. Total utility increases up through Frank's fifth trip to the club but levels off on the sixth night. Marginal utility, which has declined from the beginning, is now at zero.

Diminishing marginal utility helps explain the reason most sports have limited seasons. Even rabid fans have had enough baseball by late October. Given this fact, it would be hard to sell out ball games for a year-round season. Although diminishing marginal utility is a simple and intuitive idea, it has great power in helping us understand the economic world.

marginal utility (MU) The additional satisfaction gained by the consumption or use of *one more* unit of a good or service.

Total utility The total satisfaction a product yields.

Allocating Income to Maximize Utility

How many times in 1 week would Frank go to the club to hear his favorite band? The answer depends on three things: Frank's income, the price of admission to the club, and the alternatives available. If the price of admission was zero and no alternatives existed, he would probably go to the club five nights a week. (Remember, the sixth night does not increase his utility, so why should he bother to go?) However, Frank is also a basketball fan. His city has many good high school and college teams, and he can go to games six nights a week if he so chooses.

Let us say for now that admission to both the country music club and the basketball games is free—that is, there is no price/income constraint. There is a time constraint, however, because there are only seven nights in a week. Table 6.3 lists Frank's total and marginal utilities from attending basketball games and going to country music clubs. From column 3 of the table, we can conclude that on the first night, Frank will go to a basketball game. The game is worth far more to him (21 utils) than a trip to the club (12 utils).

On the second night, Frank's decision is not so easy. Because he has been to one basketball game this week, the second game is worth less (12 utils as compared to 21 for the first basketball game). In fact, because it is worth the same as a first trip to the club, he is indifferent as to whether he goes to the game or the club. So he splits the next two nights: One night he sees ball game number two (12 utils); the other night he spends at the club (12 utils). At this point, Frank has been to two ball games and has spent one night at the club. Where will Frank go on evening four? He will go to the club again because the marginal utility from a second trip to the club (10 utils) is greater than the marginal utility from attending a third basketball game (9 utils).

Frank is splitting his time between the two activities to maximize total utility. He does this by choosing the activity that yields the most marginal utility. Continuing with this logic, you can see that spending three nights at the club and four nights watching basketball produces

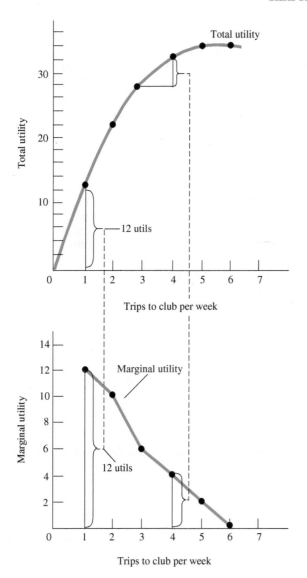

◀ **FIGURE 6.3** **Graphs of Frank's Total and Marginal Utility**
Marginal utility is the additional utility gained by consuming one additional unit of a commodity—in this case, trips to the club. When marginal utility is zero, total utility stops rising.

total utility of 76 utils each week (28 plus 48). No other combination of games and club trips can produce as much utility.

So far, the only cost of a night of listening to country music is a forgone basketball game and the only cost of a basketball game is a forgone night of country music. Now let us suppose that it costs $3 to get into the club and $6 to go to a basketball game. Suppose further that after paying rent and taking care of other expenses, Frank has only $21 left to spend on entertainment. Typically, consumers allocate limited incomes, or budgets, over a large set of goods and services. Here we have a limited income ($21) being allocated between only two goods, but the principle is the same. Income ($21) and prices ($3 and $6) define Frank's budget constraint. Within that constraint, Frank chooses to maximize utility.

Because the two activities now cost different amounts, we need to find the *marginal utility per dollar* spent on each activity. If Frank is to spend his money on the combination of activities lying within his budget constraint that gives him the most total utility, each night he must choose the activity that gives him the *most utility per dollar spent*. As you can see from column 5 in Table 6.3, Frank gets 4 utils per dollar on the first night he goes to the club (12 utils ÷ $3 = 4 utils per dollar). On night two, he goes to a game and gets 3.5 utils per dollar (21 utils ÷ $6 = 3.5 utils per dollar). On night three, it is back to the club. Then what happens? When all is said and done—work this out for yourself—Frank ends up going to two games and spending three nights at the club, which uses

TABLE 6.3	Allocation of Fixed Expenditure per Week between Two Alternatives			
(1) Trips to Club per Week	(2) Total Utility	(3) Marginal Utility (*MU*)	(4) Price (*P*)	(5) Marginal Utility per Dollar (*MU/P*)
1	12	12	$ 3.00	4.0
2	22	10	3.00	3.3
3	28	6	3.00	2.0
4	32	4	3.00	1.3
5	34	2	3.00	0.7
6	34	0	3.00	0
(1) Basketball Games per Week	(2) Total Utility	(3) Marginal Utility (*MU*)	(4) Price (*P*)	(5) Marginal Utility per Dollar (*MU/P*)
1	21	21	$ 6.00	3.5
2	33	12	6.00	2.0
3	42	9	6.00	1.5
4	48	6	6.00	1.0
5	51	3	6.00	0.5
6	51	0	6.00	0

up all his $21 budget. No other combination of activities that $21 will buy yields more total utility. Because of the added budget constraint, Frank no longer goes out seven nights a week.

The Utility-Maximizing Rule

In general, utility-maximizing consumers spread out their expenditures until the following condition holds:

$$\text{utility-maximizing rule:} \quad \frac{MU_X}{P_X} = \frac{MU_Y}{P_Y} \quad \text{for all goods,}$$

where MU_X is the marginal utility derived from the last unit of X consumed, MU_Y is the marginal utility derived from the last unit of Y consumed, P_X is the price per unit of X, and P_Y is the price per unit of Y.

utility-maximizing rule Equating the ratio of the marginal utility of a good to its price for all goods.

To see why this **utility-maximizing rule** is true, think for a moment about what would happen if it were *not* true. For example, suppose MU_X/P_X was greater than MU_Y/P_Y; that is, suppose a consumer purchased a bundle of goods so that the marginal utility from the last dollar spent on X was greater than the marginal utility from the last dollar spent on Y. This would mean that the consumer could increase his or her utility by spending a dollar less on Y and a dollar more on X. As the consumer shifts to buying more X and less Y, he or she runs into diminishing marginal utility. Buying more units of X *decreases* the marginal utility derived from consuming additional units of X. As a result, the marginal utility of another dollar spent on X falls. Now *less* is being spent on Y, and that means its marginal utility *increases*. This process continues until $MU_X/P_X = MU_Y/P_Y$. When this condition holds, there is no way for the consumer to increase his or her utility by changing the bundle of goods purchased.

You can see how the utility-maximizing rule works in Frank's choice between country music and basketball. At each stage, Frank chooses the activity that gives him the most utility per dollar. If he goes to a game, the utility he will derive from the next game—marginal utility—falls. If he goes to the club, the utility he will derive from his next visit falls, and so on.

The principles we have been describing help us understand an old puzzle dating from the time of Plato and familiar to economists beginning with Adam Smith. Adam Smith wrote about it in 1776:

The things which have the greatest value in use have frequently little or no value in exchange; and on the contrary, those which have the greatest value in exchange have frequently little or no value in use. Nothing is more useful than water: but it will

ECONOMICS IN PRACTICE

Cigarette Choice

Most states heavily tax cigarettes both as a way to raise revenue and as a way to discourage smoking. You might notice that the more taxes discourage smoking, the less revenue is raised. Thought of in another way, state tax policy in this area is always successful because either smoking is reduced a lot by the tax or a lot of revenue is raised from the tax. The effect of taxes on smoking is not only interesting from an economist's point of view but also is an important policy question.

A recent paper looked at taxes and smoking from a different angle, inquiring not how much taxes reduced smoking overall but how taxes might affect the *type* of cigarettes people smoke.[4] States tax cigarettes as a fixed price per pack or carton. In New York in 2008, the tax per carton was $15. An average branded carton in the state was $42, so the tax was a substantial part of the end price. An average generic carton cost $27, of which $15 was the tax.

The tax on cigarettes is the same for the branded and unbranded cigarettes despite their difference in pretax prices. The tax therefore changes the slope of the budget line. After tax, the slope of the budget line confronting a smoker choosing between branded and unbranded cigarettes was 1.55 (42/27). If we subtract the taxes from the two cartons, the slope rises to 2.25 (27/12). Without taxes, the relative price of the branded cigarettes has gone up.

The paper asks how much difference this makes. As it happens, there are Indian reservations in New York state that are exempt from the tax when charged to its own citizens. At least until recently, stores in these areas also sold untaxed cigarettes to non-residents, charging prices that were less than in the taxed areas by almost the full $15 value of the

tax. The relative price of branded cigarettes is thus higher in these stores. What happened when the relative price of the branded cigarettes rose? More than 20 percent of cigarette sales shifted to the generics. Changing the slope of the budget line by levying fixed per carton taxes had a large effect on what people choose to smoke.

THINKING PRACTICALLY

1. Show how the utility-maximizing rule given in the text would lead to the result described here.

[4] Phillip DeCeca, Doanld Kenkel, and FengLiu," Reservation Prices: An Economic Analysis of Cigarettes Purchased on Indian reservations," NBER Working Paper, December 2014

purchase scarce anything; scarce anything can be had in exchange for it. A diamond, on the contrary, has scarce any value in use; but a very great quantity of other goods may frequently be had in exchange for it.[5]

Although diamonds have arguably more than "scarce any value in use" today (for example, they are used to cut glass), Smith's **diamond/water paradox** is still instructive, at least where water is concerned.

The low price of water owes much to the fact that it is in plentiful supply. Even at a price of zero, we do not consume an infinite amount of water. We consume up to the point where *marginal* utility drops to zero. The *marginal* value of water is zero. Each of us enjoys an enormous consumer surplus when we consume nearly free water. At a price of zero, consumer surplus is the entire area under the demand curve. We tend to take water for granted, but imagine what would happen to its price if there were not enough for everyone. It would command a high price indeed.

diamond/water paradox A paradox stating that (1) the things with the greatest value in use frequently have little or no value in exchange and (2) the things with the greatest value in exchange frequently have little or no value in use.

[5] Adam Smith, *The Wealth of Nations*, Modern Library Edition (New York: Random House, 1937), p. 28 (1st ed. 1776). The cheapness of water is referred to by Plato in *Euthydemus*, 304 b.c.

▶ **FIGURE 6.4**
Diminishing Marginal Utility and Downward-Sloping Demand
At a price of $40, the utility gained from even the first Thai meal is not worth the price. However, a lower price of $25 lures Ann and Tom into the Thai restaurant 5 times a month. (The utility from the sixth meal is not worth $25.) If the price is $15, Ann and Tom will eat Thai meals 10 times a month—until the marginal utility of a Thai meal drops below the utility they could gain from spending $15 on other goods. At 25 meals a month, they cannot tolerate the thought of another Thai meal even if it is free.

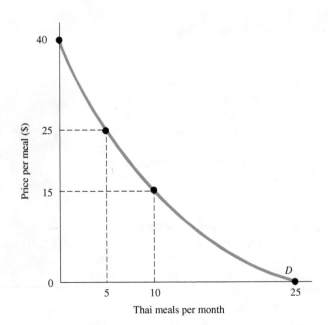

Diminishing Marginal Utility and Downward-Sloping Demand

The concept of diminishing marginal utility offers one reason people spread their incomes over a variety of goods and services instead of spending all income on one or two items. It also leads us to conclude that demand curves slope downward.

To see why this is so, let us return to our friends Ann and Tom, the struggling graduate students. Recall that they chose between meals at a Thai restaurant and trips to a jazz club. Now think about their demand curve for Thai meals, shown in Figure 6.4. When the price of a meal is $40, they decide not to buy any Thai meals. What they are really deciding is that the utility gained from even that first scrumptious meal each month is not worth the utility that would come from the other things that $40 can buy.

Now consider a price of $25. At this price, Ann and Tom buy five Thai meals. The first, second, third, fourth, and fifth meals each generate enough utility to justify the price. Tom and Ann "reveal" this by buying five meals. After the fifth meal, the utility gained from the next meal is not worth $25.

Ultimately, every demand curve hits the quantity (horizontal) axis as a result of diminishing marginal utility—in other words, demand curves slope downward. How many times will Ann and Tom go to the Thai restaurant if meals are free? Twenty-five times is the answer; and after 25 times a month, they are so sick of Thai food that they will not eat any more even if it is free. That is, marginal utility—the utility gained from the last meal—has dropped to zero. If you think this is unrealistic, ask yourself how much water you drank today.

6.3 LEARNING OBJECTIVE

Describe the income and substitution effects of a decrease in the price of food.

Income and Substitution Effects

Although the idea of utility is a helpful way of thinking about the choice process, another explanation for downward-sloping demand curves centers on income and substitution effects.

The Income Effect

Think for a moment about a price decline in a product you consume a good deal of. By itself, assuming nothing else changes, this price cut makes you better off: if you continue to buy the same amount of the good whose price has fallen, you will have income left over. In some real sense, you will feel richer. That extra income may be spent on getting more of the product whose price has declined, or on other products. The change in consumption of *the original product* due to this improvement in well-being, or your feeling richer, is called the *income effect of a price change.*

Suppose you live in Florida and four times a year you fly to Nashville to visit your mother, spending $400 for a round-trip ticket Thus, you spend a total of $1,600 per year on trips to visit Mom. This year, the price of round-trip tickets falls to $300. You can now fly home the same number of times and you will have spent $400 less for airline tickets than you did last year. That extra $400 leaves you feeling richer. What happens when you feel richer? If flying is a normal good, its demand will increase with income. So feeling richer would induce you to increase the number of times you fly home along with increasing consumption of a range of other goods. If the price of flights rose, you would feel poorer even if nothing happened to your actual income. The increase or decrease in purchases of a good when its price changes that come from a change in how rich or poor you feel as a result of that price change is called the *income effect.* Income effects are especially important when the price that changes is of a good we spend a lot on, like housing.

The Substitution Effect

The fact that a price decline leaves households better off is only part of the story. When the price of a product falls, that product also becomes *relatively* cheaper. That is, it becomes more attractive relative to potential substitutes. A fall in the price of product X might cause a household to shift its purchasing pattern away from substitutes toward X. This shift is called the *substitution effect of a price change.*

Previously we made the point that the "real" cost or price of a good is what one must sacrifice to consume it. This opportunity cost is determined by relative prices. To see why this is so, consider again the choice that you face when a round-trip ticket to Nashville costs $400. Each trip that you take requires a sacrifice of $400 worth of other goods and services. When the price drops to $300, the opportunity cost of a ticket has dropped by $100. In other words, after the price decline, you have to sacrifice only $300 (instead of $400) worth of other goods and services to visit Mom.

To clarify the distinction between the income and substitution effects, imagine how you would be affected if two things happened to you at the same time. First, the price of round-trip air travel between Florida and Nashville drops from $400 to $300. Second, your income is reduced by $400. You are now faced with new relative prices, but—assuming you flew home four times last year—you are no better off now than you were before the price of a ticket declined. The decrease in the price of air travel has offset your decrease in income.

You are still likely to take more trips home. Why? The opportunity cost of a trip home is now lower, ceteris paribus, assuming no change in the prices of other goods and services. A trip to Nashville now requires a sacrifice of only $300 worth of other goods and services, not the $400 worth that it did before. Thus, you will substitute away from other goods toward trips to see your mother.

Everything works in the opposite direction when a price rises, ceteris paribus. A price increase makes households worse off. If income and other prices do not change, spending the same amount of money buys less and households will be forced to buy less. This is the income effect. In addition, when the price of a product rises, that item becomes more expensive relative to potential substitutes and the household is likely to substitute other goods for it. This is the substitution effect.

What do the income and substitution effects tell us about the demand curve? Both the income and the substitution effects typically imply a negative relationship between price and quantity demanded—in other words, downward-sloping demand. When the price of something falls, ceteris paribus, we are better off and we are likely to buy more of that good and other goods (income effect). Because lower price also means "less expensive relative to substitutes," we are likely to buy more of the good (substitution effect). When the price of

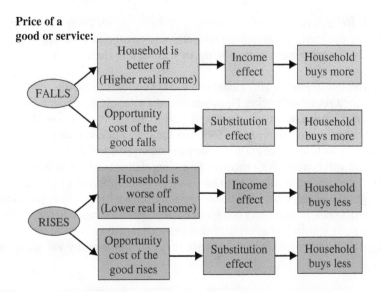

Price of a good or service:

▲ **FIGURE 6.5**   **Income and Substitution Effects of a Price Change**
For normal goods, the income and substitution effects work in the same direction. Higher prices lead to a lower quantity demanded, and lower prices lead to a higher quantity demanded.

something rises, we are worse off and we will buy less of it (income effect). Higher price also means "more expensive relative to substitutes," and we are likely to buy less of it and more of other goods (substitution effect).[6]

Figure 6.5 summarizes the income and substitution effects of a price change of a normal good.

If you recall the example of gasoline prices from early in the chapter, income and substitution effects help us answer the question posed. When gas prices rise, the income effect can cause a fall in the demand for other goods. Because gas is a big part of many budgets, these income effects can be large. It is the income effect from gasoline price increases that some people argue causes consumers to switch away from high-priced brand name products in other categories.

6.4 LEARNING OBJECTIVE

Discuss factors that affect the labor and saving decisions of households.

Household Choice in Input Markets

So far, we have focused on the decision-making process giving rise to output demand curves. Households with limited incomes allocate those incomes across various combinations of goods and services that are available and affordable. In looking at the factors affecting choices in the output market, we assumed that income was fixed, or given. But, of course, income is in fact partially determined by choices that households make in input markets. (Look back at Figure II.1 on p. 109.) We now turn to a brief discussion of the two decisions that households make in input markets: the labor supply decision and the saving decision.

---

[6] For some goods, the income and substitution effects work in opposite directions. When our income rises, we may buy less of some goods. In Chapter 3, we called such goods *inferior goods*. When the price of an inferior good rises, it is, like any other good, more expensive relative to substitutes and we are likely to replace it with lower-priced substitutes. However, when we are worse off, we increase our demand for inferior goods. Thus, the income effect could lead us to buy more of the good, partially offsetting the substitution effect.

Even if a good is "very inferior," demand curves will slope downward as long as the substitution effect is larger than the income effect. It is possible, at least in theory, for the income effect to be larger. In such a case, a price increase would actually lead to an increase in quantity demanded. This possibility was pointed out by Alfred Marshall in *Principles of Economics*. Marshall attributes the notion of an upward-sloping demand curve to Sir Robert Giffen; for this reason, the notion is often referred to as *Giffen's paradox*. Fortunately or unfortunately, no one has ever demonstrated that a Giffen good has ever existed.

ECONOMICS IN PRACTICE

Substitution and Market Baskets

In driving to work one day, one of the authors of this text heard the following advertisement for a local grocery store, which we will call Harry's Food.

"Harry's has the best prices in town, and we can prove it! Yesterday, we chose Mr. Smith out of our checkout line for a comparison test. Mr. Smith is an average consumer, much like you and me. In doing his weekly grocery shopping yesterday at Harry's, he spent $125. We then sent Mr. Smith to the neighboring competitor with instructions to buy the same market basket of food. When he returned with his food, he saw that his grocery total was $134. You too will see that Harry's can save you money!"

Advertisements like this one are commonplace. As you evaluate the claims in the ad, several things may come to mind. Perhaps Mr. Smith is not representative of consumers or is not much like you. That might make Harry's a good deal for him but not for you. (So your demand curves look different from Mr. Smith's demand curves.) Or perhaps yesterday was a sale day, meaning yesterday was not typical of Harry's prices. But there is something more fundamentally wrong with the claims in this ad even if you are just like Mr. Smith and Harry's offers the same prices every day. The fundamental error in this ad is revealed by the work you have done in this chapter.

When Mr. Smith shopped, he presumably looked at the prices of the various food choices offered at the market and tried to do the best he could for his family given those prices and his family's tastes. If we go back to the utility-maximizing rule that you learned in this chapter, we see that Mr. Smith was comparing the marginal utility of each product he consumes relative to its price in deciding what bundle to buy. In pragmatic terms, if Mr. Smith likes apples and pears about the same, while he was shopping in Harry's, he would have bought the cheaper of the two. When he was sent to the neighboring store, however, he was constrained to buy the

same goods that he bought at Harry's. (So he was forced to buy pears even if they were more expensive just to duplicate the bundle.) When we artificially restrict Mr. Smith's ability to substitute goods, we almost inevitably give him a more expensive bundle. The real question is this: Would Mr. Smith have been more happy or less happy with his market basket after spending $125 at Harry's or at its rival? Without knowing more about the shape of Mr. Smith's utility curve and the prices he faces, we cannot answer that question. The dollar comparison in the ad doesn't tell the whole story!

THINKING PRACTICALLY

1. An employer decides to transfer one of her executives to Europe. "Don't worry," she says, "I will increase your salary so that you can afford exactly the same things in your new home city as you can buy here." Is this the right salary adjustment?

The Labor Supply Decision

Most income in the United States is wage and salary income paid as compensation for labor. Household members supply labor in exchange for wages or salaries. They make decisions about whether to work at all, and, if they do work, what kinds of jobs to take. As in output markets, households face constraints as they make these decision. In labor markets, these constraints include what their skills are, available jobs and market wage levels. In addition, we are all constrained by the fact that there are only 168 hours in a week.

As with decisions in output markets, the labor supply decision involves a set of trade-offs. There are basically two alternatives to working for a wage: (1) not working and (2) doing unpaid work. If you do not work, you sacrifice income for the benefits of staying home and reading, watching TV, swimming, or sleeping. Another option is to work, but not for a money wage. In this case, you sacrifice money income for the benefits of growing your own food, watching your children, or taking care of your house.

As with the trade-offs in output markets, your final choice depends on how you value the alternatives available. If you work, you earn a wage that you can use to buy things. In not working,

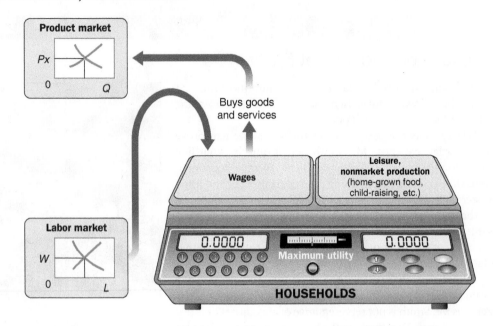

▶ **FIGURE 6.6** **The Trade-Off Facing Households**
The decision to enter the workforce involves a trade-off between wages (and the goods and services that wages will buy) on the one hand and leisure and the value of nonmarket production on the other hand.

you receive the value of things you can produce at home, such as child care, or the value you place on leisure. This choice is illustrated in Figure 6.6. In general, the wage rate can be thought of as the price—or the opportunity cost—of the benefits of either unpaid work or leisure. Just as you choose among different goods by comparing the marginal utility of each relative to its price, you also choose between leisure and other goods by comparing the marginal utility of leisure relative to its price (the wage rate) with the marginal utility of other goods relative to their prices.

The Price of Leisure

In our analysis in the early part of this chapter, households had to allocate a limited budget across a set of goods and services. Now they must choose among goods, services, and *leisure*.

When we add leisure to the picture, we do so with one important distinction. Trading one good for another involves buying less of one and more of another, so households simply reallocate *income* from one good to the other. "Buying" more leisure, however, means reallocating time between work and nonwork activities. For each hour of leisure that you decide to consume, you give up one hour's wages. Thus, the wage rate is the *price of leisure*.

Conditions in the labor market determine the budget constraints and final opportunity sets that households face. The availability of jobs and these job wage rates determine the final combinations of goods and services that a household can afford. The final choice within these constraints depends on the unique tastes and preferences of each household.

Income and Substitution Effects of a Wage Change

labor supply curve A curve that shows the quantity of labor supplied at different wage rates. Its shape depends on how households react to changes in the wage rate.

A **labor supply curve** shows the quantity of labor supplied at different wage rates. The shape of the labor supply curve depends on how households react to changes in the wage rate.

How would we expect individuals to react to a possible increase in their hourly wages? First, an increase in wages makes them better off. If they work the same number of hours—that is, if they supply the same amount of labor—they will earn higher incomes and be able to buy more goods and services. They can also buy more leisure. If leisure is a normal good—that is, a good for which demand increases as income increases—an increase in income will lead to a higher demand for leisure and a lower labor supply. This is the *income effect of a wage increase*.

However, there is also a potential *substitution effect of a wage increase*. A higher wage rate means that leisure is more expensive. If you think of the wage rate as the price of leisure, each individual hour of leisure consumed at a higher wage costs more in forgone wages. As a result, we would expect households to substitute other goods for leisure. This means working more, or a lower quantity demanded of leisure and a higher quantity supplied of labor.

ECONOMICS IN PRACTICE

Uber Drivers

Recent years have seen an increase in what has been termed the "sharing economy," in which people use their own personal goods to produce services for sale to others. Common examples include apartment and car sharing of one sort or another, typically mediated by some third party. Among the fastest growing of these shared economy companies is Uber.

Uber began in early 2012 with a simple idea. A central coordinator, using information technology, would match people who were available to use their own cars to drive people around with people who wanted a ride. The central coordinator would set some rules, including prices and qualifications, and in turn would share proceeds with the drivers (or driver-partners as Uber termed them). A new occupation was born with features that appealed to a different set of people than traditional cab driving.

By the end of 2014, 160,000 people were driving for Uber. Two economists, Alan Krueger and Jonathan Hall, studied the drivers and learned a good deal about their labor supply.[7] As the text suggests, Uber drivers choose whether to work for Uber and how much to work based on job characteristics. For these drivers, in addition to the wages, a key differentiator is the job flexibility. Because Uber relies on driver cars and does not need to supply cars themselves, they do not need to worry about whether those cars are working or idle as they would have to if they owned those cars. So Uber drivers gain flexibility, able to work as many or as few hours as they want per day or week. Nor need they schedule in advance; drivers simply click on when they wish to accept a passenger. This flexibility has large implications for who wants to work as a driver. Uber drivers are more likely to be

women than traditional cab drivers (14 percent versus 8 percent) and have more college education (37 percent versus 15 percent) than traditional cabbies. Most importantly, a majority of Uber drivers have another job.

Redefining what it means to provide passenger service in an area and the use of technology has changed the composition of the labor force in this traditional market.

THINKING PRACTICALLY

1. Why is Uber willing to let drivers be flexible in the number of hours they work?

[7] Jonathan Hall and Alan Krueger, "An analysis of the labor market for Uber's Driver-Partners in the United States," Working paper, January 2015.

Note that in the labor market, the income and substitution effects work in *opposite* directions when leisure is a normal good. The income effect of a wage increase implies buying more leisure and working less; the substitution effect implies buying less leisure and working more. Whether households will supply more labor overall or less labor overall when wages rise depends on the relative strength of both the income and the substitution effects.

If the substitution effect is greater than the income effect, the wage increase will increase labor supply. This suggests that the labor supply curve slopes upward, or has a positive slope, like the one in Figure 6.7(a). If the income effect outweighs the substitution effect, however, a higher wage will lead to added consumption of leisure and labor supply will decrease. This implies that the labor supply curve "bends back," as the one in Figure 6.7(b) does.

During the early years of the Industrial Revolution in late eighteenth-century Great Britain, the textile industry operated under what was called the "putting-out" system. Spinning and weaving were done in small cottages to supplement the family farm income—hence the term *cottage industry*. During that period, wages and household incomes rose considerably. Some economic historians claim that this higher income actually led many households to take more leisure and work fewer hours; the empirical evidence suggests a backward-bending labor supply curve.

▶ FIGURE 6.7 **Two Labor Supply Curves**
When the substitution effect outweighs the income effect, the labor supply curve slopes upward (a). When the income effect outweighs the substitution effect, the result is a "backward-bending" labor supply curve: The labor supply curve slopes downward (b).

a. Substitution effect dominates

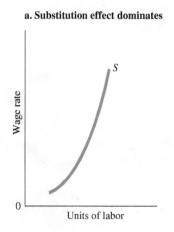

b. Income effect dominates

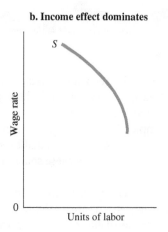

Just as income and substitution effects helped us understand household choices in output markets, they now help us understand household choices in input markets. The point here is simple: When leisure is added to the choice set, the line between input and output market decisions becomes blurred. In fact, households decide simultaneously how much of each good to consume and how much leisure to consume.

Saving and Borrowing: Present versus Future Consumption

So far, in considering how households make decisions we have talked about only the current period—the allocation of current income among alternative uses and the work/leisure choice *today*. Households can also use present income to finance future spending—they can *save*—or use future income to finance present spending—they can *borrow*.

When a household decides to save, it is using current income to finance future consumption. Individuals put money into a pension plan while they are young, and use the earnings from those plans when they are older and perhaps no longer working. Most people cannot finance large purchases—a house or condominium, for example—out of current income and savings. They almost always borrow money and sign a mortgage. When a household borrows, it is in essence financing a current purchase with future income. It pays back the loan out of future income. Saving and borrowing move income over different time periods in one's life.

Even in simple economies such as the two-person desert-island economy of Colleen and Bill (see Chapter 2), people must make decisions about *present versus future consumption*. Colleen and Bill could produce goods for today's consumption by hunting and gathering, consume leisure by sleeping on the beach, or work on projects to enhance future consumption opportunities. Building a house or a boat that will last many years is trading present consumption for future consumption. As with all of the other choices we have examined in this chapter, the broad principle will be to look at marginal utilities and prices. How much do individuals and households value having something now versus waiting for the future? How much do they gain by waiting?

When a household saves, it usually puts the money into something that will generate income, for example savings accounts, money market funds, or corporate and government bonds. A number of these financial instruments are nearly risk free. When you put your money in any of these places, you are actually lending it out and the borrower pays you a fee for its use. This fee usually takes the form of *interest*.

Just as changes in wage rates affect household behavior in the labor market, changes in interest rates affect household behavior in capital markets. Higher interest rates mean that borrowing is more expensive—required monthly payments on a newly purchased house or car will be higher. Higher interest rates also mean that saving will earn a higher return: $1,000 deposited in a 5 percent savings account or bond yields $50 per year. If rates rise to 10 percent, the annual interest will rise to $100.

What impact do interest rates have on saving behavior? As with the effect of wage changes on labor supply, the effect of changes in interest rates on saving can best be understood in terms of income and substitution effects. Suppose, for example, that I have been saving for a number of years for retirement. Will an increase in interest rates lead to an increase or a decrease in my saving? The answer is not obvious. First, because each dollar saved will earn a higher rate of return, the "price" of spending today in terms of forgone future spending is higher. That is, each dollar that I spend today (instead of saving) costs me more in terms of future consumption because my saving will now earn a higher return. On this score, I will be led to *save more*, which is the substitution effect at work.

However, higher interest rates mean more than that. Higher interest rates mean that it will take less saving today to reach a specific target amount of savings tomorrow. I will not need to save as much for retirement or future consumption as I did before. One hundred dollars put into a savings account with 5 percent compound interest will double in 14 years. If interest was paid at a rate of 10 percent, I would have my $200 in just 7 years. Consequently, I may be led to save less, which is the income effect at work. Higher interest rates mean savers are better off; so higher interest rates may lead to less saving. The final impact of a change in interest rates on saving depends on the relative size of the income and substitution effects. Most empirical evidence indicates that saving tends to increase as the interest rate rises. In other words, the substitution effect is larger than the income effect.

Saving and investment decisions involve a huge and complex set of institutions, the **financial capital market**, in which the suppliers of capital (households that save) and the demand for capital (firms that want to invest) interact. The amount of capital investment in an economy is constrained in the long run by that economy's saving rate. You can think of household *saving* as the economy's supply of capital. When a firm borrows to finance a capital acquisition, it is almost as if households have supplied the capital in exchange for the fee we call interest. We treat capital markets in detail in Chapter 11.[8]

financial capital market The complex set of institutions in which suppliers of capital (households that save) and the demand for capital (firms wanting to invest) interact.

A Review: Households in Output and Input Markets

In probing the behavior of households in both input and output markets and examining the nature of constrained choice, we went behind the household demand curve using the simplifying assumption that income was fixed and given. Income, wealth, and prices set the limits, or *constraints*, within which households make their choices in output markets. Within those limits, households make their choices on the basis of personal tastes and preferences.

The notion of *utility* helps explain the process of choice. The law of *diminishing marginal utility* partly explains why people seem to spread their incomes over many different goods and services and why demand curves have a negative slope. Another important explanation behind the negative relationship between price and quantity demanded lies in *income effects* and *substitution effects*.

As we turned to input markets, we relaxed the assumption that income was fixed and given. In the labor market, households are forced to weigh the value of leisure against the value of goods and services that can be bought with wage income. Once again, we found household preferences for goods and leisure operating within a set of constraints imposed by the market. Households also face the problem of allocating income and consumption over more than one period of time. They can finance spending in the future with today's income by saving and earning interest, or they can spend tomorrow's income today by borrowing.

We now have a rough sketch of the factors that determine output demand and input supply. (You can review these in Figure II.1 on p. 109.) In the next three chapters, we turn to firm behavior and explore in detail the factors that affect output supply and input demand.

---

[8] Here in Chapter 6, we are looking at a country as if it were isolated from the rest of the world. Often, however, capital investment is financed by funds loaned or provided by foreign citizens or governments. For example, in recent years, a substantial amount of foreign savings has found its way into the United States for the purchase of stocks, bonds, and other financial instruments. In part, these flows finance capital investment. Also, the United States and other countries that contribute funds to the World Bank and the International Monetary Fund have provided billions in outright grants and loans to help developing countries produce capital. For more information on these institutions, see Chapter 21.

SUMMARY

6.1 HOUSEHOLD CHOICE IN OUTPUT MARKETS *p. 113*

1. Every household must make three basic decisions: (1) how much of each product, or output, to demand; (2) how much labor to supply; and (3) how much to spend today and how much to save for the future.

2. Income, wealth, and prices define a household *budget constraint*. The budget constraint separates those combinations of goods and services that are available from those that are not. All the points below and to the left of a graph of a household budget constraint make up the *choice set*, or *opportunity set*.

3. It is best to think of the household choice problem as one of allocating income over a large number of goods and services. A change in the price of one good may change the entire allocation. Demand for some goods may rise, while demand for others may fall.

4. As long as a household faces a limited income, the real cost of any single good or service is the value of the next preferred *other* goods and services that could have been purchased with the same amount of spending.

5. Within the constraints of prices, income, and wealth, household decisions ultimately depend on preferences—likes, dislikes, and tastes.

6.2 THE BASIS OF CHOICE: UTILITY *p. 117*

6. Whether one item is preferable to another depends on how much *utility*, or satisfaction, it yields relative to its alternatives.

7. The *law of diminishing marginal utility* says that the more of any good we consume in a given period of time, the less satisfaction, or utility, we get out of each additional (or marginal) unit of that good.

8. Households allocate income among goods and services to maximize utility. This implies choosing activities that yield the highest marginal utility per dollar. In a two-good world,

households will choose to equate the marginal utility per dollar spent on *X* with the marginal utility per dollar spent on *Y*. This is the *utility-maximizing rule*.

6.3 INCOME AND SUBSTITUTION EFFECTS *p. 122*

9. The fact that demand curves have a negative slope can be explained in two ways: (1) Marginal utility for all goods diminishes. (2) For most normal goods, both the *income and the substitution effects* of a price decline lead to more consumption of the good.

6.4 HOUSEHOLD CHOICE IN INPUT MARKETS *p. 124*

10. In the labor market, a trade-off exists between the value of the goods and services that can be bought in the market or produced at home and the value that one places on leisure. The opportunity cost of paid work is leisure and unpaid work. The wage rate is the price, or opportunity cost, of the benefits of unpaid work or leisure.

11. The income and substitution effects of a change in the wage rate work in opposite directions. Higher wages mean that (1) leisure is more expensive (likely response: people work *more*—substitution effect) and (2) more income is earned in a given number of hours, so some time may be spent on leisure (likely response: people work *less*—income effect).

12. In addition to deciding how to allocate its present income among goods and services, a household may also decide to save or borrow. When a household decides to save part of its current income, it is using current income to finance future spending. When a household borrows, it finances current purchases with future income.

13. An increase in interest rates has a positive effect on saving if the substitution effect dominates the income effect and a negative effect if the income effect dominates the substitution effect. Most empirical evidence shows that the substitution effect dominates here.

REVIEW TERMS AND CONCEPTS

PROBLEMS

All problems are available on MyEconLab.

6.1 HOUSEHOLD CHOICE IN OUTPUT MARKETS

LEARNING OBJECTIVE: Explain where the budget constraint comes from and the role it plays in household demand.

1.1 Sketch the following budget constraints:

	P_X	P_Y	Income
a.	$ 100	$ 25	$ 5,000.00
b.	200	125	5,000.00
c.	50	400	2,000.00
d.	40	16	800.00
e.	3	2	12.00
f.	0.125	0.75	3.00
g.	0.75	0.125	3.00

1.2 On January 1, Professor Smith made a resolution to lose some weight and save some money. He decided that he would strictly budget $100 for lunches each month. For lunch, he has only two choices: the faculty club, where the price of a lunch is $5, and Alice's Restaurant, where the price of a lunch is $10. Every day that he does not eat lunch, he runs 5 miles.

    a. Assuming that Professor Smith spends the $100 each month at either Alice's or the club, sketch his budget constraint. Show actual numbers on the axes.

    b. Last month Professor Smith chose to eat at the club 10 times and at Alice's 5 times. Does this choice fit within his budget constraint? Explain your answer.

    c. Last month Alice ran a half-price lunch special all month. All lunches were reduced to $5. Show the effect on Professor Smith's budget constraint.

1.3 Assume that Diego has $400 per month to divide between playing paintball and playing golf. Assume that playing paintball costs $40 and playing golf costs $20. Suppose Diego plays paintball six times per month and plays golf eight times per month.

    a. Draw Diego's budget constraint and show that he can afford six games of paintball and eight rounds of golf.

    b. Assume that Diego has some unexpected expenses one month and can only spend $320 that month. Draw his new budget constraint.

    c. As a result of the decrease in income, Diego decides to play 11 rounds of golf and two games of paintball. What kind of a good is paintball? What kind of a good is golf?

    d. Assume Diego has his original $400 per month to spend and the price of paintball is still $40, but the price of golf doubles. Draw his new budget constraint.

1.4 Suppose the price of X is $5 and the price of Y is $10 and a hypothetical household has $500 to spend per month on goods X and Y.

    a. Sketch the household budget constraint.

    b. Assume that the household splits its income equally between X and Y. Show where the household ends up on the budget constraint.

    c. Suppose the household income doubles to $1,000. Sketch the new budget constraint facing the household.

    d. Suppose after the change the household spends $200 on Y and $800 on X. Does this imply that X is a normal or an inferior good? What about Y?

1.5 Katarina and Ivanna are sisters and plant lovers and have saved a total of $640 to spend on plants for their new apartment in Miami. They have decided to use this money on orchids and ferns. Their original budget constraint is shown in the graph below. Let X represent orchids and Y represent ferns.

    a. What is the equation of the original budget constraint?

    b. What is the price of an orchid? a fern?

    c. Assume a price change occurs and Katarina and Ivanna now face the new budget constraint. What is the equation of the new budget constraint?

    d. With the new budget constraint, what is the price of an orchid? a fern?

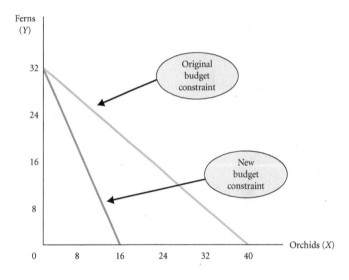

6.2 THE BASIS OF CHOICE: UTILITY

LEARNING OBJECTIVE: Understand how the utility maximizing rule works in household choice of products.

2.1 The following table gives a hypothetical total utility schedule for the Cookie Monster (CM):

# Of Cookies Per Day	Total Utility Per Day
0	0
1	100
2	200
3	275
4	325
5	350
6	360
7	360

Calculate the CM's marginal utility schedule. Draw a graph of total and marginal utility. If cookies cost the CM 5 cents each and CM had a good income, what is the maximum number of cookies he would most likely eat in a day?

2.2 [Related to the *Economics in Practice* on p. 121] Excise taxes on cigarettes vary widely by state, from 17 cents a pack in Missouri to $4.35 a pack in New York. (See http://www.taxadmin.org/fta/rate/cigarette.pdf for a list of excise taxes for all states.) Federal law allows Indian reservations to sell cigarettes to tribal members without paying state excise taxes, and because the U.S. Supreme Court ruled that states do not have the authority to enter reservations to collect taxes, many tribal smoke shops do not charge excise taxes to nontribal members as well. In the state of New York, a pack of name-brand cigarettes sells for about $10, and a pack of generic cigarettes sells for about $8. These prices include the state excise tax of $4.35 per pack. Assuming that the marginal utility for the last pack of name-brand cigarettes consumed is equal to 5 and the marginal utility for the last pack of generic cigarettes consumed is equal to 4, show that the utility-maximizing rule holds for cigarette purchases that include the excise tax, but does not hold for purchases at tribal smoke shops that do not charge the excise tax. What would need to happen to make the utility-maximizing rule hold for cigarettes sold at the tribal smoke shops?

2.3 For this problem, assume that Kendrick has $144 to spend on cigars and brandy each month and that both goods must be purchased whole (no fractional units). Cigars cost $6 each, and brandy costs $30 per bottle. Kendrick's preferences for cigars and brandy are summarized by the following information:

Cigars				Brandy			
No. Per Month	TU	MU	MU/S	Bottles Per Month	TU	MU	MU/S
1	28	—	—	1	150	—	—
2	46	—	—	2	270	—	—
3	62	—	—	3	360	—	—
4	74	—	—	4	420	—	—
5	80	—	—.	5	450	—	—
6	84	—	—	6	470	—	—
7	86	—	—	7	480	—	—

a. Fill in the figures for marginal utility and marginal utility per dollar for both cigars and brandy.

b. Are these preferences consistent with the law of diminishing marginal utility? Explain briefly.

c. Given the budget of $144, what quantity of cigars and what quantity of brandy will maximize Kendrick's level of satisfaction? Explain briefly.

d. Now suppose the price of cigars rises to $8. Which of the columns in the table must be recalculated? Do the required recalculations.

e. After the price change, how many cigars and how many bottles of brandy will Kendrick purchase?

2.4 Thomas has allocated $48 per month for entertainment expenses, which he uses either to go bowling or to play billiards. One night of bowling costs Thomas $8, and one

night of billiards costs Thomas $4. Use the information in the following graphs to determine how many nights Thomas should spend bowling and how many nights he should play billiards in order to maximize his utility. Explain your answer.

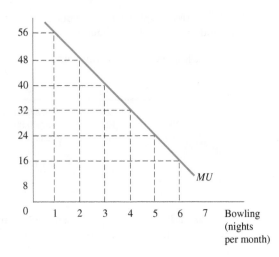

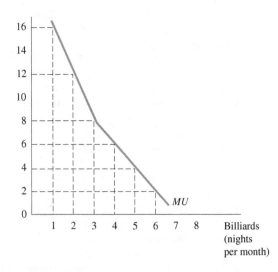

2.5 Adrian has $21 to spend on energy drinks and protein bars and wants to maximize his utility on his purchase. Based on the data in the table, how many energy drinks and protein bars should Adrian purchase, and what is his total utility from the purchase? Does the utility-maximizing rule hold true for his purchase? Explain.

Energy Drinks $3.00			Protein Bars $1.50		
Quantity	MU	TU	Quantity	MU	TU
1	84	84	1	36	36
2	72	156	2	30	66
3	60	216	3	24	90
4	48	264	4	18	108
5	36	300	5	12	120
6	24	324	6	6	126
7	12	336	7	0	126
8	0	336	8	–6	120

2.6 The table shows Darlene's marginal utility numbers for ice cream sundaes and milkshakes. Darlene is trying to decide which item to purchase first, a sundae or a milkshake, knowing that she wants to receive the most utility for each dollar she spends. Assuming she has enough money in her budget to purchase either item, which item should she purchase first? Explain.

Ice Cream Sundaes $6		Milkshakes $4	
Quantity	MU	Quantity	MU
1	24	1	16
2	16	2	6
3	6	3	2

6.3 INCOME AND SUBSTITUTION EFFECTS

LEARNING OBJECTIVE: Describe the income and substitution effects of a decrease in the price of food.

3.1 Remy is a New Orleans native who has lived for the past 7 years in Boston. For each of the last 7 years, he has made trips back to New Orleans for Mardi Gras, Jazz Fest, and Halloween. During 2015, the price of a round-trip ticket from Boston to New Orleans decreased from $575 to $350. As a result, Remy decided to buy new Mardi Gras and Halloween costumes that year and also decided to purchase tickets to see Harry Connick, Jr. perform at the TD Garden Arena in Boston.
   a. Explain how Remy's demand for costumes and concert tickets can be affected by a decrease in air travel prices.
   b. By using this example, explain why both income and substitution effects might be expected to increase Remy's number of trips to New Orleans.

3.2 [Related to the *Economics in Practice* on p. 125] The average cost of living is approximately the same in the following four cities: Sarasota, FL; Cleveland, OH; Cheyenne, WY; and Phoenix, AZ. Use the information you have learned about marginal utility and the substitution effect to explain whether you believe your purchasing choices would remain the same in each of these cities. Assume that your income would be the same in each city.

3.3 For most normal goods, the income effect and the substitution effect work in the same direction; so when the price of a good falls, both the income and substitution effects lead to a higher quantity demanded. How would this change if the good is an inferior good?

6.4 HOUSEHOLD CHOICE IN INPUT MARKETS

LEARNING OBJECTIVE: Discuss factors that affect the labor and saving decisions of households.

4.1 For each of the following events, consider how you might react. What things might you consume more or less of? Would you work more or less? Would you increase or decrease your saving? Are your responses consistent with the discussion of household behavior in this chapter?
   a. The price of gasoline falls by 50 percent, and you drive 40 miles each way to and from school.
   b. Your 98-year-old great aunt passes away and, much to your surprise, leaves you an inheritance of $50,000.
   c. Your mother's employer transfers her to an office in another state, and the rest of your family stays behind so you can continue to live at home while going to school. She returns to visit every other weekend.
   d. You are awarded a scholarship that will pay half of your tuition for the next 3 years.
   e. The 100 shares of Apple stock you bought for $20 per share in 2004 with your babysitting money have turned into 1,400 shares after stock splits and are now worth $130 per share.
   f. The small company where you work part time has a banner year, and the boss gives all part-time employees a 25 percent raise.

4.2 During 2010, Congress debated the advisability of retaining some or all of the tax cuts signed into law by former President George W. Bush in 2001 and 2003 and set to expire at the end of 2010. By reducing tax rates across the board, take-home pay for all taxpaying workers would increase. The purpose, in part, was to encourage work and increase the supply of labor. Households would respond the way the president hoped, but only if income effects were stronger than substitution effects. Do you agree or disagree? Explain your answer.

4.3 Explain why in product markets the substitution and income effects work in the same direction for normal goods, but in the labor market, the income and substitution effects work in opposite directions when leisure is considered a normal good.

4.4 [Related to the *Economics in Practice* on p. 127] As Uber continues to become a more convenient, and in many cases, less costly alternative to traditional taxi service for many of its customers, the income and substitution effects have an impact on the demand side of the market. Also, because a majority of Uber drivers have another job and therefore driving for Uber becomes a way to supplement their income, the income and substitution effects impact the labor supply market. Discuss the income and substitution effects generated by Uber from both the customers' demand perspective and the drivers' labor supply perspective.

CHAPTER 6 APPENDIX: Indifference Curves

Understand how to derive a demand curve from indifference curves and budget constraints.

Early in this chapter, we saw how a consumer choosing between two goods is constrained by the prices of those goods and by his or her income. This Appendix returns to that example and analyzes the process of choice more formally. (Before we proceed, carefully review the text under the heading "The Budget Constraint More Formally," p. 115)

Assumptions

We base the following analysis on four assumptions:

1. We assume that this analysis is restricted to goods that yield positive marginal utility, or, more simply, that "more is better." One way to justify this assumption is to say that when more of something makes you worse off, you can simply throw it away at no cost. This is the assumption of *free disposal.*

Marginal rate of substitution MU_X/MU_Y; the ratio at which a household is willing to substitute good Y for good X.

2. The **marginal rate of substitution** is defined as MU_X/MU_Y, or the ratio at which a household is willing to substitute X for Y. When MU_X/MU_Y is equal to 4, for example, I would be willing to trade 4 units of Y for 1 additional unit of X. We assume a diminishing marginal rate of substitution. That is, as more of X and less of Y are consumed, MU_X/MU_Y declines. As you consume more of X and less of Y, X becomes less valuable in terms of units of Y, or Y becomes more valuable in terms of X. This is almost but not precisely equivalent to assuming diminishing marginal utility.

3. We assume that consumers have the ability to choose among the combinations of goods and services available. Confronted with the choice between two alternative combinations of goods and services, A and B, a consumer responds in one of three ways: (1) She prefers A over B, (2) she prefers B over A, or (3) she is indifferent between A and B—that is, she likes A and B equally.

4. We assume that consumer choices are consistent with a simple assumption of rationality. If a consumer shows that he prefers A to B and subsequently shows that he prefers B to a third alternative, C, he should prefer A to C when confronted with a choice between the two.

Deriving Indifference Curves

Indifference curve A set of points, each point representing a combination of goods X and Y, all of which yield the same total utility.

If we accept these four assumptions, we can construct a "map" of a consumer's preferences. These preference maps are made up of indifference curves. An **indifference curve** is a set of points, each point representing a combination of goods X and Y, all of which yield the same total utility.

Figure 6A.1 shows how we might go about deriving an indifference curve for a hypothetical consumer. Each point in the diagram represents some amount of X and some amount of Y. Point A in the diagram, for example, represents X_A units of X and Y_A units of Y. Now suppose we take some amount of Y away from our hypothetical consumer, moving him or her to A'. At A', the consumer has the same amount of X—that is, X_A units—but less Y and now has only Y_C units of Y. Because "more is better," our consumer is unequivocally worse off at A' than at A.

To compensate for the loss of Y, we begin giving our consumer some more X. If we give the individual just a little, he or she will still be worse off than at A. If we give this individual a great deal of X, he or she will be better off. There must be some quantity of X that will just compensate for the loss of Y. By giving the consumer that amount, we will have put together a bundle, Y_C and X_C, that yields the same total utility as bundle A. This is bundle C in Figure 6A.1. If confronted with a choice between bundles A and C, our consumer will say, "Either one; I do not care." In other words, the consumer is *indifferent* between A and C. When confronted with

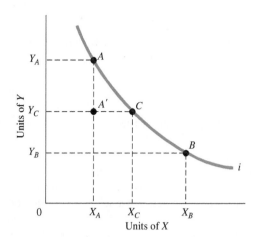

◀ **FIGURE 6A.1 An Indifference Curve**
An indifference curve is a set of points, each representing a combination of some amount of good X and some amount of good Y, that all yield the same amount of total utility. The consumer depicted here is indifferent between bundles A and B, B and C, and A and C.

a choice between bundles C and B (which represent X_B and Y_B units of X and Y), this person is also indifferent. The points along the curve labeled i in Figure 6A.1 represent all the combinations of X and Y that yield the same total utility to our consumer. That curve is thus an indifference curve.

Each consumer has a whole set of indifference curves. Return for a moment to Figure 6A.1. Starting at point A again, imagine that we give the consumer a tiny bit more X *and* a tiny bit more Y. Because more is better, we know that the new bundle will yield a higher level of total utility and the consumer will be better off. Now just as we constructed the first indifference curve, we can construct a second one. What we get is an indifference curve that is *higher* and to the *right* of the first curve. Because utility along an indifference curve is constant at all points, every point along the new curve represents a higher level of total utility than every point along the first.

Figure 6A.2 shows a set of four indifference curves. The curve labeled i_4 represents the combinations of X and Y that yield the highest level of total utility among the four. Many other indifference curves exist between those shown on the diagram; in fact, their number is infinite. Notice that as you move up and to the right, utility increases.

The shapes of the indifference curves depend on the preferences of the consumer, and the whole set of indifference curves is called a **preference map**. Each consumer has a unique preference map.

preference map A consumer's set of indifference curves.

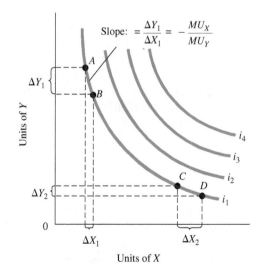

◀ **FIGURE 6A.2
A Preference Map: A Family of Indifference Curves**
Each consumer has a unique family of indifference curves called a preference map. Higher indifference curves represent higher levels of total utility.

Properties of Indifference Curves

The indifference curves shown in Figure 6A.2 are drawn bowing in toward the origin, or zero point, on the axes. In other words, the absolute value of the slope of the indifference curves decreases, or the curves get flatter, as we move to the right. Thus, we say that indifference curves are convex toward the origin. This shape follows directly from the assumption of diminishing marginal rate of substitution and makes sense if you remember the law of diminishing marginal utility.

To understand the convex shape, compare the segment of curve i_1 between A and B with the segment of the same curve between C and D. Moving from A to B, the consumer is willing to give up a substantial amount of Y to get a small amount of X. (Remember that total utility is constant along an indifference curve; the consumer is therefore indifferent between A and B.) Moving from C and D, however, the consumer is willing to give up only a small amount of Y to get more X.

This changing trade-off makes complete sense when you remember the law of diminishing marginal utility. Notice that between A and B, a great deal of Y is consumed and the marginal utility derived from a unit of Y is likely to be small. At the same time, though, only a little of X is being consumed; so the marginal utility derived from consuming a unit of X is likely to be high.

Suppose, for example, that X is pizza and Y is soda. Near A and B, a thirsty, hungry football player who has 10 sodas in front of him but only one slice of pizza will trade several sodas for another slice. Down around C and D, however, he has 20 slices of pizza and a single soda. Now he will trade several slices of pizza to get an additional soda.

We can show how the trade-off changes more formally by deriving an expression for the slope of an indifference curve. Let us look at the arc (that is, the section of the curve) between A and B. We know that in moving from A to B, total utility remains constant. That means that the utility lost as a result of consuming less Y must be matched by the utility gained from consuming more X. We can approximate the loss of utility by multiplying the marginal utility of Y (MU_Y) by the number of units by which consumption of Y is curtailed (Δ_Y). Similarly, we can approximate the utility gained from consuming more X by multiplying the marginal utility of X (MU_X) by the number of additional units of X consumed (Δ_X). Remember: Because the consumer is indifferent between points A and B, total utility is the same at both points. Thus, these two must be equal in magnitude—that is, the gain in utility from consuming more X must equal the loss in utility from consuming less Y. Because ΔY is a negative number (because consumption of Y decreases from A to B), it follows that

$$MU_X \cdot \Delta X = -(MU_Y \cdot \Delta Y)$$

When we divide both sides by MU_Y and by ΔX, we obtain

$$\frac{\Delta Y}{\Delta X} = -\left(\frac{MU_X}{MU_Y}\right)$$

Recall that the slope of any line is calculated by dividing the change in Y—that is, ΔY—by the change in X—that is, ΔX. Thus, the slope of an indifference curve is the ratio of the marginal utility of X to the marginal utility of Y, and it is negative.

Now let us return to our pizza (X) and soda (Y) example. As we move down from the A:B area to the C:D area, our football player is consuming less soda and more pizza. The marginal utility of pizza (MU_X) is falling, and the marginal utility of soda (MU_Y) is rising. That means that MU_X/MU_Y (the marginal rate of substitution) is falling and the absolute value of the slope of the indifference curve is declining. Indeed, it does get flatter.

Consumer Choice

As you recall, demand depends on income, the prices of goods and services, and preferences or tastes. We are now ready to see how preferences as embodied in indifference curves interact with budget constraints to determine how the final quantities of X and Y will be chosen.

In Figure 6A.3, a set of indifference curves is superimposed on a consumer's budget constraint. Recall that the budget constraint separates those combinations of X and Y that are

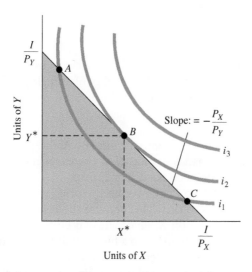

▲ FIGURE 6A.3 **Consumer Utility-Maximizing Equilibrium**
Consumers will choose the combination of X and Y that maximizes total utility. Graphically, the consumer will move along the budget constraint until the highest possible indifference curve is reached. At that point, the budget constraint and the indifference curve are tangent. This point of tangency occurs at X* and Y* (point B).

available from those that are not. The constraint simply shows those combinations that can be purchased with an income of I at prices P_X and P_Y. The budget constraint crosses the X-axis at I/P_X, or the number of units of X that can be purchased with I if nothing is spent on Y. Similarly, the budget constraint crosses the Y-axis at I/P_Y, or the number of units of Y that can be purchased with an income of I if nothing is spent on X. The shaded area is the consumer's opportunity set. The slope of a budget constraint is $-P_X/P_Y$.

Consumers will choose from among available combinations of X and Y the one that maximizes utility. In graphic terms, a consumer will move along the budget constraint until he or she is on the highest possible indifference curve. Utility rises by moving from points such as A or C (which lie on i_1) toward B (which lies on i_2). Any movement away from point B moves the consumer to a lower indifference curve—a lower level of utility. In this case, utility is maximized when our consumer buys X* units of X and Y* units of Y. At point B, the budget constraint is just tangent to—that is, just touches—indifference curve i_2. As long as indifference curves are convex to the origin, utility maximization will take place at that point at which the indifference curve is just tangent to the budget constraint.

The tangency condition has important implications. Where two curves are tangent, they have the same slope, which implies that the slope of the indifference curve is equal to the slope of the budget constraint at the point of tangency:

$$\underbrace{-\frac{MU_X}{MU_Y}}_{\text{slope of indifference curve}} = \underbrace{-\frac{P_X}{P_Y}}_{\text{slope of budget constraint}}$$

slope of indifference curve = slope of budget constraint

By multiplying both sides of this equation by MU_Y and dividing both sides by P_X, we can rewrite this utility-maximizing rule as

$$\frac{MU_X}{P_X} = \frac{MU_Y}{P_Y}$$

This is the same rule derived in our previous discussion without using indifference curves. We can describe this rule intuitively by saying that consumers maximize their total utility by equating the marginal utility per dollar spent on X with the marginal utility per dollar spent on Y. If this rule did not hold, utility could be increased by shifting money from one good to the other.

Deriving a Demand Curve from Indifference Curves and Budget Constraints

We now turn to the task of deriving a simple demand curve from indifference curves and budget constraints. A demand curve shows the quantity of a single good, X in this case, that a consumer will demand at various prices. To derive the demand curve, we need to confront our consumer with several alternative prices for X while keeping other prices, income, and preferences constant.

Figure 6A.4 shows the derivation. We begin with price P_X^1. At that price, the utility-maximizing point is A, where the consumer demands X_1 units of X. Therefore, in the right-hand diagram, we plot P_X^1 against X_1. This is the first point on our demand curve.

Now we lower the price of X to P_X^2. Lowering the price expands the opportunity set, and the budget constraint swivels to the right. Because the price of X has fallen, when our consumer spends all of the income on X, he or she can buy more of it. Our consumer is also better off because of being able to move to a higher indifference curve. The new utility-maximizing point is B, where the consumer demands X_2 units of X. Because the consumer demands X_2 units of X at a price of P_X^2, we plot P_X^2 against X_2 in the right-hand diagram. A second price cut to P_X^3 moves our consumer to point C, with a demand of X_3 units of X, and so on. Thus, we see how the demand curve can be derived from a consumer's preference map and budget constraint.

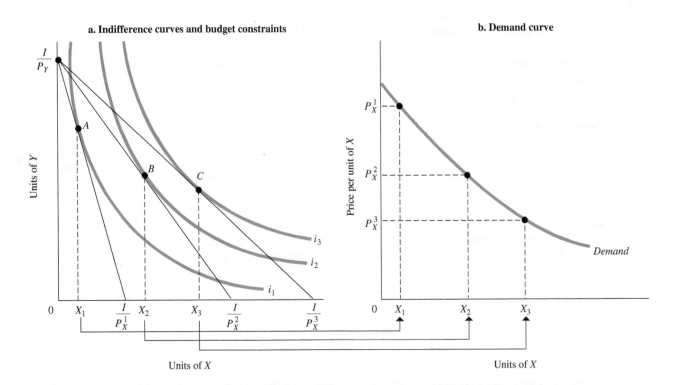

a. Indifference curves and budget constraints   **b. Demand curve**

▲ **FIGURE 6A.4   Deriving a Demand Curve from Indifference Curves and Budget Constraint**
Indifference curves are labeled i_1, i_2, and i_3; budget constraints are shown by the three diagonal lines from I/P_Y to I/P_X^1, I/P_X^2, and I/P_X^3. Lowering the price of X from P_X^1 to P_X^2 and then to P_X^3 swivels the budget constraint to the right. At each price, there is a different utility-maximizing combination of X and Y. Utility is maximized at point A on i_1, point B on i_2, and point C on i_3. Plotting the three prices against the quantities of X chosen results in a standard downward-sloping demand curve.

APPENDIX SUMMARY

1. An *indifference curve* is a set of points, each point representing a combination of goods X and Y, all of which yield the same total utility. A particular consumer's set of indifference curves is called a *preference map*.

2. The slope of an indifference curve is the ratio of the marginal utility of X to the marginal utility of Y, and it is negative.

3. As long as indifference curves are convex to the origin, utility maximization will take place at that point at which the indifference curve is just tangent to—that is, just touches—the budget constraint. The utility-maximizing rule can also be written as $MU_X/P_X = MU_Y/P_Y$.

APPENDIX REVIEW TERMS AND CONCEPTS

Indifference curve, *p. 134*

Marginal rate of substitution, *p. 134*

Preference map, *p. 135*

APPENDIX PROBLEMS

All problems are available on MyEconLab.

APPENDIX 6A: INDIFFERENCE CURVES

LEARNING OBJECTIVE: Understand how to derive a demand curve from indifference curves and budget constraints.

1A.1 Which of the four assumptions made at the beginning of the Appendix are violated by the indifference curves in Figure 1? Explain.

1A.2 Assume that a household receives a weekly income of $100. If Figure 2 represents the choices of that household as the price of X changes, plot three points on the household demand curve.

1A.3 If Tony's marginal rate of substitution of X for Y is 12—that is, $MU_X / MU_Y = 12$—the price of X is $39, and the price of Y is $3, he is spending too much of his income on Y. Do you agree or disagree? Explain.

▶ FIGURE 1

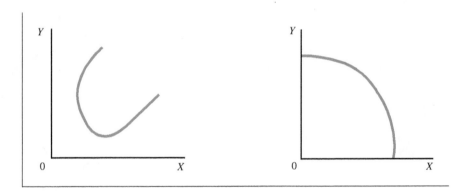

▶ FIGURE 2

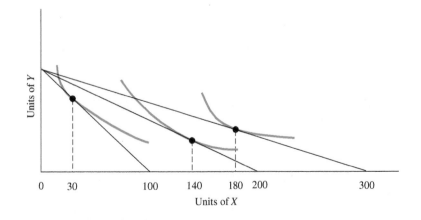

*1A.4 Assume that Jim is a rational consumer who consumes only two goods, apples (A) and nuts (N). Assume that his marginal rate of substitution of apples for nuts is given by the following formula:

$$MRS = MU_N/MU_A = A/N$$

That is, Jim's MRS is equal to the ratio of the number of apples consumed to the number of nuts consumed.

a. Assume that Jim's income is $100, the price of nuts is $5, and the price of apples is $10. What quantities of apples and nuts will he consume?

b. Find two additional points on his demand curve for nuts ($P_N = $10 and $P_N = $2).

c. Sketch one of the equilibrium points on an indifference curve graph.

1A.5 Carmen has $84 to spend on California rolls and eel sashimi, and the data in the following table represent an indifference curve for these two products. If California rolls are $4.00 each and eel sashimi is $6.00 each, draw a graph showing Carmen's indifference curve and her budget constraint, putting California rolls on the vertical axis and eel sashimi on the horizontal axis. What combination of California rolls and eel sashimi will Carmen purchase? Will this combination maximize Carmen's total utility? Explain.

California Rolls	Eel Sashimi
16	5
10	8
6	10
2	18

1A.6 The following graph shows three indifference curves and the accompanying budget constraints for products X and Y. The graph represents the price of product X falling from P_{1x} to P_{2x} and then to P_{3x}. Explain how a demand curve for product X can be derived from this graph and draw a graph showing the demand curve for product X.

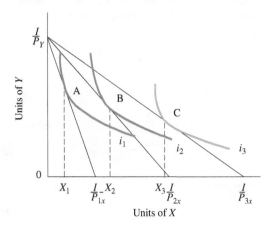

*Note: Problems marked with an asterisk are more challenging.

The Production Process: The Behavior of Profit-Maximizing Firms

7

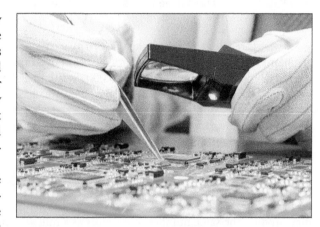

In Chapter 6, we looked at how households choose among the wide range of goods and services available to them. We also looked at household choices in the labor market as they thought about how much to work. Our goal in that chapter was to better understand household demand and labor supply decisions.

We now turn to the other side of the system and examine the behavior of firms. Firms purchase inputs to produce and sell outputs that range from computers to string quartet performances. In other words, they *demand* factors of production in input markets and *supply* goods and services in output markets. In this chapter, we look inside the firm at the production process that transforms inputs into outputs. Although Chapters 7 through 12 describe the behavior of perfectly competitive firms, much of what we say in these chapters also applies to firms that are not perfectly competitive. All firms, whether competitive or not, demand inputs, engage in production, and produce outputs. All firms have an incentive to maximize profits and thus to minimize costs.

Central to our analysis is **production**, the process by which inputs are combined, transformed, and turned into outputs. Firms vary in size and internal organization, but they all take inputs and transform them into goods and services for which there is some demand. For example, an independent accountant combines labor, computers, telephone and e-mail service, time, learning, and a Web site to provide help to confused taxpayers. An automobile plant uses steel, labor, plastic, electricity, machines, and countless other inputs to produce cars. If we want to understand a firm's costs, we first need to understand how it efficiently combines inputs to produce goods and services.

Although our discussions in the next several chapters focus on profit-making business firms, it is important to understand that production and productive activity are not confined to private business firms. Households also engage in transforming factors of production (labor, capital, energy, natural resources, and so on) into useful things. When you work in your garden, you are combining land, labor, fertilizer, seeds, and tools (capital) into the vegetables you eat and the flowers you enjoy. The government also combines land, labor, and capital to produce public services for which demand exists: national defense, homeland security, police and fire protection, and education, to name a few.

Private business firms are set apart from other producers, such as households and government, by their purpose. A **firm** exists when a person or a group of people decides to produce a good or service to meet a perceived demand. Firms engage in production—that is, they transform inputs into outputs—because they can sell their products for more than it costs to produce them.

Understand the importance of opportunity costs to economic profits and how these profits feed into firm decision making.

production   The process by which inputs are combined, transformed, and turned into outputs.

firm   An organization that comes into being when a person or a group of people decides to produce a good or service to meet a perceived demand.

The Behavior of Profit-Maximizing Firms

All firms must make several basic decisions to achieve their primary objective—maximum profits.

As Figure 7.1 states, the three decisions that all firms must make include:

1. How much output to supply (quantity of product)
2. How to produce that output (which production technique/technology to use)
3. How much of each input to demand

1. How much output to supply	2. Which production technology to use	3. How much of each input to demand

▲ **FIGURE 7.1   The Three Decisions That All Firms Must Make**

These three decisions are linked. If a firm knows how much it wants to produce, and has a given production technology, it automatically knows how many of any of its inputs it needs. If a sweater company decides to produce 5,000 sweaters this month in its current factory, it knows how many production workers it will need, how much electricity it will use, and how much raw yarn to purchase. Similarly, if that sewing factory specifies a number of workers and an amount of yarn to use, the maximum number of sweaters it can make follows.

Changing the *technology* of production will change the relationship between input and output quantities. If the sewing factory's machines could be adjusted to use less yarn and fewer workers per sweater, the number of sweaters the firm could get with its inputs would increase. It is also possible that within a market, there may be different technologies that can make the same product. A fully computerized textile mill with only a few workers running the machines may produce the same number of sweaters as a mill with no sophisticated machines but many workers. A profit-maximizing firm chooses the technology that minimizes its costs for a given level of output.

In this chapter, we focus on production in a market in which all firms make the same product. In later chapters, we will expand to look at how firms choose product type and how prices are set.

Profits and Economic Costs

profit   The difference between total revenue and total cost.

Firms make their decisions with the goal of maximizing profits. **Profit** is the difference between total revenue and total cost:

$$\text{profit} = \text{total revenue} - \text{total cost}$$

total revenue   The amount received from the sale of the product ($q \times P$).

total cost   The total of (1) out-of-pocket costs and (2) opportunity cost of all factors of production.

economic profit   Profit that accounts for both explicit costs and opportunity costs.

Total revenue is the amount received from the sale of the product; it is equal to the number of units sold (q) times the price received per unit (P). **Total cost** is less straightforward to define. We define total cost here to include (1) out-of-pocket costs and (2) opportunity cost of all inputs or factors of production. *Out-of-pocket costs* are sometimes referred to as *explicit costs* or *accounting costs*. These refer to costs as an accountant would calculate them. *Economic costs* include the opportunity cost of every input. These opportunity costs are often referred to as *implicit costs*. The term *profit* will from here on refer to **economic profit**. So whenever we say profit = total revenue − total cost, what we really mean is

$$\text{economic profit} = \text{total revenue} - \text{total economic cost}$$

Most of the inputs that firms use they buy in a market and have out-of-pocket costs. In some cases, however, firms use resources that are not explicitly priced and yet have value.

Good decision making requires that we consider these factors as well; in economics we value these factors at their opportunity cost. When I think about how to run my business, whether to expand or contract, or even whether to enter a new business, I need to consider the *full* costs of production.

If a family business employs three family members but pays them no wage, there is still a cost: the opportunity cost of their labor. A decision to expand the business clearly needs to take the opportunity cost of those family workers into account. The most important factor of production for which we use opportunity cost is capital. The opportunity cost of capital is that amount that could be earned on invested capital adjusted for the riskiness of that investment.

Normal Rate of Return   If you decide to start a firm, you will need resources. To operate a manufacturing firm, you need a plant and some equipment. To start an e-business, you need a host site, some computer equipment, some software, and a Web site design. These investments require resources that stay tied up in the firm as long as it operates. Even firms that have been around a long time must continue to invest. Plant and equipment wear out and must be replaced. Firms that decide to expand must put new capital in place. This is as true of proprietorships, where the resources come directly from the proprietor, as it is of corporations, where the resources needed to make investments come from shareholders.

Whenever resources are used to invest in a business, there is an opportunity cost. Instead of opening a candy store, you could put your funds into an alternative use such as a certificate of deposit or a government bond, both of which earn interest. Instead of using its retained earnings to build a new plant, a firm could earn interest on those funds or pay them out to shareholders as dividends.

A simple example will illustrate the importance of accounting for the opportunity cost of capital in a business. Suppose that Sue and Ann decide to start a small business selling turquoise belts in the Denver airport. To get into the business, they need to invest in a fancy pushcart. The price of the pushcart is $20,000 with all the displays and attachments included. Suppose that Sue and Ann estimate that they will sell 3,000 belts each year for $10 each. Further assume that each belt costs $5 from the supplier. Finally, the cart must be staffed by one clerk, who works for an annual wage of $14,000. Should Sue and Ann go ahead with this business? Is this business going to make a profit?

To answer this question, we must determine total revenue and total cost. First, annual revenue is $30,000 (3,000 belts × $10). Total cost includes the cost of the belts—$15,000 (3,000 belts × $5)—plus the labor cost of $14,000, for a total of $29,000. Thus, on the basis of the annual revenue and cost flows, the firm *seems* to be making a profit of $1,000 ($30,000 − $29,000).

What about the $20,000 initial investment in the pushcart? This investment is *not* a direct part of the cost of Sue and Ann's firm. If we assume that the cart maintains its value over time, *the only thing that Sue and Ann are giving up is the interest they might have earned had they not tied up their funds in the pushcart.* That is, the only real cost is the opportunity cost of the investment, which is the forgone interest on the $20,000.

Now suppose that Sue and Ann could have gotten an interest rate of 10 percent on their invested funds by purchasing corporate bonds. This implies an opportunity cost of their capital of $2,000 annually (= $20,000 × 0.10). As we determined previously, Sue and Ann will earn only $1,000 annually. Thus, they are really earning less than the opportunity cost of their capital. The total cost in this case is $31,000 ($29,000 + $2,000 in forgone interest on the investment). The level of profit is negative: $30,000 minus $31,000 equals − $1,000. These calculations are summarized in Table 7.1. Because the level of profit is negative, Sue and Ann are actually suffering a loss on their belt business.

We can think more generally about the opportunity cost of capital in a business. *Rate of return* is the annual flow of net income generated by an investment expressed as a percentage of the total investment. If someone makes a $100,000 investment in capital to start a small restaurant and the restaurant produces a flow of profit of $15,000 every year, we say the project has a "rate of return" of 15 percent. Sometimes we refer to the rate of return as the *yield* of the investment.

A **normal rate of return** is the rate that is just sufficient to keep owners and investors satisfied between the investment they are doing and their next-best alternative investments. In other words, the normal rate of return is the opportunity cost of capital. If the rate of return were to fall below

normal rate of return   A rate of return on capital that is just sufficient to keep owners and investors satisfied. For relatively risk-free firms, it should be nearly the same as the interest rate on risk-free government bonds.

TABLE 7.1 Calculating Total Revenue, Total Cost, and Profit	
Initial Investment:	$20,000
Market Interest Rate Available:	0.10, or 10%
Total revenue (3,000 belts × $10 each)	**$30,000**
Costs	
Belts from supplier	$15,000
Labor cost	14,000
Normal return/opportunity cost of capital ($20,000 × 0.10)	2,000
Total Cost	**$31,000**
Profit = total revenue − total cost	**−$1,000ᵃ**

ᵃ There is a loss of $1,000.

normal, it would be difficult or impossible for managers to raise resources needed to purchase new capital. Owners of the firm would be receiving a rate of return that was lower than what they could receive elsewhere in the economy, and they would have no incentive to invest in the firm.

If the firm has fairly steady revenues and the future looks secure, the normal rate of return should be close to the interest rate on risk-free government bonds. A firm certainly will not keep investors interested in it if it does not pay them a rate of return at least as high as they can get from a risk-free government or corporate bond. If a firm is rock solid and the economy is steady, it may not have to pay a much higher rate. However, if a firm is in a speculative industry and the future of the economy is shaky, it may have to pay substantially more to keep its shareholders happy. In exchange for a risk that the business may falter or even fail, the shareholders will expect a higher return.

A normal rate of return is considered a part of the total cost of a business. Adding a normal rate of return to total cost has an important implication: When a firm earns a normal rate of return, it is earning a zero profit as we have defined profit. If the level of economic profit is positive, the firm is earning an above-normal rate of return on capital. Positive profits, as we will see in a later chapter, are likely to attract new investors. If a firm earns less than its opportunity cost or the normal return, as did Sue and Anne, we expect exit from the industry.

Short-Run versus Long-Run Decisions

The decisions made by a firm—how much to produce, how to produce it, and what inputs to demand—all take time to implement. If a firm decides that it wants to double or triple its output, it may need time to arrange financing, hire architects and contractors, and build a new plant. Planning for a major expansion can take years. In the meantime, the firm must decide how much to produce within the constraint of its existing plant. If a firm decides to get out of a particular business, it may take time to arrange an orderly exit. There may be contract obligations to fulfill, equipment to sell, and so on. Once again, the firm must decide what to do in the meantime.

A firm's immediate response to a change in the economic environment may differ from its response over time. Consider, for example, a small restaurant with 20 tables that becomes popular. The immediate problem for the owners is getting the most profit within the constraint of the existing space. The owner might consider adding a few tables or speeding up service to squeeze in a few more customers, but it will be hard to increase the number of customers substantially. At the same time the restaurant owner is trying to squeeze in more tables, he or she may also be thinking of expanding the current facility or moving to a larger facility. But expansion typically involves either construction or finding and setting up a new facility and this takes time.

In economics we distinguish these two situations by using the terms short run versus long run. The **short run** is a decision period during which the business has a fixed scale or a fixed factor of production and there is neither exit nor entry from the business. In the restaurant example, the short run is a period of time in which there is an inability to rent new space or expand the owner's ability to serve many new customers.

Which factor or factors of production are fixed in the short run differs from industry to industry. For a manufacturing firm, the size of the physical plant is often the greatest limitation. A

short run The period of time for which two conditions hold: The firm is operating under a fixed scale (fixed factor) of production, and firms can neither enter nor exit an industry.

factory is built with a given production rate in mind. Although that rate can be increased, output cannot increase beyond a certain limit in the short run. The restaurant similarly had a facility size constraint. For a private physician, the limit may be the capacity to see patients; the day has only so many hours. In the long run, the doctor may invite others to join the practice and expand; but for now, in the short run, this sole physician is the firm, with a capacity that is the firm's only capacity.

The **long run** is defined as the decision period over which firms can choose to expand or contract all of their factors of production. Firms can plan for any output level they find desirable. They can double or triple output, for example, building new factories, or closing old ones. In addition, new firms can start up operations (enter the industry) and/or existing firms can go out of business (exit the industry).

No hard-and-fast rule specifies how long the short run is. In the restaurant business it might be possible to build an extension in a few months; if so, we would say that those months are the short run. For those months, the restaurant owner has to manage his or her existing space as best he or she can. But all the while, that owner is also thinking about and planning for the long-run future. Firms make two basic kinds of decisions: those that govern the day-to-day operations of the firm and those that involve longer-term strategic planning. Sometimes major decisions can be implemented in weeks. Often, however, the process takes years. In many large firms, different people often make the short- and long-run decisions. A production manager might well be charged with trying to do the best he or she can with the plant and equipment that he or she has, while her boss, the division head, figures out whether expansion of the plant is a good idea. In a single proprietorship, one person may wear both hats, thinking simultaneously about how to make the most out of the present while taking steps to improve the future of the business.

long run That period of time for which there are no fixed factors of production: Firms can increase or decrease the scale of operation, and new firms can enter or existing firms can exit the industry.

The Bases of Decisions: Market Price of Outputs, Available Technology, and Input Prices

As we said previously, a firm's three fundamental decisions are made with the objective of maximizing profits. Because profits equal total revenues minus total costs, each firm needs to know how much it costs to produce its product and how much its product can be sold for in order to make the right decision.

To know how much it costs to produce a good or service, a firm needs to know something about the production techniques that are available and about the prices of the inputs required. To estimate how much it will cost to operate a gas station, for instance, a firm needs to know equipment needs, number of workers, kind of building, and so on. The firm also needs to know the going wage rates for mechanics and unskilled laborers, the cost of gas pumps, interest rates, the rents per square foot of land on high-traffic corners, and the wholesale price of gasoline. Once we know the input prices and the production technique, we can figure out the costs of making our product.

The rest of this chapter and the next chapter focus on costs of production. We begin at the heart of the firm, with the production process. Faced with a set of input prices, firms must decide on the best, or optimal, method of production (Figure 7.2). The **optimal method of production** is the one that minimizes cost for a given level of output.

optimal method of production The production method that minimizes cost for a given level of output.

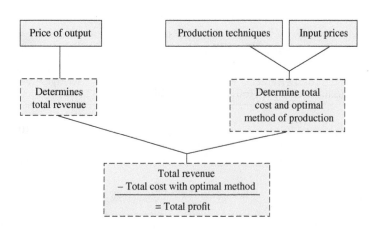

◀ FIGURE 7.2
Determining the Optimal Method of Production

The Production Process

Be able to describe how total, marginal, and average products relate to one another.

production technology The quantitative relationship between inputs and outputs.

Production is the process through which inputs are combined and transformed into outputs. A **production technology** tells us the specific quantities of inputs needed to produce any given service or good. A loaf of bread requires certain amounts of water, flour, and yeast; some kneading and patting; and an oven and gas or electricity. A trip from downtown New York to Newark, New Jersey, can be produced with a taxicab, 45 minutes of a driver's labor, some gasoline, and so on.

Most outputs can be produced by a number of different techniques. You can tear down an old building and clear a lot to create a park in several ways, for example. Five hundred men and women could descend on the building with sledgehammers and carry the pieces away by hand; this would be a **labor-intensive technology**. The same park could be produced by two people with a wrecking crane, a steam shovel, a backhoe, and a dump truck; this would be a **capital-intensive technology**. Similarly, different inputs can be combined to transport people from Oakland to San Francisco. The Bay Area Rapid Transit system carries thousands of people simultaneously under San Francisco Bay and uses a massive amount of capital relative to labor. Cab rides to San Francisco require more labor relative to capital; a driver is needed for every few passengers.

labor-intensive technology Technology that relies heavily on human labor instead of capital.

capital-intensive technology Technology that relies heavily on capital instead of human labor.

In choosing a technology, firms try to minimize the cost of production of a given quantity of output. For a firm in an economy with a plentiful supply of inexpensive labor but not much capital, the optimal method of production will involve labor-intensive techniques. For example, assembly of items such as running shoes is done most efficiently by hand. That is why Nike produces virtually all its shoes in developing countries where labor costs are low. In contrast, firms in an economy with high labor costs have an incentive to substitute away from labor and to use more capital-intensive, or labor-saving, techniques. Suburban office parks use more land and have more open space in part because land in the suburbs is more plentiful and less expensive than land in the middle of a big city and so it is cheaper to build wide buildings than tall ones.

Production Functions: Total Product, Marginal Product, and Average Product

production function *or* total product function A numerical or mathematical expression of a relationship between inputs and outputs. It shows units of total product as a function of units of inputs.

The relationship between inputs and outputs—that is, the production technology—expressed numerically or mathematically is called a **production function (*or* total product function)**. A production function shows units of total product as a function of units of inputs.

Imagine, for example, a small sandwich shop. All the sandwiches made in the shop are grilled, and the shop owns only one grill, which can accommodate only two workers comfortably. As columns 1 and 2 of the production function in Table 7.2 show, one person working alone can produce only 10 sandwiches per hour in addition to answering the phone, waiting on customers, keeping the tables clean, and so on. The second worker can stay at the grill full-time and not worry about anything except making sandwiches. The two workers together can produce 25 sandwiches, so the second worker adds $25 - 10 = 15$ sandwiches per hour to the total. The grill becomes crowded when a third person joins the team, but with careful use of space,

TABLE 7.2 Production Function

(1) Labor Units (Employees)	(2) Total Product (Sandwiches per Hour)	(3) Marginal Product of Labor	(4) Average Product of Labor (Total Product ÷ Labor Units)
0	0	—	—
1	10	10	10.0
2	25	15	12.5
3	35	10	11.7
4	40	5	10.0
5	42	2	8.4
6	42	0	7.0

10 more sandwiches can be produced. Note that the added output from hiring a third worker is less because of the capital constraint of the grill, *not* because the third worker is somehow less efficient or hardworking. We assume that all workers are equally capable.

The fourth and fifth workers add even less to the total output of sandwiches, as crowding at the grill increases. Worker four adds five sandwiches per hour to the total, and worker five adds just two. Adding a sixth worker adds no output at all: The current maximum capacity of the shop is 42 sandwiches per hour.

Figure 7.3(a) graphs the total product data from Table 7.2. As you look at Table 7.2 and think about marginal product, you should begin to see how important it is to a firm to know its production function. We see that the sandwich firm that hires a fourth worker will be expanding its sandwich production by five. Is it worth it? That will in turn depend on how much the worker costs and for how much the shop can sell the sandwich. As we proceed to analyze the firm's decision in the next few chapters, we will explore this further.

Marginal Product and the Law of Diminishing Returns   **Marginal product** is the additional output that can be produced by hiring one more unit of a specific input, holding all other inputs constant. As column 3 of Table 7.2 shows, the marginal product of the first unit of labor in the sandwich shop is 10 sandwiches; the marginal product of the second is 15; the third, 10; and so on. The marginal product of the sixth worker is zero. Figure 7.3(b) graphs the marginal product of labor curve from the data in Table 7.2.

The **law of diminishing returns** states that *after a certain point, when additional units of a variable input are added to fixed inputs* (in this case, the building and grill), *the marginal product of the variable input* (in this case, labor) *declines.* The British economist David Ricardo first formulated the law of diminishing returns on the basis of his observations of agriculture in nineteenth-century England. Within a given area of land, he noted, successive "doses" of labor and capital yielded smaller and smaller increases in crop output. The law of diminishing returns in agriculture means that only so much more can be produced by farming the same land more intensely. In manufacturing, diminishing returns set in when a firm begins to strain the capacity of its existing plant.

At our sandwich shop, diminishing returns set in when the third worker is added. The marginal product of the second worker is actually higher than the first (Figure 7.3[b]). The first worker takes care of the phone and the tables, thus freeing the second worker to concentrate exclusively on sandwich making. From that point on, the grill gets crowded. It is important to note here that diminishing returns are setting in not because the third worker is worse than

marginal product   The additional output that can be produced by adding one more unit of a specific input, *ceteris paribus.*

law of diminishing returns   When additional units of a variable input are added to fixed inputs, after a certain point, the marginal product of the variable input declines.

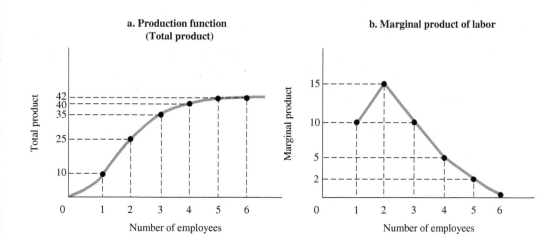

▲ **FIGURE 7.3   Production Function for Sandwiches**
A *production function* is a numerical representation of the relationship between inputs and outputs. In Figure 7.3(a), total product (sandwiches) is graphed as a function of labor inputs. The *marginal product* of labor is the additional output that one additional unit of labor produces. Figure 7.3(b) shows that the marginal product of the second unit of labor at the sandwich shop is 15 units of output; the marginal product of the fourth unit of labor is 5 units of output.

workers one or two (we assume they are identical), but because as we add staff, each has a smaller amount of capital (here a grill) to work with.

Diminishing returns, or *diminishing marginal product*, begin to show up when more and more units of a variable input are added to a fixed input, such as the scale of the plant. Recall that we defined the short run as that period in which some fixed factor of production constrains the firm. It then follows that diminishing returns always apply in the short run and that in the short run, every firm will eventually face diminishing returns. This means that every firm finds it progressively more difficult to increase its output as it approaches capacity production.

average product The average amount produced by each unit of a variable factor of production.

Marginal Product versus Average Product **Average product** is the average amount produced by each unit of a variable factor of production. At our sandwich shop with one grill, that variable factor is labor. In Table 7.2, you saw that the first two workers together produce 25 sandwiches per hour. Their average product is therefore 12.5 (25 ÷ 2). The third worker adds only 10 sandwiches per hour to the total. These 10 sandwiches are the *marginal* product of labor. The *average product* of the first three units of labor, however, is 11.7 (the average of 10, 15, and 10). Stated in equation form, the average product of labor is the *total* product divided by total units of labor:

$$\text{average product of labor} = \frac{\text{total product}}{\text{total units of labor}}$$

Average product "follows" marginal product, but it does not change as quickly. If marginal product is above average product, the average rises; if marginal product is below average product, the average falls. Suppose, for example, that you have had six exams and that your average is 86. If you score 75 on the next exam, your average score will fall, but not all the way to 75. In fact, it will fall only to 84.4. If you score a 95 instead, your average will rise to 87.3. As columns 3 and 4 of Table 7.2 show, marginal product at the sandwich shop declines continuously after the third worker is hired. Average product also decreases, but more slowly.

Figure 7.4 shows a typical production function and the marginal and average product curves derived from it. The marginal product curve is a graph of the slope of the total product curve—that is, of the production function. Average product and marginal product start out equal, as they do in Table 7.2. As marginal product climbs, the graph of average product follows it, but more slowly, up to L_1 (point A).

Notice that marginal product starts out increasing. (It did so in the sandwich shop as well.) Most production processes are designed to be run well by more than one worker. Take an assembly line, for example. To work efficiently, an assembly line needs a worker at every station; it's a cooperative process. The marginal product of the first workers is low or zero. As workers are added, the process starts to run more efficiently and marginal product rises.

At point A (L_1 units of labor), marginal product begins to fall. Because every plant has a finite capacity, efforts to increase production will always run into the limits of that capacity. At point B (L_2 units of labor), marginal product has fallen to equal the average product, which has been increasing. Between point B and point C (between L_2 and L_3 units of labor), marginal product falls below average product and average product begins to follow it *down*. Average product is at its maximum at point B, where it is equal to marginal product. At L_3, more labor yields no more output and marginal product is zero—the assembly line has no more positions, the grill is jammed.

Production Functions with Two Variable Factors of Production

So far, we have considered production functions with only one variable factor of production. However, inputs work together in production. In general, additional capital increases the productivity of labor. Because capital—buildings, machines, and so on—is of no use without people to operate it, we say that capital and labor are *complementary inputs*.

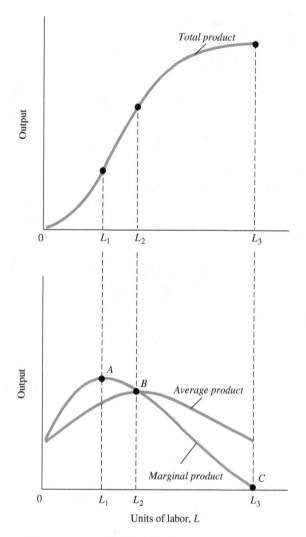

▲ **FIGURE 7.4   Total, Average, and Marginal Product**
Marginal and average product curves can be derived from total product curves. Average product is at its maximum at the point of intersection with marginal product.

A simple example will clarify this point. Consider again the sandwich shop. If the demand for sandwiches began to exceed the capacity of the shop to produce them, the shop's owner might decide to expand capacity. This would mean purchasing more capital in the form of a new grill.

A second grill would essentially double the shop's productive capacity. The new higher capacity would mean that the sandwich shop would not run into diminishing returns as quickly. With only one grill, the third and fourth workers are less productive because the single grill gets crowded. With two grills, however, the third and fourth workers could produce 15 sandwiches per hour using the second grill. In essence, the added capital raises the *productivity* of labor—that is, the amount of output produced per worker per hour.

Just as the new grill enhances the productivity of workers in the sandwich shop, new businesses and the capital they put in place raise the productivity of workers in countries such as Malaysia, India, and Kenya.

This simple relationship lies at the heart of discussions about productivity at the national and international levels. Building new, modern plants and equipment enhances a nation's productivity. In the last decade, China has accumulated capital (that is, built plants and equipment) at a high rate. The result is growth in the average quantity of output per worker in China.

ECONOMICS IN PRACTICE

Learning about Growing Pineapples in Ghana

In this chapter we have focused on the way in which labor, capital, and other inputs are used to produce outputs of various sorts. We have described a somewhat abstract production function, linking specific combinations of inputs and output levels. In reading this chapter, you might have wondered where real people interested in producing something learn about production functions. How does an entrepreneur know what the ideal combination of inputs is to produce a given output?

In a recent interesting article, Timothy Conley from Chicago and Christopher Udry from Yale asked precisely this question in thinking about the production of pineapples in Ghana. What they learned helps us think about the production process more generally.

In farming, as in manufacturing, we need a given combination of labor and capital to produce output, here a crop. The capital doesn't come in the form of a grill, as in the sandwich shop, but tractors, plows, or shovels. Raw materials include seeds and fertilizer. There are clearly substitution possibilities among these inputs; farmers can weed more and fertilize or water less, for example. How does a farmer know what the right mix of inputs is, given input prices?

Ghana proved to be an interesting place to ask this question. In the 1990s, an area of Ghana changed from an exclusive reliance on maize as the agricultural crop to the development of pineapple farms. This transformation happened slowly over time to various neighborhoods. Conley and Udry found that social learning was key in the process of technology adoption. For farmers in Ghana, the choice of how much fertilizer to use was highly dependent on how much fertilizer their more successful neighbor farmers used.

Social learning was especially important for novice pineapple farmers located near more veteran producers.[1]

Social learning obviously plays a role in the diffusion of manufacturing technology as well. It is no accident that many high-tech entrepreneurs began their careers in other high-tech firms where they learned much about the right production techniques.

THINKING PRACTICALLY

1. In many high-tech firms, executives must sign non-compete agreements, preventing them from working for a competitor after they stop working for their current firm. These agreements are much less common in mature manufacturing firms. Why?

[1] Timothy Conley and Christopher Udry, "Learning About a New Technology: Pineapples in Ghana," *American Economic Review*, March 2010, 35–69.

7.3 LEARNING OBJECTIVE

Discuss the factors that firms consider when choosing among production techniques.

Choice of Technology

As our sandwich shop example shows, inputs (factors of production) are complementary. Capital enhances the productivity of labor. Workers in the sandwich shop are more productive when they are not crowded at a single grill. Similarly, labor enhances the productivity of capital. When more workers are hired at a plant that is operating at 50 percent of capacity, previously idle machines suddenly become productive.

However, inputs can also be substituted for one another. If labor becomes expensive, firms can adopt labor-saving technologies; that is, they can substitute capital for labor. Assembly lines can be automated by replacing human beings with machines, and capital can be substituted for land when land is scarce. If capital becomes relatively expensive, firms can substitute labor for capital. In short, most goods and services can be produced in a number of ways through the use of alternative technologies. One of the key decisions that all firms must make is which technology to use.

How Fast Should a Truck Driver Go?

The trucking business gives us an opportunity to think about choice among technologies in a concrete way.

Suppose you own a truck and use it to haul merchandise for retailers such as Target and Sears. Your typical run is 200 miles, and you hire one person to drive the truck at a cost of $20 per hour. How fast should you instruct him to drive the truck? Consider the cost per trip.

Notice that even with fixed inputs of one truck and one driver, you still have some choices to make. In the language of this chapter, you can think of the choice as one of slow-drive technology (let's say 50 mph) versus fast-drive technology (say, 60 mph).

If the driver's time were the only input, the problem would be simple: Labor costs are minimized if you tell him to drive fast. At 60 mph, a trip takes the driver only 3.33 hours (200 miles divided by 60 mph) and costs you $66.67 given his $20 wage rate. However, at a speed of 50 mph, it takes four hours and costs you $80. With one variable input, the best technology is the one that uses that input most efficiently. In fact, with only one variable input, you would tell the driver to speed regardless of his wage rate.

But, of course, trucks require not only drivers but also fuel, which is where the question gets more interesting. As it turns out, the fuel mileage that a truck gets diminishes with speed beyond about 50 mph. Let's say in this case that the truck gets 15 miles per gallon at 50 mph but only 12 miles per gallon at 60 mph. Now we have a trade-off. When you tell the driver to go fast, your labor costs are lower but your fuel costs are higher.

So what instructions do you give? It should be clear that your instructions depend on the price of fuel. First suppose that fuel costs $3.50 per gallon. If the trucker drives fast, he will get 12 miles per gallon. Because the trucker has to drive 200 miles per trip, he burns 16.66 gallons (200 divided by 12) and total fuel cost is $58.31. Driving fast, the trucker goes 60 miles per hour. You have to pay him for 3.33 hours (200 divided by 60), which at $20 per hour, is a total of $66.67. The total for the trip is $124.98.

On the other hand, if your trucker drives slowly, he will get 15 miles per gallon, which means you need only 13.33 gallons, which costs $46.67. But now it takes more time. He takes four hours, and you must pay him 4 × 20, or $80 per trip. Total cost is now $126.67. Thus, the cost-minimizing solution is to have him drive fast.

Now try a price of $4.50 per gallon. Doing the same calculations, you should be able to show that when driving

slowly, the total cost is $139.99; when driving fast, the cost is $141.63. Thus, the higher fuel price means that you tell the driver to slow down.

Going one step further, you should be able to show that at a fuel price of $4, the trip costs the same whether your trucker drives fast or slowly.

In fact, you should be able to see that at fuel prices in excess of $4 per gallon, you tell your driver to slow down, whereas at cheaper prices, you tell him to speed up. With more than one input, the choice of technologies often depends on the unit cost of those inputs.

The observation that the optimal "technology" to use in trucking depends on fuel prices is one reason we might expect accident rates to fall with rises in fuel prices (in addition to the fact that everyone drives less when fuel is expensive). Modern technology, in the form of on-board computers, allows a modern trucking firm to monitor driving speed and instruct drivers.

Here is a summary of the cost per trip.

Fuel Price	$ 3.50	$ 4.00	$ 4.50
Drive Fast	$124.98	$133.33	$141.63
Drive Slowly	$126.67	$133.33	$139.99

THINKING PRACTICALLY

1. When gasoline prices rise, accident rates fall. Provide two reasons this might be true.

TABLE 7.3	Inputs Required to Produce 100 Diapers Using Alternative Technologies	
Technology	Units of Capital (*K*)	Units of Labor (*L*)
A	2	10
B	3	6
C	4	4
D	6	3
E	10	2

Consider the choices available to the diaper manufacturer in Table 7.3. Five different techniques of producing 100 diapers are available. Technology *A* is the most labor-intensive, requiring 10 hours of labor and 2 units of capital to produce 100 diapers. (You can think of units of capital as machine hours.) Technology *E* is the most capital-intensive, requiring only 2 hours of labor but 10 hours of machine time.

To choose a production technique, the firm must look to input markets to learn the current market prices of labor and capital. What is the wage rate (P_L), and what is the cost per hour of capital (P_K)? The right choice among inputs depends on how productive an input is and what its price is.

Suppose that labor and capital are both available at a price of $1 per unit. Column 4 of Table 7.4 presents the calculations required to determine which technology is best. We see that a firm will minimize its costs by choosing technology C., which produces 100 diapers for $8. All four of the other technologies produce 100 diapers at a higher cost. If the firm wishes to produce 100 diapers, it will make the highest profits by using technology C.

Now suppose that the wage rate (P_L) were to rise sharply, from $1 to $5. You might guess that this increase would lead the firm to substitute labor-saving capital for workers, and you would be right. As column 5 of Table 7.4 shows, the increase in the wage rate means that technology *E* is now the cost-minimizing choice for the firm. Using 10 units of capital and only 2 units of labor, the firm can produce 100 diapers for $20. All other technologies are now more costly. Notice too from the table that the firm's ability to shift its technique of production softened the impact of the wage increase on its costs. The flexibility of a firm's techniques of production is an important determinant of its costs.

Looking Ahead: Cost and Supply

So far, we have looked only at a *single* level of output. That is, we have determined how much it will cost to produce 100 diapers using the best available technology at a set of prices. The best technique for producing 1,000 diapers or 10,000 diapers may be entirely different. The next chapter explores the relationship between cost and the level of output in some detail. One of our main objectives in that chapter is to determine the amount that a competitive firm will choose to *supply* during a given time period.

TABLE 7.4	Cost-Minimizing Choice among Alternative Technologies (100 Diapers)			
			Cost = $(L \times P_L) + (K \times P_K)$	
(1) Technology	(2) Units of Capital (K)	(3) Units of Labor (L)	(4) $P_L = \$1$ $P_K = \$1$	(5) $P_L = \$5$ $P_K = \$1$
A	2	10	$ 12	$ 52
B	3	6	9	33
C	4	4	8	24
D	6	3	9	21
E	10	2	12	20

SUMMARY

1. Firms vary in size and internal organization, but they all take inputs and transform them into outputs through a process called *production*.

2. In perfect competition, no single firm has any control over prices. This follows from two assumptions: (1) Perfectly competitive industries are composed of many firms, each small relative to the size of the industry, and (2) each firm in a perfectly competitive industry produces *homogeneous products*.

3. The demand curve facing a competitive firm is perfectly elastic. If a single firm raises its price above the market price, it will sell nothing. Because it can sell all it produces at the market price, a firm has no incentive to reduce price.

7.1 THE BEHAVIOR OF PROFIT-MAXIMIZING FIRMS *p. 142*

4. Profit-maximizing firms in all industries must make three choices: (1) how much output to supply, (2) how to produce that output, and (3) how much of each input to demand.

5. *Profit* equals total revenue minus total cost. Total cost (economic cost) includes (1) out-of-pocket costs and (2) the opportunity cost of each factor of production, including a normal rate of return on capital.

6. A *normal rate of return* on capital is included in total cost because tying up resources in a firm's capital stock has an opportunity cost. If you start a business or buy a share of stock in a corporation, you do so because you expect to make at least a normal rate of return. Investors will not invest their money in a business unless they expect to make at least a normal rate of return.

7. A positive profit level occurs when a firm is earning an above-normal rate of return on capital.

8. Two assumptions define the *short run*: (1) a fixed scale or fixed factor of production and (2) no entry to or exit from the industry. In the *long run*, firms can choose any scale of operations they want and firms can enter and leave the industry.

9. To make decisions, firms need to know three things: (1) the market price of their output, (2) the production techniques that are available, and (3) the prices of inputs.

7.2 THE PRODUCTION PROCESS *p. 146*

10. The relationship between inputs and outputs (the *production technology*) expressed numerically or mathematically is called a *production function* or *total product function*.

11. The *marginal product* of a variable input is the additional output that an added unit of that input will produce if all other inputs are held constant. According to the *law of diminishing returns*, when additional units of a variable input are added to fixed inputs, after a certain point, the marginal product of the variable input will decline.

12. *Average product* is the average amount of product produced by each unit of a variable factor of production. If marginal product is above average product, the average product rises; if marginal product is below average product, the average product falls.

13. Capital and labor are at the same time complementary and substitutable inputs. Capital enhances the productivity of labor, but it can also be substituted for labor.

7.3 CHOICE OF TECHNOLOGY *p. 150*

14. One of the key decisions that all firms must make is which technology to use. Profit-maximizing firms will choose the combination of inputs that minimizes costs of producing any given level of output and therefore maximizes profits.

REVIEW TERMS AND CONCEPTS

average product, *p. 148*
capital-intensive technology, *p. 146*
economic profit, *p. 142*
firm, *p. 141*
labor-intensive technology, *p. 146*
law of diminishing returns, *p. 147*
long run, *p. 145*
marginal product, *p. 147*

normal rate of return, *p. 143*
optimal method of production, *p. 145*
production, *p. 141*
production function *or* total product function, *p. 146*
production technology, *p. 146*
profit, *p. 142*
short run, *p. 144*

total cost (total economic cost), *p. 142*
total revenue, *p. 142*
Equations:
profit = *total revenue* − *total cost*, *p. 142*

$$Average\ product\ of\ labor = \frac{total\ product}{total\ units\ of\ labor},$$

p. 148

PROBLEMS

All problems are available on MyEconLab.

7.1 THE BEHAVIOR OF PROFIT-MAXIMIZING FIRMS

LEARNING OBJECTIVE: Understand the importance of opportunity costs to economic profits and how these profits feed into firm decision making.

1.1 Consider a firm that uses capital and labor as inputs and sells 20,000 units of output per year at the going market price of $15. Also assume that total labor costs to the firm are $250,000 annually. Assume further that the total capital stock of the firm is currently worth $400,000, that the return available to investors with comparable risks is 7 percent annually, and that there is no depreciation. Is this a profitable firm? Explain your answer.

1.2 After working for 25 years as personal fitness trainers while raising their kids, three sisters cashed in a total of $120,000 in bonds and decided to open a small, neighborhood fitness center. They spent the $120,000 on exercise equipment, advertising, computer equipment, and other furnishings for the business. For the next 3 years, they took in $150,000 in revenue each year, paid themselves $35,000 annually each, and rented a space in a strip mall for $36,000 per year. Before the investment, their $120,000 in bonds were earning interest at a rate of 8 percent. Are they now earning economic profits? Explain your answer.

1.3 Suppose that in 2015, you inherited from your grandfather a small planetarium that had been closed for several years. Your planetarium has a maximum capacity of 75 people and all the equipment is in working order. You decide to reopen the planetarium on the weekends as a new laser-tag venture called Shoot for the Stars, and much to your delight it has become an instant success, with admission tickets selling out quickly for each day you are open. Describe some of the decisions that you must make in the short run. What might you consider to be your "fixed factor"? What alternative decisions might you be able to make in the long run? Explain.

1.4 A firm earning zero economic profits is probably suffering losses from the standpoint of general accounting principles. Do you agree or disagree with this argument? Explain why.

1.5 Ben Cartwright runs the Wild West Wax Museum in Carson City, Nevada. The museum has been in business for 40 years and is a major tourist attraction. The total value of the museum's capital stock is $3.5 million, which Ben owns outright. This year, the museum earned a total of $1.4 million after out-of-pocket expenses. Without taking the opportunity cost of capital into account, this means that Ben is earning a 40 percent return on his capital. Suppose that risk-free bonds are currently paying a rate of 12 percent to those who buy them.

a. What is meant by the "opportunity cost of capital"?
b. Explain why opportunity costs are "real" costs even though they do not necessarily involve out-of-pocket expenses.
c. What is the opportunity cost of Ben's capital?
d. How much excess profit is Ben earning?

1.6 An article on cnet.com reported on the findings of the marketing research firm IHS in its investigation of the cost of the components used to produce the 128GB Apple iPad Air 2 model with wifi + cellular. The firm found that this iPad model costs $358 to produce, 57 percent less than its retail price of $829. Does this mean that Apple is making a profit of $471 on each of these iPad Air2 models? Briefly explain.

Source: Don Reisinger, "iPad Air 2 models cost Apple $275 to $358, teardowns reveal," *cnet.com*, October 29, 2014.

1.7 Which of the following are short-run decisions and which are long-run decisions?
a. Berkshire Hathaway acquires battery-maker Duracell from Procter and Gamble.
b. The city of Santa Barbara, California, builds a water desalinization plant to help alleviate the water shortage problem arising from severe drought conditions.
c. Disney closed its Maelstrom ride at its Epcot theme park in 2014 and is replacing it with an attraction based on its mega-hit animated film *Frozen*.
d. American Express announced it will lay off 4,000 employees in 2015.
e. Boeing announced it will increase production of its 737 jetliners at its Renton, Washington factory from the current 42 per month to 52 per month in 2018.
f. Toyota announced in 2014 that it is moving its North American headquarters from Torrance, California, to Plano, Texas.

1.8 The data in the table represents annual costs and revenue for Ted's Vintage Threads, a used clothing store in Key West, Florida. Ted works 72 hours a week at the store. He also owns the building that houses his business, and if he closed the store, he could rent out the building for $75,000 per year and go to work for his cross-town rival, Cassie's Classic Couture and earn a salary of $23,000 per year. Calculate the economic profit and economic cost for Ted's Vintage Threads. Are these figures the same as the accounting cost and accounting profit? Explain.

Wages Paid	$ 38,000
Interest Paid on Loans	6,000
Other Expenditures for Factors of Production	18,000
Total Revenue	132,000

7.2 THE PRODUCTION PROCESS

LEARNING OBJECTIVE: Be able to describe how total, marginal, and average products relate to one another.

2.1 The following table gives total output or total product as a function of labor units used.

Labor	Total Output
0	0
1	30
2	54
3	72
4	84
5	90

a. Define diminishing returns.
b. Does the table indicate a situation of diminishing returns? Explain your answer.

2.2 The following is a production function.

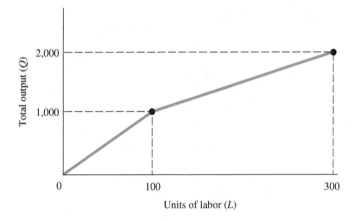

a. Draw a graph of marginal product as a function of output. (*Hint:* Marginal product is the additional number of units of output per unit of labor at each level of output.)
b. Does this graph exhibit diminishing returns? Explain your answer.

2.3 **[Related to the *Economics in Practice* on p. 150]** Identical sweaters can be made in one of two ways. With a machine that can be rented for $50 per hour and a person to run the machine who can be hired at $25 per hour, five sweaters can be produced in an hour using $10 worth of wool. Alternatively, I can run the machine with a less-skilled worker, producing only four sweaters in an hour with the same $10 worth of wool. (The less-skilled worker is slower and wastes material.) At what wage rate would I choose the less-skilled worker?

2.4 During the early phases of industrialization, the number of people engaged in agriculture usually drops sharply, even as agricultural output is growing. Given what you know about production technology and production functions, explain this seeming inconsistency.

2.5 The number of oil changes conducted by a service station depends on the number of workers as follows:

Number of Workers	Number of oil changes (Per Day)
0	0
1	6
2	14
3	26
4	40
5	52
6	58
7	61
8	60
9	48

Assume that all inputs (service bins, telephone, and utilities) other than labor are fixed in the short run.
a. Add two additional columns to the table and enter the marginal product and average product for each number of workers.
b. Over what range of labor input are there increasing returns to labor? diminishing returns to labor? negative returns to labor?
c. Over what range of labor input is marginal product greater than average product? What is happening to average product as employment increases over this range?
d. Over what range of labor input is marginal product smaller than average product? What is happening to average product as employment increases over this range?

2.6 The following table represents data for Randle's Candles. Draw a graph showing the total product, marginal product of labor, and average product of labor. Identify where increasing returns, diminishing returns, and negative returns set in on the total product curve.

Labor Units (Employees)	Total Product (Candles Per Hour)	Marginal Product of Labor	Average Product of Labor
0	0	–	–
1	18	18	18.0
2	42	24	21.0
3	78	36	26.0
4	112	34	28.0
5	140	28	28.0
6	161	21	26.8
7	173	12	24.7
8	173	0	21.6
9	165	–8	18.3
10	150	–15	15.0

2.7 Assume that we have a production process that exhibits increasing and then decreasing marginal productivity. That is, as we increase output, the marginal product of labor starts at some level above zero, rises to a maximum, and then eventually falls to zero. Which of the following statements is true? Briefly explain.
a. Total product reaches its highest level where marginal product is equal to average product.
b. Marginal product and average product are equal when marginal product is at its maximum.

c. When marginal product is equal to zero, average product is rising.

d. When marginal product is above average product, average product is rising.

e. When marginal product is equal to average product, output is maximized.

2.8 Following is information on the production levels of three different firms.

Firm A is currently producing at a quantity where it is experiencing increasing returns.

Firm B is currently producing at a quantity where it is experiencing diminishing returns.

Firm C is currently producing at a quantity where it is experiencing negative returns.

a. If each of the firms cut back on its labor force, what will happen to its marginal product of labor? Why?

b. If each of the firms adds to its labor force, what will happen to its marginal product of labor? Why?

7.3 CHOICE OF TECHNOLOGY

LEARNING OBJECTIVE: Discuss the factors that firms consider when choosing among production techniques.

3.1 Suppose that widgets can be produced using two different production techniques, A and B. The following table provides the total input requirements for each of five different total output levels.

Tech.	Q = 1		Q = 2		Q = 3		Q = 4		Q = 5	
	K	L	K	L	K	L	K	L	K	L
A	4	1	6	2	9	4	12	7	11	8
B	1	3	2	5	4	8	5	12	7	15

a. Assuming that the price of labor (P_L) is \$2 and the price of capital (P_K) is \$3, calculate the total cost of production for each of the five levels of output using the optimal (least-cost) technology at each level.

b. How many labor hours (units of labor) would be employed at each level of output? How many machine hours (units of capital)?

c. Graph total cost of production as a function of output. (Put cost on the y-axis and output, q, on the x-axis.) Again assume that the optimal technology is used.

d. Repeat a. through c. under the assumption that the price of labor (P_L) remains at \$2 while the price of capital (P_K) falls from \$3 to \$2.

3.2 A female student who lives on the fourth floor of Bates Hall is assigned to a new room on the seventh floor during her junior year. She has 11 heavy boxes of books and "stuff" to move. Discuss the alternative combinations of capital and labor that might be used to make the move. How would your answer differ if the move were to a new dorm 3 miles across campus and to a new college 400 miles away?

3.3 [**Related to the *Economics in Practice* on p. 151**] Darius has entered a competition in which he must drive from his home town of Memphis, Tennessee, to New Orleans, Louisiana, a distance of approximately 420 miles. If he arrives in 6 hours (an average speed of 70 mph), he will receive a prize of \$250. If he arrives in 7 hours (an average speed of 60 mph), he receives \$225. One of the competition rules is he must pay for his own gasoline, and Darius has calculated that he will average 24 miles per gallon at 70 mph and 30 miles per gallon at 60 mph. To maximize his winnings (prize money minus the cost of gasoline), at what speed should Darius drive if the price of gasoline is \$4.00 per gallon? What if the price of gasoline is \$5.00 per gallon? At what gasoline price would Darius be indifferent to arriving in either 6 hours or 7 hours if he wants to maximize his winnings? Other than maximizing winnings, are there any other considerations Darius should take into account when deciding on how fast to drive? Briefly explain.

3.4 Since the end of World War II, manufacturing firms in the United States and in Europe have been moving farther and farther outside of central cities. At the same time, firms in finance, insurance, and other parts of the service sector have been locating near downtown areas in tall buildings. One major reason seems to be that manufacturing firms find it difficult to substitute capital for land, whereas service-sector firms that use office space do not.

a. What kinds of buildings represent substitution of capital for land?

b. Why do you think that manufacturing firms might find it difficult to substitute capital for land?

c. Why is it relatively easier for a law firm or an insurance company to substitute capital for land?

d. Why is the demand for land likely to be high near the center of a city?

*e. One of the reasons for substituting capital for land near the center of a city is that land is more expensive near the center. What is true about the relative supply of land near the center of a city? (*Hint:* What is the formula for the area of a circle?)

3.5 A firm can use three different production technologies, with capital and labor requirements at each level of output as follows:

Daily Output	Technology 1		Technology 2		Technology 3	
	K	L	K	L	K	L
100	4	6	2	8	5	3
150	5	9	3	10	7	5
200	6	12	5	14	8	8
250	7	15	6	18	10	12

a. Suppose the firm is operating in a high-wage country, where capital cost is \$150 per unit per day and labor cost is \$100 per worker per day. For each level of output, which technology is cheapest?

b. Now suppose the firm is operating in a low-wage country, where capital cost is \$150 per unit per day but labor cost is only \$60 per unit per day. For each level of output, which technology is cheapest?

c. Suppose the firm moves from a low-wage to a high-wage country but its level of output remains constant at 100 units per day. How will its total employment change?

*Note: Problems marked with an asterisk are more challenging.

CHAPTER 7 APPENDIX: Isoquants and Isocosts

This chapter has shown that the cost structure facing a firm depends on two key pieces of information: (1) input (factor) prices and (2) technology. This appendix presents a more formal analysis of technology and factor prices and their relationship to cost.

LEARNING OBJECTIVE

Derive a cost curve from isoquants and isocost lines.

New Look at Technology: Isoquants

Table 7A.1 is expanded from Table 7.3 to show the various combinations of capital (K) and labor (L) that can be used to produce three different levels of output (q). For example, 100 units of X can be produced with 2 units of capital and 10 units of labor, with 3 units of K and 6 units of L, or with 4 units of K and 4 units of L, and so on. Similarly, 150 units of X can be produced with 3 units of K and 10 units of L, with 4 units of K and 7 units of L, and so on.

TABLE 7A.1   Alternative Combinations of Capital (K) and Labor (L) Required to Produce 50, 100, and 150 Units of Output

	$Q_X = 50$		$Q_X = 100$		$Q_X = 150$	
	K	L	K	L	K	L
A	1	8	2	10	3	10
B	2	5	3	6	4	7
C	3	3	4	4	5	5
D	5	2	6	3	7	4
E	8	1	10	2	10	3

A graph that shows all the combinations of capital and labor that can be used to produce a given amount of output is called an **isoquant**. Figure 7A.1 graphs three isoquants, one each for $q_X = 50$, $q_X = 100$, and $q_X = 150$ based on the data in Table 7A.1. Notice that all the points on the graph have been connected, indicating that there are an infinite number of combinations of labor and capital that can produce each level of output. For example, 100 units of output can

isoquant   A graph that shows all the combinations of capital and labor that can be used to produce a given amount of output.

◀ FIGURE 7A.1
Isoquants Showing All Combinations of Capital and Labor That Can Be Used to Produce 50, 100, and 150 Units of Output

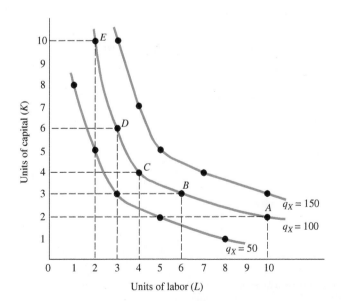

also be produced with 3.50 units of labor and 4.75 units of capital. (Verify that this point is on the isoquant labeled $q_X = 100$.)

Figure 7A.1 shows only three isoquants, but many more are not shown. For example, there are separate isoquants for $q_X = 101$, $q_X = 102$, and so on. If we assume that producing fractions of a unit of output is possible, there must be an isoquant for $q_X = 134.57$, for $q_X = 124.82$, and so on. One could imagine an infinite number of isoquants in Figure 7A.1. The higher the level of output, the farther up and to the right the isoquant will lie.

Figure 7A.2 derives the slope of an isoquant. Because points F and G are both on the $q_X = 100$ isoquant, the two points represent two different combinations of K and L that can be used to produce 100 units of output. In moving from point F to point G along the curve, less capital is employed, but more labor is used. An approximation of the amount of output lost by using less capital is ΔK times the marginal product of capital (MP_K). The *marginal product of capital* is the number of units of output produced by a single marginal unit of capital. Thus, $\Delta K \cdot MP_K$ is the total output lost by using less capital.

For output to remain constant (as it must because F and G are on the same isoquant), the loss of output from using less capital must be matched by the added output produced by using more labor. This amount can be approximated by ΔL times the marginal product of labor (MP_L). Because the two must be equal, it follows that[1]

$$\Delta K \cdot MP_K = -\Delta L \cdot MP_L$$

If we then divide both sides of this equation by ΔL and then by MP_K, we arrive at the following expression for the slope of the isoquant:

$$\text{slope of isoquant:} \quad \frac{\Delta K}{\Delta L} = -\frac{MP_L}{MP_K}$$

marginal rate of technical substitution   The rate at which a firm can substitute capital for labor and hold output constant.

The ratio of MP_L to MP_K is called the **marginal rate of technical substitution**. It is the rate at which a firm can substitute capital for labor and hold output constant.

Factor Prices and Input Combinations: Isocosts

isocost line   A graph that shows all the combinations of capital and labor available for a given total cost.

A graph that shows all the combinations of capital and labor that are available for a given total cost is called an **isocost line**. (Recall that total cost includes opportunity costs and normal rate of return.) Just as there are an infinite number of isoquants (one for every possible level of output), there are an infinite number of isocost lines, one for every possible level of total cost.

▶ **FIGURE 7A.2**   **The Slope of an Isoquant Is Equal to the Ratio of MP_L to MP_K**

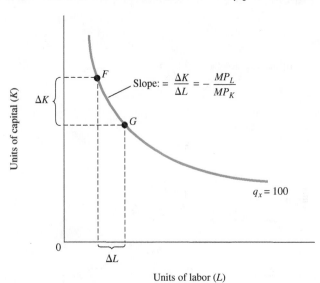

[1] We need to add the negative sign to ΔL because in moving from point F to point G, ΔK is a negative number and ΔL is a positive number. The minus sign is needed to balance the equation.

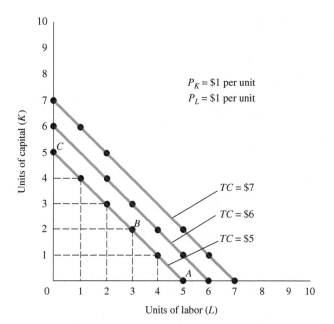

◀ FIGURE 7A.3   **Isocost Lines Showing the Combinations of Capital and Labor Available for $5, $6, and $7**

An isocost line shows all the combinations of capital and labor that are available for a given total cost.

Figure 7A.3 shows three simple isocost lines assuming that the price of labor (P_L) is $1 per unit and the price of capital (P_K) is $1 per unit. The lowest isocost line shows all the combinations of K and L that can be purchased for $5. For example, $5 will buy 5 units of labor and no capital (point A), 3 units of labor and 2 units of capital (point B), or no units of labor and 5 units of capital (point C). All these points lie along a straight line. The equation of that straight line is

$$(P_K \cdot K) + (P_L \cdot L) = TC$$

Substituting our data for the lowest isocost line into this general equation, we get

$$(\$1 \cdot K) + (\$1 \cdot L) = \$5, \text{ or } (K + L) = 5$$

Remember that the X- and Y-scales are units of labor and units of capital, not dollars.

On the same graph are two additional isocosts showing the various combinations of K and L available for a total cost of $6 and $7. These are only three of an infinite number of isocosts. At any total cost, there is an isocost that shows all the combinations of K and L available for that amount.

Figure 7A.4 shows another isocost line. This isocost assumes a different set of factor prices, $P_L = \$5$ and $P_K = \$1$. The diagram shows all the combinations of K and L that can be bought for $25. One way to draw the line is to determine the endpoints. For example, if the entire $25 were spent on labor, how much labor could be purchased? The answer is, of course, 5 units ($25 divided by $5 per unit). Thus, point A, which represents 5 units of labor and no capital, is on the isocost line. Similarly, if all of the $25 were spent on capital, how much capital could be purchased? The answer is 25 units ($25 divided by $1 per unit). Thus, point B, which represents 25 units of capital and no labor, is also on the isocost line. Another point on this particular isocost is 3 units of labor and 10 units of capital, point C.

The slope of an isocost line can be calculated easily if you first find the endpoints of the line. In Figure 7A.4, we can calculate the slope of the isocost line by taking $\Delta K / \Delta L$ between points B and A. Thus,

$$\text{slope of isocost line: } \frac{\Delta K}{\Delta L} = -\frac{TC / P_K}{TC / P_L} = -\frac{P_L}{P_K}$$

Plugging in the endpoints from our example, we get

$$\text{slope of line } AB = -\frac{\$5}{\$1} = -5$$

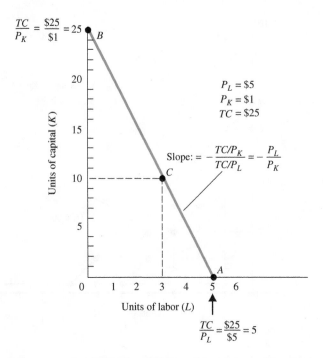

$$\frac{TC}{P_K} = \frac{\$25}{\$1} = 25$$

$P_L = \$5$
$P_K = \$1$
$TC = \$25$

$$\text{Slope:} = -\frac{TC/P_K}{TC/P_L} = -\frac{P_L}{P_K}$$

Units of capital (K)

Units of labor (L)

$$\frac{TC}{P_L} = \frac{\$25}{\$5} = 5$$

▲ FIGURE 7A.4 **Isocost Line Showing All Combinations of Capital and Labor Available for $25**
One way to draw an isocost line is to determine the endpoints of that line and draw a line connecting them.

Finding the Least-Cost Technology with Isoquants and Isocosts

Figure 7A.5 superimposes the isoquant for $q_X = 50$ on the isocost lines in Figure 7A.3, which assume that $P_K = \$1$ and $P_L = \$1$. The question now becomes one of choosing among the combinations of K and L that can be used to produce 50 units of output. Recall that each point on the isoquant (labeled $q_X = 50$ in Figure 7A.5) represents a different technology—a different combination of K and L.

We assume that our firm is a perfectly competitive, profit-maximizing firm that will choose the combination that minimizes cost. Because every point on the isoquant lies on some particular isocost line, we can determine the total cost for each combination along the isoquant. For example, point D (5 units of capital and 2 units of labor) lies along the isocost for a total cost of $7. Notice that 5 units of capital and 2 units of labor cost a total of $7. (Remember, $P_K = \$1$ and $P_L = \$1$.) The same amount of output (50 units) can be produced at lower cost. Specifically, by using 3 units of labor and 3 units of capital (point C), total cost is reduced to $6. *No other combination of K and L along isoquant $q_X = 50$ is on a lower isocost line.* In seeking to maximize profits, the firm will choose the combination of inputs that is least costly. The least costly way to produce any given level of output is indicated by the point of tangency between an isocost line and the isoquant corresponding to that level of output.[2]

In Figure 7A.5, the least-cost technology of producing 50 units of output is represented by point C, the point at which the $q_X = 50$ isoquant is just tangent to—that is, just touches—the isocost line.

Figure 7A.6 adds the other two isoquants from Figure 7A.1 to Figure 7A.5. Assuming that $P_K = \$1$ and $P_L = \$1$, the firm will move along each of the three isoquants until it finds the least-cost combination of K and L that can be used to produce that particular level of output. The result is plotted in Figure 7A.7. The minimum cost of producing 50 units of X is $6, the minimum cost of producing 100 units of X is $8, and the minimum cost of producing 150 units of X is $10.

---

[2] This assumes that the isoquants are continuous and convex (bowed) toward the origin.

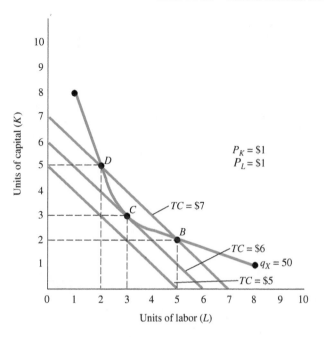

◀ FIGURE 7A.5   **Finding the Least-Cost Combination of Capital and Labor to Produce 50 Units of Output**
Profit-maximizing firms will minimize costs by producing their chosen level of output with the technology represented by the point at which the isoquant is tangent to an isocost line. Here the cost-minimizing technology—3 units of capital and 3 units of labor—is represented by point C.

The Cost-Minimizing Equilibrium Condition

At the point where a line is just tangent to a curve, the two have the same slope. (We have already derived expressions for the slope of an isocost and the slope of an isoquant.) At each point of tangency (such as at points A, B, and C in Figure 7A.6), the following must be true:

$$\text{slope of isoquant} = -\frac{MP_L}{MP_K} = \text{slope of isocost} = -\frac{P_L}{P_K}$$

Thus,

$$\frac{MP_L}{MP_K} = \frac{P_L}{P_K}$$

Dividing both sides by P_L and multiplying both sides by MP_K, we get

$$\frac{MP_L}{P_L} = \frac{MP_K}{P_K}$$

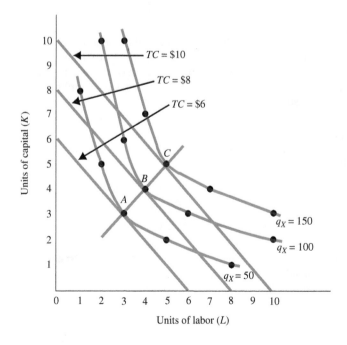

◀ FIGURE 7A.6
Minimizing Cost of Production for $q_X = 50$, $q_X = 100$, and $q_X = 150$
Plotting a series of cost-minimizing combinations of inputs—shown in this graph as points A, B, and C—on a separate graph results in a *cost curve* like the one shown in Figure 7A.7.

▶ FIGURE 7A.7 **A Cost Curve Shows the *Minimum* Cost of Producing Each Level of Output**

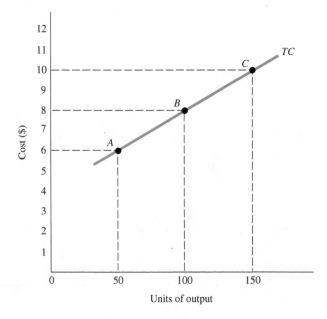

This is the firm's cost-minimizing equilibrium condition.

This expression makes sense if you think about what it says. The left side of the equation is the marginal product of labor divided by the price of a unit of labor. Thus, it is the product derived from the last dollar spent on labor. The right-hand side of the equation is the product derived from the last dollar spent on capital. If the product derived from the last dollar spent on labor was not equal to the product derived from the last dollar spent on capital, the firm could decrease costs by using more labor and less capital or by using more capital and less labor.

Look back to Chapter 6 and see if you can find a similar expression and some similar logic in our discussion of household behavior. In fact, there is great symmetry between the theory of the firm and the theory of household behavior.

─────────── **APPENDIX SUMMARY** ───────────

1. An *isoquant* is a graph that shows all the combinations of capital and labor that can be used to produce a given quantity of output. The slope of an isoquant is equal to $-MP_L / MP_K$. The ratio of MP_L to MP_K is the *marginal rate of technical substitution*. It is the rate at which a firm can substitute capital for labor and hold output constant.

2. An *isocost line* is a graph that shows all the combinations of capital and labor that can be purchased for a given total cost. The slope of an isocost line is equal to $-P_L/P_K$.

3. The least-cost method of producing a given amount of output is found graphically at the point at which an isocost line is just tangent to the isoquant corresponding to that level of production. The firm's cost-minimizing equilibrium condition is $MP_L / P_L = MP_K / P_K$.

─────── **APPENDIX REVIEW TERMS AND CONCEPTS** ───────

isocost line, *p. 158*

isoquant, *p. 157*

marginal rate of technical substitution, *p. 158*

Equations
Slope of isoquant:
$$\frac{\Delta K}{\Delta L} = -\frac{MP_L}{MP_K}, p.\ 158$$

Slope of isocost line
$$\frac{\Delta K}{\Delta L} = -\frac{TC/P_K}{TC/P_L} = -\frac{P_L}{P_K}, p.\ 159$$

APPENDIX PROBLEMS

All problems are available on MyEconLab.

APPENDIX 7A: ISOQUANTS AND ISOCOSTS

LEARNING OBJECTIVE: Derive a cost curve from isoquants and isocost lines.

1A.1 Assume that $MP_L = 10$ and $MP_K = 6$. Assume also that $P_L = 4$ and $P_K = 2$. This implies that the firm should substitute capital for labor. Explain why.

1A.2 In the isoquant/isocost diagram (Figure 1), suppose the firm is producing 1,000 units of output at point A using 100 units of labor and 200 units of capital. As an outside consultant, what actions would you suggest to management to improve profits? What would you recommend if the firm were operating at point B, using 100 units of capital and 200 units of labor?

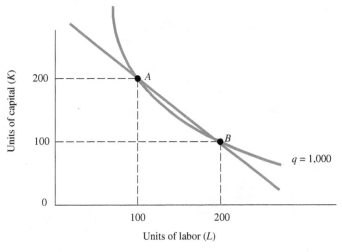

▲ FIGURE 1

1A.3 Using the information from the isoquant/isocost diagram (Figure 2) and assuming that $P_L = P_K = \$2$, complete Table 1.

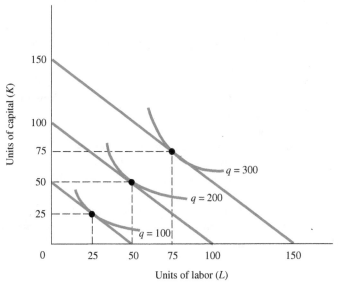

▲ FIGURE 2

TABLE 1

Output Units	Total Cost of Output	Units of Labor Demanded	Units of Capital Demanded
100	――	――	――
200	――	――	――
300	――	――	――

1A.4 Each month, a company can rent capital for $7,500 per unit and can hire workers for $2,500 each. Currently, the company is using 4 units of capital and 6 workers to produce 10,000 units of output. This combination of capital and labor represents a cost-minimizing equilibrium. Draw an isoquant/isocost diagram to illustrate this situation.

1A.5 The Red Racer Company and the Blue Bomber Company are each capable of minimizing cost and producing 4,000 bicycles per month. Red Racer's factory is located in an area where the cost of labor is significantly less and the cost of capital is significantly more than the costs of labor and capital for Blue Bomber. Assume that each company has access to the same technology to produce bicycles and draw an isoquant/isocost diagram to illustrate why the cost-minimizing combinations of inputs for these companies are different. Be sure to identify the isocost line, amount of capital, amount of labor, and cost-minimizing combination of inputs for each company.

8 Short-Run Costs and Output Decisions

This chapter continues our examination of the economic decisions made by firms. You have seen that firms make three specific decisions (Figure 8.1) involving their production:

1. How much output to supply
2. How to produce that output—that is, which production technique/technology to use
3. What quantity of each input to demand

This chapter focuses on the *costs* of production. To calculate costs, a firm must know two things: what quantity and combination of inputs it needs to produce its product and how much those inputs cost. (Do not forget that economic costs include a normal return to capital—the opportunity cost of capital.) We have already examined the production process in the last chapter. It remains to add input prices to the picture to move to production costs.

Take a moment and look back at the circular flow diagram, Figure II.1 on p. 109. There you can see where we are in our study of the competitive market system. The goal of this chapter is to look behind the supply curve in output markets. Producing output implies demanding inputs at the same time. You can also see in Figure II.1 two of the information sources that firms use in their output supply and input demand decisions: Firms look to *output markets* for the price of output and to *input markets* for the prices of capital and labor.

DECISIONS	are based on	INFORMATION
1. The quantity of output to *supply*		1. The price of output
2. How to produce that output (which technique to use)		2. Techniques of production available*
3. The quantity of each input to *demand*		3. The price of inputs*
		*Determines production costs

◀ **FIGURE 8.1** **Decisions Facing Firms**

Costs in the Short Run

Be able to describe and graph the major components of firm costs.

Our emphasis in this chapter is on costs *in the short run only*. Recall that the short run is that period during which two conditions hold: (1) existing firms face limits imposed by some fixed factor of production, and (2) new firms cannot enter and existing firms cannot exit an industry.

In the short run, all firms (competitive and noncompetitive) have costs that they must bear regardless of their output. In fact, some costs must be paid even if the firm stops producing— that is, even if output is zero. These costs are called **fixed costs**, and firms can do nothing in the short run to avoid them or to change them. In contrast, firms in the long run can leave the business completely, eliminating all their costs if they wish to produce nothing. In the long run, there is thus no category of costs labeled *fixed costs*.

Firms also have certain costs in the short run that depend on the level of output they have chosen. These kinds of costs are called **variable costs**. Total fixed costs and total variable costs together make up **total costs**:

fixed cost Any cost that does not depend on the firms' level of output. These costs are incurred even if the firm is producing nothing. There are no fixed costs in the long run.

variable cost A cost that depends on the level of production chosen.

$$TC = TFC + TVC$$

total cost (*TC*) Total fixed costs plus total variable costs.

where *TC* denotes total costs, *TFC* denotes total fixed costs, and *TVC* denotes total variable costs. We will return to this equation after discussing fixed costs and variable costs in detail.

Fixed Costs

In discussing fixed costs, we must distinguish between total fixed costs and average fixed costs.

Total Fixed Cost (*TFC*) Total fixed cost is sometimes called *overhead*. If you operate a factory, you must heat the building to keep the pipes from freezing in the winter. Even if no production is taking place, you may have to keep the roof from leaking, pay a guard to protect the building from vandals, and make payments on a long-term lease.

Fixed costs represent a larger portion of total costs for some firms than for others. Electric companies, for instance, maintain generating plants, thousands of miles of distribution wires, poles, transformers, and so on. Usually, such plants are financed by issuing bonds to the public—that is, by borrowing. The interest that must be paid on these bonds represents a substantial part of the utilities' operating cost and is a fixed cost in the short run, no matter how much (if any) electricity they are producing.

For the purposes of our discussion in this chapter, we will assume that firms use only two inputs, labor and capital, as they go about producing output. Although this may seem unrealistic, virtually everything that we will say about firms using these two factors can easily be generalized to firms that use many factors of production. Recall that capital yields services over time in the production of other goods and services. It is the plant and equipment of a manufacturing firm and the computers, desks, chairs, doors, and walls of a law office; it is the software of a Web-based firm and the boat that Bill and Colleen built on their desert island. It is sometimes assumed that capital is a fixed input in the short run and that labor is the only variable input. To be more realistic, however, we will assume that capital has both a fixed *and* a variable component. After all, some capital can be purchased in the short run.

TABLE 8.1	Short-Run Fixed Cost (Total and Average) of a Hypothetical Firm	
(1) q	(2) TFC	(3) AFC (TFC/q)
0	$ 100	$ –
1	100	100
2	100	50
3	100	33
4	100	25
5	100	20

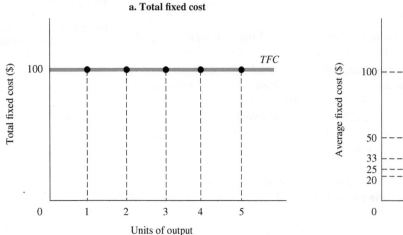
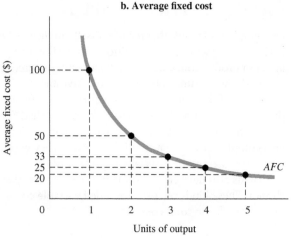

▲ **FIGURE 8.2** **Short-Run Fixed Cost (Total and Average) of a Hypothetical Firm**
Average fixed cost is simply total fixed cost divided by the quantity of output. As output increases, average fixed cost declines because we are dividing a fixed number by a larger and larger quantity.

Consider a small consulting firm that employs several economists, research assistants, and secretaries. It rents space in an office building and has a 5-year lease. The rent on the office space can be thought of as a fixed cost in the short run. The monthly electric and heating bills are also essentially fixed (although the amounts may vary slightly from month to month). So are the salaries of the basic administrative staff who work under contract. Payments on some capital equipment—a large copying machine and the main word-processing system, for instance—can also be thought of as fixed.

The same firm also has costs that vary with output. When there is a great deal of work, the firm hires temporary employees at both the professional and research assistant levels. The capital used by the consulting firm may also vary, even in the short run. Payments on the computer system do not change, but the firm may be able to buy or rent additional personal computers, network terminals, or databases quickly if needed. It must pay for the copy machine, but the machine costs more when it is running than when it is not.

total fixed cost (*TFC*) or overhead The total of all costs that do not change with output even if output is zero.

Total fixed costs (*TFC*) *or overhead* are those costs that do not change with output even if output is zero. Column 2 of Table 8.1 presents data on the fixed costs of a hypothetical firm. Fixed costs are $100 at all levels of output (*q*). Figure 8.2(a) shows total fixed costs as a function of output. Because *TFC* does not change with output, the graph is simply a straight horizontal line at $100. Firms have no control over fixed costs in the short run.

average fixed cost (*AFC*) Total fixed cost divided by the number of units of output; a per-unit measure of fixed costs.

Average Fixed Cost (*AFC*) **Average fixed cost (*AFC*)** is total fixed cost (*TFC*) divided by the number of units of output (*q*):

If the firm in Figure 8.2 produced 3 units of output, average fixed costs would be $33 ($100 ÷ 3). If the same firm produced 5 units of output, average fixed cost would be $20 ($100 ÷ 5). *Average fixed cost falls as output rises* because the same total is being spread over, or divided by, a larger number of units (see column 3 of Table 8.1). This phenomenon is sometimes called **spreading overhead**.

Graphs of average fixed cost, like that in Figure 8.2(b) (which presents the average fixed cost data from Table 8.1), are downward-sloping curves. Notice that AFC approaches zero as the quantity of output increases. If output were 10,000 units, average fixed cost would equal only 1 cent per unit in our example. AFC never actually reaches zero. We can see in this picture one of the advantages a firm might have in selling more output: it allows that firm to spread its fixed costs over more units.

spreading overhead The process of dividing total fixed costs by more units of output. Average fixed cost declines as quantity rises.

Variable Costs

Total Variable Cost (*TVC*) **Total variable cost (*TVC*)** is the sum of those costs that vary with the level of output in the short run. To produce more output, a firm uses more inputs. The cost of additional output depends directly on what additional inputs are required and how much they cost.

total variable cost (*TVC*) The total of all costs that vary with output in the short run.

As you saw in Chapter 7, input requirements are determined by technology. Firms generally have a number of production techniques available to them even in the short run, and they choose the one that produces the desired level of output at the least cost. To find out which technology involves the least cost, a firm must compare the total variable costs of producing that level of output using different production techniques. Notice the firm's fixed costs do not come into the decision process: those costs stay the same no matter what the firm does and so can be put to the side when making a decision.

Suppose you own a small farm. A certain amount of work has to be done to plant and harvest your 120 acres. You might hire four farmhands and divide up the tasks, or you might rent several pieces of complex farm machinery (capital) and do the work single-handedly. Your final choice depends on a number of things. What machinery is available? What does it do? Will it work on small fields such as yours? How much will it cost to buy each piece of equipment? What wage will you have to pay farmhands? How many will you need to hire to get the job done? If machinery is expensive and labor is cheap, you will probably choose the labor-intensive technology. If farm labor is expensive and the local farm equipment dealer is going out of business, you might get a good deal on some machinery and choose the capital-intensive method.

The **total variable cost curve** is a graph that shows the relationship between total variable cost and the level of a firm's output (q). At any given level of output, total variable cost depends on (1) the techniques of production that are available and (2) the prices of the inputs required by each technology. To examine this relationship in more detail, let us look at some hypothetical production figures.

total variable cost curve A graph that shows the relationship between total variable cost and the level of a firm's output.

Table 8.2 presents an analysis that might lie behind three points on a typical firm's total variable cost curve. In this case, there are two production techniques available, A and B, one somewhat more capital-intensive than the other. We will assume that the price of labor is $1 per unit and the price of capital is $2 per unit. For the purposes of this example, we focus on

TABLE 8.2 Derivation of Total Variable Cost Schedule from Technology and Factor Prices

Produce	Using Technique	Units of Input Required (Production Function) K	L	Total Variable Cost Assuming $P_K = \$2, P_L = \$1$ $TVC = (K \times P_K) + (L \times P_L)$
1 unit of	A	10	7	$(10 \times \$2) + (7 \times \$1) = \$27$
output	B	6	8	$(6 \times \$2) + (8 \times \$1) = \$20$
2 units of	A	16	8	$(16 \times \$2) + (8 \times \$1) = \$40$
output	B	11	16	$(11 \times \$2) + (16 \times \$1) = \$38$
3 units of	A	19	15	$(19 \times \$2) + (15 \times \$1) = \$53$
output	B	18	22	$(18 \times \$2) + (22 \times \$1) = \$58$

▶ FIGURE 8.3 **Total Variable Cost Curve**

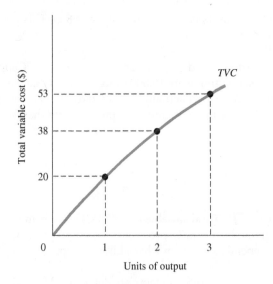

variable capital—that is, on capital that can be changed in the short run, such as a rented piece of equipment. The farmer's other capital, such as buildings and land, is fixed in the short run and thus not relevant for his short run decision. In our example, we will use K to denote variable capital.

In Table 8.2, total variable cost is derived from production requirements and input prices. A total variable cost curve expresses the relationship between TVC and total output.

Looking at Figure 8.3, we see that to produce 1 unit of output, the labor-intensive technique is least costly. Technique A requires 6 units of capital and 8 of labor, which would cost a total of $27. Technique B has a total cost of only $20. To maximize profits, the firm would use technique B if it planned to produce 1 unit.

The relatively labor-intensive technique B is also the best method of production for 2 units of output. If the firm decides to produce 3 units of output, however, technique A is cheaper.

Figure 8.3 graphs the relationship between total variable cost and output based on the data in Table 8.2, assuming the firm chooses the least-cost technology for each output. The total variable cost curve embodies information about both factor, or input, prices and technology. It shows the cost of production using the best available technique at each output level given current factor prices.

marginal cost (MC) The increase in total cost that results from producing 1 more unit of output. Marginal costs reflect changes in variable costs.

Marginal Cost (MC)   The most important of all cost concepts is that of **marginal cost (MC)**, the increase in total cost that results from the production of 1 more unit of output. Let us say, for example, that a firm is producing 1,000 units of output per period and decides to raise its rate of output to 1,001. Producing the extra unit raises total costs, and the increase—that is, the added cost of producing the 1,001st unit—is the marginal cost. Focusing on the "margin" is one way of looking at variable costs: marginal costs reflect changes in variable costs because they vary when output changes. Fixed costs do not change when output changes.

Table 8.3 shows how marginal cost is derived from total variable cost by simple subtraction. The total variable cost of producing the first unit of output is $20. Raising production from 1 unit to 2 units increases total variable cost from $20 to $38; the difference is the marginal cost of the second unit, or $18. Raising output from 2 to 3 units increases total variable cost from $38 to $53. The marginal cost of the third unit, therefore, is $15.

It is important to think for a moment about the nature of marginal cost. Specifically, marginal cost is the cost of the added inputs, or resources, needed to produce 1 additional unit of output. Look back at Table 8.2 and think about the additional capital and labor needed to go from 1 unit to 2 units. The second unit requires 5 *additional* units of capital and 8 *additional* units of labor. What, then, is the added, or marginal, cost of the second unit? Five units of capital cost $2 each ($10 total) and 8 units of labor cost $1 each (another $8), for a total marginal cost of $18, which is the number we derived in Table 8.3. Although the easiest way to derive marginal cost is

TABLE 8.3 Derivation of Marginal Cost from Total Variable Cost

Units of Output	Total Variable Costs ($)	Marginal Costs ($)
0	0	
1	20	20
2	38	18
3	53	15

to look at total variable cost and subtract, do not lose sight of the fact that when a firm increases its output level, it hires or demands more inputs. *Marginal cost* measures the *additional* cost of inputs required to produce each successive unit of output.

The Shape of the Marginal Cost Curve in the Short Run   The assumption of a fixed factor of production in the short run means that a firm is stuck at its current maximum scale of operation (in our example, the size of the plant). As a firm tries to increase its output, it will eventually find itself trapped by that scale. Thus, our definition of the short run also implies that *marginal cost eventually rises with output.* The firm can hire more labor or variable capital and use more materials—that is, it can add variable inputs—but diminishing returns eventually set in as those variable inputs add less and less to total output.

Recall from Chapter 7 the sandwich shop with one grill and too many workers trying to prepare sandwiches on it. With a fixed grill capacity, more laborers could make more sandwiches, but the marginal product of each successive cook declined as more people tried to use the grill. If each additional unit of labor adds less and less to total output, but input prices remain the same, *it follows that each additional unit of output costs more to produce.* In other words, *diminishing returns, or decreasing marginal product, imply increasing marginal cost* as illustrated in Figure 8.4.

To reiterate:

> In the short run, every firm is constrained by some fixed input that (1) leads to diminishing returns to variable inputs and (2) limits its capacity to produce. As a firm approaches that capacity, it becomes increasingly costly to produce successively higher levels of output. Marginal costs ultimately increase with output in the short run.

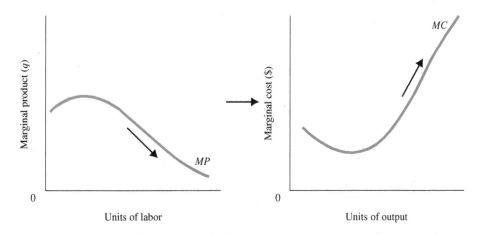

▲ **FIGURE 8.4   Declining Marginal Product Implies That Marginal Cost Will Eventually Rise with Output**
In the short run, every firm is constrained by some fixed factor of production. A fixed factor implies diminishing returns (declining marginal product) and a limited capacity to produce. As that limit is approached, marginal costs rise.

Graphing Total Variable Costs and Marginal Costs   Figure 8.5 shows the total variable cost curve and the marginal cost curve of a typical firm. We see in the top panel, that total variable costs (TVC) increase with output. To make more output requires more inputs and therefore more costs. The slope of the TVC is thus positive.

We aslo see from the graph that the shape of the marginal cost curve is consistent with short-run diminishing returns. At first, MC declines, but eventually the fixed factor of production begins to constrain the firm and marginal cost rises. Up to q units of output, producing each successive unit of output costs slightly less than producing the one before. Beyond this level, however, the cost of each successive unit is greater than the one before.

Remember that the slope of a line is equal to the change in the units measured on the y-axis divided by the change in the units measured on the x-axis. The slope of a total variable cost curve is thus the change in total variable cost divided by the change in output ($\Delta TVC/\Delta q$). Because marginal cost is by definition the change in total variable cost resulting from an increase in output of one unit ($\Delta q = 1$), *marginal cost actually is the slope of the total variable cost curve:*

$$\text{slope of TVC} = \frac{\Delta\, TVC}{\Delta q} = \frac{\Delta\, TVC}{1} = \Delta\, TVC = MC$$

Notice that up to q, marginal cost decreases and the variable cost curve becomes flatter. The slope of the total variable cost curve is declining—that is, total variable cost increases, but at a

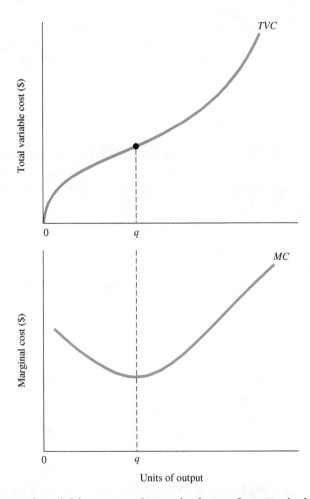

▲ **FIGURE 8.5   Total Variable Cost and Marginal Cost for a Typical Firm**
Total variable costs always increase with output. Marginal cost is the cost of producing each additional unit. Thus, the marginal cost curve shows how total variable cost changes with single-unit increases in total output.

TABLE 8.4   Short-Run Costs of a Hypothetical Firm

(1) q	(2) TVC	(3) MC (Δ TVC)	(4) AVC (TVC/q)	(5) TFC	(6) TC (TVC + TFC)	(7) AFC (TFC/q)	(8) ATC (TC/q or AFC + AVC)
0	$ 0.00	$ —	$ —	$100.00	$100.00	$ —	$ —
1	20.00	20.00	20.00	100.00	120.00	100.00	120.00
2	38.00	18.00	19.00	100.00	138.00	50.00	69.00
3	53.00	15.00	17.66	100.00	153.00	33.33	51.00
4	65.00	12.00	16.25	100.00	165.00	25.00	41.25
5	75.00	10.00	15.00	100.00	175.00	20.00	35.00
6	83.00	8.00	13.83	100.00	183.00	16.67	30.50
7	94.50	11.50	13.50	100.00	194.50	14.28	27.78
8	108.00	13.50	13.50	100.00	208.00	12.50	26.00
9	128.50	20.50	14.28	100.00	228.50	11.11	25.39
10	168.50	40.00	16.85	100.00	268.50	10.00	26.85

decreasing rate. Beyond *q* units of output, marginal cost increases and the total variable cost curve gets steeper—total variable costs continue to increase, but at an *increasing rate*.

Average Variable Cost (AVC)

Average variable cost (AVC) is total variable cost divided by the number of units of output (*q*):

$$AVC = \frac{TVC}{q}$$

In Table 8.4, we calculate AVC in column 4 by dividing the numbers in column 2 (TVC) by the numbers in column 1 (*q*). For example, the AVC of 2 units is $19.00, or $38.00 ÷ 2. Marginal cost of the second unit is $18.00.

Graphing Average Variable Costs and Marginal Costs

Figure 8.6 provides a graph of the marginal cost and average variable cost of a firm using the data in Table 8.4. We have smoothed out the curve, acting as though the firm can make fractional units, to simplify the graph. As the graph illustrates, average variable cost *follows* marginal cost but lags behind. As we increase output from 0 to 6 units, marginal cost falls from $20.00 to $8.00. This decrease in marginal cost pulls down average variable costs. At these levels of production, adding workers allows each to coordinate better, as we showed in the sandwich shop. As we push production further beyond 6 units, workers begin to interfere with one another as they find themselves, as in the sandwich shop, making do with less room to work or less machinery to use. At output levels above 6, we are seeing diminishing returns and the marginal cost curve rises. However,

average variable cost (AVC)   Total variable cost divided by the number of units of output; a per-unit measure of variable costs.

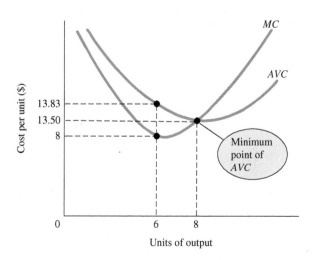

◀ FIGURE 8.6   **More Short-Run Costs**
When marginal cost is *below* average cost, average cost is declining. When marginal cost is *above* average cost, average cost is increasing. Rising marginal cost intersects average variable cost at the minimum point of *AVC*.

ECONOMICS IN PRACTICE

The Cost Structure of a Rock Concert: Welcome to New York

In the late spring and summer of 2015 Taylor Swift went on tour in part to promote her *1989* album. As economists we might want to think a bit about the cost structure of that tour.

For a rock concert, the output in question is a seat at a concert. Swift's tour took place in indoor venues, large arenas like the MetLife Stadium in East Rutherford, New Jersey. These venues have a maximum capacity, so there is a fixed number of seats that could be produced at a maximum. What are the fixed costs of producing a concert in a venue in New Jersey, say on July 15, 2015?

Any costs—and they are likely to be considerable—associated with producing the material for the concert are clearly fixed from the point of view of the specific concert on the 15th. So too is the cost of the stadium. Whether I sell one ticket or 500 tickets I still have to pay to rent the stadium. A large stadium might well cost $20,000 per night. Swift would also have to contract and pay for an elaborate lighting show, paying sound and lighting engineers. A group of roadies to move the baggage and get the instruments on stage also is a fixed cost. Publicity is also a fixed cost. None of these costs would vary with the number of tickets sold. If Swift sells only one ticket to that concert, she still has to pay all of these costs.

What about variable costs? Once Swift decides to put on a concert on that date, what is her cost of selling one more ticket, assuming there is room in the house? At first you might think it was zero, that adding another member to the audience costs nothing if there is a vacant seat. But that is not quite true. Some of the concert costs depend on how many tickets are sold.

Adding customers may increase the cost of security. Ticket sellers often charge a fee per ticket sale. Back up band members may get a fixed fee (and thus be a fixed cost) or take a fee that depends on the size of the audience, becoming a variable cost. So variable costs of one more ticket are not zero, but they are low relative to the fixed costs. For this reason, if the Swift concert is not sold out by performance time (unlikely!) you should expect a last minute ticket to be very cheap.

THINKING PRACTICALLY

1. Can you think of other products or services that have low marginal costs and high fixed costs and conversely?

notice that average variable cost continues to fall until 8 units because marginal cost is still below average variable cost until this point is reached.

The graph shows us that the marginal cost curve intersects the AVC curve when the AVC is at a minimum, which we see from our earlier table is at 8 units of output. At output levels less than 8, the fact that marginal cost is below average variable cost brings the average down. When marginal cost rises to be above AVC, after 8 units, the average begins to increase.

An example using test scores should help you understand the relationship between MC and AVC. Consider the following sequence of test scores: 95, 85, 92, 88. The average of these four scores is 90. Suppose you get an 80 on your fifth test. This score will drag down your average to 88. Now suppose you get an 85 on your sixth test. This score is higher than 80, but its still *below* your 88 average. As a result, your average continues to fall (from 88 to 87.5) even though your marginal test score rose. If instead of an 85 you get an 89—just one point over your average— you have turned your average around; it is now rising. You will recall that we saw this same pattern when we looked at marginal product and average product in the last chapter.

Total Costs

We are now ready to complete the cost picture by adding total fixed costs to total variable costs. Recall that

$$TC = TFC + TVC$$

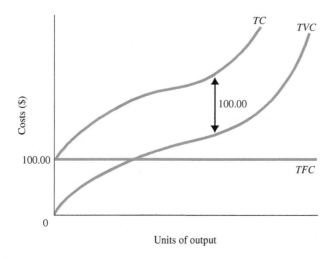

◀ FIGURE 8.7 **Total Cost = Total Fixed Cost + Total Variable Cost**
Adding *TFC* to *TVC* means adding the same amount of total fixed cost to every level of total variable cost. Thus, the total cost curve has the same shape as the total variable cost curve; it is simply higher by an amount equal to *TFC*.

In Table 8.4, column 6 adds the total fixed cost of $100.00 to total variable cost to arrive at total cost. Figure 8.7 graphs total cost. At each level of output, the total cost line is a vertical distance of $100 from the *TVC* line.

Average Total Cost (*ATC*)

Average total cost (*ATC*) is total cost divided by the number of units of output (*q*):

average total cost (*ATC*) Total cost divided by the number of units of output; a per-unit measure of total costs.

$$ATC = \frac{TC}{q}$$

Column 8 in Table 8.4 shows the average total costs of the firm. For example, at 5 units of output, *total* cost is $175.00; *average* total cost is $175.00 ÷ 5, or $35.00. So, the per unit total cost of producing each of these 5 units is $35.00 apiece.

Another, more revealing, way of writing average total cost is as the sum of average fixed cost and average variable cost. We see that column 8 in Table 8.4 is the sum of column 4 (*AVC*) and column 7 (*AFC*).

Figure 8.8 graphs these data. The bottom part of the figure shows average fixed cost. At 5 units of output, average fixed cost is *TFC*/*q* = $100,00 ÷ 5 = $20.00. At 10 units of output, *AFC* = $100.00 ÷ 10 = $10.00. The top part of Figure 8.8 shows the declining *AFC* added to *AVC* at each level of output. Because *AFC* gets smaller and smaller as output increases, *ATC* gets closer and closer to *AVC* as output increases, but the two lines never meet.

The Relationship between Average Total Cost and Marginal Cost

The relationship between average *total* cost and marginal cost is exactly the same as the relationship between average *variable* cost and marginal cost. The average total cost curve follows the marginal cost curve but lags behind because it is an average over all units of output. The average total cost curve lags behind the marginal cost curve even more than the average variable cost curve does because the cost of each added unit of production is now averaged not only with the variable cost of all previous units produced but also with fixed costs.

Fixed costs equal $100.00 and are incurred even when the output level is zero. The first unit of output in the example in Table 8.4 costs $20.00 in variable cost to produce, so the average total cost of 1 unit is $120.00. The second unit costs only $18.00 more in variable cost to produce so the average total cost of 2 units is $69 ($138.00/2) Over this region, average total cost is falling rapidly as we increase output because we are spreading the fixed costs. Average total cost is minimized at 9 units, where the cost is $25.39.[1] Of this $100.00/9 or $11.11 are fixed costs and the rest are variable.

As you saw with the test scores example, marginal cost is what drives changes in average total cost. If marginal cost is *below* average total cost, average total cost will *decline* toward

---

[1] *ATC* is in fact minimized at just over 9 units, and just below $25.39 where MC = AC. Notice from Table 8.4 that at 9 units MC is still pulling *ATC* down. Treating the units as integers creates this difficulty.

▶ FIGURE 8.8 **Average Total Cost = Average Variable Cost + Average Fixed Cost**

To get average total cost, we add average fixed and average variable costs at all levels of output. Because average fixed cost falls with output, an ever-declining amount is added to *AVC*. Thus, *AVC* and *ATC* get closer together as output increases, but the two lines never meet.

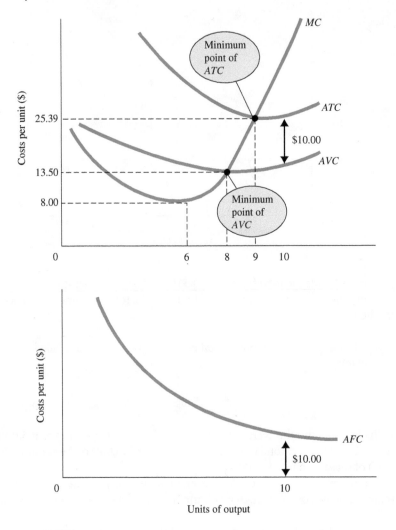

marginal cost. If marginal cost is *above* average total cost, average total cost will *increase*. As a result, marginal cost intersects average *total* cost at *ATC*'s minimum point for the same reason that it intersects the average *variable* cost curve at its minimum point.

Short-Run Costs: A Review

Let us now pause to review what we have learned about the behavior of firms. We know that firms make three basic choices: how much product or output to produce or supply, how to produce that output, and how much of each input to demand to produce what they intend to supply. Firms make these decisions to maximize profits. Profits are equal to the difference between a firm's revenue from the sale of its product and the costs of producing that product: profit = total revenue − total cost.

So far, we have looked only at costs, but costs are just one part of the profit equation. To complete the picture, we must turn to the output market and see how these costs compare with the price that a product commands in the market. Before we do so, however, it is important to consolidate what we have said about costs.

Before a firm does anything else, it needs to know the different methods that it can use to produce its product. The technologies available determine the combinations of inputs that are needed to produce each level of output. Firms choose the technique that produces the desired level of output at the least cost. The cost curves that result from the analysis of all this information show the cost of producing each level of output using the best available technology.

Remember that so far, we have talked only about short-run costs. The curves we have drawn are therefore *short-run cost curves*. The shape of these curves comes largely from the diminishing

TABLE 8.5	A Summary of Cost Concepts	
Term	Definition	Equation
Accounting costs	Out-of-pocket costs or costs as an accountant would define them. Sometimes referred to as *explicit costs*.	—
Economic costs	Costs that include the full opportunity costs of all inputs. These include what are often called *implicit costs*.	—
Total fixed costs (*TFC*)	Costs that do not depend on the quantity of output produced. These must be paid even if output is zero.	—
Total variable costs (*TVC*)	Costs that vary with the level of output.	—
Total cost (*TC*)	The total economic cost of all the inputs used by a firm in production.	$TC = TFC + TVC$
Average fixed costs (*AFC*)	Fixed costs per unit of output.	$AFC = TFC/q$
Average variable costs (*AVC*)	Variable costs per unit of output.	$AVC = TVC/q$
Average total costs (*ATC*)	Total costs per unit of output.	$ATC = TC/q$ $ATC = AFC + AVC$
Marginal costs (*MC*)	The increase in total cost that results from producing 1 additional unit of output.	$MC = \Delta TC/\Delta q$

returns created by the fixed factor of production With diminishing returns, marginal costs eventually rise and average cost curves are likely to be U-shaped. Table 8.5 summarizes the cost concepts that we have discussed.

After gaining a complete knowledge of how to produce a product and how much it will cost to produce it at each level of output, the firm turns to the market to find out what it can sell its product for. We now turn our attention to the output market.

Output Decisions: Revenues, Costs, and Profit Maximization

To calculate potential profits, firms must combine their cost analyses with information on potential revenues from sales. After all, if a firm cannot sell its product for more than the cost of production, it will not be in business long. In contrast, if the market gives the firm a price that is significantly greater than the cost it incurs to produce a unit of its product, the firm may have an incentive to expand output. Large profits might also attract new competitors to the market.

Let us now examine in detail how a firm goes about determining how much output to produce. We will begin by examining the decisions of a perfectly competitive firm.

Perfect Competition

Perfect competition exists in an industry that contains many relatively small firms producing identical or **homogeneous products**. In a perfectly competitive industry, no single firm has any control over prices. Of course, we do not mean that firms cannot affix price tags to their merchandise; all firms have this ability. We mean that given the availability of perfect substitutes, any product priced over the market price will not be sold. Prices are set not by an individual firm, but by the interaction of all firms in the industry in ways we will shortly describe. As a result, we say that competitive firms are "price takers" in the marketplace.

Discuss how revenues and costs affect the profit-maximizing levels of output in perfectly competitive firms.

perfect competition An industry structure in which there are many firms, each small relative to the industry, producing identical products and in which no firm is large enough to have any control over prices. In perfectly competitive industries, new competitors can freely enter the market and old firms can exit.

homogeneous products Undifferentiated products; products that are identical to, or indistinguishable from, one another.

These assumptions limit the decisions open to competitive firms and simplify the analysis of competitive behavior. Firms in perfectly competitive industries do not differentiate their products and do not make decisions about price. Instead, each firm takes prices as given—that is, as determined in the market by the laws of supply and demand—and decides only how much to produce and how to produce it.

Our description of the competitive firm as a price taker also tells us that the firm faces a perfectly elastic demand curve for *its individual* product. Consider the Ohio corn farmer whose situation is shown in Figure 8.9. The left side of the diagram represents the current conditions in the market. Corn is currently selling for $5.00 per bushel.[1] The right side of the diagram shows the demand for *this individual farmer's corn*. If she were to raise her price, she would sell no corn at all; because there are perfect substitutes available, the quantity demanded of her corn would drop to zero. To lower her price would be silly because she can sell all she wants at the current price. (Remember, each farmer's production is small relative to the entire corn market.) Notice that the demand for corn as a whole is downward sloping; higher prices cut consumption somewhat but do not reduce corn consumption to zero. Although there are substitutes for corn as a category, these substitutes (like peas) are not perfect. For the individual farmer, another farmer's corn is a perfect substitute and this gives rise to the perfectly elastic demand curve. It is important to distinguish the firm or individual from the market as a whole.

In perfect competition, we also assume easy entry and exit in the long run—that firms can easily enter and exit the industry. We will discuss this feature of competition in the next chapter as we look at the long run.

Total Revenue and Marginal Revenue

total revenue (*TR*) The total amount that a firm takes in from the sale of its product: the price per unit times the quantity of output the firm decides to produce (*P* × *q*).

Profit is the difference between total revenue and total cost. **Total revenue (*TR*)** is the total amount that a firm takes in from the sale of its product. A perfectly competitive firm sells each unit of product for the same price, the market price, regardless of the individual output level it has chosen. Therefore, a firm's total revenue is simply the price per unit times the quantity of output that it produces:

$$\text{total revenue} = \text{price} \times \text{quantity}$$
$$TR = P \times q$$

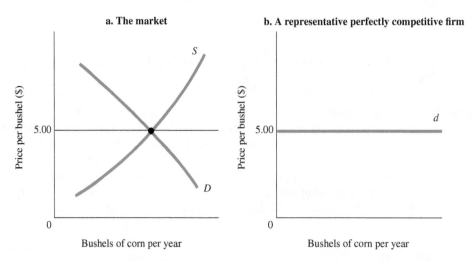

a. The market

b. A representative perfectly competitive firm

▲ FIGURE 8.9 **Demand Facing a Single Firm in a Perfectly Competitive Market**
If a representative firm in a perfectly competitive market raises the price of its output above $5.00, the quantity demanded of *that firm's* output will drop to zero. Each firm faces a perfectly elastic demand curve, *d*.

[1] Capital letters refer to the entire market, and lowercase letters refer to representative firms. For example, in Figure 8.9, the market demand curve is labeled *D* and the demand curve facing the firm is labeled *d*.

Marginal revenue (MR) is the added revenue that a firm takes in when it increases output by 1 additional unit. If a firm producing 100 units of output per month increases that output to 101 units per month, that added unit will increase the firm's revenue. If the market price for this product is $5.00 per unit, then the increase in revenue from one unit, or the marginal revenue, will be $5.00. For a competitive firm, marginal revenue is equal to the current market price of each additional unit sold.

A firm's *marginal revenue curve* shows how much revenue the firm will gain by raising output by 1 unit at every level of output. The *marginal revenue curve and the demand curve facing a competitive firm are identical*. The horizontal line in Figure 8.9(b) can be thought of as both the demand curve facing the firm and its marginal revenue curve:

$$P* = d = MR$$

marginal revenue (MR)   The additional revenue that a firm takes in when it increases output by one additional unit. In perfect competition, the marginal revenue is equal to the price.

Comparing Costs and Revenues to Maximize Profit

The discussion in the next few paragraphs conveys one of the most important concepts in all of microeconomics. As we pursue our analysis, remember that we are working under two assumptions: (1) that the industry we are examining is perfectly competitive and (2) that firms choose the level of output that yields the maximum total profit.

The Profit-Maximizing Level of Output   Look carefully at the graphs in Figure 8.10. Once again, we have the whole market, or industry, on the left and a single, typical small firm—one of the 1,000 firms in the industry—on the right. And again the current market price is $P*$.

The firm observes the market price (Figure 8.10[a]) and knows that it can sell all that it wants for $P* = \$5.00$ per unit. How much should it produce? The goal of the firm is to choose an output level that leaves it with the maximum profit possible. Let us start by looking at an output level of 100 units and ask whether expanding beyond that level would make us better off.

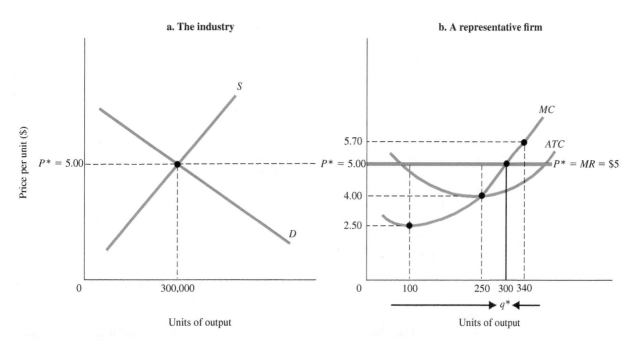

▲ FIGURE 8.10   **The Profit-Maximizing Level of Output for a Perfectly Competitive Firm**
If price is above marginal cost, as it is at every quantity less than 300 units of output, profits can be increased by raising output; each additional unit increases revenues by more than it costs to produce the additional output because $P > MC$. Beyond $q* = 300$, however, added output will reduce profits. At 340 units of output, an additional unit of output costs more to produce than it will bring in revenue when sold on the market. Profit-maximizing output is thus $q*$, the point at which $P = MC$.

Our goal is to maximize the difference between total revenue and total cost, which is equivalent to maximizing profits. What happens to profits as we move from 100 to 101 units? Think about the 101st unit. Adding that single unit to production each period adds $5.00 to revenues but adds only about $2.50 to cost. Profits each period would be higher by about $2.50. Thus, the optimal (profit-maximizing) level of output is clearly higher than 100 units.

What are we doing in this example as we try to find the optimal output? We are thinking about each possible incremental unit and asking whether it adds more to revenue than it does to cost. In other words, we compare the marginal revenue of a unit with its marginal cost. If a unit's marginal revenue exceeds its marginal costs, our profits will rise if we produce that unit. If marginal costs exceed marginal revenue, producing that unit will cause profits to decline.

Now look at an output level of 250 units. Here, once again, raising output increases profit. The revenue gained from producing the 251st unit (marginal revenue) is still $5.00, and the cost of the 251st unit (marginal cost) is only about $4. Although the difference between marginal revenue and marginal cost is shrinking, it is still positive and for that reason added output means added profit. Whenever marginal revenue exceeds marginal cost, the revenue gained by increasing output by 1 unit per period exceeds the cost incurred by doing so. This logic leads us to conclude that the optimal, profit maximizing level of output is 300 units. At 300 units, marginal cost has risen to $5.00 and $P^* = MR = MC = \$5.00$. Notice that since the competitive firm's marginal revenue is equal to its price, we can write the profit-maximizing condition as either choose output such that $MR = MC$ or $P = MC$.

Notice that if the firm were to produce *more* than 300 units, marginal cost would rise above marginal revenue. At 340 units of output, for example, the cost of the 341st unit is about $5.70, whereas that added unit of output still brings in only $5.00 in revenue, thus reducing profit. It simply does not pay to increase output above the point where marginal cost rises above marginal revenue because such increases will *reduce* profit. The profit-maximizing perfectly competitive firm will produce up to the point where the price of its output is just equal to short-run marginal cost—the level of output at which $P^* = MC$. Thus, in Figure 8.10, the profit-maximizing level of output, q^*, is 300 units.

You have likely noticed that at the optimum output level of 300 units, the firm's average total costs are not as low as they could be (those costs are lowest at 250 units). We will return to this issue next chapter.

Important note: The key idea here is that firms will produce as long as marginal revenue exceeds marginal cost. When marginal cost rises smoothly, as it does in Figure 8.10, the profit-maximizing condition is that *MR* (or *P*) *exactly equals* MC. If marginal cost moves up in increments—as it does in the following numerical example—marginal revenue or price may not exactly equal marginal cost at a whole integer value. Optimal output will be a fractional unit, if possible. The key idea of finding output where $P = MC$ still holds.

A Numerical Example Table 8.6 presents some data for a hypothetical firm. The market has set a $15 unit price for the firm's product. Total revenue in column 6 is the product $p \times q$ (the numbers in column 1 times $15). The table derives total, marginal, and average costs exactly as Table 8.4 did. Here, however, we have included revenues, and we can calculate the profit, which is shown in column 8.

Column 8 shows that a profit-maximizing firm would choose to produce 4 units of output assuming the firm produces only whole units. At this level, profits are $20. At all other output levels, they are lower. Now let us see if "marginal" reasoning leads us to the same conclusion.

First, should the firm produce at all? If it produces nothing, it suffers losses equal to $10. If it increases output to 1 unit, marginal revenue is $15 (remember that it sells each unit for $15) and marginal cost is $10. Thus, it gains $5, reducing its loss from $10 each period to $5.

Should the firm increase output to 2 units? The marginal revenue from the second unit is again $15, but the marginal cost is only $5. Thus, by producing the second unit, the firm gains $10 ($15 − $5) and turns a $5 loss into a $5 profit. The third unit adds $10 to profits. Again, marginal revenue is $15 and marginal cost is $5, an increase in profit of $10, for a total profit of $15.

The fourth unit offers still more profit. Price is still above marginal cost, which means that producing that fourth unit will increase profits. Price, or marginal revenue, is $15, and marginal cost is just $10. Thus, the fourth unit adds $5 to profit. At unit number five, however, diminishing returns push marginal cost above price. The marginal revenue from producing the fifth unit

(1)	(2)	(3)	(4)	(5)	(6) TR	(7) TC	(8) Profit
q	TFC	TVC	MC	P = MR	(P × q)	(TFC + TVC)	(TR − TC)
0	$10	$ 0	$−	$15	$ 0	$10	$−10
1	10	10	10	15	15	20	− 5
2	10	15	5	15	30	25	5
3	10	20	5	15	45	30	15
4	10	30	10	15	60	40	20
5	10	50	20	15	75	60	15
6	10	80	30	15	90	90	0

is $15, whereas marginal cost is now $20. As a result, profit per period drops by $5, to $15 per period. Clearly, the firm will not produce the fifth unit. If firms can produce fractional units, it is optimal to produce between 4 and 5 units. The profit-maximizing level of output is thus between 4 and 5 units. The firm continues to increase output as long as price (marginal revenue) is greater than marginal cost.

The Short-Run Supply Curve

In the preceding numerical example, we determined how much a firm would produce by comparing its marginal cost with the price it would receive for its output. Let us now return to the simpler firm graphed in Figure 8.10 on page 177 to see how a firm responds to changes in the prices it faces.

Figure 8.11b replicates Figure 8.10b with a fuller range of values noted so that we can look at the effect of a price change. As we noted previously, at a price of $5.00, this firm produces 300 units and the industry of 1,000 firms produces in total 300,000 units. On the left panel, Figure 8.11a, we see that

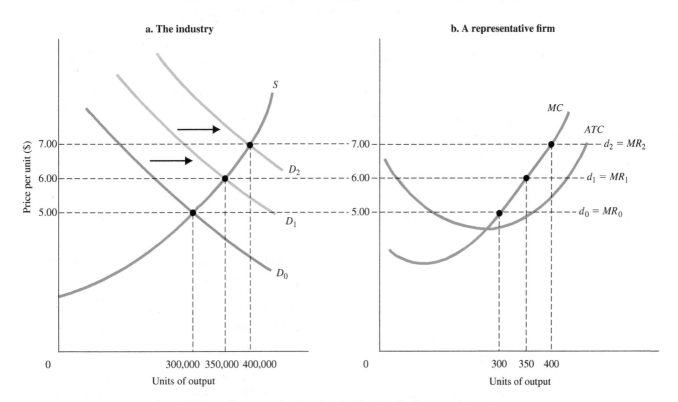

a. The industry   **b. A representative firm**

▲ FIGURE 8.11   **Marginal Cost Is the Supply Curve of a Perfectly Competitive Firm**
At any market price,[a] the marginal cost curve shows the output level that maximizes profit. Thus, the marginal cost curve of a perfectly competitive profit-maximizing firm is the firm's short-run supply curve.

[a] This is true except when price is so low that it benefits a firm to shut down—a point that will be discussed in Chapter 9.

with demand at level D_0 that level of production is an equilibrium in that demand just equals supply at the $5.00 price. At a price of $5.00; the firm *supplied* 300 units and the industry *supplied* 300,000 units, so the point $5.00, 300 is on the firm's supply curve, and the point $5.00, 300,000 is on the industry's supply curve. If demand now shifts to D_1 and the price rises, the firm will find it worthwhile to increase output. Its marginal cost curve tells us that if the price rises to $6.00, this firm—and all the other firms like this firm will produce 350 units. So at a price of $6.00, the industry output is 350,000. And at a price of $7.00, output rises for the firm to 400 and for the industry to 400,000.

All of these are points on the supply curve of the firm because they tell us how much the firm will supply at each price. What determines the firm's willingness to supply various levels of output at these prices? Its marginal cost curve. In fact, the marginal cost curve of the competitive firm is the firm's short-run supply curve, and the industry supply curve is derived from these firm supply curves.

We will return to this story in the next chapter as we turn to look at long-run costs. There we will spell out the dynamics of price changes and also consider an important exception to the rule that the firm's supply curve is its marginal cost curve, which is when a firm decides to shut down.

Looking Ahead

At the beginning of this chapter, we set out to combine information on technology, factor prices, and output prices to understand the supply curve of a competitive firm. We have now accomplished that goal.

Because marginal cost is such an important concept in microeconomics, you should carefully review any sections of this chapter that were unclear to you. Above all, keep in mind that the *marginal cost curve* carries information about both *input prices* and *technology*. The firm looks to output markets for information on potential revenues, and the current market price defines the competitive firm's marginal revenue curve. The point where price (which is equal to marginal revenue in perfect competition) is just equal to marginal cost is the perfectly competitive firm's profit-maximizing level of output. Thus, with one important exception we will examine in the next chapter, the marginal cost curve *is* the perfectly competitive firm's supply curve in the short run.

In the next chapter, we turn to the long run. What happens when firms are free to choose their scale of operations without being limited by a fixed factor of production? Without diminishing returns that set in as a result of a fixed scale of production, what determines the shape of cost curves? What happens when new firms can enter industries in which profits are being earned? How do industries adjust when losses are being incurred? How does the structure of an industry evolve over time?

SUMMARY
---

1. Profit-maximizing firms make decisions to maximize profit (total revenue minus total cost).

2. To calculate production costs, firms must know two things: (1) the quantity and combination of inputs they need to produce their product and (2) the cost of those inputs.

8.1 COSTS IN THE SHORT RUN *p. 165*

3. *Fixed costs* are costs that do not change with a firm's output. In the short run, firms cannot avoid fixed costs or change them even if production is zero.

4. *Variable costs* are those costs that depend on the level of output chosen. Fixed costs plus variable costs equal *total costs* ($TC = TFC + TVC$).

5. *Average fixed cost* (AFC) is total fixed cost divided by the quantity of output. As output rises, average fixed cost declines steadily because the same total is being spread over a larger and larger quantity of output. This phenomenon is called *spreading overhead*.

6. Numerous combinations of inputs can be used to produce a given level of output. The least-cost combinations are optimal. *Total variable cost* (TVC) is the sum of all costs that vary with output in the short run.

7. *Marginal cost* (MC) is the increase in total cost that results from the production of 1 more unit of output. If a firm is producing 1,000 units, the additional cost of increasing output to 1,001 units is marginal cost. Marginal cost measures the cost of the additional inputs required to produce each

successive unit of output. Because fixed costs do not change when output changes, marginal costs reflect only changes in variable costs.

8. In the short run, a firm is limited by a fixed factor of production or a fixed scale of a plant. As a firm increases output, it will eventually find itself trapped by that scale. Because of the fixed scale, marginal cost eventually rises with output.

9. Marginal cost is the slope of the total variable cost curve. The total variable cost curve always has a positive slope because total variable costs always rise with output. However, increasing marginal cost means that total variable costs and therefore total costs ultimately rise at an increasing rate.

10. *Average variable cost* (AVC) is equal to total variable cost divided by the quantity of output.

11. When marginal cost is above average variable cost, average variable cost is *increasing*. When marginal cost is below average variable cost, average variable cost is *declining*. Marginal cost intersects average variable cost at AVC's minimum point.

12. *Average total cost* (ATC) is equal to total cost divided by the quantity of output. It is also equal to the sum of average fixed cost and average variable cost.

13. When marginal cost is below average total cost, average total cost is declining toward marginal cost. When marginal cost is above average total cost, average total cost is increasing. Marginal cost intersects average total cost at ATC's minimum point.

8.2 OUTPUT DECISIONS: REVENUES, COSTS, AND PROFIT MAXIMIZATION *p. 175*

14. A perfectly competitive firm faces a demand curve that is a horizontal line (in other words, perfectly elastic demand).

15. *Total revenue* (TR) is simply price times the quantity of output that a firm decides to produce and sell. *Marginal revenue* (MR) is the additional revenue that a firm takes in when it increases output by 1 unit.

16. For a perfectly competitive firm, marginal revenue is equal to the current market price of its product.

17. A profit-maximizing firm in a perfectly competitive industry will produce up to the point at which the price of its output is just equal to short-run marginal cost: $P = MC$. The more general profit-maximizing formula is $MR = MC$ (where $P = MR$ in perfect competition). The marginal cost curve of a perfectly competitive firm is the firm's short-run supply curve, with one exception (discussed in Chapter 9).

—————— REVIEW TERMS AND CONCEPTS ——————

average fixed cost (AFC), *p. 166*

average total cost (ATC), *p. 173*

average variable cost (AVC), *p. 171*

fixed cost, *p. 165*

homogeneous products, *p. 175*

marginal cost (MC), *p. 168*

marginal revenue (MR), *p. 177*

perfect competition, *p. 175*

spreading overhead, *p. 167*

total cost (TC), *p. 165*

total fixed costs (TFC) *or* overhead, *p. 166*

total revenue (TR), *p. 176*

total variable cost (TVC), *p. 167*

total variable cost curve, *p. 167*

variable cost, *p. 165*

Equations:

$TC = TFC + TVC$, *p. 165*

$AFC = TFC/q$, *p. 166*

Slope of $TVC = MC$, *p. 170*

$AVC = TVC/q$, *p. 171*

$ATC = TC/q = AFC + AVC$, *p. 173*

$TR = P \times q$, *p. 176*

Profit-maximizing level of output for all firms: $MR = MC$, *p. 178*

Profit-maximizing level of output for perfectly competitive firms: $P = MC$, *p. 178*

—————— PROBLEMS ——————

All problems are available on MyEconLab.

8.1 COSTS IN THE SHORT RUN

LEARNING OBJECTIVE: Be able to describe and graph the major components of firm cost.

1.1 Consider the following costs of owning and operating a car. An $18,000 Fiat 500 Pop financed over 60 months at 4 percent interest means a monthly payment of $331.50. Insurance costs $120 a month regardless of how much you drive. The car gets 35 miles per gallon and uses regular-grade gasoline that costs $2.60 per gallon. Finally, suppose that wear and tear on the car costs about 20 cents a mile. Which costs are fixed, and which

are variable? What is the marginal cost of a mile driven? In deciding whether to drive from Atlanta to Las Vegas (about 2,000 miles round-trip), which costs would you consider? Why?

1.2 As of June 2014, John Green's international bestselling novel, *The Fault in Our Stars*, had sold more than 10.7 million copies. In book publishing, fixed costs are high and marginal costs are low and fairly constant. Suppose that the fixed cost of producing *The Fault in Our Stars* is $4 million. What is the *average fixed cost* if the publisher produces 1 million copies? 5 million copies? 15 million copies?

Now suppose that the marginal cost of the print version of *The Fault in Our Stars* is $2.50 per book and is the same for each book up to 20 million copies. Assume that this includes all variable costs. Explain why in this case marginal cost (MC) is a horizontal line, as is average variable cost (AVC). What is the *average total cost* of the book if the publisher produces 1 million copies? 5 million copies? 15 million copies?

Sketch the average fixed cost (AFC) curve and the average total cost (ATC) curve facing the publisher.

1.3 While charging a general admission price of $15 for adults most days of the week, the Museum of Fine Arts in Houston offers free admission every Thursday. Why do you suppose that museums often price this way, offering free admission on one day during the week? Why would they choose a day like Thursday rather than Saturday?

1.4 The following table gives capital and labor requirements for 10 different levels of production.

q	K	L
0	0	0
1	6	1
2	10	3
3	13	5
4	16	7
5	20	9
6	25	11
7	31	13
8	38	15
9	46	17
10	55	19

a. Assuming that the price of labor (P_L) is $6 per unit and the price of capital (P_K) is $4 per unit, compute and graph total cost, marginal cost, and average variable cost for the firm.
b. Do the graphs have the shapes that you might expect? Explain.
c. Using the numbers here, explain the relationship between marginal cost and average variable cost.
d. Using the numbers here, explain the meaning of "marginal cost" in terms of additional inputs needed to produce a marginal unit of output.

1.5 For each of the following businesses, what is the likely fixed factor of production that defines the short run?
a. Golf course
b. Movie theater
c. Law office
d. Brewery
e. Amusement park

1.6 Explain which of the following is a fixed cost or a variable cost for General Motors.
a. The cost of aluminum used for its automobiles.
b. The property taxes on its Bowling Green, Kentucky assembly plant.

c. The cost of labor for its assembly line workers.
d. The yearly payments for the naming rights for the General Motors Centre sports arena in Oshawa, Ontario, Canada
e. The salary paid to Mary Barra, the Chief Executive Officer of General Motors.
f. The cost of tires it purchases from Goodyear for its trucks and SUVs.

1.7 Use the information in the graph to find the values for the following costs at an output level of 500.
a. Total fixed cost
b. Total variable cost
c. Total cost
d. Marginal cost

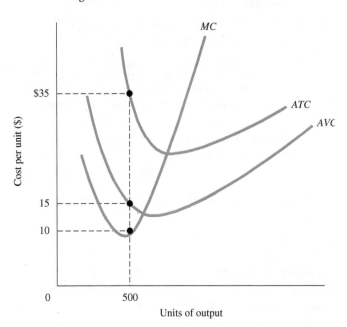

1.8 Explain how the following events would affect the cost curves in the graph from the previous question.
a. Hourly wages for employees increase.
b. The company signs a new 3-year contract with its landlord, which lowers its monthly rent by 10 percent.
c. The company employs a new technology, which lowers its utility costs.
d. The company receives notice of a 5 percent increase in its property insurance rate.
e. The company's primary supplier of resources implements a 3 percent price increase for all of its supplies.

1.9 Evaluate the following statement. If the total variable cost of production is the sum of the marginal cost of each additional unit of output, we can calculate the marginal cost by taking the total variable cost of production and dividing it by the quantity of output produced.

8.2 OUTPUT DECISIONS: REVENUES, COSTS, AND PROFIT MAXIMIZATION

LEARNING OBJECTIVE: Discuss how revenues and costs affect the profit-maximizing levels of output in perfectly competitive firms.

2.1 [**Related to the *Economics in Practice* on p. 172**] In addition to gambling, Las Vegas is famous for its live production shows. Close to 100 shows are performed at various venues across the city on any given day, and many of the shows are multi-million dollar productions with months-long waiting lists for the best seats. Box office ticket prices range from less than $10 for a few of the smaller shows to over $200 for some of the major productions. In recent years, a number of these shows have begun offering tickets for sale at half price through discount ticket outlets. These half-price tickets are only available on the day of the show, on a first-come, first-served basis. Using the concept of marginal cost, explain why many of these productions have begun to offer these half-price tickets. Who do you suppose are the most- and least-likely customers to purchase show tickets through these discount ticket outlets? Can you think of any reasons why a production show would choose to not offer tickets in this manner?

2.2 Do you agree or disagree with this statement? Firms minimize costs; thus, a firm earning short-run economic profits will choose to produce at the minimum point on its average total cost curve.

2.3 You are given the following cost data:
Total fixed costs are $60.

q	TVC
0	0
1	25
2	40
3	60
4	90
5	130
6	185

How many units of output will this firm produce at a price of $22 and at a price of $42? What is the total revenue and total cost at each price? What is the profit at each price? Briefly explain using the concept of marginal cost.

2.4 Do you agree or disagree with each of the following statements? Explain your reasons.
a. For a competitive firm facing a market price above average total cost, the existence of economic profits means that the firm should increase output in the short run even if price is below marginal cost.
b. If marginal cost is rising with increasing output, average cost must also be rising.

c. Fixed cost is constant at every level of output except zero. When a firm produces no output, fixed costs are zero in the short run.

2.5 A firm's costs are given in the following table.

q	TC	TFC	TVC	AVC	ATC	MC
0	$50	—	—	—	—	—
1	70	—	—	—	—	—
2	80	—	—	—	—	—
3	90	—	—	—	—	—
4	110	—	—	—	—	—
5	140	—	—	—	—	—
6	175	—	—	—	—	—
7	220	—	—	—	—	—
8	280	—	—	—	—	—
9	360	—	—	—	—	—
10	450	—	—	—	—	—

a. Complete the table.
b. Graph AVC, ATC, and MC on the same graph. What is the relationship between MC and ATC and between MC and AVC?
c. Suppose market price is $20. How much will the firm produce in the short run? How much are total profits?
d. Suppose market price is $60. How much will the firm produce in the short run? What are total profits?

2.6 Isabel runs her family's small pineapple processing plant, which takes fresh pineapples and cuts them into pineapple rings, spears, and chunks. The capital stock of the firm consists of three machines of various vintages, each of which can process the pineapples into any of the three different forms. All of the machines are in excellent condition, and all machines can be running at the same time.

	Cost of Processing per Pineapple	Maximum Total Capacity (Pineapples) per Day
Machine 1	$ 0.10	250
Machine 2	0.25	400
Machine 3	0.50	500

a. Assume that "cost of processing" includes *all* labor and materials, including the owner's wages. Assume further that Isabel's family signed a long-term contract (20 years) with a service company to keep the machines in good repair for a fixed fee of $1,825 per year, or $5 per day.
(1) Derive the firm's marginal cost curve.
(2) Derive the firm's total cost curve.
b. At a price of $0.40, how many pineapples would the company process? What would total revenues, total costs, and total profits be?

2.7 The following is a total cost curve. Sketch the corresponding marginal cost curve. If the price of output is $3 and there are no fixed costs, what is the profit-maximizing level of output?

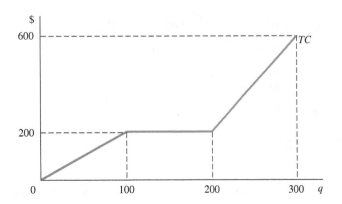

2.8 The following curve is a production function for a firm that uses just one variable factor of production, labor. It shows total output, or product, for every level of labor input.
   a. Derive and graph the marginal product curve.
   b. Suppose the wage rate is $4. Derive and graph the firm's marginal cost curve.
   c. If output sells for $6, what is the profit-maximizing level of output? How much labor will the firm hire?

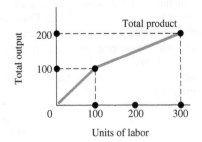

2.9 Fill in the columns in the following table. What quantity should a profit-maximizing firm produce? Verify your answer with marginal reasoning.

q	TFC	TVC	MC	$P = MR$	TR	TC	Profit
0	$5	$ 0		$5			
1	5	3		5			
2	5	5		5			
3	5	9		5			
4	5	16		5			
5	5	25		5			
6	5	36		5			

2.10 Use the information from your answer to the previous question to construct a rough plot showing marginal revenue, marginal cost, and average total cost. Also identify the profit-maximizing quantity of output on the graph. You will have to calculate average total cost from the information in the table.

2.11 Marginal cost represents the increase in total cost that results from producing one more unit of output. Marginal product represents the additional output that can be produced by adding one more unit of a specific input, holding all other inputs constant. What does this imply about the relationship between marginal cost and marginal product?

Long-Run Costs and Output Decisions

9

The last two chapters discussed the behavior of profit-maximizing competitive firms in the short run. In Chapter 8 we saw how cost curves can be derived from production functions and input prices. Once a firm has a clear picture of its short-run costs, the price at which it sells its output determines the quantity of output that will maximize profits. Specifically, a profit-maximizing perfectly competitive firm will supply output up to the point that price (marginal revenue)

equals marginal cost. The marginal cost curve of such a firm is thus the same as its supply curve.

In this chapter we turn from the short run to the long run. A firm's short-run position (Are they making profits? Are they incurring losses?) determines what is likely to happen in the long run. Output (supply) decisions in the long run are less constrained than in the short run, for two reasons. First, in the long run firms can choose their scale of plant; the firm can increase any or all of its inputs and thus has no fixed factor of production that confines its production to a given scale. Second, firms are free to enter industries to seek profits and to leave industries to avoid losses.

In thinking about the relationship between the short run and long run, it is useful to put yourself in the position of a manager of a firm. At times, you will be making what we term *short-run* decisions: You are stuck with a particular factory and set of machines, and your decisions involve asking how best to use those assets to produce output. At the same time, you or another manager at the firm will be doing more strategic *long-run* thinking: Should you be in this business at all, or should you close up shop? In better times, you might consider expanding the operation. In thinking about the long run, you will also have to reckon with other firms entering and exiting the industry. Managers simultaneously make short- and long-run decisions, making the best of the current constraints while planning for the future.

In making decisions or understanding industry structure, costs are important. As we saw in the short run, a fixed factor of production eventually causes marginal cost to increase along with output. In the long run, all factors can be varied. Under these circumstances, it is no longer inevitable that increased volume comes with higher costs. In fact, as we will see, long-run cost curves need not slope up at all. You might have wondered why there are only a few automobile and steel companies in the United States but dozens of firms producing software apps and furniture. Differences in the shapes of the long-run cost curves in those industries do a good job of explaining these differences in the industry structures.

We begin our discussion of the long run by looking at firms in three short-run circumstances: (1) firms that earn economic profits, (2) firms that suffer economic losses but continue to operate to reduce or minimize those losses, and (3) firms that decide to shut down and bear losses just equal to fixed costs. We then examine how these firms make their long-run decisions in response to conditions in their markets.

Although we continue to focus on perfectly competitive firms, *all* firms are subject to the spectrum of short-run profit or loss situations regardless of *market structure*. Assuming perfect competition allows us to simplify our analysis and provides us with a strong background for understanding the discussions of imperfectly competitive behavior in later chapters.

9.1 LEARNING OBJECTIVE

Discuss how short-run conditions affect a firm's short-run and long-run behavior.

Short-Run Conditions and Long-Run Directions

Before beginning our examination of firm behavior, let us review the concept of profit. Recall that a normal rate of return is included in the definition of total cost (Chapter 7). Because we define *profit* as total revenue minus total cost and because total cost includes a normal rate of return, our concept of profit takes into account the opportunity cost of capital. When a firm is earning an above-normal rate of return, it has a positive profit level and, as a result, new firms are likely to be attracted to the industry. When firms earn below normal rates of return, they tend to leave the industry seeking profits elsewhere. A firm that is **breaking even**, or earning a zero level of profit, is one that is earning exactly a normal rate of return. New investors are not attracted, but current ones are not running away either.

breaking even   The situation in which a firm is earning exactly a normal rate of return.

With these distinctions in mind, we can say that for any firm, one of three conditions holds at any given moment: (1) The firm is making positive profits, (2) the firm is suffering losses, or (3) the firm is just breaking even. Each of these conditions leads firms and industry to different long run actions,which we will now explore.

Maximizing Profits

The best way to understand the behavior of a firm that is currently earning economic profits is by way of example.

Example: The Blue Velvet Car Wash   Let us consider as an example the Blue Velvet Car Wash. Looking at a few numbers will help you see how the specifics of a business operation translate into action by managers.

Car washes require a facility. In the case of Blue Velvet, suppose the owners have put up $500,000 to construct a building and purchase all the equipment required to wash cars. If the car wash closes, the building and equipment can be sold for its original purchase price, but as long as the firm is in business, that capital is tied up. If the investors could get 10 percent return on their investment in another business, then for them to keep their money in this business, they will also expect 10 percent from Blue Velvet. Thus, the annual cost of the capital needed for the business is $50,000 (10 percent of $500,000).

The car wash is currently servicing 800 cars a week and can be open 50 weeks a year (2 weeks are needed for maintenance). The cost of the basic maintenance contract on the equipment is $50,000 per year, and Blue Velvet has a contract to pay for those services for a year whether it opens the car wash or not. The fixed costs then for the car wash are $100,000 per year: $50,000 for the capital costs and $50,000 for the equipment contract. On a weekly basis, these costs amount to $2,000 per week. If the car wash operates at the level of 800 cars per week, fixed costs are $2.50 per car ($2,000/800).

There are also variable costs associated with the business. To run a car wash, one needs workers and soap and water. Workers can be hired by the hour for $10.00 an hour, and at a customer level of 800 cars per week, on average a worker can wash 8 cars an hour. At this service level, then, Blue Velvet hires 100 hours worth of workers and has a wage bill of $1,000. The labor cost of each car wash, when Blue Velvet serves 800 customers, is $1.25 ($10/8).

The number of cars each worker can service depends on the number of cars being worked on. When there is too little business and few workers, no specialization is possible and cars washed per worker fall. With many cars to service, workers start getting in one another's way. We saw that at 800 cars per week, workers could wash an average of 8 cars per hour. If the facility tries to expand the number of cars served beyond this level, there will be a dramatic reduction in

TABLE 9.1   Blue Velvet Car Wash Weekly Costs

TFC Total Fixed Cost		TVC Total Variable Cost (800 Washes)		TC Total Cost (800 Washes)	TR Total Revenue (P = \$5)
1. Normal return to investors	\$ 1,000	1. Labor 2. Soap	\$ 1,000 600	$TC = TFC + TVC$ $= \$2,000 + \$1,600$ $= \$3,600$	$TR = \$5 \times 800$ $= \$4,000$
2. Other fixed costs (maintenance contract)			**\$ 1,600**		$Profit = TR - TC$ $= \$400$
	1,000 **\$ 2,000**				

worker productivity. As we will see when we look at the graphs, worker productivity is higher at somewhat lower volumes of car washes.

Every car that is washed costs \$0.75 in soap, adding \$600 to the weekly bill if 800 car washes are done. Table 9.1 summarizes the costs of Blue Velvet at the 800 washes per week level.

The market price for car washes in Blue Velvet's neighborhood is \$5. Blue Velvet is just like every other car wash in the area and so cannot charge any more than \$5 or all the customers will go elsewhere. At a price of \$5, we see that Blue Velvet is making money in excess of all of its costs, including the opportunity cost of its capital investment in the business (the \$1,000 per week). At a high price like \$5, excess profits are earned. At this price, the owners of Blue Velvet—and other car wash entrepreneurs in the area—are likely to start thinking about expanding, given that they are reaping excess returns.

What happens when the price falls? Eventually, as prices fall, the firm's excess profits also fall. At some point, prices fall enough that even if they make all the adjustments they can in terms of service levels, price will be less than the firm's average total costs. At this point, Blue Velvet's owners may start to think about closing their business in the *long run*. But in the *short run*, Blue Velvet's owners face a hard choice: If they shut down, they lose the \$1,000 per week that they have contracted to spend on the maintenance contract and still will not be able to recover their investment in the building, given that selling that building will likely take some time. If Blue Velvet can *lose less* than \$2,000 per week (their weekly fixed costs) by operating, then they should continue to do so. When the price falls below average variable cost, then the firm is better off shutting down. For Blue Velvet to produce at all, the price must at least cover the \$0.75 for soap per car and the labor costs.

In the short run, then, there are a range of prices that we might see in the marketplace and at which Blue Velvet will continue to produce. In the short run, when owners cannot exit a business, they will do the best they can and minimize losses. When times are good, they may earn excess returns. But when prices are either very high or very low, managers start to think about long-run strategy. At a price of \$5, our managers were starting to think about expanding their business, maybe buying a plot of land next door and building a new facility. When the price falls below average total cost, and they begin to lose money, they soon think of leaving the business.

Later in this chapter, we look at what happens as managers begin to think about these longer-run decisions. But first, we will look at a graphical presentation for the general case of firms making short-run decisions as prices move from super-normal levels, generating excess returns, down to the point at which they shut down completely, even in the short run.

Graphic Presentation   Figure 9.1 graphs the performance of an industry and a representative firm at a point in which prices are high enough that it is earning excess returns.

The industry price is \$5.00, and there are 10 firms producing 800 units each in a competitive marketplace all earning economic profits. There are three key cost curves shown in the graph. The average variable cost (AVC) curve shows what happens to the per unit costs of workers and the other variable factors as we change output. In this example, we see that worker productivity improves at first as we expand output, driving the AVC down, but productivity then declines as diminishing returns set in, driving the AVC up. Now look at

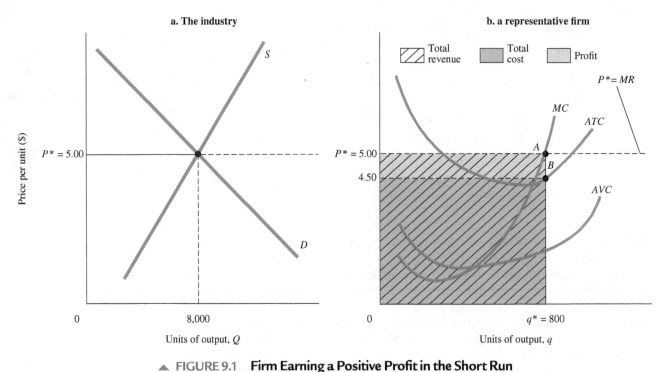

a. The industry

b. a representative firm

▲ FIGURE 9.1 **Firm Earning a Positive Profit in the Short Run**
A profit-maximizing perfectly competitive firm will produce up to the point where $P^* = MC$. Profit is the difference between total revenue and total cost. At $q^* = 800$, total revenue is $\$5.00 \times 800 = \$4,000$, total cost is $\$4.50 \times 800 = \$3,600$, and profit $= \$4,000 - \$3,600 = \$400$.

the average total cost (ATC) curve. The average total cost curve falls at first in response to the spreading of the fixed costs over more and more units and eventually begins to rise as the inefficiencies in labor take their toll. Finally, we see the marginal cost (MC) curve, which rises after a certain point because of the fixed factors of production.

With a price of $5.00, firms are making a profit (the gray box). Each firm maximizes profits by producing up to the point where price equals marginal cost, here 800. Any units produced beyond 800 would add more to cost than they would bring in revenue. Notice the firm is producing at a level that is larger than the output that minimizes average costs. The high price in the marketplace has induced it to increase its service level even though the result is slightly less labor productivity and thus higher per unit costs.

Both revenues and costs are shown graphically. *Total revenue* (TR) is simply the product of price and quantity: $P^* \times q^* = \$5.00 \times 800 = \$4,000$. On the diagram, total revenue is equal to the area of the rectangle P^*Aq^*0. (The area of a rectangle is equal to its length times its width.) At output q^*, average total cost is $4.50 (point B). Numerically, it is equal to the length of line segment q^*B. Because average total cost is derived by dividing total cost by q, we can get back to total cost by *multiplying* average total cost by q. That is,

$$ATC = \frac{TC}{q}$$

and so

$$TC = ATC \times q$$

Total cost (TC), then, is $\$4.50 \times 800 = \$3,600$, the area shaded blue in the diagram. *Profit* is simply the difference between total revenue (TR) and total cost (TC), or $400. This is the area that is shaded gray in the diagram. This firm is earning positive profits.

A firm that is earning a positive profit in the short run and expects to continue doing so has an incentive to expand its scale of operation in the long run. Managers in these firms will likely be planning to expand even as they concentrate on producing 800 units. We expect greater output to be produced in the long run as firms react to profits they are earning.

Minimizing Losses

A firm that is not earning a positive profit or breaking even is suffering a loss. Firms suffering losses fall into two categories: (1) those that find it advantageous to shut down operations immediately and bear losses equal to total fixed costs and (2) those that continue to operate in the short run to minimize their losses. The most important thing to remember here is that firms cannot exit the industry in the short run. The firm can shut down, but it cannot get rid of its fixed costs by going out of business. Fixed costs must be paid in the short run no matter what the firm does. In the case of Blue Velvet, shutting down results in a $2,000 loss per week—the unavoidable cost of the capital for the building and maintenance contract. As long as Blue Velvet can sell car washes for more than it has to spend on labor and soap, the two variable factors, it is worth staying open and reducing its losses. Sometimes the best strategy still results in losing money!

Whether a firm suffering losses decides to produce or not to produce in the short run depends on the advantages and disadvantages of continuing production. If a firm shuts down, it earns no revenue and has no variable costs to bear. If it continues to produce, it both earns revenue and incurs variable costs. Because a firm must bear fixed costs *whether or not* it shuts down, its decision depends *solely on whether total revenue from operating is sufficient to cover total variable cost.*

- If total revenue exceeds total variable cost, the excess revenue can be used to offset fixed costs and reduce losses, and it will pay the firm to keep operating.
- If total revenue is smaller than total variable cost, the firm that operates will suffer losses in excess of fixed costs. In this case, the firm can minimize its losses by shutting down.

Producing at a Loss to Offset Fixed Costs If price is less than average variable cost at its lowest point, the firm will not only lose its initial investment but also have added losses on every unit produced. For Blue Velvet, prices must be higher than the costs of soap and labor for the firm to continue to operate. Economists call this the **shutdown point**. At all prices above this shutdown point, the marginal cost curve shows the profit-maximizing level of output. At all points below this point, optimal short-run output is zero.

We can now refine our previous statement from Chapter 8, that a perfectly competitive firm's marginal cost curve is its short-run supply curve. As we have just seen, a firm will shut down when the market price is less than the minimum point on the *AVC* curve. Also recall (or notice from the graph) that the marginal cost curve intersects the *AVC* at *AVC*'s lowest point. It therefore follows that the short-run supply curve of a competitive firm is that portion of its marginal cost curve that lies above its average variable cost curve.

Figure 9.2 shows the short-run supply curve for the general case of a perfectly competitive firm like Blue Velvet.

shutdown point The lowest point on the average variable cost curve. When price falls below the minimum point on *AVC*, total revenue is insufficient to cover variable costs and the firm will shut down and bear losses equal to fixed costs.

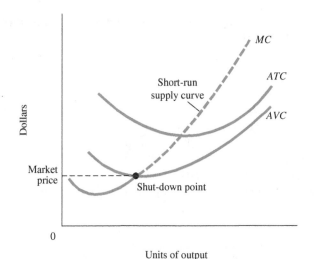

◀ **FIGURE 9.2 Short-Run Supply Curve of a Perfectly Competitive Firm**
At prices below average variable cost, it pays a firm to shut down rather than continue operating. Thus, the short-run supply curve of a competitive firm is the part of its marginal cost curve that lies *above* its average variable cost curve.

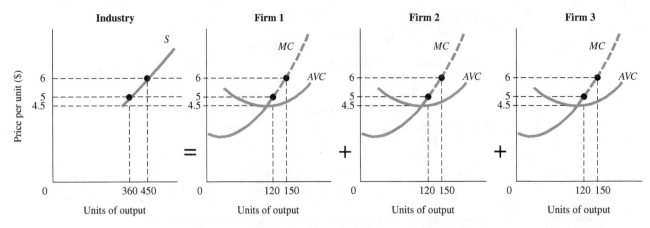

▲ **FIGURE 9.3**   **The Industry Supply Curve in the Short Run Is the Horizontal Sum of the Marginal Cost Curves (above *AVC*) of All the Firms in an Industry**
If there are only three firms in the industry, the industry supply curve is simply the sum of all the products supplied by the three firms at each price. For example, at $6 each firm supplies 150 units, for a total industry supply of 450.

The Short-Run Industry Supply Curve

short-run industry supply curve
The sum of the marginal cost curves (above *AVC*) of all the firms in an industry.

Supply in a competitive industry is the sum of the quantity supplied by the individual firms in the industry at each price level. The **short-run industry supply curve** is the sum of the individual firm supply curves—that is, the marginal cost curves (above *AVC*) of all the firms in the industry. Because quantities are being added—that is, because we are finding the total quantity supplied in the industry at each price level—the curves are added horizontally.

Figure 9.3 shows the supply curve for an industry with three identical firms.[1] At a price of $6, each firm produces 150 units, which is the output where $P = MC$. The total amount supplied on the market at a price of $6 is thus 450. At a price of $5, each firm produces 120 units, for an industry supply of 360. Below $4.50, all firms shut down; *P* is less than *AVC*.

Two things can cause the industry supply curve to shift. In the short run, the industry supply curve shifts if something—a decrease in the price of some input, for instance—shifts the marginal cost curves of all the individual firms simultaneously. For example, when the cost of producing components of home computers decreased, the marginal cost curves of all computer manufacturers shifted downward. Such a shift amounted to the same thing as an outward shift in their supply curves. Each firm was willing to supply more computers at each price level because computers were now cheaper to produce.

In the long run, an increase or decrease in the number of firms—and, therefore, in the number of individual firm supply curves—shifts the total industry supply curve. If new firms enter the industry, the industry supply curve moves to the right; if firms exit the industry, the industry supply curve moves to the left.

We return to shifts in industry supply curves and discuss them further when we take up long-run adjustments later in this chapter.

Long-Run Directions: A Review

Table 9.2 summarizes the different circumstances that perfectly competitive firms may face as they plan for the long run. Profit-making firms will produce up to the point where price and marginal cost are equal in the short run. If there are positive profits, in the long run, there is an incentive for firms to expand their scales of plant and for new firms to enter the industry.

A firm suffering losses will produce if and only if revenue is sufficient to cover total variable cost. Such firms, like profitable firms, will also produce up to the point where $P = MC$. Thus, in

---

[1] Perfectly competitive industries are assumed to have many firms. Many is, of course, more than three. We use three firms here simply for purposes of illustration. The assumption that all firms are identical is often made when discussing a perfectly competitive industry.

TABLE 9.2	Profits, Losses, and Perfectly Competitive Firm Decisions in the Long and Short Run		
	Short-Run Condition	Short-Run Decision	Long-Run Decision
Profits	$TR > TC$	$P = MC$: operate	Expand: new firms enter
Losses	1. $TR \geq TVC$	$P = MC$: operate (loss < total fixed cost)	Contract: firms exit
	2. $TR < TVC$	Shut down: loss = total fixed cost	Contract: firms exit

the short run we expect output to fall as prices fall. If a firm suffering losses cannot cover total variable cost by operating, it will shut down and bear losses equal to total fixed cost. Whether a firm that is suffering losses decides to shut down in the short run or not, the losses create an incentive to contract in the long run. When firms are suffering losses, they generally exit the industry in the long run.

Thus, the short-run profits of firms cause them to expand or contract when opportunities exist to change their scale of plant. If expansion is desired because economic profits are positive, firms must consider what their costs are likely to be at different scales of operation. (When we use the term "scale of operation," you may find it helpful to picture factories of varying sizes.) Just as firms have to analyze different technologies to arrive at a cost structure in the short run, they must also compare their costs at different scales of plant to arrive at long-run costs. Perhaps a larger scale of operation will reduce average production costs and provide an even greater incentive for a profit-making firm to expand, or perhaps large firms will run into problems that constrain growth. The analysis of long-run possibilities is even more complex than the short-run analysis because more things are variable—scale of plant is not fixed, for example, and there are no fixed costs because firms can exit their industry in the long run. In theory, firms may choose *any* scale of operation; so they must analyze many possible options.

Now let us turn to an analysis of cost curves in the long run.

Long-Run Costs: Economies and Diseconomies of Scale

9.2 LEARNING OBJECTIVE

Explain the causes and effects of economies and diseconomies of scale.

The shapes of short-run cost curves follow directly from the diminishing returns associated with a fixed factor of production. In the long run, however, there is no fixed factor of production. Firms can choose any scale of production. They can build small or large factories, double or triple output, or go out of business completely.

The shape of a firm's **long-run average cost curve** shows how costs vary with scale of operation. In some firms, production technology is such that increased scale, or size, reduces average or per unit costs. For others, increased scale leads to higher per-unit costs. When an increase in a firm's scale of production leads to lower average costs, we say that there are **increasing returns to scale, *or* economies of scale**. When average costs do not change with the scale of production, we say that there are **constant returns to scale**. Finally, when an increase in a firm's scale of production leads to higher average costs, we say that there are **decreasing returns to scale, *or* diseconomies of scale**. Economies of scale are a property of production characteristics of the individual firm and are sometimes referred to as *internal* economies of scale. In the Appendix to this chapter, we talk about *external* economies of scale, which describe economies or diseconomies of scale on an industry-wide basis.

long-run average cost curve (LRAC) Shows the way per unit costs change with output in the long run.

increasing returns to scale, *or* economies of scale An increase in a firm's scale of production leads to lower costs per unit produced.

constant returns to scale An increase in a firm's scale of production has no effect on costs per unit produced.

decreasing returns to scale, *or* diseconomies of scale An increase in a firm's scale of production leads to higher costs per unit produced.

Increasing Returns to Scale

Technically, the phrase *increasing returns to scale* refers to the production relationship. When we say that a production function exhibits increasing returns, we mean that a given percentage increase in inputs leads to a *larger* percentage increase in the production of output. For example, if a firm doubled or tripled inputs, it would more than double or triple output.

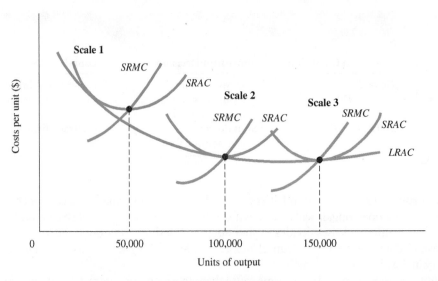

▲ FIGURE 9.4 **A Firm Exhibiting Economies of Scale**
The long-run average cost curve of a firm shows the different scales on which the firm can choose to operate in the long run. Each scale of operation defines a different short run. Here we see a firm exhibiting economies of scale; moving from scale 1 to scale 2 reduces average cost.

minimum efficient scale (MES) The smallest size at which long-run average cost is at its minimum.

When the firm experiences economies of scale, its *LRAC* will decline with output. Figure 9.4 shows short-run and long-run average cost curves for a firm that realizes economies of scale up to about 100,000 units of production. The 100,000 unit output level in Figure 9.4 is sometimes called the **minimum efficient scale (MES)** of the firm. The MES is the smallest size at which long-run average cost is at its minimum. Essentially, it is the answer to this question: how large does a firm have to be to have the best per-unit cost position possible? Consider a firm operating in an industry in which all of the firms in that industry face the long-run average cost curve shown in Figure 9.4. If you want your firm to be cost-competitive in that market, you need to produce at least 100,000 units. At smaller volumes, you will have higher costs than other firms in the industry, which makes it hard for you to stay in the industry. Policy makers are often interested in learning how large MES is relative to the total market for a product because when MES is large relative to the total market size, we typically expect fewer firms to be in the industry. And, as we will see in the next chapter, competition may be reduced.

Figure 9.4 shows three potential scales of operation, each with its own set of short-run cost curves. Each point on the *LRAC* curve represents the minimum cost at which the associated output level can be produced, assuming an ability to adjust scale. Once the firm chooses a scale on which to produce, it becomes locked into one set of cost curves in the short run. If the firm were to settle on scale 1, it would not realize the major cost advantages of producing on a larger scale. By roughly doubling its scale of operations from 50,000 to 100,000 units (scale 2), the firm reduces average costs per unit significantly.

Figure 9.4 shows that at every moment, firms face two different cost constraints. In the long run, firms can change their scale of operation, and costs may be different as a result. However, at any *given* moment, a particular scale of operation exists, constraining the firm's capacity to produce in the short run. That is why we see both short- and long-run curves in the same diagram.

The Sources of Economies of Scale Most of the economies of scale that immediately come to mind are technological in nature. Automobile production, for example, would be more costly per unit if a firm were to produce 100 cars per year by hand. In the early 1900s, Henry Ford introduced standardized production techniques that increased output volume, reduced costs per car, and made the automobile available to almost everyone. The new technology is not cost effective at small volumes of cars, but at larger volumes costs are greatly reduced. Ford's innovation provided a source of scale economics at the plant level of the auto firm. Coors originally produced all its beer in Golden, Colorado, in what was, at the time, one of the largest U.S. brewing plants; the firm believed that large size at the plant level brought cost savings.

ECONOMICS IN PRACTICE

Economies of Scale in the Search Business

The latest estimates from ComScore suggest that almost two thirds of all searches are done via Google. Microsoft's Bing, the next highest competitor, has less than 20 percent of the searches. What accounts for Google's success in this business?

One element of Google's success story comes from the cost side of the picture. Search has been called the ultimate scale driven business. Think about what a firm needs to compete in the search business. To convince people to use your search engine, it must be the case that when someone types in a term like "Economies of Scale," he or she gets back a reasonable set of sites. Likely, you would want to make sure that the search picks up related terms, terms like "Scale Economies" or "Economies to Scale" or even "Diseconomies of Scale." Surely you should also make sure the search accepts spelling mistakes. If the search is productive for the first person typing in the term, it can be used more or less costlessly for the millions of others who search for the same term. In fact, the search behavior of that first user can be used in turn to improve the search of future users. To provide any search at all, we need data centers, engineers to develop better and better search algorithms and support staff. Doubling your output may involve some increase in these inputs but the evidence suggests that the increase will be relatively modest. Google, for example, has more than three times the searches of Bing, but it employs only about twice as many engineers to work on algorithms for search. Similarly the number of data centers increases only modestly with search numbers,

so that Google can spend less per search on these centers than its smaller rivals. Economies of scale in search help support Google's product quality and make it difficult for other firms, even firms with the experience and size of Microsoft, to challenge them in this market.

THINKING PRACTICALLY

1. Google was an early pioneer in the search business. How did that early lead interact with the fact of scale economies in Google's favor?

Some economies of scale result not from technology but from firm-level efficiencies and bargaining power that can come with size. Very large companies, for instance, can buy inputs in volume at discounted prices. Large firms may also produce some of their own inputs at considerable savings, and they can certainly save in transport costs when they ship items in bulk. Wal-Mart has become the largest retailer in the United States in part because of scale economies of this type. Economics of scale have come from advantages of larger *firm* size rather than gains from plant size. Most electronic companies produce their output in multiple moderate-sized plants and hope to achieve cost savings in part through large firm size.

Constant Returns to Scale

Technically, the term *constant returns* means that the quantitative relationship between input and output stays constant, or the same, when output is increased. If a firm doubles inputs, it doubles output; if it triples inputs, it triples output; and so on. Furthermore, *if input prices are fixed*, constant returns imply that average cost of production does not change with scale. In other words, constant returns to scale mean that the firm's long-run average cost curve remains flat.

The firm in Figure 9.4 exhibits roughly constant returns to scale between scale 2 and scale 3. The average cost of production is about the same in each. If the firm exhibited constant returns at levels above 150,000 units of output, the *LRAC* would continue as a flat, straight line.

Economists have studied cost data extensively over the years to estimate the extent to which economies of scale exist. Evidence suggests that in most industries, firms do not have to be gigantic to realize cost savings from scale economies. In other words, the MES is moderate relative to market size. Perhaps the best example of efficient production on a small scale is the manufacturing sector in Taiwan. Taiwan has enjoyed rapid growth based on manufacturing firms that employ fewer than 100 workers.

Most industries seem to exhibit constant returns to scale (a flat *LRAC*) after some level of output at least at the level of the plant. A firm that wants to grow when it has reached its "optimal" size can do so by building another identical plant. It thus seems logical to conclude that most firms face constant returns to scale at the plant level *as long as* they can replicate their existing plants.

Diseconomies of Scale

When average cost increases with scale of production, a firm faces *diseconomies of scale*. Under these conditions, the *LRAC* curve slopes up. The most often cited example of a diseconomy of scale is bureaucratic inefficiency. As size increases beyond a certain point, operations tend to become more difficult to manage. Large size often entails increased bureaucracy, affecting both managerial incentives and control. The coordination function is more complex for larger firms than for smaller ones, and the chances that it will break down are greater. You can see that this diseconomy of scale is firm-level in type.

U-Shaped Long-Run Average Costs

As we have seen, the shape of a firm's long-run average cost curve depends on how costs react to changes in scale. Some firms see economies of scale, and their long-run average cost curves slope downward. Most firms seem to have flat long-run average cost curves at least at some output level. Still others encounter diseconomies, and their long-run average cost curves slope upward.

Figure 9.5 describes a firm that exhibits both economies of scale and diseconomies of scale. Average costs decrease with scale of plant up to *q** and increase with scale after that. The *Economics in Practice* on the next page discusses the history of the U-shaped curve.

The U-shaped average cost curve looks very much like the short-run average cost curves we have examined in the last two chapters, but do not confuse the two. All short-run average cost curves are U-shaped because the fixed scale of plant constrains production and drives marginal cost upward as a result of diminishing returns. In the long run, the scale of plant can be changed and the U-shape instead comes from the changing way in which this scale translates into first cost saving and then later cost increases.

optimal scale of plant The scale of plant that minimizes long-run average cost.

The **optimal scale of plant** is the scale of plant that minimizes long-run average cost. In fact, as we will see next, competition forces firms to use the optimal scale assuming there is sufficient demand. In Figure 9.5, *q** is the unique optimal scale.

▶ **FIGURE 9.5** **A Firm Exhibiting Economies and Diseconomies of Scale**

Economies of scale push this firm's average costs down to *q**. Beyond *q**, the firm experiences diseconomies of scale; *q** is the level of production at lowest long-run average costs, using optimal scale.

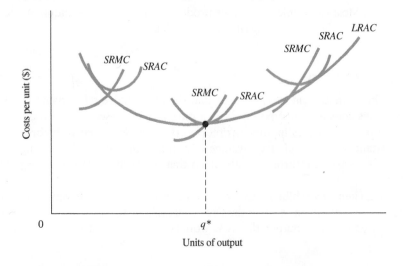

ECONOMICS IN PRACTICE

The Long-Run Average Cost Curve: Flat or U-Shaped?

The long-run average cost curve has been a source of controversy in economics for many years. A long-run average cost curve was first drawn as the "envelope" of a series of short-run curves in a classic article written by Jacob Viner in 1931.[1] In preparing that article, Viner gave his draftsman the task of drawing the long-run curve through the minimum points of all the short-run average cost curves.

In a supplementary note written in 1950, Viner commented:

> ...the error in Chart IV is left uncorrected so that future teachers and students may share the pleasure of many of their predecessors of pointing out that if I had known what an envelope was, I would not have given my excellent draftsman the technically impossible and economically inappropriate task of drawing an *AC* curve which would pass through the lowest cost points of all the *AC* curves yet not rise above any *AC* curve at any point....[2]

While this story is an interesting part of the lore of economics, a more recent debate concentrates on the economic content of this controversy. In 1986, Professor Herbert Simon of Carnegie-Mellon University stated bluntly in an interview for *Challenge* magazine that most textbooks are wrong to use the U-shaped long-run cost curve to predict the size of firms. Simon explained that studies show the firm's cost curves are not U-shaped but instead slope down to the right and then level off.[3]

What difference does it make if the long-run average cost curve has a long flat section with no upturn? In this case, there

is no single point on the long-run curve that is the best. Once a firm achieves some scale, it has the same costs no matter how much larger it gets. As Simon tells us, this means we can't predict firm size. But we can still predict industry size: In this situation, we still have forces of profit seeking causing firms to enter and exit until excess profits are zero. The unique industry output is the one that corresponds to a price equal to long-run average cost that also equates supply and demand. Simon is right that this type of cost curve means the economic theory doesn't explain everything, but it still tells us a good deal.

THINKING PRACTICALLY

1. Some have argued that even if long-run *AC* curves do eventually slope up, we would not likely see many firms operating at this size. Why not?

[1] Jacob Viner, "Cost Curves and Supply Curves," *Zeitschrift fur Nationalokonomie*, 3 (1–1931): 23–46.
[2] George J. Stigler and Kenneth E. Boulding, eds., *AEA Readings in Price Theory*, Vol. 6 (Chicago: Richard D. Irwin, 1952), p. 227.
[3] Based on interview with Herbert A. Simon, "The Failure of Armchair Economics," *Challenge* (November–December 1986): 23–24.

Long-Run Adjustments to Short-Run Conditions

9.3 LEARNING OBJECTIVE

Describe long-run adjustments for short-run profits and losses.

We began this chapter by discussing the different short-run positions in which firms like Blue Velvet may find themselves. Firms can be operating at a profit or suffering economic losses; they can be shut down or producing. When firms are earning economic profits (profits above normal, or positive) or are suffering economic losses (profits below normal, or negative), the industry is not at long-run equilibrium and firms have an incentive to change their behavior. What firms are likely to do under these circumstances depends in part on the shape of the long run cost curve.

Short-Run Profits: Moves In and Out of Equilibrium

Consider a competitive market in which demand and costs have been stable for some period and the industry is in long-run equilibrium. The market price is such that firms are earning a normal rate of return and the flow of firms in and out of the industry balances out. Firms are producing as efficiently as possible, and supply equals demand. Figure 9.6 shows this situation at a price of $6 and an output of 200,000 units for an industry with a U-shaped long-run cost curve.

Now suppose demand increases. Perhaps this is the market for green tea, and there has been a news report on the health benefits of the tea. What happens? Managers at the firms notice the

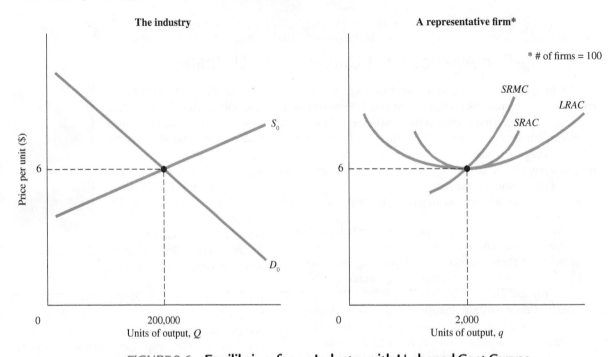

▲ **FIGURE 9.6   Equilibrium for an Industry with U-shaped Cost Curves**
The individual firm on the right is producing 2,000 units, and we also know that the industry consists of 100 firms. All firms are identical, and all are producing at the uniquely best output level of 2,000 units.

demand increase—they too read the paper! But each firm has a fixed capital stock—it owns a set tea plantation, for example. Entry also is impossible in the short run. But existing firms can do something to meet the new demand, even within the constraints of their existing plant. They can hire overtime workers, for example, to increase yield by more careful picking of the leaves. But this increases average costs. In Figure 9.7, firms will move up their SRMC curves as they produce output beyond the level of 2,000. Why do firms do this? Because the increased demand

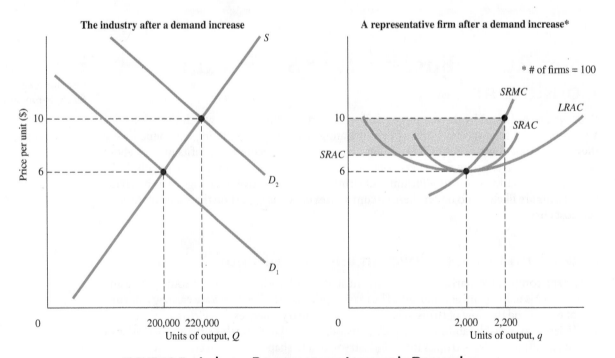

▲ **FIGURE 9.7   Industry Response to an Increase in Demand**

has increased the price. The new higher price makes it worthwhile for the firms to increase their output even though in the short run it is expensive to do so. In fact, the firms increase output as long as the new price is greater than the short-run marginal cost curve. We have noted the new short-run equilibrium in Figure 9.7.

Again supply equals demand. But there are two important differences. First, and most important, firms are making profits. The profits are noted in the gray-shaded rectangle in Figure 9.7 and are the difference between the new higher price and the new higher average cost. Second, firms are also operating inefficiently, with per-unit cost well above the minimum. Managers in these firms are scrambling to get increased output from a plantation designed for a smaller output level.

What happens next? Other entrepreneurs observing the industry see the excess profits and enter. Each one enters at a scale of 2,000 because that is the optimal scale in this industry. Perhaps existing firms also build new plants (which will also have a scale of 2,000). With each new entry, the industry supply curve (which is just the sum of all the individual firms' supply curves) shifts to the right. More supply is available because there are more firms. Price begins to fall. As long as the price is above $6, each of the firms, both old and new, is making economic profits and more entry will occur. Once price is back to $6, there are no longer economic profits and thus no further entry. Figure 9.8 shows this new equilibrium where supply has shifted sufficiently to return the industry to the original price of $6 at a new quantity level.

Again, notice the characteristics of the final equilibrium: Each individual firm chooses a scale of operations that minimizes its long-run average cost. It operates this plant at an output level that minimizes short-run average cost. In equilibrium, each firm has

$$SRMC = SRAC = LRAC$$

Firms make no economic profits so that

$$P = SRMC = SRAC = LRAC$$

and there are enough firms so that supply equals demand.

Suppose instead of a positive demand shock, the industry experiences an unexpected cut in demand. Precisely the same economic logic holds. When demand falls (shifts to the left), the

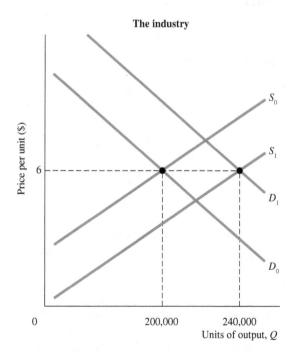
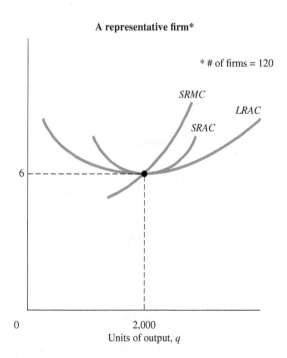

▲ FIGURE 9.8 **New Equilibrium with Higher Demand**

price falls. In the short run, firms cannot shrink plants, nor can they exit. But with the lower price, firms begin to produce less in their plants than before. In fact, firms cut back production so long as the price they receive is less than their short-run marginal cost. At this point, firms earn losses and are producing at too small a level and thus have higher average cost than before. Some firms drop out, and when they do so, the supply curve shifts to the left. How many firms leave? Enough so that the equilibrium is restored with the price again at $6 and the industry output has fallen, to reflect the reduced demand for the product.

The Long-Run Adjustment Mechanism: Investment Flows Toward Profit Opportunities

The central idea in our discussion of entry, exit, expansion, and contraction is this: In efficient markets, investment capital flows toward profit opportunities. The actual process is complex and varies from industry to industry.

We talked about efficient markets in Chapter 1. In efficient markets, profit opportunities are quickly eliminated as they develop. To illustrate this point, we described choosing among the lines in a grocery store and suggested that shorter-than-average lines are quickly eliminated as people shift lines. Profits in competitive industries also are eliminated as new competing firms move into open slots, or perceived opportunities, in the industry. The **long-run competitive equilibrium** occurs when entry and exit have moved the industry back into a position of earning normal returns. Of course, a dynamic economy experiences frequent changes both in demand conditions and in technology and we will see frequent moves in and out of industries, all with the intention of exploiting profit opportunities while they last.

In practice, the entry and exit of firms in response to profit opportunities usually involve the financial capital market. In capital markets, people are constantly looking for profits. When firms in an industry do well, capital is likely to flow into that industry in a variety of forms. Entrepreneurs start new firms, and firms using entirely new technologies may break into markets.

long-run competitive equilibrium When $P = SRMC = SRAC = LRAC$ and profits are zero.

> Investment—in the form of new firms and expanding old firms—will over time tend to favor those industries in which profits are being made; and over time, industries in which firms are suffering losses will gradually contract from disinvestment.

Output Markets: A Final Word

In the last four chapters, we have been building a model of a simple market system under the assumption of perfect competition. Let us provide just one more example to review the actual response of a competitive system to a change in consumer preferences.

Over the past two decades, Americans have developed a taste for wine in general and for California wines in particular. We know that household demand is constrained by income, wealth, and prices and that income is (at least in part) determined by the choices that households make. Within these constraints, households increasingly choose—or demand—wine. The demand curve for wine has shifted to the right, causing excess demand followed by an increase in price.

With higher prices, wine producers find themselves earning positive profits. *This increase in price and consequent rise in profits is the basic signal that leads to a reallocation of society's resources.* In the short run, wine producers are constrained by their current scales of operation. California has only a limited number of vineyards and only a limited amount of vat capacity, for example.

In the long run, however, we would expect to see resources flow in to compete for these profits, and this is exactly what happens. New firms enter the wine-producing business. New vines are planted, and new vats and production equipment are purchased and put in place. Vineyard owners move into new states—Rhode Island, Texas, and Maryland—and established

ECONOMICS IN PRACTICE

Why Are Hot Dogs So Expensive in Central Park?

Recently, one of the authors of this textbook was walking in Central Park in New York City. Because it was lunchtime and she was hungry, she decided to indulge her secret passion for good old-fashioned hot dogs. Because she did this frequently, she was well aware that the standard price for a hot dog in New York City was $1.50. So she was surprised when she handed the vendor $2 that she received no change back. As it turned out, the price of a hot dog inside the park was $2.00, not the $1.50 vendors charged elsewhere in the city. Since she was trained as an economist, she wanted to know what caused the difference in price.

First, she looked to the demand side of the market. If hot dogs are selling for $2.00 in the park but only $1.50 outside the park, people must be willing and able to pay more for them in the park. Why? Perhaps hot dogs are more enjoyable to people when eaten while walking through Central Park. Hot dogs and "walking through the park" may be complementary goods. Or maybe people who walk in the park at noon are richer.

You might ask, if hot dogs are available outside the park for $1.50, why don't people buy them there and bring them to the park? The fact is that hot dogs are good only when they are hot, and they get cold very quickly. A hot dog purchased 5 minutes away from Central Park will be stone cold by the time someone reaches the park.

But looking at the demand side is not enough to understand a market. We also have to explain the behavior of the hot dog vendors who comprise the supply side of the market. On the supply side, the author knew that the market for hot dogs was virtually perfectly competitive outside the park. First, the product is homogeneous. Essentially all vendors supply the same product: a standard quality certified hot dog and two varieties of mustard. Second, there is free entry. Because most vendors have wheels on their carts, if the price of hot dogs rises above $1.50 in one part of town, we would expect vendors to move there. The added supply would then push prices back to Price (P) = short-run marginal cost ($SRAC$) = long-run average cost ($LRAC$). At $P = \$1.50$, individual vendors around the city must be earning enough to cover average costs including a normal rate of return (see the discussion in the text on p. 186). If the market price produces

excess profits, new vendors will show up to compete those excess profits away.

All of this would suggest that the price of hot dogs should be the same everywhere in New York City. If a vendor is able to charge $2 in the park and has the same costs as a vendor outside the park, he must be earning above-normal profits. After all, the vendor makes $.50 more on each hot dog. Something must be preventing the outside vendors from rolling their carts into the park, which would increase the supply of hot dogs and drive the price back to $1.50.

That something is a more expensive license. In New York, you need a license to operate a hot dog cart, and a license to operate in the park costs more. Since hot dogs are $0.50 more in the park, the added cost of a license each year must be roughly $0.50 per hot dog sold. In fact, in New York City, licenses to sell hot dogs in the park are auctioned off for many thousands of dollars, whereas licenses to operate in more remote parts of the city cost only about $1,000.

THINKING PRACTICALLY

1. Show on a graph how a higher-priced license increases hot dog prices.
2. Who is the woman in the coat?

---

growers increase production. Overall, more wine is produced to meet the new consumer demand. At the same time, competition is forcing firms to operate using the most efficient technology available.

What starts as a shift in preferences thus ends up as a shift in resources. Land is reallocated, and labor moves into wine production. All this is accomplished without any central planning or direction.

You have now seen what lies behind the demand curves and supply curves in competitive output markets. The next two chapters take up competitive *input* markets and complete the picture.

SUMMARY

1. For any firm, one of three conditions holds at any given moment: (1) The firm is earning positive profits, (2) the firm is suffering losses, or (3) the firm is just breaking even—that is, earning a normal rate of return and thus zero profits.

9.1 SHORT-RUN CONDITIONS AND LONG-RUN DIRECTIONS *p. 186*

2. A firm that is earning positive profits in the short run and expects to continue doing so has an incentive to expand in the long run. Profits also provide an incentive for new firms to enter the industry.

3. In the short run, firms suffering losses are stuck in the industry. They can shut down operations ($q = 0$), but they must still bear fixed costs. In the long run, firms suffering losses can exit the industry.

4. A firm's decision about whether to shut down in the short run depends solely on whether its total revenue from operating is sufficient to cover its total variable cost. If total revenue exceeds total variable cost, the excess can be used to pay some fixed costs and thus reduce losses.

5. Any time price is below the minimum point on the average variable cost curve, total revenue will be less than total variable cost, and the firm will shut down. The minimum point on the average variable cost curve (which is also the point where marginal cost and average variable cost intersect) is called the *shutdown point*. At all prices above the shutdown point, the *MC* curve shows the profit-maximizing level of output. At all prices below it, optimal short-run output is zero.

6. The *short-run supply curve* of a firm in a perfectly competitive industry is the portion of its marginal cost curve that lies above its average variable cost curve.

7. Two things can cause the industry supply curve to shift: (1) in the short run, anything that causes marginal costs to change across the industry, such as an increase in the price of a particular input, and (2) in the long run, entry or exit of firms.

9.2 LONG-RUN COSTS: ECONOMIES AND DISECONOMIES OF SCALE *p. 191*

8. When an increase in a firm's scale of production leads to lower average costs, the firm exhibits *increasing returns to scale*, or *economies of scale*. When average costs do not change with the scale of production, the firm exhibits *constant returns to scale*. When an increase in a firm's scale of production leads to higher average costs, the firm exhibits *decreasing returns to scale*, or *diseconomies of scale*.

9. A firm's *long-run average cost curve* (LRAC) shows the costs associated with different scales on which it can choose to operate in the long run.

9.3 LONG-RUN ADJUSTMENTS TO SHORT-RUN CONDITIONS *p. 195*

10. When short-run profits exist in an industry, firms enter and existing firms expand. These events shift the industry supply curve to the right. When this happens, price falls and ultimately, economic profits are eliminated.

11. When short-run losses are suffered in an industry, some firms exit and some firms reduce scale. These events shift the industry supply curve to the left, raising price and eliminating losses.

12. *Long-run competitive equilibrium* is reached when $P = SRMC = SRAC = LRAC$ and profits are zero.

13. In efficient markets, investment capital flows toward profit opportunities.

REVIEW TERMS AND CONCEPTS

breaking even, *p. 186*

constant returns to scale, *p. 191*

decreasing returns to scale *or diseconomies of scale, p. 191*

increasing returns to scale *or economies of scale, p. 191*

long-run average cost curve (*LRAC*), *p. 191*

long-run competitive equilibrium, *p. 198*

minimum efficient scale (MES), *p. 192*

optimal scale of plant, *p. 194*

short-run industry supply curve, *p. 190*

shutdown point, *p. 189*

Equation:

long-run competitive equilibrium, $P = SRMC = SRAC = LRAC$, *p. 197*

— PROBLEMS —

All problems are available on MyEconLab.

9.1 SHORT-RUN CONDITIONS AND LONG-RUN DIRECTIONS

LEARNING OBJECTIVE: Discuss how short-run conditions affect a firm's short-run and long-run behavior.

1.1 For each of the following, decide whether you agree or disagree and explain your answer:
   a. A firm earning positive profits in the short run always has an incentive to increase its scale of operation in the long run.
   b. A firm suffering losses in the short run will continue to operate as long as total revenue at least covers fixed cost.

1.2 Megatron is a competitive firm operating under the following conditions: Price of output is $15, the profit-maximizing level of output is 40,000 units, and the total cost (full economic cost) of producing 40,000 units is $650,000. The firm's *only* fixed factor of production is a $750,000 stock of capital (a building). If the interest rate available on comparable risks is 8 percent, should this firm shut down immediately in the short run? Explain your answer.

1.3 For cases A through F in the following table, would you (1) operate or shut down in the short run and (2) expand your plant or exit the industry in the long run?

	A	B	C	D	E	F
Total revenue	1,000	2,500	4,000	7,500	7,500	7,500
Total cost	1,400	1,500	5,500	7,000	7,500	8,000
Total fixed cost	300	1,000	500	2,500	2,500	2,500

1.4 You are given the following cost data:

q	TFC	TVC
0	25	0
1	25	7
2	25	12
3	25	18
4	25	25
5	25	34
6	25	46
7	25	62
8	25	88

If the price of output is $15, how many units of output will this firm produce? What is the total revenue? What is the total cost? Will the firm operate or shut down in the short run? in the long run? Briefly explain your answers.

1.5 Construct a graph with AVC, ATC, and MC curves. On this graph add a marginal revenue curve for a representative firm in a perfectly competitive industry that is maximizing profits at a price of $p*_1$. Add a second marginal

revenue curve for a firm that is minimizing losses but continues to produce when the price is $p*_2$. Add a third marginal revenue curve for a firm that is shutting down when the price is $p*_3$. Explain where you decided to place each of the marginal revenue curves and identify the shutdown point on the graph.

9.2 LONG-RUN COSTS: ECONOMIES AND DISECONOMIES OF SCALE

LEARNING OBJECTIVE: Explain the causes and effects of economies and diseconomies of scale.

2.1 For each of the following, decide whether you agree or disagree and explain your answer:
   a. Firms that exhibit constant returns to scale have U-shaped long-run average cost curves.
   b. Firms that exhibit increasing returns to scale are on the part of the long-run average cost curve that is upsloping.

2.2 Explain why it is possible that a firm with a production function that exhibits increasing returns to scale can run into diminishing returns at the same time.

2.3 [**Related to the *Economics in Practice* on p. 193**] One of the more recent innovations in computer technology is called "cloud computing." With cloud computing, information and software are provided to computers on an "as-needed" basis, much like utilities are provided to homes and businesses. At the beginning of 2015, Amazon and Microsoft were ranked number 1 and 2 in terms of size for cloud services providers. In a statement advocating the advantages of large, public cloud providers like Amazon.com over smaller enterprise data centers, James Hamilton, a vice president at Amazon claimed that "server, networking and administration costs the average enterprise five to seven times what it costs a large provider." What does Hamilton's statement imply about the returns to scale in the cloud computing industry, and what does it indicate about the size of the companies that will most likely dominate this industry in the long run?

Source: James Urquhart, "James Hamilton on cloud economies of scale," *cnet.com,* April 28, 2010.

2.4 [**Related to the *Economics in Practice* on p. 195**] Do you agree or disagree with the following statements? Explain in a sentence or two.
   a. A firm will never sell its product for less than it costs to produce it.
   b. If the short-run marginal cost curve is U-shaped, the long-run average cost curve is likely to be U-shaped as well.

2.5 Lafourche Parish, Louisiana, is the home to three crawfish farms. Thibodeaux Crawfish Farm harvests 40,000 pounds of crawfish per month at a total cost of $50,000. The Mardi Gras Mud Bug Cooperative harvests 25,000 pounds of crawfish per month at a total cost of $35,000. Lafourche Farms harvests 90,000 pounds of crawfish per month at a total cost of $140,000. These data suggest that there are significant economies of scale in crawfish production. Do you agree or disagree with this statement? Explain your answer.

2.6 Indicate whether you agree or disagree with the following statements. Briefly explain your answers.
  a. Increasing returns to scale refers to a situation where an increase in a firm's scale of production leads to higher costs per unit produced.
  b. Constant returns to scale refers to a situation where an increase in a firm's scale of production has no effect on costs per unit produced.
  c. Decreasing returns to scale refers to a situation where an increase in a firm's scale of production leads to lower costs per unit produced.

2.7 The concept of economies of scale refers to lower per-unit production costs at higher levels of output. The easiest way to understand this is to look at whether long-run average cost decreases with output (economies of scale) or whether long-run average cost increases with output (diseconomies of scale). If average cost is constant as output rises, there are constant returns to scale. But the concept of falling unit costs is all around us. Explain how the concept of economies of scale helps shed light on each of the following:
  a. aircraft production
  b. satellite television providers
  c. ebooks versus printed books
  d. a retired couple downsizing from a 4,000 sq. ft. house to a 1,500 sq. ft. condo
  e. buying a season pass to an amusement park

2.8 The shape of a firm's long-run average cost curve depends on how costs vary with scale of operation. Draw a long-run average cost curve for a firm that exhibits economies of scale, constant returns to scale, and diseconomies of scale. Identify each of these sections of the cost curve and explain why each section exemplifies its specific type of returns to scale.

2.9 The long-run average cost curve for an industry is represented in the following graph. Add short-run average cost curves and short-run marginal cost curves for three firms in this industry, with one firm producing an output of 10,000 units, one firm producing an output of 20,000, and one firm producing an output of 30,000. Label these as Scale 1, Scale 2, and Scale 3, respectively. What is likely to happen to the scale of each of these three firms in the long run?

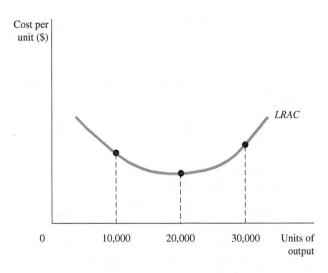

9.3 LONG-RUN ADJUSTMENTS TO SHORT-RUN CONDITIONS

LEARNING OBJECTIVE: Describe long-run adjustments for short-run profits and losses.

3.1 From 2000 to 2005, the home building sector was expanding and new housing construction as measured by housing starts was approaching an all-time high. (At www.census.gov, click "Housing," then click "Construction data.") Big builders such as Lennar Corporation were making exceptional profits. The industry was expanding. Existing home building firms invested in more capacity and raised output. New home building firms entered the industry. From 2006 to 2009, demand for new and existing homes dropped. The inventory of unsold homes grew sharply. Home prices began to fall. Home builders suffered losses, and the industry contracted. Many firms went out of business, and many workers in the construction industry lost their jobs. From 2009 to 2013, the industry expanded again, with demand for new and existing homes once again increasing. Use the Internet to verify that all of these events happened. Access www.bls.gov for employment data and www.bea.gov for information on residential construction as part of gross domestic product. What has happened since the beginning of 2014? Has the housing market continued to recover? Have housing starts continued to rise? If so, at what level? Write a short essay about whether the housing sector is continuing to expand or if it, yet again, appears to be contracting.

3.2 Each year, lists of the fastest-growing and fastest-dying industries in the United States are published by various sources. Do some research to find three industries from each of these two lists for the current year and briefly explain why you think these industries are either growing or dying. For each industry, explain what is likely happening in capital markets and what the likely effect will be on the industry's long-run average cost curve.

3.3 **[Related to the *Economics in Practice* on p. 199]** St. Mark's Square is a beautiful plaza in Venice that is often frequented by both tourists and pigeons. Ringing the piazza are many small, privately-owned cafes. In these cafes, a cappuccino costs 9 euros despite the fact that an equally good cappuccino costs only 3 euros a block away. What is going on here?

3.4 The following problem traces the relationship between firm decisions, market supply, and market equilibrium in a perfectly competitive market.

a. Complete the following table for a single firm in the short run.

OUTPUT	TFC	TVC	TC	AVC	ATC	MC
0	$150	$ 0	–	–	–	–
1	–	40	–	–	–	–
2	–	100	–	–	–	–
3	–	180	–	–	–	–
4	–	280	–	–	–	–
5	–	400	–	–	–	–
6	–	560	–	–	–	–
7	–	760	–	–	–	–
8	–	1,000	–	–	–	–
9	–	1,300	–	–	–	–
10	–	1,850	–	–	–	–

b. Using the information in the table, fill in the following supply schedule for this individual firm under perfect competition and indicate profit (positive or negative) at each output level. (*Hint:* At each hypothetical price, what is the *MR* of producing 1 more unit of output? Combine this with the *MC* of another unit to figure out the quantity supplied.)

Price	Quantity Supplied	Profit
$ 40	–	–
70	–	–
110	–	–
140	–	–
180	–	–
220	–	–
260	–	–
400	–	–

c. Now suppose there are 100 firms in this industry, all with identical cost schedules. Fill in the market quantity supplied at each price in this market.

Price	Market Quantity Supplied	Market Quantity Demanded
$ 40	–	1,700
70	–	1,500
110	–	1,300
140	–	1,100
180	–	900
220	–	700
260	–	500
400	–	**300**

d. Fill in the blanks: From the market supply and demand schedules in c., the equilibrium market price for this good is ____ and the equilibrium market quantity is ____. Each firm will produce a quantity of ____ and earn a ____ (profit/loss) equal to ____.

e. In d., your answers characterize the short-run equilibrium in this market. Do they characterize the long-run equilibrium as well? If so, explain why. If not, explain why not (that is, what would happen in the long run to change the equilibrium and why?).

*3.5 Assume that you are employed as an analyst at an international consulting firm. Your latest assignment is to do an industry analysis of the fast-growing "telemonica" industry. After extensive research on this combination cell phone and harmonica, you have obtained the following information:

■ *Long-run costs:*
   Capital costs: $40 per unit of output
   Labor costs: $25 per unit of output
■ No economies or diseconomies of scale
■ Industry currently earning a normal return to capital (profit of zero)
■ Industry perfectly competitive, with each of 100 firms producing the same amount of output
■ *Total industry output:* 800,000 telemonicas. Demand for telemonicas is expected to grow rapidly over the next few years, especially in foreign markets, to a level four times as high as it is now, but (due to short-run diminishing returns) each of the 100 existing firms is likely to be producing only 100 percent more.

a. Sketch the long-run cost curve of a representative firm.

b. Show the current conditions by drawing two diagrams, one showing the industry and one showing a representative firm.

c. Sketch the increase in demand and show how the industry is likely to respond in the short run and in the long run.

3.6 The following graph shows the supply curve and three different demand curves for a perfectly competitive industry. The table represents cost data for a representative firm in the industry.

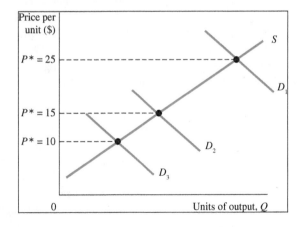

MyEconLab Visit www.myeconlab.com to complete these exercises online and get instant feedback. Exercises that update with real-time data are marked with art 🌐.

Market Price	q^* @ p^* = MC	ATC @ p^* = MC	AVC @ p^* = MC
P^* = 25	600	$ 15	$10
P^* = 15	400	18	10.50
P^* = 10	300	21	11

a. Use the data in the table and draw a graph for the representative firm in the industry when the industry demand curve is represented by D_1. What is the profit or loss for this firm? Shade in the profit or loss area on the graph.

b. Draw a graph for the representative firm when the industry demand curve falls to D_2. What is the profit or loss for this firm? Shade in the profit or loss area on the graph.

c. Draw a graph for the representative firm when the industry demand curve falls to D_3. What is the profit or loss for this firm? Shade in the profit or loss area on the graph.

3.7 For each of the three scenarios in the previous question (P^* = 25, P^* = 15, and P^* = 10), explain the long-run incentives for each representative firm in the industry. Also explain what should happen to the size of the industry as a whole.

3.8 On the following graph for a purely competitive industry, Scale 1 represents the short-run production for a representative firm. Explain what is currently happening with firms in this industry in the short run and what will likely happen in the long run.

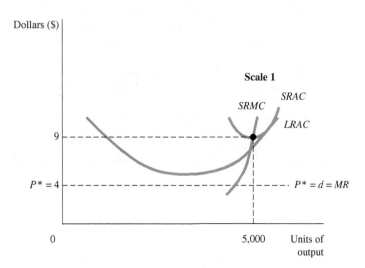

CHAPTER 9 APPENDIX

LEARNING OBJECTIVE

Understand how external economies and diseconomies impact the slope of long run industry supply curves.

external economies and diseconomies When industry growth results in a decrease of long-run average costs, there are *external economies*; when industry growth results in an increase of long-run average costs, there are *external diseconomies*.

External Economies and Diseconomies

Sometimes average costs increase or decrease with the size of the industry, in addition to responding to changes in the size of the firm itself. When long-run average costs decrease as a result of industry growth, we say that there are **external economies**. When average costs increase as a result of industry growth, we say that there are **external diseconomies**. (Remember the distinction between internal and external economies: *Internal* economies of scale are found within firms, whereas *external* economies occur on an industry-wide basis.)

The expansion of the home building sector of the economy between 2000 and 2005 illustrates how external diseconomies of scale arise and how they imply a rising long-run average cost curve.

Beginning in 2000, the overall economy suffered a slowdown as the dot-com exuberance turned to a bursting stock market bubble, and the events of 9/11 raised the specter of international terrorism.

One sector, however, came alive between 2000 and 2005: housing. Very low interest rates lowered the monthly cost of home ownership, immigration increased the number of households, millions of baby boomers traded up and bought second homes, and investors who had been burned by the stock market bust turned to housing as a "real" asset.

All of this increased the demand for single-family homes and condominiums around the country. Table 9A.1 shows what happened to house prices, output, and the costs of inputs during the first 5 years of the decade.

First, house prices began to rise faster than other prices while the cost of construction materials stayed flat. Profitability in the home building sector took off. Next, as existing builders expanded their operations, new firms started up. The number of new housing units "started" stood at just over 1.5 million annually in 2000 and then rose to more than 2 million by 2005. All of this put pressure on the prices of construction materials such as lumber and

| | | | | Construction | |
Year	House Prices % Over the Previous Year	Housing Starts (Thousands)	Housing Starts % Change Over the Previous Year	Materials Prices % Change Over the Previous Year	Consumer Prices %Change Over the Previous Year
2000	–	1,573	–	–	–
2001	7.5	1,661	56%	0%	2.8%
2002	7.5	1,710	2.9%	1.5%	1.5%
2003	7.9	1,853	8.4%	1.6%	2.3%
2004	12.0	1,949	5.2%	8.3%	2.7%
2005	13.0	2,053	5.3%	5.4%	2.5%

TABLE 9A.1 Construction of New Housing and Construction Materials Costs, 2000–2005

Source: Economy.com and the Office of Federal Housing Enterprise Oversight (OFHEO).

wallboard. The table shows that construction materials costs rose more than 8 percent in 2004. These input prices increased the costs of home building. The expanding *industry* caused external diseconomies of scale.

The Long-Run Industry Supply Curve

Recall that long-run competitive equilibrium is achieved when entering firms responding to profits or exiting firms fleeing from losses drive price to a level that just covers long-run average costs. Profits are zero, and $P = LRAC = SRAC = SRMC$. At this point, individual firms are operating at the most efficient scale of plant—that is, at the minimum point on their $LRAC$ curve.

As we saw in the text, long-run equilibrium is not easily achieved. Even if a firm or an industry does achieve long-run equilibrium, it will not remain at that point indefinitely. Economies are dynamic. As population and the stock of capital grow and as preferences and technology change, some sectors will expand and some will contract. How do industries adjust to long-term changes? The answer depends on both internal and external factors.

The extent of *internal* economies (or diseconomies) determines the shape of a firm's long-run average cost curve ($LRAC$). If a firm changes its scale and either expands or contracts, its average costs will increase, decrease, or stay the same *along* the $LRAC$ curve. Recall that the $LRAC$ curve shows the relationship between a firm's output (q) and average total cost (ATC). A firm enjoying internal economies will see costs decreasing as it expands its scale; a firm facing internal diseconomies will see costs increasing as it expands its scale.

However, external economies and diseconomies have nothing to do with the size of *individual* firms in a competitive market. Because individual firms in perfectly competitive industries are small relative to the market, other firms are affected only minimally when an individual firm changes its output or scale of operation. *External* economies and diseconomies arise from industry expansions; that is, they arise when many firms increase their output simultaneously or when new firms enter an industry. If industry expansion causes costs to increase (external diseconomies), the $LRAC$ curves facing individual firms shift upward; costs increase regardless of the level of output finally chosen by the firm. Similarly, if industry expansion causes costs to decrease (external economies), the $LRAC$ curves facing individual firms shift downward; costs decrease at all potential levels of output.

An example of an expanding industry facing external economies is illustrated in Figure 9A.1. Initially, the industry and the representative firm are in long-run competitive equilibrium at the price P_0 determined by the intersection of the initial demand curve D_0 and the initial supply curve S_0. P_0 is the long-run equilibrium price; it intersects the initial long-run average cost curve ($LRAC_0$) at its minimum point. At this point, economic profits are zero.

Let us assume that as time passes, demand increases—that is, the demand curve shifts to the right from D_0 to D_1. This increase in demand will push price all the way to P_1. Without drawing the short-run cost curves, we know that economic profits now exist and that firms are likely to enter the industry to compete for them. In the absence of external economies or diseconomies,

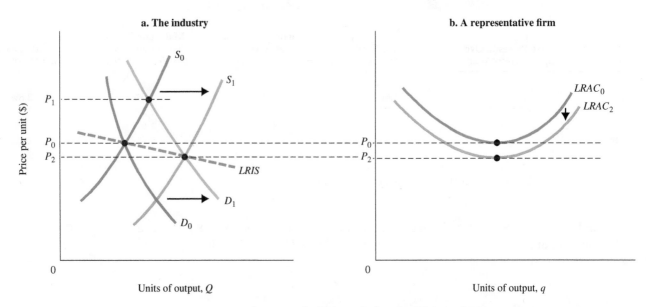

a. The industry

b. A representative firm

▲ **FIGURE 9A.1   A Decreasing-Cost Industry: External Economies**
In a decreasing-cost industry, average cost declines as the industry expands. As demand expands from D_0 to D_1, price rises from P_0 to P_1. As new firms enter and existing firms expand, supply shifts from S_0 to S_1, driving price down. If costs decline as a result of the expansion to $LRAC_2$, the final price will be below P_0 at P_2. The long-run industry supply curve (*LRIS*) slopes downward in a decreasing-cost industry.

long-run industry supply curve (LRIS)   A graph that traces out price and total output over time as an industry expands.

decreasing-cost industry   An industry that realizes external economies—that is, average costs decrease as the industry grows. The long-run supply curve for such an industry has a negative slope.

increasing-cost industry   An industry that encounters external diseconomies—that is, average costs increase as the industry grows. The long-run supply curve for such an industry has a positive slope.

constant-cost industry   An industry that shows no economies or diseconomies of scale as the industry grows. Such industries have flat, or horizontal, long-run supply curves.

firms would enter the industry, shifting the supply curve to the right and driving price back to the bottom of the long-run average cost curve, where profits are zero. Nevertheless, the industry in Figure 9A.1 enjoys external economies. As firms enter and the industry expands, costs decrease; and as the supply curve shifts to the right from S_0 toward S_1, the long-run average cost curve shifts downward to $LRAC_2$. Thus, to reach the new long-run equilibrium level of price and output, the supply curve must shift all the way to S_1. Only when the supply curve reaches S_1 is price driven down to the new equilibrium price of P_2, the minimum point on the *new* long-run average cost curve.

Presumably, further expansion would lead to even greater savings because the industry encounters external economies. The red dashed line in Figure 9A.1(a) that traces out price and total output over time as the industry expands is called the **long-run industry supply curve (LRIS)**. When an industry enjoys external economies, its long-run supply curve slopes down. Such an industry is called a **decreasing-cost industry**.

Figure 9A.2 shows the long-run industry supply curve for an industry that faces external *diseconomies*. (These were suffered in the construction industry, you will recall, when increased house building activity drove up lumber prices.) As demand expands from D_0 to D_1, price is driven up from P_0 to P_1. In response to the resulting higher profits, firms enter, shifting the short-run supply schedule to the right and driving price down. However, this time, as the industry expands, the long-run average cost curve shifts up to $LRAC_2$ as a result of external diseconomies. Now, price has to fall back only to P_2 (the minimum point on $LRAC_2$), not all the way to P_0, to eliminate economic profits. This type of industry, whose long-run industry supply curve slopes up to the right, is called an **increasing-cost industry**.

It should not surprise you to know that industries in which there are no external economies or diseconomies of scale have flat, or horizontal, long-run industry supply curves. These industries are called **constant-cost industries**.

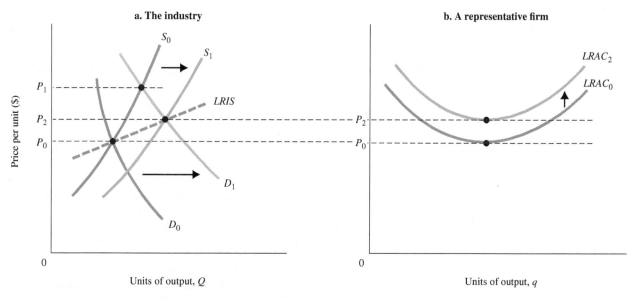

▲ FIGURE 9A.2   **An Increasing-Cost Industry: External Diseconomies**
In an increasing-cost industry, average cost increases as the industry expands. As demand shifts from D_0 to D_1, price rises from P_0 to P_1. As new firms enter and existing firms expand output, supply shifts from S_0 to S_1, driving price down. If long-run average costs rise, as a result, to $LRAC_2$, the final price will be P_2. The long-run industry supply curve (LRIS) slopes up in an increasing-cost industry.

APPENDIX SUMMARY

EXTERNAL ECONOMIES AND DISECONOMIES   p. 204

1. When long-run average costs decrease as a result of industry growth, we say that the industry exhibits *external economies*. When long-run average costs increase as a result of industry growth, we say that the industry exhibits *external diseconomies*.

THE LONG-RUN INDUSTRY SUPPLY CURVE   p. 205

1. The *long-run industry supply curve (LRIS)* is a graph that traces out price and total output over time as an industry expands. A *decreasing-cost industry* is an industry in which

average costs fall as the industry expands. It exhibits external economies, and its long-run industry supply curve slopes downward. An *increasing-cost industry* is an industry in which average costs rise as the industry expands. It exhibits external diseconomies, and its long-run industry supply curve slopes upward. A *constant-cost industry* is an industry that shows no external economies or diseconomies as the industry grows. Its long-run industry supply curve is horizontal, or flat.

APPENDIX REVIEW TERMS AND CONCEPTS

constant-cost industry, *p. 206*
decreasing-cost industry, *p. 206*

external economies and diseconomies, *p. 204*
increasing-cost industry, *p. 206*

long-run industry supply curve (LRIS), *p. 206*

MyEconLab Visit **www.myeconlab.com** to complete these exercises online and get instant feedback. Exercises that update with real-time data are marked with art 🌐.

APPENDIX PROBLEMS

All problems are available on MyEconLab.

APPENDIX 9A: EXTERNAL ECONOMIES AND DISECONOMIES AND THE LONG-RUN INDUSTRY SUPPLY CURVE

LEARNING OBJECTIVE: Understand how external economies or diseconomies shift the long-run supply curves.

1A.1 In deriving the short-run industry supply curve (the sum of firms' marginal cost curves), we assumed that input prices are constant because competitive firms are price-takers. This same assumption holds in the derivation of the long-run industry supply curve. Do you agree or disagree? Explain.

1A.2 Consider an industry that exhibits external diseconomies of scale. Suppose that over the next 10 years, demand for that industry's product increases rapidly. Describe in detail the adjustments likely to follow. Use diagrams in your answer.

1A.3 A representative firm producing watermelons is earning a normal profit at a price of $35 per hundred pounds. Draw a supply and demand diagram showing equilibrium at this price. Assuming that the industry is a constant-cost industry, use the diagram to show the long-term adjustment of the industry as demand falls over time. Explain the adjustment mechanism.

1A.4 Evaluate the following statement. If a firm is facing internal diseconomies of scale, it must be in an industry which is experiencing external diseconomies.

1A.5 Assume demand is decreasing in a contracting industry. Draw three supply and demand diagrams that reflect this, with the first representing an increasing-cost industry, the second representing a decreasing-cost industry, and the third representing a constant-cost industry. Assume that prior to the decrease in demand, the industry is in competitive long-run equilibrium. Include the long-run industry supply curve in each diagram and explain what is happening in each scenario. Specify whether each diagram represents external economies or external diseconomies.

Input Demand: The Labor and Land Markets

10

In 2014 the average yearly wage for a welder was $38,000, while the average yearly wage for a computer programmer was $56,000. What determines these wages? *Why* is the price for an acre of land in Toledo, Ohio, less than it is in San Francisco, California? It should not surprise you to learn that the same forces of supply and demand that determine the prices of the goods and services we consume can also be used to explain what happens in the markets for inputs like labor, land, and capital. These input markets are the subject of our next two chapters. In this chapter we set out a basic framework and discuss labor and land, whereas in Chapter 11 we tackle the more complicated topic of capital and investment.

Define the basic concepts of input markets.

Input Markets: Basic Concepts

Demand for Inputs: A *Derived* Demand

When we looked at the Blue Velvet Car Wash in Chapter 9, we saw that the number and price of car washes depended on, among other things, how much drivers liked getting their cars washed (the demand curve). If we want to explain the price of ice cream, knowing that most people have a sweet tooth would be helpful. Now think about the demand for a welder. Why might someone have a demand for a welder? In input markets, the reason we demand something is not because it is itself useful, but because it can be used to produce something else that we want. We, or more precisely a firm, demands a welder because he or she is needed to make a car and that car has value. The central difference between the demand for final goods and services and the demand for an input is that input demand is a **derived demand**. The higher the demand for cars, the higher the demand for welders.

derived demand The demand for resources (inputs) that is dependent on the demand for the outputs those resources can be used to produce.

> Inputs are demanded by a firm if and only if households demand the good or service provided by that firm.

In the press we often read about conflicts between labor unions and manufacturing firms. But understanding that labor demand is a derived demand shows us the common ground between labor and management: An increase in the demand for a product potentially improves the position not only of owners of the firm producing that good, but also the position of workers providing labor input.

The demand that a firm or industry has for a worker of a particular type depends then on how much value that worker can produce for the firm. This value, in turn, depends on how many physical units the worker can produce, his or her **productivity**, and how much those physical units can be sold for.

productivity of an input The amount of output produced per unit of that input.

Marginal Revenue Product

In Chapter 7 we defined the **marginal product of labor (MP_L)** as the additional output produced if a firm hires 1 additional unit of labor. For example, if a firm pays for 400 hours of labor per week—10 workers working 40 hours each—and asks one worker to stay an extra hour, the product of the 401st hour is the marginal product of labor for that firm. In that chapter, we used as an example the declining marginal product at a sandwich shop as the workers tried to manage with only one grill. The first three columns of Table 10.1 reproduce some of the production data from that shop.

marginal product of labor (MP_L) The additional output produced by 1 additional unit of labor.

TABLE 10.1	Marginal Revenue Product per Hour of Labor in Sandwich Production (One Grill)			
(1) Total Labor Units (Employees)	(2) Total Product (Sandwiches per Hour)	(3) Marginal Product of Labor (MP_L) (Sandwiches per Hour)	(4) Price (P_X) (Value Added per Sandwich)[a]	(5) Marginal Revenue Product ($MP_L \times P_X$) (per Hour)
0	0	—	—	—
1	10	10	$0.50	$5.00
2	25	15	0.50	7.50
3	35	10	0.50	5.00
4	40	5	0.50	2.50
5	42	2	0.50	1.00
6	42	0	0.50	0.00

[a] The "price" is essentially profit per sandwich; see discussion in text.

ECONOMICS IN PRACTICE

Do Managers Matter?

Many of you will likely someday go on to work as managers in firms. As you study productivity and think about your future, you might wonder about how managers, like the one you will become, can affect the productivity of the people who work for them. A recent field experiment run by several economists (and former consultants) has some interesting things to say about this.

Bloom, Eifert, Mahajan, McKenzie, and Roberts, economists from a range of places including Stanford University and the World Bank, recently published a paper describing a field experiment they ran on a group of large Indian textile firms.[1] Using a sample of several dozen firms, the researchers randomly sorted those firms into one of two groups. In the treatment group firm managers received five months of extensive management training from a large international consulting group. They were taught a range of operational practices that earlier research had suggested might be effective. A second, control group received a shorter period of diagnostic consulting, with no training.

The results? Within the first year after treatment, productivity in the treated plants increased by 17%. One of the authors of this textbook teaches MBA students and was pleased to read these results!

THINKING PRACTICALLY

1. Many of the firms treated had multiple plants. After the researchers left, what do you think they did about training in their other plants?

[1] Nicholas Bloom, Benn Eifert, Aprajit Mahajan, David McKenzie, and John Roberts, "Does Management Matter: Evidence from India." *Quarterly Journal of Economics* (2013): 1–51.

We see in this case the number of sandwiches that can be made by the first, second, third worker and so on, but to see how many workers this firm wants to hire at a given wage, we also need to know how much those sandwiches sell for. After all, we will be paying our workers in dollars, not in sandwiches!

The **marginal revenue product (MRP)** of a variable input is the additional revenue a firm earns by employing 1 additional unit of that input, *ceteris paribus*. If labor is the variable factor, for example, hiring an additional unit will lead to added output (the *marginal product* of labor). The sale of that added output will yield revenue. *Marginal revenue product* is the revenue produced by selling the good or service that is produced by the marginal unit of labor. In a competitive firm, marginal revenue product is the value of a factor's marginal product. The marginal revenue product is also called the **value of the marginal product**.

> **marginal revenue product (MRP)** *or* **the value of marginal product (VMP)**   The additional revenue a firm earns by employing 1 additional unit of an input, *ceteris paribus*.

By using labor as our variable factor, we can state this proposition more formally by saying that if MP_L is the marginal product of labor and P_X is the price of output, then the marginal revenue product of labor is

$$MRP_L = MP_L \times P_X$$

When calculating marginal revenue product, we need to be precise about what is being produced. A sandwich shop sells sandwiches, but it does not produce the bread, meat, cheese, mustard, and mayonnaise that go into the sandwiches. What the shop is producing is "sandwich cooking and assembly services." The shop is "adding value" to the meat, bread, and other ingredients by preparing and putting them all together in ready-to-eat form. With this in mind, let us assume that each finished sandwich in our shop sells for $0.50 over and above the costs of its ingredients. Thus, the *price of the service* the shop is selling is $0.50 per sandwich, and the only variable cost of providing that service is that of the labor used to put the sandwiches together. Thus, if X is the product of our shop, $P_X = \$0.50$.

Table 10.1, column 5, calculates the marginal revenue product of each worker if the shop charges $0.50 per sandwich over and above the costs of its ingredients. The first worker produces 10 sandwiches per hour, which at $0.50 each, generates revenues of $5.00 per hour. The addition of a second worker yields $7.50 an hour in revenues. After the second worker, diminishing returns drive MRP_L down. The marginal revenue product of the third worker is $5.00 per hour, of the fourth worker is only $2.50, and so on.

Figure 10.1 graphs the data from Table 10.1. Notice that the marginal revenue product curve has the same downward slope and shape as the marginal product curve but that MRP is measured in dollars, not units of output. The MRP curve shows the dollar value of labor's marginal product.

We can look at the MRP curve to ask how many workers the sandwich shop should hire. Suppose the going wage for sandwich makers is $4 per hour. A profit-maximizing firm would hire three workers. The first worker would yield $5 per hour in revenue, and the second would yield $7.50, but they each would cost only $4 per hour. The third worker would bring in $5 per hour, but still cost only $4 in marginal wages. The marginal product of the fourth worker, however, would not bring in enough revenue ($2.50) to pay this worker's salary. Total profit is thus maximized by hiring three workers. If the wage were instead $2.00, the firm would hire four workers. So we see that the curve in the lower panel of Figure 10.1 tells us how much labor our sandwich owner will hire at each potential market wage. If the market wage falls,

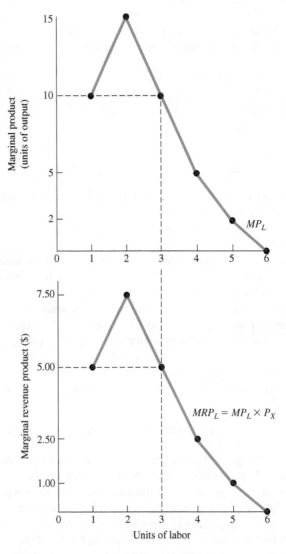

▲ **FIGURE 10.1** **Deriving a Marginal Revenue Product Curve from Marginal Product**

The marginal revenue product of labor is the price of output, P_X, times the marginal product of labor, MP_L.

the quantity of labor hours demanded rises. If the market wage rises, the quantity of labor demanded will fall. Therefore, we can now say that the factor's marginal revenue product curve is its demand curve for that factor in the short run. It tells us how many workers the firm will hire at different wage rates.

Labor Supply

In Chapter 6 we introduced the individual labor supply decision in the context of household choice. As we saw in that chapter, the choice to work, and how much to work, essentially involves a trade-off between leisure and the goods that can be purchased with wages earned from working. To maximize utility, an individual worker chooses work hours so that the marginal utility from an additional dollar earned from that work exactly offsets the marginal utility lost from not enjoying the leisure benefits of that hour. For most people, as their wage rate increases, the number of hours they are willing to work also increases, at least up to a point.[1] Thus, for an individual, the labor supply curve, which shows the number of hours the individual is willing to work at different wage rates, slopes up.

How do we derive a **market labor supply** curve? Here we proceed just as we did in the case of the move from an individual firm supply curve to a market supply curve in the output market. If we are interested in the labor supply of workers facing firms in a given location, we simply "add up" all the individual labor supply curves of the workers in that area. If the individual supply curves slope up, then so will the market supply curves.

market labor supply curve
the horizontal aggregation of the individual labor supply curves for workers in an area.

The labor supply curve traces the relationship between wage rates and the number of hours workers are willing to supply, holding other things constant. The number of hours people are willing to work clearly depends on factors other than wage rates, factors that *shift* the supply curve. At the individual level, preferences and norms play a role in the decision to work. In the United States, the labor force participation rate of working-age women grew dramatically in the 1970s, a change most people attribute to cultural change rather than economics. Changes in attitudes toward work, as well as opportunities for leisure, also can shift the labor supply curve. A change in wealth can also shift the labor supply curve. As individuals get richer, from nonwage income, the marginal utility of a dollar typically falls, thus reducing hours worked for a given wage rate. With more wealth, the typical individual "buys" more leisure. Finally, population change shifts the supply curve. The market labor supply curve is the sum of all the individual supply curves. If we increase the number of individuals in a market, this naturally shifts the labor supply curve to the right.

Labor Markets

The Firm's Labor Market Decision

We can now put demand and supply together to look at how firms determine how many workers to hire. We have seen that an individual firm's demand for an input depends on that input's marginal revenue product and its unit cost, or price. The market demand for labor is simply the aggregation of the demands from all of the firms in the area who want that particular type of worker. For the sandwich shop, using largely unskilled workers, their demand for those workers is added to the demand for that type of worker by all the other firms in that region. In this sense, a sandwich shop shares a work force with numerous other, perhaps quite different, firms.

The left side of Figure 10.2 shows a typical supply and demand curve in the labor market for a type of worker in a particular region. The demand curve comes from aggregating the demand curves of area firms, and reflects the marginal revenue products of labor to those firms. The supply curve comes from aggregating the individual supply curves of the workers in that area. The *market price* or the wage is determined in the labor market as a whole. We see in Figure 10.2 that the market clears at a wage of $10 and 560,000 hours of labor.

10.2 LEARNING OBJECTIVE

Discuss the conditions that affect supply and demand in labor markets.

---

[1] For a labor supply curve to slope up, the substitution effect must dominate the income effect. See Chapter 6 for a review.

▶ **FIGURE 10.2**

Marginal Revenue Product and Factor Demand for a Firm Using One Variable Input (Labor)

A competitive firm will use that factor as long as its marginal revenue product exceeds its unit cost. A perfectly competitive firm will hire labor as long as MRP_L is greater than the going wage, W^*. The hypothetical firm will demand 210 units or hours of labor.

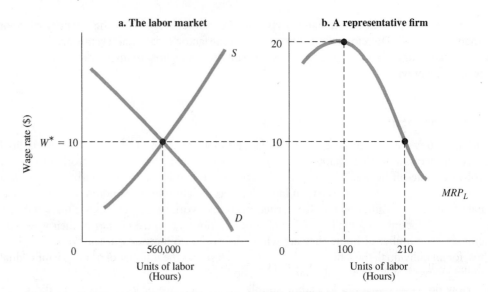

On the right side of Figure 10.2, we have shown a representative firm in this input market. This firm is a small part of the overall demand for labor. It is contemplating hiring only a few hundred hours of workers in a market with hundreds of thousands of hours. As a small player, this firm acts in the input market, just as it does in the output market, as a price-taker. Such firms can hire all the labor they want to hire as long as they pay the market wage. How many workers does the firm want to hire? Each worker hour costs the firm $10, the hourly wage. We can think of the hourly wage as the marginal cost of a unit of labor. The firm's value from hiring workers is the marginal revenue product curve, or its demand curve. A profit-maximizing firm will hire workers as long as the marginal revenue product of that labor exceeds its market price (or wage).

As long as MRP_L remains above $10, the firm will earn positive value from each worker hired. In this case, the firm hires labor up to 210 hours. At that point, the wage rate is equal to the marginal revenue product of labor, or $W^* = MRP_L = 10$. The firm will not demand labor beyond 210 hours because the cost of hiring the 211th hour of labor would be greater than the value of what that hour produces.

Comparing Marginal Revenue and Marginal Cost to Maximize Profits   In Chapter 8, we saw that a competitive firm's marginal cost curve is the same as its supply curve. That is, at any output price, the marginal cost curve determines how much output a profit-maximizing firm will produce. We came to this conclusion by comparing the marginal revenue that a firm would earn by producing one more unit of output with the marginal cost of producing that unit of output.

There is no difference between the reasoning in Chapter 8 and the reasoning in this chapter. The only difference is that what is being measured at the margin has changed. In Chapter 8, the firm was comparing the marginal revenues and costs of producing *another unit of output*. Here the firm is comparing the marginal revenues and costs of employing *another unit of input*.

In both cases, the firm is comparing the cost of production with potential revenues from the sale of product *at the margin*. In Chapter 8, the firm compared the price of output (*P*, which is equal to *MR* in perfect competition) directly with cost of production (*MC*), where cost was derived from information on factor prices and technology. (Review the derivation of cost curves in Chapter 8 if this is unclear.) Here information on output price and technology is contained in the marginal revenue product curve, which the firm compares with information on input price to determine the optimal level of input to demand.

Many Labor Markets

Although Figure 10.1 depicts "*the* labor market," many labor markets exist. There is a market for baseball players, for carpenters, for chemists, for college professors, and for unskilled workers. Still other markets exist for taxi drivers, assembly-line workers, secretaries, and corporate executives. Each market has a set of skills associated with it and a supply of people with the requisite skills.

ECONOMICS IN PRACTICE

The National Football League Predicts Marginal Products

The market for new, fresh-from-college football players has an unusual structure relative to the labor markets we have been discussing. Rather than being part of an open market in which, say, teams directly approach college players with salary offers, teams engage in an annual player draft under the auspices of the National Football League. The annual draft is held as a way to try to keep team quality more even, rather than allow one rich team to hire all of the best players year after year. Instead, teams are given draft numbers, allowing them to choose a player, with whom they then negotiate salary and so on. For football fans, watching the "draft" each year to see which promising college player goes first is an exciting event.

Teams are given draft numbers based on their record in the prior year. But they are allowed to trade numbers. So the Philadelphia Eagles could if given number 2, trade that for picks 4 and 7 if they chose to. This feature of the draft has allowed two creative economists, Richard Thaler and Cade Massey, to see how well football teams predict future productivity of football players.[1] How closely do the prices implicit in trades made match player productivity, taking into account salary? If the Eagles do trade pick 2 for picks 4 plus 7, does performance on the field of the combination of the lower-ranked players make up for the lost performance of pick 2? Thaler and Massey find that teams tend to "overpay" for the top pick in terms of the trades they make, displaying overconfidence in their

ability to predict skill differences between two closely ranked players. Before the next draft, you might want to look at their paper!

THINKING PRACTICALLY

1. How would you measure the marginal productivity of one professional football player versus another?

[1] Richard Thaler and Cade Massey, "Loser's Curse: Overconfidence versus Market Efficiency in the National Football League," *Management Science* (forthcoming).

If labor markets are competitive, the wages in those markets are determined by the interaction of supply and demand. As we have seen, firms will hire additional workers only as long as the value of their product exceeds the relevant market wage. This is true in all competitive labor markets.

Land Markets

10.3 LEARNING OBJECTIVE

Describe the relationship between supply and demand in land markets.

Unlike labor and capital, land has a special feature that we have not yet considered: It is in strictly fixed (perfectly inelastic) supply in total. The only real questions about land thus center around how much it is worth and how it will be used.

Because land is fixed in supply, we say that its price is **demand determined**. In other words, the price of land is determined exclusively by what households and firms are willing to pay for it. The return to any factor of production in fixed supply is called a **pure rent.**

Thinking of the price of land as demand determined can be confusing because all land is not the same. Some land is clearly more valuable than other land. What lies behind these differences? As with any other factor of production, land will presumably be sold or rented to the user who is willing to pay the most for it. The value of land to a potential user may depend on the characteristics of the land or on its location. For example, more fertile land should produce more farm products per acre and thus command a higher price than less fertile land. A piece of property located at the intersection of two highways may be of great value as a site for a gas station because of the volume of traffic that passes the intersection daily.

demand-determined price
The price of a good that is in fixed supply; it is determined exclusively by what households and firms are willing to pay for the good.

pure rent   The return to any factor of production that is in fixed supply.

▶ **FIGURE 10.3**   **The Rent on Land Is Demand Determined**
Because land in general (and each parcel in particular) is in fixed supply, its price is demand determined. Graphically, a fixed supply is represented by a vertical, perfectly inelastic supply curve. Rent, R_0, depends exclusively on demand—what people are willing to pay.

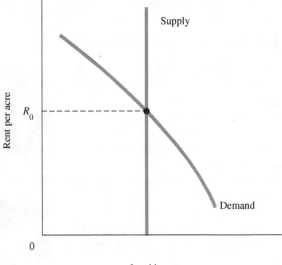

A numerical example may help to clarify our discussion. Consider the potential uses of a corner lot in a suburb of Kansas City. Alan wants to build a clothing store on the lot. He anticipates that he can earn economic profits of $10,000 per year because of the land's excellent location. Bella, another person interested in buying the corner lot, believes that she can earn $35,000 per year in economic profit if she builds a pharmacy there. Because of the higher profit that she expects to earn, Bella will be able to outbid Alan, and the landowner will sell (or rent) to the highest bidder.

Because location is often the key to profits, landowners are frequently able to "squeeze" their renters. One of the most popular locations in the Boston area, for example, is Harvard Square. There are dozens of restaurants in and around the square, and most of them are full a good deal of the time. Despite this seeming success, most Harvard Square restaurant owners are not getting rich. Why? Because they must pay very high rents on the location of their restaurants. A substantial portion of each restaurant's revenues goes to rent the land that (by virtue of its scarcity) is the key to unlocking those same revenues.

Although Figure 10.3 shows that the supply of land is perfectly inelastic (a vertical line), the supply of land in a *given use* may not be perfectly inelastic or fixed. Think, for example, about farmland available for housing developments. As a city's population grows, housing developers find themselves willing to pay more for land. As land becomes more valuable for development, some farmers sell out, and the supply of land available for development increases. This analysis would lead us to draw an upward-sloping supply curve (not a perfectly inelastic supply curve) for land in the land-for-development category.

Nonetheless, our major point—that land earns a pure rent—is still valid. The supply of land of a *given quality* at a *given location* is truly fixed in supply. Its value is determined exclusively by the amount that the highest bidder is willing to pay for it. Because land cannot be reproduced, supply is perfectly inelastic.

Rent and the Value of Output Produced on Land

Because the price of land is demand determined, rent depends on what the potential users of the land are willing to pay for it. As we have seen, land will end up being used by whoever is willing to pay the most for it. What determines this willingness to pay? Let us now connect our discussion of land markets with our earlier discussions of factor markets in general.

As our example of two potential users bidding for a plot of land shows, the bids depend on the land's potential for profit. Alan's plan would generate $10,000 a year; Bella's would generate $35,000 a year. Nevertheless, these profits do not just materialize. Instead, they come from producing and selling an output that is valuable to households. Land in a popular downtown location is expensive because of what can be produced on it. Note that land is needed as an input into the production of nearly all goods and services. A restaurant located next to a popular theater can charge a premium price because it has a relatively captive clientele.

ECONOMICS IN PRACTICE

Valuing Land

The *New York Times*, as well as a number of other newspapers and magazines, now and again run columns showing us what some price—say $350,000—would buy us in the way of a house in various parts of the United States. The range in size and quality of houses is quite large. In New York City or San Francisco $350,000 buys one very little, perhaps a small one-bedroom apartment. In New Haven, CT, you would fare better and likely could buy a small attractive house. In some parts of the country, $350,000 buys a six-bedroom mansion. And yet, construction costs are actually quite similar across the country. Housing price differences are driven much more by differences in land prices. Land, after all, in a particular location is inelastically supplied. We have not yet figured out how to move an acre of land from Toledo, Ohio, to Scarsdale, NY. Price differences are demand determined, given the fixed supply.

So what determines people's demand for one location versus another? Nice weather helps, as does proximity to high-paying employment. More recently economists have begun estimating how much more people will pay for environmental quality, not only in the United States but increasingly in Chinese cities.[1]

THINKING PRACTICALLY

1. Europe has been expanding its range of high-speed trains. What do you think this might do to land prices in the areas served by these trains?

[1] For new work on the United States see Bajari, Cooley, Kim, and Timmins, "A Theory Based Approach to Hedonic Price Regressions with Time Varying Unobservable Product Attributes," NBER Working paper, November 2010. For some work on China, see Zheng, Siqi, Fu Yuming, and Liu, Hongyu, "Demand for Urban Quality of Living in China," *Journal of Real Estate Finance* (2009).

The restaurant must produce a quality product to stay in business, but the location alone provides a substantial profit opportunity.

It should come as no surprise that the demand for land follows the same rules as the demand for inputs in general. A profit-maximizing firm will employ an additional factor of production as long as its marginal revenue product exceeds its market price. For example, a profit-maximizing firm will hire labor as long as the revenue earned from selling labor's product is sufficient to cover the cost of hiring additional labor—which for perfectly competitive firms, equals the wage rate. The same thing is true for land. A firm will pay for and use land as long as the revenue earned from selling the product produced on that land is sufficient to cover the price of the land. Stated in equation form, the firm will use land up to the point at which $MRP_A = P_A$, where A is land (acres).

Just as the demand curve for labor reflects the value of labor's product as determined in output markets, so the demand for land depends on the value of land's product in output markets. The profitability of the restaurant located next to the theater results from the fact that the meals produced there command a price in the marketplace.

The allocation of a given plot of land among competing uses thus depends on the trade-off between competing products that can be produced there. Agricultural land becomes developed when its value in producing housing or manufactured goods (or providing space for a mini mall) exceeds its value in producing crops. A corner lot in Kansas City becomes the site of a pharmacy instead of a clothing store because the people in that neighborhood have a greater need for a pharmacy.

One final word about land: Because land cannot be moved physically, the value of any one parcel depends to a large extent on the uses to which adjoining parcels are put. A factory belching acrid smoke will probably reduce the value of adjoining land, while a new highway that increases accessibility may enhance it.

10.4 LEARNING OBJECTIVE

Identify factors that trigger shifts in factor demand curves.

Input Demand Curves

In Chapter 3, we considered the factors that shift the demand curves for products or outputs. We have not yet talked about *input* demand curves in any detail, however, so we now need to say more about what lies behind them.

Shifts in Factor Demand Curves

Factor (input) demand curves are derived from information on technology—that is, production functions—and output price. A change in the demand for outputs, a change in the quantity of complementary or substitutable inputs, changes in the prices of other inputs, and technological change all can cause factor demand curves to shift. These shifts in demand are important because they directly affect the allocation of resources among alternative uses as well as the level and distribution of income.

The Demand for Outputs   A firm will demand an input as long as its marginal revenue product exceeds its market price. Marginal revenue product, which in perfect competition is equal to a factor's marginal product times the price of output, is the value of the factor's marginal product. In the case of labor we have:

$$MRP_L = MP_L \times P_X$$

The amount that a firm is willing to pay for a factor of production depends directly on the value of the things the firm produces, and the marginal productivity of that factor of production. It follows that if product demand increases, product price will rise and marginal revenue product (factor demand) will increase—the *MRP* curve will shift to the right. If product demand declines, product price will fall and marginal revenue product (factor demand) will decrease—the *MRP* curve will shift to the left.

Go back and raise the price of sandwiches from $0.50 to $1.00 in the sandwich shop example examined in Table 10.1 on p. 210 to see that this is so.

To the extent that an input is used intensively in the production of some product, changes in the demand for that product cause factor demand curves to shift and the prices of those inputs to change. Land prices are a good example. Forty years ago, the area in Manhattan along the west side of Central Park from about 80th Street north was a run-down neighborhood full of abandoned houses. The value of land there was virtually zero. During the mid-1980s, increased demand for housing caused rents to hit record levels. Some single-room apartments, for example, rented for as much as $1,400 per month. With the higher price of output (rent), input prices increased substantially. By 2015, small one-bedroom apartments on 80th Street and Central Park West sold for well over $700,000, and the value of the land figures importantly in these prices. In essence, a shift in demand for an output (housing in the area) pushed up the marginal revenue product of land from zero to very high levels.

The Quantity of Complementary and Substitutable Inputs   In our sandwich shop example, the marginal product of labor was derived assuming there was only one grill available. As we showed in another chapter, expanding the number of grills increases the marginal product of workers on those grills. The productivity of, and thus the demand for, any one factor of production depends on the quality and quantity of the other factors with which it works.

The effect of capital accumulation on wages is one of the most important themes in all of economics. In general, the production and use of capital enhances the productivity of labor and normally increases the demand for labor and drives up wages. Consider as an example transportation. In a poor country such as Bangladesh, one person with an ox cart can move a small load over bad roads very slowly. By contrast, the stock of capital used by workers in the transportation industry in the United States is enormous. A truck driver in the United States works with a substantial amount of capital. The typical 18-wheel tractor trailer, for example, is a piece of capital worth more than $100,000. The roads themselves are capital that was put in place by the government. The amount of material that a single driver can move between distant points in a short time is staggering relative to what it was 100 years ago.

The Prices of Other Inputs When a firm has a choice among alternative technologies, the choice it makes depends to some extent on relative input prices.

In recent years, the large increase in energy prices relative to prices of other factors of production had a number of effects on the demand for those other inputs. Insulation of new buildings, installation of more efficient heating plants, and similar efforts substantially raised the demand for capital as capital was substituted for energy in production. It has also been argued that an energy crisis can lead to an increase in demand for labor. If capital and energy are complementary inputs—that is, if technologies that are capital-intensive are also energy-intensive—the argument goes, the higher energy prices tended to push firms away from capital-intensive techniques toward more labor-intensive techniques. A new highly automated technique, for example, might need fewer workers, but it would also require a vast amount of electricity to operate. High electricity prices could lead a firm to reject the new techniques and stick with an old, more labor-intensive method of production.

Technological Change Closely related to the impact of capital accumulation on factor demand is the potential impact of **technological change**—that is, the introduction of new methods of production or new products. New technologies usually introduce ways to produce outputs with fewer inputs by increasing the productivity of existing inputs or by raising marginal products. Because marginal revenue product reflects productivity, increases in productivity directly shift input demand curves. If the marginal product of labor rises, for example, the demand for labor shifts to the right (increases). Technological change can and does have a powerful influence on factor demands. As new products and new techniques of production are born, so are demands for new inputs and new skills. As old products become obsolete, so do the labor skills and other inputs needed to produce them.

technological change The introduction of new methods of production or new products intended to increase the productivity of existing inputs or to raise marginal products.

Profit-Maximizing Condition in Input Markets

10.5 LEARNING OBJECTIVE

Understand how the prices of the different inputs relate to their relative productivity.

Thus far, we have discussed the labor and land markets in some detail. Although we will put off a detailed discussion of capital until the next chapter, it is now possible to generalize about competitive demand for factors of production. Every firm has an incentive to use variable inputs as long as the revenue generated by those inputs covers the costs of those inputs at the margin. More formally, firms will employ each input up to the point that its price equals its marginal revenue product. This condition holds for all factors at all levels of output.

The profit-maximizing condition for the perfectly competitive firm is

$$P_L = MRP_L = (MP_L \times P_X)$$
$$P_K = MRP_K = (MP_K \times P_X)$$
$$P_A = MRP_A = (MP_A \times P_X)$$

where L is labor, K is capital, A is land (acres), X is output, and P_X is the price of that output.

When all these conditions are met, the firm will be using the optimal, or least costly, combination of inputs. If all the conditions hold at the same time, it is possible to rewrite them another way:

$$\frac{MP_L}{P_L} = \frac{MP_K}{P_K} = \frac{MP_A}{P_A}$$

Your intuition tells you much the same thing that these equations do: The marginal product of the last dollar spent on labor must be equal to the marginal product of the last dollar spent on capital, which must be equal to the marginal product of the last dollar spent on land, and so on. If this was not the case, the firm could produce more with less and reduce cost. Suppose, for example, that $MP_L/P_L > MP_K/P_K$. In this situation, the firm can produce more output by shifting dollars out of capital and into labor. Hiring more labor drives down the marginal product of labor, and using less capital increases the marginal product of capital. This means that the ratios come back to equality as the firm shifts out of capital and into labor.

Looking Ahead

We now have a complete, but simplified picture of household and firm decision making. We have also examined some of the basic forces that determine the allocation of resources and the mix of output in perfectly competitive markets.

In this competitive environment, profit-maximizing firms make three fundamental decisions: (1) how much to produce and supply in output markets, (2) how to produce (which technology to use), and (3) how much of each input to demand. Chapters 7 through 9 looked at these three decisions from the perspective of the output market. We derived the supply curve of a competitive firm in the short run and discussed output market adjustment in the long run. Deriving cost curves, we learned, involves evaluating and choosing among alternative technologies. Finally, we saw how a firm's decision about how much product to supply in output markets implicitly determines input demands. Input demands, we argued, are also derived demands. That is, they are ultimately linked to the demand for output.

To show the connection between output and input markets, this chapter took these same three decisions and examined them from the perspective of input markets. Firms hire up to the point at which each input's marginal revenue product is equal to its price.

The next chapter takes up the complexity of what we have been loosely calling the "capital market." There we discuss the relationship between the market for physical capital and financial capital markets and look at some of the ways that firms make investment decisions. Once we examine the nature of overall competitive equilibrium in Chapter 12, we can finally begin relaxing some of the assumptions that have restricted the scope of our inquiry—most importantly, the assumption of perfect competition in input and output markets.

——————— SUMMARY ———————

1. The same set of decisions that lies behind output supply curves also lies behind input demand curves. Only the perspective is different.

10.1 INPUT MARKETS: BASIC CONCEPTS *p. 210*

2. Demand for inputs depends on demand for the outputs that they produce; input demand is thus a *derived demand*. *Productivity* is a measure of the amount of output produced per unit of input.

3. In general, firms will demand workers as long as the value of what those workers produce exceeds what they must be paid. Households will supply labor as long as the wage exceeds the value of leisure or the value that they derive from nonpaid work.

4. In the short run, some factor of production is fixed. This means that all firms encounter diminishing returns in the short run. Stated somewhat differently, diminishing returns means that all firms encounter declining marginal product in the short run.

5. The *marginal revenue product* (MRP) of a variable input is the additional revenue a firm earns from the output produced by employing one additional unit of the input, *ceteris paribus*. MRP is equal to the input's marginal product times the price of output.

6. An individual's labor supply curve is determined by his or her choice between leisure and the value of goods that can be purchased with wages earned.

7. A market labor supply curve is the horizontal aggregation of individual labor supply curves.

8. Labor supply curves shift as a result of changes in preferences, wealth, and population.

10.2 LABOR MARKETS *p. 213*

9. Demand for an input depends on that input's marginal revenue product. Profit-maximizing perfectly competitive firms will buy an input (for example, hire labor) up to the point where the input's marginal revenue product equals its price. For a firm employing only one variable factor of production, the *MRP* curve is the firm's demand curve for that factor in the short run.

10. For a perfectly competitive firm the condition $W = MRP_L$ is exactly the same as the condition $P = MC$. Firms weigh the value of outputs as reflected in output price against the value of inputs as reflected in marginal costs.

10.3 LAND MARKETS *p. 215*

11. Because land is in strictly fixed supply, its price is *demand determined*—that is, its price is determined exclusively by

what households and firms are willing to pay for it. The return to any factor of production in fixed supply is called a *pure rent*. A firm will pay for and use land as long as the revenue earned from selling the product produced on that land is sufficient to cover the price of the land. The firm will use land up to the point at which $MRP_A = P_A$, where A is land (acres).

10.4 INPUT DEMAND CURVES *p. 218*

12. A shift in a firm's demand curve for a factor of production can be influenced by the demand for the firm's product, the quantity of complementary and substitutable inputs, the prices of other inputs, and changes in technology.

10.5 THE FIRM'S PROFIT-MAXIMIZING CONDITION IN INPUT MARKETS *p. 219*

13. Every firm has an incentive to use variable inputs as long as the revenue generated by those inputs covers the costs of those inputs at the margin. Therefore, firms will employ each input up to the point that its price equals its marginal revenue product. This profit-maximizing condition holds for all factors at all levels of output.

REVIEW TERMS AND CONCEPTS

demand-determined price, *p. 215*

derived demand, *p. 210*

marginal product of labor (*MP_L*), *p. 210*

marginal revenue product (*MRP*), *p. 211*

market labor supply curve, *p. 213*

productivity of an input, *p. 210*

pure rent, *p. 215*

technological change, *p. 219*

Equation:
$MRP_L = MP_L \times P_X$, *p. 211, 218*

PROBLEMS

All Problems are Available on MyEconLab.

10.1 INPUT MARKETS: BASIC CONCEPTS

LEARNING OBJECTIVE: Define the basic concepts of input markets.

1.1 According to the Bureau of Labor Statistics, the average weekly earnings of production and nonsupervisory employees in education and health services was $822 in March 2015, up from $671 in March 2006. All else equal, such an increase in wages would be expected to reduce the quantity of labor demanded and employment should fall. Instead, the quantity demanded for labor has increased dramatically with more than 3.7 million jobs being created between 2006 and 2015. How can you explain this seeming discrepancy?

1.2 The following schedule shows the technology of production at Mahalo Macadamia Nut Farm for 2015:

Workers	Total Pounds of Macadamia Nuts Per Week
0	0
1	1,200
2	2,000
3	2,500
4	2,700
5	2,800
6	2,400

If macadamia nuts sell for $3.50 per pound and workers can be hired in a competitive labor market for $800 per week, how many workers should be hired? What if workers unionized and the weekly wages doubled? (*Hint:* Create marginal product and marginal revenue product columns for the table.) Explain your answers clearly.

1.3 Consider the following information for a soccer ball manufacturing firm that can sell as many soccer balls as it wants for $12 per ball.

Number of Workers	Number of Soccer Balls Produced Per Week	MP_L	TR	MRP_L
0	0	—	—	—
1	20	—	—	—
2	50	—	—	—
3	90	—	—	—
4	—	50	—	—
5	180	—	—	—
6	—	—	2,520	—
7	—	—	—	336
8	—	—	—	216
9	—	14	—	—
10	280	—	—	—

a. Fill in all the blanks in the table.
b. Verify that MRP_L for this firm can be calculated in two ways: (1) change in TR from adding another worker and (2) MP_L times the price of output.
c. If this firm must pay a wage rate of $320 per worker per week, how many workers should it hire? Briefly explain why.
d. Suppose the wage rate rises to $400 per worker per week. How many workers should be hired now? Why?
e. Suppose the firm adopts a new technology that increases output at each level of employment by 50 percent and the price of soccer balls remains at $12. What is the effect of this new technology on MP_L and on MRP_L? At a wage of $400, how many workers should the firm hire now?

1.4 **[Related to the *Economics in Practice* on p. 211]** According to the Organization for Economic Cooperation and Development (OECD), labor productivity increased and unemployment also increased in Australia from 2013 to 2014. Explain why an increase in labor productivity and an increase in unemployment are not likely to coincide in the long run. Can you think of any explanation for these changes to simultaneously occur in the long run?

1.5 On October 29, 2012, Hurricane Sandy's storm surge hit the Northeast United States, causing more than $65 billion in damage. The hurricane was devastating to many east coast industries, with one of the hardest-hit being the shellfish industry. Explain the effect this hurricane most likely had on the following:
a. Price of shellfish
b. Marginal product of shellfishermen
c. Demand for shelfishermen

1.6 For a perfectly competitive firm, the marginal cost curve determines how much output a profit-maximizing firm will produce. For input markets, the marginal revenue

product curve determines how much labor a profit-maximizing firm will hire in a perfectly competitive labor market. Explain how the reasoning behind these two concepts is related.

1.7 Each year in New Orleans, Carnival season begins on January 6 and culminates with the city's biggest celebration of the year, Mardi Gras. This wildly popular celebration attracts people from around the world, and the city of New Orleans estimates that more than one million people attended the festivities in 2015. The Tuesday on which Mardi Gras falls each year has been declared a state holiday in Louisiana, with banks, post offices, and many private businesses closing for the day. On the basis of labor productivity, explain why you think Mardi Gras has been declared a state holiday in Louisiana and why so many businesses in New Orleans are closed on that day.

10.2 LABOR MARKETS

2.1 The following graph is the production function for a firm using only one variable factor of production, labor.
a. Graph the marginal product of labor for the firm as a function of the number of labor units hired.
b. Assuming the price of output, P_X, is equal to $6, graph the firm's marginal revenue product schedule as a function of the number of labor units hired.
c. If the current equilibrium wage rate is $4 per hour, how many hours of labor will you hire? How much output will you produce?

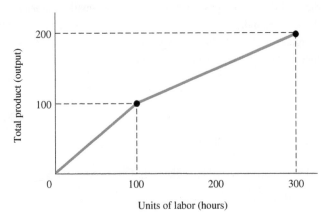

2.2 Assume that you are living in a house with two other people and that the house has a big lawn that must be mowed. One of your roommates, who dislikes working outdoors, suggests hiring a neighbor's daughter to mow the grass for $40 per week instead of sharing the work and doing it yourselves. How would you go about deciding who will mow the lawn? What factors would you raise in deciding? What are the trade-offs here?

2.3 At many colleges and universities, the highest paid member of the faculty is an athletic coach. At Duke

University in Durham, North Carolina, basketball coach Mike Krzyzewski earned a salary of more than $7.2 million during the 2013-2014 academic year, while the average total compensation for full professors at Duke was $240,300. How would you explain this?

Sources: "The 20 Highest-Paid College Coaches," *thebestschools.org* and "2013-14 AAUP Faculty Salary Survey," *Chronicle of Higher Education*, April 7, 2014.

2.4 In 2013, the CEO of Procter & Gamble, A. G. Lafley, earned $1,800,000 in total compensation (salary, bonuses, and other compensation) and Reynold Levy, the president of the non-profit Lincoln Center for the Performing Arts, earned $1,725,493. How can a non-profit organization like the Lincoln Center justify compensating its chief executive at a similar level to the CEO of a successful for-profit company like Procter & Gamble?

Sources: "Executive Compensation: How CEOs Rank," *wsj.com* and Kurumi Fukushima, "These 9 Nonprofit Executives Made Over $1-Million," *The Street.com*, September 15, 2014.

10.3 LAND MARKETS

LEARNING OBJECTIVE: Describe the relationship between supply and demand in land markets.

3.1 The demand for land is a derived demand. Think of a popular location near your school. What determines the demand for land in that area? What outputs are sold by businesses located there? Discuss the relationship between land prices and the prices of those products.

3.2 Antoinette's coastal property in Mississippi has five major ponds that she uses to raise shrimp. The productivity of each pond follows:

Annual Yield, Pounds

Pond 1	18,000
Pond 2	11,000
Pond 3	8,000
Pond 4	5,000
Pond 5	4,000

Assume that each pond is the same size and that the variable costs of raising shrimp are $18,000 per year per pond. The variable costs cover labor and machinery time, which is rented.

Antoinette must decide each year how many ponds to stock. In 2014, Shrimp farmers received $3.50 per pound. How many ponds did Antoinette stock? Explain. By 2015, the price of shrimp had fallen to $2.00 per pound. How will this price decrease change Antoinette's decision? How will it affect her demand for labor? How will it affect the value of Antoinette's land?

3.3 [**Related to the *Economics in Practice* on p. 217**] In Orlando, Florida, the land value went up dramatically when Disney built its theme park there. How do you explain this land price increase?

3.4 The price of land is said to be "demand-determined." Explain what this means and draw a graph to exemplify your explanation.

3.5 Houston, Texas, is the only major U.S. city with virtually no zoning laws. This means that single-family homes, apartment buildings, shopping centers, high-rise buildings, and industrial complexes can all be built in the same neighborhood. Of the major U.S. cities, Houston was also one of the least impacted by the housing market crisis of 2008. In 2009, Houston issued 42,697 building permits and was the top-ranked city in the list of healthiest housing markets. How might the lack of zoning laws have played a part in Houston's healthy housing and building markets?

Source: La Familia, "Zoning in on Zoning Laws," *El Gato*, June 2, 2010.

10.4 INPUT DEMAND CURVES

LEARNING OBJECTIVE: Identify factors that trigger shifts in factor demand curves.

4.1 Assume that a firm that manufactures gizmos can produce them with one of three processes used alone or in combination. The following table indicates the amounts of capital and labor required by each of the three processes to produce one gizmo.

	Units of Labor	Units of Capital
Process 1	5	2
Process 2	3	3
Process 3	1	6

a. Assuming capital costs $5 per unit and labor costs $3 per unit, which process will be employed?

b. Plot the three points on the firm's *TVC* curve corresponding to $q = 25$, $q = 50$, and $q = 100$.

c. At each of the three output levels, how much *K* and *L* will be demanded?

d. Repeat parts a. through c. assuming the price of labor is still $3 per unit and the price of capital has risen to $7 per unit.

4.2 Since 1980, wage inequality in the United States has increased substantially. According to the U.S. Census Bureau, income received by the top 20 percent of households rose from 44 percent of total aggregate income in the economy in 1980 to 51 percent in 2013, whereas the income received by the bottom 20 percent of households fell from 4.2 percent to 3.2 percent. Using the logic of marginal revenue product, give an explanation for this change in the distribution of income. In your explanation, you may want to consider the rise of the high-technology, high-skill sector and the decline of industries requiring low-skill labor.

4.3 Describe how each of the following events would affect (1) demand for auto workers and (2) auto workers' wages in the country of Astoria, home of the all-electric car, the Astro Galactica. Illustrate with supply and demand curves.

a. A sharp decrease in interest rates on new automobiles increases the demand for new automobiles.

b. The government of Astoria offers a 20 percent tax credit on the purchase of electric cars.

c. The Astorian economy falters, and the overall unemployment rate rises from 5 percent to 15 percent.

d. Gasoline prices fall by 30 percent, decreasing the demand for electric vehicles.

4.4 Many states provide firms with an "investment tax credit" that effectively reduces the price of capital. In theory, these credits are designed to stimulate new investment and thus create jobs. Critics have argued that if there are strong factor substitution effects, these subsidies could *reduce* employment in the state. Explain their arguments.

10.5 THE FIRM'S PROFIT-MAXIMIZING CONDITION IN INPUT MARKETS

LEARNING OBJECTIVE: Understand how the prices of the different inputs relate to their relative productivity.

5.1 For a given firm, $MRP_L = \$75$ and $MRP_K = \$150$ while $P_L = \$50$ and $P_K = \$200$.

a. Is the firm maximizing profits? Why or why not?

b. Identify a specific action that would increase this firm's profits.

*5.2 The following data represents output for a perfectly competitive firm with a product price of $2 per unit. Assume that the productivity of each resource is independent of the quantity of the other two.

a. Fill in the table.

b. If the price of labor is $4 per unit, the price of capital is $10 per unit, and the price of land is $80 per unit, what is the profit-maximizing combination of resources? Explain in terms of marginal revenue product.

Total Labor Units	Total Product	MP_L	TR ($)	MRP_L ($)	Total Capital Units	Total Product	MP_K	TR ($)	MRP_K ($)	Total Land Units	Total Product	MP_A	TR ($)	MRP_A ($)
0	0				0	0				0	0			
1	12				1	20				1	100			
2	20				2	35				2	180			
3	26				3	45				3	240			
4	30				4	50				4	280			
5	32				5	52				5	300			
6	32				6	53				6	310			

*Note: Problems marked with an asterisk are more challenging.

Input Demand: The Capital Market and the Investment Decision

11

In Chapter 10 we explored the labor and land markets in some detail. In this chapter, we consider the capital market more fully. Transactions between households and firms in the labor and land markets are direct. In the labor market, households offer their labor directly to firms in exchange for wages. In the land market, landowners rent or sell their land directly to firms in exchange for rent or an agreed-to price. In the capital market, though, households often *indirectly* supply the financial resources necessary for firms to purchase capital. When households save and add funds to their bank accounts, for example, firms can borrow those funds from the bank to finance their capital purchases.

The importance of the movement of capital from individuals to firms in a market economy cannot be overemphasized. For firms to enter new industries or produce new products, capital is required. In market capitalist systems, decisions about which enterprises to support via capital are made by private citizens seeking private gain. The *Economics in Practice* on p. 228 describes this process for one firm, Tesla, maker of electric cars. These decisions are risky—it is hard to know which new firms will succeed and which will fail. Understanding the institutions through which capital flows from households to firms is the subject of this chapter.

Define the concepts of capital, investment, and depreciation.

Capital, Investment, and Depreciation

Before we proceed with our analysis of the capital market, we need to review some basic economic principles and introduce some related concepts.

Capital

capital Those goods produced by the economic system that are used as inputs to produce other goods and services in the future.

One of the most important concepts in all of economics is the concept of **capital**. Capital goods are those goods produced by the economic system that are used as inputs to produce other goods and services in the future. Capital goods thus yield valuable productive services over time. The value of capital is only as great as the value of the services it renders over time.

physical, *or* tangible, capital
Material things used as inputs in the production of future goods and services. The major categories of physical capital are nonresidential structures, durable equipment, residential structures, and inventories.

Tangible Capital When we think of capital, we generally think of the physical, material capital employed by firms. The major categories of **physical, *or* tangible, capital** are (1) nonresidential structures (for example, office buildings, power plants, factories, shopping centers, warehouses, and docks), (2) durable equipment (for example, machines, trucks, computers, sandwich grills, and automobiles), (3) residential structures, and (4) inventories of inputs and outputs that firms have in stock.

Most firms need tangible capital, along with labor and land, to produce their products. A restaurant's capital requirements include a kitchen, ovens and grills, tables and chairs, silverware, dishes, and light fixtures. These items must be purchased up front and maintained if the restaurant is to function properly. A manufacturing firm must have a plant, specialized machinery, trucks, and inventories of parts. A winery needs casks, vats, piping, temperature-control equipment, and cooking and bottling machinery.

The capital stock of a retail pharmacy is made up mostly of inventories. Pharmacies do not produce the aspirin, vitamins, and toothbrushes that they sell. Instead, they buy those items from manufacturers and put them on display. The product actually produced and sold by a pharmacy is convenience. Like any other product, convenience is produced with labor and capital in the form of a store with many products, or inventory, displayed on the sales floor and kept in storerooms. The inventories of inputs and outputs that manufacturing firms maintain are also capital. To function smoothly and meet the demands of buyers, for example, the Ford Motor Company maintains inventories of both auto parts (tires, windshields, and so on) and completed cars.

An apartment building is also capital. Produced by the economic system, it yields valuable services over time and it is used as an input to produce housing services, which are rented.

social capital, *or* infrastructure
Capital that provides services to the public. Most social capital takes the form of public works (roads and bridges) and public services (police and fire protection).

Social Capital: Infrastructure Some physical or tangible capital is owned by the public instead of by private firms. **Social capital**, sometimes called **infrastructure**, is capital that provides services to the public. Most social capital takes the form of public works such as highways, roads, bridges, mass transit systems, and sewer and water systems. Police stations, fire stations, city halls, courthouses, and police cars are all forms of social capital that are used as inputs to produce the services that government provides.

All firms use some forms of social capital in producing their outputs. Recent economic research has shown that a country's infrastructure plays an important role in helping private firms produce their products efficiently. When public capital is not properly cared for—for example, when roads deteriorate or when airports are not modernized to accommodate increasing traffic—private firms that depend on efficient transportation networks suffer.

intangible capital
Nonmaterial things that contribute to the output of future goods and services.

human capital A form of intangible capital that includes the skills and other knowledge that workers have or acquire through education and training and that yields valuable services to a firm over time.

Intangible Capital Not all capital is physical. Some things that are intangible (nonmaterial) satisfy every part of our definition of capital. When a firm invests in advertising to establish a brand name, it is producing a form of **intangible capital** called *goodwill*. This goodwill yields valuable services to the firm over time.

When a firm establishes a training program for employees, it is investing in its workers' skills. We can think of such an investment as the production of an intangible form of capital called **human capital**. It is produced with labor (instructors) and capital (classrooms, computers, projectors, and books). Human capital in the form of new or augmented skills is an input—it will yield valuable productive services for the firm in the future. Learning economics increases your human capital!

When research produces valuable results, such as a new production process that reduces costs or a new formula that creates a new product, the new technology can be considered capital. Furthermore, even intellectual property can be patented and the rights to it can be sold.

A large number of "new economy" start-up technology companies have responded to the growth of the Internet. These dot-com and e-commerce companies generally start with limited tangible capital. Instead most of their capital is in the skills and knowledge of their employees: human capital.

Measuring Capital Labor is measured in hours, and land is measured in square feet or acres. Because capital comes in so many forms, it is virtually impossible to measure it directly in physical terms. The indirect measure generally used is *current market value*. The measure of a firm's **capital stock** is the current market value of its plant, equipment, inventories, and intangible assets. By using value as a measuring stick, business managers, accountants, and economists can, in a sense, add buildings, barges, and bulldozers into a measure of total capital.

capital stock For a single firm, the current market value of the firm's plant, equipment, inventories, and intangible assets.

Capital is measured as a *stock* value. That is, it is measured at a point in time: According to Department of Commerce estimates, the capital stock of the U.S. economy in 2013 was about $50.9 trillion. Of that amount, $12.9 trillion was owned by the federal, state, and local governments (for example, aircraft carriers and school buildings). Of the remaining $38.0 trillion, $17.4 trillion was residential capital and $20.6 trillion was nonresidential capital.

Although it is measured in terms of money, or value, it is important to think of the actual capital stock. When we speak of capital, we refer not to money or to financial assets such as bonds and stocks, but instead to the firm's physical plant, equipment, inventory, and intangible assets.

Investment and Depreciation

Recall the difference between stock and flow measures discussed in previous chapters. *Stock measures* are valued at a particular point in time, whereas *flow measures* are valued over a period of time. The easiest way to think of the difference between a stock and a flow is to think about a tub of water. The volume of water in the tub is measured at a point in time and is a stock. The amount of water that flows into the tub *per hour* and the amount of water that evaporates out of the tub *per day* are flow measures. Flow measures have meaning only when the time dimension is added. Water flowing into the tub at a rate of 5 gallons per hour is different from water flowing at a rate of 5 gallons per year.

Capital stocks are affected over time by two flows: investment and depreciation. When a firm produces or puts in place new capital—a new piece of equipment, for example—it has invested. **Investment** is a flow that increases the stock of capital. Because it has a time dimension, we speak of investment per period (by the month, quarter, or year).

investment New capital additions to a firm's capital stock. Although capital is measured at a given point in time (a stock), investment is measured over a period of time (a flow). The flow of investment increases the capital stock.

As you proceed, keep in mind that the term *investing* is *not* used in economics to describe the act of buying a share of stock or a bond. Although people commonly use the term this way ("I invested in some Facebook stock" or "he invested in Treasury bonds"), the term *investment* when used correctly refers *only to an increase in capital*.

Table 11.1 presents data on private investment in the U. S. economy in 2014. About 60 percent of the total was equipment and intellectual property products (like software). Almost all the rest was investment in structures, both residential (apartment buildings, condominiums, houses, etc.) and nonresidential (factories, shopping malls, etc.). Inventory investment was small. Column 3 looks at private investment as a percent of gross domestic product (GDP), a measure of the total output of the economy.

Depreciation is the decline in an asset's economic value over time. If you have ever owned a car, you are aware that its resale value falls with age. Suppose you bought a new Toyota Prius for $30,500 and you decide to sell it 2 years and 25,000 miles later. Checking the newspaper and talking to several dealers, you find out that, given its condition and mileage, you can expect to get $22,000 for it. It has depreciated $8,500 ($30,500 − $22,000). Table 11.1 shows that in 2014, private depreciation in the U.S. economy was $2,216.3 billion.

depreciation The decline in an asset's economic value over time.

A capital asset can depreciate because it wears out physically or because it becomes obsolete. Take, for example, a computer control system in a factory. If a new, technologically superior system does the same job for half the price, the old system may be replaced even if it still functions well. The Prius depreciated because of wear and tear *and* because new models had become available.

ECONOMICS IN PRACTICE

Investment Banking, IPOs, and Electric Cars

Automobile production is, as we noted in Chapter 9, subject to economies of scale. Becoming a new car manufacturer requires considerable capital, well beyond what most individuals can put together. In the summer of 2010, Tesla Motors, a new electric car manufacturer, turned to the public to seek capital.

How did Tesla do this? Tesla decided to become a *public company*, with shares offered to the public on a stock exchange. The process of doing this is called an initial public offering (IPO). Tesla initially offered the public 13.3 million shares, each for a price of $17, for a total increase in capital for the firm of $226 million. In mounting its IPO, Tesla, like most other firms, relied on investment banks to help figure out the right price and manage the sales. In Tesla's case, a number of firms were involved, including Goldman Sachs, J. P. Morgan, and Morgan Stanley. Managing IPOs is one of the functions of investment banks, as they help move capital from households to entrepreneurs with new ideas.[1]

You might be interested to know that the Tesla share price had risen to $182.00 by 2015!

THINKING PRACTICALLY

1. Stock prices after an IPO are often quite volatile. Why?

[1] For a further discussion of this see *The Wall Street Journal Online*, "TSLA: What Does Tesla's IPO Mean for the Future of Electric Cars?" by Jonathan Welsh. Copyright 2010 by *Dow Jones & Company, Inc.* Reproduced with permission of *Dow Jones & Company, Inc.* via Copyright Clearance Center.

TABLE 11.1   Private Investment in the U.S. Economy, 2014

GDP $17,418.9 billion	Billions of Current Dollars	As a Percentage of Total Gross Investment	As a Percentage of GDP
Nonresidential structures	506.9	17.8	2.9
Equipment and intellectual property products	1,703.6	59.7	9.8
Change in private inventories	82.0	2.9	0.5
Residential structures	559.1	19.6	3.2
Total gross private investment	2851.6	100.0	16.4
− depreciation	−2,216.3	−77.7	−12.7
Net investment = gross investment − depreciation	635.3	22.2	3.6

Source: U.S. Department of Commerce, Bureau of Economic Analysis, March 27, 2015

11.2 LEARNING OBJECTIVE

Describe the forms and functions of capital income and discuss the fundamentals of financial markets and mortgage markets.

capital market The market in which households supply their savings to firms that demand funds to buy capital goods.

The Capital Market

Where does capital come from? How and why is it produced? How much and what kinds of capital are produced? These questions are answered in the complex set of institutions in which households supply their savings to firms that demand funds to buy capital goods. Collectively, these institutions are called the **capital market.**

Although governments and households make some capital investment decisions, most decisions to produce new capital goods—that is, to invest—are made by firms. However, a firm cannot invest unless it has the funds to do so. Although firms can invest in many ways, it is always the case that the funds that firms use to buy capital goods come, directly or indirectly, from households. When a household decides not to consume a portion of its income, it saves.

Investment by firms is the *demand for capital*. Saving by households is the *supply of capital*. Various financial institutions facilitate the transfer of households' savings to firms that use them for capital investment.

Let us use a simple example to see how the system works. Suppose a firm wants to purchase a machine that costs $1,000 and a household decides at the same time to save $1,000 from its income. Figure 11.1 shows one way that the household's decision to save might connect with the firm's decision to invest.

Either directly or through a financial intermediary (such as a bank), the household agrees to loan its savings to the firm. In exchange, the firm contracts to pay the household interest at some agreed-to rate each period. Interest is the fee paid by a borrower to a lender or by a bank to a depositor for the use of funds. The interest rate is that fee paid annually, and it is expressed as a percentage of the loan or deposit. If the household lends directly to the firm, the firm gives the household a **bond**, which is nothing more than a contract promising to repay the loan at some specific time in the future. The bond also specifies the flow of interest to be paid in the meantime.

The new saving adds to the household's stock of wealth. The household's *net worth* has increased by the $1,000, which it holds in the form of a bond.[1] The bond represents the firm's promise to repay the $1,000 at some future date with interest. The firm uses the $1,000 to buy a new $1,000 machine, which it adds to its capital stock. In essence, the household has supplied the capital demanded by the firm. It is almost as if the household bought the machine and rented it to the firm for an annual fee. Presumably, this investment will generate added revenues that will facilitate the payment of interest and principal to the household.

Sometimes the transfer of household savings through the capital market into investment occurs without a financial intermediary. An *entrepreneur* is one who organizes, manages, and assumes the risk of a new firm. When entrepreneurs start a new business by buying capital with their own savings, they are both demanding capital and supplying the resources (that is, their savings) needed to purchase that capital. No third party is involved in the transaction. Most investment, however, is accomplished with the help of financial intermediaries (third parties such as banks, insurance companies, and pension funds) that stand between the supplier (saver) and the demander (investing firm). The part of the capital market in which savers and investors interact through intermediaries is often called the **financial capital market**.

bond   A contract between a borrower and a lender, in which the borrower agrees to pay the loan at some time in the future. Some bonds also make regular, constant payments once or twice a year.

financial capital market
The part of the capital market in which savers and investors interact through intermediaries.

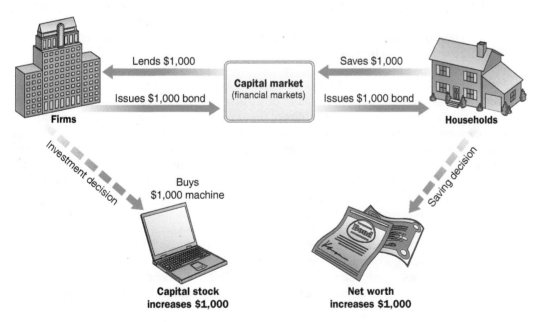

▲ FIGURE 11.1   **$1,000 in Savings Becomes $1,000 of Investment**

---

[1] Note that the *act of saving* increases the household's wealth, not the act of buying the bond. Buying the bond simply transforms one financial asset (money) into another (a bond). The household could simply have held on to the money.

Capital Income: Interest and Profits

It should now be clear to you how capital markets fit into the circular flow: They facilitate the movement of household savings into the most productive investment projects. When households allow their savings to be used to purchase capital, they receive payments, and these payments (along with wages and salaries) are part of household incomes. Income that is earned on savings that have been put to use through financial capital markets is called **capital income**. Capital income is received by households in many forms, the two most important of which are *interest* and *profits*.

capital income Income earned on savings that have been put to use through financial capital markets.

Interest The most common form of capital income received by households is interest. In simplest terms, **interest** is the payment made for the use of money. Banks pay interest to depositors, whose deposits are loaned out to businesses or individuals who want to make investments.[2] Banks also *charge* interest to those who borrow money. Corporations pay interest to households that buy their bonds. The government borrows money by issuing bonds, and the buyers of those bonds receive interest payments.

interest The payments made for the use of money.

The **interest rate** is almost always expressed as an annual rate. It is the annual interest payment expressed as a percentage of the loan or deposit. For example, a $1,000 bond (representing a $1,000 loan from a household to a firm) that carries a fixed 10 percent interest rate will pay the household $100 per year ($1,000 × .10) in interest. A savings account that carries a 5 percent annual interest rate will pay $50 annually on a balance of $1,000. Those of you with savings accounts will know that in the last few years, interest rates paid have been low.

interest rate Interest payments expressed as a percentage of the loan.

The interest rate is usually agreed to at the time a loan or deposit is made. Sometimes borrowers and lenders agree to periodically adjust the level of interest payments depending on market conditions. These types of loans are called *adjustable* or *floating-rate loans*. (*Fixed rate loans* are loans in which the interest rate never varies.) A loan's interest rate depends on a number of factors. A loan that involves more risk will generally pay a higher interest rate than a loan with less risk. Similarly, firms that are considered bad credit risks will pay higher interest rates than firms with good credit ratings. You have probably heard radio or TV advertisements by finance companies offering to loan money to borrowers "regardless of credit history." This means that they will loan to people or businesses that pose a relatively high risk of *defaulting*, or not paying off the loan. What they do not tell you is that the interest rate will be quite high.

It is generally agreed that the safest borrower is the U.S. government. With the "full faith and credit" of the U.S. government pledged to buyers of U.S. Treasury bonds and bills, most people believe that there is little risk that the government will not repay its loans. For this reason, the U.S. government can borrow money at a lower interest rate than any other borrower.

Profits *Profits* is another word for the net income of a firm: revenue minus costs of production. Some firms are owned by individuals or partners who try to sell their products for more than it costs to produce them. The profits of proprietors or partnerships generally go directly to the owner or owners who run the firm. Corporations are firms owned by shareholders who usually are not otherwise connected with the firms. Most corporations are organized and chartered under state laws that grant limited liability status to their owners or shareholders. Essentially, that means that shareholders cannot lose more than they have invested if the company incurs liabilities it cannot pay.

common stock A share of stock is an ownership claim on a firm, entitling its owner to a profit share.

dividend Payment made to shareholders of a corporation.

A share of **common stock** is a certificate that represents the ownership of a share of a business, almost always a corporation. For example, Merck is a large pharmaceutical company based in New Jersey. Merck has almost 3 billion shares of stock outstanding that are owned by individuals, including its own employees, pension funds, and other institutions. When profits are paid directly to shareholders, the payment is called a **dividend**. Merck made a profit of almost $16 billion in 2014 or more than $4.00 per share of which they paid $1.80 per share in dividends.

---

[2] Although we are focusing on investment by businesses, households can and do make investments also. The most important form of household investment is the construction of a new house, usually financed by borrowing in the form of a mortgage. A household may also borrow to finance the purchase of an existing house, but when it does so, no new investment is taking place.

In discussing profit, it is important to distinguish between profit as defined by generally accepted *accounting* principles (GAAP) and *economic* profits as we defined them in Chapter 7. Recall that our definition of profit is total revenue minus total cost, where total cost includes the normal rate of return on capital. We defined profit this way because true economic cost includes the opportunity cost of capital.

Functions of Interest and Profit   Capital income serves several functions. First, interest may function as an incentive to postpone gratification. When you save, you pass up the chance to buy things that you want right now. One view of interest holds that it is the reward for postponing consumption.

Second, profit serves as a reward for innovation and risk taking. Every year, *Forbes* magazine publishes the names of the richest people in the United States, and virtually every major fortune listed there is traceable to the founding of some business enterprise that "made it big." In recent years, big winners have included retail stores (the Walton family of Walmart), high-tech companies (Bill Gates of Microsoft and Larry Ellison of Oracle), and finance (Warren Buffet and Michael Bloomberg).

Many argue that rewards for innovation and risk taking are the essence of the U.S. free enterprise system. Innovation is at the core of economic growth and progress. More efficient production techniques mean that the resources saved can be used to produce new things. There is another side to this story, however: Critics of the free enterprise system claim that such large rewards are not justified and that accumulations of great wealth and power are not in society's best interests.

Financial Markets in Action

When a firm issues a fixed-interest-rate bond, it borrows funds and makes payments at an agreed on rate to the bond owner. Many other mechanisms, four of which are illustrated in Figure 11.2, also channel household savings into investment projects.

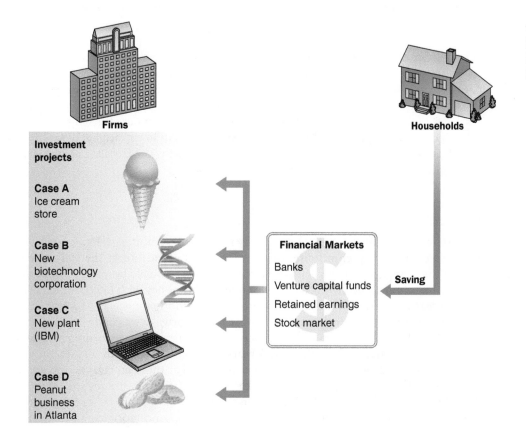

◀ FIGURE 11.2
Financial Markets Link Household Saving and Investment by Firms

Case A: Business Loans As I look around my hometown, I see several ice cream stores doing very well; but I think that I can make better ice cream than they do. To go into the business, I need capital: ice cream-making equipment, tables, chairs, freezers, signs, and a store. Because I put up my house as collateral, I am not a big risk, so the bank grants me a loan at a fairly reasonable interest rate. Banks have these funds to lend only because households deposit their savings there.

Case B: Venture Capital A scientist at a leading university develops an inexpensive method of producing an important family of virus-fighting drugs, using microorganisms created through gene splicing. The business could very well fail within 12 months, but if it succeeds, the potential for profit is huge.

Our scientist goes to a *venture capital fund* for financing. Such funds take household savings and put them into high-risk ventures in exchange for a share of the profits if the new businesses succeed. By investing in many different projects, the funds reduce the risk of going broke. Once again, household funds make it possible for firms to undertake investments. If a venture succeeds, those owning shares in the venture capital fund receive substantial profits. In the United States, the biggest venture capital funds include Kleiner Perkins, Sequioa Capital, and Greylock.

Case C: Retained Earnings IBM decides in 2009 to build a new plant in Dubuque, Iowa, and it discovers that it has enough funds to pay for the new facility. The new investment is thus paid for through internal funds, or *retained earnings*.

The result is the same as if the firm had gone to households via some financial intermediary and borrowed the funds. If IBM uses its profits to buy new capital, it does so only with the shareholders' implicit consent. When a firm takes its own profit and uses it to buy capital assets instead of paying it out to its shareholders, the total value of the firm goes up, as does the value of the shares held by stockholders. As in our other examples, IBM capital stock increases and so does the net worth of households.

When a household owns a share of stock that *appreciates*, or increases in value, the appreciation is part of the household's income. Unless the household sells the stock and consumes the gain, that gain is part of saving. In essence, when a firm retains earnings for investment purposes, it is actually saving on behalf of its shareholders.

Case D: The Stock Market A former high-ranking government official decides to start a new peanut-processing business in Atlanta; he also decides to raise the funds needed by issuing shares of stock. Households buy the shares with income that they decide not to spend. In exchange, they are entitled to a share of the peanut firm's profits.

The shares of stock become part of households' net worth. The proceeds from stock sales are used to buy plant equipment and inventory. Savings flow into investment, and the firm's capital stock goes up by the same amount as household net worth. The *Economics in Practice* on p. 228 describes how Tesla raised funds in this way.

Mortgages and the Mortgage Market

Most real estate in the United States is financed by mortgages. A mortgage, like a bond, is a contract in which the borrower promises to repay the lender in the future. The real estate is collateral for the mortgage. When a household buys a home, it usually borrows most of the money by signing a mortgage in which it agrees to repay the money with interest often over as long as 30 years. Historically, the most common form of mortgage was the 30-year fixed rate mortgage. In 2015 the interest rate on a 30-year fixed mortgage was under 4 percent to qualified buyers. Many current home buyers instead use Adjustable Rate Mortgages (ARMs) in which the rate is guaranteed for the first 5 years and then adjusts with market interest rates. In 2015 ARM rates were in the mid 3 percent range. For these mortgages, the home buyer pays less in the beginning but has the risk that his or her interest rates will go up in the future if market rates rise. ARMs have proven to be especially attractive to people who plan to sell their homes within the 5-year period and thus face no mortgage rate risk. All

ECONOMICS IN PRACTICE

Stocks in the United States

In the text we describe how households buy shares of stock to invest in businesses and to generate hoped-for returns. In some cases these shares of stock come with dividends. For example, in 2015 General Electric, a large, diversified manufacturing firm, paid a dividend of 3.7 percent. Other firms, like Google, pay no dividends, and people benefit from their ownership of the stock if they end up selling it for more than they paid for it. In some years returns from stock appreciation are quite high: between February 2014 and February 2015, the Standard and Poor's 500 index, which tracks 500 large U.S. companies, rose more than 14 percent. In other years, for example 2009, stock prices on average fell.

Firms differ a lot in their stock performance. Some stocks are quite volatile, others less so. Firms also differ in who owns them. Some firms, like General Electric and Google have a lot of institutional owners. About a third of Google's stock is owned by institutions, which includes many pension funds. Other companies have a substantial amount of their stock owned by their own executives. Pandora, an Oakland-based Internet radio company, has about 5 percent of its stock owned by its executives. For larger, more established companies this share is typically much lower; Google's executives, for example, own only 0.2 percent of its stock.

The Census Bureau estimates that about half of U.S. households own stock, either as individuals or through their pension funds. Higher income, more well-educated households are more likely to own stock than poorer, less educated families.

THINKING PRACTICALLY

1. Why do you think executives in firms like Pandora own a lot of stock in their own company?

mortgages require the home owner to pay a monthly fee which pays off the house and the interest over the term of the loan.

Until the last decade, most mortgage loans were made by banks and savings and loans. The lenders used depositors' money to make the loans, and the signed promissory notes were kept by the lenders who collected the payment every month.

Recently, the mortgage market changed dramatically and became more complicated. Most mortgages are now written by mortgage brokers or mortgage bankers who immediately sell the mortgages to a secondary market. The secondary market is run by governmental agencies such as Fannie Mae and Freddie Mac and large investment banks. Loans in this market are "securitized," which means that the mortgage documents are pooled and then mortgage-backed securities are sold to investors who want to take different degrees of risk.

The risk of owning mortgages is primarily the risk that the borrower will default on the obligation. When default occurs, the house may be taken through foreclosure, a procedure in which the lender takes possession of the borrower's house and sells it to get back at least some of the amount that the lender is owed. In 2007 and for some years afterwards, the housing market was hit with a large number of loan defaults and foreclosures. In some areas of the country, many foreclosed houses remain in 2015.

Capital Accumulation and Allocation

You can see from the preceding examples that various connections between households and firms facilitate the movement of savings into productive investment. The methods may differ, but the results are the same. Industrialized or agrarian, small or large, simple or complex, all societies exist through time and must allocate resources over time. In simple societies, investment and saving decisions are made by the same people. However:

> In modern industrial societies, investment decisions (capital production decisions) are made primarily by firms. Households decide how much to save, and in the long run, savings limit or constrain the amount of investment that firms can undertake. The capital market exists to direct savings into profitable investment projects.

11.3 LEARNING OBJECTIVE

Discuss the demand for new capital and explain the investment decision process.

The Demand for New Capital and the Investment Decision

We saw in Chapter 9 that firms have an incentive to expand in industries that earn positive profits—that is, a rate of return above normal—and in industries in which economies of scale lead to lower average costs at higher levels of output. We also saw that positive profits in an industry stimulate the entry of new firms. The expansion of existing firms and the creation of new firms both involve investment in new capital.

Even when there are no profits in an industry, firms must still do some investing. First, equipment wears out and must be replaced if the firm is to stay in business. Second, firms are constantly changing. A new technology may become available, sales patterns may shift, or the firm may expand or contract its product line.

With these points in mind, we now turn to a discussion of the investment decision process within the individual firm. In the end, we will see that a perfectly competitive firm invests in capital up to the point at which the marginal revenue product of capital is equal to the price of capital, mirroring our discussion in Chapter 10 about labor and land decisions.

Forming Expectations

The most important dimension of capital is time. Capital produces useful services over *some period of time*. In building an office tower, a developer makes an investment that will be around for decades. In deciding where to build a branch plant, a manufacturing firm commits a large amount of resources to purchase capital that will be in place for a long time. Often the decision to build a building or purchase a piece of equipment must be made years before the actual project is completed. Although the acquisition of a small business computer may take only days, the planning process for downtown development projects in big U.S. cities has been known to take decades.

The Expected Benefits of Investments   Decision makers must have expectations about what is going to happen in the future. A new plant will be valuable—that is, it will produce much profit—if the market for a firm's product grows and the price of that product remains high. The same plant will be worth little if the economy goes into a slump or consumers grow tired of the firm's product. The Tesla's success will depend not only on consumer tastes for electric cars, but also on the government's energy policy. The investment process requires that the potential investor evaluate the expected flow of future productive services that an investment project will yield.

An official of the General Electric Corporation (GE) once described the difficulty involved in making such predictions. GE subscribes to a number of different economic forecasting services. In the early 1980s, those services provided the firm with 10-year predictions of new housing construction that ranged from a low of 400,000 new units per year to a high of 4 million new units per year. Because GE sells millions of household appliances to contractors building new houses, condominiums, and apartments, the forecast was critical. If GE decided that the high number was more accurate, it would need to spend billions of dollars on new plant and equipment to prepare for the extra demand. If GE decided that the low number was more accurate, it would need to begin closing several of its larger plants and disinvesting. In fact, GE took the middle road. It assumed that housing production would be between 1.5 and 2 million units—which, in fact, it was.

GE is not an exception. All firms must rely on forecasts to make sensible investment and production decisions, but forecasting is an inexact science because so much depends on events that cannot be foreseen.

The Expected Costs of Investments   The benefits of any investment project take the form of future profits. Revenues must be forecast, and costs must also be evaluated. Like households, firms have access to financial markets, both as borrowers and as lenders. If a firm borrows, it must *pay* interest over time. If it lends, it will *earn* interest. If the firm borrows to finance a project, the interest on the loan is part of the cost of the project.

Even if a project is financed with the firm's own retained earnings instead of through borrowing, an opportunity cost is involved. A thousand dollars put into a capital investment project will generate an expected flow of future profit; the same $1,000 put into the financial market (in essence, loaned to another firm) will yield a flow of interest payments. The project will not be undertaken unless it is expected to yield more than the market interest rate. The cost of an investment project may thus be direct or indirect because the ability to lend at the market rate of interest means that there is an *opportunity cost* associated with every investment project. The evaluation process thus involves not only estimating future benefits but also comparing them with the possible alternative uses of the funds required to undertake the project.

Comparing Costs and Expected Return

Once expectations have been formed, firms must quantify them—that is, they must assign some dollars-and-cents value to them. One way to quantify expectations is to calculate an **expected rate of return** on the investment project. For example, if a new computer network that costs $400,000 is likely to save $100,000 per year in data processing costs forever after, the expected rate of return on that investment is 25 percent per year. Each year the firm will save $100,000 as a result of the $400,000 investment. The expected rate of return will be less than 25 percent if the computer network wears out or becomes obsolete after a while and the cost saving ceases.[3] The expected rate of return on an investment project depends on the price of the investment, the expected length of time the project provides additional cost savings or revenue, and the expected amount of revenue attributable each year to the project.

Table 11.2 presents a menu of investment choices and expected rates of return that a hypothetical firm faces. Because expected rates of return are based on forecasts of future profits attributable to the investments, any change in expectations would change all the numbers in column 2.

expected rate of return   The annual rate of return that a firm expects to obtain through a capital investment.

TABLE 11.2	Potential Investment Projects and Expected Rates of Return for a Hypothetical Firm, Based on Forecasts of Future Profits Attributable to the Investment	
Project	(1) Total Investment (Dollars)	(2) Expected Rate of Return (Percent)
A. New computer network	400,000	25
B. New branch plant	2,600,000	20
C. Sales office in another state	1,500,000	15
D. New automated billing system	100,000	12
E. Ten new delivery trucks	400,000	10
F. Advertising campaign	1,000,000	7
G. Employee cafeteria	100,000	5

---

[3] We have simplified this example considerably by not explicitly dealing with the planning period. The Appendix to this chapter has a more advanced discussion.

▶ **FIGURE 11.3** **Total Investment as a Function of the Market Interest Rate**

The demand for new capital depends on the interest rate. When the interest rate is low, firms are more likely to invest in new plant and equipment than when the interest rate is high. This is so because the interest rate determines the direct cost (interest on a loan) or the opportunity cost (alternative investment) of each project.

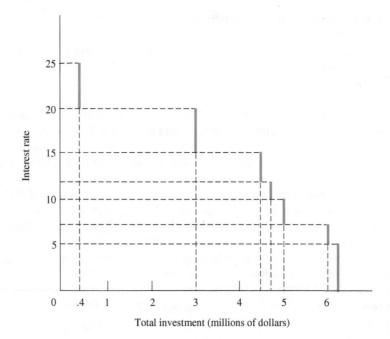

Figure 11.3 graphs the total amount of investment in millions of dollars that the firm would undertake at various interest rates. If the interest rate were 24 percent, the firm would fund only project A, the new computer network. It can borrow at 24 percent and invest in a computer that is expected to yield 25 percent. At 24 percent, the firm's total investment is $400,000. The first vertical red line in Figure 11.3 shows that at any interest rate above 20 percent and below 25 percent, only $400,000 worth of investment (that is, project A) will be undertaken.

If the interest rate were 18 percent, the firm would fund projects A and B, and its total investment would rise to $3 million ($400,000 + $2,600,000). If the firm could borrow at 18 percent, the flow of additional profits generated by the new computer and the new plant would more than cover the costs of borrowing, but none of the other projects would be justified. The rates of return on projects A and B (25 percent and 20 percent, respectively) both exceed the 18 percent interest rate. Only if the interest rate fell below 5 percent would the firm fund all seven investment projects.

The investment schedule in Table 11.2 and its graphic depiction in Figure 11.3 describe the firm's demand for new capital, expressed as a function of the market interest rate. If we add the total investment undertaken by *all* firms at every interest rate, we arrive at the demand for new capital in the economy as a whole. In other words, like any other demand curve, the market demand curve for new capital is the sum of all the individual demand curves for new capital in the economy (Figure 11.4). In a sense, the investment demand schedule is a ranking of all the investment opportunities in the economy in order of expected yield. Only those investment projects in the economy that are expected to yield a rate of return higher than the market interest rate will be funded. At lower market interest rates, more investment projects are undertaken.

The most important thing to remember about the investment demand curve is that its shape and position depend critically on the *expectations* of those making the investment decisions. Because many influences affect these expectations, they are usually volatile and subject to frequent change. Thus, although lower interest rates tend to stimulate investment and higher interest rates tend to slow it, many other hard-to-measure and hard-to-predict factors also affect the level of investment spending.

The Expected Rate of Return and the Marginal Revenue Product of Capital The concept of the expected rate of return on investment projects is analogous to the concept of the marginal revenue product of capital (MRP_K). Recall that we defined an input's marginal revenue product as the additional revenue a firm earns by employing one additional unit of that input, *ceteris paribus*.

Now think carefully about the return on an additional unit of new capital (the marginal revenue product of capital). Suppose that the rate of return on an investment in a new machine

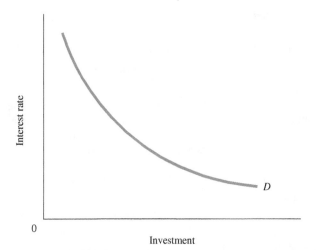

Investment Demand
Lower interest rates are likely to stimulate investment in the economy as a whole, whereas higher interest rates are likely to slow investment.

is 15 percent. This means that the investment project yields the same return as a bond yielding 15 percent. If the current interest rate is less than 15 percent, the investment project will be undertaken because a perfectly competitive profit-maximizing firm will keep investing in new capital up to the point at which the expected rate of return is equal to the interest rate. This is analogous to saying that the firm will continue investing up to the point at which the marginal revenue product of capital is equal to the price of capital, or $MRP_K = P_K$, which is what we learned in Chapter 10.

A Final Word on Capital

The concept of capital is one of the central ideas in economics. Capital is produced by the economic system itself. Capital generates services over time, and it is used as an input in the production of goods and services. The enormous productivity of modern industrial societies is due in part to the tremendous amount of capital that they have accumulated over the years. Most of this chapter described the institutions and processes that determine the amount and types of capital produced in a market economy. Existing firms in search of increased profits, potential new entrants to the markets, and entrepreneurs with new ideas are continuously evaluating potential investment projects. At the same time, households are saving. Each year, households save some portion of their after-tax incomes. These new savings become part of their net worth, and they want to earn a return on those savings. Each year, a good portion of the savings finds its way into the hands of firms that use it to buy new capital goods.

Between households and firms is the financial capital market. Millions of people participate in financial markets every day. There are literally thousands of financial managers, pension funds, mutual funds, brokerage houses, options traders, and banks whose sole purpose is to earn the highest possible rate of return on people's savings.

Brokers, bankers, and financial managers are continuously scanning the financial horizons for profitable investments. What businesses are doing well? What businesses are doing poorly? Should we lend to an expanding firm? All the analysis done by financial managers seeking to earn a high yield for clients, by managers of firms seeking to earn high profits for their stockholders, and by entrepreneurs seeking profits from innovation serves to channel capital into its most productive uses. Within firms, the evaluation of individual investment projects involves forecasting costs and benefits and valuing streams of potential income that will be earned only in future years.

We have now completed our discussion of competitive input and output markets. We have looked at household and firm choices in output markets, labor markets, land markets, and capital markets.

We now turn to a discussion of the allocative process that we have described. How do all the parts of the economy fit together? Is the result good or bad? Can we improve on it? All of this is the subject of Chapter 12.

SUMMARY

11.1 CAPITAL, INVESTMENT, AND DEPRECIATION *p. 226*

1. In market capitalist systems, the decision to put capital to use in a particular enterprise is made by private citizens putting their savings at risk in search of private gain. The set of institutions through which such transactions occur is called the *capital market*.

2. *Capital goods* are those goods produced by the economic system that are used as inputs to produce other goods and services in the future. Capital goods thus yield valuable productive services over time.

3. The major categories of *physical*, or *tangible, capital* are nonresidential structures, durable equipment, residential structures, and inventories. *Social capital* (or *infrastructure*) is capital that provides services to the public. *Intangible (nonmaterial) capital* includes *human capital* and goodwill.

4. The most important dimension of capital is that it exists through time. Therefore, its value is only as great as the value of the services it will render over time.

5. The most common measure of a firm's *capital stock* is the current market value of its plant, equipment, inventories, and intangible assets. However, in thinking about capital, it is important to focus on the actual capital stock instead of its simple monetary value.

6. In economics, the term *investment* refers to the creation of new capital, not to the purchase of a share of stock or a bond. Investment is a flow that increases the capital stock.

7. *Depreciation* is the decline in an asset's economic value over time. A capital asset can depreciate because it wears out physically or because it becomes obsolete.

11.2 THE CAPITAL MARKET *p. 228*

8. Income that is earned on savings that have been put to use through *financial capital markets* is called *capital income*. The two most important forms of capital income are *interest* and *dividends*. Interest is the fee paid by a borrower to a lender.

Interest rewards households for postponing gratification, and profit rewards entrepreneurs for innovation and risk taking.

9. In modern industrial societies, investment decisions (capital production decisions) are made primarily by firms. Households decide how much to save, and in the long run, saving limits the amount of investment that firms can undertake. The capital market exists to direct savings into profitable investment projects.

11.3 THE DEMAND FOR NEW CAPITAL AND THE INVESTMENT DECISION *p. 234*

10. Before investing, investors must evaluate the expected flow of future productive services that an investment project will yield.

11. The interest rate is the opportunity cost of investment. This cost must be weighed against the stream of earnings that a project is expected to yield.

12. A firm will decide whether to undertake an investment project by comparing costs with expected returns. The *expected rate of return* on an investment project depends on the price of the investment, the expected length of time the project provides additional cost savings or revenue, and the expected amount of revenue attributable each year to the project.

13. The investment demand curve shows the demand for capital in the economy as a function of the market interest rate. Only those investment projects that are expected to yield a rate of return higher than the market interest rate will be funded. Lower interest rates should stimulate investment.

14. A perfectly competitive profit-maximizing firm will keep investing in new capital up to the point at which the expected rate of return is equal to the interest rate. This is equivalent to saying that the firm will continue investing up to the point at which the marginal revenue product of capital is equal to the price of capital, or $MRP_K = P_K$.

REVIEW TERMS AND CONCEPTS

bond, *p. 229*
capital, *p. 226*
capital income, *p. 230*
capital market, *p. 228*
capital stock, *p. 227*
common stock, *p. 230*

depreciation, *p. 227*
dividend, *p. 230*
expected rate of return, *p. 235*
financial capital market, *p. 229*
human capital, *p. 226*
intangible capital, *p. 226*

interest, *p. 230*
interest rate, *p. 230*
investment, *p. 227*
physical, *or* tangible, capital, *p. 226*
social capital, *or* infrastructure, *p. 226*

PROBLEMS

All problems are available on MyEconLab.

11.1 CAPITAL, INVESTMENT, AND DEPRECIATION

LEARNING OBJECTIVE: Define the concepts of capital, investment, and depreciation.

1.1 Which of the following are capital, and which are not? Explain your answers.
  a. Lifeguard training and certification from the Red Cross
  b. The Ben and Jerry's Waterbury, Vermont, ice cream factory
  c. The Texas Giant roller coaster at Six Flags Over Texas
  d. An individual retirement account (IRA) at Wells Fargo Bank
  e. The Smithsonian National Air and Space Museum
  f. 40 shares of Apple stock
  g. An all-terrain vehicle used by park rangers at Yellowstone National Park
  h. Cans of paint at Home Depot
  i. A roll of 20 Kennedy half dollar coins
  j. Wrigley Field, home of the Chicago Cubs

1.2 For each of the following, decide whether you agree or disagree and explain your answer:
  a. *Capital and investment* are just two words for the same thing.
  b. For a capital asset to depreciate, it must physically become worn out and can no longer be used.
  c. Social capital provides services to the public, so it is a form of intangible capital.

1.3 Describe the capital stock of your college or university. How would you go about measuring its value? Has your school made any major investments in recent years? If so, describe them. What does your school hope to gain from these investments?

11.2 THE CAPITAL MARKET

LEARNING OBJECTIVE: Describe the forms and functions of capital income and discuss the fundamentals of financial markets and mortgage markets

2.1 The Federal Reserve Board of Governors has the power to raise or lower short-term interest rates. Between 2005 and 2006, the Fed aggressively increased the benchmark federal funds interest rate from 2.5 percent in February 2005 to 5.25 percent in June 2006, where it remained until July 2007. From July 2007 to December 2008, the Fed rapidly decreased the federal funds rate, where it dropped to 0.16 percent and has remained between 0.07 percent and 0.20 percent through the middle of 2015. Assuming that other interest rates also increased and then decreased along with the federal funds rate, what effects do you think those moves had on investment spending in the economy? Explain your answer. What do you think the Fed's objective was in increasing, and then decreasing, the federal

funds rate? When and why might the Fed decide to start raising the federal funds rate?

2.2 Give at least three examples of how savings can be channeled into productive investment. Why is investment so important for an economy? What do you sacrifice when you save today?

2.3 From a newspaper such as *The Wall Street Journal*, from the business section of your local daily, or from the Internet, look up the prime interest rate, the corporate bond rate, and the interest rate on 10-year U.S. government bonds today. List some of the reasons these three rates are different.

2.4 Explain what we mean when we say that "households supply capital and firms demand capital."

2.5 [**Related to the *Economics in Practice* on p. 228**] On January 30, 2015 Spark Therapeutics, a gene therapy company based in Philadelphia that started operations in October 2013, offered 7 million shares of stock at an introductory price of $23 per share (an initial value of over $160 million) through an IPO on the NASDAQ stock exchange. At the end of the same day, Spark Therapeutics stock had closed at a price of $50.00 per share, 117 percent above its IPO price. Why might a company like Spark Therapeutics choose the IPO route to raise funds? What are some of the other options that the company might have considered before deciding on the IPO, and why might these options have been less attractive to Spark Therapeutics?

2.6 On October 28, 2011, the St. Louis Cardinals won game 7 of the World Series. For the next month the stock market fell. The S&P 500 index (an index of the stock prices of the 500 largest corporations in the United States) dropped from 1,285.96 to 1161.41 on November 25. Ten-year Treasury notes were paying 2.31% on 10-year obligations of the government. The Fed had recently announced its intentions to keep its target for the federal funds rate between 0 and 0.25 percent for at least another year.

Look up today's S&P index, the 10-year Treasury interest rate, and the fed funds rate. You can find them at http://money.cnn.com. Provide an explanation for what has happened to those three numbers since 2011.

2.7 Lending institutions charge different interest rates for different classifications of mortgages. Two of these mortgage types are Alt-A mortgages and subprime mortgages. Alt-A mortgages generally carry a higher interest rate than a typical "prime rate" mortgage, and subprime mortgage rates are generally even higher than Alt-A rates. What is the likely economic justification for the higher interest rates for these two types of mortgages?

2.8 [**Related to the *Economics in Practice* on p. 233**] The text states that in terms of value, the majority of stock in the United States is held by households through institutions and the percentage of institutional holding of stock (as well as the percentage of insider holding) often varies based on the maturity of the company. Choose two publicly traded companies based in your local area, one relatively new and the other relatively mature. Go to www.finance.yahoo.com and enter each company in the "GET QUOTES" dialog box; then click on "Key Statistics" to find trading information. Look at the Share Statistics for each company. Describe the variation in the percentage of shares held by institutions and the percentage of shares held by insiders for the two companies.

2.9 For each of the following, decide whether you agree or disagree and explain your answer:
   a. *Savings* and *investment* are just two words for the same thing.
   b. When I buy a share of Microsoft stock, I have invested; when I buy a government bond, I have not.
   c. Higher interest rates lead to more investment because those investments pay a higher return.

11.3 THE DEMAND FOR NEW CAPITAL AND THE INVESTMENT DECISION

LEARNING OBJECTIVE: Discuss the demand for new capital and explain the investment decision process.

3.1 You and nine of your softball teammates are offered the chance to buy a pool hall. Each partner would put up $50,000. The revenues from the operation of the pool hall have been steady at $125,000 per year for several years and are projected to remain steady into the future. The costs (not including opportunity costs) of operating the pool hall (including maintenance and repair, depreciation, and salaries) have also been steady at $50,000 per year. Currently, 5-year Treasury bills are yielding 3.5 percent interest. Would you go in on the deal? Explain your answer.

3.2 The board of directors of the Estelar Company in Brazil was presented with the following list of investment projects for implementation in 2016:

Project	Total Cost (Brazilian Reais Converted to U.S. Dollars)	Estimated Rate of Return
Factory in Buenos Aires, Argentina	$ 22,480,000	17%
Factory in Caracas, Venezuela	16,550,000	9
A new headquarters in Rio de Janeiro	6,450,000	13
New logistics software	8,000,000	12
A new distribution warehouse	4,200,000	14
A new fleet of delivery trucks	3,650,000	11

Sketch total investment as a function of the interest rate (with the interest rate on the y-axis). Currently, the interest rate in Brazil is 12.5 percent. How much investment would you recommend to Estelar's board?

3.3 In March 2015, the Willis Tower in Chicago was sold to the Blackstone Group, a global investment firm, for $1.3 billion, the highest price ever paid for a U.S. office building outside of New York City. If you were a real estate investment company considering bidding on this building, what would you want to know first? What specific factors would you need to form expectations about? What information would you need to form those expectations?

3.4 Abigail, an analyst with a venture capital firm, is approached by Tomas about financing his new business venture, a company which will produce solar-powered hydroponic growing equipment for light industrial use. What information should Abigail have before making a decision about financing Tomas's new company?

3.5 Draw a graph showing an investment demand curve and explain the slope of the curve.

3.6 The Blume quintuplets, Aster, Dahlia, Iris, Jasmine, and Poppy, have an opportunity to purchase a wholesale florist company. Each of the women would have to put up $300,000 to make the purchase. The revenue from the business is expected to remain constant at $650,000 per year for the next several years. The costs (not including the opportunity costs of the investment) of operating the florist are expected to remain constant at $530,000 for the next several years. The current market interest rate on enterprises with comparable risks is 9.25% per year. Should the Blume quintuplets purchase the wholesale florist? Explain.

CHAPTER 11 APPENDIX

Calculating Present Value

LEARNING OBJECTIVE

Be able to caluculate the present value of $100 that you receive in 5 years for various interest rates.

We have seen in this chapter that a firm's major goal in making investment decisions is to evaluate revenue streams that will not materialize until the future. One way for the firm to decide whether to undertake an investment project is to compare the expected rate of return from the investment with the current interest rate available (assuming comparable risk) in the financial market. We discussed this procedure in the text. The purpose of this Appendix is to present a more complete method of evaluating future revenue streams through present-value analysis.

Present Value

Consider the investment project described in Table 11A.1. We use the word *project* in this example to refer to buying a machine or a piece of capital for $1,200 and receiving the cash flow given in the right-hand column of the table. Would you do the project? At first glance, you might answer yes. After all, the total flow of cash that you will receive is $1,600, which is $400 greater than the amount that you have to pay. But be careful: The $1,600 comes to you over a 5-year period, and your $1,200 must be paid right now. You must consider the alternative uses and opportunity costs of the $1,200. At the same time, you must consider the risks that you are taking.

What are these alternatives? At a bare minimum, the same $1,200 could be put in a bank account, where it would earn interest. In addition, there are other things that you could do with the same money. You could buy Treasury bonds from the federal government that guarantee you interest of 4 percent for 5 years. Or you might find other projects with a similar degree of risk that produce more than $1,600.

Recall that the *interest rate* is the amount of money that a borrower agrees to pay a lender or a bank agrees to pay a depositor each year, expressed as a percentage of the deposit or the loan. For example, if I deposited $1,000 in an account paying 10 percent interest, I would receive $100 per year for the term of the deposit. Sometimes we use the term *rate of return* to refer to the amount of money that the lender receives from its investment each year, expressed as a percentage of the investment.

The idea is that in deciding to do any project, you must consider the opportunity costs: What are you giving up? If you did not do this project but put the money to use elsewhere, would you do better?

Almost all investments that you might consider involve risks: The project might not work out the way you anticipate, the economy may change, or market interest rates could go up or down. To assess the opportunity costs and to decide whether this project is worth it, you first have to think about those risks and decide on the rate of return that you require to compensate yourself for taking the risks involved.

If there were no risk, the opportunity cost of investing in a project would be the government-guaranteed or bank-guaranteed interest rate. But in considering a project that involves risk, you would want more profit in return for bearing that risk. For example, you might invest in a sure

TABLE 11A.1	Expected Profits from a $1,200 Investment Project
Year 1	$ 100
Year 2	100
Year 3	400
Year 4	500
Year 5	500
All later years	0
Total	1,600

deal if you received a 3 percent annual return comparable to what you might earn with a bank account or certificate of deposit, whereas you might demand 15 percent or even 20 percent on a very risky investment.

Evaluating the opportunity costs of any investment project requires taking the following steps:

Step 1: The first step in evaluating the opportunity costs of an investment project is to look at the market. What are interest rates today? What rates of interest are people earning by putting their money in bank accounts? If there is risk that something could go wrong, what interest rate is the market paying to those who accept that risk? The *discount rate* used to evaluate an investment project is the interest rate that you could earn by investing a similar amount of money in an alternative investment *of comparable risk*.

Let's suppose that the investment project described in Table 11A.1 involved some risk. While you are quite certain that the expected flow of profits in years 1–5 ($100, $100, $400, and so on) is a very good estimate, the future is always uncertain. Let's further suppose that alternative investments of comparable risks are paying a 10 percent rate of interest (rate of return). So you will not do this project unless it earns at least 10 percent per year. We will thus use a 10 percent discount rate in evaluating the project.

Step 2: Now comes the trick. Is your investment worth it? By doing the project, you must consider the opportunity cost of the money. To do this, imagine a bank that will pay 10 percent on deposits. The question that you must answer is, how much would you have to put in a bank paying 10 percent interest on deposits to get the same flow of profits that you would get if you did the project?

If it turns out that you can replicate the flow of profits for *less* money up front than the project costs—$1,200—you will *not* do the project. The project would be paying you less than a 10 percent rate of return. On the other hand, if it turns out that you would have to put *more* than $1,200 in the bank to replicate the flow of profits from the project, the project would be earning more than 10 percent, and you would do it.

The amount of money that you would have to put in the imaginary bank to replicate the flow of profits from an investment project is called the **present discounted value (PDV)** or simply the **net present value (NPV)** of the expected flow of profits from the project. To determine that flow, we have to look at the flow *1 year at a time*.

At the end of a year, you will receive $100 if you do the project. To receive $100 a year from now from your hypothetical bank, how much would you have to deposit now? The answer is clearly less than $100 because you will earn interest. Let's call the interest rate r. In the example, $r = .10$ (10 percent). To get back $100 next year, you need to deposit X, where X plus a year's interest on X is equal to $100. That is,

$$X + rX = \$100 \text{ or } X(1 + r) = \$100$$

And if we solve for X, we get

$$X = \frac{\$100}{(1 + r)}$$

and that means if $r = .10$,

$$X = \frac{\$100}{1.1}$$

or

$$X = \$90.91$$

To convince yourself that this is right, think of putting $90.91 into your hypothetical bank and coming back in a year. You get back your $90.91 plus interest of 10 percent, which is $9.09. When you add the interest to the initial deposit, you get $90.91 + 9.09, or exactly $100. *We say that the present value of $100 a year from now at a discount rate of 10 percent (r = .10) is $90.91.*

Notice that if you paid more than $90.91 for the $100 that you will receive from the project after a year, you would be receiving *less than a 10 percent return.* For example, suppose that you paid $95. If you put $95 in an account and came back after a year and found exactly $100, you would have received $5 in interest. Since $5 is just about .0526 (or 5.26 percent) of $95, the interest rate that the bank paid you is only 5.26 percent, not 10 percent.

What about the next year and the years after that? At the end of year 2, you get another $100. How much would you have to put in the bank today to be able to come back in 2 years and take away $100? Assume that you put amount X in the bank today. Then at the end of year 1, you have $X + rX$, which you keep in the account. At the end of year 2, you have $X + rX$ *plus* interest on $X + rX$; so at the end of year 2 you have[1]

$$(X + rX) + r(X + rX)$$

which can be written

$$X(1 + r) + rX(1 + r) \quad \text{or} \quad X(1 + r)(1 + r) \text{ or } X(1 + r)^2$$

Therefore,

$$X = \frac{\$100}{(1 + r)^2}$$

is the amount you must deposit today to get back $100 in 2 years.

If $r = .10$, then

$$X = \frac{\$100}{(1.1)^2} \quad \text{or} \quad X = \$82.65$$

To convince yourself that this calculation is right, if you put $82.65 in your hypothetical bank today and came back to check the balance after a year, you would have $82.65 plus interest of 10 percent, or $8.26, which is $90.91. But this time you leave it in the bank and receive 10 percent on the entire balance during the second year, which is $9.09. Adding the additional 10 percent, you get back to $100. Thus, if you deposit $82.65 in an account and come back in 2 years, you will have $100. The present value of $100 two years from now is $82.65.

Now on to year 3. This time you receive a check for $400, but you don't get it until 3 years have passed. Again, how much would you have to put in your hypothetical bank to end up with $400? Without doing all the math, you can show that X, the amount that you must deposit to get back $400 in 3 years, is

$$X = \frac{\$400}{(1 + r)^3}$$

and if $r = .10$,

$$X = \frac{\$400}{(1.1)} \quad \text{or} \quad X = \$300.53$$

In general, the present value, or present discounted value (PDV), of R dollars to be received in t years is

$$PDV = \frac{R}{(1 + r)^t}$$

---

[1]We have assumed annual compounding.

TABLE 11A.2		Calculation of Total Present Value of a Hypothetical Investment Project (Assuming $r = 10$ Percent)	
End of...	(r)	Divided by $(1 + r)^t$	= Present Value ($)
Year 1	100	(1.1)	90.91
Year 2	100	$(1.1)^2$	82.64
Year 3	400	$(1.1)^3$	300.53
Year 4	500	$(1.1)^4$	341.51
Year 5	500	$(1.1)^5$	**310.46**
Total present value			1,126.05

Step 3: Once you have looked at the project 1 year at a time, you must add up the total present value to see what the whole project is worth. In Table 11A.2, the right-hand column shows the present value of each year's return. If you add up the total, you have arrived at the amount that you would have to put in your hypothetical bank (that pays interest on deposits at 10 percent) today to receive the exact flow that is expected to come from the project. That total is $1,126.05.

So if you go to the bank today and put in $1,126.05, then come back in a year and withdraw $100, then come back after 2 years and withdraw another $100, then come back in 3 years and withdraw $400, and so on, until 5 years have passed, when you show up to close the account at the end of the fifth year, there will be exactly $500 left to withdraw. Lo and behold, you have figured out that you can receive the exact flow of profit that the project is expected to yield for $1,126.05. If you were looking for a 10 percent yield, you would *not* spend $1,200 for it. You would not do the project.

What you have done is to convert an expected *flow* of dollars from an investment project that comes to you over some extended period of time to a *single number*: the present value of the flow.

We can restate the point this way: If the present value of the income stream associated with an investment is less than the full cost of the investment project, the investment should not be undertaken. This is illustrated in Figure 11A.1.

It is important to remember that we are discussing the *demand for new capital.* Business firms must evaluate potential investments to decide whether they are worth undertaking. This involves predicting the flow of potential future profits arising from each project and comparing those future profits with the return available in the financial market at the current interest rate. The present-value method allows firms to calculate how much it would *cost today* to purchase a contract for the same flow of earnings in the financial market.

Lower Interest Rates, Higher Present Values

Now consider what would happen if you used a lower interest rate in calculating the present value of a flow of earnings. You might use a lower rate in the analysis because interest rates in general have gone down in financial markets, making the opportunity cost of investment lower in general. You might also find out that the project is less risky than you believed previously. For whatever reason, let's say that you would now do the project if it produced a return of 5 percent.

In evaluating the present value, the firm now looks at each year's flow of profit and asks how much it would cost to earn that amount if it were able to earn exactly 5 percent on its money in a hypothetical bank. With a lower interest rate, the firm will have to *pay more* now to purchase the same number of future dollars. Consider, for example, the present value of $100 in 2 years. We saw that if the firm puts aside $82.65 at 10 percent interest, it will have $100 in

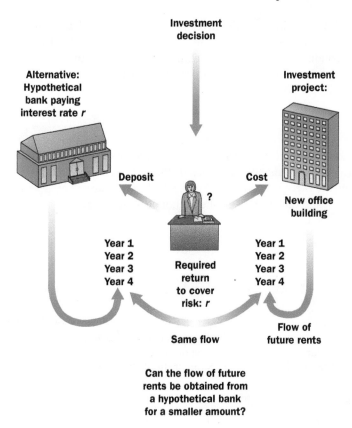

▲ FIGURE 11A.1   **Investment Project: Go or No? A Thinking Map**

2 years—at a 10 percent interest rate, the present discounted value (or current market price) of $100 in 2 years is $82.65. However, $82.65 put aside at a 5 percent interest rate would generate only $4.13 in interest in the first year and $4.34 in the second year, for a total balance of $91.11 after 2 years. To get $100 in 2 years, the firm needs to put aside more than $82.65 now. Solving for X as we did before,

$$X = \frac{\$100}{(1 + r)^2} = \frac{\$100}{(1.05)^2} = \$90.70$$

When the interest rate falls from 10 percent to 5 percent, the present value of $100 in 2 years rises by $8.05 ($90.70 − $82.65).

Table 11A.3 recalculates the present value of the full stream at the lower interest rate; it shows that a decrease in the interest rate from 10 percent to 5 percent causes the total present

TABLE 11A.3	Calculation of Total Present Value of a Hypothetical Investment Project (Assuming $r = 5$ Percent)		
End of...	$	Divided by $(1 + r)^t$	= Present Value ($)
Year 1	100	(1.05)	95.24
Year 2	100	$(1.05)^2$	90.70
Year 3	400	$(1.05)^3$	345.54
Year 4	500	$(1.05)^4$	411.35
Year 5	500	$(1.05)^5$	391.76
Total present value			1,334.59

value to rise to $1,334.59. Because the investment project costs less than this (only $1,200), it should be undertaken. It is now a better deal than can be obtained in the financial market.

Under these conditions, a profit-maximizing firm will make the investment. As discussed in the chapter, a lower interest rate leads to more investment.

The basic rule is as follows:

> If the present value of an expected stream of earnings from an investment exceeds the cost of the investment necessary to undertake it, the investment should be undertaken. However, if the present value of an expected stream of earnings falls short of the cost of the investment, the financial market can generate the same stream of income for a smaller initial investment and the investment should not be undertaken.

APPENDIX SUMMARY

1. The present value (PV) of R dollars to be paid t years in the future is the amount you need to pay today, at current interest rates, to ensure that you end up with R dollars t years from now. It is the current market value of receiving R dollars in t years.

2. If the present value of the income stream associated with an investment is less than the full cost of the investment

project, the investment project should not be undertaken. If the present value of an expected stream of income exceeds the cost of the investment necessary to undertake it, the investment should be undertaken.

APPENDIX REVIEW TERMS AND CONCEPTS

present discounted value (PDV) *or* net present value (NPV), *p. 242*

Equation: $PDV = \dfrac{R}{(1 + r)^{t}}$, *p. 243*

APPENDIX PROBLEMS

All problems are available on MyEconLab.

APPENDIX 11A: CALCULATING PRESENT VALUE

LEARNING OBJECTIVE: Be able to calculate the present value of $100 that you receive in 5 years for various interest rates.

1A.1 Suppose you were offered $5,000 to be delivered in 1 year. Further suppose you had the alternative of putting money into a safe certificate of deposit paying annual interest at 8 percent. Would you pay $4,800 in exchange for the $5,000 after 1 year? What is the *maximum* amount you would pay for the offer of $5,000? Suppose the offer was $5,000, but delivery was to be in 3 years instead of 1 year. What is the maximum amount you would be willing to pay?

1A.2 Your Godmother left you an inheritance of $75,000, payable to you when you turn 26 years old. You are now 21. Currently, the annual rate of interest that can be obtained by buying 5-year bonds is 2.5 percent. Your mother offers you

$60,000 cash right now to sign over your inheritance. Should you do it? Explain your answer.

1A.3 The town council's finance committee has evaluated data and determined that the present discounted value of the benefits from a proposed dog park comes to $3,250,000. The total construction cost of the dog park is $3,500,000. This implies that the dog park should be built. Do you agree with this conclusion? Explain your answer. What impact could a substantial decrease in interest rates have on your answer?

1A.4 Calculate the present value of the income streams A to E in Table 1 at an 8 percent interest rate and again at a 10 percent rate.

Suppose the investment behind the flow of income in E is a machine that cost $1,235 at the beginning of year 1. Would you buy the machine if the interest rate were 8 percent? if the interest rate were 10 percent?

TABLE 1

End of Year	A	B	C	D	E
1	$ 80	$ 80	$ 100	$ 100	$500
2	80	80	100	100	300
3	80	80	1,100	100	400
4	80	80	0	100	300
5	1,080	80	0	100	0
6	0	80	0	1,100	0
7	0	1,080	0	0	0

1A.5 Determine what someone should be willing to pay for each of the following bonds when the market interest rate for borrowing and lending is 3.5 percent.
  a. A bond that promises to pay $15,000 in a lump-sum payment after 1 year
  b. A bond that promises to pay $15,000 in a lump-sum payment after 2 years
  c. A bond that promises to pay $5,000 per year for 3 years

1A.6 What should someone be willing to pay for each of the bonds in question 1A.5 if the interest rate doubled to 7 percent?

1A.7 Based on your answers to questions 1A.5 and 1A.6, state whether each of the following is true or false:
  a. Ceteris paribus, the price of a bond increases when the interest rate increases.
  b. Ceteris paribus, the price of a bond increases when any given amount of money is received sooner rather than later.

1A.8 Assume that the present discounted value of an investment project (commercial development) at a discount rate of 7 percent is $825,445,000. Assume that the building just sold for $850 million. Will the buyer earn a rate of return of more than 4 percent, exactly 4 percent, or less than 4 percent? Briefly explain.

1A.9 Assume that I promise to pay you $100 at the end of each of the next 3 years. Using the following formula,

$$X = 100/(1 + r) + 100/(1 + r)^2 + 100/(1 + r)^3$$

if $r = 0.075$, then $X = \$260.06$.
  Assuming that somebody of roughly comparable reliability offers to pay out 7.5 percent on anything you let him or her borrow from you, would you be willing to pay me $270 for my promise? Explain your answer.

1A.10 Teresa won the Florida lottery and was given the option of receiving $22 million immediately or $1,250,000 at the end of each year for 30 years.
  a. If Teresa opts for the 30 annual payments, how much in total will she receive?
  b. What is the present value of the 30 annual payments if the interest rate is 4 percent? Based on this value, should Teresa opt for the up-front payment or the 30 installments?
  c. What is the present value of the 30 annual payments if the interest rate is 8 percent? Based on this value, should Teresa opt for the up-front payment or the 30 installments?

1A.11 How would your answers to the previous question change if the annual payments changed to $2,000,000 per year for 15 years?

1A.12 Explain what will happen to the present value of money 1 year from now if the market interest rate falls? What if the market interest rate rises?

12 General Equilibrium and the Efficiency of Perfect Competition

In the last nine chapters, we have built a model of a simple, perfectly competitive economy. Our discussion has revolved around the two fundamental decision-making units, *households* and *firms*, which interact in two basic market arenas, *input markets* and *output markets*. (Look again at the circular flow diagram, shown in Figure II.1 on p. 109.) By limiting our discussion to perfectly competitive firms, we have been able to examine how the basic decision-making units interact in the two basic market arenas.

Output and input markets are connected because firms and households make simultaneous choices in both arenas, but there are other connections among markets as well. Firms buy in both capital and labor markets, for example, and they can substitute capital for labor and vice versa. A change in the price of one factor can easily change the demand for other factors. Buying more *capital*, for instance, usually changes the marginal revenue product of *labor* and shifts the labor demand curve. Similarly, a change in the price of a single good or service usually affects household demand for other goods and services, as when a price decrease makes one good more attractive than other close substitutes. The same change also makes households better off when they find that the same amount of income will buy more. Such additional "real income" can be spent on any of the other goods and services that the household buys.

The point here is simple:

> Input and output markets cannot be considered as if they were separate entities or as if they operated independently. Although it is important to understand the decisions of individual firms and households and the functioning of individual markets, we now need to add it all up so we can look at the operation of the system as a whole.

You have seen the concept of equilibrium applied both to markets and to individual decision-making units. In individual markets, supply and demand determine an equilibrium price. Perfectly competitive firms are in short-run equilibrium when price and marginal cost are equal ($P = MC$). In the long run, however, equilibrium in a competitive market is achieved only when economic profits are eliminated. Households are in equilibrium when they have equated the marginal utility per dollar spent on each good to the marginal utility per dollar spent on all other goods. This process of examining the equilibrium conditions in individual markets and for individual households and firms separately is called **partial equilibrium analysis**.

A **general equilibrium** exists when all markets in an economy are in simultaneous equilibrium. An event that disturbs the equilibrium in one market may disturb the equilibrium in many other markets as well. The ultimate impact of the event depends on the way *all* markets adjust to it. Thus, partial equilibrium analysis, which looks at adjustments in one isolated market, may not tell the full story. When we consider policy changes, like increasing taxes on a specific good or encouraging investment in a sector, these general equilibrium effects may be quite important.

In talking about general equilibrium in the beginning of this chapter, we continue our exercise in *positive economics*—that is, we seek to understand how systems operate without making value judgments about outcomes. Later in the chapter, we turn from positive economics to *normative economics* as we begin to judge the economic system. Are its results good or bad? Can we make them better?

In judging the performance of any economic system, you will recall, it is essential first to establish specific criteria by which to judge. In this chapter, we use two such criteria: *efficiency* and *equity* (fairness). First, we demonstrate the **efficiency** of the allocation of resources—that is, the system produces what people want and does so at the least possible cost—if all the assumptions that we have made thus far hold. When we begin to relax some of our assumptions, however, it will become apparent that free markets may *not* be efficient. Several sources of inefficiency naturally occur within an unregulated market system. In the final part of this chapter, we introduce the potential role of government in correcting market inefficiencies and achieving fairness.

partial equilibrium analysis The process of examining the equilibrium conditions in individual markets and for households and firms separately.

general equilibrium The condition that exists when all markets in an economy are in simultaneous equilibrium.

efficiency The condition in which the economy is producing what people want at the least possible cost.

Market Adjustment to Changes in Demand

12.1 LEARNING OBJECTIVE

Discuss the relationship between general equilibrium and demand shifts.

All economies, particularly market systems, are dynamic. Markets experience shifts of demand, both up and down; costs and technology change; and prices and outputs change. We have spent a lot of time looking at how these changes affect individual markets. But markets are also connected to one another. If capital flows into one market, often that means it is flowing out of another market. If consumers ride trains, often that means they stay off the bus. How do we think about connections across markets?

As we look at the general case, you might find it helpful to keep an example in mind. In 2007, Amazon introduced the Kindle, the first e-reader. We could analyze this product introduction in a partial equilibrium setting, considering the responsiveness of potential buyers to price or quality changes in the Kindle. But the introduction of the Kindle and subsequent pricing decisions by Amazon and Apple affect other markets as well. E-books substitute in part for printed books. The introduction of the Kindle and subsequent price reductions in the device thus shift the demand for printed books to the left. When the demand for printed books falls, storefront booksellers like Barnes and Noble suffer lower profits or even losses. Likely their sales of other products in the stores—complements to their book sales—also decline. Many printed books are ordered over the Web, many in fact through Amazon itself. When demand for these books falls, shipping services like UPS lose business. Printed books are produced using paper. When the demand for books falls, so does the demand for paper, and through that channel the demand for forest products falls.

Nor is the story over there. When Amazon prices the Kindle, it must take into account what is going on in the marketplace for printed books. If Barnes and Noble responds to the shift in its demand by lowering prices of printed books, that move will influence the optimal price for the Kindle. If the fall in demand for paper reduces the cost of paper, the costs of printing books will fall, and that too will lead to a lower price for printed books. Amazon will need to respond to that as well. In a general equilibrium analysis, one needs to work through all the feedback loops and connections across industries to get to a final answer.

Figure 12.1 begins our discussion of the more general case of market connections. In the figure we assume that there are two sectors in the economy, X and Y, and that both are currently in long-run equilibrium. Total output in sector X is Q_X^0, the product is selling for a price of P_X^0, and each firm in the industry produces up to where P_X^0 is equal to marginal cost—q_X^0. At that point, price is just equal to average cost and economic profits are zero. The same condition holds initially in sector Y. The market is in zero profit equilibrium at a price of P_Y^0.

Now assume that a change in consumer preferences (or in the age distribution of the population or in something else) shifts the demand for X out to the right from D_X^0 to D_X^1. That shift drives the price up to P_X^1. If households decide to buy more X, without an increase in income,

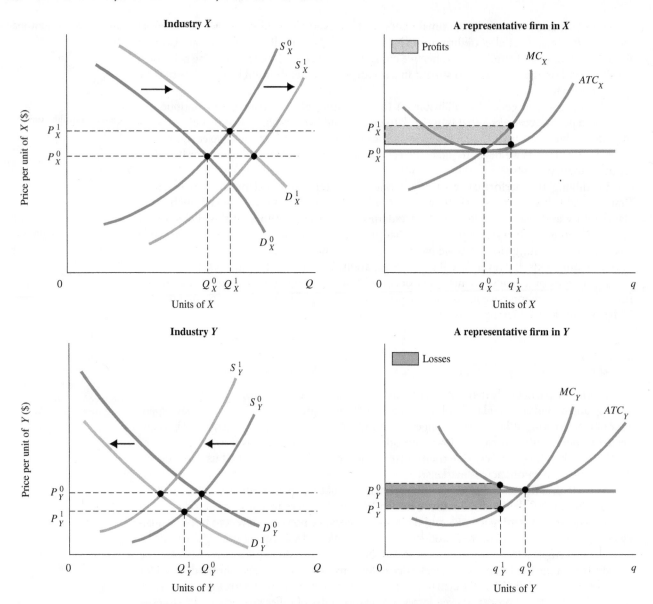

▲ **FIGURE 12.1** **Adjustment in an Economy with Two Sectors**
Initially, demand for X shifts from D_X^0 to D_X^1. This shift pushes the price of X up to P_X^1, creating profits. Demand for Y shifts down from D_Y^0 to D_Y^1 pushing the price of Y down to P_Y^1 and creating losses. Firms have an incentive to leave sector Y and an incentive to enter sector X. Exiting sector Y shifts supply in that industry to S_Y^1 raising price and eliminating losses. Entry shifts supply in X to S_X^1 thus reducing and eliminating profits.

they must buy *less* of something else. Because everything else is represented by Y in this example, the demand for Y must decline and the demand curve for Y shifts to the left, from D_Y^0 to D_Y^1.

With the shift in demand for X, price rises to P_X^1 and profit-maximizing firms increase output to q_X^1 (the point where $P_X^1 = MC_X$). However, now there are positive profits in X. With the downward shift of demand in Y, price falls to P_Y^1. Firms in sector Y cut back to q_Y^1 (the point where $P_Y^1 = MC_Y$), and the lower price causes firms producing Y to suffer losses.

In the short run, adjustment is simple. Firms in both industries are constrained by their current scales of plant. Firms can neither enter nor exit their respective industries. Each firm in industry X raises output somewhat, from q_X^0 to q_X^1. Firms in industry Y cut back from q_Y^0 to q_Y^1.

In response to the existence of profit in sector X, the capital market begins to take notice. In Chapter 9, we saw that new firms are likely to enter an industry in which there are profits to be earned. Financial analysts see the profits as a signal of future healthy growth, and entrepreneurs may become interested in moving into the industry.

Adding all of this together, we would expect to see investment begin to favor sector X. This is indeed the case: Capital begins to flow into sector X. As new firms enter, the supply curve in the industry shifts to the right and continues to do so until all profits are eliminated. In the top-left diagram in Figure 12.1, the supply curve shifts out from S_X^0 to S_X^1, a shift that drives the price back down to P_X^0.

We would also expect to see a movement out of sector Y because of losses. Some firms will exit the industry. In the bottom-left diagram in Figure 12.1, the supply curve shifts back from S_Y^0 to S_Y^1, a shift that drives the price back up to P_Y^0. At this point, all losses are eliminated.

Note that a new general equilibrium is not reached until equilibrium is reestablished in all markets. If we have constant returns to scale as in Figure 12.1, this equilibrium occurs at the initial product prices, but with more resources and production in X and fewer in Y. In contrast, if an expansion in X drives up the prices of resources used specifically in X, the cost curves in X will shift upward and the final postexpansion zero-profit equilibrium will occur at a higher price. Such an industry is called an *increasing-cost industry*.

Allocative Efficiency and Competitive Equilibrium

12.2 LEARNING OBJECTIVE
Explain the principles of economic efficiency.

As we have built models of a competitive economic system, we have often referred to the efficiency of that system. How do we think about efficiency in a general equilibrium world, in which many markets are interconnected?

Pareto Efficiency

In Chapter 1, we introduced several specific criteria used by economists to judge the performance of economic systems and to evaluate alternative economic policies. These criteria are (1) efficiency, (2) equity, (3) growth, and (4) stability. In Chapter 1, you also learned that an *efficient* economy is one that produces the things that people want at the least cost. The idea behind the efficiency criterion is that the economic system exists to serve the wants and needs of people. If resources somehow can be reallocated to make people "better off," then they should be. We want to use the resources at our disposal to produce maximum well-being. The trick is defining *maximum well-being*.

For many years, social philosophers wrestled with the problem of "aggregation," or "adding up." When we say "maximum well-being," we mean maximum *for society*. Societies are made up of many people, and the problem has always been how to maximize satisfaction, or well-being, for all members of society. What has emerged is the now widely accepted concept of *allocative efficiency*, first developed by the Italian economist Vilfredo Pareto in the nineteenth century. Pareto's precise definition of efficiency is often referred to as **Pareto efficiency** *or* **Pareto optimality**.

Specifically, a change is said to be efficient when it makes some members of society better off without making other members of society worse off. An efficient, or *Pareto optimal*, system is one in which no such changes are possible. An example of a change that makes some people better off and nobody worse off is a simple voluntary exchange. I have apples and you have nuts. I like nuts and you like apples. We trade. We both gain, and no one loses.

For a definition of efficiency to have practical meaning, we must answer two questions: (1) What do we mean by "better off"? and (2) How do we account for changes that make some people better off and others worse off?

The answer to the first question is simple. People decide what "better off" and "worse off" mean. I am the only one who knows whether I am better off after a change. If you and I exchange one item for another because I like what you have and you like what I have, we both "reveal" that we are better off after the exchange because we agreed to it voluntarily. If everyone in the neighborhood wants a park and the residents all contribute to a fund to build one, they have consciously changed the allocation of resources and they all are better off for it.

The answer to the second question is more complex. Nearly every change that one can imagine leaves some people better off and some people worse off. If some gain and some lose as the result of a change, and it can be demonstrated that the value of the gains exceeds the value

Pareto efficiency *or* **Pareto optimality** A condition in which no change is possible that will make some members of society better off without making some other members of society worse off.

ECONOMICS IN PRACTICE

More Corn to Burn, Less to Eat

For decades, the United States has struggled to find alternative fuels so as to reduce its reliance on oil. For some, the issue is environmental. Others are worried about dependence on foreign producers, though as we have seen throughout this book, most economists see much value in trade between nations. In the hunt for alternatives, corn has come to play a central role

Ethanol can be made from either sugar or corn. In the United States, given its climate and weather, corn production is mush less costly than is sugar production. So for the United States, interest in ethanol as an alternative fuel has been corn-based. Over the years, the government has used several mechanisms to encourage the use of corn-based ethanol. Until January 2012, refiners were given a subsidy of $0.45 for every gallon of ethanol they blended into their fuel. Refiners also face mandates requiring them to blend some corn-based ethanol into their fuel. So historically, both carrots and sticks were used to promote this alternative fuel.

One might object to this program because it is expensive for the government budget, and many have done so. This is one reason the subsidy was finally allowed to expire in January 2012. But the general equilibrium effects of the corn mandates have also caused some to doubt the wisdom of pushing ethanol. When corn is moved into fuel, the price of corn for food rises. Most corn actually is used as feed for cows and pigs. You may have noticed the prices of beef and pork rising. This is due, in part, to higher corn prices. Many have worried about the cost of this to people throughout the world for whom small food price increases carry big costs. On environmental grounds, some scientists have found that

emissions from corn-based ethanol are lower than other fuels (though not all agree), but other environmentalists note that increased corn production from ethanol mandates may come at the expensive of open land which is better for the environment. There is considerable debate around this topic, and clearly good answers require system-wide thinking.

THINKING PRACTICALLY

1. Use general equilibrium supply and demand analysis to show the impact of requiring more corn ethanol on the market for food. Treat corn as good X and all other foods as Y.

of the losses, then the change is said to be *potentially efficient*. In practice, however, the distinction between a *potentially* and an *actually* efficient change is often ignored and all such changes are simply called *efficient*.

Example: Budget Cuts in Massachusetts   Several years ago, in an effort to reduce state spending, the budget of the Massachusetts Registry of Motor Vehicles was cut substantially. Among other things, the state sharply reduced the number of clerks in each office. Almost immediately, Massachusetts residents found themselves waiting in line for hours when they had to register their automobiles or get their driver's licenses.

Drivers and car owners began paying a price: standing in line, which used time and energy that could otherwise have been used more productively. However, before we can make sensible efficiency judgments, we must be able to measure, or at least approximate, the value of both the gains and the losses produced by the budget cut. To approximate the losses to car owners and drivers, we might ask how much people would be willing to pay to avoid standing in those long lines.

One office estimated that 500 people stood in line every day for about 1 hour each. If each person were willing to pay just $2 to avoid standing in line, the damage incurred would be $1,000 (500 × $2) per day. If the registry were open 250 days per year, the reduction in labor force at that office alone would create a cost to car owners, conservatively estimated, of $250,000 (250 × $1,000) per year.

Estimates also showed that taxpayers in Massachusetts saved about $80,000 per year by having fewer clerks at that office. If the clerks were reinstated, there would be some gains and some losses. Car owners and drivers would gain, and taxpayers would lose. However, because we can show that the value of the gains would substantially exceed the value of the losses, it can be argued that reinstating the clerks would be an efficient change. Note that the only *net* losers would be those taxpayers who do not own a car and do not hold driver's licenses.[1]

The Efficiency of Perfect Competition

All societies answer these basic questions in the design of their economic systems:

1. *What gets produced?* What determines the final mix of output?
2. *How is it produced?* How do capital, labor, and land get divided up among firms? In other words, what is the allocation of resources among producers?
3. *Who gets what is produced?* What determines which households get how much? What is the distribution of output among consuming households?

The following discussion of efficiency uses these three questions and their answers to prove informally that perfect competition is efficient. To demonstrate that the perfectly competitive system leads to an efficient, or Pareto optimal, allocation of resources, we need to show that no changes are possible that will make some people better off without making others worse off. Specifically, we will show that under perfect competition, (1) resources are allocated among firms efficiently, (2) final products are distributed among households efficiently, and (3) the system produces the things that people want.

Efficient Allocation of Resources Among Firms   The simple definition of efficiency holds that firms must produce their products using the best available—that is, lowest-cost—technology. If more output could be produced with the same amount of inputs, it would be possible to make some people better off without making others worse off.

The perfectly competitive model we have been using rests on several assumptions that assure us that resources in such a system would indeed be efficiently allocated among firms. Most important of these is the assumption that individual firms maximize profits. To maximize profit, a firm must minimize the cost of producing its chosen level of output. With a full knowledge of existing technologies, firms will choose the technology that produces the output they want at the least cost.

There is more to this story than meets the eye, however. Inputs must be allocated *across* firms in the best possible way. If we find that it is possible, for example, to take capital from firm A and swap it for labor from firm B and produce more product in both firms, then the original allocation was inefficient. This condition might strike you as being difficult to attain. Firms A and B are, after all, independent decision makers. When A is deciding whether or not to hire more workers or invest in a machine, it does not ask itself if those inputs would be more productive at another firm. So how is it that with independent decision-making firms in a market economy we end up with an optimal allocation of inputs across firms?

The answer lies in the price mechanism. Recall from Chapter 10 that perfectly competitive firms will hire additional factors of production as long as their marginal revenue product exceeds their market price. As long as all firms have access to the *same* factor markets and the *same* factor prices, the last unit of a factor hired will produce the same value in each firm. Each firm will be making its own independent decision, choosing input levels so that marginal revenue products *(MRP)* equals the input price, but the fact that each faces the same prices for those inputs tells us that in equilibrium, their marginal revenue products will also be equal. Certainly, firms will use different technologies and factor combinations, but at the margin, no single

---

[1] You might wonder whether there are other gainers and losers. What about the clerks? In analysis like this, it is usually assumed that the citizens who pay lower taxes spend their added income on other things. The producers of those other things need to expand to meet the new demand, and they hire more labor. Thus, a contraction of 100 jobs in the public sector will open up 100 jobs in the private sector. If the economy is fully employed, the transfer of labor to the private sector is assumed to create no net gains or losses to the workers.

profit-maximizing firm can get more value out of a factor than that factor's current market price. For example, if workers can be hired in the labor market at a wage of $6.50, *all* firms will hire workers as long as the marginal revenue product produced by the marginal worker (MRP_L) remains above $6.50. *No* firms will hire labor beyond the point at which MRP_L falls below $6.50. Thus, at equilibrium, additional workers are not worth more than $6.50 to any firm, and switching labor from one firm to another will not produce output of any greater value to society. Each firm has hired the profit-maximizing amount of labor. In short:

> The assumptions that factor markets are competitive and open, that all firms pay the same prices for inputs, and that all firms maximize profits lead to the conclusion that the allocation of resources among firms is efficient.

You should now have a greater appreciation for the power of the price mechanism in a market economy. Each individual firm needs only to make decisions about which inputs to use by looking at its own labor, capital, and land productivity relative to their prices. But because all firms face identical input prices, the market economy achieves efficient input use among firms. Prices are the instrument of Adam Smith's "invisible hand," allowing for efficiency without explicit coordination or planning.

Efficient Distribution of Outputs Among Households   Even if the system is producing the right things and is doing so efficiently, these things still have to get to the right people. Just as open, competitive factor markets ensure that firms do not end up with the wrong inputs, open, competitive output markets ensure that households do not end up with the wrong goods and services.

Within the constraints imposed by income and wealth, households are free to choose among all the goods and services available in output markets. A household will buy a good as long as that good generates utility, or subjective value, greater than its market price. Utility value is revealed in market behavior. You do not go out and buy something unless you are willing to pay *at least* the market price.

Remember that the value you place on any one good depends on what you must give up to have that good. The trade-offs available to you depend on your budget constraint. The trade-offs that are desirable depend on your preferences. If you buy a $300 iPhone, you may be giving up a trip home. If I buy it, I may be giving up four new tires for my car. We have both revealed that the iPhone is worth at least as much to us as all the other things that $300 can buy. As long as we are free to choose among all the things that $300 can buy, we will not end up with the wrong things; it is not possible to find a trade that will make us both better off. Again, the price mechanism plays an important role. Each of us faces the same price for the goods that we choose, and that in turn leads us to make choices that ensure that goods are allocated efficiently among consumers.

> We all know that people have different tastes and preferences and that they will buy different things in different combinations. As long as everyone shops freely in the same markets, no redistribution of final outputs among people will make them better off. If you and I buy in the same markets and pay the same prices and I buy what I want and you buy what you want, we cannot possibly end up with the wrong combination of things. Free and open markets are essential to this result.

Producing What People Want: The Efficient Mix of Output   It does no good to produce things efficiently or to distribute them efficiently if the system produces the wrong things. Will competitive markets produce the things that people want?

If the system is producing the wrong mix of output, we should be able to show that producing more of one good and less of another will make people better off. To show that perfectly competitive markets are efficient, we must demonstrate that no such changes in the final mix of output are possible.

If $P_X > MC_X$, society gains value by producing *more X*.

If $P_X < MC_X$, society gains value by producing *less X*.

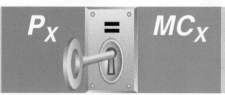

The value placed on good *X* by society through the market, or the social value of a marginal unit of *X*.

Market-determined value of resources needed to produce a marginal unit of *X*. MC_X is equal to the opportunity cost of those resources: lost production of other goods or the value of the resources left unemployed (leisure, vacant land, and so on).

▲ FIGURE 12.2 **The Key Efficiency Condition: Price Equals Marginal Cost**

The condition that ensures that the right things are produced is $P = MC$. That is, in both the long run and the short run, a perfectly competitive firm will produce at the point where the price of its output is equal to the marginal cost of production. As long as price is above marginal cost, it pays for a firm to increase output. When a firm weighs price and marginal cost, it weighs the value of its product to society *at the margin* against the value of the things that could otherwise be produced with the same resources. Figure 12.2 summarizes this logic.

The argument is quite straightforward. *First, price reflects households' willingness to pay.* By purchasing a good, individual households reveal that it is worth at least as much as the other goods that the same money could buy. Thus, current price reflects the value that households place on a good.

Second, marginal cost reflects the opportunity cost of the resources needed to produce a good. If a firm producing *X* hires a worker, it must pay the market wage. That wage must be sufficient to attract that worker out of leisure or away from firms producing other goods. The same argument holds for capital and land.

Thus, if the price of a good ends up greater than marginal cost, producing more of it will generate benefits to households in excess of opportunity costs, and society gains. Similarly, if the price of a good ends up below marginal cost, resources are being used to produce something that households value less than opportunity costs. Producing less of it creates gains to society.[2]

Society will produce the efficient mix of output if all firms equate price and marginal cost.

Figure 12.3 shows how a simple competitive market system leads individual households and firms to make efficient choices in input and output markets. For simplicity, the figure assumes only one factor of production, labor. Households weigh the market wage against the value of leisure and time spent in unpaid household production. However, the wage is a measure of labor's potential product because firms weigh labor cost (wages) against the value of the product produced and hire up to the point at which $W = MRP_L$. Households use wages to buy market-produced goods. Thus, households implicitly weigh the value of market-produced goods against the value of leisure and household production.

When a firm's scale is balanced, it is earning maximum profit; when a household's scale is balanced, it is maximizing utility. Under these conditions, no changes can improve social welfare.

Perfect Competition versus Real Markets

So far, we have built a model of a perfectly competitive market system that produces an efficient allocation of resources, an efficient mix of output, and an efficient distribution of output. The perfectly competitive model is built on a set of assumptions, all of which must hold for our conclusions to be fully valid. We have assumed that all firms and households are price-takers in input and output markets, that firms and households have perfect information, and that all firms maximize profits.

---

[2] It is important to understand that firms do not act *consciously* to balance social costs and benefits. In fact, the usual assumption is that firms are self-interested private profit maximizers. It just works out that in perfectly competitive markets, when firms are weighing private benefits against private costs, they are actually (perhaps without knowing it) weighing the benefits and costs to society as well.

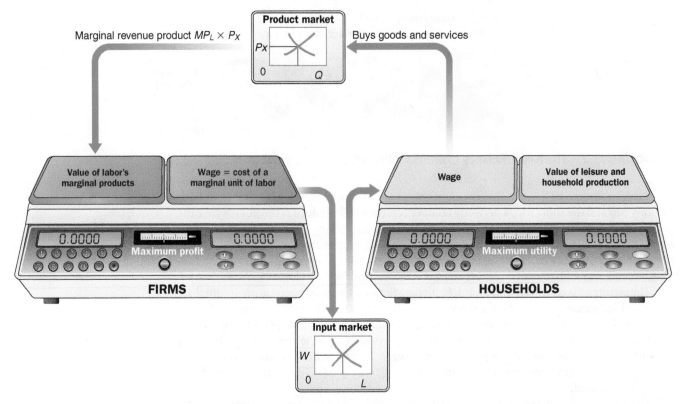

▲ FIGURE 12.3 **Efficiency in Perfect Competition Follows from a Weighing of Values by Both Households and Firms**

These assumptions often do not hold in real-world markets. When this is the case, the conclusion breaks down that free, unregulated markets will produce an efficient outcome. The remainder of this chapter discusses some inefficiencies that occur naturally in markets and some of the strengths, as well as the weaknesses, of the market mechanism. We also discuss the usefulness of the competitive model for understanding the real economy.

12.3 LEARNING OBJECTIVE

Describe four sources of market failure.

market failure Occurs when resources are misallocated, or allocated inefficiently. The result is waste or lost surplus.

The Sources of Market Failure

In suggesting some of the problems encountered in real markets and some of the possible solutions to these problems, the rest of this chapter previews the next part of this book, which focuses on the economics of market failure and the potential role of government in the economy.

Market failure occurs when resources are misallocated, or allocated inefficiently. The result is waste or lost surplus. In this section, we briefly describe four important sources of market failure: (1) *imperfect competition*, or noncompetitive behavior; (2) the existence of *public goods*; (3) the presence of *external costs and benefits*; and (4) *imperfect information*. Each condition results from the failure of one of the assumptions basic to the perfectly competitive model, and each is discussed in more detail in later chapters. Each also points to a potential role for government in the economy. The desirability and the extent of actual government involvement in the economy are hotly debated subjects. In some cases, government action helps improve market failures; in other cases, there are other problems created by the government intervention itself.

Imperfect Competition

One of the elements of the efficiency of a perfectly competitive market that we described is the efficient mix of outputs. Society produces the right mix of goods given their costs and the preferences of households in the economy. Efficient mix comes because products are sold at prices equal to their marginal costs.

Think back to two goods, nuts and apples. For efficiency, we would like, in equilibrium, to find that the relative prices of nuts and apples reflect their relative costs. If the marginal costs of apples is twice that of nuts, efficiency means that consumption should be adjusted so that the relative price of apples is twice that of nuts. Otherwise, society does better in using its resources differently. In a perfectly competitive market, this comes easily. If both goods are sold at prices equal to their marginal costs, then the ratio of the prices of the two goods will also equal the ratio of the marginal costs. Equilibrium in separate markets gives us efficiency in the general equilibrium setting. But suppose one of the two goods is priced for some reason at a level in excess of its marginal costs. Now relative prices will no longer reflect relative costs.

So we can see that efficiency of output mix comes from marginal cost pricing. As we will learn in the next few chapters, however, in imperfectly competitive markets, with fewer firms competing and limited entry by new firms, prices will not typically equal marginal costs. As a consequence, in a market with firms that have some market power, where firms do not behave as price-takers, we are not guaranteed an efficient mix of output.

Public Goods

A second major source of inefficiency lies in the fact that private producers may not find it in their best interest to produce everything that members of society want because for one reason or another they are unable to charge prices to reflect values people place on those goods. More specifically, there is a whole class of goods and services called **public goods *or* social goods** that will be underproduced or not produced at all in a completely unregulated market economy.[3]

Public goods are goods and services that bestow collective benefits on society; they are, in a sense, collectively consumed. The classic example is national defense, but there are countless others—police protection, homeland security, preservation of wilderness lands, and public health, to name a few. These things are "produced" using land, labor, and capital just like any other good. Some public goods, such as national defense, benefit the whole nation. Others, such as clean air, may be limited to smaller areas—the air may be clean in a Kansas town but dirty in a Southern California city. Public goods are consumed by everyone, not just by those who pay for them. The inability to exclude nonpayers from consumption of a public good makes it, not surprisingly, hard to charge people a price for the good.

If the provision of public goods were left to private profit-seeking producers with no power to force payment, a serious problem would arise. Suppose, for example, you value some public good, *X*. If there were a functioning market for *X*, you would be willing to pay for *X*. Suppose you are asked to contribute voluntarily to the production of *X*. Should you contribute? Perhaps you should on moral grounds, but not on the basis of pure self-interest.

At least two problems can get in the way. First, because you cannot be excluded from using *X* for not paying, you get the good whether you pay or not. Why should you pay if you do not have to? Second, because public goods that provide collective benefits to large numbers of people are expensive to produce, any one person's contribution is not likely to make much difference to the amount of the good ultimately produced. Would the national defense suffer, for example, if you did not pay your share of the bill? Probably not. Thus, nothing happens if you do not pay. The output of the good does not change much, and you get it whether you pay or not. Private provision of public goods fails. A completely laissez-faire market system will not produce everything that all members of a society might want. Citizens must band together to ensure that desired public goods are produced, and this is generally accomplished through government spending financed by taxes. Public goods are the subject of Chapter 16.

public goods, *or* social goods   Goods and services that bestow collective benefits on members of society. Generally, no one can be excluded from enjoying their benefits. The classic example is national defense.

Externalities

A third major source of inefficiency is the existence of external costs and benefits. An **externality** is a cost or benefit imposed or bestowed on an individual or a group that is outside, or external to, the transaction—in other words, something that affects a third party. In a city, external costs

externality   A cost or benefit imposed or bestowed on an individual or a group that is outside, or external to, the transaction.

---

[3] Although they are normally referred to as public *goods*, many of the things we are talking about are *services*.

are pervasive. The classic example is air or water pollution, but there are thousands of others, such as noise, congestion, and your house painted a color that the neighbors think is ugly. Global warming is a worldwide externality.

Not all externalities are negative, however. For example, improving your house or yard may benefit your neighbors. A farm located near a city provides residents in the area with nice views and a less congested environment.

Externalities are a problem only if decision makers do not take them into account. The logic of efficiency presented previously in this chapter required that firms weigh social benefits against social costs. If a firm in a competitive environment produces a good, it is because the value of that good to society exceeds the social cost of producing it—this is the logic of $P = MC$. If social costs or benefits are overlooked or left out of the calculations, inefficient decisions result. In essence, if the calculation of either MC or P in the equation is "wrong," equating the two will clearly not lead to an optimal result.

The effects of externalities can be enormous. For years, companies piled chemical wastes indiscriminately into dump sites near water supplies and residential areas. In some locations, those wastes seeped into the ground and contaminated the drinking water. In response to the evidence that smoking damages not only the smoker but also others, governments have increased prohibitions against smoking on airplanes and in public places.

Imperfect Information

imperfect information   The absence of full knowledge concerning product characteristics, available prices, and so on.

The fourth major source of inefficiency is **imperfect information** on the part of buyers and sellers. The conclusion that markets work efficiently rests heavily on the assumption that consumers and producers have full knowledge of product characteristics, available prices, and so on. The absence of full information can lead to transactions that are ultimately disadvantageous.

Some products are so complex that consumers find it difficult to judge the potential benefits and costs of purchase. Buyers of life insurance have a difficult time sorting out the terms of the more complex policies and determining the true "price" of the product. Consumers of almost any service that requires expertise, such as plumbing and medical care, have a hard time evaluating what is needed, much less how well it is done. With imperfect information, prices may no longer reflect individual preferences.

Some forms of misinformation can be corrected with simple rules such as truth-in-advertising regulations. In some cases, the government provides information to citizens; nutrition labeling is a good example. In certain industries, there is no clear-cut solution to the problem of noninformation or misinformation. We discuss all these topics in detail in Chapter 16.

12.4 LEARNING OBJECTIVE

Understand the way that market imperfections may interfere with the ability of the market to achieve efficiency.

Evaluating the Market Mechanism

Is the market system good or bad? Should the government be involved in the economy, or should it leave the allocation of resources to the free market? So far, our information is mixed and incomplete. To the extent that the perfectly competitive model reflects the way markets really operate, there seem to be some clear advantages to the market system. When we relax our assumptions and expand our discussion to include noncompetitive behavior, public goods, externalities, and the possibility of imperfect information, we see at least a potential role for government.

The market system may not provide participants with the incentive to weigh costs and benefits and to operate efficiently. If there are no externalities or if such costs or benefits are properly internalized, firms *will* weigh social benefits and costs in their production decisions. Under these circumstances, the profit motive should provide competitive firms with an incentive to minimize cost and to produce their products using the most efficient technologies. Likewise, competitive input markets should provide households with the incentive to weigh the value of their time against the social value of what they can produce in the labor force.

However, markets are far from perfect. Freely functioning markets in the real world do not always produce an efficient allocation of resources, and this result provides a potential role for government in the economy. Many have called for government involvement in the economy to correct for market failure—that is, to help markets function more efficiently. As you will see, however, others believe that government involvement in the economy creates more inefficiency than it cures.

In addition, we have thus far discussed only the criterion of efficiency, but economic systems and economic policies must be judged by many other criteria, not the least of which is *equity*, or fairness. Indeed, some contend that the outcome of any free market is ultimately unfair because some become rich while others remain poor.

Part III, which follows, explores in greater depth the issue of market imperfections and government involvement in the economy.

SUMMARY

1. Both firms and households make simultaneous choices in input and output markets. For example, input prices determine output costs and affect firms' output supply decisions. Wages in the labor market affect labor supply decisions, income, and ultimately the amount of output households can and do purchase.

2. A *general equilibrium* exists when all markets in an economy are in simultaneous equilibrium. An event that disturbs the equilibrium in one market may disturb the equilibrium in many other markets as well. *Partial equilibrium* analysis can be misleading because it looks only at adjustments in one isolated market.

12.1 MARKET ADJUSTMENT TO CHANGES IN DEMAND *p. 249*

3. General equilibrium is reached when equilibrium is established in all markets.

12.2 ALLOCATIVE EFFICIENCY AND COMPETITIVE EQUILIBRIUM *p. 251*

4. An *efficient* economy is one that produces the goods and services that people want at the least possible cost. A change is said to be efficient if it makes some members of society better off without making others worse off. An efficient, or *Pareto optimal*, system is one in which no such changes are possible.

5. If a change makes some people better off and some people worse off but it can be shown that the value of the gains exceeds the value of the losses, the change is said to be *potentially efficient* or simply *efficient*.

6. If all the assumptions of perfect competition hold, the result is an efficient, or Pareto optimal, allocation of resources. To prove this statement, it is necessary to show that resources are allocated efficiently among firms, that final products are distributed efficiently among households, and that the system produces what people want.

7. The assumptions that factor markets are competitive and open, that all firms pay the same prices for inputs, and that all firms maximize profits lead to the conclusion that the allocation of resources among firms is efficient.

8. People have different tastes and preferences, and they buy different things in different combinations. As long as everyone shops freely in the same markets, no redistribution of outputs among people will make them better off. This leads to the conclusion that final products are distributed efficiently among households.

9. Because perfectly competitive firms will produce as long as the price of their product is greater than the marginal cost of production, they will continue to produce as long as a gain for society is possible. The market thus guarantees that the right things are produced. In other words, the perfectly competitive system produces what people want.

12.3 THE SOURCES OF MARKET FAILURE *p. 256*

10. When the assumptions of perfect competition do not hold, the conclusion that free, unregulated markets will produce an efficient allocation of resources breaks down.

11. An imperfectly competitive industry is one in which single firms have some control over price and competition. Imperfect competition is a major source of market inefficiency because prices do not necessarily equal marginal cost.

12. *Public*, or *social*, *goods* bestow collective benefits on members of society. Because the benefits of social goods are collective, people cannot, in most cases, be excluded from enjoying them. Thus, private firms usually do not find it profitable to produce public goods. The need for public goods is thus another source of inefficiency.

13. An *externality* is a cost or benefit that is imposed or bestowed on an individual or a group that is outside, or external to, the transaction. If such social costs or benefits are overlooked, the decisions of households or firms are likely to be wrong or inefficient.

14. Market efficiency depends on the assumption that buyers have perfect information on product quality and price and that firms have perfect information on input quality and price. *Imperfect information* can lead to wrong choices and inefficiency.

12.4 EVALUATING THE MARKET MECHANISM *p. 258*

15. Sources of market failure—such as imperfect markets, public goods, externalities, and imperfect information—are considered by many to justify the existence of government and governmental policies that seek to redistribute costs and income on the basis of efficiency, equity, or both.

——— REVIEW TERMS AND CONCEPTS ———

efficiency, *p. 249*

externality, *p. 257*

general equilibrium, *p. 248*

imperfect information, *p. 258*

market failure, *p. 256*

Pareto efficiency *or* Pareto optimality, *p. 251*

partial equilibrium analysis, *p. 248*

public goods *or* social goods, *p. 257*

Equation:

Key efficiency condition in perfect competition: $P_X = MC_X$, *p. 255*

——— PROBLEMS ———

All problems are available on MyEconLab.

12.1 MARKET ADJUSTMENTS TO CHANGES IN DEMAND

LEARNING OBJECTIVE: Discuss the relationship between general equilibrium and demand shifts.

1.1 [**Related to the *Economics in Practice* on p. 252**] The *Economics in Practice* in this chapter describes the adjustment of the corn market in the United States to the federal mandate requiring refiners to use corn-based ethanol in the production of fuel. Up until January 2012, refiners were given a subsidy of $0.45 for every gallon of ethanol they blended into their fuel. This subsidy drove up the prices of other agricultural goods such as wheat and substantially raised the value of farmland. Assuming the subsidy was still in place, what would happen to the prices of these other agricultural goods and to the value of farmland if oil prices were to rise extensively at the same time? What if oil prices were to fall? Trace these changes on the economy using supply and demand curves.

1.2 For each of the following, tell a story about what is likely to happen in labor and capital markets using the model of the whole economy that we developed over the first 11 chapters.
   a. After several years of a sluggish economy, home values have begun to rapidly rise in response to a large increase in demand in the housing market.
   b. As the baby boomers age, the demand for medical care is rapidly increasing. Healthcare costs, including the cost of prescription drugs, are also significantly increasing. At the same time, the health care industry is experiencing rapid growth.
   c. Mortgage rates continue to fall and credit restrictions have significantly eased, making it easier for potential home buyers to gain access to credit and take advantage of the low mortgage rates.

1.3 A major source of chicken feed in the United States is anchovies, small fish that can be scooped out of the ocean at low cost. Every 7 years, when the anchovies disappear to spawn, producers must turn to grain, which is more expensive, to feed their chickens. What is likely to happen to the cost of chicken when the anchovies disappear? What are substitutes for chicken? How are the markets for these substitutes affected? Name some complements to chicken. How are the markets for

these complements affected? How might the allocation of farmland be changed as a result of the disappearance of anchovies?

12.2 ALLOCATIVE EFFICIENCY AND COMPETITIVE EQUILIBRIUM

LEARNING OBJECTIVE: Explain the principles of economic efficiency.

2.1 Numerous times in history, the courts have issued consent decrees requiring large companies to break up into smaller competing companies for violating the antitrust laws. The two best-known examples are American Telephone and Telegraph (AT&T) in the 1980s and Microsoft 20 years later. (AT&T was broken up into the "Baby Bells"; but the Microsoft breakup was successfully appealed, and the breakup never occurred.)

   Many argue that breaking up a monopoly is a Pareto-efficient change. This interpretation cannot be so because breaking up a monopoly makes its owners (or shareholders) worse off. Do you agree or disagree? Explain your answer.

2.2 A gourmet food truck selling vegetarian hot dogs has just opened in Seattle. A vegi-dog is currently selling for $5 over and above the cost of intermediate goods (condiments, gluten-free bun, and so on). Assuming that labor is the only variable factor of production, the following table gives the production function for the vegi-dog.

Workers	Vegi-Dogs
0	0
1	12
2	20
3	26
4	30
5	32
6	33
7	30

   a. Suppose the current wage rate is $14 per hour. How many workers will the food truck employ?
   b. Suppose the economy begins to grow, incomes rise, and the price of a vegi-dog is pushed up to $7. Assuming no increase in the price of labor, how many workers will the food truck hire?

c. An increase in the demand for labor pushes up wages to $20 per hour. What impact will this increase in cost have on employment and output in the food truck at the $9 price of vegi-dogs?

d. If all firms behaved like our food truck, would the allocation of resources in Seattle be efficient? Explain your answer.

2.3 Emerald Island has a climate that is suited to banana production and yields 840 pounds per acre. Tropical Springs has a climate that is not well-suited for bananas and yields only 250 pounds per acre. Emerald Island has a climate that is not well-suited for mango production and yields 325 pounds per acre. Tropical Springs has a climate that is suited for mangoes and yields 950 pounds per acre. In 2015, there was no trade between Emerald Island and Tropical Springs because of high tariffs and both countries together produced huge quantities of bananas and mangoes. In 2016, tariffs were eliminated because of a new trade agreement. What is likely to happen? Can you justify the trade agreement on the basis of Pareto efficiency? Why or why not?

2.4 The point of scalping is to find someone who wants a ticket more than the person who presently has it. Whenever two different prices exist in a market, arbitrage opportunities (buy and then sell at a higher price) are there. Professional scalpers buy up tickets when they are first offered to the public, while some buy them on the street the night of the event. They can sell any ticket, even those in short supply, *at some price*. When many people want to go to an event that has a limited supply of tickets, the scalping price can be quite high. Go online and find scalping agencies like StubHub and Ace Ticket. See if you can find an event for which the scalping price is much higher than the original price. What determines whether the event is worth the higher price?

It is argued that scalping is efficient. Explain that argument. Others ask how could it be efficient "if only rich people can afford to go to most games?" Do you agree? Why or why not?

2.5 Which of the following are examples of Pareto-efficient changes? Explain your answers.

a. The Hooterville Police Department implements cost-saving programs without having to sacrifice the quality of their services.

b. Competition is introduced into the satellite television industry, and monthly rates drop. A study shows that benefits to consumers are larger than the lost monopoly profits.

c. James trades his Harley-Davidson motorcycle to Lola for her John Deere tractor.

d. The government eliminates an international transportation tax on airline tickets when airlines complain that the tax was costing them business.

2.6 Suppose two passengers end up with a reservation for the last seat on a train from San Francisco to Los Angeles. Two alternatives are proposed:

a. Toss a coin.

b. Sell the ticket to the highest bidder.

Compare the two options from the standpoint of efficiency and equity.

2.7 Assume that there are two sectors in an economy: goods (G) and services (S). Both sectors are perfectly competitive, with large numbers of firms and constant returns to scale. As income rises, households spend a larger portion of their income on S and a smaller portion on G. Using supply and demand curves for both sectors and a diagram showing a representative firm in each sector, explain what would happen to output and prices in the short run and the long run in response to an increase in income. (Assume that the increase in income causes demand for G to shift left and demand for S to shift right.) In the long run, what would happen to employment in the goods sector? in the service sector? (*Hint:* See Figure 12.2 on p. 255.)

2.8 Which of the following are actual Pareto-efficient changes? Explain briefly.

a. You blast your MP3 player at full volume through your car speakers while driving your convertible through Chicago.

b. Your neighbor never returns the lawnmower he borrowed from you.

c. You use a store coupon to save $1.50 on a jar of peanut butter.

d. You pay a ticket scalper $250 for a ticket to a Green Bay Packer's game at Lambeau Field. The ticket has a face value of $125.

2.9 Three golf courses in the same resort town hire groundskeepers with the same skills. Ocean Oaks pays its workers $12 per hour, Luxury Links pays $11 per hour, and Pacific Paradise pays $14 per hour. Each golf course hires the profit-maximizing number of workers. Is the allocation of labor between these three golf courses efficient? Explain why or why not.

2.10 Explain why resources are allocated efficiently among firms and why output is distributed efficiently among households in perfectly competitive markets.

2.11 Under what condition would society benefit from more of a good being produced, and under what condition would society benefit from less of a good being produced?

12.3 THE SOURCES OF MARKET FAILURE

LEARNING OBJECTIVE: Describe four sources of market failure.

3.1 Do you agree or disagree with each of the following statements? Explain your answer.

a. Nutritional food is a public good and should be produced by the public sector because private markets will fail to produce it efficiently.

b. Imperfect markets are inefficient because as price-makers, firms in these markets can guarantee that price will always be less than marginal cost.

c. Financial planning service is an example of a potentially inefficient market because consumers do not have perfect information about the service.

3.2 Each instance that follows is an example of one of the four types of market failure discussed in this chapter. In each case, identify the type of market failure and defend your choice briefly.
  a. Everyone in town would benefit from the acquisition of two new fire engines, but the town does not have the money to pay for them and no one is willing to purchase and donate them to the town.
  b. The only three gas stations in a small town all agree to raise their prices.
  c. Your electrician convinces you that you need to replace your entire breaker box when all you really need is a new breaker switch.
  d. Your neighbor refuses to vaccinate his children for measles.

3.3 After suffering from three floods in 5 years, Clarice decided to have a new drainage ditch installed at the front of her property. This new ditch not only keeps water from flooding her home, but also channels some of the water away from neighboring properties, where it flows directly into the city sewer. Explain why the installation of the drainage ditch might lead to an inefficient outcome.

3.4 Briefly explain whether each of the following represents a public good.
  a. The Krewe of Endymion parade as it travels down Canal Street in New Orleans during Mardi Gras
  b. A therapeutic stone massage at the Sahra Spa in the Cosmopolitan Hotel and Casino in Las Vegas
  c. A fireworks show in Downtown Minneapolis on the Fourth of July
  d. A drinking fountain at Grand Central Station in New York
  e. Clothing purchased at a charity thrift store
  f. A ticket for a seat on a Virgin Galactic SpaceShipTwo spaceliner

3.5 Explain the difference between a positive externality and a negative externality. Can both types of externalities result in market failure? Why or why not?

Monopoly and Antitrust Policy

13

In 1911 the U.S. Supreme Court found that Standard Oil of New Jersey, the largest oil company in the United States, was a monopoly and ordered that it be divided up. In 1999 a U.S. court similarly found that Microsoft had exercised monopoly power and ordered it to change a series of its business practices. From 2010 to early 2013 the Federal Trade Commission—one of the government agencies empowered to protect consumers—investigated whether Google possessed monopoly power and should also be restrained by the government in its business practices. What do we mean by a monopoly, and why might the government and the courts try to control monopolists? Have our ideas on what constitutes a monopoly changed over time with new technology?

In previous chapters, we described in some detail the workings and benefits of perfect competition. Market competition among firms producing undifferentiated or homogeneous products limits the choices of firms. Firms decide how much to produce and how to produce, but in setting prices, they look to the market. Moreover, because of entry and competition, firms do no better than earn the opportunity cost of capital in the long run. For firms such as Google and Microsoft, economic decision making is richer and so is the potential for profit making.

In the next three chapters, we explore markets in which competition is limited, either by the fewness of firms or by product differentiation. After a brief discussion of market structure in general, this chapter will focus on monopoly markets. Chapter 14 will cover oligopolies, and Chapter 15 will deal with monopolistic competition.

Explain the fundamentals of imperfect competition and market power.

imperfectly competitive industry An industry in which individual firms have some control over the price of their output.

market power An imperfectly competitive firm's ability to raise price without losing all of the quantity demanded for its product.

Imperfect Competition and Market Power: Core Concepts

In the competitive markets we have been studying, all firms charge the same price. With many firms producing identical or homogeneous products, consumers have many choices of firms to buy from, and those choices constrain the pricing of individual firms. This same competition also means that firms in the long run earn only a normal return on their capital. In **imperfectly competitive industries**, on the other hand, the absence of numerous competitors or the existence of product differentiation creates situations in which firms can at times raise their prices and not lose all their customers. Firms are no longer price takers, but price makers. These firms can be said to have **market power.** In these markets we may observe firms earning excess profits, and we may see firms producing different variants of a product and charging different prices for those variants. Studying these markets is especially interesting because we now have to think not only about pricing behavior, but also about how firms choose product quality and type.

Forms of Imperfect Competition and Market Boundaries

Once we move away from perfectly competitive markets, with its assumption of many firms and undifferentiated products, there is a range of other possible market structures. At one extreme lies the monopoly. A *monopoly* is an industry with a single firm in which the entry of new firms is blocked. An *oligopoly* is an industry in which there is a small number of firms, each large enough so that its presence affects prices. Firms that differentiate their products in industries with many producers and free entry are called *monopolistic competitors.* We begin our discussion in this chapter with monopoly.

What do we mean when we say that a monopoly firm is the only firm in the industry? In practice, given the prevalence of branding, many firms, especially in the consumer products markets, are alone in producing a specific product. Procter & Gamble (P&G), for example, is the only producer of Ivory soap. Coca-Cola is the only producer of Coke Classic. And yet we would call neither firm monopolistic because for both, many other firms produce products that are *close substitutes.* Instead of drinking Coke, we could drink Pepsi; instead of washing with Ivory, we could wash with Dove. To be meaningful, therefore, our definition of a monopolistic industry must be more precise. We define a **pure monopoly** as an industry (1) with a single firm that produces a product for which there are *no close substitutes* and (2) in which significant barriers to entry prevent other firms from entering the industry to compete for profits.

pure monopoly An industry with a single firm that produces a product for which there are no close substitutes and in which significant barriers to entry prevent other firms from entering the industry to compete for profits.

As we think about the issue of product substitutes and market power, it is useful to recall the structure of the competitive market. Consider a firm producing an undifferentiated brand of hamburger meat, Brand X hamburger. As we show in Figure 13.1, the demand this firm faces is horizontal, perfectly elastic. The demand for hamburgers as a whole, however, likely slopes down. Although there are substitutes for hamburgers, they are not perfect and some people will continue to consume hamburgers even if they cost more than other foods. As we broaden the category we are considering, the substitution possibilities *outside* the category decline, and demand becomes quite inelastic, as for example for food in general. If a firm were the only producer of Brand X hamburger, it would have no market power: If it raised its price, people would just switch to Brand Z hamburger. A firm that produced all the hamburgers in the United States, on the other hand, might have some market power: It could perhaps charge more than other beef-product producers and still sell hamburgers. A firm that controlled all of the food in the United States would likely have substantial market power because we all must eat!

In practice, figuring out which products are close substitutes for one another to determine market power can be difficult. Are hamburgers and hot dogs close substitutes so that a hamburger monopoly would have little power to raise prices? Are debit cards and checks close substitutes for credit cards so that credit card firms have little market power? The courts in a recent antitrust case said no. Is Microsoft a monopoly, or does it compete with Linux and Apple for software users? These are questions that occupy considerable time for economists, lawyers, and the antitrust courts.

◀ FIGURE 13.1 **The Boundary of a Market and Elasticity**
We can define an industry as broadly or as narrowly as we like. The more broadly we define the industry, the fewer substitutes there are; thus, the less elastic the demand for that industry's product is likely to be. A monopoly is an industry with one firm that produces a product for which there are *no close substitutes*. Therefore, monopolies face relatively inelastic demand curves. The producer of Brand X hamburger cannot properly be called a monopolist because this producer has no control over market price and there are many substitutes for Brand X hamburger.

Price and Output Decisions in Pure Monopoly Markets

13.2 LEARNING OBJECTIVE

Discuss revenue and demand in monopolistic markets.

Consider a market with a single firm producing a good for which there are few substitutes. How does this profit-maximizing monopolist choose its output levels? At this point we assume the monopolist cannot price discriminate. It sells its product to all demanders at the same price. (*Price discrimination* means selling the same product to different consumers or groups of consumers at different prices and will be discussed later in this chapter.)

Assume initially that our pure monopolist buys in competitive input markets. Even though the firm is the only one producing for its product market, it is only one among many firms buying factors of production in input markets. The local cable company must hire labor like any other firm. To attract workers, the company must pay the market wage; to buy fiber-optic cable, it must pay the going price. In these input markets, the monopolistic firm is a price-taker.

On the cost side of the profit equation, a pure monopolist does not differ from a perfect competitor. Both choose the technology that minimizes the cost of production. The cost curve of each represents the minimum cost of producing each level of output. The difference arises on the revenue, or selling side of the equation, where we begin our analysis.

Demand in Monopoly Markets

A perfectly competitive firm, you will recall, can sell all it wants to sell at the market price. The firm is a small part of the market. The demand curve facing such a firm is thus a horizontal line; it is perfectly elastic. Raising the price of its product means losing all demand because many perfect substitutes are available. The perfectly competitive firm has no incentive to charge a lower price either because it can sell all it wants at the market price.

A monopolist is different. It does not constitute a small part of the market; it *is* the market. The firm no longer looks at a market price to see what it can charge; it sets the market price. How does it do so? Even a firm that is a monopolist in its own market will nevertheless compete with other firms in other markets for a consumer's dollars. Even a monopolist thus loses some customers when it raises its price. The monopolist sets its price by looking at the trade-off in terms of profit earned between getting more money for each unit sold versus selling fewer units.

ECONOMICS IN PRACTICE

Figuring out the Right Price

A new firm entering an existing market may have a hard time making money, given levels of competition, but it is relatively easy to figure out what the best price is to charge: Just look at what everyone else is doing. But how does an entrepreneur bringing a completely new product to market figure out what people are willing to pay?

Sometimes trial and error turn out to be pretty helpful. Suppose you develop a new drink that with one sip turns the drinker's hair a golden shade of blond. How much could you charge for this? One approach might be to experiment with one price in one market and another in a second otherwise similar market and compare sales levels. Firms call this approach "test marketing," and it is commonly used. Suppose, however, you want to know what price you can charge before you invest a lot of money into developing the product. After all, if you learn that the most anyone would pay is $5 and the average cost of producing this miracle drink is $10, then it would be nice to know that before you build an expensive factory! Oftentimes firms try to learn about the demand of potential customers by getting a representative group together, describing the product, and asking about price response. Marketers call such groups "focus groups," and they, too, are common. Another approach is to look at other products currently serving a need similar to your new product. In this case, an alternative way to turn one's hair blond is dye. Of course it is not a perfect substitute, and so your price need not be the same. But common

sense tells us that prices of similar products, satisfying similar needs, will have prices in the same ballpark. Some call this using "benchmark" pricing.

THINKING PRACTICALLY

1. What kind of benchmarks do you think were used in the pricing of the Kindle when it was first brought to market?

Shortly we will look at exactly how a monopolist thinks about this trade-off. But before we become more formal, it is interesting to think about the business decisions of the competitive firm versus a monopolist. For a competitive firm, the market provides a lot of information; in effect, all the firm needs to do is figure out if, given its costs, it can make money at the current market price. A monopolist needs to learn about the demand curve for its product. When the iPod first came out, Apple had to figure out how much individuals would be willing to pay for this new product. What did its demand curve look like? Firms like Apple have quite sophisticated marketing departments that survey potential consumers, collect data from related markets, and even do a bit of trial and error to learn what their demand curves really look like.

Marginal Revenue and Market Demand We learned in Chapter 7 that the competitive firm maximizes its profit by continuing to produce output so long as marginal revenue exceeds marginal cost. Under these conditions, incremental units add more to the plus, or revenue, side than they add to the minus, or cost, side. The same general rule is true for the monopolist: A monopolist too will maximize profits by expanding output so long as marginal revenue exceeds marginal cost. The key difference in the two cases lies in the definition of marginal revenue.

For a competitive firm marginal revenue is simply the price, as we discussed in Chapter 7. Every unit that the firm sells, it sells at the going market price. The competitive firm is a small part of the overall market, and its behavior has no effect on the overall market price. So the incremental or marginal revenue from each new unit sold is simply the price. In the case of a monopolist, however, the monopolist is the market. If that firm decides to double its output, market output will double, and it is easy to see that the only way the firm will be able to sell

TABLE 13.1	Marginal Revenue Facing a Monopolist		
(1) Quantity	(2) Price	(3) Total Revenue	(4) Marginal Revenue
0	$11	0	—
1	10	$10	$ 10
2	9	18	8
3	8	24	6
4	7	28	4
5	6	30	2
6	5	30	0
7	4	28	−2
8	3	24	−4
9	2	18	−6
10	1	10	−8

twice the output is to lower its price. The fact that a monopolist's output decisions influence market prices means that price and marginal revenue will diverge. The simplest way to see this is via a bit of arithmetic.

Consider the hypothetical demand schedule in Table 13.1. Column 3 lists the total revenue that the monopoly would take in at different levels of output. If it were to produce 1 unit, that unit would sell for $10, and total revenue would be $10. Two units would sell for $9 each, in which case total revenue would be $18. As column 4 shows, marginal revenue from the second unit would be $8 ($18 minus $10). Notice that the marginal revenue from increasing output from 1 unit to 2 units ($8) is *less* than the price of the second unit ($9).

Now consider what happens when the firm considers setting production at 4 units instead of 3. The fourth unit would sell for $7, but because the firm cannot price discriminate, it must sell *all* 4 units for $7 each. Had the firm chosen to produce only 3 units, it could have sold those 3 units for $8 each. Thus, offsetting the revenue gain of $7 from the fourth unit is a revenue loss of $3— that is, $1 for each of the 3 units that would have sold at the higher price. The marginal revenue of the fourth unit is $7 minus $3, or $4, which is considerably below the price of $7. (Remember, unlike a monopoly, a perfectly competitive firm does not have to charge a lower price to sell more. Thus, $P = MR$ in competition.) For a monopolist, an increase in output involves not only producing more and selling it, but also reducing the overall price of its output.

Marginal revenue can also be derived by looking at the change in total revenue as output changes by 1 unit. At 3 units of output, total revenue is $24. At 4 units of output, total revenue is $28. Marginal revenue is the difference, or $4.

Moving from 6 to 7 units of output actually reduces total revenue for the firm. At 7 units, marginal revenue is negative. Although it is true that the seventh unit will sell for a positive price ($4), the firm must sell all 7 units for $4 each (for a total revenue of $28). If output had been restricted to 6 units, each would have sold for $5. Thus, offsetting the revenue gain of $4 from the seventh unit is a revenue loss of $6—that is, $1 for each of the 6 units that the firm would have sold at the higher price. Increasing output from 6 to 7 units actually decreases revenue by $2. Figure 13.2 graphs the marginal revenue schedule derived in Table 13.1. Notice that at every level of output except 1 unit, marginal revenue is *below* price. Marginal revenue turns from positive to negative after 6 units of output. When the demand curve is a straight line, and quantity is continuous, the marginal revenue curve bisects the quantity axis between the origin and the point where the demand curve hits the quantity axis, as in Figure 13.3.

Look carefully at Figure 13.3. The marginal revenue curve shows the change in total revenue that results as a firm moves along the segment of the demand curve that lies directly above it. Consider starting at a price in excess of point A per period in the top panel of Figure 13.3. Here total revenue (shown in the bottom panel) is zero because nothing is sold. To begin selling, the firm must lower the product price. At prices below A, marginal revenue is positive, and total revenue begins to increase. To sell increasing quantities of the good, the firm must lower its price more and more. As output increases between zero and

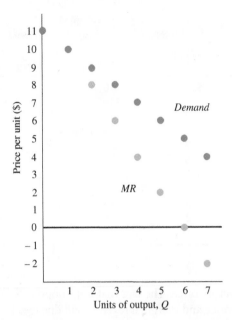

▲ FIGURE 13.2 **Marginal Revenue Curve Facing a Monopolist**

At every level of output except 1 unit, a monopolist's marginal revenue (MR) is below price. This is so because (1) we assume that the monopolist must sell all its product at a single price (no price discrimination) and (2) to raise output and sell it, the firm must lower the price it charges. Selling the additional output will raise revenue, but this increase is offset somewhat by the lower price charged for all units sold. Therefore, the increase in revenue from increasing output by 1 (the marginal revenue) is less than the price.

Q* and the firm moves down its demand curve from point A to point B, marginal revenue remains positive and total revenue continues to increase. The quantity of output (Q) is rising, which tends to push total revenue (P × Q) *up*. At the same time, the price of output (P) is falling, which tends to push total revenue (P × Q) *down*. Up to point B, the effect of increasing Q dominates the effect of falling P and total revenue rises: Marginal revenue is positive (above the quantity axis).

What happens as we look at output levels greater than Q*—that is, farther down the demand curve from point B toward point C? We are still lowering P to sell more output, but at levels greater than Q*, marginal revenue is negative, and total revenue in the bottom panel starts to fall. Beyond Q*, the effect of cutting price on total revenue is larger than the effect of increasing quantity. As a result, total revenue (P × Q) falls. At point C, revenue once again is at zero, this time because price has dropped to zero.[1]

The Monopolist's Profit-Maximizing Price and Output   We have spent much time defining and explaining marginal revenue because it is an important factor in the monopolist's choice of profit-maximizing price and output. Figure 13.4 superimposes a demand curve and the marginal revenue curve derived from it over a set of cost curves. In determining price and output, a monopolistic firm must go through the same basic decision process that a competitive firm goes through. Any profit-maximizing firm will raise its production as long as the added revenue from the increase outweighs the added cost. All firms, including monopolies, raise output as long as marginal revenue is greater than marginal cost. Any positive difference between marginal revenue and marginal cost can be thought of as marginal profit.

---

[1] Recall from Chapter 5 that if the percentage change in P is greater than the percentage change in P as you move along a demand curve, the absolute value of elasticity of demand is greater than 1. Thus, as we move along the demand curve in Figure 13.3 between point A and point B, demand is *elastic*. Beyond Q*, between points B and C on the demand curve in Figure 13.3, the decline in price must be bigger in percentage terms than the increase in quantity. Thus, the absolute value of elasticity beyond point B is less than 1: Demand is inelastic. At point B, marginal revenue is zero; the decrease in P exactly offsets the increase in Q, and elasticity is unitary or equal to −1.

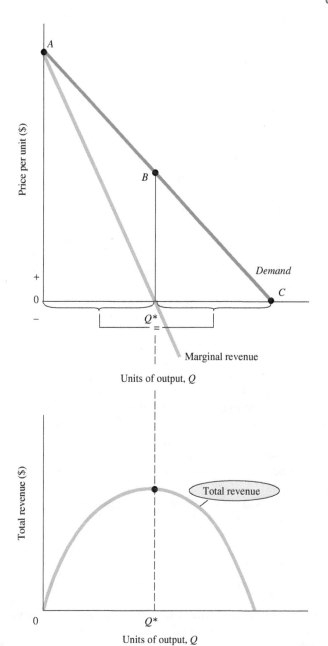

◀ FIGURE 13.3
**Marginal Revenue
and Total Revenue**
A monopoly's marginal revenue
curve bisects the quantity axis
between the origin and the point
where the demand curve hits the
quantity axis. A monopoly's MR
curve shows the change in total
revenue that results as a firm
moves along the segment of the
demand curve that lies exactly
above it.

The optimal price/output combination for the monopolist in Figure 13.4 is $P_m = \$6$ and $Q_m = 5$ units, the quantity at which the marginal revenue curve and the marginal cost curve intersect. At any output below 5, marginal revenue is greater than marginal cost. At any output above 5, increasing output would reduce profits because marginal cost exceeds marginal revenue. This leads us to conclude that the profit-maximizing level of output for a monopolist is the one at which marginal revenue equals marginal cost: $MR = MC$.

Because marginal revenue for a monopoly lies below the demand curve, the final price chosen by the monopolist will be above marginal cost. ($P_m = \$6.00$ is greater than $MC = \$2.00$.) At 5 units of output, price will be fixed at $6 (point A on the demand curve), which is as much as the market will bear, and total revenue will be $P_m \times Q_m = \$6 \times 5 = \$30$ (area P_mAQ_m0). Total cost is the product of average total cost and units of output, $\$4.50 \times 5 = \$22.50$ (area CBQ_m0). Total profit is the difference between total revenue and total cost, $\$30 - \$22.50 = \$7.50$. In Figure 13.4, total profit is the area of the gray rectangle P_mABC.

Our discussion about the optimal output level for a monopolist points to a common misconception. Even monopolists face constraints on the prices they can charge. Suppose a single firm controlled the production of bicycles. That firm would be able to charge more than could

▶ **FIGURE 13.4** **Price and Output Choice for a Profit-Maximizing Monopolist**

A profit-maximizing monopolist will raise output as long as marginal revenue exceeds marginal cost. Maximum profit is at an output of 5 units per period and a price of $6. Above 5 units of output, marginal cost is greater than marginal revenue; increasing output beyond 5 units would reduce profit. At 5 units, $TR = P_m A Q_m 0$, $TC = CBQ_m 0$, and profit $= P_m ABC$.

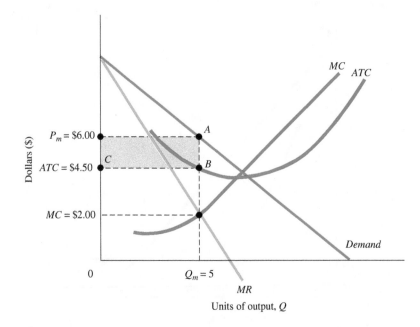

be charged in a competitive marketplace, but its power to raise prices has limits. As the bike price rises, we will see more people buying inline skates or walking. A particularly interesting case comes from monopolists who sell durable goods, goods that last for some period of time. Microsoft is the only producer for Windows, the operating system that dominates the personal computer (PC) market. But when Microsoft tries to sell a new version of that operating system, its price is constrained by the fact that many of the potential consumers it seeks already have an old operating system. If the new price is too high, consumers will stay with the older version. Some monopolists may face quite elastic demand curves as a result of the characteristics of the product they sell.

The Absence of a Supply Curve in Monopoly In perfect competition, the supply curve of a firm in the short run is the same as the portion of the firm's marginal cost curve that lies above the average variable cost curve. As the price of the good produced by the firm changes, the perfectly competitive firm simply moves up or down its marginal cost curve in choosing how much output to produce.

As you can see, however, Figure 13.4 contains nothing that we can point to and call a supply curve. The amount of output that a monopolist produces depends on its marginal cost curve *and* on the shape of the demand curve that it faces. In other words, the amount of output that a monopolist supplies is not independent of the shape of the demand curve. A monopoly firm has no supply curve that is independent of the demand curve for its product.

To see why, consider what a firm's supply curve means. A supply curve shows the quantity of output the firm is willing to supply at each price. If we ask a monopolist how much output she is willing to supply at a given price, the monopolist will say that her supply behavior depends not only on marginal cost but also on the marginal revenue associated with that price. To know what that marginal revenue would be, the monopolist must know what her demand curve looks like.

In sum, in perfect competition, we can draw a firm's supply curve without knowing anything more than the firm's marginal cost curve. The situation for a monopolist is more complicated: A monopolist sets both price and quantity, and the amount of output that it supplies depends on its marginal cost curve and the demand curve that it faces. In other words, firms in imperfectly competitive markets have no supply curves.

Perfect Competition and Monopoly Compared

One way to understand monopoly is to compare equilibrium output and price in a perfectly competitive industry with the output and price that would be chosen if the same industry were organized as a monopoly. To make this comparison meaningful, let us exclude from consideration any technological or other cost advantage that a single large firm might enjoy.

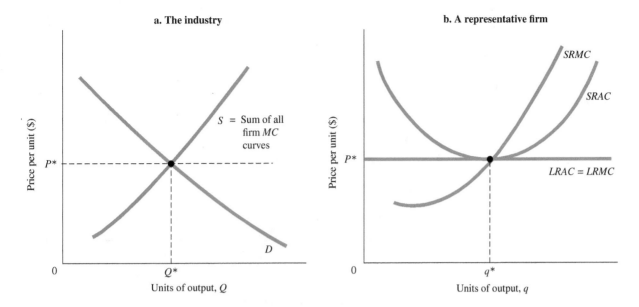

a. The industry

b. A representative firm

▲ FIGURE 13.5 **A Perfectly Competitive Industry in Long-Run Equilibrium**
In a perfectly competitive industry in the long run, price will be equal to long-run average cost. The market supply curve is the sum of all the short-run marginal cost curves of the firms in the industry. Here we assume that firms are using a technology that exhibits constant returns to scale: *LRAC* is flat. Big firms enjoy no cost advantage.

We begin our comparison with a perfectly competitive industry made up of a large number of firms operating with a production technology that exhibits constant returns to scale in the long run. (Recall that *constant returns to scale* means that average cost is the same whether the firm operates one large plant or many small plants.) Figure 13.5 shows a perfectly competitive industry at long-run equilibrium, a condition in which price is equal to long-run average costs and in which there are no profits. We also show the short-run marginal and average cost curves.

Suppose the industry were to fall under the control of a single price monopolist. The monopolist now owns one firm with many plants. However, technology has not changed, only the location of decision-making power has. To analyze the monopolist's decisions, we must derive the consolidated cost curves now facing the monopoly.

The marginal cost curve of the new monopoly will be the horizontal sum of the marginal cost curves of the smaller firms, which are now branches of the larger firm. That is, to get the large firm's *MC* curve, at each level of *MC*, we add together the output quantities from each separate plant. In the case at hand, with constant returns to scale technology, all firms, whether large or small, have the same long-run average and marginal cost curves. So, the monopolist will also have the same long-run average cost curve because it can use any or all of its plants to produce output at this cost.

Figure 13.6 illustrates the cost curves, marginal revenue curve, and demand curve of the consolidated monopoly industry. If the industry were competitively organized, total industry output would have been $Q_c = 4{,}000$ and price would have been \$2.00. These price and output decisions are determined by the intersection of the competitive long-run marginal cost curve and the market demand curve.

On the other hand, facing no competition, the monopolist can choose any price/quantity combination along the demand curve. Of course, even without direct competition, the monopolist knows it will lose some customers when it raises price. The output level that maximizes profits to the monopolist is $Q_m = 2{,}000$—the point at which marginal revenue intersects marginal cost. Output will be priced at $P_m = \$4$. To increase output beyond 2,000 units or to charge a price below \$4 (which represents the amount consumers are willing to pay) would reduce profit. Relative to a perfectly competitive industry, a monopolist restricts output, charges higher prices, and earns positive profits. In the case of constant returns to scale, as we have here, the monopoly output will be one-half that of the competitive industry. In the long run, the monopolist will close plants.

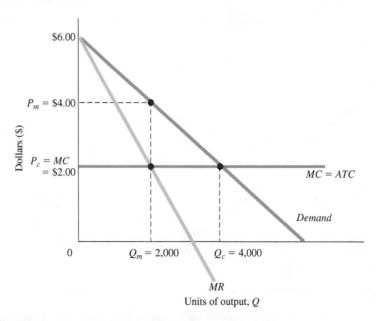

▲ **FIGURE 13.6**   **Comparison of Monopoly and Perfectly Competitive Outcomes for a Firm with Constant Returns to Scale**

In the newly organized monopoly, the marginal cost curve is the same as the supply curve that represented the behavior of all the independent firms when the industry was organized competitively. Quantity produced by the monopoly will be less than the perfectly competitive level of output, and the monopoly price will be higher than the price under perfect competition. Under monopoly, $P = P_m = \$4$ and $Q = Q_m = 2,000$. Under perfect competition, $P = P_c = \$2$ and $Q = Q_c = 4,000$.

Also remember that all we did was transfer decision-making power from the individual small firms to a consolidated owner. The new firm gains nothing technologically by being big given that we have constant returns to scale

Monopoly in the Long Run: Barriers to Entry

What will happen to a monopoly in the long run? Of course, it is possible for a monopolist to suffer losses. Just because a firm is the only producer in a market does not guarantee that anyone will buy its product. Monopolists can end up going out of business just like competitive firms. If, on the contrary, the monopolist is earning positive profits (a rate of return above the normal return to capital), as in Figure 13.4, we would expect other firms to enter as they do in competitive markets. In fact, many markets that end up competitive begin with an entrepreneurial idea and a short-lived monopoly position. In the mid-1970s, a California entrepreneur named Gary Dahl "invented" and marketed the Pet Rock. Dahl had the market to himself for about 6 months, during which time he earned millions before scores of competitors entered, driving down the price and profits. (In the end, this product, perhaps not surprisingly, disappeared). *For a monopoly to persist, some factor or factors must prevent entry.* We turn now to a discussion of those factors, commonly termed **barriers to entry**.

barriers to entry Factors that prevent new firms from entering and competing in imperfectly competitive industries.

Return for a moment to Figure 13.4 on p. 270 or Figure 13.6 on this page. In these graphs, we see that the monopolist is earning a positive economic profit. Such profits can persist only if other firms cannot enter this industry and compete them away. The term *barriers to entry* is used to describe the set of factors that prevent new firms from entering a market with excess profits. Monopoly can persist only in the presence of entry barriers. Let's examine some barriers to entry.

Economies of Scale   In Chapter 9, we described production technologies in which average costs fall with output increases. In situations in which those scale economies are large relative to the overall market, the cost advantages associated with size can give rise to monopoly power.

Scale economies come in a number of different forms. Providing cable service requires laying expensive cable; conventional telephones require the installation of poles and wires. For these cases, there are clear cost advantages in having only one set of physical apparatuses. Once a firm has laid the wire, providing service to one more customer is inexpensive. In the search

ECONOMICS IN PRACTICE

Managing the Internet: Net Neutrality

In February 2015 the Federal Communications Commission (FCC), the Federal body that regulates communications, ruled that broadband Internet service providers (ISPs), like Comcast, Verizon, and AT&T, would be reclassified as common carriers. The new designation allows the FCC to regulate these firms more closely.

The key debate surrounding this reclassification involves the issue of "net neutrality." Under net neutrality, ISPs would be prevented from offering some content providers, like Netflix, faster Internet service to their customers in return for higher rates. In the current language of the debate, ISPs would be unable to offer a "fast lane" to companies like Netflix to send their videos to customers for a higher price. Nor could they "throttle" or slow down other companies. Of course, there is no real fast lane in the Internet, as it is a highway only in a metaphorical sense. Nevertheless it is technically possible for ISPs to favor some content providers over others and speed or slow down their streams. Net neutrality requires that all traffic over the network managed by the ISPs be treated the same. Of course, households can pay ISPs for faster services, and a number currently do so.

Why do some people, including the majority of the FCC commissioners and content providers like Netflix, think we need to regulate the ISPs as common carriers to give us net neutrality? The answer lies in the market structure. In most areas, these ISP's are monopolies over what is often called the "last mile," that is, the connection to the individual household. This market power limits the choice of the customers as we have seen in this chapter and tells us that the market itself will not automatically yield the right outcomes. To make the problem more complex, some of the ISPs have services that compete with

those of their buyers, most particularly with video providers like Netflix. Common carrier status prevents these ISPs from favoring their own subsidiaries to gain an advantage over outside rivals by requiring that all content providers, even those owned by the ISPs, are given the same service.

THINKING PRACTICALLY

1. What ISP subsidiaries currently compete with Netflix?

---

business we also see economies of scale, which helps to explain the dominance of one firm, Google, in this market. In some cases, scale economies come from marketing and advertising. Breakfast cereal can be produced efficiently on a small scale, for example; large-scale production does not reduce costs. However, to compete, a new firm would need an advertising campaign costing millions of dollars. The large front-end investment requirement in advertising is risky and likely to deter would-be entrants to the cereal market.

When scale economies are so large relative to the size of the market that costs are minimized with only one firm in the industry, we have a **natural monopoly**.

Figure 13.7 shows a natural monopoly. One large-scale plant (Scale 2) can produce 500,000 units of output at an average unit cost of $1. If the industry were restructured into five firms, each producing on a smaller scale (Scale 1), the industry could produce the same amount, but average unit cost would be five times as high ($5). Consumers potentially see a considerable gain when economies of scale are realized. The critical point here is that for a natural monopoly to exist, economies of scale must be realized at a scale that is close to total demand in the market.

Notice in Figure 13.7 that the long-run average cost curve continues to decline until it almost hits the market demand curve. If at a price of $1 market demand is 5 *million* units of output, there would be no reason to have only one firm in the industry. Ten firms could each produce 500,000 units, and each could reap the full benefits of the available economies of scale.

natural monopoly An industry that realizes such large economies of scale that single-firm production of that good or service is most cost-efficient.

▶ **FIGURE 13.7 A Natural Monopoly**

A natural monopoly is a firm in which the most efficient scale is large. Here, average total cost declines until a single firm is producing nearly the entire amount demanded in the market. With one firm producing 500,000 units, average total cost is $1 per unit. With five firms each producing 100,000 units, average total cost is $5 per unit.

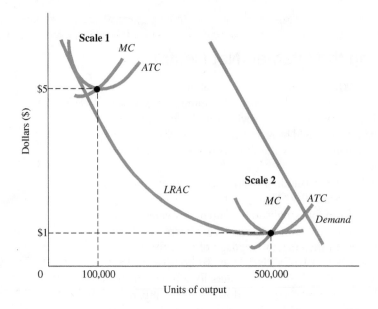

patent A barrier to entry that grants exclusive use of the patented product or process to the inventor.

Historically, natural monopolies in the United States have been regulated by the state. Public utility commissions in each state monitor electric companies and locally operating cable companies, regulating prices with the objective of ensuring that the benefits of scale economies are realized without the inefficiencies of monopoly power.

Patents **Patents** are legal barriers that prevent entry into an industry by granting exclusive use of the patented product or process to the inventor. Patents are issued in the United States under the authority of Article I, Section 8 of the Constitution, which gives Congress the power to "promote the progress of science and the useful arts, by securing for limited times to authors and inventors the exclusive right to their respective writings and discoveries." Patent protection in the United States is currently granted for a period of 20 years from the date the patent application was filed.

Patents provide an incentive for invention and innovation. New products and new processes are developed through research undertaken by individual inventors and by firms. Research requires resources and time, which have opportunity costs. Without the protection that a patent provides, the results of research would become available to the general public quickly. If research did not lead to expanded profits, less research would be done. On the negative side though, patents do serve as a barrier to competition and they slow down the benefits of research flowing through the market to consumers.

The expiration of patents after a given number of years represents an attempt to balance the benefits of firms and the benefits of households: On the one hand, it is important to stimulate invention and innovation; on the other hand, invention and innovation do society less good when their benefits to the public are constrained.[2]

Government Rules Patents provide one example of a government-enforced regulation that creates monopoly. For patents, the justification for such intervention is to promote innovation. In some cases, governments impose entry restrictions on firms as a way of controlling activity. In most parts of the United States, governments restrict the sale of alcohol. In fact, in some states (Iowa, Maine, New Hampshire, Ohio, and Pennsylvania), liquor can be sold only through state-controlled and managed stores. Most states operate lotteries as monopolists. However, when large economies of scale do not exist in an industry or when equity is not a concern, the

---

[2] Another alternative is *licensing*. With licensing, the new technology is used by all producers and the inventor splits the benefits with consumers. Because forcing the nonpatent–producers to use an inefficient technology results in waste, some analysts have proposed adding mandatory licensing to the current patent system. A key question here involves determining the right licensing fee.

arguments in favor of government-run monopolies are much weaker. One argument is that the state wants to prevent private parties from encouraging and profiting from "sin," particularly in cases in which society at large can be harmed. Government monopolies can also be a convenient source of revenues.

Ownership of a Scarce Factor of Production

You cannot enter the diamond-producing business unless you own a diamond mine. There are not many diamond mines in the world, and most are already owned by a single firm, the DeBeers Company of South Africa. At one time, the Aluminum Company of America (now Alcoa) owned or controlled virtually 100 percent of the known bauxite deposits in the world and until the 1940s monopolized the production and distribution of aluminum. Obviously, if production requires a particular input and one firm owns the entire supply of that input, that firm will control the industry. Ownership alone can be a barrier to entry.

Network Effects

How much value do you get from a telephone or a fax machine? It will depend on how many other people own a machine that can communicate with yours. Products such as these, in which benefits of ownership are a function of how many other people are part of the network, are subject to **network externalities**. For phones and faxes, the network effects are direct. Social sites, like Facebook, similarly have network effects. For products such as the Windows operating system and the Xbox, network effects may be indirect. Having a large consumer base increases consumer valuation by encouraging the development of complementary goods. When many people own an Xbox, game developers have an incentive to create games for the system. Good games increase the value of the system. In the case of online interactive games, some observers have argued that the size of the playing community creates large network effects.

How does the existence of network effects create a barrier to entry? In this situation, a firm that starts early and builds a large product base will have an advantage over a newcomer. Microsoft's dominant position in the operating system market reflects network effects in this business. The high concentration in the game console market (Microsoft, Nintendo, and Sony control this market) also comes in part from network effects.

network externalities The value of a product to a consumer increases with the number of that product being sold or used in the market.

The Social Costs of Monopoly

13.3 LEARNING OBJECTIVE

Explain the source of the social costs for a monopoly.

So far, we have seen that a monopoly produces less output and charges a higher price than a competitively organized industry if no large economies of scale exist for the monopoly. We have also seen the way in which barriers to entry can allow monopolists to persist over time. You are probably thinking at this point that producing less and charging more to earn positive profits is not likely to be in the best interests of consumers, and you are right.

Inefficiency and Consumer Loss

One obvious consequence of the higher prices charged by a monopolist is that, relative to the competitive case, consumers pay more for their goods and the monopoly firm earns more in profits. A less obvious, but in some ways a more troubling consequence of the higher prices, is that those high prices *distort* consumer choice. Because of this distortion, monopoly pricing causes not only a transfer of money from consumer to monopolist, but actually creates an added social loss, captured by no one.

In the absence of externalities (costs incurred but not borne by the firm, like pollution costs), the marginal cost of production tells us the social opportunity cost of a product. The price in the market, in turn, tells us about consumer's valuation or willingness to pay for a good. If a pizza sells for $5 a slice, and you buy a slice, we know it is worth at least $5 to you. In fact, the marginal buyer values that slice at exactly $5. Putting these two factors together, we see that when prices are equal to marginal costs, consumers are paying the opportunity cost of making that good and no more. Every unit of the good that can be made for equal or less than its value to consumers is, in fact, made. In this way, as we saw in Chapter 12, the right goods are produced from society's perspective.

deadweight loss or excess burden of a monopoly The social cost associated with the distortion in consumption from a monopoly price.

Now suppose, instead, that pizza were produced by a monopolist charging $7. Only consumers who valued the slice at $7 or more would buy. All of the consumers who valued it at more than $5 but less than $7 now go hungry or perhaps eat falafel. These lost customers valued the pizza at more than its marginal cost and yet were excluded from the market by the monopoly price. The monopolist's ability to raise its price above marginal cost means that some transactions that would have been advantageous from an overall perspective are not made. Economists call this *loss*, a loss associated with the fact that higher prices discourage consumption by people whose value of a good exceeds its social cost of production, the **deadweight loss or excess burden of a monopoly**. You have seen deadweight loss in Chapter 4 when we looked more generally at the underproduction of goods.

The monopoly diagram we introduced appears in Figure 13.8 and allows us to make a rough estimate of the size of the loss to social welfare that arises from monopoly. Recall we have constant returns to scale. Under competitive conditions, firms would produce output up to $Q_c = 4{,}000$ units and price would ultimately settle at $P_c = \$2$, equal to long-run average cost. Any price above $2 will mean positive profits, which would be eliminated by the entry of new competing firms in the long run. (You should remember this from Chapter 9.)

A monopoly firm in the same industry, however, would produce only $Q_m = 2{,}000$ units per period and charge a price of $P_m = \$4$ because $MR = MC$ at $Q_m = 2{,}000$ units. The monopoly would make a profit equal to total revenue minus total cost, or $P_m \times Q_m$ minus $ATC \times Q_m$. Profit to the monopoly is thus equal to the area P_mACP_c, or $4,000. [(\$4 \times 2{,}000) - (\$2 \times 2{,}000) = \$8{,}000 - \$4{,}000 = \$4{,}000$. Remember that $P_c = ATC$ in this example.]

Now consider the gains and losses associated with increasing price from $2 to $4 and cutting output from 4,000 units to 2,000 units. As you might guess, the winner will be the monopolist and the loser will be the consumer, but let us see how it works out.

At $P_c = \$2$, the price under perfect competition, there are no profits. Consumers are paying a price of $2, but the demand curve shows that many are willing to pay more than that. For example, a substantial number of people would pay $4 or more. Those people willing to pay more than $2 are receiving what we previously called a *consumer surplus*. Consumer surplus is the difference between what households are willing to pay for a product and the current market price. The demand curve shows approximately how much households are willing to pay at each level of output. Thus, the area of triangle DBP_c gives us a rough measure of the

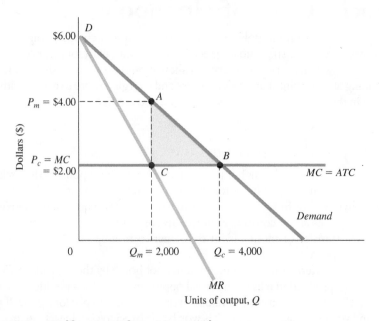

▲ **FIGURE 13.8** **Welfare Loss from Monopoly**

A demand curve shows the amounts that people are willing to pay at each potential level of output. Thus, the demand curve can be used to approximate the benefits to the consumer of raising output above 2,000 units. *MC* reflects the marginal cost of the resources needed. The triangle *ABC* roughly measures the net social gain of moving from 2,000 units to 4,000 units (or the loss that results when monopoly decreases output from 4,000 units to 2,000 units).

"consumer surplus" being enjoyed by households when the price is $2. Consumers willing to pay exactly $4 get a surplus equal to $2. Those who place the highest value on this good—that is, those who are willing to pay the most ($6)—get a surplus equal to DP_c, or $4.

Now the industry is reorganized as a monopoly that cuts output to 2,000 units and raises price to $4. The big winner is the monopolist, who ends up earning profits equal to $4,000. The big losers are the consumers. Their "surplus" now shrinks from the area of triangle DBP_c to the area of triangle DAP_m. Part of that loss (which is equal to $DBP_c - DAP_m$ or the area P_mABP_c) is covered by the monopolist's gain of P_mACP_c, but not all of it. The loss to consumers exceeds the gain to the monopoly by the area of triangle $ABC(P_mABP_c - P_mACP_c)$, which roughly measures the net loss in social welfare associated with monopoly power in this industry. Because the area of a triangle is half its base times its height, the welfare loss is $1/2 \times 2,000 \times \$2 = \$2,000$. If we could push price back down to the competitive level and increase output to 4,000 units, consumers would gain more than the monopolist would lose and the gain in social welfare would approximate the area of ABC, or $2,000.

Notice the deadweight loss comes about because the price increase has led some people to leave the market. The deadweight loss is the consumer surplus no longer reaped by the 2,000 units of consumption that left the market when faced with the monopoly price. Monopoly imposes the largest deadweight loss in markets with elastic demands because under these circumstances the higher price causes more change in consumer behavior.

Rent-Seeking Behavior

Economists have another concern about monopolies. Triangle ABC in Figure 13.8 represents a real net loss to society, but part of rectangle P_mACP_c (the $4,000 monopoly profit) may also end up lost. To understand why, we need to think about the incentives facing potential monopolists.

The area of rectangle P_mACP_c shows positive profits. If entry into the market were easy and competition were open, these profits would eventually be competed to zero. Owners of businesses earning profits have an incentive to prevent this development. In fact, the graph shows how much they would be willing to pay to prevent it. A rational owner of a monopoly firm would be willing to pay any amount less than the entire rectangle. Any portion of profits left over after expenses is better than zero, which would be the case if free competition eliminated all profits.

Potential monopolists can do many things to protect their profits. One obvious approach is to push the government to impose restrictions on competition. A classic example is the market for cabs in New York and other large cities. To operate a cab legally in New York City, you need a license. The city tightly controls the number of licenses available. If entry into the taxi business were open, competition would hold down cab fares to the cost of operating cabs. However, owners of the taxi medallions have become a powerful lobbying force and have recently fought against the introduction of a potential rival, Uber, into various cities.

There are countless other examples. The steel industry and the automobile industry spend large sums lobbying Congress for tariff protection.[3] Some experts claim that establishment of the now-defunct Civil Aeronautics Board in 1937 to control competition in the airline industry and extensive regulation of trucking by the Interstate Commerce Commission (ICC) before deregulation in the 1970s came about partly through industry efforts to restrict competition and preserve profits.

This kind of behavior, in which households or firms take action to preserve economic profits, is called **rent-seeking behavior**. Recall from Chapter 10 that rent is the return to a factor of production in strictly limited supply. Rent-seeking behavior has two important implications.

First, this behavior consumes resources. Lobbying and building barriers to entry are not costless activities. Lobbyists' wages, expenses of the regulatory bureaucracy, and the like must be paid. Periodically faced with the prospect that the city of New York will issue new taxi licenses, cab owners and drivers have become so well organized that they can bring the city to a standstill with a strike or even a limited job action. Indeed, economic profits may be completely consumed through rent-seeking behavior that produces nothing of social value; all it does is help to preserve the current distribution of income.

rent-seeking behavior
Actions taken by households or firms to preserve economic profits.

---

[3] A tariff is a tax on imports designed to give a price advantage to domestic producers.

government failure Occurs when the government becomes the tool of the rent seeker and the allocation of resources is made even less efficient by the intervention of government.

Second, the frequency of rent-seeking behavior leads us to another view of government. So far, we have considered only the role that government might play in helping to achieve an efficient allocation of resources in the face of market failure—in this case, failures that arise from imperfect market structure. Later in this chapter we survey the measures government might take to ensure that resources are efficiently allocated when monopoly power arises. However, the idea of rent-seeking behavior introduces the notion of **government failure**, in which the government becomes the tool of the rent seeker and the allocation of resources is made even less efficient than before.

13.4 LEARNING OBJECTIVE

Discuss the conditions under which we find price discrimination and its results.

Price Discrimination

So far in our discussion of monopoly, we have assumed that the firm faces a known downward-sloping demand curve and must choose a *single price* and a single quantity of output. Indeed, the reason that price and marginal revenue are different for a monopoly and the same for a perfectly competitive firm is that if a monopoly compared to a perfectly competitive firm is that if a monopoly decides to sell more output, it must lower price to do so.

In the real world, however, there are many examples of firms that charge different prices to different groups of buyers, where these price differences are not an inflection of cost differences. Charging different prices to different buyers for identical products is called **price discrimination**. The motivation for price discrimination is fairly obvious: If a firm can identify those who are willing to pay a higher price for a good, it can earn more profit from them by charging a higher price. The idea is best illustrated using the extreme case in which a firm knows what each buyer is willing to pay. A firm that charges the maximum amount that buyers are willing to pay for each unit is practicing **perfect price discrimination**.

price discrimination

Charging different prices to different buyers for identical products, where these price differences are not a inflection of cost differences.

perfect price discrimination

Occurs when a firm charges the maximum amount that buyers are willing to pay for each unit.

Figure 13.9 is similar to Figure 13.8. For simplicity, assume a firm with a constant marginal cost equal to $2 per unit. A nonprice–discriminating monopolist would have to set one and only one price. That firm would face the marginal revenue curve shown in the diagram and would produce as long as MR is above MC: Output would be Q_m, and price would be set at $4 per unit. The firm would earn an economic profit of $2 per unit for every unit up to Q_m. Consumers would enjoy a consumer surplus equal to the shaded area. Consumer A, for example, is willing to pay $5.75 but has to pay only $4.00.

Now consider what would happen if the firm could charge each consumer the maximum amount that that consumer was willing to pay. In Figure 13.9(a), if the firm could charge consumer A a price of $5.75, the firm would earn $3.75 in profit on that unit and the consumer would get no consumer surplus. Going on to consumer B, if the firm could determine B's maximum willingness to pay and charge $5.50, profit would be $3.50 and consumer surplus for B would again be zero. This would continue all the way to point C on the demand curve, where total profit would be equal to the entire area under the demand curve and above the $MC = ATC$ line, as shown in Figure 13.9(b).

Another way to look at the diagram in Figure 13.9(b) is to notice that the demand curve actually becomes the same as the marginal revenue curve. When a firm can charge the maximum that anyone is willing to pay *for each unit*, that price *is* marginal revenue. There is no need to draw a separate MR curve as there was when the firm could charge only one price to all consumers. Once again, profit is the entire shaded area and consumer surplus is zero.

It is interesting to note that a perfectly price-discriminating monopolist will actually produce the *efficient* quantity of output—Q_c in Figure 13.9(b), which is the same as the amount that would be produced had the industry been perfectly competitive. The firm will continue to produce as long as benefits to consumers exceed marginal cost; it does not stop at Q_m in Figure 13.9(a). But when a monopolist can perfectly price discriminate, it reaps all the net benefits from higher production. There is no deadweight loss, but there is no consumer surplus either.

Examples of Price Discrimination

Examples of price discrimination are all around us. It used to be that airlines routinely charged those who stayed over Saturday nights a much lower fare than those who did not. On any given flight, one can find dozens of different prices being charged for seats in the same

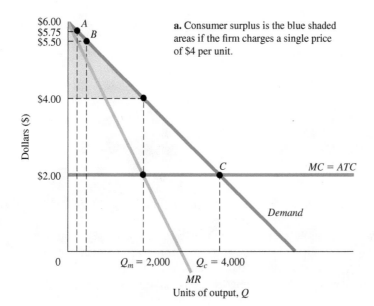

a. Consumer surplus is the blue shaded areas if the firm charges a single price of $4 per unit.

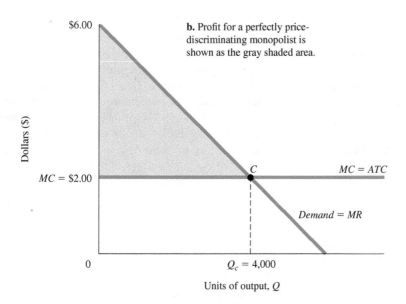

b. Profit for a perfectly price-discriminating monopolist is shown as the gray shaded area.

◀ FIGURE 13.9 **Price Discrimination**
In Figure 13.9(a), consumer A is willing to pay $5.75. If the price-discriminating firm can charge $5.75 to A, profit is $3.75. A monopolist who cannot price discriminate would maximize profit by charging $4. At a price of $4.00, the firm makes $2.00 in profit and consumer A enjoys a consumer surplus of $1.75. In Figure 13.9(b), for a perfectly price-discriminating monopolist, the demand curve is the same as marginal revenue. The firm will produce as long as $MR > MC$, up to Q_c. At Q_c, profit is the entire shaded area and consumer surplus is zero.

section of a plane. Movie theaters, restaurants, hotels, and many other industries routinely charge a lower price for the elderly. The *Economics in Practice* box on page 280 gives an example of price discrimination in Laotian temples.

How do we explain the patterns of price discrimination that we see? When a firm raises its price, it earns more revenue on the customers it keeps, but of course it loses other customers. Naturally, when a firm is able to price discriminate, it will look for customers to whom it can raise prices without losing their business. As we already know, these are the customers with *inelastic demand*. These customers may well be unhappy about a price increase, but they will not stop buying! Governments follow the same strategy in setting taxes: look for inelastic markets.

Return to our examples. Business travelers have fewer choices about when or if to travel and this makes them more inelastic. They often travel back and forth in one day and rarely spend a weekend, so airlines can identify them by patterns of travel and charge more for that type of ticket. Older people tend to be more flexible in their travel and often have less income; this makes them more elastic and more likely to get cheaper deals. Amtrak, for example, offers discount tickets for those over 65 years of age, but does not allow these tickets to be used on the fast train, the Acela. Tourists visiting a shrine are typically more inelastic in demand than locals, as we see in the *Economics in Practice* box. Price discrimination

ECONOMICS IN PRACTICE

Price Discrimination at Work: Laos's Wat SisKent

If at some point you are visiting one of the many impressive Buddhist temples, or wats, in Laos, you will likely see a sign like the one at the left.

Notice the prices: Foreigners pay 2.5 times the price of Laotians to enter the temple. (The Laotian currency is the kip, and in 2015 one dollar exchanged for about 8,000 kip.) Many people looking at this price list might well think about the fairness of this price discrimination. Laotians likely contribute alms for the upkeep of the temple and perhaps taxes as well. In this sense, it seems fair that they pay less than a foreign visitor to enter. But there is also some good economics behind the differential pricing.

Foreign visitors to the temples are typically much richer than the local Laotians. The average per capita income of a North American, for example, is about 10 times that of a Laotian. Higher income tends to make foreign visitors less sensitive to high prices; they are less elastic buyers. Foreign tourists are also looking at the price of entry as a single event:

Is the price so high that having traveled all the way from New York or Toronto I am now going to remain outside the wat? Local visitors are more likely to make multiple visits. For them, the question is: Given the price, do I want to visit the temple again? This difference in perspective also tells us that a high price is less likely to discourage tourist visits than it is to discourage local visits. In other words, foreign visitor demand is more inelastic than local demand. To maximize revenue, the optimal strategy is to charge a higher price to the more inelastic customers. And that is precisely what the temples in Laos are doing.

THINKING PRACTICALLY

1. Many countries follow the local/foreigner price discrimination strategy. Why do you think it is unusual in the United States?

requires that a firm be able to identify the inelastic versus elastic users and then to make sure that those buyers cannot trade between them. We can see how this works in all the examples we have given.

13.5 LEARNING OBJECTIVE

Summarize the functions and guidelines of federal antitrust laws.

Remedies for Monopoly: Antitrust Policy

As we have just seen, the exercise of monopoly power can bring with it considerable social costs. On the other hand, as our discussion of entry barriers suggested, at times, monopolies may bring with them benefits associated with scale economies or innovation gains. Sometimes monopolies result from the natural interplay of market and technological forces, while at other times firms actively and aggressively pursue monopoly power, doing their best to eliminate the competition. In the United States, the rules set out in terms of what firms can and cannot do in their markets are contained in two pieces of antitrust legislation: the Sherman Act passed in 1890 and the Clayton Act passed in 1914.

Major Antitrust Legislation

The following are some of the major antitrust legislation that have been passed in the United States.

The Sherman Act of 1890   The substance of the Sherman Act is contained in two short sections:

> *Section 1.* Every contract, combination in the form of trust or otherwise, or conspiracy, in restraint of trade or commerce among the several States, or with foreign nations, is hereby declared to be illegal....
>
> *Section 2.* Every person who shall monopolize, or attempt to monopolize, or combine or conspire with any other person or persons, to monopolize any part of the trade or commerce among the several States, or with foreign nations, shall be deemed guilty of a misdemeanor, and, on conviction thereof, shall be punished by fine not exceeding five thousand dollars, or by imprisonment not exceeding one year, or by both said punishments, in the discretion of the court.

For our treatment of monopoly, the relevant part of the Sherman Act is Section 2, the rule against monopolization or attempted monopolization. The language of the act is quite broad, so it is the responsibility of the courts to judge conduct that is legal and conduct that is illegal. As a firm competes in the hopes of winning business, what kind of behavior is acceptable hard competition and what is not? Two different administrative bodies have the responsibility for initiating actions on behalf of the U.S. government against individuals or companies thought to be in violation of the antitrust laws. These agencies are the Antitrust Division of the Justice Department and the Federal Trade Commission (FTC). In addition, private citizens can initiate antitrust actions.

In 1911, two major antitrust cases were decided by the Supreme Court. The two companies involved, Standard Oil and American Tobacco, seemed to epitomize the textbook definition of monopoly, and both appeared to exhibit the structure and the conduct outlawed by the Sherman Act. Standard Oil controlled about 91 percent of the refining industry, and although the exact figure is still disputed, the American Tobacco Trust probably controlled between 75 percent and 90 percent of the market for all tobacco products except cigars. Both companies had used tough tactics to swallow up competition or to drive competitors out of business. Not surprisingly, the Supreme Court found both firms guilty of violating Sections 1 and 2 of the Sherman Act and ordered their dissolution.[4]

The Court made clear, however, that the Sherman Act did not outlaw every action that seemed to restrain trade, only those that were "unreasonable." In enunciating this **rule of reason**, the Court seemed to say that structure alone was not a criterion for unreasonableness. Thus, it was possible for a near-monopoly not to violate the Sherman Act as long as it had won its market using "reasonable" tactics.

Subsequent court cases confirmed that a firm could be convicted of violating the Sherman Act only if it had exhibited *unreasonable conduct*. Between 1911 and 1920, cases were brought against Eastman Kodak, International Harvester, United Shoe Machinery, and United States Steel. The first three companies controlled overwhelming shares of their respective markets, and the fourth controlled 60 percent of the country's capacity to produce steel. Nonetheless, all four cases were dismissed on the grounds that these companies had shown no evidence of "unreasonable conduct."

New technologies have also created challenges for the courts in defining reasonable conduct. Perhaps the largest antitrust case recently has been the case launched by the U.S. Department of Justice against Microsoft. By the 1990s, Microsoft had more that 90 percent of the market in operating systems for PCs. The government argued that Microsoft had achieved this market share through illegal dealing, while Microsoft argued that the government failed to understand the issues associated with competition in a market with network externalities and dynamic competition. In the end, the case was settled with a *consent decree* in July 1994. A consent decree is a formal agreement between a prosecuting government and defendants that must be approved by the courts. Such decrees can be signed before, during, or after a trial and are often used to save litigation costs. In the case of Microsoft, under the consent decree, it agreed to give computer manufacturers more freedom to install software from other software companies.

rule of reason The criterion introduced by the Supreme Court in 1911 to determine whether a particular action was illegal ("unreasonable") or legal ("reasonable") within the terms of the Sherman Act.

---

[4] *United States v. Standard Oil Co. of New Jersey,* 221 U.S. 1 (1911); *United States v. American Tobacco Co.,* 221 U.S. 106 (1911).

ECONOMICS IN PRACTICE

What Happens When You Google: The FTC Case against Google

In January 2012 the Federal Trade Commission settled a suit against Google. The original case involved several matters, including some involving the patents Google acquired through its purchase of Motorola. But a core part of the case was an allegation that Google had abused its monopoly behavior in some of its practices.

So one question you might ask is: Is Google a monopolist? And, if so, what is it a monopolist of? In antitrust cases this pair of related questions is key. For Google, the market at issue was the market for search. Although there are other search engines, Microsoft's Bing for example, Google clearly has the bulk of the market. It is no surprise we usually say, "I will Google that," as opposed to, "I will Bing that." Moreover, barriers to entry into search are high. Microsoft has spent huge resources on Bing and yet it is far behind Google. The intellectual property associated with search is considerable. But just being a monopolist is no offense. The question is what you do with that power. In the Google case the charge was that Google manipulated its search results to favor its own subsidiaries. Try Googling a flight question. Likely the first thing that will pop up is not Expedia or Kayak, but the Google

travel site. Is this an abuse of power? At the moment, it appears that the FTC says no.

THINKING PRACTICALLY

1. Why would Google want to manipulate its search results, particularly on cell phone searches?

In 1997, Microsoft found itself charged with violating the terms of the consent decree and was back in court. In 2000, the company was found guilty of violating the antitrust laws and a judge ordered it split into two companies. But Microsoft appealed; and the decision to split the company was replaced with a consent decree requiring Microsoft to behave more competitively, including a provision that computer makers would have the ability to sell competitors' software without fear of retaliation. In the fall of 2005, Microsoft finally ended its antitrust troubles in the United States after agreeing to pay RealNetworks $761 million to settle one final lawsuit.

In 2005, Advanced Micro Devices (AMD) brought suit against Intel, which has an 80 percent share of the x-86 processors used in most of the world's PCs. AMD alleged anticompetitive behavior and attempted monopolization. At present in the United States, private antitrust cases, brought by one firm against another, are 20-plus times more common than government-led cases.

Clayton Act   Passed by Congress in 1914 to strengthen the Sherman Act and clarify the rule of reason, the act outlawed specific monopolistic behaviors such as tying contracts, price discrimination, and unlimited mergers.

The Clayton Act and the Federal Trade Commission, 1914   Designed to strengthen the Sherman Act and to clarify the rule of reason, the **Clayton Act** of 1914 outlawed a number of specific practices. First, it made *tying contracts* illegal. Such contracts force a customer to buy one product to obtain another. Second, it limited mergers that would "substantially lessen competition or tend to create a monopoly." Third, it banned *price discrimination*—charging different customers different prices for reasons other than changes in cost or matching competitors' prices. This provision is rarely enforced.

Federal Trade Commission (FTC)   A federal regulatory group created by Congress in 1914 to investigate the structure and behavior of firms engaging in interstate commerce, to determine what constitutes unlawful "unfair" behavior, and to issue cease-and-desist orders to those found in violation of antitrust law.

The **Federal Trade Commission (FTC)**, created by Congress in 1914, was established to investigate "the organization, business conduct, practices, and management" of companies that engage in interstate commerce. At the same time, the act establishing the commission added another vaguely worded prohibition to the books: "Unfair methods of competition in commerce are hereby declared unlawful." The determination of what constituted "unfair" behavior was left up to the commission. The FTC was also given the power to issue "cease-and-desist orders" where it found behavior in violation of the law.

Nonetheless, the legislation of 1914 retained the focus on *conduct*; thus, the rule of reason remained central to all antitrust action in the courts.

Imperfect Markets: A Review and a Look Ahead

A firm has *market power* when it exercises some control over the price of its output or the prices of the inputs that it uses. The extreme case of a firm with market power is the pure monopolist. In a pure monopoly, a single firm produces a product for which there are no close substitutes in an industry in which all new competitors are barred from entry.

Our focus in this chapter on pure monopoly (which occurs rarely) has served a number of purposes. First, the monopoly model describes a number of industries quite well. Second, the monopoly case shows that imperfect competition leads to an inefficient allocation of resources. Finally, the analysis of pure monopoly offers insights into the more commonly encountered market models of monopolistic competition and oligopoly, which we discussed briefly in this chapter and will discuss in detail in the next two chapters.

SUMMARY

1. A number of assumptions underlie the logic of perfect competition. Among them: (1) A large number of firms and households are interacting in each market; (2) firms in a given market produce undifferentiated, or homogeneous, products; and (3) new firms are free to enter industries and compete for profits. The first two imply that firms have no control over input prices or output prices; the third implies that opportunities for positive profit are eliminated in the long run.

13.1 IMPERFECT COMPETITION AND MARKET POWER: CORE CONCEPTS *p. 264*

2. A market in which individual firms have some control over price is imperfectly competitive. Such firms exercise *market power*. The three forms of *imperfect competition* are monopoly, oligopoly, and monopolistic competition.

3. A *pure monopoly* is an industry with a single firm that produces a product for which there are no close substitutes and in which there are significant *barriers to entry*.

4. Market power means that firms must make four decisions instead of three: (1) how much to produce, (2) how to produce it, (3) what quantity of each input to buy, and (4) *what price to charge for their output*.

5. Market power does not imply that a monopolist can charge any price it wants. Monopolies are constrained by market demand. They can sell only what people will buy and only at a price that people are willing to pay.

13.2 PRICE AND OUTPUT DECISIONS IN PURE MONOPOLY MARKETS *p. 265*

6. In perfect competition, many firms supply homogeneous products. With only one firm in a monopoly market, however, there is no distinction between the firm and the industry—the firm *is* the industry. The market demand curve is thus the firm's demand curve, and the total quantity supplied in the market is what the monopoly firm decides to produce.

7. For a monopolist, an increase in output involves not just producing more and selling it but also reducing the price of its output to sell it. Thus, marginal revenue, to a monopolist, is not equal to product price, as it is in competition. Instead, marginal revenue is lower than price because to raise output 1 unit *and to be able to sell* that 1 unit, the firm must lower the price it charges to all buyers.

8. A profit-maximizing monopolist will produce up to the point at which marginal revenue is equal to marginal cost ($MR = MC$).

9. Monopolies have no identifiable supply curves. They simply choose a point on the market demand curve. That is, they choose a price and quantity to produce, which depend on the shapes of both the marginal cost and demand curves.

10. In the short run, monopolists are limited by a fixed factor of production, just as competitive firms are. Monopolies that do not generate enough revenue to cover costs will go out of business in the long run.

11. Compared with a competitively organized industry, a monopolist produces too little output, charges higher prices, and earns economic profits. Because MR always lies below the demand curve for a monopoly, monopolists always charge a price higher than MC (the price that would be set by perfect competition).

12. Barriers to entry prevent new entrants from competing away industry excess profits.

13. Forms of barriers to entry include economies of scale, patents, government rules, ownership of scarce factors, and network effects.

14. When a firm exhibits economies of scale so large that average costs continuously decline with output, it may be efficient to have only one firm in an industry. Such an industry is called a *natural monopoly*.

13.3 THE SOCIAL COSTS OF MONOPOLY *p. 275*

15. When firms price above marginal cost, the result is an inefficient mix of output. The decrease in consumer surplus is larger than the monopolist's profit, thus causing a net loss in social welfare.

16. Actions that firms take to preserve positive profits, such as lobbying for restrictions on competition, are called rent seeking. *Rent-seeking behavior* consumes resources and adds to social cost, thus reducing social welfare even further.

13.4 PRICE DISCRIMINATION *p. 278*

17. Charging different prices to different buyers is called *price discrimination*. The motivation for price discrimination is fairly obvious: If a firm can identify those who are willing to pay a higher price for a good, it can earn more profit from them by charging a higher price.

18. A firm that charges the maximum amount that buyers are willing to pay for each unit is practicing *perfect price discrimination*.

19. A perfectly price-discriminating monopolist will actually produce the *efficient* quantity of output.

20. Examples of price discrimination are all around us. Airlines routinely charge travelers who stay over Saturday nights a much lower fare than those who do not. Business travelers generally travel during the week, often are unwilling to stay over Saturdays, and generally are willing to pay more for tickets.

13.5 REMEDIES FOR MONOPOLY: ANTITRUST POLICY *p. 280*

21. Governments have assumed two roles with respect to imperfectly competitive industries: (1) They *promote* competition and restrict market power, primarily through antitrust laws and other congressional acts; and (2) they *restrict* competition by regulating industries.

22. In 1914, Congress passed the *Clayton Act*, which was designed to strengthen the Sherman Act and to clarify what specific forms of conduct were "unreasonable" restraints of trade. In the same year, the *Federal Trade Commission* was established and given broad power to investigate and regulate unfair methods of competition.

REVIEW TERMS AND CONCEPTS

barriers to entry, *p. 272*

Clayton Act, *p. 282*

deadweight loss or excess burden
of a monopoly, *p. 276*

Federal Trade Commission (FTC), *p. 282*

government failure, *p. 278*

imperfectly competitive industry, *p. 264*

market power, *p. 264*

natural monopoly, *p. 273*

network externalities, *p. 275*

patent, *p. 274*

perfect price discrimination, *p. 278*

price discrimination, *p. 278*

pure monopoly, *p. 264*

rent-seeking behavior, *p. 277*

rule of reason, *p. 281*

PROBLEMS

All problems are available on MyEconLab.

13.1 IMPERFECT COMPETITION AND MARKET POWER: CORE CONCEPTS

LEARNING OBJECTIVE: Explain the fundamentals of imperfect competition and market power.

1.1 Suppose Vincent has the only franchise for a 7-Eleven convenience store in Oxford, Mississippi, a city with a population of roughly 21,000. Does the fact that Vincent has the only 7-Eleven in town necessarily mean this represents a monopoly? Explain.

13.2 PRICE AND OUTPUT DECISIONS IN PURE MONOPOLY MARKETS

LEARNING OBJECTIVE: Discuss revenue and demand in monopolistic markets.

2.1 Do you agree or disagree with each of the following statements? Explain your reasoning.
   a. For a monopoly, price is equal to marginal revenue because a monopoly has the power to control price.
   b. Because a monopoly is the only firm in an industry, it can charge virtually any price for its product.
   c. It is always true that when demand elasticity is equal to −1, marginal revenue is equal to 0.

2.2 Explain why the marginal revenue curve facing a competitive firm differs from the marginal revenue curve facing a monopolist.

2.3 Assume that the craft beer industry in Hawaii in 2014 was competitively structured and in long-run competitive equilibrium; firms were earning a normal rate of return. In 2015, a young entrepreneur quietly bought up all the breweries and began operations as a monopoly called "Tropical Suds." To operate efficiently, Tropical Suds hired a management consulting firm, which estimated long-run costs and demand. These results are presented in the following figure.

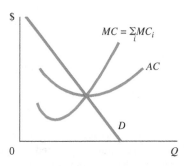

($\Sigma_i MC_i$ = the horizontal sum of the marginal cost curves of the individual branches/firms.)

a. Indicate 2014 output and price on the diagram.

b. By assuming that the monopolist is a profit-maximizer, indicate on the graph total revenue, total cost, and total profit after the consolidation.

c. Compare the perfectly competitive outcome with the monopoly outcome.

d. In 2015, a bar owner files a complaint with the Antitrust Division of the Justice Department claiming that Tropical Suds has monopolized the craft beer industry. Justice concurs and prepares a civil suit. Suppose you work in the White House and the president asks you to prepare a brief memo (two or three paragraphs) outlining the issues. In your response, be sure to include:
  (1) The economic justification for action.
  (2) A proposal to achieve an efficient market outcome.

2.4 Edible Entomology, a monopoly, faces the following demand schedule for its chocolate-covered grasshoppers (sales in pounds per week):

PRICE	$15	$30	$45	$60	$75	$90	$105	$120	$135
QUANTITY DEMANDED	80	70	60	50	40	30	20	10	0

Calculate marginal revenue over each interval in the schedule—for example, between $q = 50$ and $q = 40$. Recall that marginal revenue is the added revenue from an additional *unit* of production/sales and assume that MR is constant within each interval.

If marginal cost is constant at $25 and fixed cost is $800, what is the profit-maximizing level of output? (Choose one of the specific levels of output from the schedule.) What is the level of profit? Explain your answer using marginal cost and marginal revenue.

Repeat the exercise for $MC = 50$.

2.5 The following diagram illustrates the demand curve facing a monopoly in an industry with no economies or diseconomies of scale and no fixed costs. In the short and long run, $MC = ATC$. Copy the diagram and indicate the following:

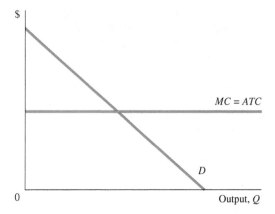

a. Optimal output
b. Optimal price
c. Total revenue
d. Total cost
e. Total monopoly profits
f. Total "excess burden" or "welfare costs" of the monopoly (briefly explain)

2.6 The following diagram shows the cost structure of a monopoly firm as well as market demand. Identify on the graph and calculate the following:

a. Profit-maximizing output level
b. Profit-maximizing price
c. Total revenue
d. Total cost
e. Total profit or loss

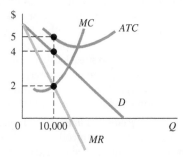

*2.7 Prior to 1995, Taiwan had only one beer producer, a government-owned monopoly called Taiwan Beer. Suppose that while it was a monopoly, the company was run in a way to maximize profit for the government. That is, assume that it behaved like a private, profit-maximizing monopolist. Assuming demand and cost conditions are given on the following diagram, at what level would Taiwan Beer have targeted output and what price would it have charged?

Suppose that while it was a monopoly, Taiwan Beer decided to compete in the highly competitive U.S. market. Assume further that Taiwan maintained import barriers so that U.S. producers could not sell in Taiwan

*Note: Problems marked with an asterisk are more challenging.

but that they were not immediately reciprocated. Assuming Taiwan Beer could sell all that it could produce in the U.S. market at a price $P = P_{US}$, indicate the following:

a. Total output
b. Output sold in Taiwan
c. New price in Taiwan
d. Output sold in the United States
e. Total profits
f. Total profits on U.S. sales
g. Total profits on Taiwan sales

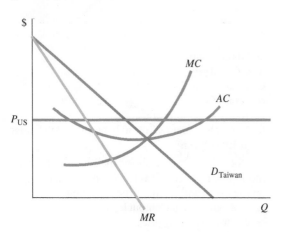

2.8 [**Related to the *Economics in Practice* on p. 273**] Part of the net neutrality rules passed by the Federal Communications Commission includes the prohibition of "paid prioritization", which is the practice of favoring some Internet content over other Internet content in exchange for payment. This applies to Internet advertising as well as entire Web sites. Explain how banning the practice of paid prioritization for Internet advertising could be viewed as reducing or even eliminating a barrier to entry into some industries for some firms.

2.9 [**Related to the *Economics in Practice* on p. 266**] When the 2001 Toyota Prius was introduced in the United States, it was the first mass-produced hybrid gas/electric car in the U.S. market. At the time of its introduction, almost 2,000 cars had been pre-sold at the manufacturer's suggested retail price (MSRP) of $19,995. Three years later, the 2004 Prius was larger than the original model and featured an upgraded power train, yet the MSRP was still $19,995, and due to growing demand, customers were put on waiting lists to be able to purchase the car. Explain some of the ways you think Toyota may have arrived at the MSRP of $19,995 for the (then) unique 2001 Prius. Why might Toyota have kept the same MSRP for the more advanced and larger 2004 Prius that it had for the original 2001 model, given that demand had significantly increased to the point where customers were put on waiting lists at dealerships?

2.10 Taylor Swift is a singer-songwriter whose pop album *1989* was the top-selling album of 2014, with 3.66 million copies sold in just its first 9 weeks of release. The path to success for pop musicians involves reducing the elasticity of demand that they face and building barriers

to entry. That sounds like economic babble, but it has a lot of meaning. Using the language of economics and the concepts presented in this chapter, explain why lowering the elasticity of demand and building barriers to entry are exactly what Taylor Swift is trying to do.

2.11 Explain why a monopoly faces no supply curve.

13.3 THE SOCIAL COSTS OF MONOPOLY

LEARNING OBJECTIVE: Explain the source of the social costs for a monopoly.

3.1 The diagram below shows a firm (industry) that earns a normal return to capital if organized competitively. Price in the market place is P_c under competition. We assume at first that marginal cost is fixed at $250 per unit of output and that there are no economies or diseconomies of scale. [The equation of the demand curve facing the industry is $P = 500 - 1/20\ Q$].

Calculate the total revenue to the competitive firms, assuming free entry. What is total cost under competition? Calculate consumer surplus under competition.

Now assume that you bought all the firms in this industry, combining them into a single-firm monopoly protected from entry by a patent. Calculate the profit-maximizing price, P_m, total revenue from the monopoly, total cost, profit, and consumer surplus. Also compare the competitive and monopoly outcomes. Calculate the dead-weight loss from monopoly. What potential remedies are available?

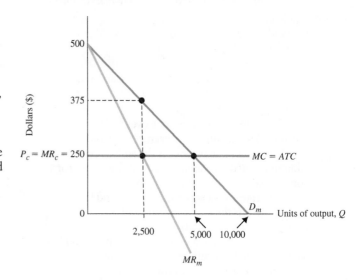

13.4 PRICE DISCRIMINATION

LEARNING OBJECTIVE: Discuss the conditions under which we find price discrimination and its results.

4.1 The following diagram illustrates the demand and marginal revenue curves facing a monopoly in an industry with no economies or diseconomies of scale. In the short and long run, $MC = ATC$.

a. Calculate the values of profit, consumer surplus, and deadweight loss, and illustrate these on the graph.

b. Repeat the calculations in part a, but now assume the monopoly is able to practice perfect price discrimination.

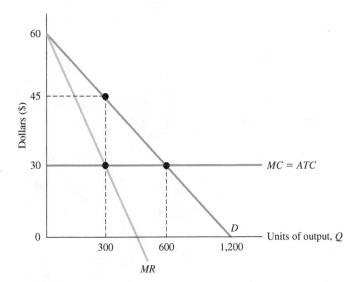

4.2 **[Related to the *Economics in Practice* on p. 280]** One of the most popular tourist destinations in the United States is Las Vegas, famous for its casinos, hotels, shopping, dining, and live entertainment. Unlike many other destinations in the United States, price discrimination is common in Las Vegas, with many businesses regularly offering discounts to local residents for food and drink, entertainment, and even hotel rooms. Why do you suppose these "local's discounts" are common in Las Vegas but not in most other U.S. cities? How is this pricing policy in Las Vegas similar to the one described in your text for the Buddhist temple in Laos?

13.5 REMEDIES FOR MONOPOLY: ANTITRUST POLICY

LEARNING OBJECTIVE: Summarize the functions and guidelines of federal antitrust laws.

5.1 **[Related to the *Economics in Practice* on p. 282]** One of the big success stories of recent years has been Google. Research the firm and write a memorandum to the head of the Antitrust Division of the Justice Department presenting the case for and against antitrust action against Google. In what ways has Google acted to suppress competition? What private suits have been brought? What are the benefits of a strong, profitable Google?

14 Oligopoly

We have now examined two "pure" market structures. At one extreme is *perfect competition*, a market structure in which many firms, each small relative to the size of the market, produce undifferentiated products and have no market power at all. Each competitive firm takes price as given and faces a perfectly elastic demand for its product. At the other extreme is *pure monopoly*, a market structure in which only one firm is the industry. The monopoly holds the power to set price and is protected against competition by barriers to entry. Its market power would be complete if it did not face the discipline of the market demand curve. Even a monopoly, however, must produce a product that people want and are willing to pay for.

Most industries in the United States fall somewhere between these two extremes. In the next two chapters, we focus on two types of industries in which firms exercise some market power but at the same time face competition: oligopoly and monopolistic competition. In this chapter, we cover oligopolies, and in Chapter 15, we turn to monopolistic competition.

An **oligopoly** is an industry dominated by a few firms that, by virtue of their individual sizes, are large enough to influence the market price. Oligopolies exist in many forms. Consider the following cases:

In the United States, 90 percent of the music produced and sold comes from one of three studios: Universal, Sony, or Warner. The competition among these three firms is intense, but most of it involves the search for new talent and the marketing of that talent.

Smartphones are a large and growing global business. Of the 1.3 billion smartphones sold in 2014, more than 50 percent are sold by one of two firms, Samsung and Apple. Part of the competition between these two behemoths involve the choice of operating systems for these firms. Competition in product design and innovative features also play a large role.

Airlines are another oligopolistic industry, but price competition can be fierce. When Southwest enters a new market, travelers often benefit from large price drops.

What we see in these examples is the complexity of competition among oligopolists. Oligopolists compete with one another not only in price but also in developing new products, marketing and advertising those products, and developing complements to use with the products. At times, in some industries, competition in any of these areas can be fierce; in the other industries, there seems to be more of a "live-and-let-live" attitude. The complex interdependence among oligopolists combined with the wide range of strategies that they use to compete makes them difficult to analyze. To find the right strategy, firms need to anticipate the reactions of their customers and their rivals. If I raise my price, will my rivals follow me? If they do not, how many of my customers will leave? If Universal decides to dramatically cut prices of its music and redo its contracts with artists so that they earn more revenue from concerts, will Sony imitate that strategy? If Sony does, how will that affect Universal? As you can see, these are hard, and important, questions. This chapter will introduce you to a range of different models from the fields of game theory and competitive strategy to help you answer these questions.

The cases just described differ not only in how firms compete but also in some of the fundamental features of their industries. Before we describe the formal models of the way oligopoly firms interact, it is useful to provide a few tools that can be used to analyze the *structure* of the industries to which those firms belong. Knowing more of the structure of an industry can help us figure out which of the models we describe will be most helpful. For this exercise, we will rely on some of the tools developed in the area of competitive strategy used in business schools and in management consulting.

oligopoly   A form of industry (market) structure characterized by a few dominant firms. Products may be homogeneous or differentiated.

Market Structure in an Oligopoly

14.1 LEARNING OBJECTIVE

One of the standard models used in the competitive strategy area to look at the structure of an oligopoly industry is the **Five Forces model** developed by Michael Porter of Harvard University. Figure 14.1 illustrates the model.

Describe the structure and characteristics of oligopolistic industries.

The five forces help us explain the relative profitability of an industry and identify in which area firm rivalry is likely to be most intense.

Five Forces model   A model developed by Michael Porter that helps us understand the five competitive forces that determine the level of competition and profitability in an industry.

The center box of the figure focuses on the competition among the existing firms in the industry. In the competitive market, that box is so full of competitors that no individual firm needs to think strategically about any other individual firm. In the case of monopoly, the center box has only one firm. In an oligopoly, there are a small number of firms and each of those firms will spend time thinking about how it can best compete against the other firms.

What characteristics of the existing firms should we look at to see how that competition will unfold? An obvious structural feature of an industry to consider is the number and size distribution of those firms. Do the top two firms have 90 percent of the market or only 20 percent? Is there one large firm and a few smaller competitors, or are firms similar in size? Table 14.1 shows the distribution of market shares in a range of different U.S. industries, based on census data using value of shipments. Market share can also be constructed using employment data. We can see that even within industries that are highly *concentrated*, there are differences. Ninety percent of U.S. beer is made by the top four firms (Anheuser-Busch itself produces 50 percent of the beer sold in the United States), but there is a relatively large fringe of much smaller firms. In the copper industry, we find only large firms. As we will see shortly in the models, with fewer firms, all else being equal, competition is reduced.

We are also interested in the size distribution of firms among the top firms. Again, looking at the beer industry, although Anheuser-Busch produces half of the U.S. beer consumed, under many different labels, MillerCoors (a recently merged pair) is now up to 30 percent of the market, giving us a two-firm **concentration ratio** of 80 percent. When we discuss the price leadership model of oligopoly, we will highlight this question of size distribution. In our discussion of government merger policy, we will discuss measures other than the concentration ratio that can be used to measure firm shares.

concentration ratio   The share of industry output in sales or employment accounted for by the top firms.

The final feature of existing firms that we want to look at is the amount of product differentiation we see in the industry. Are the firms all making the same product, or are the products

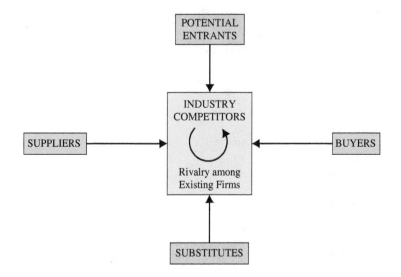

◀ FIGURE 14.1   **Forces Driving Industry Competition**

ECONOMICS IN PRACTICE

Patents in the Smartphone Industry

As we have suggested, the smartphone industry is highly concentrated. It is also profitable and growing. One of the key weapons in the smartphone wars turns out to be patent litigation.

In the last several years, hundreds of patent cases have been filed in the U.S. courts. Many others have been filed all around the world. Apple has filed 7 cases since 2006 and has been named as a defendant in more than 100. At one time we find Apple suing Samsung for infringing several of its patents, while Samsung simultaneously charges Apple with violating its patents. Google, Microsoft, Nokia, HTC, Blackberry, even universities like Cornell, have all joined the game. Indeed, there are firms started that do nothing more than buy up patents from other firms and hire lawyers to sue large firms for infringing those patents. These firms have been disparagingly referred to as "patent trolls," and even the distinguished Chief Justice of the Second Circuit Court of the United States, Richard Posner, has complained about the social cost of these trolls.[1] Nor are all suits about technical details. In a case in which Apple sued Samsung for its Galaxy Pad, the key issue was the design of the product. In that case, a United Kingdom court ruled that Samsung did not violate Apple's design patent because the Galaxy product was not "cool" enough to be a copycat![2]

Many economists, lawyers, judges, and industry people believe that we are likely to see major changes in patent law,

largely as a consequence of the use of competitive patent litigation in the smart phone oligopoly.

THINKING PRACTICALLY

1. Smartphones all rely on technology covered by a number of different patents, owned by many different firms. How does this complicate the competitive picture?

[1] Richard Posner, "Why There are Too Many Patents in America," *Atlantic Monthly*, July 12, 2012.
[2] *Bloomberg News*, October 18, 2012.

different from one another? This takes us back to the issue of how close products are as substitutes, a topic introduced in Chapter 13 in the description of monopoly. How different are Activision's Guitar Hero and Electronic Arts' Rock Band? Does Farmville compete, or are there really different markets for casual and dedicated gamers as some claim? The more differentiated products made by oligopolists are, the more their behavior will resemble that of the monopolist.

TABLE 14.1	Percentage of Value of Shipments Accounted for by the Largest Firms in High-Concentration Industries, 2002		
Industry Designation	Four Largest Firms	Eight Largest Firms	Number of Firms
Primary copper	99	100	10
Cigarettes	95	99	15
Household laundry equipment	93	100	13
Cellulosic man-made fiber	93	100	8
Breweries	90	94	344
Electric lamp bulbs	89	94	57
Household refrigerators and freezers	85	95	18
Small arms ammunition	83	89	109
Cereal breakfast foods	82	93	45
Motor vehicles	81	91	308

Source: U.S. Department of Commerce, Bureau of the Census, 2002 Economic Census, *Concentration Ratios: 2002* ECO2-315R-1, May 2006.

Now look at the boxes to the north and south of the competitive rivalry box in Figure 14.1. To the north, we see potential entrants. In the last chapter, we described the major sources of entry barriers. When entry barriers are low, new firms can come in to compete away any excess profits that existing firms are earning. In an oligopoly, we find that the threat of entry by new firms can play an important role in how competition in the industry unfolds. In some cases, the threat alone may be enough to make an industry with only a few firms behave like a perfectly competitive firm. Markets in which entry and exit are easy so that the threat of potential entry holds down prices to a competitive level are known as **contestable markets**.

contestable markets Markets in which entry and exit are easy enough to hold prices to a competitive level even if no entry actually occurs.

Consider, for example, a small airline that can move its capital stock from one market to another with little cost. Cape Air flies between Boston, Martha's Vineyard, Nantucket, and Cape Cod during the summer months. During the winter, the same planes are used in Florida, where they fly up and down that state's west coast between Naples, Fort Meyers, Tampa, and other cities. A similar situation may occur when a new industrial complex is built at a fairly remote site and a number of trucking companies offer their services. Because the trucking companies' capital stock is mobile, they can move their trucks somewhere else at no great cost if business is not profitable. Existing firms in this market are continuously faced with the threat of competition. In contestable markets, even large oligopolistic firms may end up behaving like perfectly competitive firms. Prices can be pushed to long-run average cost by competition, and positive profits may not persist.

To the south of the competitor box, we see substitutes. For oligopolists—just like the monopolists described in the last chapter—the availability of substitute products outside the industry will limit the ability of firms to earn high profits.

Now take a look at the horizontal boxes in Figure 14.1. One of the themes in this book has been the way in which input and output markets are linked. Firms that sell in the product market also buy in the input market. Conditions faced by firms in their input markets are described in the left-hand box, suppliers. The circular flow diagram in Chapter 3 emphasizes this point. We see this same point in the Five Forces horizontal boxes. Airlines, which have some market power in the airline industry, face strong oligopolists when they try to buy or lease airplanes. In the airplane market, Boeing and Airbus control almost the entire market for commercial airplanes. In the market for leasing planes, General Electric (GE) has a dominant position. When a firm with market power faces another firm with market power in the input markets, interesting bargaining dynamics may result in terms of who ends up with the profits.

Finally, on the right side of the Five Forces diagram, we see the buyer or consumer—in some ways the most important part of the schema. Buyer preferences, which we studied as we looked at individual demand and utility functions—help to determine how successful a firm will be when it tries to differentiate its products. Some buyers can also exert bargaining power, even when faced with a relatively powerful seller. When people think of buyers, they usually think of the retail buyer of consumer goods. These buyers typically have little power. But many products in the U.S. economy are sold to other firms, and in many of these markets firms face highly concentrated buyers. Intel sells its processors to the relatively concentrated personal computer market, in which Lenovo and Dell have large shares. Proctor & Gamble (P&G) sells its consumer products to Walmart, which currently controls 25 percent of the retail grocery market. Walmart's power has enormous effects on how P&G can compete in its markets.

We have now identified a number of the key features of an oligopolistic industry. Understanding these features will help us predict the strategies firms will use to compete with their rivals for business. We turn now to some of the models of oligopolistic behavior.

Oligopoly Models

14.2 LEARNING OBJECTIVE

Compare and contrast three oligopoly models.

Because many different types of oligopolies exist, a number of different oligopoly models have been developed. The following provides a sample of the alternative approaches to the behavior (or conduct) of oligopolistic firms. As you will see, all kinds of oligopolies have one thing in common: The behavior of any given oligopolistic firm depends on the behavior of the other firms in the industry composing the oligopoly.

The Collusion Model

In Chapter 13, we examined what happens when a perfectly competitive industry falls under the control of a single profit-maximizing firm. We saw that when many competing firms act independently, they produce more, charge a lower price, and earn less profit than if they had acted as a single unit. If these firms get together and agree to cut production and increase price—that is, if firms can agree *not* to price compete—they will have a bigger total-profit pie to carve up. When a group of profit-maximizing oligopolists colludes on price and output, the result is the same as it would be if a monopolist controlled the entire industry. That is, the colluding oligopoly will face market demand and produce only up to the point at which marginal revenue and marginal cost are equal ($MR = MC$) and price will be set above marginal cost.

A group of firms that gets together and makes price and output decisions jointly is called a **cartel**. Perhaps the most familiar example of a cartel today is the Organization of Petroleum Exporting Countries (OPEC). The OPEC cartel consists of 13 countries, including Saudi Arabia and Kuwait, that agree on oil production levels. As early as 1970, the OPEC cartel began to cut petroleum production. Its decisions in this matter led to a 400 percent increase in the price of crude oil on world markets during 1973 and 1974.

OPEC is a cartel of governments. Cartels consisting of firms, by contrast, are illegal under U.S. antitrust laws described in Chapter 13. Price-fixing has been defined by courts as any agreement among individual competitors concerning prices. All agreements aimed at fixing prices or output levels, regardless of whether the resulting prices are high, are illegal. Moreover, price-fixing is a criminal offense, and the penalty for being found guilty often involves jail time as well as fines. The *Economics in Practice* box on the next page describes a recent case of price-fixing.

For a cartel to work, a number of conditions must be present. First, demand for the cartel's product must be inelastic. If many substitutes are readily available, the cartel's price increases may become self-defeating as buyers switch to substitutes. Here we see the importance of understanding the substitutes box in Figure 14.1. Second, the members of the cartel must play by the rules. If a cartel is holding up prices by restricting output, there is a big incentive for members to cheat by increasing output. Breaking ranks can mean temporary huge profits. Entry into the industry by non-cartel members must also be difficult.

Incentives of the various members of a cartel to "cheat" on the cartel rather than cooperate highlights the role of the size distribution of firms in an industry. Consider an industry with one large firm and a group of small firms that has agreed to charge relatively high prices. For each firm, the price will be above its marginal cost of production. Gaining market share by selling more units is thus appealing. On the other hand, if every firm drops prices to gain a market share, the cartel will collapse. For small players in an industry, the attraction of the added market share is often hard to resist, while the top firms in the industry have more to lose if the cartel collapses and have less added market share to gain. In most cartels, it is the small firms that begin pricing at below cartel prices.

Collusion occurs when price- and quantity-fixing agreements are explicit, as in a cartel. **Tacit collusion** occurs when firms end up fixing prices without a specific agreement or when such agreements are implicit. A small number of firms with market power may fall into the practice of setting similar prices or following the lead of one firm without ever meeting or setting down formal agreements. The fewer and more similar the firms, the easier it will be for tacit collusion to occur. As we will see later in this chapter, antitrust laws also play a role in trying to discourage tacit collusion.

The Price-Leadership Model

In another form of oligopoly, one firm dominates an industry and all the smaller firms follow the leader's pricing policy—hence its name **price leadership**. If the dominant firm knows that the smaller firms will follow its lead, it will derive its own demand curve by subtracting from total market demand the amount of demand that the smaller firms will satisfy at each potential price.

The price-leadership model is best applied when the industry is made up of one large firm and a number of smaller competitive firms. Under these conditions, we can think of

cartel A group of firms that gets together and makes joint price and output decisions to maximize joint profits.

tacit collusion Collusion occurs when price- and quantity-fixing agreements among producers are explicit. *Tacit collusion* occurs when such agreements are implicit.

price leadership A form of oligopoly in which one dominant firm sets prices and all the smaller firms in the industry follow its pricing policy.

ECONOMICS IN PRACTICE

Price-Fixing Can Send You to Jail!

Price-fixing is a criminal offense, and the Department of Justice (DOJ) vigorously attacks price-fixing. Although economists often disagree about government policies, it is hard to find an economist who does not support vigorous prosecution of price fixers.

In 2011 the Department of Justice filed 90 cases against firms for allegedly fixing their prices. The largest case, completed in September 2012, was a price-fixing case against a Taiwanese firm, AU Optronics. All firms who do business on U.S. soil are subject to U.S. antitrust laws, regardless of where their owners live. In this case, the firm's executive officers were accused of price-fixing in the liquid crystal display (LCD) screen business. LCDs are used in televisions and monitors for computers. The company paid $500 million in fines to the government and its chief executive was sentenced to 3 years in jail. Scott Hammond, the Deputy Assistant General of the DOJ, put it this way,

"This long-running price-fixing conspiracy resulted in every family, school, business, charity and government agency who bought notebook computers, computer monitors and LCD televisions during the conspiracy to pay more for these products. The Antitrust Division will continue to pursue vigorously international cartels that target American consumers and rob them of their hard earned money."[1]

THINKING PRACTICALLY

1. Suppose you believed that the size of the fine levied in price-fixing cases was an important deterrent to price-fixing. What market factors would you want to look at to figure out what fine to charge?

[1] U.S. Department of Justice, Web page, September 20, 2012. "Taiwan Based AU Optronics Corporation Sentenced to Pay $500 Million Criminal Fine for Role in LCD Price-Fixing Conspiracy."

the dominant firm as maximizing profit subject to the constraint of market demand *and* subject to the behavior of the smaller competitive firms. Smaller firms then can essentially sell all they want at this market price. The difference between the quantity demanded in the market and the amount supplied by the smaller firms is the amount that the dominant firm will produce.

Under price leadership, the quantity demanded in the market will be produced by a mix of the smaller firms and the dominant firm. Contrast this situation with that of the monopolist. For a monopolist, the only constraint it faces comes from consumers, who at some price will forgo the good the monopolist produces. In an oligopoly, with a dominant firm practicing price leadership, the existence of the smaller firms (and their willingness to produce output) is also a constraint. For this reason, the output expected under price leadership lies between that of the monopolist and the competitive firm, with prices also set between the two price levels.

The fact that the smaller firms constrain the behavior of the dominant firm suggests that the firm might have an incentive to try to push those smaller firms out of the market by buying up or merging with the smaller firms. We have already seen in the monopoly chapter how moving from many firms to one firm can help a firm increase profits, even as it reduces social welfare. Antitrust rules governing mergers, discussed later in this chapter, reflect the potential social costs of such mergers. An alternative way for a dominant firm to reduce the number of smaller firms in its industry is through aggressive price setting. Rather than accommodate the small firms, as is done in the price-leadership situation, the dominant firm can try cutting prices aggressively, even below their own costs, to create such large losses for weaker, smaller firms until the smaller firms leave. The practice by which a large, powerful firm tries to drive smaller firms out of the market by temporarily selling at an artificially low price is called *predatory pricing*. Such behavior can be expensive for the larger firm and is often ineffective. Charging prices below average variable costs to push other firms out of an industry in the expectation of later recouping through price increases is also illegal under antitrust laws.

The Cournot Model

A simple model that illustrates the idea of interdependence among firms in an oligopoly is the Cournot model, introduced in the nineteenth century by the mathematician Antoine Augustin Cournot. The model is based on Cournot's observations of competition between two producers of spring water. Despite the age of the model and some of its restrictive assumptions, the intuition that emerges from it has proven to be helpful to economists and policy makers.

duopoly   A two-firm oligopoly.

The original Cournot model focused on an oligopoly with only two firms producing identical products and not colluding. A two-firm oligopoly is known as a **duopoly**. The key feature of an oligopoly, compared to the competitive firm, is that a firm's optimal decisions depend on the actions of the other individual firms in its industry. In a duopoly, the right output choice for each of the two firms will depend on what the other firm does. Cournot provides us with one way to model how firms take each other's behavior into account.

Return to the monopoly example that we used in the previous chapter in Figure 13.8 on p. 276, reproduced here as Figure 14.2(a). Marginal cost is constant at $2, and the demand curve facing the monopolist firm is the downward-sloping market demand curve. Recall that the marginal revenue curve lies below the demand curve because to increase sales the monopoly firm must lower its per-unit price on all units sold. In this example, the marginal revenue curve hits zero at an output of 3,000 units. In this market, the monopolist maximizes profits at a quantity of 2,000 units and a price of $4 as we saw in the last chapter. What happens in this market if, instead of having one monopoly firm, we have a Cournot duopoly? What does the duopoly equilibrium look like?

In choosing the optimal output, the monopolist had only to consider its own costs and the demand curve that it faced. The duopolist has another factor to consider: how much output will its rival produce? The more the rival produces, the less market is left for the other firm in the duopoly. In the Cournot model, each firm looks at the market demand, subtracts what it expects

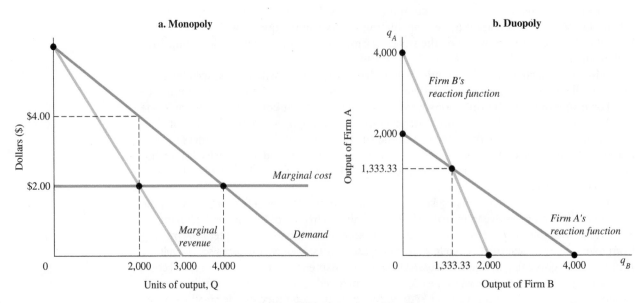

▲ FIGURE 14.2   **Graphical Depiction of the Cournot Model**
The left graph shows a profit-maximizing output of 2,000 units for a monopolist with marginal cost of $2.00. The right graph shows output of 1,333.33 units *each* for two duopolists with the same marginal cost of $2.00, facing the same demand curve. Total industry output increases as we go from the monopolist to the Cournot duopolists, but it does not rise as high as the competitive output (here 4,000 units).

the rival firm to produce, and chooses its output to maximize its profits based on the market that is left.

Let's illustrate the Cournot duopoly solution to this problem with two firms, Firm A and Firm B. Recall the key feature of the duopoly: Firms must take each other's output into account when choosing their own output. Given this feature, it is helpful to look at how each firm's optimal output might vary with its rival's output. In Figure 14.2(b), we have drawn two *reaction functions*, showing each firm's optimal, profit-maximizing output as it depends on its rival's output. The vertical axis shows levels of Firm A's output, denoted q_A, and the horizontal axis shows Firm B's output, denoted as q_B.

Several of the points along Firm A's reaction function should look familiar. Consider the point where Firm A's reaction function crosses the vertical axis. At this point, Firm A's task is to choose the optimal output assuming Firm B produces 0. But we know what this point is from solving the monopoly problem. If Firm B produces nothing, then Firm A is a monopolist and it optimally produces 2,000 units. So *if* Firm A expects Firm B to produce 0, it should produce 2,000 to maximize its profits.

Look at the point at which Firm A's reaction function crosses the horizontal axis. At this point Firm B is producing 4,000 units. Look back at Figure 14.2(a). At an output level of 4,000 units the market price is $2, which is the marginal cost of production. If Firm A expects Firm B to produce 4,000 units, there is no profitable market left for Firm A and it will produce 0. If you start there, where the output of Firm B (measured on the horizontal axis) is 4,000 units each period, and you let Firm B's output fall moving to the left, Firm A will find it in its interest to increase output. If you carefully figure out what Firms A's profit-maximizing output is at every possible level of output for Firm B, you will discover that Firm A's reaction function is just a downward-sloping line between 2,000 on the vertical axis and 4,000 on the horizontal axis. The downward slope reflects the way in which firm A chooses its output. It looks at the market demand, subtracts its rival's output, and then chooses its own optimal output. The more the rival produces, the less market is profitably left for the other firm in the duopoly.

Next, we do the same thing for Firm B. How much will Firm B produce if it maximizes profit and accepts Firm A's output as given? Because the two firms are exactly alike in costs and type of product, Firm B's reaction function looks just like Firm A's: When Firm B thinks it is alone in the market (Firm A's output on the vertical axis is 0) it produces the monopoly output of 2,000; when Firm B thinks Firm A is going to produce 4,000 units, it chooses to produce 0.

As you can see, the two reaction functions cross. Each firm's reaction function shows what it wants to do, conditional on the other firm's output. At the point of intersection, each firm is doing the best it can, given the actual output of the other firm. This point is sometimes called the *best response equilibrium*. As you can see from the graph, the Cournot duopoly equilibrium to this problem occurs when each firm is producing 1,333.33 units for an industry total of 2,666.66. This output is more than the original monopolist produced in this market, but less than the 4,000 units that a competitive industry would produce.

It turns out that the crossing point is the only equilibrium point in Figure 14.2(b). To see why, consider what happens if you start off with a monopoly and then let a second firm compete. Suppose, for example, Firm A expected Firm B to stay out of the market, to produce nothing, leaving Firm A as a monopolist. With that expectation, Firm A would choose to produce 2,000 units. But now look at Firm B's reaction function. If Firm A is now producing 2,000 units, Firm B's profit-maximizing output is not zero, it is 1,000 units. Draw a horizontal line from Firm A's output level of 2,000 to Firm B's reaction function and then go down to the *x*-axis and you will discover that Firm B's optimal output lies at 1,000 units. So an output level for Firm A of 2,000 units is not an equilibrium because it was predicated on a production level for Firm B that was incorrect. Going one step further, with Firm B now producing 1,000 units, Firm A will cut back from 2,000. This will in turn lead to a further increase in Firm B's output and the process will go on until both are producing 1,333.33.

As we have seen, the output level predicted by the Cournot model is between that of the monopoly and that of a perfectly competitive industry. Later extensions of the Cournot model tell us that the more firms we have, behaving as Cournot predicted, the closer output (and thus prices) will be to the competitive levels. This type of intuitive result is one reason the Cournot model has been widely used despite its simplified view of firm interaction. The field of game theory, to which we now turn, offers a more sophisticated and complete view of firm interactions.

ECONOMICS IN PRACTICE

Ideology and Newspapers

In the 1920s, in contrast to the current period, many cities in the United States had multiple newspapers. In an era well before television, and in the early infancy of radio, most people got their news, including their political news, from newspapers. Perhaps, not surprisingly, most newspapers at the time were identified explicitly as having either a Republican or a Democratic bent. It should not surprise you to learn that economists studying this period have identified economic forces governing the political affiliation of these newspapers.[1]

Think about a simple economic model of newspaper demand. Given what we know about people, most of us would expect that individual readers would prefer newspapers that mirrored their own ideological bent. Although political liberals might now and again enjoy Fox news and conservatives might read *The New York Times* op-ed section, most people like to read confirmatory messages. Indeed, Gentzkow and Shapiro find a strong relationship between the way a town votes and the political affiliation of papers: a 10 percent increase in a town's Republican vote share increases the demand for a Republican newspaper by 10 percent. But what happens in a world in which towns have multiple newspapers? Is it better to be the second Republican-focused newspaper in a Republican town or the first Democratic newspaper? In the terms used in this chapter, is it better to compete for advertisers and readers in the main part of the market or to differentiate and focus on the part of the market with less competition?

Gentzkow and Shapiro find strong incentives in newspaper markets for firms to soften competition by

differentiating. One Republican newspaper in an area decreases the likelihood of an added Republican newspaper by 15 percent. Even in markets that many believe to be ideological in nature, supply supply seems to respond to economic forces of demand.

THINKING PRACTICALLY

1. How would you expect the possibility of differentiating your product to change competition between oligopolists?

[1] Matthew Gentzkow and Jesse Shapiro, "Competition and ideological diversity: Historical evidence from U.S. newspapers," *American Economic Review*, October 2014

14.3 LEARNING OBJECTIVE

Explain the principles and strategies of game theory.

game theory Analyzes the choices made by rival firms, people, and even governments when they are trying to maximize their own well-being while anticipating and reacting to the actions of others in their environment.

Game Theory

The firms in Cournot's model do not anticipate the moves of the competition. Instead, they try to guess the output levels of their rivals and then choose optimal outputs of their own. But notice, the firms do not try to anticipate or influence what the rival firms will do in response to their own actions. In many situations, it does not seem realistic for firms to just take their rival's output as independent of their own. We might think that Intel, recognizing how important Advanced Micro Devices (AMD) is in the processor market, would try to influence AMD's business decisions. **Game theory** is a subfield of mathematics that analyzes the choices made by rival firms, people, and even governments when they are trying to maximize their own well-being while anticipating and reacting to the actions of others in their environment.

Game theory began in 1944 with the work of mathematician John von Neumann and economist Oskar Morgenstern who published path-breaking work in which they analyzed a set of problems, or *games*, in which two or more people or organizations pursue their own interests and in which neither one of them can dictate the outcome. Game theory has become an increasingly popular field of study and research. The notions of game theory have been applied to analyses of firm behavior, politics, international relations, nuclear war, military strategy, and foreign policy. In 1994, the Nobel Prize in Economic Science was awarded jointly to three early game theorists: John F. Nash of Princeton University, John C. Harsanyi of the University

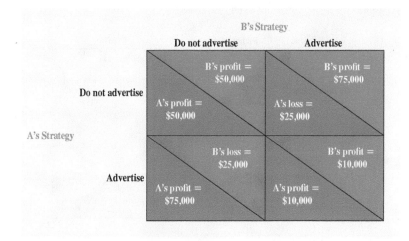

▲ FIGURE 14.3   **Payoff Matrix for Advertising Game**

Both players have a dominant strategy. If B does not advertise, A will because $75,000 beats $50,000. If B does advertise, A will also advertise because a profit of $10,000 beats a loss of $25,000. A will advertise regardless of what B does. Similarly, B will advertise regardless of what A does. If A does not advertise, B will because $75,000 beats $50,000. If A does advertise, B will too because a $10,000 profit beats a loss of $25,000.

of California at Berkeley, and Reinhard Selten of the University of Bonn. You may have seen the movie *A Beautiful Mind* about John Nash and his contribution to game theory.

Game theory begins by recognizing that in all conflict situations, there are decision makers (or players), rules of the game, and payoffs (or prizes). Players choose strategies without knowing with certainty what strategy the opposition will use. At the same time, though, some information that indicates how their opposition may be "leaning" may be available to the players. Most centrally, understanding that the other players are also trying to do their best will be helpful in predicting their actions.

Figure 14.3 illustrates what is called a payoff matrix for a simple game. Each of two firms, A and B, must decide whether to mount an expensive advertising campaign. If each firm decides not to advertise, each one will earn a profit of $50,000. If one firm advertises and the other does not, the firm that does will increase its profit by 50 percent (to $75,000) while driving the competition into the loss column. If both firms decide to advertise, they will each earn profits of $10,000. They may generate a bit more demand by advertising, but not enough to offset the expense of the advertising.

If firms A and B could collude (and we assume that they cannot), their optimal strategy would be to agree not to advertise. That solution maximizes the joint profits to both firms. If both firms do not advertise, joint profits are $100,000. If both firms advertise, joint profits are only $20,000. If only one of the firms advertises, joint profits are $75,000 − $25,000 = $50,000.

We see from Figure 14.3 that each firm's *payoff* depends on what the other firm does. In considering what firms should do, however, it is more important to ask whether a firm's *strategy* depends on what the other firm does. Consider A's choice of strategy. Regardless of what B does, it pays A to advertise. If B does not advertise, A makes $25,000 more by advertising than by not advertising. Thus, A will advertise. If B does advertise, A must advertise to avoid a loss. The same logic holds for B. Regardless of the strategy pursued by A, it pays B to advertise. A **dominant strategy** is one that is best no matter what the opposition does. In this game, both players have a dominant strategy, which is to advertise.

The result of the game in Figure 14.4 is an example of what is called a **prisoners' dilemma**. The term comes from a game in which two prisoners (call them Ginger and Rocky) are accused of robbing the local 7-Eleven together, but the evidence is shaky. Police separate the two and try to induce each to confess and implicate the other. If both confess, they each get 5 years in prison for armed robbery. If each one refuses to confess, they are convicted of a lesser charge, shoplifting, and get 1 year in prison each. The district attorney has offered each of them a deal independently. If Ginger confesses and Rocky does not, Ginger goes free and Rocky gets 7 years. If Rocky confesses and Ginger does not, Rocky goes free and Ginger gets 7 years. The payoff matrix for the prisoners' dilemma is given in Figure 14.4.

dominant strategy   In game theory, a strategy that is best no matter what the opposition does.

prisoners' dilemma   A game in which the players are prevented from cooperating and in which each has a dominant strategy that leaves them both worse off than if they could cooperate.

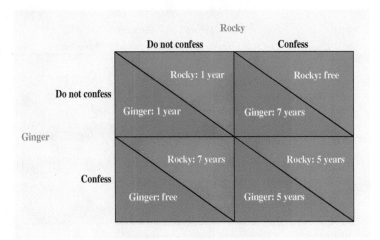

▲ **FIGURE 14.4** **The Prisoners' Dilemma**
Both players have a dominant strategy and will confess. If Rocky does *not* confess, Ginger will because going free beats a year in jail. Similarly, if Rocky *does* confess, Ginger will confess because 5 years in the slammer is better than 7. Rocky has the same set of choices. If Ginger does *not* confess, Rocky will because going free beats a year in jail. Similarly, if Ginger *does* confess, Rocky also will confess because 5 years in the slammer is better than 7. Both will confess *regardless* of what the other does.

By looking carefully at the payoffs, you may notice that both Ginger and Rocky have dominant strategies: to confess. That is, Ginger is better off confessing regardless of what Rocky does and Rocky is better off confessing regardless of what Ginger does. The likely outcome is that both will confess even though they would be better off if they both kept their mouths shut. There are many cases in which we see games like this one. In a class that is graded on a curve, all students might consider agreeing to moderate their performance. But incentives to "cheat" by studying would be hard to resist. In an oligopoly, the fact that prices tend to be higher than marginal costs provides incentives for firms to "cheat" on output—restricting agreements by selling additional units.

Is there any way out of this dilemma? There may be, under circumstances in which the game is played over and over. Look back at Figure 14.3. The best joint outcome is not to advertise. But the power of the dominant strategy makes it hard to get to the top-left corner. Suppose firms interact over and over again for many years. Now opportunities for cooperating are richer. Suppose firm A decided not to advertise for one period to see how firm B would respond. If firm B continued to advertise, A would have to resume advertising to survive. Suppose B decided to match A's strategy. In this case, both firms might—with no explicit collusion—end up not advertising after A figures out what B is doing. We return to this in the discussion of repeated games, which follows.

There are many games in which one player does not have a dominant strategy, but in which the outcome is predictable. Consider the game in Figure 14.5(a) in which C does not have a dominant strategy. If D plays the left strategy, C will play the top strategy. If D plays the right strategy, C will play the bottom strategy. What strategy will D choose to play? If C knows the options, it will see that D has a dominant strategy and is likely to play that same strategy. D does better playing the right-hand strategy regardless of what C does. D can guarantee a $100 win by choosing right and is guaranteed to win nothing by playing left. Because D's behavior is predictable (it will play the right-hand strategy), C will play bottom. When all players are playing their best strategy *given* what their competitors are doing, the result is called a **Nash equilibrium**, named after John Nash. We have already seen one example of a Nash equilibrium in the Cournot model.

In the new game (b), C had better be very sure that D will play right because if D plays left and C plays bottom, C is in big trouble, losing $10,000. C will probably play top to minimize the potential loss if the probability of D's choosing left is at all significant.

Now suppose the game in Figure 14.5(a) were changed. Suppose all the payoffs are the same except that if D chooses left and C chooses bottom, C loses $10,000, as shown in Figure 14.5(b). While D still has a dominant strategy (playing right), C now stands to lose a great deal by choosing

Nash equilibrium In game theory, the result of all players' playing their best strategy given what their competitors are doing.

a. Original Game

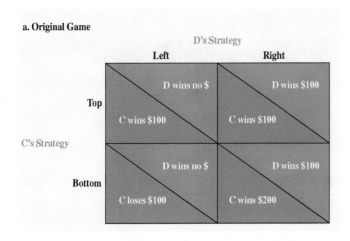

b. New Game

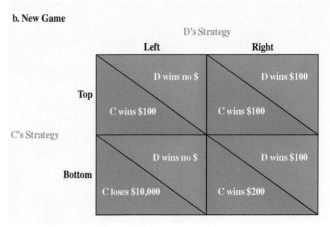

▲ FIGURE 14.5   **Payoff Matrixes for Left/Right–Top/Bottom Strategies**
In the original game (*a*), C does not have a dominant strategy. If D plays left, C plays top; if D plays right, C plays bottom. D, on the other hand, *does* have a dominant strategy: D will play right regardless of what C does. If C believes that D is rational, C will predict that D will play right. If C concludes that D will play right, C will play bottom. The result is a Nash equilibrium because each player is doing the best that it can *given* what the other is doing.

bottom on the off chance that D chooses left instead. When uncertainty and risk are introduced, the game changes. C is likely to play top and guarantee itself a $100 profit instead of playing bottom and risk losing $10,000 in the off chance that D plays left. A **maximin strategy** is a strategy chosen by a player to maximize the minimum gain that it can earn. In essence, one who plays a maximin strategy assumes that the opposition will play the strategy that does the most damage.

maximin strategy   In game theory, a strategy chosen to maximize the minimum gain that can be earned.

Repeated Games

Clearly, games are not played once. Firms must decide on advertising budgets, investment strategies, and pricing policies continuously. Pepsi and Coca-Cola have competed against each other for 100 years, in countries across the globe. Although explicit collusion violates the antitrust statutes, strategic reaction does not. Yet strategic reaction in a repeated game may have the same effect as tacit collusion.

Consider the game in Figure 14.6. Suppose British Airways and Lufthansa were competing for business on the New York to London route during the off-season. To lure travelers, they were offering low fares. The question is how much to lower fares. Both airlines were considering a deep reduction to a fare of $400 round-trip or a moderate one to $600. Suppose costs are such that each $600 ticket produces profit of $400 and each $400 ticket produces profit of $200.

Clearly, demand is sensitive to price. Assume that studies of demand elasticity have determined that if *both* airlines offer tickets for $600, they will attract 6,000 passengers per week (3,000 for each airline) and each airline will make a profit of $1.2 million per week ($400 dollar profit times 3,000 passengers). However, if both airlines offer deeply reduced fares of $400, they will attract 2,000 additional customers per week for a total of 8,000 (4,000 for each airline). Although they will have more passengers, each ticket brings in less profit and total profit falls to $800,000 per week ($200 profit times 4,000 passengers). In this example, we can make some inferences about demand elasticity. With a price cut from $600 to $400, revenues fall from $3.6 million (6,000 passengers times $600) to $3.2 million (8,000 passengers times $400). We know from Chapter 5 that if a price cut reduces revenue, we are operating on an *inelastic* portion of the demand curve.

What if the two airlines offer different prices? To keep things simple, we will ignore brand loyalty and assume that whichever airline offers the lowest fare gets all of the 8,000 passengers. If British Airways offers the $400 fare, it will sell 8,000 tickets per week and make $200 profit each, for a total of $1.6 million. Because Lufthansa holds out for $600, it sells no tickets and makes no profit. Similarly, if Lufthansa were to offer tickets for $400, it would make $1.6 million per week while British Airways would make zero.

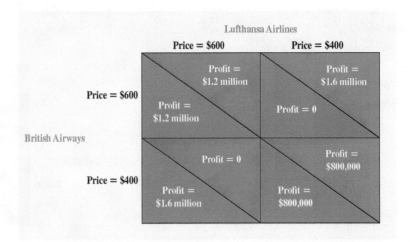

▲ FIGURE 14.6 **Payoff Matrix for Airline Game**
In a single play, both British Airways (BA) and Lufthansa Airlines (LA) have dominant strategies. If LA prices at $600, BA will price at $400 because $1.6 million beats $1.2 million. If, on the other hand, LA prices at $400, BA will again choose to price at $400 because $800,000 beats zero. Similarly, LA will choose to price at $400 regardless of which strategy BA chooses.

Looking carefully at the payoff matrix in Figure 14.6, do you conclude that either or both of the airlines have a dominant strategy? In fact, both do. If Lufthansa prices at $600, British Airways will price at the lower fare of $400 because $1.6 million per week is more than $1.2 million. On the other hand, if Lufthansa offers the deep price cut, British Airways must do so as well. If British Airways does not, it will earn nothing, and $800,000 beats nothing! Similarly, Lufthansa has a dominant strategy to offer the $400 fare because it makes more regardless of what British Airways does.

The result is that both airlines will offer the greatly reduced fare and each will make $800,000 per week. This is a classic prisoners' dilemma. If they were permitted to collude on price, they would both charge $600 per ticket and make $1.2 million per week instead—a 50 percent increase.

It was precisely this logic that led American Airlines President Robert Crandall to suggest to Howard Putnam of Braniff Airways in 1983, "I think this is dumb as hell . . . to sit here and pound the @#%* out of each other and neither one of us making a @#%* dime." . . . "I have a suggestion for you, raise your @#%* fares 20 percent. I'll raise mine the next morning."

Because competing firms are prohibited from even talking about prices, Crandall got into trouble with the Justice Department when Putnam turned over a tape of the call in which these comments were made. But could they have colluded without talking to each other? Suppose prices are announced each week at a given time. It is like playing the game in Figure 14.6 a number of times in succession, a repeated game. After a few weeks of making $800,000, British Airways raises its price to $600. Lufthansa knows that if it sits on its $400 fare, it will double its profit from $800,000 to $1.6 million per week. But what is British Airways up to? It must know that its profit will drop to zero unless Lufthansa raises its fare too. The fare increase could just be a signal that both firms would be better off at the higher price and that if one leads and can count on the other to follow, they will both be better off. The strategy to respond in kind to a competitor is called a **tit-for-tat strategy**.

If Lufthansa figures out that British Airways will play the same strategy that Lufthansa is playing, both will end up charging $600 per ticket and earning $1.2 million instead of charging $400 and earning only $800,000 per week even though there has been no explicit price-fixing.

tit-for-tat strategy A repeated game strategy in which a player responds in kind to an opponent's play.

A Game with Many Players: Collective Action Can Be Blocked by a Prisoner's Dilemma

Some games have many players and can result in the same kinds of prisoners' dilemmas as we have just discussed. The following game illustrates how coordinated collective action in everybody's interest can be blocked under some circumstances.

Suppose I am your professor in an economics class of 100 students. I ask you to bring $10 to class. In front of the room I place two boxes marked Box A and Box B. I tell you that you must put the sum of $10 split any way you would like in the two boxes. You can put all $10 in Box A and nothing in Box B. You can put all $10 in Box B and nothing in Box A. On the other hand, you can put $2.50 in Box A and $7.50 in Box B. Any combination totaling $10 is all right, and I am the only person who will ever know how you split up your money.

At the end of the class, every dollar put into Box A will be returned to the person who put it in. You get back exactly what you put in. But Box B is special. I will add 20 cents to Box B for every dollar put into it. That is, if there is $100 in the box, I will add $20. But here is the wrinkle: The money that ends up in Box B, *including* my 20 percent contribution, will be divided equally among everyone in the class regardless of the amount that an individual student puts in.

You can think of Box A as representing a private market where we get what we pay for. We pay $10, and we get $10 in value back. Think of Box B as representing something we want to do collectively where the benefits go to all members of the class regardless of whether they have contributed. In Chapter 12, we discussed the concept of a *public good*. People cannot be excluded from enjoying the benefits of a public good once it is produced. Examples include clean air, a lower crime rate from law enforcement, and national defense. You can think of Box B as representing a public good.

Now where do you put your money? If you were smart, you would call a class meeting and get everyone to agree to put his or her entire $10 in Box B. Then everybody would walk out with $12. There would be $1,000 in the box, I would add $200, and the total of $1,200 would be split evenly among the 100 students.

But suppose you were not allowed to get together, in the same way that Ginger and Rocky were kept in separate interview rooms in the jailhouse? Further suppose that everyone acts in his or her best interest. Everyone plays a strategy that maximizes the amount that he or she walks out with. If you think carefully, the dominant strategy for each class member is to put all $10 in Box A. *Regardless of what anyone else does*, you get more if you put all your money into Box A than you would get from any other split of the $10. And if you put all your money into A, no one will walk out of the room with more money than you will!

How can this be? It is simple. Suppose everyone else puts the $10 in B but you put your $10 in A. Box B ends up with $990 plus a 20 percent bonus from me of $198, for a grand total of $1,188, just $12 short of the maximum possible of $1,200. What do you get? Your share of Box B—which is $11.88, *plus* your $10 back, for a total of $21.88. Pretty slimy but clearly optimal for you. If you had put all your money into B, you would get back only $12. You can do the same analysis for cases in which the others split up their income in any way, and the optimal strategy is still to put the whole $10 in Box A.

Here is another way to think about it is: What part of what you ultimately get out is linked to or dependent upon what you put in? For every dollar you put in A, you get a dollar back. For every dollar *you yourself* put in B, you get back only 1 cent, one one-hundredth of a dollar, because your dollar gets split up among all 100 members of the class.

Thus, the game is a classic prisoners' dilemma, where collusion if it could be enforced would result in an optimal outcome but where dominant strategies result in a suboptimal outcome.

How do we break this particular dilemma? We call a town meeting (class meeting) and pass a law that requires us to contribute to the production of public goods by paying taxes. Then, of course, we run the risk that government becomes a player. We will return to this theme in Chapters 16 and 18.

To summarize, oligopoly is a market structure that is consistent with a variety of behaviors. The only necessary condition of oligopoly is that firms are large enough to have some control over price. Oligopolies are concentrated industries. At one extreme is the cartel, in which a few firms get together and jointly maximize profits—in essence, acting as a monopolist. At the other extreme, the firms within the oligopoly vigorously compete for small, contestable markets by moving capital quickly in response to observed profits. In between are a number of alternative models, all of which emphasize the interdependence of oligopolistic firms.

Oligopoly and Economic Performance

How well do oligopolies perform? Should they be regulated or changed? Are they efficient, or do they lead to an inefficient use of resources? On balance, are they good or bad?

With the exception of the contestable-markets model, all the models of oligopoly we have examined lead us to conclude that concentration in a market leads to pricing above marginal cost and output below the efficient level. When price is above marginal cost at equilibrium, consumers are paying more for the good than it costs to produce that good in terms of products forgone in other industries. To increase output would be to create value that exceeds the social cost of the good, but profit-maximizing oligopolists have an incentive not to increase output.

Entry barriers in many oligopolistic industries also prevent new capital and other resources from responding to profit signals. Under competitive conditions or in contestable markets, positive profits would attract new firms and thus increase production. This does not happen in most oligopolistic industries. The problem is most severe when entry barriers exist and firms explicitly or tacitly collude. The results of collusion are identical to the results of a monopoly. Firms jointly maximize profits by fixing prices at a high level and splitting up the profits.

On the other hand, it is useful to ask why oligopolies exist in an industry in the first place and what benefits larger firms might bring to a market. When there are economies of scale, larger and fewer firms bring cost efficiencies even as they reduce price competition.

Vigorous product competition among oligopolistic competitors may produce variety and lead to innovation in response to the wide variety of consumer tastes and preferences. The connection between market structure and the rate of innovation is the subject of some debate in research literature.

Industrial Concentration and Technological Change

One of the major sources of economic growth and progress throughout history has been technological advance. Innovation, both in methods of production and in the creation of new and better products, is one of the engines of economic progress. Much innovation starts with research and development (R&D) efforts undertaken by firms in search of profit.

Several economists, notably Joseph Schumpeter and John Kenneth Galbraith, argued in works now considered classics that industrial concentration, where a relatively small number of firms control the marketplace, actually increases the rate of technological advance. As Schumpeter put it in 1942:

> As soon as we...inquire into the individual items in which progress was most conspicuous, the trail leads not to the doors of those firms that work under conditions of comparatively free competition but precisely to the doors of the large concerns...and a shocking suspicion dawns upon us that big business may have had more to do with creating that standard of life than keeping it down.[1]

This interpretation caused the economics profession to pause and take stock of its theories. The conventional wisdom had been that concentration and barriers to entry insulate firms from competition and lead to sluggish performance and slow growth.

The evidence concerning where innovation comes from is mixed. Certainly, most small businesses do not engage in R&D and most large firms do. When R&D expenditures are considered as a percentage of sales, firms in industries with high concentration ratios spend more on R&D than do firms in industries with low concentration ratios.

Many oligopolistic companies do considerable research. In the opening segment of this chapter, we noted that Apple and Samsung dominate the smartphone market. Apple alone spent $3.4 billion on R&D in 2012. In this market, R&D plays an enormous role and favors larger firms.

---

[1] J. A. Schumpeter, *Capitalism, Socialism, and Democracy* (New York: Harper, 1942); and J. K. Galbraith, *American Capitalism* (Boston: Houghton Mifflin, 1952).

However, the "high-tech revolution" grew out of many tiny start-up operations. Companies such as Apple, Cisco Systems, and even Microsoft barely existed only a generation ago. The new biotechnology firms that use genetic engineering are often small operations that started with research done by individual scientists in university laboratories.

The Role of Government

14.5 LEARNING OBJECTIVE
Discuss the role of government in oligopolistic industries.

As we suggested previously, one way that oligopolies increase market concentration is through mergers. Not surprisingly, the government has passed laws to control the growth of market power through mergers.

Regulation of Mergers

The Clayton Act of 1914 (as mentioned in Chapter 13) had given government the authority to limit mergers that might "substantially lessen competition in an industry." The **Celler-Kefauver Act** (1950) enabled the Justice Department to monitor and enforce these provisions. In the early years of the Clayton Act, firms that wanted to merge knew there was a risk of government opposition. Firms could spend large amounts of money on lawyers and negotiation for a potential merger, only to have the government take the firms to court.

Celler-Kefauver Act Extended the government's authority to control mergers.

In 1968, the Justice Department issued its first guidelines designed to reduce uncertainty about the mergers it would find acceptable. The 1968 guidelines were strict. For example, if the largest four firms in an industry controlled 75 percent or more of a market, an acquiring firm with a 15 percent market share would be challenged if it wanted to acquire a firm that controlled as little as an additional 1 percent of the market.

In 1982, the Antitrust Division—in keeping with President Ronald Reagan's hands-off policy toward big business—issued a new set of guidelines. Revised in 1984, they remain in place today. The standards are based on a measure of market structure called the **Herfindahl-Hirschman Index (HHI)**. The HHI is calculated by expressing the market share of each firm in the industry as a percentage, squaring these figures, and summing. For example, in an industry in which two firms each control 50 percent of the market, the index is

Herfindahl-Hirschman Index (HHI) An index of market concentration found by summing the square of percentage shares of firms in the market.

$$50^2 + 50^2 = 2,500 + 2,500 = 5,000$$

For an industry in which four firms each control 25 percent of the market, the index is

$$25^2 + 25^2 + 25^2 + 25^2 = 625 + 625 + 625 + 625 = 2,500$$

Table 14.2 shows HHI calculations for several hypothetical industries. The Justice Department's courses of action, summarized in Figure 14.7, are as follows: If the HHI is less than 1,000, the industry is considered unconcentrated and any proposed merger will go unchallenged

TABLE 14.2   Calculation of a Simple Herfindahl-Hirschman Index for Four Hypothetical Industries, Each with No More Than Four Firms

	Percentage Share of:				
	Firm 1	Firm 2	Firm 3	Firm 4	Herfindahl-Hirschman Index
Industry A	50	50	–	–	$50^2 + 50^2 = 5,000$
Industry B	80	10	10	–	$80^2 + 10^2 + 10^2 = 6,600$
Industry C	25	25	25	25	$25^2 + 25^2 + 25^2 + 25^2 = 2,500$
Industry D	40	20	20	20	$40^2 + 20^2 + 20^2 + 20^2 = 2,800$

▶ **FIGURE 14.7**
Department of Justice Merger Guidelines (revised 1984)

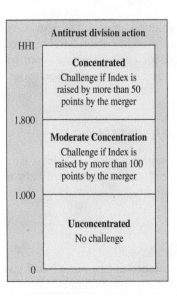

by the Justice Department. If the index is between 1,000 and 1,800, the department will challenge any merger that would increase the index by more than 100 points. Herfindahl indexes above 1,800 mean that the industry is considered concentrated already, and the Justice Department will challenge any merger that pushes the index up more than 50 points.

You should be able to see that the HHI combines two features of an industry that we identified as important in our Five Forces discussion: the number of firms in an industry and their relative sizes. Because the market shares are squared, the presence of one large firm will push the index up a bit. Compare industries C and D in Table 14.2 to see this.

In the previous arithmetic example, we looked at the share of the market controlled by each of several firms. Before we can make these calculations, however, we have to answer another question: How do we define the market? What are we taking a share of? Think back to our discussion of market power in Chapter 13. Coca-Cola has a "monopoly" in the production of Coke but is one of several firms making cola products, one of many more firms making soda in general, and one of hundreds of firms making beverages. Coca-Cola's market power depends on how much substitutability there is among cola products, among sodas in general, and among beverages in general. Before the government can calculate an HHI, it must *define the market*, a task that involves figuring out which products are good substitutes for the products in question.

An interesting example of the difficulty in defining markets and the use of the HHI in merger analysis comes from the 1997 opposition by the FTC to the proposed merger between Staples and Office Depot. At that time, Office Depot and Staples were the number one and number two firms, respectively, in terms of market share in dedicated sales of office supplies. The FTC argued that in sales of office supplies, office superstores such as Office Depot and Staples had a strong advantage in the mind of the consumer. As a result of the one-stop shopping that they offered, it was argued that other stores selling stationery were not good substitutes for the sales of these two stores. So the FTC defined the market over which it intended to calculate the HHI to decide on the merger as the sale of office supplies in office superstores. Practically, this meant that stationery sold in the corner shop or in Walmart was not part of the market, not a substantial constraint on the pricing of Office Depot or Staples. Using this definition, depending on where in the United States one looked, the HHI resulting from the proposed merger was between 5,000 and 10,000, clearly above the threshold. Economists working for Staples, on the other hand, argued that the market should include all sellers of office supplies. By that definition, a merger between Office Depot and Staples would result in a HHI well below the threshold because these two firms together controlled only 5 percent of the total market and the HHI in the overall market was well below 1,000. In the end, the merger was not allowed. You might be interested to learn that in 2015, the two firms again petitioned the government to allow them to merge,

ECONOMICS IN PRACTICE

Block that Movie Advertisement!

Many of you have no doubt been annoyed by the plethora of advertisements as you begin to eat your popcorn in most movie houses. What you may not know is that the bulk of these advertisements—almost 90 percent of them—are produced and sold to those movie theatres by only two firms, National CineMedia, Inc and the much smaller Screenvision.

In 2014, National made an offer to buy Screenvision, and the U.S. Department of Justice brought suit to block the merger. Bill Baer, the Assistant Attorney General of the United States described the merger as a "bad idea" for movie theatres, advertisers, and consumers alike. The Department of Justice argued that National CineMedia was trying to stop the aggressive price competition to serve theatres that it had faced in recent years from Screenvision by buying this competitor. National CineMedia, on the other hand, argued that there would be economic benefits in the merger, as the two merged firms could better serve the movie theatres by offering a broader product variety. One of the authors wonders how much moviegoers actually appreciate broader variety in these advertisements!

THINKING PRACTICALLY

1. Why do you think there are so few firms in this business in the first place?

perhaps feeling that the competition from firms like Amazon had changed the competitive landscape and might result in a new decision.

In Table 14.3, we present HHIs for a few different markets. Notice in one case—Las Vegas gaming—that the market has both a product and a geographic component. This definition, which was used by the government in one merger case, assumes that casinos in Las Vegas do not effectively compete with casinos in Atlantic City, for example. Other markets (for example, beer and semiconductors) are national or international in scope. In general, the broader the definition of the market, the lower the HHI.

In 1997, the Department of Justice and the FTC issued joint *Horizontal Merger Guidelines*, updating and expanding the 1984 guidelines. The most interesting part of the new provisions is that the government examines each potential merger to determine whether it enhances the firms' power to engage in "coordinated interaction" with other firms in the industry. The guidelines define "coordinated interaction" as

actions by a group of firms that are profitable for each of them only as the result of the accommodating reactions of others. This behavior includes tacit or express collusion, and may or may not be lawful in and of itself.[2]

TABLE 14.3	
Industry Definition	Some Sample HHIs
Beer	3,525
Ethanol	326
Las Vegas gaming	1,497
Critical care patient monitors	2,661

[2] U.S. Department of Justice, Federal Trade Commission, *Horizontal Merger Guidelines*, 2005.

A Proper Role for Government?

Certainly, there is much to guard against in the behavior of large, concentrated industries. For several reasons, however, economists no longer attack industry concentration with the same fervor they once did. First, even firms in highly concentrated industries can be pushed to produce efficiently under certain market circumstances. Second, the benefits of product differentiation and product competition are real. After all, a constant stream of new products and new variations of old products comes to the market almost daily. Third, the effects of concentration on the rate of R&D spending are, at worst, mixed. It is true that large firms do a substantial amount of the total research in the United States. Finally, in some industries, substantial economies of scale simply preclude a completely competitive structure. On the other side, of course, we have the higher prices that increased concentration often brings.

In addition to the debate over the desirability of industrial concentration, there is a debate concerning the role of government in regulating markets. One view is that high levels of concentration lead to inefficiency and that government should act to improve the allocation of resources—to help the market work more efficiently. This logic has been used to justify the laws and other regulations aimed at moderating noncompetitive behavior.

An opposing view holds that the clearest examples of effective barriers to entry are those created by government. This view holds that government regulation in past years has been ultimately anticompetitive and has made the allocation of resources less efficient than it would have been with no government involvement. Recall from Chapter 13 that those who earn positive profits have an incentive to spend resources to protect themselves and their profits from competitors. This rent-seeking behavior may include using the power of government.

Complicating the debate further is international competition. Increasingly, firms are faced with competition from foreign firms in domestic markets at the same time they are competing with other multinational firms for a share of foreign markets. We live in a truly global economy today. Thus, firms that dominate a domestic market may be fierce competitors in the international arena.

SUMMARY

14.1 MARKET STRUCTURE IN AN OLIGOPOLY *p. 289*

1. An *oligopoly* is an industry dominated by a few firms that, by virtue of their individual sizes, are large enough to influence market price. The behavior of a single oligopolistic firm depends on the reactions it expects of all the other firms in the industry. Industrial strategies usually are complicated and difficult to generalize about.

2. The Five Forces model is a helpful way to organize economic knowledge about the structure of oligopolistic industries. By gathering data on an industry's structure in terms of the existing rivals, new entrants, substitutes, and buyer and supplier characteristics, we can better understand the sources of excess profits in an industry.

14.2 OLIGOPOLY MODELS *p. 291*

3. When firms collude, either explicitly or tacitly, they jointly maximize profits by charging an agreed-to price or by setting output limits and splitting profits. The result is the same as it would be if one firm monopolized the industry:

The firm will produce up to the point at which $MR = MC$, and price will be set above marginal cost.

4. The *price-leadership* model of oligopoly leads to a result similar but not identical to the collusion model. In this organization, the dominant firm in the industry sets a price and allows competing firms to supply all they want at that price. An oligopoly with a dominant price leader will produce a level of output between what would prevail under competition and what a monopolist would choose in the same industry. An oligopoly will also set a price between the monopoly price and the competitive price.

5. The *Cournot model* of oligopoly is based on three assumptions: (1) that there are few firms in an industry, (2) that each firm takes the output of the other as a given, and (3) that firms maximize profits. The model holds that a series of output-adjustment decisions leads to a final level of output between that which would prevail under perfect competition and that which would be set by a monopoly.

14.3 GAME THEORY *p. 296*

6. *Game theory* analyzes the behavior of firms as if their behavior were a series of strategic moves and countermoves. It helps us understand the problem of oligopoly, focusing us on the complex interactions among firms.

14.4 OLIGOPOLY AND ECONOMIC PERFORMANCE *p. 302*

7. Concentration in markets often leads to price above marginal cost and output below the efficient level. Market concentration, however, can also lead to gains from economies of scale and may promote innovation.

14.5 THE ROLE OF GOVERNMENT *p. 303*

8. The *Clayton Act* of 1914 (see Chapter 13) gave the government the authority to limit mergers that might "substantially lessen competition in an industry." The *Celler-Kefauver Act* (1950) enabled the Justice Department to move against a proposed merger. Currently, the Justice Department uses the *Herfindahl-Hirschman Index* to determine whether it will challenge a proposed merger.

9. Some argue that the regulation of mergers is no longer a proper role for government.

REVIEW TERMS AND CONCEPTS

PROBLEMS

All problems are available on MyEconLab.

14.1 MARKET STRUCTURE IN AN OLIGOPOLY

LEARNING OBJECTIVE: Describe the structure and characteristics of oligopolistic industries.

1.1 Which of the following industries would you classify as an oligopoly? Explain your answer. If you are not sure, what information do you need to know to decide?
   a. Motorcycles
   b. Hotels
   c. Cruise lines
   d. Firearms
   e. Furniture

1.2 [**Related to the *Economics in Practice* on p. 290**] In recent years, the Federal Trade Commission (FTC) has been concerned with patent litigation settlements between brand-name and generic manufacturers in the pharmaceutical industry. A primary focus of the FTC in these cases involves agreements between brand-name and generic manufacturers to keep generics off the market in return for often sizeable payments. Use the Five Forces model to explain why brand-name pharmaceutical manufacturers would want to enter into such agreements, and explain why these patent litigation settlements have drawn the attention of the FTC.

1.3 Which of the following markets are likely to be perfectly contestable? Explain your answers.
   a. Coal mining
   b. Insurance
   c. Wind Farms
   d. Landscaping
   e. Advertising

14.2 OLIGOPOLY MODELS

LEARNING OBJECTIVE: Compare and contrast three oligopoly models.

2.1 Assume that you are in the business of providing medical insurance. You have analyzed the market carefully, and you know that at a price of $6,000 per year, you will sell 40,000 insurance policies per year. In addition, you know that at any price above $6,000, no one will buy your insurance policies because the government provides equal-quality policies to anyone who wants one at $6,000. You also know that for every $1,000 you lower your price, you will be able to sell an additional 10,000 policies. For example, at a price of $5,000, you can sell 50,000 policies; at a price of $4,000, you can sell 60,000 policies; and so on.

a. Sketch the demand curve that your firm faces.
b. Sketch the effective marginal revenue curve that your firm faces.
c. If the marginal cost of providing a health insurance policy is $5,000, how many will you sell and what price will you charge? What if $MC = \$4,500$?

2.2 [**Related to the *Economics in Practice* on p. 293**]
Between 2008 and 2014, dozens of lawsuits were brought or reinstated against U.S. firms for conspiracy to fix prices of things as diverse as pharmaceuticals, baby products, digital music, and eggs. Choose one of these lawsuits or cases and describe the economic and legal issues. What are the details of the case? What law was allegedly violated? How was the case settled? Was justice done? Explain your answer.

2.3 Explain whether you agree or disagree with the following statement. If all firms in an industry successfully engage in collusion, the resulting profit-maximizing price and output would be the same as if the industry was a monopoly.

2.4 What is the *Cournot* model? How does the output decision in the *Cournot* model differ from the output decision in a monopoly?

2.5 [**Related to the *Economics in Practice* on p. 296**]
T-Mobile is the fourth-largest wireless communication provider in the United States, behind Verizon, AT&T, and Sprint. In an effort to differentiate themselves from their three larger competitors, T-Mobile was the first major company in the industry to allow customers to bring in unlocked phones to switch to their service, pay early termination fees for new customers that were switching service to T-Mobile, and promote the idea of customers not being tied down to a specific wireless provider. Do some research to find what has happened to the market share of each of these companies over the past several years, and describe how the other major wireless communication providers have reacted to these policies from T-Mobile.

14.3 GAME THEORY

LEARNING OBJECTIVE: Explain the principles and strategies of game theory.

3.1 The matrix in Figure 1 at page bottom shows payoffs based on the strategies chosen by two firms. If they collude and hold prices at $10, each firm will earn profits of $5 million. If A cheats on the agreement, lowering its price, but B does not, A will get 75 percent of the business and earn profits of $8 million and B will lose $2 million. Similarly, if B cheats and A does not, B will earn $8 million and A will lose $2 million. If both firms cut prices, they will end up with $2 million each in profits.

Which strategy minimizes the maximum potential loss for A and for B? If you were A, which strategy would you choose? Why? If A cheats, what will B do? If B cheats, will A do? What is the most likely outcome of such a game? Explain.

3.2 The payoff matrixes in Figure 2 at page bottom show the payoffs for two games. The payoffs are given in parentheses. The values on the left refers to the payoff to A; the values on the right refers to the payoff to B. Hence, (2, 25) means a $2 payoff to A and a $25 payoff to B.
a. Is there a dominant strategy in each game for each player?
b. If game 1 were repeated a large number of times and you were A and you could change your strategy, what might you do?
c. Which strategy would you play in game 2? Why?

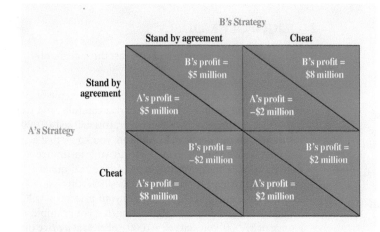

▲ FIGURE 1

Game 1: Pricing

		Firm B	
		Price high	Price low
Firm A	**Price high**	(15, 15)	(2, 25)
	Price low	(25, 2)	(5, 5)

Game 2: Chicken

		Bob (B)	
		Swerve	Do not swerve
Ann (A)	**Swerve**	(5, 5)	(3, 10)
	Do not swerve	(10, 3)	(−10, −10)

▲ FIGURE 2

3.3 Suppose we have an industry with two firms producing the same product. Acme Corporation produces 19,000 units, while Zoltar Corporation produces 1,000 units. The price in the market is $20, and both firms have marginal costs of production of $5. What incentives do the two firms have to lower prices as a way of trying to get consumers to switch to the firm from which they are not currently purchasing? Which firm is more likely to lower its price?

3.4 Bernie and Leona were arrested for money laundering and were interrogated separately by the police. Bernie and Leona were each presented with the following independent offers. If one confesses and the other doesn't, the one who confesses will go free and the other will receive a 20-year prison sentence; if both confess, each will receive a 10-year prison sentence.

Bernie and Leona both know that without any confessions, the police only have enough evidence to convict them of the lesser crime of tax evasion, and each would then receive a 2-year prison sentence.
a. Use the information to construct a payoff matrix for Bernie and Leona.
b. What is the dominant strategy for Bernie and for Leona? Why?
c. Based on your response to the previous question, what prison sentence will each receive?

14.4 OLIGOPOLY AND ECONOMIC PERFORMANCE

LEARNING OBJECTIVE: Discuss the economic performance of oligopolies.

4.1 Explain whether you agree or disagree with the following statements:
a. In all oligopoly models except the contestable-market model, market concentration leads to output below the efficient level, and increasing output would create value that exceeds the social cost of the good. Therefore, profit-maximizing oligopolists have an incentive to increase output.
b. In most oligopolistic industries, positive profits attract new firms and thus increase output.

14.5 THE ROLE OF GOVERNMENT

LEARNING OBJECTIVE: Discuss the role of government in oligopolistic industries.

5.1 The following table represents the market share percentage for each firm in a hypothetical industry.

Firm	A	B	C	D	E	F	G	H
Market Share	15	6	12	7	20	10	19	11

a. Calculate the four-firm concentration ratio for this industry.
b. Calculate the Herfindahl-Hirschman Index (HHI) for this industry.
c. Would the Justice Department consider this industry as unconcentrated, moderately concentrated, or concentrated? Why?
d. Suppose firms B, D, and F wanted to merge. What would be the value of the HHI following this merger? Would the Justice Department most likely challenge this merger? Why or why not?

15 Monopolistic Competition

We come now to our last broad type of market structure: *monopolistic competition*. Like perfect competition, a monopolistically competitive industry is an industry in which entry is easy and many firms are the norm. In contrast to the perfectly competitive firm, however, firms in this industry type do not produce homogeneous goods. Rather, each firm produces a slightly different version of a product. These product differences give rise to some market power. In the monopolistically competitive industry, a firm can charge a higher price than a competitor and not lose all of its customers. We will spend some time in this chapter looking at pricing in these industries.

But pricing is only one part of the story in these industries. When we look at firms in an industry characterized by monopolistic competition, we naturally focus on how firms make decisions about what kinds of products to sell and how to market and advertise them. Why do we see a dozen different types of shampoo in a store? Is a dozen too many, too few, or just the right number? Why are beverages and automobiles advertised a great deal but semiconductors and economics textbooks are not? Advertising is expensive: Is it a waste of money, or does it serve some social function? In this chapter, we will also explore briefly some ideas from *behavioral economics*. Can consumers ever be offered too many choices? Why does nutritional cereal sell better in the extra large size while candy sells better by the bar?

By the end of this chapter, we will have covered the four basic types of market structure. Figure 15.1 summarizes the four types: perfect competition, monopoly, oligopoly, and monopolistic competition. The behavior of firms in an industry, the key decisions facing firms, and the key policy issues government faces in dealing with those firms differ depending on the market structure we are in. Although not every industry fits neatly into one of these categories, they do provide a useful and convenient framework for thinking about industry structure and behavior.

	Number of firms	Products differentiated or homogeneous	Price a decision variable	Easy entry	Distinguished by	Examples
Perfect competition	Many	Homogeneous	No	Yes	Market sets price	Wheat farmer Textile firm
Monopoly	One	One version or many versions of a product	Yes	No	Still constrained by market demand	Public utility Patented drug
Monopolistic competition	Many	Differentiated	Yes, but limited	Yes	Price and quality competition	Restaurants Hand soap
Oligopoly	Few	Either	Yes	Limited	Strategic behavior	Automobiles Aluminum

▲ FIGURE 15.1 **Characteristics of Different Market Organizations**

Industry Characteristics

A **monopolistically competitive industry** has the following characteristics:

1. A large number of firms
2. No barriers to entry
3. Product differentiation

Although pure monopoly and perfect competition are rare, monopolistic competition is common in the United States, for example, in the restaurant business. In a Yahoo search of San Francisco restaurants, there are many thousands listed in the area. Each produces a slightly different product and attempts to distinguish itself in consumers' minds. Entry to the market is not blocked. At one location near Union Square in San Francisco, five different restaurants opened and went out of business in 5 years. Although many restaurants fail, small ones can compete and survive because there are few economies of scale in the restaurant business.

The feature that distinguishes monopolistic competition from monopoly and oligopoly is that firms that are monopolistic competitors cannot influence market price by virtue of their size. No one restaurant is big enough to affect the market price of a prime rib dinner even though all restaurants can control their *own* prices. Instead, firms gain control over price in monopolistic competition by *differentiating* their products. You make it in the restaurant business by producing a product that people want that others are not producing or by establishing a reputation for good food and good service. By producing a unique product or establishing a particular reputation, a firm becomes, in a sense, a "monopolist"—that is, no one else can produce the exact same good.

The feature that distinguishes monopolistic competition from pure monopoly is that good substitutes are available in a monopolistically competitive industry. With thousands of restaurants in the San Francisco area, there are dozens of good Italian, Chinese, and French restaurants. San Francisco's Chinatown, for example, has about 50 small Chinese restaurants, with more than a dozen packed on a single street. The menus are nearly identical, and they all charge virtually the same prices. At the other end of the spectrum are restaurants, with established names and prices far above the cost of production, that are always booked. That is the goal of every restaurateur who ever put a stockpot on the stove. They succeed by doing something different in either real or imaginary terms!

Table 15.1 presents some data on nine national manufacturing industries that have the characteristics of monopolistic competition. Each of these industries includes hundreds of individual firms, some larger than others, but all small relative to the industry. The top four firms in book printing, for example, account for 42 percent of total shipments. The top 20 firms account for 66 percent of the market, while the market's remaining 34 percent is split among 538 separate firms.

Firms in a monopolistically competitive industry are small relative to the total market. New firms can enter the industry in pursuit of profit, and relatively good substitutes for the firms' products are available. Firms in monopolistically competitive industries try to achieve a degree

15.1 LEARNING OBJECTIVE

Identify the characteristics of a monopolistically competitive industry.

monopolistic competition
A common form of industry (market) structure characterized by a large number of firms, no barriers to entry, and product differentiation.

TABLE 15.1	Percentage of Value of Shipments Accounted for by the Largest Firms in Selected Industries, 2007			
Industry Designation	Four Largest Firms	Eight Largest Firms	Twenty Largest Firms	Number of Firms
Travel trailers and campers	40	50	63	756
Games, toys	34	48	62	721
Wood office furniture	40	52	65	438
Book printing	42	54	66	558
Fresh or frozen seafood	28	41	60	481

Source: U.S. Department of Commerce, Bureau of the Census, 2007 Census of Manufacturers, *Concentration Ratios in Manufacturing.* SubjectECO731SR12, May 2009.

of market power by differentiating their products—by producing something new, different, or better or by creating a unique identity in the minds of consumers. To discuss the behavior of such firms, we begin with product differentiation and advertising.

15.2 LEARNING OBJECTIVE

Discuss the methods and implications of product differentiation and advertising in monopolistically competitive industries.

product differentiation
A strategy that firms use to achieve market power. Accomplished by producing goods that differ from others in the market.

Product Differentiation and Advertising

Monopolistically competitive firms achieve whatever degree of market power they command through **product differentiation**, by producing goods that differ from others in the market. But what determines how much differentiation we see in a market and what form it takes?

How Many Varieties?

As you look around your neighborhood, notice the sidewalks that connect individual homes with the common outside walk. In some areas, you will see an occasional brick or cobblestone walk, but in most places in the United States, these sidewalks are made of concrete. In almost every case, that concrete is gray. Now look at the houses that these sidewalks lead up to. Except in developments with tight controls, house colors vary across the palette. Why do we have one variety of concrete sidewalk while we have multiple varieties of house colors?

Whenever we see limited varieties of a product, a first thought might be that all consumers—here homeowners—have similar preferences. Perhaps everyone has a natural affection for gray, at least in concrete. The wide variety in the colors of the houses that these sidewalks lead up to might make you skeptical of this explanation, but it is possible. Another possible explanation for the common gray sidewalks might be a desire for coordination: Maybe everyone wants his or her sidewalk to look like the neighbor's, and the fact that the sidewalk connecting the houses—often provided by the city—is gray serves to make gray a focal point. In fashion, for example, coordination and conformity play an enormous role. There is no inherent reason that oversized jeans should be more or less attractive than narrow-cut, low-rise jeans except that they are made so at certain times by the fact that many people are wearing them. Again, you might wonder why conformity is important in sidewalk color but not in house color, something even more visible to the neighbors.

In explaining the narrow variety of concrete sidewalks, a better explanation may come from a review of the material we covered in Chapter 8 when we looked at cost structures. As you know, concrete is made in large mixer trucks. The average capacity of these trucks is 9 or more cubic yards, well more than you would need for a sidewalk. An obvious way to color this concrete is to mix a coloring agent in the mixer truck along with the cement and other ingredients. When done this way, however, we need to find several neighbors who want the same color cement that we want at the same time—concrete is not storable. Even doing it this way is potentially problematic because the inside of the mixer unit can be affected, leaving a residue of our purple concrete, for example, for the next customer. Alternatively, we could add dye after the concrete comes out of the truck, which is done in some places, but the resulting colors are limited, and the process is expensive. So the lack of variety in concrete and not in houses may reflect the scale economies in homogeneous production of concrete not found in house painting.

The example of the sidewalks versus the houses helps explain the wide variety in some product areas and the narrowness in others. In some cases, consumers may have *different tastes.* It should be no surprise that immigration brings with it an increase in the variety of restaurant types in an area and in the food offerings at the local grocery store. Immigration typically increases the heterogeneity of consumer tastes. Product variety is narrower when there are gains to coordination. In Chapter 13, we described products in which there are network externalities. Here *coordination needs* can dramatically narrow product choice. For example, it will be more important to most people to use the same word-processing program their friends use than to use one that suits them perfectly. Finally, scale economies that make producing different varieties more expensive than a single type can reduce variety. Some people prefer a relatively inexpensive standardized good over a more expensive custom product that perfectly suits them. The development of the Levitt house in the postwar period in Pennsylvania and New York was a testament to the cost savings in housing that came from standardization, creating uniform tract houses for affordable prices.

In sum, in well-working markets, the level of product variety reflects the underlying heterogeneity of consumers' tastes in that market, the gains if any from coordination, and cost economies from standardization. In industries that are monopolistically competitive, differences in consumer tastes, lack of need for coordination, and modest or no scale economies from standardization give rise to a large number of firms, each of which has a different product. Even within this industry structure, however, these same forces play a role in driving levels of variety.

In recent years, quite a few people have taken up the sport of running. The market has responded in a big way. Now there are numerous running magazines; hundreds of orthotic shoes designed specifically for runners with particular running styles; running suits of every color, cloth, and style; weights for the hands, ankles, and shoelaces; tiny radios to slip into sweatbands; and so on. Even physicians have differentiated their products: Sports medicine clinics have diets for runners, therapies for runners, and doctors specializing in shin splints or Morton's toe.

Why has this increase in variety in the running market taken place? More runners—each with a different body, running style, and sense of aesthetics—increase consumer heterogeneity. The increased market size also tells us that if you produce a specialized running product, it is more likely you will sell enough to cover whatever fixed costs you had in developing the product. So market size allows for more variety. New York has a wider range of ethnic restaurants than does Eden Prairie, Minnesota, not only because of the difference in the heterogeneity of the populations but also because of the relative size of the two markets.

How Do Firms Differentiate Products?

We have learned that differentiation occurs in response to demands by consumers for products that meet their individual needs and tastes, constrained by the forces of costs of coordination and scale economies. We can go one step further and characterize the kinds of differentiation we see in markets.

Return to the restaurant example we brought up earlier. Of the thousands of restaurants in San Francisco, some are French, some are Chinese, and some are Italian. Economists would call this form of differentiation across the restaurants **horizontal differentiation**. Horizontal differentiation is a product difference that improves the product for some people but makes it worse for others. If we were to poll San Francisco residents, asking for the best restaurant in town, we would undoubtedly get candidates from a number of different categories. Indeed, many people might not even consider this to be a legitimate question.

horizontal differentiation
Products differ in ways that make them better for some people and worse for others.

If you add sea salt and vinegar to potato chips, that makes them more attractive to some people and less attractive to others. Horizontal differentiation creates variety to reflect differences in consumers' tastes in the market.

For some products, people choose a type and continue with it for a long time. For many of us, breakfast cereals have this feature. Day after day we eat Cheerios or corn flakes. Brand preference for mayonnaise has the same stability. For dinner, however, most of us are *variety-seeking.*

ECONOMICS IN PRACTICE

Measuring the Benefits from Variety: How Many Different Pairs of Sandals Do You Need?

For those people who love shoes, one of the great benefits of online retailers like Zappos is the wide variety of shoes just a click away. Although the average brick-and-mortar store, even a large one, might carry a few thousand varieties of shoes, large online retailers might well stock 50,000 varieties. Indeed, one of the authors in a recent search of Zappos found 192 varieties of brown women's sandals! An economist might naturally want to know how valuable is all this variety from a consumer welfare point of view?

This is precisely the question asked in a recent paper by two economists from Minnesota and Yale.[1] Answering this question requires some careful statistical work, but the intuition behind the results is quite straightforward. Suppose the average brick and mortar store carries 1,000 pairs of shoes, whereas the online store carries 50,000 pairs. With 50 times the shoes, does the online store deliver 50 times the value? A moment's reflection will tell you this can't be true. Presumably, a smart brick-and-mortar retailer does not choose 1,000 random shoes to carry, but rather carries those shoes most likely to appeal to local customers. If customers vary a lot across areas of the country or between cities and rural areas, it could be that each brick-and-mortar store carries exactly the 1,000 pairs of shoes that anyone in their shopping area would ever want to buy. In that case, the online retailer stocks 50,000 shoes because it is dealing with many different submarkets; its advantages for consumers would be that clicking might be easier than driving, but there would be no gains from variety. If consumers across the country are all the same, however, at least some people in each of the different markets would gain from access to more unusual shoes carried by the online store.

Quan and Williams actually find quite a lot of variety in tastes across the country. If we look at online sales, the top

1,000 products in the shoe market account for 56.5 percent of the sales in that state; across the country the top 1,000 shoes account for only 11.3 percent of the sales. Failing to take account of the fact that tastes tend to differ across areas and that retailers stock their shelves in response to those differences would cause an economist to overstate the benefits to this added variety quite substantially.

THINKING PRACTICALLY

1. How would you expect a profit-maximizing retailer to choose which shoes to stock in his or her store?

[1] Thomas Quan and Kevin Williams, "Product Variety, Across Market Demand Heterogeneity, and the Value of Online Retail," Working paper, December 2014.

Even small cities can support some variety in restaurant types because people get tired of eating at the same place every week.

People who visit planned economies often comment on the lack of variety. Before the Berlin Wall came down in 1989 and East and West Germany were reunited in 1990, those who were allowed passed from colorful and exciting West Berlin into dull and gray East Berlin; variety seemed to vanish. As the wall came down, thousands of Germans from the East descended on the department stores of the West. Visitors to China since the economic reforms of the mid-1980s claim that the biggest visible sign of change is the increase in the selection of products available to the population.

Products can be distinguishable not only in terms of horizontal differentiation but also in terms of **vertical differentiation**. A new BMW with GPS is better than one without for almost everyone. A hard drive with more capacity is better than one with less. The Hilton is better than a Motel 6 if they are located in the same place. How can a product survive in a competitive marketplace when another better product is available? The answer, of course, is in the price. The better products cost more, and only some people find it worthwhile to pay the higher price to get a better product. So differences among people also give rise to vertical

vertical differentiation
A product difference that, from everyone's perspective, makes a product better than rival products.

differentiation. Some people value quality in a specific product more than others do and are willing to pay for that quality. If you are on a special date, it might be worthwhile to go to the best restaurant in town. On the other hand, while at a casual dinner with friends, watching your budget might be more important.

Recent work in the area of *behavioral economics* suggests, however, that there may be times in which too much variety is a bad thing.[1] **Behavioral economics** is a branch of economics that uses the insight of psychology and economics to investigate decision making.

Researchers set up an experiment in an upscale grocery, Draeger's, located in Menlo Park, California. Draeger's is known for its large selection, carrying, for example, 250 varieties of mustard. A tasting booth was set up in the store on two consecutive Saturdays. On one day, consumers were offered one of six exotic jams to taste, while on the other day, 24 varieties were offered. The results of the experiment were striking. Although more customers approached the 24-jam booth for a taste than approached the booth with a limited selection, almost none of the tasters at the 24-jam booth bought anything; in contrast, almost 30 percent of tasters at the six-jam booth made a purchase.[2] The researchers conclude that while some choice is highly valued by people, too much choice can reduce purchases.

The jam experiment offers a case in which individuals react to a wide range of choices by not making a choice at all. Behavioral economists also note that when the number of choices is large, individuals may avoid the decision-making burden by using a rule of thumb or by reverting to the default option. In the area of retirement savings, for example, some studies have found a tendency for people to allocate savings evenly across a range of investment options without paying much attention to the earnings characteristics of those funds. In other cases, people appear to favor whatever option is the default designated by the government body or by the firm offering the plan. For this reason, some economists have argued that one way to increase consumer savings (if that is desirable) is to make participation rather than no participation the default in pension plans. In this way, individuals would be enrolled in a retirement plan unless they chose not to be. These plans are called *opt-out plans* rather than opt-in plans.

Behavioral economics also has something to say about another form of horizontal differentiation—package size and pricing form.[3] Many consumer goods come in small, large, and extra large packages. Many goods (for example, health club visits and magazines) can be bought per visit or issue or via membership or subscription. Many of us think of these differences as matters of convenience. Firms can use these differences to create products targeted at consumer types. Small households buy small boxes of cereals, and large families purchase extra large sizes. Occasional readers buy *Us Weekly* on the newsstand, and fans subscribe to the magazine. Clearly, these kinds of differences play a role. But behavioral economists have also suggested that some of these differences survive in the market because some consumers are interested in trying to control their purchasing behavior. People buy small containers of ice cream but large bottles of vitamins. Why? Because they want to *commit* themselves to taking a vitamin every day but only occasionally eating ice cream. People buy memberships to health clubs as an incentive to work out; they make the marginal cost of a visit zero even though in the end, they may pay more than they would have by paying a per-visit fee. We subscribe to *The Economist* but buy *Us Weekly* on the newsstand at high per-issue prices in the hopes that we will read more of *The Economist* and less of *Us Weekly*. Some students choose classes that reward attendance as a way of ensuring that they go to class. Firms can be creative about using product differentiation to offer consumers commitment devices that help them control their own impulses. A **commitment device** is an action taken by an individual now to try to control his or her behavior in the future.

Behavioral economics is an exciting new field that is challenging and deepening our understanding of a number of areas of economics. New ideas from behavioral economics have entered both microeconomics and macroeconomics.

behavioral economics
A branch of economics that uses the insights of psychology and economics to investigate decision making.

commitment device Actions that individuals take in one period to try to control their behavior in a future period.

---

[1] The classic paper that describes the study reported here is Sheena S. Iyengar and Mark R. Lepper, "When Choice Is Demotivating: Can One Desire Too Much of a Good Thing?" *Journal of Personality and Social Psychology*, 2000, 995–1006.
[2] The subsample of six brands was carefully selected to be neither the best nor the worst of the flavors, and to actually buy, consumers had to go to a shelf that contained all the varieties of jam.
[3] Papers described in this paragraph include Klaus Wertenbroch, "Self-Rationing: Self-Control in Consumer Choice," INSEAD Working Paper, 2001, on the package size topic; Ulrike Malmendier and Stefano DellaVigna, "Paying Not to Go to the Gym," *AER*, June 2006, 694–719, on health club memberships; and Sharon Oster and Fiona Scott Morton, "Behavioral Biases Meet the Market," *BEPress Journal of Economic Advance and Policy*, 2005, on magazines.

ECONOMICS IN PRACTICE

An Economist Makes Tea

You have probably seen Honest Tea, a slightly sweetened bottled iced tea made from green, black, and herbal blends in your local grocery store. It is probably not the only iced tea on the shelf. In addition to the popular brands Lipton and Snapple, you may also see SoBe, Tazo, and Turkey Hill, depending on where you live. Bottled iced tea is a classic example of a monopolistically competitive market. None of the brands are exactly alike. Honest Tea, for example, prides itself on being made with high-end tea leaves and only a hint of sweetener, whereas Snapple uses lower-quality leaves and a hefty dose of sweetener. Nor are the teas priced the same. In a typical store, the retail price of Honest Tea and SoBe are likely to be about $1.89, while Snapple would likely cost about $1.39. If you spend time in the beverage aisle of a grocery store, you will notice that despite the higher price of Honest Tea, some consumers choose it over the alternatives.

What you may not know about Honest Tea is that it was started a decade ago by Seth Goldman, an entrepreneur, and Barry Nalebuff, an economist. In figuring out how to differentiate his tea from others in the industry, Nalebuff used some of the economic theory that we covered in Chapter 6 of this book. Look at the following graph, which shows the placement of one of Honest Tea's most popular flavors, Green Dragon. The graph shows how taste varies with sugar for Goldman and Nalebuff's potential customers. Tea taste improves for the first few grams of sugar, but shortly begins to flatten out and then fall. Note that Green Dragon is somewhat to the left of the taste peak. Some economists looking at this graph criticized Nalebuff for choosing too little sugar content for his tea. What were the critics thinking, and why were they wrong?

The critics clearly noticed that Green Dragon is not at the peak of the taste curve. That is, a little more sugar would

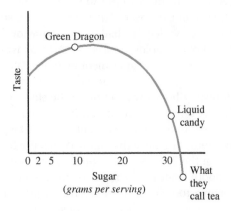

improve the taste of the tea. Why did Nalebuff stop short of that point? This is product differentiation at its best. Goldman and Nalebuff set out to produce a new product that will attract demand. That is, at a reasonable price they must attract consumers away from other products. Goldman and Nalebuff discovered that sugar beyond some point adds little taste, yet comes at a health cost—more calories. Given consumers' new awareness of healthy and natural foods, Honest Tea became an overnight success. Because Nalebuff is an economist, he couldn't resist a graph on the label of the tea bottles.

THINKING PRACTICALLY

1. What would you expect to see happen to the placement of Green Dragon Tea if we discovered sugar was good for us?

We have described the forces that help determine how much differentiation we will see in a market and the major forms that differentiation can take. We turn now to advertising, which plays a special role in the area of monopolistic competition.

Advertising

Advertising fits into the differentiation story in two different ways. One role advertising plays is to inform people about the real differences that exist among products. Advertising can also *create* or contribute to product differentiation, creating a brand image for a product that has little to do with its physical characteristics. We can all think of examples of each type.

Recent Coca-Cola ads trumpeting the "Coke Side of Life" have little to do with Coke's taste, for example. The dancers in iPod's ads create an image of hip and happy people rather than describe the technical features of the device. On the other hand, the advertising circulars in local newspapers carry specific information about what products are on sale that week in the local grocery store.

In 2014 the Kantar Media firm estimated that advertising in the United States totaled $180 billion. It may surprise you that television remains the strongest category of spending, followed by direct mail and newspapers. The fastest-growth area in media advertising, however, was mobile, tablets, and smartphones, which by 2014 was 10 percent of total media ad spending. In 2015, 30 seconds of commercial advertising time for the Super Bowl cost $4.5 million.

YouTube, part of Google, an important current player in the online advertising business, offers firms the opportunity to actively interact with customers. In addition to the standard video ads, firms can create online contests and brand channels to learn from customers about their preferences. Advertising as information has become more of a transparent two-way street as a result of the Internet.

The effects of product differentiation in general (and advertising in particular) on the allocation of resources have been hotly debated for years. Advocates claim that these forces give the market system its vitality and power. Critics argue that they cause waste and inefficiency. Before we proceed to the models of monopolistic competition output-setting, let us look at this debate.

The Case for Advertising   For product differentiation to be successful, consumers must know about product features and availability. In perfect competition, where all products are alike, we assume that consumers have perfect information; without it, the market fails to produce an efficient allocation of resources. Complete information is even more important when we allow for product differentiation. Consumers get this information through advertising, at least in part. The basic function of advertising, according to its proponents, is to assist consumers in making informed, rational choices. When we think of advertising, many of us think of the persuasive ads shown on television geared to changing our image of a product. Over the years, Budweiser has developed a reputation for clever ads of this sort, especially those delivered during the Super Bowl. But much advertising is entirely informational. In most parts of the country, one day a week the newspaper grows in size. On this day, stores advertise and promote their food sales. For many newspapers, advertisements are a big source of revenue; and it is all informational, helping consumers figure out where to buy their orange juice and chicken, for example. During the holiday season, toy advertising, both in print and on television, increases dramatically. For toys, which have a high rate of new product introduction, publicizing them is important.

Supporters of advertising also note that it can promote competition. New products can compete with old, established brands only when promoters can get their messages through to consumers. The standard of living rises when we have product *innovation*, when new and better products come on the market. Think of all the products today that did not exist 20 years ago. When consumers are informed about a wide variety of potential substitutes, their market choices help discipline older firms that may have lost touch with consumers' tastes.

Even advertising that seems to function mostly to create and reinforce a brand image can have efficiency effects. Creating a brand name such as Coca-Cola or Tide requires a huge investment in marketing and advertising. The stronger the brand name and the more a firm has invested in creating that name, the more the firm will invest in trying to protect that name. In many cases, those investments provide benefits for consumers. In reacting to the 2007 news about lead in children's toys made in China, large toy companies such as Hasbro and Mattel spent millions in new testing of those toys. Restoring parental trust in the face of the toy recalls is vital to the future of the firms.

Differentiated products and advertising give the market system its vitality and are the basis of its power. Product differentiation helps to ensure high quality and variety, and advertising provides consumers with valuable information on product availability, quality, and price that they need to make efficient choices in the marketplace.

The Case against Product Differentiation and Advertising   Product differentiation and advertising waste society's scarce resources, argue critics. They say enormous sums of money are spent to create minute, meaningless differences among products.

ECONOMICS IN PRACTICE

Green Advertising

In recent years many companies have spent resources, both in terms of advertising and in real actions, to increase their reputations for environmental stewardship. At least one of the motivations for spending resources in this way is that customers, investors, and employees value this activity, and in this way environmental investments could have a positive effect on profits. A recent paper by Barrage, Chyn, and Hastings[1] looks at the connection between market outcomes and green advertising in the oil industry.

In the years 2000 through 2008 BP Oil launched a large "green" advertising campaign, spending over those years more than $200 million. The initials BP, which once stood for British Petroleum, were recast as Beyond Petroleum, and sun symbol logos adorned the gas stations across the world. Consumer surveys taken near the end of this period found that BP was rated the most environmentally friendly of the major oil companies. The green advertising campaign received many marketing awards.

In April 2010, 206 million gallons of BP oil spilled into the Gulf of Mexico in the Deepwater Horizon oil spill. Barrage et al. found that consumers reacted strongly to the oil spill and that both sales and prices at BP gas stations fell relative to other companies, suggesting that at least some consumers hold companies accountable for environmental damage. But the paper further found that BP's previous investments in building an environmental reputation helped to cushion consumer reaction to the spill, causing sales to fall less and

recover sooner than they otherwise would have. This cushioning effect was larger in areas of the country where more consumers support environmental causes.

THINKING PRACTICALLY

1. Use supply-and-demand curves to show the effect of the oil spill as described in this example.

[1] Lint Barrage, Eric Chyn, and Justine Hastings, " Advertising, Reputation and Environmental Stewardship: Evidence from the BP Oil Spill," NBER Working Paper, January 2014.

Do we really need 50 different kinds of soap, some of whose prices are increased by the cost of advertising? For a firm producing a differentiated product, advertising is part of the everyday cost of doing business. Its price is built into the average cost curve and thus into the price of the product in the short run and the long run. Thus, consumers pay to finance advertising.

Advertising may also reduce competition by creating a barrier to the entry of new firms into an industry. One famous case study taught at many business schools calculates the cost of entering the brand-name breakfast cereal market. To be successful, a potential entrant would have to start with millions of dollars in an extensive advertising campaign to establish a brand name recognized by consumers. Entry to the breakfast cereal game is not completely blocked, but such financial requirements make entry difficult.

The bottom line, critics of product differentiation and advertising argue, is waste and inefficiency. Enormous sums are spent to create minute, meaningless, and possibly nonexistent differences among products. Advertising raises the cost of products and frequently contains little information. Often, it is merely an annoyance. Advertising can lead to unproductive warfare and may serve as a barrier to entry, thus reducing real competition.

Open Questions   You will see over and over as you study economics that many questions remain open. There are strong arguments on both sides of the advertising debate, and even the empirical evidence yields conflicting conclusions. Some studies show that advertising leads to concentration and positive profits; others, that advertising improves the functioning of the market.

Price and Output Determination in Monopolistic Competition

15.3 LEARNING OBJECTIVE

Discuss price and output determination for monopolistically competitive firms.

Recall that monopolistically competitive industries are made up of a large number of firms, each small relative to the size of the total market. Thus, no one firm can affect market price by virtue of its size alone. Firms do differentiate their products, however, in ways we have been discussing. By doing so, they gain some control over price.

Product Differentiation and Demand Elasticity

Perfectly competitive firms face a perfectly elastic demand for their product: All firms in a perfectly competitive industry produce exactly the same product. If firm A tried to raise prices, buyers would go elsewhere and firm A would sell nothing. When a firm can distinguish its product from all others in the minds of consumers, as we assume it can under monopolistic competition, it can raise its price without losing all quantity demanded. Figure 15.2 shows how product differentiation might make demand somewhat less elastic for a hypothetical firm.

A monopoly is an industry with a single firm that produces a good for which there are no close substitutes. A monopolistically competitive firm is like a monopoly in that it is the only producer of its unique product. Only one firm can produce Cheerios or Wheat Thins or Johnson's Baby Shampoo or Oreo cookies. However, unlike the product in a monopoly market, the product of a monopolistically competitive firm has many close substitutes competing for the consumer's spending. Although the demand curve that a monopolistic competitor faces is less elastic than the demand curve that a perfectly competitive firm faces, it is likely to be more elastic than the demand curve we would see if that same market were monopolized.

Price/Output Determination in the Short Run

A profit-maximizing, monopolistically competitive firm behaves much like a monopolist in the short run. First, marginal revenue is not equal to price because the monopolistically competitive firm is different enough from its rivals that small price increases over those rivals do not eliminate all customers. This firm sees its price respond to its output decisions. The monopolistic competitor's marginal revenue curve lies *below* its demand curve, intersecting the quantity axis midway between the origin and the point at which the demand curve intersects it. (If necessary,

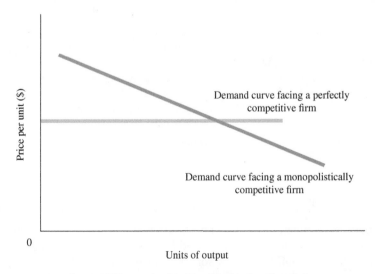

▲ FIGURE 15.2 **Product Differentiation Reduces the Elasticity of Demand Facing a Firm**
The demand curve that a monopolistic competitor faces is likely to be less elastic than the demand curve that a perfectly competitive firm faces. Demand is more elastic than the demand curve that a monopolist faces because close substitutes for the products of a monopolistic competitor are available.

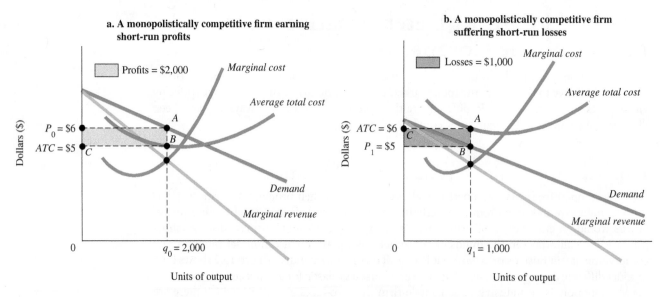

a. A monopolistically competitive firm earning short-run profits

b. A monopolistically competitive firm suffering short-run losses

▲ FIGURE 15.3 **Monopolistic Competition in the Short Run**

In the short run, a monopolistically competitive firm will produce up to the point $MR = MC$. At $q_0 = 2,000$ in panel a, the firm is earning short-run profits equal to $P_0ABC = \$2,000$. In panel b, another monopolistically competitive firm with a similar cost structure is shown facing a weaker demand and suffering short-run losses at q_1 that are equal to $CABP_1 = \$1,000$.

review Chapter 13 to make sure you understand this idea.) The firm chooses the output/price combination that maximizes profit. To maximize profit, the monopolistically competitive firm will increase production until the marginal revenue from increasing output and selling it no longer exceeds the marginal cost of producing it. This occurs at the point at which marginal revenue equals marginal cost: $MR = MC$.

In Figure 15.3(a), the profit-maximizing output is $q_0 = 2,000$, where marginal revenue equals marginal cost. To sell 2,000 units, the firm charges \$6, which is the most it can charge and still sell the 2,000 units. Total revenue is $P_0 \times q_0 = \$12,000$, or the area of P_0Aq_00. Total cost is equal to average total cost times q_0, which is \$10,000, or CBq_00. Total profit is the difference, \$2,000 (the gray-shaded area P_0ABC).

Nothing guarantees that a firm in a monopolistically competitive industry will earn positive profits in the short run. Figure 15.3(b) shows what happens when a firm faces a weaker market demand relative to its costs. Even though the firm does have some control over price, market demand is insufficient to make the firm profitable.

As in perfect competition, such a firm minimizes its losses by producing up to the point where marginal revenue is equal to marginal cost. Of course, as in perfect competition, the price that the firm charges must be sufficient to cover average variable costs. Otherwise, the firm will shut down and suffer losses equal to total fixed costs instead of increasing losses by producing more. In Figure 15.3(b), the loss-minimizing level of output is $q_1 = 1,000$ at a price of \$5. Total revenue is $P_1 \times q_1 = \$5,000$, or P_1Bq_10. Total cost is $ATC \times q_1 = \$6,000$, or CAq_10. Because total cost is greater than revenue, the firm suffers a loss of \$1,000, equal to the pink-shaded area, $CABP_1$.

Price/Output Determination in the Long Run

Under monopolistic competition, entry and exit are easy in the long run. Firms can enter an industry when there are profits to be made, and firms suffering losses can go out of business. However, entry into an industry of this sort is somewhat different from entry into perfect competition because products are differentiated in monopolistic competition. A firm that enters a monopolistically competitive industry is producing a close substitute for the good in question, *but not the same good.*

Let us begin with a firm earning positive profits in the short run, as shown on the left-hand side of Figure 15.3. Those profits provide an incentive for new firms to enter the industry.

This entry creates new substitutes for the profit-making firm, which, in turn, drives down demand for its product. For example, if several restaurants seem to be doing well in a particular location, others may start up and take business from the existing restaurants. Although firms are not perfect substitutes, they are similar enough to take business from one another.

In profitable markets, new firms continue to enter the market until profits are eliminated. As the new firms enter, the demand curve facing each old firm begins to shift to the left, pushing the marginal revenue curve along with it. With more entrants, less demand is left for older firms. This shift continues until profits are eliminated, which occurs when the demand curve slips down to the average total cost curve. Graphically, this is the point at which the demand curve and the average total cost curve are tangent (the point at which they just touch and have the same slope). Figure 15.4 shows a monopolistically competitive industry in long-run equilibrium. At q^* and P^*, price and average total cost are equal; so there are no profits or losses.

Look carefully at the tangency, which, in Figure 15.4, is at output level q^*. The tangency occurs at the profit-maximizing level of output. At this point, marginal cost is equal to marginal revenue. At any level of output other than q^*, ATC lies above the demand curve. This means that at any other level of output, ATC is greater than the price that the firm can charge. (Recall that the demand curve shows the price that can be charged at every level of output.) Hence, price equals average total cost at q^* and profits equal zero.

This equilibrium must occur at the point at which the demand curve is *just tangent* to the average total cost curve. If the demand curve cuts across the average cost curve, intersecting it at two points, the demand curve would be *above* the average total cost curve at some levels of output. Producing at those levels of output would mean positive profits. Positive profits would attract entrants, shifting the firm's demand curve to the left and lowering profits. If the firm's demand curve were always *below* the average total cost curve, all levels of output would produce losses for the firm. This would cause some firms to exit the industry, shifting the remaining firms' demand curves to the right and increasing profits (or reducing losses) for those firms still in the industry. The firm's demand curve must end up tangent to its average total cost curve for profits to equal zero. This is the condition for long-run equilibrium in a monopolistically competitive industry.

There is something else to notice about Figure 15.4: The monopolistically competitive firm is not operating at the lowest point on its average total cost curve. It is producing at a scale smaller than the one that minimizes its average total cost. In some ways this is the cost of product differentiation: The industry consists of firms that serve individualized tastes of customers, but serving those different tastes results in higher production costs than we would see if everyone liked the same thing.

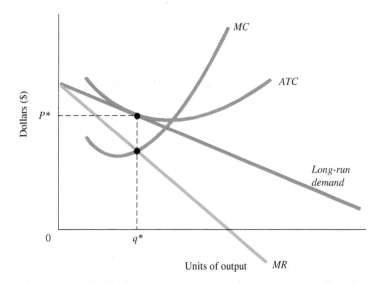

▲ FIGURE 15.4 **Monopolistically Competitive Firm at Long-Run Equilibrium**
As new firms enter a monopolistically competitive industry in search of profits, the demand curves of existing profit-making firms begin to shift to the left, pushing marginal revenue with them as consumers switch to the new close substitutes. This process continues until profits are eliminated, which occurs for a firm when its demand curve is just tangent to its average total cost curve.

Remember our example of the gray sidewalks previously in the chapter. Uniform gray sidewalks allows us to lower costs, but the cost is a gray undifferentiated product. In other cases, we see a rainbow of products, but the firms producing them are all operating at too small a scale.

15.4 LEARNING OBJECTIVE

Summarize the economic advantages and disadvantages of monopolistic competition.

Economic Efficiency and Resource Allocation

We have already noted some of the similarities between monopolistic competition and perfect competition. Because entry is easy and economic profits are eliminated in the long run, we might conclude that the result of monopolistic competition is efficient. There are two problems, however.

First, once a firm achieves any degree of market power by differentiating its product (as is the case in monopolistic competition), its profit-maximizing strategy is to hold down production and charge a price above marginal cost, as you saw in Figure 15.3 and Figure 15.4. Remember from Chapter 12 that price is the value that society places on a good and that marginal cost is the value that society places on the resources needed to produce that good. By holding production down and price above marginal cost, monopolistically competitive firms prevent the efficient use of resources. More product could be produced at a resource cost below the value that consumers place on the product.

Second, as Figure 15.4 shows, the final equilibrium in a monopolistically competitive firm is necessarily to the left of the low point on its average total cost curve. That means a typical firm in a monopolistically competitive industry will not realize all the economies of scale available. (In perfect competition, you will recall, firms are pushed to the bottom of their long-run average cost curves, and the result is an efficient allocation of resources.)

Suppose a number of firms enter an industry and build plants on the basis of initially profitable positions. As more firms compete for those profits, individual firms find themselves with smaller market shares; eventually, they end up with "excess capacity." The firm in Figure 15.4 is not fully using its existing capacity because competition drove its demand curve to the left. In monopolistic competition, we end up with many firms, each producing a slightly different product at a scale that is less than optimal. Would it not be more efficient to have a smaller number of firms, each producing on a slightly larger scale?

The costs of less-than-optimal production, however, need to be balanced against the gains that can accrue from increased product variety. If product differentiation leads to the introduction of new products, improvements in old products, and greater variety, an important gain in economic welfare may counteract (and perhaps outweigh) the loss of efficiency from pricing above marginal cost or not fully realizing all economies of scale.

Most industries that comfortably fit the model of monopolistic competition are competitive. Price competition coexists with product competition, and firms do not earn economic profits and do not violate any of the antitrust laws that we discussed in the last chapter. Monopolistically competitive firms have not been a subject of great concern among economic policy makers. Their behavior appears to be sufficiently controlled by competitive forces, and no serious attempt has been made to regulate or control them.

SUMMARY

15.1 INDUSTRY CHARACTERISTICS *p. 311*

1. A monopolistically competitive industry has the following structural characteristics: (1) a large number of firms, (2) no barriers to entry, and (3) *product differentiation*. Relatively good substitutes for a monopolistic competitor's products are available. Monopolistic competitors try to achieve a degree of market power by differentiating their products.

15.2 PRODUCT DIFFERENTIATION AND ADVERTISING *p. 312*

2. The amount of product differentiation in an industry depends on a number of features of the industry. How different are customers' tastes? Are there gains to customers in buying a product that is identical to one bought by everyone else? Are there large-scale economies associated with making only one

variety of a good? Industries with many different products reflect strong heterogeneity of consumers, low gains from coordination, and small cost gains from standardization.

3. Products can be differentiated horizontally or vertically. Horizontal differentiation produces different types of a good with different appeals to different types of people. In vertical differentiation, people agree that one product is better than another; they just may not be willing to pay for the better good.

4. *Behavioral economics* suggests that there may be times when too much variety reduces consumers' purchases.

5. Behavioral economics also suggests that there may be times when consumers prefer one form of a good over another as a way to commit themselves to different actions in the future than they would otherwise take.

6. Advocates of free and open competition believe that differentiated products and advertising give the market system its vitality and are the basis of its power. Critics argue that product differentiation and advertising are wasteful and inefficient.

15.3 PRICE AND OUTPUT DETERMINATION IN MONOPOLISTIC COMPETITION *p. 319*

7. By differentiating their products, firms will be able to raise prices without losing all demand. The demand curve facing a monopolistic competitor is less elastic than the demand curve faced by a perfectly competitive firm but more elastic than the demand curve faced by a monopoly.

8. To maximize profit in the short run, a monopolistically competitive firm will increase output as long as the marginal revenue from increasing output and selling it exceeds the marginal cost of producing it.

9. When firms enter a monopolistically competitive industry, they introduce close substitutes for the goods being produced. This attracts demand away from the firms already in the industry. Demand faced by each firm shifts left, and profits are ultimately eliminated in the long run. This long-run equilibrium occurs at the point where the demand curve is just tangent to the average total cost curve.

15.4 ECONOMIC EFFICIENCY AND RESCOURCE ALLOCATION *p. 322*

10. Monopolistically competitive firms end up pricing above marginal cost. This is inefficient, as is the fact that monopolistically competitive firms do not realize all economies of scale available. There may be offsetting gains from increased variety.

REVIEW TERMS AND CONCEPTS

behavioral economics, *p. 315*

commitment device, *p. 315*

horizontal differentiation, *p. 313*

monopolistic competition, *p. 311*

product differentiation, *p. 312*

vertical differentiation, *p. 314*

PROBLEMS

All problems are available on MyEconLab.

15.1 INDUSTRY CHARACTERISTICS

LEARNING OBJECTIVE: Identify the characteristics of a monopolistically competitive industry.

1.1 Mariano's Hacienda Ranch is a Mexican restaurant in Dallas. Founder Mariano Martinez is not only known for serving up great Mexican food, but also for being the inventor of the world's first frozen margarita machine, which he began using soon after opening his first restaurant in 1971. (His original frozen margarita machine resides in the Smithsonian's National Museum of American History!) Mariano's continues to this day to create unique varieties of margaritas as well as one-of-a-kind twists on classic Mexican cuisine. Using industry characteristics, explain in which of the four market organizations Mariano's Hacienda Ranch falls.

15.2 PRODUCT DIFFERENTIATION AND ADVERTISING

LEARNING OBJECTIVE: Discuss the methods and implications of product differentiation and advertising in monopolistically competitive industries.

2.1 Consider the local music scene in your area. Name some of the local live bands that play in clubs and music halls, both on and off campus. Look in your local newspaper for advertisements of upcoming shows or performances. How would you characterize the market for local musicians? Is there product differentiation? In what specific ways do firms (individual performers or bands) compete? To what degree are they able to exercise market power? Are there barriers to entry? How profitable do you think the musicians are?

2.2 Write a brief essay explaining the accuracy of this statement: The Beatles were once a monopolistically competitive firm that became a monopolist.

2.3 In a market in which there is vertical differentiation, we always see price differences among the products. In markets with horizontal differentiation, sometimes the products differ but prices are much the same. Why does vertical differentiation naturally bring with it price differences?

2.4 [**Related to the** *Economics in Practice* **on p. 316**] If you look at the prices listed in the *Economics in Practice* on p. 316, you will see that the more well-known brands are being sold for a lower price than the less well-known brands. Is this pattern always true? Explain your answer.

2.5 [**Related to the** *Economics in Practice* **on p. 318**] As cities go, Las Vegas is about as "over-the-top" as is imaginable. Where else in the world can you find a 350-foot tall glass pyramid, a half-scale replica of the Eiffel Tower, a fire-spewing volcano, and patrons being serenaded in Italian while riding in authentic Venetian gondolas, and all of this along one street, Las Vegas Blvd? Despite the city's numerous excesses, the four largest casino companies in the United States, all based in Las Vegas, have each spent millions of dollars on environmental sustainability programs, with the earliest program dating back to 2007. What are the positive and negative effects of engaging in such programs? Why do you suppose all four companies have chosen to implement these environmental programs?

2.6 The table shows the relationship for a hypothetical firm between its advertising expenditures and the quantity of its output that it expects it can sell at a fixed price of $12 per unit.

Advertising Expenditures (Millions)	Quantity Sold at P = $12 in Million Units
$2.5	20.0
$3.5	24.0
$4.5	26.0
$5.5	26.8
$6.5	27.2

a. In economic terms, why might the relationship between advertising and sales look the way it does?

b. Assume that the marginal costs of producing this product (not including the advertising costs) are a constant $10. How much advertising should this firm be doing? What economic principle are you using to make this decision?

2.7 Conduct an online search for "iPhone repair San Diego." You will find more than 4 million entries. Now try "iPhone screen repair San Diego." You will find about 470,000 entries. Try to estimate the total number of businesses that repair iPhone screens in San Diego. Pick some random areas in San Diego and see how many are listed nearby. See if you can find some advertisements with prices. How much variation does there seem to be in the price of a screen repair for an iPhone 5? Make the case that the iPhone repair industry is or is not well described by the model of monopolistic competition presented in this chapter. Be specific.

2.8 If you have traveled to other countries, you may have firsthand knowledge about McDonald's menu items that are available only in foreign markets, but McDonald's menus also contain regional variations in the United States. A few of these regional menu offerings include breakfast platters with Spam and rice in Hawaii, the McLobster sandwich in Maine, a crab cake sandwich in parts of the mid-Atlantic, and biscuits and gravy in the deep south. In addition to these regional items, McDonald's also offers some menu items on a limited-time basis, such as the McRib sandwich, the Cherry Berry Chiller, and the Angus Chipotle BBQ Burger. Why would a company like McDonald's offer menu items that are region-specific or available only for a limited time?

15.3 PRICE AND OUTPUT DETERMINATION IN MONOPOLISTIC COMPETITION

LEARNING OBJECTIVE: Discuss price and output determination for monopolistically competitive firms.

3.1 Every weekend more than 500 different vendors set up at the local farmers' market, selling a variety of items from homemade prepared foods to fresh produce. Yolanda rents a booth each weekend at the farmers' market to sell homemade tamales for $10 a dozen. Yolanda pays each of her four cousins $20 per hour to make the tamales on Friday evenings in the food truck she operates for weekday lunch service. Yolanda sells 60 dozen tamales each weekend at the farmers' market, which take her cousins 4 hours to make each Friday. The cost of ingredients for all the tamales totals $240 and the booth at the farmers' market rents for $150 per weekend.

a. What market structure does this business most resemble? What characteristics lead you to this conclusion?

b. What would you expect to see happen in this business? Use the data in the problem to support your conclusions.

c. How would your calculations change if Yolanda were to develop a weekend lunch business that used the food truck kitchen's capacity?

3.2 The following diagram shows the structure of cost and demand facing a monopolistically competitive firm in the short run.

a. Identify the following on the graph and calculate each one.

  i.   Profit-maximizing output level
  ii. Profit-maximizing price
  iii. Total revenue
  iv. Total cost
  v.   Total profit or loss

b. What is likely to happen in this industry in the long run?

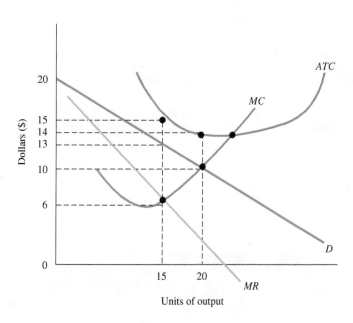

3.3 Explain the relationship between price and marginal revenue for a perfectly competitive firm and for a monopolistically competitive firm. Why is the relationship different for these markets?

15.4 ECONOMIC EFFICIENCY AND RESOURCE ALLOCATION

LEARNING OBJECTIVE: Summarize the economic advantages and disadvantages of monopolistic competition.

4.1 For each of the following, state whether you agree or disagree. Explain your answer.
   a. Monopolistically competitive firms generate economic profits because they are protected by barriers to entry.
   b. Monopolistically competitive firms are efficient because in the long run, price falls to equal marginal cost.

16 Externalities, Public Goods, and Common Resources

In Chapters 6 through 12, we built a complete model of a perfectly competitive economy. The market economy described in those chapters does a good job at providing efficient outcomes for society. In Chapters 13 to 15, we described three different market structures that impede the achievement of efficiency. In these cases it was the absence of competition that created problems for the working of the market. In this chapter we tackle a rather different set of market failures. Here we will be looking at environmental problems, issues in providing collective goods and managing common resources. In these cases, as we will see, competitive markets do not in most circumstances lead to efficient outcomes. Here we will find an enhanced role for the government in helping the economy to achieve efficiency.

As we continue our examination of market failure, we look first at *externalities* as a source of inefficiency. When you buy a car or decide how much to drive it, how much do you consider the effects on the environment of the carbon produced by that car? For many years, manufacturing firms and power plants paid little attention to the effects of the smoke they produced on the quality of the air we breathe. In both cases, the costs of these actions are borne not entirely by the decision maker, but by others in society. As a consequence, the decisions made will in general not be optimal.

Most goods we have thus far discussed are private goods. If I buy an apple and eat it, the benefits come to me alone. Some goods, however, are consumed collectively. National parks, military defense, and public education all benefit society in general. These products are called *public goods* or *social goods,* and even when they are quite valuable to a large number of people, private markets do not typically provide them. Public goods are most commonly produced or financed by governments. The process of choosing what social goods to produce is different from the process of private choice.

We will also explore common resources in this chapter. How well does the private market manage our seas? Our large fisheries? Here too we will discover a role for governments, often at the global level.

Finally, while the existence of externalities, public goods, and common resources are examples of market failure and provide an opportunity for government action, it is not necessarily true that government involvement always improves matters. Just as markets fail, so too can governments.

Externalities and Environmental Economics

An **externality** exists when the actions or decisions of one person or group impose a cost or bestow a benefit on second or third parties. Externalities are sometimes called *spillovers* or *neighborhood effects*. Inefficient decisions result when decision makers fail to consider social costs and benefits.

The presence of externalities is a significant phenomenon in modern life. Examples are everywhere: Air, water, land, sight, and sound pollution; traffic congestion; automobile accidents; abandoned housing; nuclear accidents; and secondhand cigarette smoke are only a few. Reports of melting ice caps have fueled worry among scientists and others across the world about global warming. Concern about air quality is a major political issue in much of the developing world. The study of externalities is a major concern of *environmental economics*.

The growth of China and India has put increased pressure on the environment. As new countries industrialize, strains on global air and water systems are inevitable. We have become increasingly aware of the global nature of externalities.

16.1 LEARNING OBJECTIVE

Understand the market failure associated with externalities and the possible solutions to this set of issues.

externality Actions of one party impose costs or benefits on a second party.

Marginal Social Cost and Marginal Cost Pricing

In the absence of externalities, when a firm weighs price and marginal cost to decide output, it is weighing the full benefits to society of additional production against the full costs to society of that production. Those who benefit from the production of a product are the people or households who end up consuming it. The price of a product is a good measure of what an additional unit of that product is "worth" because those who value it more highly already buy it. People who value it less than the current price are not buying it. If marginal cost includes all costs—that is, all costs *to society*—of producing a marginal unit of a good, additional production will be efficient, provided P is greater than MC. Up to the point where $P = MC$, each unit of production yields benefits in excess of cost. Figure 16.1(a) shows a firm and an industry in which no externalities exist.

Suppose, however, that the production of the firm's product imposes external costs on society as well. A firm producing detergent may dump wastewater into a local river as a byproduct of its detergent production, affecting the local community. A steel firm may produce carbon emissions as well as steel, contributing both to air pollution and global warming. These are costs of producing steel or detergent just as much as is the labor or capital costs of making those goods. What would happen to the firm and industry in Figure 16.1(a) if we made the firms responsible financially for the external costs they impose? Figure 16.1(b) shows what happens graphically when we add the external costs to the financial costs of the firm. The curve labeled *MSC*, **marginal social cost**, is the sum of the marginal cost of producing the product and the correctly measured marginal external cost involved in the process of production.

When we correctly include the external costs in the firm's budget, the firm's marginal costs rise, shifting up to the curve labeled *MSC* on the right hand side of Figure 16.1(b). The industry supply curve, which is just the sum of the marginal cost curves of the firms in the industry, also then shifts up to the curve labeled S' in the figure. A new equilibrium occurs at the intersection of the original demand curve and the new supply curve and now embeds the full cost of production of this good. The new price is P^{**}, and each firm chooses quantity q^{**}, which equates its new higher marginal cost with the industry price. Industry output at the optimum is Q^{**}.

Notice what has happened. Making the firms responsible for their external costs increases the costs they see. This reduces firm and industry output and increases the price. Fewer units will be sold, but the price they are sold at will now reflect all the costs of production, both private and social.

We can also use Figure 16.1 to show what happens when decision makers are not made responsible for the external costs they impose. Without being charged for their external costs, firms will continue to produce at q^*, and the industry will produce at Q^*, charging the price P^*. You can see that the industry is producing too much output. In particular, it overproduces by $Q^* - Q^{**}$. There is a social loss from this over production. We can see the costs of producing these units by reading along the *MSC* curve between Q^{**} and Q^*. It is labeled in the figure as

marginal social cost (*MSC*) The total cost to society of producing an additional unit of a good or service. MSC is equal to the sum of the marginal cost of producing the product and the correctly measured marginal external cost involved in the process of production.

segment *AB*. The *value* of these extra units can be seen by looking at the demand curve, which is shown in the figure as the segment *AC*. We can see easily that these added units generate more cost than their value to consumers. That is what we mean when we say there is overproduction or that the production level is inefficient. Indeed the triangle *ABC* is a measure of the efficiency loss from this overproduction. It should look familiar as it parallels the deadweight loss from underproduction in the monopoly case and was also covered in another context in Chapter 4.

The analysis thus far should give you some insight into the kinds of policy solutions likely to help in the environmental area. The central issue in externalities is that some decisions are being made without taking into account full costs. Solutions will thus involve figuring out ways to make individuals and firms take these costs into account. Sometimes this process is called "internalizing the externalities." We will discuss some policy options later in this chapter.

Acid Rain and the Clean Air Act   Acid rain is an excellent example of an externality and of the issues and conflicts involved in dealing with externalities. When manufacturing firms and power plants in the Midwest burn coal with a high-sulfur content, smoke from those plants mixes with moisture in the atmosphere. The result is a dilute acid that is windblown north to Canada and east to New York and New England, where it falls to Earth as rain. The same sources produce acid rain in Germany, Sweden, and Norway.

How does the acid rain problem look to the different parties involved? For manufacturing firms and public utilities generating the sulfur dioxide that creates acid rain, burning high-sulfur coal delivers cheap power and employment to residents of the Midwest. Paying to clean up the damage or changing the fuel mix to reduce sulfur would result in higher electricity prices. Some firms would likely go out of business, and jobs would be lost. For residents in other parts of

▶ **FIGURE 16.1 Profit Maximizing Firm With and Without Externalities**
(a) Without externalities, optimum output *Q** is produced at the level where *P* = *MC*.
(b) With externalities, *Q** is inefficient and the optimum output is *Q***. The price has risen from *P** to *P***.

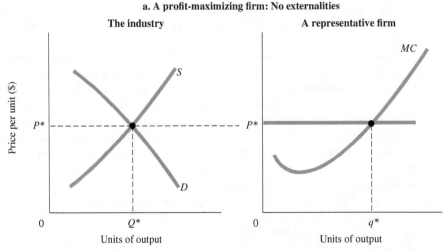

ECONOMICS IN PRACTICE

Adjusting to an Environmental Disaster: The Dust Bowl

In economics we often distinguish between short- and long-run effects of various policies or actions. Whether we think about consumer reactions to price increases or firm reactions to cost increases or demand shifts, we normally assume that the ability of people and institutions to react to these new circumstances as time passes softens their impact. The same arguments have been applied in environmental areas, including the case of global warning, where it is argued that changing patterns of agriculture and overall land use can mitigate some of the economic consequences of temperature increases. A recent, interesting study of the short- and long-run effects of the U.S. Dust Bowl in the 1930s provides a counterpoint.[1]

In the late nineteenth century, as agriculture spread through the plains in the United States, grasslands were replaced by crops. When times were good and rainfall adequate, farms and farmers thrived. But in the 1930s the U.S. plains experienced a severe drought, with large-scale crop failure. Subsequent dust storms blew topsoil off the lands, creating what some dubbed black Sundays, as valuable soil from Oklahoma, Texas, and the Dakotas ended up in the Atlantic Ocean. By the 1940s many of the plains areas had lost almost three-fourths of their topsoil cover. The consequence was an eroded landscape, with a much diminished ability to sustain crops and families. Many of you will have read John Steinbeck's *The Grapes of Wrath*, which describes the travails of the Joad family as they left their home in Oklahoma to head to California in this period.

Hornbeck's recent work asks the question: How long did it take for the U.S. plains to recover from this man-made environmental disaster? His conclusion? Large and

widespread economic effects were felt throughout the 1940s and 1950s and most of the long-run adjustment occurred not with recovery of the plains or a change in crop choice but with the movement of people out of the region much as Steinbeck described. Perhaps for environmental recovery and readjustment, the long run may be long indeed.

THINKING PRACTICALLY

1. Why do you think adjustment to the Dust Bowl was so slow?

[1] Richard Hornbeck, "The Enduring Impact of the American Dust Bowl: Short and Long Run Adjustments to Environmental Catastrophe" *American Economic Review*, June 2012, 1477–1507.

the United States and Canada, particularly those near wildlife areas, the burning of high-sulfur coal and the resulting acid rain results in fish kills and deforestation. Often these citizens are far enough away from the power plants producing the sulfur dioxide that they are not even benefiting from the cheaper power. As in many areas of economics, the hard issue here is how to balance benefits to one set of claimants with costs to another.

In complex cases of externalities, like acid rain, governments often get involved. The United States began its regulatory work in reducing acid rain with the Clean Air Act in 1990. Since then, the United States has made substantial progress in reducing the problem of acid rain, and many acidified lakes and streams now once again support fish life. Recently, the United States has employed an innovative "cap-and-trade" program to control emissions, which we will discuss later in this chapter. For acid rain, which travels across national boundaries, agreements between Canada and the United States have also played an important role.

Other Externalities   Clearly, the most significant and hotly debated issue of externalities is global warming. The 2007 Nobel Peace Prize was awarded to former Vice President Al Gore and the Intergovernmental Panel on Climate Change, a group of 2,500 researchers from 130 nations that issued a number of reports linking human activity to the recent rise of the average temperature on Earth. Although there is some disagreement, most scientists predict that absent a change in policy major adverse consequences such as dramatically rising sea levels are likely. The global nature of the problem, coupled with the fact that warming will hurt some countries—those with big coastlines and warm current temperatures—more than others makes finding a solution to this issue especially hard.

Individual actions can also create externalities. When I drive during rush hour, I increase congestion faced by other drivers. If I smoke, your health may be compromised. Again the key issue is weighing the costs and benefits to all parties.

Some Examples of Positive Externalities   Thus far we have described a series of negative externalities. But externalities can also be positive. In some cases, when other people or firms engage in an activity, there are side *benefits* from that activity. From an economics perspective, there are problems with positive externalities as well.

Ian Ayres and Steve Levitt have studied a fascinating example of a product with positive externalities, LoJack. LoJack is a device that allows police to track a car when it is stolen. When a car has a LoJack device installed, the gains to stealing that car are sharply reduced. These devices not only help recover cars but also help catch car thieves. Suppose that 90 percent of the cars in a community had LoJack installed. If all LoJack cars were identified—the way houses are that have burglar alarms—potential thieves could look for the unmarked cars. As it happens, LoJack does not come with any identifying mark. From a thief's perspective, any car has a 90 percent chance of having a LoJack installed. As a result, the benefits from stealing *any* car are reduced. With reduced benefits, fewer thefts occur. Ayres and Levitt have found that the size of these positive externalities are large; they estimate that the purchaser of a LoJack captures, as an individual, only 10 percent of the value of the device.[1]

We also see positive externalities in the case of vaccinations. The more people who are vaccinated, and thus less likely to become ill, the less likely it is that a disease will spread. But the less likely the disease, the lower the private benefits to people from getting a vaccination. With communicable diseases, health precautions taken by an individual have positive external benefits to the rest of the community.

The problem with positive externalities should now be clear. For this type of externality, the individuals in charge have too little incentive to engage in the activity. Too few LoJacks are bought; too few people wash their hands often; too few people would vaccinate their children unless forced to do so by school systems.

Costs and Benefits of Pollution

If you look back at Figure 16.1, you will see that the optimum amount of output for the pollution-emitting firm analyzed in the figure is positive. This tells us that at the optimum this firm is producing emissions, with some cost to the environment. In general, we will find that at the optimum the level of emissions of most pollutants is not zero. This may surprise you but is an important application of economics to a serious world issue.

Note that the title of this subsection has both "costs" and "benefits" in it. The social costs of pollution are likely clear to you. They might include health problems from smog or loss of fish species from water pollution. But what are the social benefits of pollution? The social benefits of pollution are the costs we avoid by not eliminating the pollution while still being able to enjoy the goods that create the pollution in the first place. You could eliminate the carbon you emit by not driving, but that would have a cost to you. Or you could turn in your gas-powered car and buy a hybrid, which would cost money. Not doing those things is a benefit to you, one that we want to weigh against the costs to society of having you drive. Similarly, a steel plant gets a benefit from pollution both from the profits it earns selling steel and from avoiding costs of refitting the steel plant. The **marginal social benefit of pollution** is the incremental benefit to society from producing one more unit of pollution. The benefit is the cost saved from polluting.

We can use this idea to determine the optimum amount of pollution in a society. The goal is to use the absorptive capacity of our environment as efficiently as possible. The principle we

marginal social benefit of pollution   The incremental benefit to society from producing one more unit of pollution.

---

[1] Ian Ayres and Steven D. Levitt, "Measuring Positive Externalities from Unobservable Victim Precautions: An Empirical Analysis of Lojack," *Quarterly Journal of Economics* 108, (1), 1998.

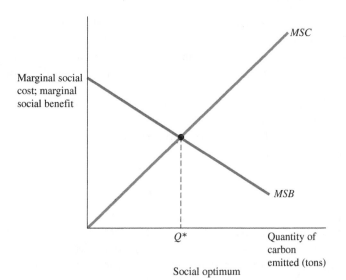

will apply should be familiar to you from other contexts. Each unit of pollution that is emitted has a marginal social cost, borne by society, perhaps in the form of health losses or lost recreational opportunities from polluted waterways. Continuing to produce that unit of pollution also has a benefit, represented by the marginal social benefit of pollution. Again, the benefit comes from resources saved in not having to eliminate the externality. We compare the two. If an incremental unit of pollution has a marginal social benefit in excess of its marginal social cost, we produce it; otherwise we do not. In other words, if on the margin society benefits more from controlling the emission than it costs to do that control, then the emission is controlled. Otherwise it is not. At the optimum, the marginal social cost of pollution emitted will exactly equal the marginal social benefit from emissions.

Figure 16.2 presents this analysis graphically. Along the horizontal axis we measure the level of pollution; here we have used tons of carbon emitted. On the vertical axis we represent the marginal social cost of experiencing carbon emissions (green line) and the marginal social benefit from pollution (purple line). It is interesting to think about the slopes of these two curves. As we increase emissions levels, the MSC increases; the *MSC* curve slopes up. This tells us that as we increase emissions the added cost of one more unit of emissions goes up. For many pollutants the environment can absorb low levels reasonably well, so marginal costs at low levels are low. As we dump more pollutants into the environment, however, the harm to nature generally increases. Adding a little bit of smoke to a clear sky may have little effect as it dissipates; adding that same smoke to an already hazy sky may have serious health consequences. In some cases the *MSC* curve may increase quite dramatically as the environment approaches a saturation point. The marginal social benefit curve shown in the figure has, by contrast, a downward slope. At high levels of emissions (to the right), there are often cheap ways to eliminate some emissions. Cutting back a ton of carbon emissions at this level may be quite cheap. Thus, the benefits from being able to pollute are small. In the driving example, it is easy to think of some trips you could avoid taking at all with little detriment. As we cut back emissions, however, moving to the left on the graph, technology for reductions may reach a limit and eliminating the last little bit of pollution may in fact be possible only by eliminating production altogether. If you had to give up driving altogether, that lost benefit might be high indeed.

We see the optimum emissions level in Figure 16.2 is Q^*, found at the intersection of the *MSC* and *MSB* curves. At this point, society is using its environment most efficiently, weighing the reduction in costs from experiencing pollution against the lost benefits from changing consumption or investing resources in mitigation.

Drawing the marginal curves as we have done and identifying the optimal level of pollution is a relatively straightforward application of the principles of marginalism that we have covered often in this text. It is a more difficult challenge to empirically measure these curves. The MSC of emissions ranges from health costs, to aesthetics, to loss of species diversity, or even to increases in risks to populations from rising sea levels. Many of these risks are uncertain. Environmental economists working with natural scientists have spent considerable time trying to provide reasonable estimates of what these costs might be. Nor is it easy to estimate the marginal social benefit curves, which requires us to assess the costs of technological solutions to emissions problems.

We have explored externalities and, focusing on pollution, have seen the characteristics of an optimal solution to the externality problem. But how do we move to the optimal level? Here there is much debate, both about how much progress can be made by private action and about the right type of government policy instruments to use.

Internalizing Externalities

A number of mechanisms are available to provide decision makers with incentives to weigh the external costs and benefits of their decisions, a process called *internalization*. In some cases, externalities are internalized through bargaining and negotiation without government involvement. In other cases, private bargains fail and the only alternative may be government action of some kind.

Four approaches have been taken to solving the problem of externalities: (1) private bargaining and negotiation, (2) environmental standards, (3) government-imposed taxes and subsidies, and (4) sale or auctioning of rights to impose externalities. Although each is best suited for a different set of circumstances, all provide decision makers with an incentive to weigh the external effects of their decisions.

Private Bargaining and Negotiation Many of you probably live in dormitories. Now and again you may have found yourself with a neighbor who is much noisier than you would like. For you the noise is an externality, one that prevents you from either sleeping or studying. For the neighbor, the noise has its benefits, likely produced by a party. How do you handle this externality? For most people in this situation, the first step is obvious: Knock on the neighbor's door and ask him to be quieter. In fact, good manners are a societal reaction to incipient externalities. As societies increase in population density, more and more activities fall under the category of "not done in public." Consider what has happened over time to the social acceptability of smoking, for example. Even fashion can create externalities. In 2010, in anticipation of its Expo, the Chinese government cracked down on the tendency of its citizens in Shanghai to wear their pajamas outside the home, believing that this attire has negative externalities for their international guests.

Even when there are no social norms against an activity, private bargains and negotiation can often solve an externality problem. The first formal model of how private negotiations might work in this setting was described by Ronald Coase in 1960.[2] The **Coase theorem**, which is a staple topic in both law and economics classes, tells us that under certain conditions, private bargaining can solve the externality problem without government action.

To see how the Coase theorem works, let us return to the problem of your noisy neighbor. Suppose your polite request has been turned down and that this neighbor parties every day. How might the Coase theorem help us here? How can we use bargaining to help us get some sleep? Coase would tell us that the first step is to learn what the rules are; it will turn out that it won't matter *what* the rules are, only that both parties to a dispute *know* the rules. Negotiations are difficult when the two parties don't agree on who has what rights. Let us assume, at least at first, that in your dormitory there are no rules against noise and that everyone in the dorm is aware of this lenient policy. In a system with no rules and a rude neighbor, do you have any recourse?

Coase would answer yes. If your neighbor has the right to make noise all the time and you object to that noise, you can try to pay him not to make so much noise. If your neighbor is partying every day, it is likely that diminishing returns have set in. His first party of the month might

Coase theorem Under certain conditions, when externalities are present, private parties can arrive at the efficient solution without government involvement.

---

[2] See Ronald Coase, "The Problem of Social Cost," *Journal of Law and Economics*, 1960. Coase won the 1991 Nobel Prize in Economics.

be worth a good deal to him, but by the time party 30 comes around, even he might be tired of the noise and mess! By day 30 of noise, you likely would value quiet a good deal. With nonstop partying, it is likely that your marginal cost from the noise of the last party exceeds your neighbor's marginal benefit from that noise. In short, current noise levels are socially inefficient and there is room for a deal! Of course, as your neighbor cuts back in his partying because of your bribes, his value of the marginal hour of noise goes up, and the marginal cost to you of listening begins to fall. At some point, you can no longer bribe the neighbor to be quiet because his marginal benefit from one more noisy party exceeds its cost to you. We have reached a socially optimal level of noise. Notice this level balances your value of silence against your neighbor's benefit from noise.

Suppose, on the other hand, your dormitory had strict noise rules. Now the neighbor who wanted to party would have to bribe you not to report him. Again we would expect payments to continue as long as there was a difference in marginal values. In the end, exactly the same amount of partying would go on, one that just balanced the interests of the people involved. Coase tells us that the optimal level, in which the marginal cost from experiencing the externality exactly equals the marginal benefit from that externality, will be achieved no matter how the original property rights are arranged. All that differs is who is paying whom.

We learn from Coase that under certain conditions, private negotiations will push society to the right level of output even with externalities. What features of a situation are required for this type of solution to work? First, as noted, basic rights must be understood by all parties. If rights are not spelled out, arguments about who has what right interfere with the bargaining process. A second condition is that people must be able to bargain without impediment or costs. When people live next to one another, bargaining is a lot easier. Finally, private negotiation works best when the number of parties involved is few in number. If one party to a bargain is a large group, such as all residents of a town or a large area as in the previous acid rain example, private negotiations work less well.

In some cases, especially involving neighbors, the offer of compensation might be made in some form other than cash. You may offer your dormmate goodwill, a favor or two, or help with his school work. In this example, rather than using bribes, you might just pay to insulate your room. Of course, your willingness to do this would depend on how much insulation costs, how much you suffered from the noise, and how long you expected to live next door.

Coase's critics are quick to point out that the conditions required for bargaining to produce the efficient result are not always present. The biggest problem with Coase's system is also a common problem. Often one party to a bargain is a large group of people, and our reasoning may be subject to a fallacy of composition.

Suppose a power company in Pittsburgh is polluting the air. The damaged parties are the 100,000 people who live near the plant. Let us assume the plant has the right to pollute. The Coase theorem predicts that the people who are damaged by the smoke will get together and offer a bribe. If the bribe is sufficient to induce the power plant to stop polluting or reduce the pollutants with air scrubbers, it will accept the bribe and cut down on the pollution. If the bribe is not sufficient, the pollution will continue, but the firm will have weighed all the costs and the result will be efficient.

However, not everyone will contribute to the bribe fund. First, each contribution is so small relative to the whole that no single contribution makes much of a difference. Making a contribution may seem unimportant or unnecessary to some. Second, all people get to breathe the cleaner air whether they contribute to the bribe or not. Many people will not participate simply because they are not compelled to, and the private bargain breaks down—the bribe that the group comes up with will be less than the full damages unless everyone participates. (We discuss these two problems—the *drop-in-the-bucket* and the *free-rider*—later in this chapter.) When the number of damaged parties is large, government taxes or regulation may be the only avenue to a remedy.

As we have just seen, for bargaining to result in an efficient outcome, the initial assignment of rights must be clear to both parties. When rights are established by law, more often than not some mechanism to protect those rights is also built into the law. In some cases where a nuisance exists, for example, there may be legal remedies. In such cases, the victim can go to court and ask for an **injunction** that forbids the damage-producing behavior from continuing.

Injunctive remedies are irrelevant when the damage has already been done. Consider accidents. If your leg has already been broken as the result of an automobile accident, enjoining the

injunction A court order forbidding the continuation of behavior that leads to damages.

liability rules Laws that require A to compensate B for damages that A imposed on B.

driver of the other car from drinking and driving will not work—it is too late. In these cases, rights must be protected by **liability rules**, rules that require A to compensate B for damages imposed. In theory, such rules are designed to do the same thing that taxing a polluter is designed to do: provide decision makers with an incentive to weigh all the consequences, actual and potential, of their decisions. Just as taxes do not stop all pollution, liability rules do not stop all accidents.

However, the threat of liability actions does induce people to take more care than they might otherwise. Product liability is a good example. If a person is damaged in some way because a product is defective, the producing company is, in most cases, held liable for the damages, even if the company took reasonable care in producing the product. Producers have a powerful incentive to be careful. If consumers know they will be generously compensated for any damages, however, they may not have as powerful an incentive to be careful when using the product.

Environmental Standards   One of the most important policy tools used to deal with externalities are standards, rules that directly govern how firms and individuals who produce externalities behave.

Direct regulation of externalities takes place at federal, state, and local levels. The Environmental Protection Agency (EPA) is a federal agency established by an act of Congress in 1970. Since the 1960s, Congress has passed a great deal of legislation that sets specific standards for permissible discharges into the air and water. Every state has a division or department charged with regulating activities that are likely to harm the environment. Most airports in the United States have landing patterns and hours that are regulated by local governments to minimize noise.

Many criminal penalties and sanctions for violating environmental regulations are like the taxes imposed on polluters. Not all violations and crimes are stopped, but violators and criminals face "costs." For the outcome to be efficient, the penalties they expect to pay should reflect the damage that their actions impose on society.

How strict should the standards be that the government imposes? This is a question we have already answered! Look back at Figure 16.2. We see from this that looking at both benefits and costs, we find the optimal level of pollution is Q^*. In setting standards, most economists believe that the government should be trying to set rules so that Q^* is achieved. The goal of policy is to set up rules such that decision makers end up producing the optimal level of emissions.

It turns out that under some common circumstances, setting standards to achieve Q^* will be difficult. Standards often involve setting rules on how firms produce. For example, we might require firms to install filters on the top of their smokestacks to reduce their emissions. But specifying what firms should do often results in higher costs for reducing pollution than we could achieve in other ways. Forcing a utility plant to install a filter might be much more expensive than allowing it to cut emissions by the same amount by changing the type of fuel it burns. It is hard to use standards to encourage firms to choose the right technology to reduce emissions. When firms creating the externality have different marginal costs of reducing their pollution, it is also difficult to find the right standard to set. In these circumstances, when methods to reduce emissions are varied, and polluters differ widely in their ability to control emissions, most economists favor managing externalities by turning to a type of price system, using either taxes or a tradable permits market.

Taxes and Subsidies   When private negotiations fail, economists have traditionally advocated marginal taxes and subsidies as a direct way of forcing firms to consider external costs or benefits. When a firm imposes an external social cost, the reasoning goes, a per-unit tax should be imposed equal to the damages of each successive unit of output produced by the firm—the tax should be *exactly equal* to marginal external costs.[3]

---

[3] As we discuss later in this chapter, damage costs are difficult to measure. It is often assumed that they are proportional to the volume of pollutants discharged into the air or water. Instead of taxes, governments often impose *effluent charges*, which make the cost to polluters proportional to the amount of pollution caused. We will use *tax* to refer to both taxes and effluent charges.

Return to look at Figure 16.1(b). We saw in this figure how a firm would do the right thing in terms of emissions if only it faced the right marginal cost curve, the MSC. We can use the tax system to do exactly this! Suppose we impose a tax on this firm exactly equal to the marginal external cost it imposes on society. The firm now faces a marginal cost curve that is the same as the marginal social cost curve—its marginal cost curve is now MSC. It experiences the externality cost as a financial cost; it pays the government taxes to "use" the environment, just as it pays workers to use their labor. Remember that the industry supply curve is the sum of the marginal cost curves of the individual firms. This means that as a result of the tax, the industry supply curve shifts to the left, driving output down to the optimal level and the price up. Because a profit-maximizing firm equates price with marginal cost, the new price to consumers covers the resource costs of producing the product *and* the external costs created by the pollution that results from these goods being produced. The consumer decision process is once again efficient at the margin because marginal social benefit as reflected in market price is equal to the full social marginal cost of the product.

We argued previously that standards sometimes created problems when there are multiple ways to reduce emissions and when firms differ in the marginal benefits they received from polluting (or thought of another way, their marginal costs of cleaning up). Emission taxes will work much better in this regard. Suppose in drawing the marginal social benefit curve in Figure 16.2 we were combining information from two different polluters. One firm, A, finds it easy to avoid polluting. Perhaps it is a new plant, easily able to switch to a different type of fuel. For A, the marginal benefit of polluting is relatively low because avoiding that pollution is easy. A second firm, B, is old and can stop polluting only at great expense. Ideally, if we want to reduce as much pollution as possible per dollar, we should have the firm that can reduce pollution cheaply do more of it. And that is exactly what a tax will do. If the government sets a tax at $10 per ton of carbon emitted, both firms will take actions that reduce carbon as long as those actions cost them less than $10 per ton. For Firm A, there may be many such actions, so it will cut back a lot before it becomes too expensive to do any more. For Firm B, perhaps little reduction will occur. Both firms will look across technological solutions to find the ones that reduce emissions at the lowest costs. In the end, the key policy goal is to make sure the right amount of total reduction occurs, and taxes will accomplish this at lower costs than will a standard.

Figure 16.3 shows us how a tax would work for Firms A and B. Before we impose a tax, each firm is polluting at its maximum level, thinking of pollution as free. *Each* firm produces Q_0 worth of emissions. Total industry emissions is thus $2Q_0$. Suppose now the government, based on information about both firms and about the MSCs of emissions, wants to reduce emissions in half to Q_0. Looking at the information it has gathered, it sets the tax at T*. Every unit of emissions produced by the firm costs it T*, so you can think of T* as the per-unit price of emissions.

Look first at Firm A. At its original level of emissions, Q_0, the tax per unit is quite a bit higher than the marginal benefit it gets from polluting. So it starts to cut back using whatever

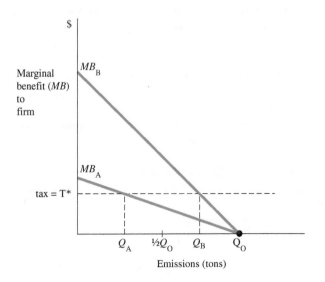

Emissions (tons)

Optimal Emissions Taxes for Firms with Different Marginal Benefit Curves

If a per-unit tax exactly equal to marginal external costs is imposed on a firm, the firm will weigh the tax against its marginal benefits from polluting and choose an optimal emissions level. Here two firms differ in their marginal benefits and thus choose different levels. In equilibrium each firm chooses a level so that the MSB = the tax. The result is that the optimal pollution level is achieved at the lowest costs.

technological opportunities it has. As long as the price of the emission is more than the benefit to the firm of not cleaning up, the firm reduces its emissions. For firm A, emissions fall all the way to Q_A. At that point, it is too expensive to cut back any further. Firm B, with much higher benefits from polluting, ends up producing Q_B emissions. If the tax has been set right, the sum of Q_A and Q_B will be Q_0, or one half the original emission level of $2Q_0$. The tax has accomplished its task of reducing emission levels.

Suppose we had instead used standards to achieve the emissions reduction, requiring each firm to produce $\frac{1}{2}Q_0$ rather than allowing firms to choose emissions based on their costs? Firm B is now producing more emissions than the standards would have required and would need to reduce further. We can see from the marginal benefit curve of Firm B how much it would lose by having to cut back its emissions further. Firm A's emissions under the tax system are lower than $\frac{1}{2}Q_0$, the standard allowance, so Firm A could increase its emissions. So a common standard benefits Firm A and costs Firm B. But notice, Firm A gains *less* from the ability to have higher emissions than Firm B loses in having to reduce its emissions. Therefore, on net, using a standard to achieve the desired emissions level gives us higher costs. The emissions tax has not only reduced emissions as firms face the true price of those emissions, but it has also done so at minimum cost by encouraging firms with the lower benefits from polluting to do less of it relative to other firms.

The control of carbon emissions is one area in which many economists have argued strongly for the use of a tax, though we have not yet seen one at the federal level. Carbon emissions come from many different industries and consumers, with different marginal social benefit curves. Automobiles and airplanes create considerable emissions; power plants also emit considerable carbon. Moreover, each of these actors has multiple ways to reduce emissions, from fuel choice to filters to technology choice. As we have seen, with big differences in marginal benefit curves taxes can achieve the same results as standards but at lower costs. The *Economics in Practice* box on the next page describes the carbon taxes that some firms have begun to impose on their own divisions to improve their environmental performance.

Measuring Social Costs   To use taxes and subsidies, social costs from externalities must be estimated in financial terms. For the detergent plant polluting the nearby river to be properly taxed, the government must evaluate the costs done to residents downstream in money terms. This evaluation is difficult but not impossible. When legal remedies are pursued, judges are forced to make such estimates as they decide on compensation to be paid. Surveys of "willingness to pay," studies of property values in affected versus nonaffected areas, and sometimes the market value of recreational activities can provide basic data.[4]

In the case of some externalities, social costs involve health problems or loss of life. Here, monetary costs are more difficult to estimate. Nevertheless, in many settings policy makers make judgments that implicitly set values on life and health. In making choices about traffic safety or occupational hazards, government agencies routinely put a dollar value on lives. As individuals, when we decide the risks to take, we too are implicitly valuing our health and lives.

Subsidizing External Benefits   Sometimes activities or decisions generate external benefits instead of costs, as in the LoJack example. Investors who revitalize a downtown area—an old theater district in a big city, for example—provide benefits to many people, both in the city and in surrounding areas.

Activities that provide such external social benefits may be subsidized at the margin to give decision makers an incentive to consider them. Just as ignoring social costs can lead to inefficient decisions, so too can ignoring social benefits. Government subsidies for housing and other development, either directly through specific expenditure programs or indirectly through tax exemptions, have been justified on such grounds.

Tradeable Emissions Permits: Selling or Auctioning Pollution Rights   As we have
seen, the right to impose environmental externalities is beneficial to the parties causing the external costs. In a sense, the right to dump in a river or to pollute the air or the ocean is a valuable resource as it permits a firm to produce its goods and avoid any costs of cleanup. Thinking of the

---

[4] Kenneth Arrow et al., "Report of the NOAA Panel on Contingent Valuations," January 1993.

ECONOMICS IN PRACTICE

Imposing Internal Carbon Prices

As we have seen in this chapter, many economists favor the use of carbon prices to reflect the social cost of carbon emissions on the environment. Although we do not yet have a nationwide tax on carbon, we have seen a number of organizations using their own internal carbon "taxes" to change the behavior of their workers.

Walt Disney and Microsoft are two of the leaders among U.S. companies in using carbon taxes. As you likely know, Disney runs a number of parks and also has a sizeable fleet of cruise ships. The potential for carbon emissions from these businesses is large, especially from the cruise ships, which use a good deal of fuel. Beginning in 2009, Disney decided to try to make its own executives more sensitive to the way their decisions affected carbon emissions by imposing an internal carbon fee. For a range of corporate activities and investments, carbon emissions were calculated and then a division running an operation or planning an investment was charged by the center for the carbon their operations or investments produced. This fee increased the perceived costs to those decision makers of high-carbon-emission choices and made those emissions much more salient to these executives. Next time you visit a Disney park, pay attention to the trains. Many of them are run using vegetable oil recycled from the Disney kitchens.

Microsoft similarly uses internal carbon prices. For the Microsoft executives one major source of carbon emissions is air travel. It is now Microsoft practice to charge divisions carbon fees for the trips taken by their executives. The clear hope is that these fees will incentivize executives to substitute video meetings for in-person meetings when possible.

There are a number of universities that are also experimenting with the use of internal carbon fees to make both students and faculty more aware of the social costs of carbon. Yale University is one of these universities.

A key question in the use of these internal fees is what price to use. A number of agencies in the federal government, including the Environmental Protection Agency, use the social cost of carbon as their fee. In 2015, at a 3 percent discount rate, that price was $39 per ton of carbon when they consider the costs of various policies.

THINKING PRACTICALLY

1. Why might the social cost of capital be a good carbon fee to use from an economic efficiency perspective?

privilege to dump in this way suggests an alternative mechanism for controlling pollution: selling or auctioning the pollution rights to the highest bidder. The Clean Air Act of 1990 takes this cap-and-trade approach to controlling the emissions from our nation's power plants. Emissions related to acid rain from each plant are capped; that is, emissions are limited to a specified level. The lower the level specified, the more air quality will improve. The plant is issued a permit allowing it to emit only at that level. This permit can be used or can be traded to another firm in what has developed into a large auction market. For a firm with low costs of abating pollution, it is often in the firm's best interest to cut back below its permit levels and sell its unused permits to a firm with higher abatement costs. In this way, the given level of emissions chosen by the government will be achieved at the lowest possible costs as a result of market trades. Environmentalists can also buy up permits and leave them unused, resulting in improvements in air quality beyond what the government mandated. These cap-and-trade programs are being used around the world in an attempt to reduce greenhouse gases responsible for global warming.

A simple example will help illustrate the potential gains from a cap-and-trade system, picking up from the two firm example we discussed previously but using a bit of arithmetic. Table 16.1 shows the situation facing the two polluting firms. Assume that each firm emits 5 units of pollution per period and the government wants to reduce the total amount of pollution from the

TABLE 16.1 Permit Trading					
Firm A	Firm A	Firm A	Firm B	Firm B	Firm B
Reduction of pollution by Firm A (in units of pollution)	MC of reducing pollution for Firm A	TC of reducing pollution for Firm A	Reduction of pollution by Firm B (in units of pollution)	MC of reducing pollution for Firm B	TC of reducing pollution for Firm B
1	$ 5	$ 5	1	$ 8	$ 8
2	7	12	2	14	22
3	9	21	3	23	45
4	12	33	4	35	80
5	17	50	5	50	130

current level of 10 to 4. To do this, the government caps each firm's allowed pollution level at 2. Thus, each firm must pay to cut its pollution levels by 3 units. The process of reducing pollution is sometimes called *pollution abatement*. The table shows the marginal cost of abatement for each firm and the total costs. (In our language, the marginal cost of abatement is just the marginal benefit to the firm of not abating). For Firm A, for example, the first unit of pollution reduced or abated costs only $5. So the marginal benefit from being allowed to pollute is $5. As the firm tries to abate more pollution, doing so becomes more costly; the marginal costs of reducing pollution rise. If Firm A wants to reduce its pollution levels from 5 units to 2, as the government requires, it must spend $21, $5 for the first unit, $7 for the second unit, and $9 for the third unit. Firm B finds reducing pollution to be more expensive. If it tries to reduce pollution by 3 units, it will have costs of $45. A cap-and-trade policy gives each of these firms two permits and allows them to trade permits if they so choose. What will the firms want to do?

Firm A can reduce its emissions from 2 units to 1 unit by spending $12 more on abatement. It would then have a permit to sell to Firm B. How much would Firm B be willing to pay for this permit? At the moment, the firm is abating 3 units, and the marginal cost of that third unit is $23. This tells us that Firm B would be willing to pay up to $23 to buy a permit to allow it to continue polluting up to a level of 3. So there is room for a deal. Indeed, the permit price will be somewhere between the $12 demanded by Firm A and the $23 that Firm B is willing to spend. Because Firm A's marginal costs of abatement are lower than Firm B's, we expect Firm A to do more abatement and sell its extra permit to B. You should be able to see from the numbers that Firm A will not sell its last permit to B. To abate another unit, Firm A would have marginal costs of $17. To avoid abatement, however, Firm B would pay only $14. There is no room for a deal. Once the trade of one permit by A to B has occurred, there are still only 4 units of pollution, but now Firm A is emitting 1 unit and Firm B is emitting 3 units. What are the total costs of this pollution reduction? When both firms were reducing their emission levels equally, the total costs were $21 for Firm A and $45 for Firm B, for a total of $66. Now costs are $33 for A and $22 for B, for a total of $55. (Of course, A will also be receiving a payment for the permit.)

Europe implemented the world's first mandatory trading scheme for carbon dioxide emissions in 2005 in response to its concern for global warming. Carbon dioxide emissions are a major source of global warming. The first phase of the plan, which was over at the end of 2007, involved around 12,000 factories and other facilities. The participating firms were oil refineries; power generation facilities; and glass, steel, ceramics, lime, paper, and chemical factories. These 12,000 plants represented 45 percent of total European Union (EU) emissions. The EU set an absolute cap on carbon dioxide emissions and then allocated allowances to governments. The nations in turn distributed the allowances to the separate plants. In the second phase from 2008 through 2012, a number of large sectors were added, including agriculture and petrochemicals.

In both the United States and Europe, the allowances are given out to the selected plants free of charge even though the allowances will trade at a high price once they are distributed. Many are now questioning whether the government should sell them in the market or collect a fee from the firms. As it is, many of the firms that receive the allocations get a huge windfall. During the second phase in Europe, the governments are allowed to auction more than 10 percent of the allowances issued.

ECONOMICS IN PRACTICE

Emissions and Electricity Prices

The cap-and-trade program introduced in Europe and described in the text effectively resulted in a price for carbon in Europe, thus increasing the costs for carbon-producing firms. Electricity firms are among the largest of the carbon producers, and one might therefore expect increases in electricity prices to be a result. A recent study with Spanish data provides some evidence on this.

We can use the supply and demand analysis we have already learned to look at this question from a theoretical perspective. The carbon tax increases the marginal costs of electricity producers. Thus, the supply curve for the electricity market is shifted upward to the left. With stable demand, we would expect prices to rise for electricity. The question is by how much. And, we already know the answer to that as well: It depends on the elasticity of supply and demand!

Fortunately, our researchers were able to use excellent data from Spain to estimate quite precisely the marginal costs for the electricity market. They also know a good deal about the structure of the Spanish market, so that the firm interactions in this oligopoly market could also be modeled well. In this market, Fabra and Mar found almost a complete pass through: for a one Euro cost increase, electricity prices rose by 0.86 Euros. This is a high pass through and likely comes from two features of this market: quite inelastic aggregate demand for electricity and the fact that all firms faced similar cost increases, so that the firms had little incentive to compete by altering markups.

THINKING PRACTICALLY

1. What do you think would have happened to pass through if the largest of the electricity providers had been heavily invested in solar power, which does not produce carbon?

Natalia Fabra and Mar Reguant, "Pass-Through of Emissions Costs in Electricity Markets," *American Economic Review*, September, 2014, 2872–2899.

Another example of selling externality rights comes from Singapore, where the right to buy a car is auctioned each year. Despite high taxes and the need for permits to drive in downtown areas, the roads in Singapore have become congested. The government decided to limit the number of new cars on the road because the external costs associated with them (congestion and pollution) were becoming high. With these limits imposed, the decision was made to distribute car ownership rights to those who place the highest value on them. It seems likely that taxi drivers, trucking companies, bus lines, and traveling salespeople will buy the licenses; families who drive for convenience instead of taking public transportation will find the licenses too expensive. Congestion and pollution are not the only externalities that Singapore takes seriously: In 2005 the fine for littering was as high as $1,000; for failing to flush a public toilet, more than $100; and for eating on a subway, $300.

Public (Social) Goods

16.2 LEARNING OBJECTIVE

Another source of market failure lies in **public goods**, often called **social *or* collective goods**. Public goods are defined by two closely related characteristics: They are nonrival in consumption, and their benefits are nonexcludable. As we will see, these goods represent a market failure because they have characteristics that make it difficult for the private sector to produce them profitably. In an unregulated market economy with no government to see that they are produced, public goods would at best be produced in insufficient quantity and at worst not produced at all.

Discuss the characteristics and provision of public goods.

public goods (social *or* collective goods) Goods that are nonrival in consumption and their benefits are nonexcludable.

The Characteristics of Public Goods

nonrival in consumption A characteristic of public goods: One person's enjoyment of the benefits of a public good does not interfere with another's consumption of it.

A good is **nonrival in consumption** when A's consumption of it does not interfere with B's consumption of it. This means that the benefits of the goods are collective; they accrue to everyone. National defense, for instance, benefits us all. The fact that I am protected in no way detracts from the fact that you are protected; every citizen is protected just as much as every other citizen. If the air is cleaned up, my breathing that air does not interfere with your breathing it, and (under ordinary circumstances) that air is not used up as more people breathe it. Private goods, in contrast, are *rival in consumption*. If I eat a hamburger, you cannot eat it too.

Goods can sometimes generate collective benefits and still be rival in consumption. This happens when crowding occurs. A park or a pool can accommodate many people at the same time, generating collective benefits for everyone. However, when too many people crowd in on a hot day, they begin to interfere with each other's enjoyment.

nonexcludable A characteristic of public goods: Once a good is produced, no one can be excluded from enjoying its benefits.

Public goods are also **nonexcludable**. Once the good is produced, people cannot be excluded for any reason from enjoying its benefits. Once a national defense system is established, it protects everyone.

Before we go on, it is important to note that goods are either public or private by virtue of their characteristics (nonrival and nonexcludable) and *not* by virtue of whether they are produced by the public sector. If the government decided to make it a law that hamburgers were an entitlement (that is, all people could have all the hamburgers they wanted at government expense), that decision would not make hamburgers into public goods. It is an example of the government's providing a private good free of charge to all. The government's decision not to exercise the power to exclude doesn't change the nature of a hamburger.

The real problem with public goods is that private producers may simply not have any incentive to produce them or to produce the right amount. For a private profit-making firm to produce a good and make a profit, it must be able to withhold that good from those who do not pay. McDonald's can make money selling chicken sandwiches only because customers do not get the chicken sandwich unless they pay for it first. If payment were optional, McDonald's would not be in business for long.

Consider an entrepreneur who decides to offer better police protection to the city of Metropolis. Careful (and we assume correct) market research reveals that the citizens of Metropolis want high-quality protection and are willing to pay for it. Not everyone is willing to pay the same amount. Some can afford more, others less. People also have different preferences and different feelings about risk. Our entrepreneur hires a sales force and begins to sell his service. Soon he encounters a problem. Because his company is private, payment is optional. He cannot force anyone to pay. Payment for a hamburger is voluntary too, but a hamburger can be withheld for nonpayment. The good that our new firm is selling, however, is by nature a public good.

free-rider problem A problem intrinsic to public goods: Because people can enjoy the benefits of public goods whether or not they pay for them, they are usually unwilling to pay for them.

As a potential consumer of a public good, you face a dilemma. You want more police protection, and let us say that you are even willing to pay $50 a month for it. But nothing is contingent on your payment. First, if the good is produced, the crime rate falls and all residents benefit. You get that benefit whether or not you pay for it. You get a free ride. That is why this dilemma is called the **free-rider problem**. Second, your payment is small relative to the amount that must be collected to provide the service. Thus, the amount of police protection actually produced will not be significantly affected by how much you contribute or whether you contribute at all. This is the **drop-in-the-bucket problem**. Consumers acting in their own self-interest have no incentive to contribute voluntarily to the production of public goods. Some will feel a moral responsibility or social pressure to contribute, and those people indeed may do so. Nevertheless, the economic incentive is missing, and most people do not find room in their budgets for many voluntary payments. The public goods problem can also be thought of as a large-number, prisoners' dilemma game theory problem. (For a full discussion, see Chapter 14.)

drop-in-the-bucket problem A problem intrinsic to public goods: The good or service is usually so costly that its provision generally does not depend on whether any single person pays.

Public Provision of Public Goods

All societies, past and present, have had to face the problem of providing public goods. When members of society get together to form a government, they do so to provide themselves with goods and services that will not be provided if they act separately. Like any other good or service, a body of laws (or system of justice) is produced with labor, capital, and other inputs. Law and the courts yield social benefits, and they must be set up and administered by some sort of collective, cooperative effort.

Notice that we are talking about public *provision*, not public *production*. Once the government decides what service it wants to provide, it often contracts with the private sector to produce the good. Much of the material for national defense is produced by private defense contractors. Highways, government offices, data processing services, and so on, are usually produced by private firms.

One of the immediate problems of public provision is that it frequently leads to public dissatisfaction. It is easy to be angry at government. Part, but certainly not all, of the reason for this dissatisfaction lies in the nature of the goods that government provides. Firms that produce or sell private goods post a price—we can choose to buy any quantity we want, or we can walk away with nothing. It makes no sense to get angry at a shoe store because no one can force you to shop there.

You cannot shop for collectively beneficial public goods. When it comes to national defense, the government must choose one and only one kind and quantity of (collective) output to produce. Because none of us can choose how much should be spent or what it should be spent on, most of us are dissatisfied. Even if the government does its job with reasonable efficiency, at any given time, about half of us think we have too much national defense and about half of us think we have too little.

Optimal Provision of Public Goods

In the early 1950s, economist Paul Samuelson, building on the work of Richard Musgrave, demonstrated that there exists an *optimal*, or a *most efficient*, level of output for every public good. The discussion of the Samuelson and Musgrave solution that follows leads us straight to the thorny problem of how societies, as opposed to individuals, make choices.

The Samuelson–Musgrave Theory An efficient economy produces what people want. Private producers, whether perfect competitors or monopolists, are constrained by the market demand for their products. If they cannot sell their products for more than it costs to produce them, they will be out of business. Because private goods permit exclusion, firms can withhold their products until households pay. Buying a product at a posted price reveals that it is "worth" at least that amount to you and to everyone who buys it.

Market demand for a private good is the sum of the quantities that each household decides to buy (as measured on the horizontal axis) at each price. The diagrams in Figure 16.4 review the derivation of a market demand curve. Assume that society consists of two people, A and B. At a price of $1, A demands 9 units of the private good and B demands 13. Market demand at a

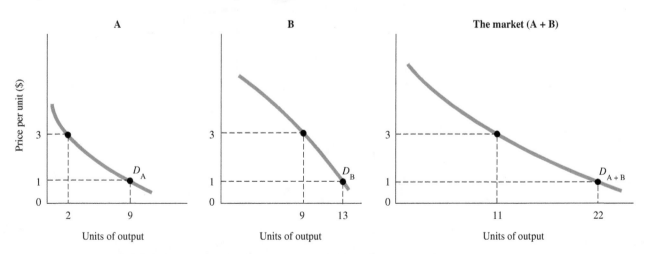

▲ FIGURE 16.4 **With Private Goods, Consumers Decide What Quantity to Buy; Market Demand Is the Sum of Those Quantities at Each Price**
At a price of $3, A buys 2 units and B buys 9 for a total of 11. At a price of $1, A buys 9 units and B buys 13 for a total of 22. We all buy the quantity of each private good that we want. Market demand is the horizontal sum of all individual demand curves.

price of $1 is 22 units. If price were to rise to $3, A's quantity demanded would drop to 2 units and B's would drop to 9 units; market demand at a price of $3 is 2 + 9 = 11 units. The point is that the price mechanism forces people to reveal what they want, and it forces firms to produce only what people are willing to pay for, but it works this way only because exclusion is possible.

People's preferences and demands for public goods are conceptually no different from their preferences and demands for private goods. You may want fire protection and be willing to pay for it in the same way you want to listen to music. To demonstrate that an efficient level of production exists, Samuelson assumes that we know people's preferences. Figure 16.5 shows demand curves for buyers A and B. If the public good were available in the private market at a price of $6, A would buy X_1 units. Put another way, A is willing to pay $6 per unit to obtain X_1 units of the public good. B is willing to pay only $3 per unit to obtain X_1 units of the public good.

Remember, public goods are nonrival or nonexcludable—benefits accrue simultaneously to everyone. One and only one quantity can be produced, and that is the amount that everyone gets. When X_1 units are produced, A gets X_1 and B gets X_1. When X_2 units are produced, A gets X_2 and B gets X_2.

To arrive at market demand for public goods, we do not sum quantities. Instead, *we add the amounts that individual households are willing to pay for each potential level of output.* In Figure 16.5, A is

▶ **FIGURE 16.5** **With Public Goods, There Is Only One Level of Output and Consumers Are Willing to Pay Different Amounts for Each Potential Level**

A is willing to pay $6 per unit for X_1 units of the public good. B is willing to pay only $3 for X_1 units. Society—in this case A and B—is willing to pay a total of $9 for X_1 units of the good. Because only one level of output can be chosen for a public good, we must add A's contribution to B's to determine market demand. This means adding demand curves vertically.

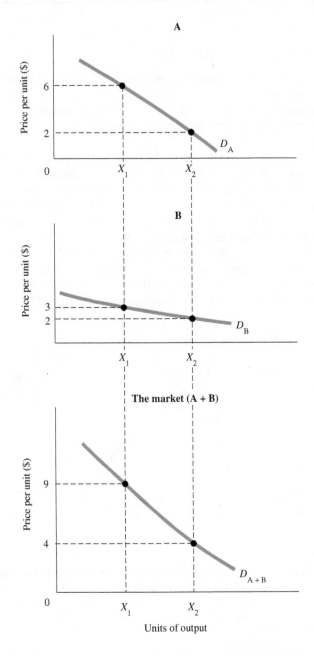

willing to pay $6 per unit for X_1 units and B is willing to pay $3 per unit for X_1 units. Thus, if society consists only of A and B, society is willing to pay $9 per unit for X_1 units of public good X. For X_2 units of output, society is willing to pay a total of $4 per unit.

For private goods, market demand is the horizontal sum of individual demand curves; we add the different *quantities* that households consume (as measured on the *horizontal* axis). For public goods, market demand is the vertical sum of individual demand curves—we add the different *amounts* that households are willing to pay to obtain each level of output (as measured on the *vertical* axis).

Samuelson argued that once we know how much society is willing to pay for a public good, we need only compare that amount to the cost of its production. Figure 16.6 reproduces A's and B's demand curves and the total demand curve for the public good. As long as society (in this case, A and B) is willing to pay more than the marginal cost of production, the good should be produced. If A is willing to pay $6 per unit of public good and B is willing to pay $3 per unit, society is willing to pay $9.

Given the MC curve as drawn in Figure 16.6, the efficient level of output is X_1 units. If at that level A is charged a fee of $6 per unit of X produced and B is charged a fee of $3 per unit of X, everyone should be happy. Resources are being drawn from the production of other goods and services only to the extent that people want the public good and are willing to pay for it. We have arrived at the **optimal level of provision for public goods**. At the optimal level, society's total willingness to pay per unit is equal to the marginal cost of producing the good.

The Problems of Optimal Provision One major problem exists, however. To produce the optimal amount of each public good, the government must know something that it cannot possibly know—everyone's preferences. Because exclusion is impossible, nothing forces households to reveal their preferences. Furthermore, if we ask households directly about their willingness to pay, we run up against the same problem encountered by our protection-services salesperson mentioned previously. If your actual payment depends on your answer, you have an incentive to hide your true feelings. Knowing that you cannot be excluded from enjoying the benefits of the good and that your payment is not likely to have an appreciable influence on the level of output finally produced, what incentive do you have to tell the truth—or to contribute?

How does society decide which public goods to provide? We assume that members of society want certain public goods. Private producers in the market cannot make a profit by producing these goods, and the government cannot obtain enough information to measure society's demands accurately. No two societies have dealt with this dilemma in the same way. In some countries, dictators simply decide for the people. In other countries, representative political bodies speak for the people's preferences. In still other countries, people vote directly. None of these solutions works perfectly.

optimal level of provision for public goods The level at which society's total willingness to pay per unit is equal to the marginal cost of producing the good.

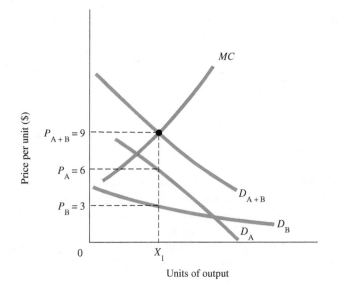

◀ **FIGURE 16.6**
Optimal Production of a Public Good
Optimal production of a public good means producing as long as society's total willingness to pay per unit (D_{A+B}) is greater than the marginal cost of producing the good.

Local Provision of Public Goods: Tiebout Hypothesis

In 1956, economist Charles Tiebout made this point: To the extent that local governments are responsible for providing public goods, an efficient market-choice mechanism may exist. Consider a set of towns that are identical except for police protection. Towns that choose to spend a great deal of money on police are likely to have a lower crime rate. A lower crime rate will attract households who are risk-averse and who are willing to pay higher taxes for a lower risk of being a crime victim. Those who are willing to bear greater risk or have fewer resources may choose to live in the low-tax/high-crime towns. Also, if some town is efficient at crime prevention, it will attract residents—given that each town has limited space, property values will be bid up in this town. The higher home price in this town is the "price" of the lower crime rate.

According to the **Tiebout hypothesis**, an efficient mix of public goods is produced when local prices (in the form of taxes or higher housing costs) come to reflect consumer preferences just as they do in the market for private goods. What is different in the Tiebout world is that people exercise consumer sovereignty not by "buying" different combinations of goods in a market, but by "voting with their feet" (choosing among bundles of public goods and tax rates produced by different towns and participating in local government).

Tiebout hypothesis An efficient mix of public goods is produced when local land/housing prices and taxes come to reflect consumer preferences just as they do in the market for private goods.

Understand why the market undersupplies common resources.

Common Resources

In the seventeenth century and previously in England, many villages had large common green areas in which villagers grazed their sheep. The areas were unowned, but in some sense held in common, and indeed these areas were called commons. Some of you may have learned about the enclosure movement in which many of these common areas were privatized and common grazing eliminated.

In most parts of the world, the open sea, beyond territorial limits around individual countries, is currently common area, available and open to all to fish, subject to a handful of international fishing rules. Like the original grazing grounds, the sea has no owner. Economists refer to areas like the commons and fishing grounds as **common resources**. Common resources, like public goods, are nonexcludeable. One cannot keep someone from setting out a fishing line in open sea, nor from sending their sheep to graze in the common pasture. But, in contrast to public goods, the consumption of a common resource by one person has an effect on the availability of that resource to others. If I catch too many fish, the population will suffer and there will be none left for future generations. If I breed too many sheep, the grass will not regenerate and your sheep will starve.

common resource A resource that is nonexcludeable but rival in consumption.

Economists have worried for a long time about the management of commons. Of central concern is overuse. Suppose I own a lake stocked with fish. If I overfish it and there are not enough fish to reproduce, I suffer the consequences. My children and I lose the pleasure of fishing and my lake loses value. To a large extent, I have the right incentives to protect my fish stock. If I overfish, I alone bear the consequences. But if we all own the lake in common, as a community, then when I fish too much, we share the costs, while I get all the benefits of catching more fish. It should not surprise you to learn that, under these conditions, overuse is common.

When is overuse most problematic? In agrarian England, there is some evidence of overgrazing of the commons, especially in larger villages. But not all commons are overused. In some communities, both grazing and fishing are controlled by custom and mutual forbearance. If there is low productivity in extraction methods, overuse is also less of a problem. But where a common resource is shared by many, and technology is well developed, overuse is more likely. In modern times, overfishing of the sea is a problem that worries many policy makers.

As with externalities, there are several policy instruments we can use to control overuse of a commons. Standards are common; there are in most areas times of the year one cannot fish and limits on the size of fish that can be landed. Taxes are also common, typically levied by limiting and charging for fishing licenses. For some commons problems, a solution is found by privatizing the resource, as England did in the enclosure movement. If a common area is turned into a private resource, the owner will have incentives for using that resource efficiently.

— SUMMARY —

16.1 EXTERNALITIES AND ENVIRONMENTAL ECONOMICS *p. 327*

1. Often when we engage in transactions or make economic decisions, second or third parties suffer consequences that decision makers have no incentive to consider. These are called *externalities*. A classic example of an external cost is pollution.

2. When external costs are not considered in economic decisions, we may engage in activities or produce products that are not "worth it." When external benefits are not considered, we may fail to do things that are indeed "worth it." The result is an inefficient allocation of resources.

3. A number of alternative mechanisms have been used to control externalities: (1) private bargaining and negotitiations, (2) environmental standards, (3) government-imposed taxes and subsidies, and (4) sale or auctioning of rights to impose externalities.

16.2 PUBLIC (SOCIAL) GOODS *p. 339*

4. In an unfettered market, certain goods and services that people want will not be produced in adequate amounts. These *public goods* have characteristics that make it difficult or impossible for the private sector to produce them profitably.

5. Public goods are *nonrival in consumption* (their benefits fall collectively on members of society or on groups of members), and their benefits are *nonexcludable* (it is generally impossible to exclude people who have not paid from enjoying the benefits of public goods). An example of a public good is national defense.

6. One of the problems of public provision is that it leads to public dissatisfaction. We can choose any quantity of private goods that we want, or we can walk away without buying any. When it comes to public goods such as national defense, the government must choose one and only one kind and quantity of (collective) output to produce.

7. Theoretically, there exists an *optimal level of provision* for each public good. At this level, society's willingness to pay per unit equals the marginal cost of producing the good. To discover such a level, we would need to know the preferences of each individual citizen.

8. According to the *Tiebout hypothesis*, an efficient mix of public goods is produced when local land/housing prices and taxes come to reflect consumer preferences just as they do in the market for private goods.

16.3 COMMON RESOURCES *p. 344*

9. Common resources are nonexcludeable but rival in consumption. A central problem with common resources is overuse.

— REVIEW TERMS AND CONCEPTS —

Coase theorem, *p. 332*

common resource, *p. 344*

drop-in-the-bucket problem, *p. 340*

externality, *p. 327*

free-rider problem, *p. 340*

injunction, *p. 333*

liability rules, *p. 334*

marginal social cost (MSC), *p. 327*

marginal social benefit of pollution, *p. 330*

nonexcludable, *p. 340*

nonrival in consumption, *p. 340*

optimal level of provision for public goods, *p. 343*

public goods (social *or* collective goods), *p. 339*

Tiebout hypothesis, *p. 344*

— PROBLEMS —

All problems are available on MyEconLab.

16.1 EXTERNALITIES AND ENVIRONMENTAL ECONOMICS

LEARNING OBJECTIVE: Understand the market failure associated with externalities and the possible solutions to this set of issues.

1.1 If government imposes on the firms in a polluting industry penalties (taxes) that exceed the actual value of the damages done by the pollution, the result is an inefficient and unfair imposition of costs on those firms and on the consumers of their products. Discuss that statement. Use a graph to show how consumers are harmed.

1.2 [Related to the *Economics in Practice* on p. 337] The kingdom of Freedonia is divided into two countries: East Babalu and West Babalu. In an effort to reduce carbon dioxide emissions, the kingdom has enacted a carbon tax on all electricity providers. In East Babalu, a gloomy country with cloudy skies and rain every day of the year, 90 percent of households rely on electricity to power their homes. In West Babalu, a tropical paradise where the sun shines bright every day, only 10 percent of households get power from electricity providers, with the rest using solar panels to directly power their homes. Use supply and demand curves to

MyEconLab Visit **www.myeconlab.com** to complete these exercises online and get instant feedback. Exercises that update with real-time data are marked with art ⓜ.

show the effect of this carbon tax on the residents of both East Babalu and West Babalu, and explain which country's residents will bear a greater burden of the tax. Assume that all electricity providers in the kingdom of Freedonia will face similar cost increases as a result of the carbon tax.

1.3 Many people are concerned with the problem of urban sprawl. As the development of new housing tracts and suburban shopping malls continues over time, metropolitan areas have become more congested and polluted. Open space disappears, and the quality of life changes. Think of your own metropolitan area, city, or town. Using the concept of externalities, consider the issue of land use and development. What are the specific decisions made in the development process that lead to externalities? On whom are the externalities imposed? Do you think that they are measurable? In what specific ways can decision makers be given the incentive to consider them? One of the cities that has paid the most attention to urban sprawl is Portland, Oregon. Search the Web to see what you can find out about Portland's approach.

1.4 A paper factory dumps polluting chemicals into the Snake River. Thousands of citizens live along the river, and they bring suit, claiming damages. You are asked by the judge to testify at the trial as an impartial expert. The court is considering four possible solutions, and you are asked to comment on the potential efficiency and equity of each. Your testimony should be brief.
   a. Deny the merits of the case and affirm the polluter's right to dump. The parties will achieve the optimal solution without government.
   b. Find in favor of the plaintiff. The polluters will be held liable for damages and must fully compensate citizens for all past and future damages imposed.
   c. Order an immediate end to the dumping, with no damages awarded.
   d. Refer the matter to the Environmental Protection Agency, which will impose a tax on the factory equal to the marginal damage costs. Proceeds will not be paid to the damaged parties.

1.5 **[Related to the *Economics in Practice* on p. 337]** Microsoft and Disney are just two of a growing number of organizations using internal carbon taxes in an attempt to reduce carbon emissions, and the carbon prices being used to set the internal taxes vary widely. (In 2015, Microsoft priced carbon at $6-$7 per metric ton, and Disney used a price of $10 - $20 per metric ton.) Do some research to find three other companies or organizations that have also implemented an internal carbon tax. What are these companies or organizations doing with the revenue from these internal taxes? What price has each assigned to carbon, and how do the prices compare to the social cost of carbon as set by the Environmental Protection Agency?

1.6 The Coase theorem implies that we never need to worry about regulating externalities because the private individuals involved will reach the efficient outcome through negotiations. Is that statement true or false? Justify your answer and use examples.

1.7 **[Related to the *Economics in Practice* on p. 329]** The *Economics in Practice* suggests that economists often distinguish between short-run and long-run effects of policies or actions when adjusting to environmental disasters. Research a recent environmental disaster (such as the New England blizzard in early 2015, Hurricane Sandy in 2012, the 2015 earthquake in Nepal, or the BP oil spill in 2010.) Explain the major environmental impact the disaster had on the affected area, how long you think it will take for the area to recover from the disaster, and why you believe the adjustment to the disaster will take either a relatively short or long time.

1.8 The following diagram represents the profit-maximizing price and output for a firm in a perfectly competitive industry with no externalities. Use this diagram to explain what will happen if the production of the product imposes external costs on society and these costs are not factored into production decisions.

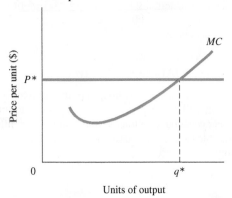

1.9 Refer to the previous question but assume that the government has imposed a per-unit tax on this product that is exactly equal to the marginal damage costs. Use the diagram to show what will happen to production, output, and price.

1.10 Two firms, Vesuvius and Etna, are each emitting 9 units of pollution, and the government wants to reduce the total level of pollution from the current level of 18 to 6. To do this, the government caps each firm's allowed pollution level at 3. Each firm must now pay to cut pollution levels by 6 units. A cap-and-trade policy gives each of these firms three permits and allows them to trade permits if they choose. Based on the table below which represents the situation faced by these two firms, what will the firms want to do?

Vesuvius			Etna		
Pollution Reduction, Units	MC of Reducing Pollution	TC of Reducing Pollution	Pollution Reduction, Units	MC of Reducing Pollution	TC of Reducing Pollution
1	$ 5	$ 5	1	$10	$ 10
2	6	11	2	13	23
3	8	19	3	17	40
4	11	30	4	22	62
5	15	45	5	28	90
6	22	67	6	37	127
7	31	98	7	48	175
8	42	140	8	60	235
9	57	197	9	75	310

1.11 Velma, a book editor for a local publishing company, and Daphne, an opera singer in a local opera company, share a townhouse in Miami. Velma enjoys reading and editing books at home, and Daphne enjoys rehearsing her arias at home. Daphne is willing to pay Velma $200 per week if she will find another place to read and edit books. Velma offers Daphne $240 per week to find someplace else to rehearse. If Daphne has the right to rehearse in her home, explain why the townhouse will be free of aria rehearsals. If Velma has the right to read and edit books in her home, explain why the townhouse will still be free of aria rehearsals.

16.2 PUBLIC (SOCIAL) GOODS

LEARNING OBJECTIVE: Discuss the characteristics and provision of public goods.

2.1 The existence of "public goods" is an example of potential market failure and suggests that a government or public sector can *improve* the outcome of completely free markets. Write a brief summary of the arguments *for* government provision of public goods. (Make sure you consider the discussion of a prisoners' dilemma in Chapter 14.) The following three arguments suggest that government may not improve the outcome as much as we might anticipate.

   a. *Public goods theory:* Because public goods are collective, the government is constrained to pick a single level of output for all of us. National defense is an example. The government must pick one level of defense expenditure. Some will think it is too much, some will think it is too little, and no one is happy.

   b. *Problems of social choice:* It is impossible to choose collectively in a rational way that satisfies voters/consumers of public goods.

   c. *Public choice and public officials:* Once elected or appointed, public officials tend to act in accordance with their own preferences and not out of concern for the public.

   Which of the three arguments do you find to be most persuasive?

2.2 It has been argued that the following are examples of "mixed goods." They are essentially private but partly public. For each example, describe the private and public components and discuss briefly why the government should or should not be involved in their provision.

   a. Public housing
   b. Public transportation
   c. Trash collection
   d. Fire protection

2.3 Explain why you agree or disagree with each of the following statements:

   a. The government should be involved in providing health care for all citizens because health care is a "public good."

   b. From the standpoint of economic efficiency, an unregulated market economy tends to underproduce public goods.

2.4 Society is made up of two individuals, Bert and Ernie, whose demands for public good A are given in Figure 1. Assuming that the public good can be produced at a constant marginal cost of $7, what is the optimal level of output? How much would you charge Bert and Ernie?

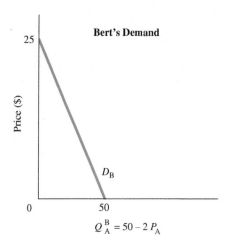

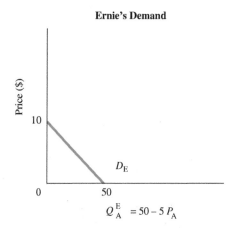

▲ FIGURE 1

2.5 Government involvement in general scientific research has been justified on the grounds that advances in knowledge are public goods—once produced, information can be shared at virtually no cost. A new production technology in an industry could be made available to all firms, reducing costs of production, driving down price, and benefiting the public. The patent system, however, allows private producers of "new knowledge" to exclude others from enjoying the benefits of that knowledge. Inventors would have little incentive to produce new knowledge if there was no possibility of profiting from their inventions. If one company holds exclusive rights to an advanced production process, it produces at lower cost but can use the exclusion to acquire monopoly power and charge the monopoly price.

a. On balance, is the patent system a good or bad thing? Explain.

b. Is government involvement in scientific research a good idea? Discuss.

2.6 The recent economic growth resulting from government policies of newly industrializing nations such as India and China has increased environmental strains on global air and water systems. The negative externalities associated with this economic growth demonstrate that the best economic system is one in which *all* economic decisions are made by individual households and firms without *any* government involvement. Comment briefly.

16.3 COMMON RESOURCES

LEARNING OBJECTIVE: Understand why the market undersupplies common resources.

3.1 The overuse of a common resource is often referred to as the tragedy of the commons, and traffic congestion has been described as a modern example of this problem. Explain how traffic congestion exemplifies the overuse of a common resource, how consumption of that resource affects the availability of that resource to others, and what solution, if any, is possible to alleviate this problem.

Uncertainty and Asymmetric Information

17

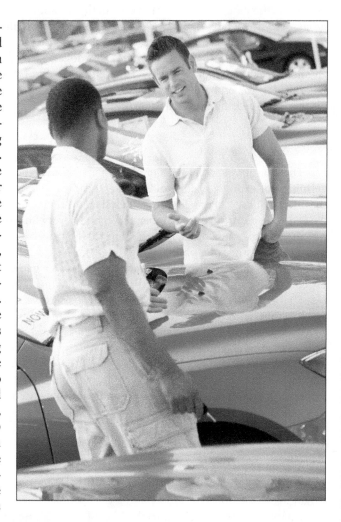

In previous chapters, we assumed that consumers and firms made choices based on perfect information about the qualities of the goods they were choosing among. Under these circumstances, we could interpret their choices as revealing to us their true preferences. Similarly, when firms choose how many workers to hire or how much capital to use, we assumed that they know the productivity of those workers or that capital. Of course, in many settings, perfect information seems to be a reasonable assumption to make. Every day you may choose whether to have cereal or eggs for breakfast. Every evening you may decide what to have for dinner and whether to go to the movies or stay home and study. Even for these choices, a little uncertainty can creep in; perhaps a new cereal is on the market or a new movie has been released. But assuming that these choices are made with perfect information does not seem too far a stretch.

In some markets, however, consumers and firms clearly make decisions with quite limited information. When you decide to insure your car against theft, you don't know whether the car will be stolen. When you decide to buy a used car, it is not easy to figure out how good that car really is. If you are choosing between a sales job that pays a flat salary and one that pays a commission for every sale you make, you have to predict how good your sales skills will be to determine which is the better offer. In many markets, including some important markets, consumers as well as firms make decisions while having only some of the information they need. In this chapter, we will explore the economics of these markets. As we go through this chapter, you will see how both the recent healthcare reform discussion and the 2008–2009 banking crisis can be understood using economic tools.

17.1 LEARNING OBJECTIVE

Define the concepts of expected value and expected utility and how these measures relate to risk attitudes.

Decision Making Under Uncertainty: The Tools

In Chapter 6, we laid out the fundamental principles of consumer choice assuming perfect information. To adapt this model to cases in which there is uncertainty, we need to develop a few more tools.

Expected Value

payoff The amount that comes from a possible outcome or result.

expected value The sum of the payoffs associated with each possible outcome of a situation weighted by its probability of occurring.

Suppose I offer you the following deal: You flip a coin 100 times. Every time the coin is a head, you pay me $1. Whenever the coin lands on tails, I pay you a dollar. We call the amount that one player—in this case, me—receives in each of the situations the **payoff**. Here my payoff is +$1 for heads and −$1 for tails. In the case of a coin toss, the probability of heads is ½, as is the probability of tails. This tells us that the financial value of this deal to me, or its expected value, is $0. Half the time I win a dollar, and half the time I lose a dollar. Formally, we define the **expected value** of an uncertain situation or deal as the sum of the payoffs associated with each possible outcome multiplied by the probability that outcome will occur. Again, in the case of a coin toss with the payoffs described, the expected value (EV) is

$$EV = 1/2(\$1) + 1/2(-\$1) = 0$$

The coin toss is an easy example, in part because there are only two outcomes. But the definition of expected value holds for any deal in which I can describe both the payoffs and the probabilities of all possible outcomes. If I play a game in which I receive $1 every time I roll a die and end up with an even number and I pay $1 every time the die comes up odd, this deal also has an expected value of $0. Half the time (3 of 6 possible outcomes) I receive $1, and half the time (3 of 6 possible outcomes) I pay $1.

fair game *or* fair bet A game whose expected value is zero.

The two games just described are known as **fair games *or* fair bets**. A fair game has an expected value of $0. The expected financial gains from playing a fair game are equal to the financial costs of that game. In the two fair games we described, the stakes are quite low. Suppose instead of $1 payoffs, we made the payoffs $1,000 for heads and −$1,000 for tails. As you can see, the expected value of that deal is $0 just as it was in the $1 game. But we have learned in watching people's behavior that although some people might be willing to play a fair game with $1 payoffs, few people will play $1,000-payoff fair games. What is it about people that makes them change their minds about taking a fair bet when the stakes get high? We will explore this question next using some of the tools already covered in Chapter 6.

Expected Utility

Recall from Chapter 6 that consumers make choices to maximize utility. The idea of maximizing utility will also help us understand the way in which those consumers make choices in risky situations.

diminishing marginal utility The more of any one good consumed in a given period, the less incremental satisfaction is generated by consuming a marginal or incremental unit of the same good.

Chapter 6 introduced you to the idea of **diminishing marginal utility**—the more of any one good consumed in a period, the less incremental satisfaction (utility) will be generated by each additional (marginal) unit of that good. Review Figure 6.3 on p. 119 and notice the form the utility curve takes when we have diminishing marginal utility for a good. The curve flattens as we increase units of the good consumed. Now think about what happens to your utility level when we increase not the number of units of a particular good, but your overall income. Figure 17.1 graphs the total utility of a typical consumer, Jacob, as a function of his income. On the y-axis, we have assigned units of total utility, while on the x-axis we have annual income. The shape of the utility curve tells us that Jacob has diminishing marginal utility from income. The first $20,000 of income is important to Jacob, moving him from a total utility level of 0 to 10; this first $20,000 might allow him to buy food and shelter, for example. Moving from $20,000 to $40,000 brings an increase in well-being from 10 to 15. Notice that the second $20,000 adds 5 to the total utility level, whereas the first $20,000

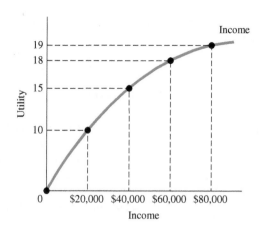

◀ FIGURE 17.1 **The Relationship Between Utility and Income**
The figure shows the way in which utility increases with income for a hypothetical person, Jacob. Notice that utility increases with income but at a decreasing rate: the curve gets flatter as income increases. This curve shows diminishing marginal utility of income.

adds 10. And the pattern continues as we add $20,000 increments to income. Each dollar increases total utility, but at a decreasing rate. The result is a curve as shown in Figure 17.1 that flattens as we move from left to right, with smaller gains in total utility from equal gains in income.

You should see that the assumption of diminishing marginal utility of income reflects the diminishing marginal utility of goods that we talked about in Chapter 6. Income counts for less the more we have because the value of what we can buy with that money on the margin falls as we buy more.

As you think about Figure 17.1, remember that we are describing the relationship between utility and income for a *given individual*. The figure does not tell us that rich people get less utility from an incremental dollar than do poor people. Indeed, it might be argued that one reason some rich people work so hard to make money is that they get a great deal of utility from increases in income relative to the average person. But rich or poor, Figure 17.1 tells us that as your income increases, the marginal utility of another dollar falls.

How does Figure 17.1 help us explain people's unwillingness to play fair games with larger stakes? Suppose Jacob, the individual whose preferences are shown in Figure 17.1, is currently earning $40,000. We see that $40,000 corresponds to a total utility level of 15. Now a firm offers Jacob a different type of salary structure. Rather than earning $40,000 for sure, at the end of the year, a manager will toss a coin. If it is heads, Jacob will earn $60,000; but if the coin turns up tails, his earnings will fall to $20,000. This is a high stakes game of the sort described previously. Notice that the expected value of the two salaries is the same. With one, Jacob earns $40,000 with certainty. With the second, he earns $20,000 half the time and $60,000 half the time, for an expected value of

$$EV = 1/2 (\$20,000) + 1/2 (\$60,000) = \$40,000$$

From an expected value perspective, the two salary offers are identical. So if we simply looked at the expected values, we might expect Jacob to be indifferent between the two wage offers. But if you put yourself in Jacob's shoes, probably you would not find the coin-tossing salary to be as attractive as the fixed $40,000 wage. If we think back to the model introduced in Chapter 6, we can see why. Consumers make choices not to maximize income per se but to maximize their utility levels. Figure 17.1 tells us that although utility increases with income, the relationship is not linear. So to decide what Jacob will do, we need to look at his utility under the two contracts.

What can we say about Jacob's utility under the two salary contracts? With a fixed $40,000 salary, total utility is at a level of 15, as we saw previously. If his income falls to $20,000, that utility level falls from 15 to 10, a substantial drop. With a possible earnings level of $60,000, the total utility level goes up; but notice that it only increases from 15 to 18. The drop in income causes a bigger loss in utility than comes from a gain in income. Of course, this results from the diminishing marginal utility of income. In fact, we can define **expected utility** as the sum of the utilities coming from all possible outcomes of a deal, weighted by the probability of each occurring. You can see that the expected utility is like the expected value, but the payoffs

expected utility The sum of the utilities coming from all possible outcomes of a deal, weighted by the probability of each occurring.

are in utility terms rather than in dollars. In the coin-toss salary offer, if you look again at Figure 17.1, the expected utility (EU) is

$$EU = 1/2\,U(\$20{,}000) + 1/2\,U(60{,}000), \text{ which reduces to}$$

$$EU = 1/2\,(10) + 1/2\,(18) = 14$$

Because Jacob's utility from a fixed salary of $40,000 is 15, he will not take the coin-toss salary alternative.

Of course, in practice, workers are not paid wages based on the toss of a coin. Nevertheless, many wage contracts contain some uncertainty. Many of you have probably had jobs where your wages were uncertain in ways you could not control. Understanding the difference between expected value maximization and expected utility maximization helps us understand these job contracts.

In uncertain situations, consumers make choices to maximize their expected utility. Looking at Figure 17.1, you should now see why people may take small fair bets but will avoid fair games with high stakes. For small games, both alternatives lie within a small region of the utility curve. The utility of gaining one more dollar or losing it is almost identical. When we compare outcomes at different points on the utility curve, the differences in marginal utility become more pronounced. This makes large fair bets quite unattractive. The prospect of losing and moving down the marginal utility (MU) curve is much more troublesome to you than the prospect of moving up the curve is pleasurable.

Attitudes Toward Risk

risk-averse   Refers to a person's preference of a certain payoff over an uncertain one with the same expected value.

risk-neutral   Refers to a person's willingness to take a bet with an expected value of zero.

risk-loving   Refers to a person's willingness to take bets with negative expected values.

We have now seen that diminishing marginal utility of income means that the typical individual will not play a large stakes fair game. Individuals, like Jacob, who prefer a certain payoff to an uncertain payoff with an equal expected value are called **risk-averse**. Risk aversion thus comes from the assumption of diminishing marginal utility of income and can be seen in the shape of the utility curve. You are unwilling to take a risk because the costs of losing in terms of your well-being or utility exceed the gains of possibly winning. People who are willing to take a fair bet, one that has an expected value of zero, are known as **risk-neutral**. For these individuals, the marginal utility of income is constant so that the relationship between total utility and income in a graph like Figure 17.1, for example, would be a straight, upward-sloping line. Again, we have seen that some people will be risk-neutral when the stakes are low. Finally, some people, in some circumstances, may actually prefer uncertain games to certain outcomes. Individuals who pay to play a game with an expected value of zero *or less* are known as **risk-loving**. Since most people are risk-averse in most situations, we will concentrate on this case.

The fact that people are, in general, risk-averse is seen in many markets. Most people who own houses buy fire insurance even when not required to do so. In general, a fire insurance policy costs a homeowner more than it is worth in terms of expected value; this is how insurance companies make money. People pay for this insurance because they are risk-averse: The possible loss of their home is important relative to the value of the premiums they have to pay to protect it. When people invest in a risky business, there has to be some chance that they will "make it big" to induce them to put up their money. The riskier the business in the sense that it may fail, the bigger the upside potential needs to be. This too is an indication of risk aversion. The presence of risk and uncertainty do not by themselves pose a problem for the workings of the market. The risk that your house might burn down does not prevent you from buying a house; it simply encourages you, if you are risk-averse, to buy insurance. In fact, many markets are designed to allow people to trade risk. Individuals who are risk-averse seek out other individuals (or more commonly firms) who are willing to take on those risks for a price.

What is the maximum price a risk-averse person will pay to avoid taking a risk? Figure 17.2 gives us another look at the same individual, Jacob, we examined in Figure 17.1. Suppose Jacob is currently earning $40,000 but faces a 50 percent chance of suffering an unpreventable disability that will reduce his income level to $0. Thus, the expected value of Jacob's income is

$$EV = 1/2(\$40{,}000) + 1/2(\$0) = \$20{,}000$$

Suppose further that there are many individuals just like Jacob. On average, in any year, half would become disabled and half would not. If an insurance company offered policies to all of them, offering to replace their $40,000 salaries should they become disabled, on average, this policy would cost the company $20,000 per person. In other words, the expected value tells us what, on average, it would cost a firm that pooled large numbers of identical people to offer them insurance against an income loss of this size. If the individuals are willing to pay the insurance company more than this expected value, there is a potential deal to be made. In fact, looking at Figure 17.2 shows us that the deal offered by the insurance company to cover earnings losses in the case of a disability is worth more than $20,000 to a risk-averse individual like Jacob. Uninsured, Jacob faces a 50 percent chance of earning $0 and a 50 percent chance of earning $40,000. Looking at the graph, we see that the expected utility of Jacob in his uninsured state is

$$EU = 1/2\,U(\$0) + 1/2\,U(\$40,000)$$
$$EU = 1/2(0) + 1/2(15) = 7.5$$

But a utility level of 7.5 corresponds, as we look at Figure 17.2, to a certain income level of x, which is below the $20,000 level. In other words, Jacob would be indifferent between a certain income of $x and remaining uninsured. But because $x is less than $20,000, we know that Jacob is willing to pay a premium to avoid this disability risk. So there is room for a deal between the insurance company and risk-averse individuals. Because insurance companies can pool risks across many different people, they will be risk-neutral, willing to take on the risks of individuals for a price. In this example, the distance between $20,000, the expected value of the risk, and $x tells us the bargaining range between Jacob and the insurers.

You may now be wondering how economists explain gambling. Every day people throughout the United States buy lottery tickets even though they know that lotteries are not a fair bet. The Powerball lottery in Connecticut is one example. The winning number is generated by choosing 5 numbers out of a pool of 59, then choosing another number from a pool of 35. The probability of getting all 6 numbers correct and winning the lottery's top prize is 1 in 175 million. The top prize in the lottery varies but is typically in the $10 million to $150 million range. The prize is taxable, and winning the top prize would push a winner into the top tax bracket with a tax rate of almost 40 percent. When the prize level is high, many people play the lottery and there is a risk of multiple winners, with prize sharing. Thus, in all cases, the expected value of the typical lottery is highly negative. Playing the slots at a casino also has a negative expected value, as do all professional games of chance. If this were not true, casinos would go out of business and the state would not make money from its lottery. Nevertheless, individuals buy lottery tickets and gamble in a range of forms. One explanation for this risk-taking behavior may, of course, be that some people find gambling fun and gamble not just in the hopes of winning but for the experience. For other people, gambling may be an addiction. Trying to understand more fully why people gamble while they seem to be risk-averse in most other ways remains an interesting research area in economics.

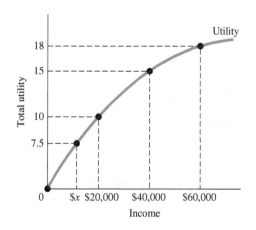

◀ FIGURE 17.2   **Risk Aversion and Insurance Markets**

With a 50 percent chance of earning $40,000 and a 50 percent chance of becoming disabled and earning $0, Jacob has an EV of income of $20,000. But his expected utility is halfway between the utility of $40,000 (15) and the utility of 0 (0), or 7.5. $x is the amount of certain earnings Jacob would accept to avoid a 50 percent chance of earning $0.

Asymmetric Information

In the discussion so far, we have described the way people behave in situations in which everyone involved in the deal is equally uncertain. Again, the coin toss is a classic case. When you offer me a coin toss game, neither you nor I know how the coin will fall. Unless you have somehow fixed the coin, it is an unknowable game of chance. In these situations, we have seen how to use the idea of expected utility to understand choices and we have seen how markets arise to enable risk trading. In other situations, though, the playing field may be less even, with one party to the transaction having more information relevant to the transaction than the other party. Economists refer to these circumstances as ones of **asymmetric information**. Asymmetric information creates possibilities of market failure by making it harder for individuals to make deals that would otherwise be attractive.

asymmetric information One of the parties to a transaction has information relevant to the transaction that the other party does not have.

We are surrounded by situations with asymmetric information. A homeowner has better information than does his or her insurance company about how careful his or her family is, how often family members use candles, and whether anyone smokes. All of these factors are important to an insurance company trying to set an insurance price. When you applied to college, you likely knew more about your work ethic than did the colleges to which you applied.

In this section, we will explore several classic types of asymmetric situations. We will look at the nature of the market failure that arises when we have asymmetric information, and we will consider some of the mechanisms that individuals and markets use to deal with these problems.

Adverse Selection

A common saying in the car market is that once you drive a new car off the lot, it loses a substantial part of its original value. Why might this be true? Physical depreciation is likely small after only a few miles, for example. The answer can be found in the theory of adverse selection, a theory whose development was cited by the Nobel Committee in its award to George Akerlof in 2001. **Adverse selection** is a category of asymmetric information problems. In adverse selection, the quality of what is being offered in a transaction matters and is not easily demonstrated. For example, consumers might be willing to pay for high-quality used cars. But it is hard to tell which cars are good and which cars are not, and sellers will not, in general, have an incentive to be completely truthful. Insurance companies might be willing to offer inexpensive health insurance to people who take good care of themselves. But it is not easy to figure out who those people are, and insurance buyers are not likely to want to tell the company about their bad habits. As we will see, under these conditions, high-quality products and high-quality consumers are often squeezed out of markets, giving rise to the term *adverse selection*. In the *Economics in Practice* on page 356, we will explore some issues in adverse selection and genetic testing. But first we will explore the used car market, the setting Akerlof first wrote about.

adverse selection A situation in which asymmetric information results in high-quality goods or high-quality consumers being squeezed out of transactions because they cannot demonstrate the quality of the product they are offering for sale.

Adverse Selection and Lemons Suppose you were in the market for a slightly used car of a particular make, perhaps from 2009. Having read a number of automotive magazines, you learned that half of these cars are lemons (bad cars) and half are peaches (good cars). Given your own tastes, a peach of this model year is worth $12,000 to you, whereas a lemon is worth only $3,000. What would you pay if you were unable to tell a peach from a lemon?

One possible solution to this problem might involve thinking back to the lesson on expected value. The data we described suggest that the expected value of this type of used car is $7,500, which we calculate as $\frac{1}{2}(\$12,000) + \frac{1}{2}(\$3,000)$. From expected utility theory, you might conclude that as a risk averse person you would pay somewhat less than this—let's say $7,000.

The problem with this calculation, however, is that you have forgotten that you will be trying to buy this car from a rational, utility-maximizing car seller. Under these circumstances, it will not be equally likely that the car offered will be a peach or a lemon. So the original calculation you made of the expected values will not be right. Let us see how a potential seller of a used car sees the situation.

Suppose you offer current owners of a random 2009 car the $7,000 that we calculated. Which owners will want to sell? Owners of cars likely know whether they have peaches or lemons. After all, they have been driving these cars for a while. The game we are playing here is different from the coin toss. Owners of the peaches will not, on average, find your offer attractive because their cars are worth $12,000 and you are offering only $7,000. Owners of lemons, on the other hand, will leap at the chance of unloading their cars at that price. In fact, with an offer of only $7,000, only lemon owners will offer their cars for sale. Over time, buyers come to understand that the probability of getting a lemon on the used market is greater than the probability of getting a peach and the price of the used cars will fall. In fact, in this situation, because you know with certainty that only lemons will be offered for sale, the most you will offer for the 2009 car is $3,000, the value to you of a lemon. In the end, Akerlof suggests, only lemons will be left in the market. Indeed, Akerlof called his paper "The Market for Lemons."

The used car example highlights the market failure associated with adverse selection. Because one party to the transaction—the seller here—has better information than the other party and because people behave opportunistically, owners of high-quality used cars will have difficulty selling them. Buyers who are interested in peaches will find it hard to buy one because they cannot tell a lemon from a peach and thus are not willing to offer a high enough price to make the transaction. Thus, although there are buyers who value a peachy used car more than it is valued by its current seller, no transaction will occur. The market, which is normally so good at moving goods from consumers who place a lower value on a good to consumers with higher values, does not work properly.

You should now see why the simple act of driving a car off the lot reduces its price dramatically: Potential buyers assume you are selling the car because you must have bought a lemon, and it is hard for you to prove otherwise.

Adverse Selection and Insurance   Adverse selection is a problem in a number of markets. Consider the important market for insurance. We have already seen that risk aversion causes people to want to buy health insurance. But individuals often know more about their own health than anyone else, even with required medical exams. For a given premium level, those who know themselves to be most in need of medical care will be most attracted to health insurance. As unhealthy people swell the ranks of the insured, premiums will rise. The higher the rates, the less attractive healthy people will find such insurance. Similar problems are likely in markets for insurance on auto theft and fire. As with used cars, it will be difficult for insurance companies to transact business with lower-risk (high-quality) individuals.

Reducing Adverse Selection Problems   In practice, there are a number of ways in which individuals and markets try to respond to adverse selection problems. Mechanics offer would-be used car buyers an inspection service that levels the information playing field a bit. Of course, these inspection services have a price. Buyers can also look for other clues to quality. Some buyers have come to recognize that the best used cars to buy are from individuals who have to relocate to another state. Many students buy used cars from graduating seniors for example. People who need to relocate, like graduating seniors, often want to sell their cars even if they are peaches, and they may be willing to do so at prices that do not quite reflect what they know to be the high quality of the car they are selling. If a car is being sold by a dealer, he or she can offer a warranty that covers repairs for the first few years. The fact that a dealer is willing to offer a warranty tells the potential buyer that the car is not likely to be a lemon. Dealers also develop reputations for selling peaches or lemons. The government also plays a role in trying to reduce adverse selection problems in the used car market. All states have lemon laws that allow buyers to return a used car for a full refund within a few days of purchase on the grounds that some major problems can be detected after modest driving.

Insurance markets also employ strategies to reduce the problem of adverse selection. Companies require medical exams, for example, and often impose restrictions on their willingness to pay for treatment for preexisting conditions. Some companies offer better prices to people based on verifiable health-related behavior such as not smoking.

Understanding the problem of adverse selection is also useful when we think about the policy issue of universal health coverage. In the United States, health coverage is provided by a mix of the private sector (through employers and private purchase) and by the government through Medicare and Medicaid programs. Under the traditional U.S. system, many people had a choice about what, if any, kind of health insurance they wanted to purchase given the premiums that insurers offer. By contrast, in some countries, including much of Western Europe, everyone

ECONOMICS IN PRACTICE

Adverse Selection in the Healthcare Market

Health care is one area in which insurers worry about the problem of adverse selection. A recent study on long-term care insurance and Huntington's disease (HD) illustrates the issue.[1]

Huntington's disease is a degenerative neurological disorder. It is caused by a genetic mutation and affects 1 in 10,000 individuals. Onset typically occurs between ages 30 and 50 and individuals become increasingly disabled as the disease progresses. Death typically occurs about 20 years after onset.

Given the inheritability of HD, any individual with a parent who has the disease knows they have a 50 percent chance of having HD. Moreover, since 1993, there has been a test that perfectly predicts HD. Thus, individuals—because they know their family history and because they can be tested—have or could have substantial information about their likelihood of eventually suffering from HD. Insurers, on the other hand, although they can and typically do ask about health status, do not ask about family history and are not at this point permitted to inquire about the results of genetic tests. The Affordable Care Act of 2010 similarly requires the government to provide a long-term care option with premiums based only on age, not family or genetic history. Thus, we have clear conditions of asymmetric information favoring potential insurance buyers. As indicated, HD also results in a prolonged period of severe disability, so that there is considerable benefit to owning insurance.

In a long-term study of patients with HD, Oster et al. found that individuals who carry the HD genetic mutation are up to five times as likely as the general population to buy long-term care insurance, indicating that adverse selection is both present and strong. For this population, the study finds that at current premiums, long-term care insurance is a bargain: For

an individual who knows for sure that he or she will contract HD, the payout is almost $4 for every $1 of premiums paid. As genetic testing increases, situations of adverse selection in the healthcare area are likely to increase and we will be confronted with harder choices on how much genetic testing to reveal.

THINKING PRACTICALLY

1. Economists have found that many young single people do not buy healthcare insurance. Why not?

[1] Emily Oster, Kimberly Quaid, Ira Shoulson, E. Ray Dorsey, "Genetic Adverse Selection: Evidence from Long-Term Care Insurance and Huntington Disease," *Journal of Public Economics*, December 2010, 1048–1050.

receives health insurance, typically through a government program. A government program in which everyone is covered, at least at some level, is known as *universal health coverage*. The Affordable Care Act of 2010 (sometimes called Obamacare) moved the United States toward universal health coverage by *requiring* that everyone get health insurance or face a substantial tax. This requirement prevented healthy people from opting out of the insurance market. Although there is considerable debate about the merits of moving to a universal health coverage system, most economists agree that universal coverage reduces problems of adverse selection. When individuals can choose whether to be covered, on average, those who expect to most need medical care will be most attracted to the insurance offer. To the extent that universal coverage reduces choice, it reduces the adverse selection problem.

Market Signaling

market signaling Actions taken by buyers and sellers to communicate quality in a world of uncertainty.

We have discussed how asymmetric information between buyers and sellers can lead to adverse selection. However, there are many things that can be done to overcome or at least reduce the information problem. Michael Spence, who shared the Nobel Prize in Economics with George Akerlof and Joseph Stiglitz in 2001, used the concept of **market signaling** to help explain how buyers and sellers communicate quality in a world of uncertainty.

The college admission process is a good example of how signaling works. In the year 2008–2009, the age group applying to college in the United States peaked. This is the result of 4.1 million births in 1990, record immigration, and an economy that provided young people with an incentive to get a good education. Thus, the demand for spaces at the top schools far exceeded the spaces available, a condition which continues.

In selective admissions, the student is clearly "selling" in the admissions process and the colleges and universities are buying. Signaling results because the matching between students and colleges involves communicating quality in a world of uncertainty.

The selective colleges and universities have uncertain information about the students that they admit. Although schools have concrete information such as test scores and grades, they do not have concrete measures for other qualities that they are seeking. Thus, schools must look for *signals* of those characteristics.

First, selective schools want students who are likely to be successful. They are seeking students who are willing to work hard and who will do well academically. But schools also want students who will contribute to society by becoming good scientists, artists, humanists, dancers, musicians, businesspeople, and leaders. In their admissions forms, brochures, and Web sites, many selective colleges and universities explain that they are "seeking students who will make a difference."

Developing a set of signals for identifying quality in admissions candidates is a difficult task, but there are some generally accepted signals that the colleges and universities look at. Clearly, they look beyond grades and standardized tests. "Quality of the program" is a term used to describe the difficulty of the classes that the applicant took in high school. How many advanced placement courses did the student take? How many years of math, science, and foreign language? Did the student challenge himself or herself?

In addition to courses, extracurricular activities serve as a signal for future success. Admissions professionals also see hours of practicing the violin or piano or soccer as signals of students who dedicate energy to difficult challenges. Admissions professionals make these assumptions about students because they have imperfect information.

Even without knowing about the theory of signals, most high school students recognize that colleges reward extracurricular activities. Not surprisingly, this knowledge increases the incentive of all students to engage in such activities. But how can extracurricular activities be a good signal of interests and productivity if everyone begins to do them? If every high school senior belongs to the French Club, membership ceases to have a signaling effect.

For extracurricular activities to remain useful as a good signal, they must be more easily done by well-rounded and productive students than by other students. If a student who is truly interested in writing and is well-organized about time management finds it easier to write for the school paper, colleges can correctly infer that the newspaper writer is more likely to be interested in writing and is a good manager. It would be too costly in terms of lost time and fun for someone who dislikes writing and is disorganized to join the newspaper staff just to signal colleges. For signals to work, they must be costly and the cost of using them must be less for people who have the trait that is valued. College admissions committees are, for this reason, beginning to think about things like how many hours a given activity takes. Time-intensive activities are more painful if a student does not really like the activity, and they involve more of a trade-off with other academic pursuits.

For a signal to reduce the problem of adverse selection, then, it must be less costly for the high quality-type person to obtain. Extracurricular activities work as a signal when the most committed and brightest students are most able to do the activities and do well at school. Under those conditions, these activities are thought of as a *strong signal*. In the job market, education is a strong signal. Of course, education improves your life in many ways, as a consumer, a citizen, and a worker. Education can directly improve your productivity in most jobs. But it can also signal a potential employer that you are a productive person. Why is education a good signal? Education, like extracurricular activities, is most easily attained by people who are disciplined, bright, and hard-working. All of those qualities are valued in the workplace but are hard to certify—hence, the need for a signal.

Signals are everywhere. Return for a moment to the used car example and the discussion of warranties. We argued that a car for which a dealer offered a warranty was likely to be a peach. Why? A warranty is a promise to pay for repairs for any defects. For a dealer, the warranty is expensive to live up to only if the car is a lemon. Because a lemon will require more repairs than a peach, providing a warranty for it will end up costing the dealer more. So the fact that a seller offers a warranty is a strong signal that the car is a peach.

How to Read Advertisements

Many high-end magazines, including alumni magazines for colleges, have a section at the back with advertisements for rentals of vacation homes. Consider the following ad recently found in one of those magazines.

St. Thomas Rental: "Lovely villa on the Caribbean island of St. Thomas. Sleeps 6. Beautiful garden and pool area. Covered veranda and barbecue. Available by the week or month."

What conclusion should a discerning reader of this ad draw about the property beyond what is written? The obvious conclusion to be drawn from this ad by anyone who has studied economics is that the property is not on or even near the beach.

Why do we conclude this? Ads are designed by people who want to attract customers. So a first step in our deduction is to recognize that the villa owner will mention any attractive and important positive feature that the villa has. On a Caribbean island, beachfront is a key attraction; thus, no mention of the beach tells us that this villa is not on or near the beach. Recognizing that profit-seeking individuals place the ad lets us draw conclusions about the information they do not provide.

This same logic can be used in a corporate setting. In 2002, Congress and the president passed new accounting rules that require firms to inform shareholders of the stock options they give to their executives and the effect of those options on the firms' costs. Information could be embedded in the financial statements or placed in the footnotes. Not

surprisingly, those firms—typically the dot-com firms—for whom options costs were large chose the less transparent method of putting the information in the footnotes, although more traditional firms, with fewer options to disclose, were more forthcoming.

Sometimes the lack of information serves as a signal.

THINKING PRACTICALLY

1. If a box of raisins claims it contains at least 100 raisins, do you think it is likely that there are 200?

Under some conditions, a firm's name can signal quality to consumers. Many airports now have nail salons offering manicures to travelers with spare time. On the surface, though, it appears that there might be a problem with adverse selection in the nail salon business. In a community, a nail salon that does a poor job for the money it charges is likely to go out of business. The salon will have few return visitors, and word of mouth of its poor quality is likely to spread. In an airport salon, return business is infrequent; thus, one might think that low-quality nail salons would not be forced out of business. Given that quality is more expensive in terms of labor costs and that consumers do not know whether a salon is good before they have a manicure, one might expect bad salons to crowd out good salons in airports. Savvy consumers would come to realize that only the desperate or those unconcerned with quality should get their nails done in an airport. In fact, there is an offset to this story about the crowding out of good salons. What we see in many airports is a shop that is part of a large chain of salons. The firm that owns the chain recognizes that providing good care in a shop at the Dallas-Fort Worth airport, for example, will have positive reputation effects in the same-named shop at the St. Louis airport. This gives the firm an incentive to provide better quality care at each airport. As a result, airport visitors can view the brand name of the salon as a signal of its quality. One of the economic advantages of a chain is its ability to provide some assurance to customers who are not local of a common level of product quality at different locations. Next time you are traveling along the interstate, look at the hotel and food choices at the rest stops. Most are chains for the reasons we just described.

Moral Hazard

Another information problem that arises in insurance markets is *moral hazard*. Often people enter into contracts in which the result of the contract, at least in part, depends on one of the parties' future behavior. A **moral hazard** problem arises when one party to a contract changes behavior in response to that contract and thus passes the cost of its behavior on to the other party to the contract. For example, accident insurance policies are contracts that agree to pay for repairs to your car if it is damaged in an accident. Whether you have an accident depends in part on whether you drive cautiously. Similarly, diet, exercise and risky behavior all affect how much you will need to use health insurance. If the potential for moral hazard is large, contracts will be difficult to write.

Moral hazard can lead to inefficient behavior. Insurance creates a type of externality problem in which firms and households have inadequate incentives to consider the full costs of their behavior. If your car is fully insured against theft, why should you lock it? If health insurance provides new glasses whenever you lose a pair, it is likely that you will be less careful.

In 2009, the U.S. government "bailed out" a number of firms in danger of failing: many of the largest banks, AIG, and General Motors. Many economists who looked at these bailouts warned about moral hazard. If the government is around to bail out banks when they fail, what will govern the risks those banks will take? If General Motors and AIG are kept from bankruptcy, will they too behave imprudently in the future? "Moral hazard" became part of many headlines in 2009.

Like adverse selection, the moral hazard problem is an information problem. Contracting parties cannot always determine the future behavior of the person with whom they are contracting, and this reduces their willingness to write contracts or increases the price of those contracts. If all future behavior could be predicted, contracts could be written to try to eliminate undesirable behavior. Sometimes this is possible. Life insurance companies do not pay off in the case of suicide during the first two years the policy is in force. Fire insurance companies will not write a policy unless you have smoke detectors. If you cause unreasonable damage to an apartment, your landlord can retain your security deposit. But it is impossible to know everything about behavior and intentions. If a contract absolves one party of the consequences of his or her action and people act in their own self-interest, the result is inefficient.

moral hazard Arises when one party to a contract changes behavior in response to that contract and thus passes on the costs of that behavior change to the other party.

Incentives

The discussion of moral hazard provides us with a number of examples in which individuals who buy insurance may have the wrong *incentives* when they make decisions. Incentives play an important role in other areas of life as well. When firms hire, they want to make sure that their workers have the incentive to work hard. Many employers provide bonuses for exemplary performance to create incentives for their employees. In class, teachers try to provide incentives in the form of feedback (both positive and negative) and grades to encourage students to learn the material. In designing policies to deal with unemployment, poverty, and even international relations, governments constantly worry about designing appropriate incentives.

In fact, most of our interest in incentives comes because of uncertainty. Because your teacher or employer cannot always see how hard you are working, he or she wants to design incentives to ensure that you work even when no one is watching. Grades and salary bonuses play this role. Because insurance companies cannot monitor whether you lock your car door, they would like to create incentives to encourage you to lock your doors even though you have theft insurance.

Within economics, the area of **mechanism design** explores how transactions and contracts can be designed so that, even under conditions of asymmetric information, self-interested people have the incentive to behave properly. In 2007, Leonid Hurwicz, Roger Myerson, and Eric Maskin won the Nobel Prize for their work in this area. Although the field of mechanism design is a complex one, a simple idea in the field is that different incentive schemes can cause people to *reveal* the truth about themselves. In the following discussion, we will look at a few examples in the labor market and the healthcare market to see how incentives can help reduce both adverse selection and moral hazard in this way.

Discuss the benefits of effective incentive design.

mechanism design An area of economics that explores how contract or transaction structures can overcome asymmetric information problems.

ECONOMICS IN PRACTICE

How's the Snow?

Most skiers enjoy fresh or newly fallen snow. For those traveling some distance to a ski area, knowing snow conditions is clearly important. Two researchers at Dartmouth (likely skiers themselves) decided to take a look at how accurate ski resorts were in their snow reports.[1]

We can see why resorts might have an incentive to exaggerate the frequency of snowfall. More fresh snow in the report entices more skiers, at least until they wise up to you! But Zinman and Zitzewitz realized that the incentive to over-report snow was especially prominent on weekends, when more opportunistic one day skiers are likely to be enticed to a particular area. So they looked for ski resort reporting by day of the week. Sure enough, there are 23 percent more reports of natural, new, or fresh snow by resorts on weekends than on weekdays. On average, of course, it snows more or less equally on each day of the week. Most of the reports were for modest amounts; presumably reports of blizzards are harder to fabricate.

But take heart skiers: Zinman and Zitzewitz also found that a new iPhone app that allows skiers at a slope to report conditions to others has dramatically reduced the over-reporting problem.

THINKING PRACTICALLY

1. What do you think stimulated the demand for this new iPhone app?

[1] Jonathan Zinman and Eric Zitzewitz, "Wintertime for Deceptive Advertising," Dartmouth Working Paper, January 2012.

Labor Market Incentives

In the section on expected utility versus expected value, we described an employee trying to choose between a job that offered a wage of $40,000 versus a coin toss that could bring him either $20,000 or $60,000. We suggested that few employees would take such a deal, given risk aversion. And yet many people do have wage contracts that contain some uncertainty. For many CEOs of large U.S. companies, less than half of their compensation is in the form of a fixed salary. Most of their pay comes from bonuses based on the firm's profits or its stock market performance. Some factory jobs pay piece wages that depend on how fast the worker is. Sales jobs often pay commissions for sales made. Why do we see these contracts, given the risk aversion of most people?

These types of contracts occur because variable compensation can help firms get better performance from their workforce. Suppose you are hiring one individual as a salesperson and have two candidates, George and Harry. Both men seem to be affable, good with people, and hard-working. How can you tell who will be a better salesperson? In this case, incentives can play a powerful role. Suppose you offer George and Harry the following deal: The base pay for this job is $25,000, but for every sale made beyond a certain level, a large commission is paid. How valuable is this salary offer? That depends on how good George and Harry are as salespeople. If George knows he is an excellent salesperson, whereas Harry recognizes that despite his good nature, he is not good at selling, only George will want to take this salary offer. The way the incentive package is designed has caused the right person, the better salesperson, to *select* into the job. Notice that in contrast to the problem of adverse selection described previously in this chapter, this incentive scheme creates *beneficial* selection dynamics. One reason that many companies design compensation with a component that varies with performance is that they want to attract the right kind of employees. In this case, the compensation scheme has *screened out* the poor worker. Harry has revealed his own skills and abilities by his job choice, as a result of the design of the incentive.

Performance compensation plays another role as well. Once George has taken the job, the fact that some of his salary depends on his hard work will encourage him to work even harder. Of course, it is important that his compensation depend on things he can, in part, control. This is one reason that in most companies, the CEO's compensation is tied more to firm profitability than is the salary of his or her executive assistant. Because the CEO has more control over profitability, he or she should face the strongest performance incentives.

At the top levels in the investment banking industry, most compensation is performance-based. In 2008, just before the financial meltdown, Lloyd Blankfein, the CEO of Goldman Sachs, received $73 million in compensation. Of that, $600,000 was in base pay! Many have argued that compensation in the financial industry provides an incentive to take excessive risks.

In recent years, there have been efforts in some states to use more incentive compensation for public school teachers. In some cases, bonuses have been tied to student performance on standardized tests. In a related set of experiments, New York City had a pilot program to reward students who earn good grades with gifts such as cell phones. There has been a lot of debate about the efficacy of both programs. Some people think that public school teachers are already highly motivated and that monetary compensation is not likely to have much effect. Others worry that teachers will "teach to the test," suggesting that the wrong behavior will be stimulated. Some worry that incentive pay will screen out committed teachers, whereas other people believe it will improve retention of hard-working teachers. In the case of public school students, critics worry that these incentives will turn learning from a matter of love to one of commerce. These issues will likely be debated for some time to come.

SUMMARY

17.1 DECISION MAKING UNDER UNCERTAINTY: THE TOOLS *p. 350*

1. To find the expected value of a deal, you identify all possible outcomes of the deal and find the payoffs associated with those outcomes. *Expected value* is the weighted average of those payoffs where the weights are the probability of each payoff occurring.

2. In general, people do not accept uncertain deals with the same expected value as certain deals.

3. *Risk aversion* exists when people prefer a certain outcome to an uncertain outcome with an equal expected value. *Risk-neutral* people are indifferent between these two deals, and *risk-loving* people prefer the uncertain deal to its certain equivalent.

4. Most people are risk-averse unless the bet is small.

5. Income is subject to *diminishing marginal utility*, and this diminishing marginal utility explains risk aversion.

17.2 ASYMMETRIC INFORMATION *p. 354*

6. Choices made in the presence of imperfect information may not be efficient. Problems are particularly important when information is asymmetric. *Asymmetric information* occurs when one of the parties to a transaction has information relevant to the transaction that the other party does not have. Under these conditions, we may have *adverse selection*.

Opportunistic behavior on the part of the better informed buyer or seller prevents some welfare-enhancing transactions from occurring. *Moral hazard* arises when one party to a contract changes behavior in response to incentives in the contract so as to pass some of the cost of his or her behavior on to the other party. Under these conditions, it will also be difficult to write some welfare-enhancing contracts.

7. Market signaling is a process by which sellers can communicate to buyers their quality. For a signal to be meaningful, it must be less expensive for high-quality types to acquire the signal than for low-quality types.

8. In many cases, the market provides solutions to information problems. Profit-maximizing firms will continue to gather information as long as the marginal benefits from continued search are greater than the marginal costs. Consumers will do the same: More time is afforded to the information search for larger decisions. In other cases, government must be called on to collect and disperse information to the public.

17.3 INCENTIVES *p. 359*

9. Correct incentive design can improve the selection mechanism along with reducing the moral hazard problem.

10. Performance contracts in the labor market and co-pays in the health insurance market are two examples of incentive contracts.

REVIEW TERMS AND CONCEPTS

adverse selection, *p. 354*

asymmetric information, *p. 354*

diminishing marginal utility, *p. 350*

expected utility, *p. 351*

expected value, *p. 350*

fair game *or* fair bet, *p. 350*

market signaling, *p. 356*

mechanism design, *p. 359*

moral hazard, *p. 359*

payoff, *p. 350*

risk-averse, *p. 352*

risk-loving, *p. 352*

risk-neutral, *p. 352*

PROBLEMS

All problems are available on MyEconLab.

17.1 DECISION MAKING UNDER UNCERTAINTY: THE TOOLS

LEARNING OBJECTIVE: Define the concepts of expected value and expected utility and how these measures relate to risk attitudes.

1.1 The following table shows the relationship between utility and income for three individuals. Show each relationship graphically and explain whether each person is risk-averse, risk-neutral, or risk-loving.

Alexandra		Bianca		Caleb	
Income	Utility	Income	Utility	Income	Utility
$ 25,000	15	$ 25,000	10	$ 25,000	3
50,000	27	50,000	20	50,000	8
75,000	35	75,000	30	75,000	20
100,000	40	100,000	40	100,000	40

*1.2 Your current salary is a fixed sum of $115,600 per year. You have an offer for another job. The salary there is a flat $75,000 plus a chance to earn $350,000 if the company does well. Assume that your utility from income can be expressed as $U = \sqrt{\text{Income}}$. So, for example, at an income level of $100, your utility level is 10; your utility level from the current salary of $115,600 is 340. How high does the probability of success for the company have to be to induce you to take this job?

1.3 At the beginning of 2015 I bought a fire insurance policy for my vacation home in Aspen; at the end of the year, my vacation home had not burned down. Was my purchase a mistake? Explain.

1.4 Video poker is a popular form of gambling in casinos, second only to slot machines. Some video poker games offer a "double-up" feature, where players receiving a paying hand are offered the chance to double their winnings. If a player chooses to play the double-up feature, the machine deals one card from a 52-card deck to the player and one to the "dealer." If the player's card is higher than the dealer's (with an ace being the highest card), the player doubles his or her winnings. If the player's card is lower than the dealer's card, the player loses his or her winnings. If both are dealt cards of the same value (a

push), the player keeps his or her original bet. Explain whether the double-up feature is an example of a fair game.

17.2 ASYMMETRIC INFORMATION

LEARNING OBJECTIVE: Describe the characteristics, implications, and solutions for asymmetric situations.

2.1 Explain how imperfect information problems such as adverse selection and moral hazard might affect the following markets or situations:
   a. The market for wireless internet connectivity at large international airports
   b. The market for renter's insurance
   c. The market for used automobile tires
   d. The market for pharmaceuticals purchased over the Internet

2.2 Many colleges offer pass/fail classes. Use the ideas of adverse selection and moral hazard to explain why teachers in these classes find that pass/fail students rarely score at the top of the class.

2.3 Signals are also used in social settings. In a new place, what signals do you look for to find people who share your interests?

2.4 [**Related to the *Economics in Practice* on p. 358**] Find a product advertisement in a magazine, in a newspaper, or on a Web site, for which the missing information tells you something important about this product. Explain what information is missing, why you think it is missing, and what it is telling you about the product.

2.5 [**Related to the *Economics in Practice* on p. 356**] Do you think companies that issue health insurance should be allowed to inquire about family medical history and the results of genetic testing before deciding to issue insurance policies? Why or why not?

2.6 Valentino wants to purchase a classic motorcycle and sees a 1974 Triumph Bonneville T140 listed on Cycletrader.com for $5,950. He is willing to pay $7,500 if the motorcycle is reliable, but only $2,000 if the motorcycle is not reliable. What additional information might Valentino find helpful in making his decision about the purchase?

Note: Problems with an asterisk are more challenging.

2.7 One way insurance companies reduce adverse selection problems is by offering group medical coverage to large firms and requiring all employees to participate in the coverage. Explain how this reduces adverse selection.

17.3 INCENTIVES

LEARNING OBJECTIVE: Discuss the benefits of effective incentive design.

3.1 Mona Stangley owns an organic egg farm just outside of Gilbert, Texas. At present, she pays her workers an hourly wage to inspect and package her organic eggs in egg cartons. She is considering changing to a piece rate, in which workers would be paid based on how many eggs they inspect and package during a day. Assume on any given day that there are more eggs than the work staff can handle. What effect would you expect this change in compensation to have on Mona's operations?

3.2 The five busiest airports in the United States are in Atlanta, Chicago, Los Angeles, Dallas-Ft. Worth, and Denver. At these airports there are more than 450 food outlets, with each airport offering a number of dining options that feature regional cuisines. Passengers will also see many familiar names like McDonald's, Starbucks, Jamba Juice, Burger King, Subway, and Chili's. Why might these national chains find it beneficial to locate inside these large airports?

3.3 [**Related to the *Economics in Practice* on p. 360**] The *Economics in Practice* discusses a new iPhone app that allows skiers to report snow conditions directly from a ski resort, and this app has dramatically reduced inaccurate reports of snowfall issued by the resorts. Describe another smartphone app that can be used to reduce misinformation about a product or service and explain the current or potential popularity of this app.

3.4 Simon likes to watch movies and his Internet service provider offers streaming movies on a pay-per-view basis for $3 each. The provider also offers a service for unlimited streaming of movies for $15 per month. Simon predicts that he will watch three movies per month, so the value of the movies he would watch is not enough to opt for the unlimited streaming option. Therefore, Simon decides to stream movies on a pay-per-view basis.

  a. At the end of six months, Simon finds that he only streamed movies an average of two times per month rather than the three times per month he predicted. He is still sure, however, that with the unlimited streaming option, he would watch 3 movies per month and insists that economic logic supports his prediction. What principle is he thinking about?

  b. Simon's brother Andrew likes to come to Simon's apartment and watch movies on his 70-inch television, but being a broke college student, Andrew has very little extra money each month. Andrew would like to watch more than two movies per month, but all he has to offer Simon is $2 per month for the additional movies. Do you think Andrew's offer would convince Simon to pay for additional movies? If not, suggest an alternative that would achieve Andrew's goal.

3.5 Most casino game dealers in Las Vegas are paid minimum wage, and therefore rely on tips for a large portion of their income. Within the past few years, a majority of Las Vegas casinos have instituted tip-pooling policies for their dealers, whereby dealers are not allowed to keep the tips they earn; instead, they must pool all of their tips to be evenly distributed to all dealers. How would the tip-pooling system affect the productivity of the dealers?

Glossary

ability-to-pay principle A theory of taxation holding that citizens should bear tax burdens in line with their ability to pay taxes. *p. 400*

absolute advantage A producer has an absolute advantage over another in the production of a good or service if he or she can produce that product using fewer resources (a lower absolute cost per unit). *p. 25*

absolute advantage The advantage in the production of a good enjoyed by one country over another when it uses fewer resources to produce that good than the other country does. *p. 411*

adverse selection A situation in which asymmetric information results in high-quality goods or high-quality consumers being squeezed out of transactions because they cannot demonstrate the quality of the product they are offering for sale. *p. 354*

after-tax income Before-tax income minus taxes paid. *p. 365*

asymmetric information One of the parties to a transaction has information relevant to the transaction that the other party does not have. *p. 354*

average fixed cost (AFC) Total fixed cost divided by the number of units of output; a per-unit measure of fixed costs. *p. 166*

average product The average amount produced by each unit of a variable factor of production. *p. 148*

average tax rate Total amount of tax paid divided by total income. *p. 390*

average total cost (ATC) Total cost divided by the number of units of output; a per unit measure of total costs. *p. 173*

average variable cost (AVC) Total variable cost divided by the number of units of output; a per unit measure of variable costs. *p. 171*

barriers to entry Factors that prevent new firms from entering and competing in imperfectly competitive industries. *p. 272*

before-tax income Market income plus transfers. *p. 365*

behavioral economics A branch of economics that uses the insights of psychology and economics to investigate decision making. *p. 315*

benefits-received principle A theory of fairness holding that taxpayers should contribute to government (in the form of taxes) in proportion to the benefits they receive from public expenditures. *p. 400*

black market A market in which illegal trading takes place at market-determined prices. *p. 77*

bond A contract between a borrower and a lender, in which the borrower agrees to pay the loan at some time in the future. Some bonds also make regular, constant payments once or twice a year. *p. 229*

brain drain The tendency for talented people from developing countries to become educated in a developed country and remain there after graduation. *p. 438*

breaking even The situation in which a firm is earning exactly a normal rate of return. *p. 186*

budget constraint The limits imposed on household choices by income, wealth, and product prices. *p. 113*

capital Those goods produced by the economic system that are used as inputs to produce other goods and services in the future. *pp. 22, 226*

capital flight The tendency for both human capital and financial capital to leave developing countries in search of higher expected rates of return elsewhere with less risk. *p. 437*

capital gain An increase in the value of an asset. *p. 585*

capital income Income earned on savings that have been put to use through financial capital markets. *p. 230*

capital market The input/factor market in which households supply their savings, for interest or for claims to future profits, to firms that demand funds to buy capital goods. *pp. 44, 228*

capital stock For a single firm, the current market value of the firm's plant, equipment, inventories, and intangible assets. *p. 227*

capital-intensive technology Technology that relies heavily on capital instead of human labor. *p. 146*

cartel A group of firms that gets together and makes joint price and output decisions to maximize joint profits. *p. 292*

Celler-Kefauver Act Extended the government's authority to control mergers. *p. 303*

ceteris paribus*, or *all else equal A device used to analyze the relationship between two variables while the values of other variables are held unchanged. *p. 8*

choice set *or* opportunity set The set of options that is defined and limited by a budget constraint. *p. 114*

Clayton Act Passed by Congress in 1914 to strengthen the Sherman Act and clarify the rule of reason, the act outlawed specific monopolistic behaviors such as tying contracts, price discrimination, and unlimited mergers. *p. 282*

Coase theorem Under certain conditions, when externalities are present, private parties can arrive at the efficient solution without government involvement. *p. 332*

command economy An economy in which a central government either directly or indirectly sets output targets, incomes, and prices. *p. 36*

commitment device Actions that individuals take in one period to try to control their behavior in a future period. *p. 315*

common resource A resource that is nonexcludeable but rival in consumption. *p. 344*

common stock A share of stock is an ownership claim on a firm, entitling its owner to a profit share. *p. 230*

comparative advantage A producer has a comparative advantage over another in the production of a good or service if he or she can produce that product at a lower *opportunity cost*. *p. 26*

comparative advantage The advantage in the production of a good enjoyed by one country over another when that good can be produced at lower cost in terms of other goods than it could be in the other country. *p. 412*

compensating differentials Differences in wages that result from differences in working conditions. Risky jobs usually pay higher wages; highly desirable jobs usually pay lower wages. *p. 369*

complements, complementary goods Goods that "go together"; a decrease in the price of one results in an increase in demand for the other and vice versa. *p. 49*

concentration ratio The share of industry output in sales or employment accounted for by the top firms. *p. 289*

constant returns to scale An increase in a firm's scale of production has no effect on costs per unit produced. *p. 191*

consumer goods Goods produced for present consumption. *p. 28*

consumer sovereignty The idea that consumers ultimately dictate what

will be produced (or not produced) by choosing what to purchase (and what not to purchase). *p. 36*

consumer surplus The difference between the maximum amount a person is willing to pay for a good and its current market price. *p. 82*

contestable markets Markets in which entry and exit are easy enough to hold prices to a competitive level even if no entry actually occurs. *p. 291*

Corn Laws The tariffs, subsidies, and restrictions enacted by the British Parliament in the early nineteenth century to discourage imports and encourage exports of grain. *p. 411*

correlated Two variables are correlated if their values tend to move together. *p. 453*

cross-price elasticity of demand A measure of the response of the quantity of one good demanded to a change in the price of another good. *p. 101*

dead weight loss *or* excess burden of a monopoly The social cost associated with the distortion in consumption from a monopoly price. *p. 276*

deadweight loss The total loss of producer and consumer surplus from underproduction or overproduction. *p. 84*

decreasing returns to scale, *or* diseconomies of scale An increase in a firm's scale of production leads to higher costs per unit produced. *p. 191*

deflation A decrease in the overall price level. *p. 413*

demand curve A graph illustrating how much of a given product a household would be willing to buy at different prices. *p. 47*

demand schedule Shows how much of a given product a household would be willing to buy at different prices for a given time period. *p. 46*

demand-determined price The price of a good that is in fixed

supply; it is determined exclusively by what households and firms are willing to pay for the good. *p. 215*

depreciation of a currency The fall in value of one currency relative to another. *p. 687*

depreciation The decline in an asset's economic value over time, or the amount by which an asset's value falls in a given period. *p. 227*

derived demand The demand for resources (inputs) that is dependent on the demand for the outputs those resources can be used to produce. *p. 210*

diamond/water paradox A paradox stating that (1) the things with the greatest value in use frequently have little or no value in exchange and (2) the things with the greatest value in exchange frequently have little or no value in use. *p. 121*

difference-in-differences Difference-in-differences is a method of identifying causality by looking at the way in which the average change over time in the outcome variable is compared to the average change in a control group. *p. 458*

diminishing marginal utility The more of any one good consumed in a given period, the less incremental satisfaction is generated by consuming a marginal or incremental unit of the same good. *p. 350*

dividend Payment made to shareholders of a corporation. *p. 230*

dividends The portion of a firm's profits that the firm pays out each period to its shareholders. *p. 416*

Doha Development Agenda An initiative of the World Trade Organization focused on issues of trade and development. *p. 423*

dominant strategy In game theory, a strategy that is best no matter what the opposition does. *p. 297*

drop-in-the-bucket problem A problem intrinsic to public goods: The good or service is usually so costly that its provision generally does not depend on whether any single person pays. *p. 340*

dumping A firm's or an industry's sale of products on the world market at prices below its own cost of production. *p. 420*

duopoly A two-firm oligopoly. *p. 294*

economic growth An increase in the total output of an economy. Growth occurs when a society acquires new resources or when it learns to produce more using existing resources. *pp. 10, 32*

economic integration Occurs when two or more nations join to form a free-trade zone. *p. 665*

economic profit Profit that accounts for both explicit costs and opportunity costs. *p. 142*

economics The study of how individuals and societies choose to use the scarce resources that nature and previous generations have provided. *p. 1*

efficiency In economics, allocative efficiency. An efficient economy is one that produces what people want at the least possible cost. *pp. 10, 249*

efficient market A market in which profit opportunities are eliminated almost instantaneously. *p. 3*

elastic demand A demand relationship in which the percentage change in quantity demanded is larger than the percentage change in price in absolute value (a demand elasticity with an absolute value greater than 1). *p. 91*

elasticity A general concept used to quantify the response in one variable when another variable changes. *p. 90*

elasticity of labor supply A measure of the response of labor supplied to a change in the price of labor. *p. 101*

elasticity of supply A measure of the response of quantity of a good supplied to a change in price of that good. Likely to be positive in output markets. *p. 101*

empirical economics The collection and use of data to test economic theories. *p. 8*

entrepreneur A person who organizes, manages, and assumes the risks of a firm, taking a new idea or a new product and turning it into a successful business. *p. 43*

equilibrium The condition that exists when quantity supplied and quantity demanded are equal. At equilibrium, there is no tendency for price to change. In the macroeconomic goods market, equilibrium occurs when planned aggregate expenditure is equal to aggregate output. *p. 60*

equity Fairness *p. 10*

estate The property that a person owns at the time of his or her death. *p. 402*

estate tax A tax on the total value of a person's estate. *p. 402*

excess burden The amount by which the burden of a tax exceeds the total revenue collected. Also called *deadweight loss. p. 397*

excess demand *or* **shortage** The condition that exists when quantity demanded exceeds quantity supplied at the current price. *p. 60*

excess supply *or* **surplus** The condition that exists when quantity supplied exceeds quantity demanded at the current price. *p. 62*

exchange rate The price of one country's currency in terms of another country's currency; the ratio at which two currencies are traded for each other. *p. 417*

excise tax A per unit tax on a specific good. *p. 103*

exogenous variable A variable that is assumed not to depend on the state of the economy—that is, it does not change when the economy changes. *p. 473*

expansion or boom The period in the business cycle from a trough up to a peak during which output and employment grow. *p. 412*

expected rate of return The annual rate of return that a firm expects to obtain through a capital investment. *p. 235*

expected utility The sum of the utilities coming from all possible outcomes of a deal, weighted by the probability of each occurring. *p. 351*

expected value The sum of the payoffs associated with each possible outcome of a situation weighted by its probability of occurring. *p. 350*

export promotion A trade policy designed to encourage exports. *p. 443*

export subsidies Government payments made to domestic firms to encourage exports. *p. 662*

externality A cost or benefit imposed or bestowed on an individual or a group that is outside, or external to, the transaction. *pp. 257, 327*

factor endowments The quantity and quality of labor, land, and natural resources of a country. *p. 419*

factors of production (*or* factors) The inputs into the process of production. Another term for *resources*. Land, labor, and capital are the three key factors of production. *pp. 23, 44*

fair game or fair bet A game whose expected value is zero. *p. 350*

favored customers Those who receive special treatment from dealers during situations of excess demand. *p. 76*

Federal Trade Commission (FTC) A federal regulatory group created by Congress in 1914 to investigate the structure and behavior of firms engaging in interstate commerce, to determine what constitutes unlawful "unfair" behavior, and to issue cease-and-desist orders to those found in violation of antitrust law. *p. 282*

financial capital market The complex set of institutions in which suppliers of capital (households that save) and the demand for capital (firms wanting to invest) interact. *pp. 129, 229*

firm An organization that comes into being when a person or a group of people decides to produce a good or service to meet a perceived demand. *p. 141*

firm An organization that transforms resources (inputs) into products (outputs). Firms are the primary producing units in a market economy. *p. 43*

Five Forces model A model developed by Michael Porter that helps us understand the five competitive forces that determine the level of competition and profitability in an industry. *p. 289*

fixed cost Any cost that does not depend on the firms' level of output. These costs are incurred even if the firm is producing nothing. There are no fixed costs in the long run. *p. 165*

free-rider problem A problem intrinsic to public goods: Because people can enjoy the benefits of public goods whether or not they pay for them, they are usually unwilling to pay for them. *p. 340*

game theory Analyzes the choices made by rival firms, people, and even governments when they are trying to maximize their own well-being while anticipating and reacting to the actions of others in their environment. *p. 296*

General Agreement on Tariffs and Trade (GATT) An international agreement signed by the United States and 22 other countries in 1947 to promote the liberalization of foreign trade. *p. 422*

general equilibrium The condition that exists when all markets in an economy are in simultaneous equilibrium. *p. 248*

Gini coefficient A commonly used measure of the degree of inequality of income derived from a Lorenz curve. It can range from 0 to a maximum of 1. *p. 367*

Global South Developing nations in Asia, Africa, and Latin America. *p. 435*

government failure Occurs when the government becomes the tool of the rent seeker and the allocation of resources is made even less efficient by the intervention of government. *p. 278*

Heckscher-Ohlin theorem A theory that explains the existence of a country's comparative advantage by its factor endowments: A country has a comparative advantage in the production of a product if that country is relatively well endowed with inputs used intensively in the production of that product. *p. 419*

Herfindahl-Hirschman Index (HHI) An index of market concentration found by summing the square of percentage shares of firms in the market. *p. 303*

homogeneous products Undifferentiated outputs; products that are identical to or indistinguishable from one another. *pp. 111, 175*

horizontal differentiation Products differ in ways that make them better for some people and worse for others. *p. 313*

households The consuming units in an economy. *p. 43*

human capital A form of intangible capital that includes the skills and other knowledge that workers have or acquire through education and training and that yields valuable services to a firm over time. *p. 226*

human capital The stock of knowledge, skills, and talents that people possess; it can be inborn or acquired through education and training. *p. 368*

imperfect information The absence of full knowledge concerning product characteristics, available prices, and so on. *p. 258*

imperfectly competitive industry An industry in which individual firms have some control over the price of their output. *p. 264*

import substitution An industrial trade strategy that favors developing local industries that can manufacture goods to replace imports. *p. 443*

impossibility theorem A proposition demonstrated by Kenneth Arrow showing that no system of aggregating individual preferences into social decisions will always yield consistent, nonarbitrary results. *p. 403*

income The sum of all a household's wages, salaries, profits, interest payments, rents, and other forms of earnings in a given period of time. It is a flow measure. *p. 49*

income elasticity of demand A measure of the responsiveness of quantity demanded to changes in income. *p. 100*

increasing returns to scale, *or* **economies of scale** An increase in a firm's scale of production leads to lower costs per unit produced. *p. 191*

Industrial Revolution The period in England during the late eighteenth and early nineteenth centuries in which new manufacturing technologies and improved transportation gave rise to the modern factory system and a massive movement of the population from the countryside to the cities. *p. 3*

inelastic demand Demand that responds somewhat, but not a great deal, to changes in price. Inelastic demand always has a numerical value between zero and 1. *p. 91*

infant industry A young industry that may need temporary protection from competition from the established industries of other countries to develop an acquired comparative advantage. *p. 428*

inferior goods Goods for which demand tends to fall when income rises. *p. 49*

injunction A court order forbidding the continuation of behavior that leads to damages. *p. 333*

input *or* **factor markets** The markets in which the resources used to produce goods and services are exchanged. *p. 44*

inputs *or* resources Anything provided by nature or previous generations that can be used directly or indirectly to satisfy human wants. *p. 23*

intangible capital Nonmaterial things that contribute to the output of future goods and services. *p. 226*

intention to treat A method in which we compare two groups based on whether they were part of an initially specified random sample subjected to an experimental protocol. *p. 455*

interest The payments made for the use of money. *p. 230*

interest rate Interest payments expressed as a percentage of the loan. *p. 230*

investment The process of using resources to produce new capital. New capital additions to a firm's capital stock. Although capital is measured at a given point in time (a stock), investment is measured over a period of time (a flow). The flow of investment increases the capital stock. *pp. 28, 227*

labor market The input/factor market in which households supply work for wages to firms that demand labor. *p. 44*

labor supply curve A curve that shows the quantity of labor supplied at different wage rates. Its shape depends on how households react to changes in the wage rate. A graph that illustrates the amount of labor that households want to supply at each given wage rate. *p. 126*

labor-intensive technology Technology that relies heavily on human labor instead of capital. *p. 146*

laissez-faire economy Literally from the French: "allow [them] to do." An economy in which individual people and firms pursue their own self-interest without any central direction or regulation. *p. 36*

land market The input/factor market in which households supply land or other real property in exchange for rent. *p. 44*

law of demand The negative relationship between price and quantity demanded: *Ceteris paribus*, as price rises, quantity demanded decreases; as price falls, quantity demanded increases. *p. 47*

law of diminishing marginal utility The more of any one good consumed in a given period, the less satisfaction (utility) generated by consuming each additional (marginal) unit of the same good. *p. 117*

law of diminishing returns When additional units of a variable input are added to fixed inputs, after a certain point, the marginal product of the variable input declines. *p. 147*

law of supply The positive relationship between price and quantity of a good supplied: An increase in market price will lead to an increase in quantity supplied, and a decrease in market price will lead to a decrease in quantity supplied. *p. 56*

least squares estimates Least squares estimates are those that correspond to the smallest sum of squared distances, or errors. *p. 462*

liability rules Laws that require A to compensate B for damages that A imposed on B. *p. 334*

logrolling Occurs when Congressional representatives trade votes agreeing to help each other get certain pieces of legislation passed. *p. 404*

long run That period of time for which there are no fixed factors of production: Firms can increase or decrease the scale of operation, and new firms can enter and/or existing firms can exit the industry. *p. 145*

long-run average cost curve (*LRAC*) Shows the way per unit costs change with output in the long run. *p. 191*

long-run competitive equilibrium When $P = SRMC = SRAC = LRAC$ and profits are zero. *p. 198*

Lorenz curve A widely used graph of the distribution of income, with cumulative percentage of households plotted along the horizontal axis and cumulative percentage of income plotted along the vertical axis. *p. 366*

macroeconomics Deals with the economy as a whole. Macroeconomics focuses on the determinants of total national income, deals with aggregates such as aggregate consumption and investment, and looks at the overall level of prices instead of individual prices. The branch of economics that examines the economic behavior of aggregates—income, employment, output, and so on—on a national scale. *p. 4*

marginal cost (*MC*) The increase in total cost that results from producing 1 more unit of output. Marginal costs reflect changes in variable costs. *p. 168*

marginal product The additional output that can be produced by adding one more unit of a specific input, *ceteris paribus*. *p. 147*

marginal product of labor (*MP*$_L$) The additional output produced by 1 additional unit of labor. *p. 210*

marginal rate of transformation (*MRT*) The slope of the production possibility frontier (ppf). *p. 30*

marginal revenue (*MR*) The additional revenue that a firm takes in when it increases output by one additional unit. In perfect competition, the marginal revenue is equal to the price. *p. 177*

marginal revenue product (*MRP*) *or* the value of marginal product (*VMP*) The additional revenue a firm earns by employing 1 additional unit of an input, *ceteris paribus*. *p. 211*

marginal social benefit of pollution The incremental benefit to society from producing one more unit of pollution. *p. 330*

marginal social cost (*MSC*) The total cost to society of producing an additional unit of a good or service. *MSC* is equal to the sum of the marginal cost of producing the product and the correctly measured marginal external cost involved in the process of production. *p. 327*

marginal tax rate   The tax rate paid on the next dollar earned. *p. 390*

marginal utility (MU)   The additional satisfaction gained by the consumption or use of *one more* unit of a good or service. *p. 118*

marginalism   The process of analyzing the additional or incremental costs or benefits arising from a choice or decision. *p. 2*

market   The institution through which buyers and sellers interact and engage in exchange. *p. 36*

market demand   The sum of all the quantities of a good or service demanded per period by all the households buying in the market for that good or service. *p. 53*

market failure   Occurs when resources are misallocated, or allocated inefficiently. The result is waste or lost surplus. *p. 256*

market income   Wage and property income before transfers and taxes. *p. 365*

market labor supply curve   The horizontal aggregation of the individual labor supply curves for workers in an area. *p. 213*

market power   An imperfectly competitive firm's ability to raise price without losing all of the quantity demanded for its product. *p. 264*

market signaling   Actions taken by buyers and sellers to communicate quality in a world of uncertainty. *p. 356*

market supply   The sum of all that is supplied each period by all producers of a single product. *p. 59*

maximin strategy   In game theory, a strategy chosen to maximize the minimum gain that can be earned. *p. 299*

mechanism design   An area of economics that explores how contract or transaction structures can overcome asymmetric information problems. *p. 359*

Medicaid *and* Medicare   In-kind government transfer programs that provide health and hospitalization benefits: Medicare to the aged and their survivors and to certain of the disabled, regardless of income, and Medicaid to people with low incomes. *p. 377*

microeconomics   Examines the functioning of individual industries and the behavior of individual decision-making units—firms and households. The branch of economics that examines the functioning of individual industries and the behavior of individual decision-making units—that is, firms and households. *p. 4*

midpoint formula   A more precise way of calculating percentages using the value halfway between P_1 and P_2 for the base in calculating the percentage change in price and the value halfway between Q_1 and Q_2 as the base for calculating the percentage change in quantity demanded. *p. 94*

minimum efficient scale (MES)   The smallest size at which long-run average cost is at its minimum. *p. 192*

minimum wage   A price floor set for the price of labor. The lowest wage that firms are permitted to pay workers. *pp. 79, 380*

model   A formal statement of a theory, usually a mathematical statement of a presumed relationship between two or more variables. *p. 7*

monopolistic competition   A common form of industry (market) structure characterized by a large number of firms, no barriers to entry, and product differentiation. *p. 311*

moral hazard   Arises when one party to a contract changes behavior in response to that contract and thus passes on the costs of that behavior change to the other party. *p. 359*

movement along a demand curve   The change in quantity demanded brought about by a change in price. *p. 53*

movement along a supply curve   The change in quantity supplied brought about by a change in price. *p. 58*

Nash equilibrium   In game theory, the result of all players' playing their best strategy given what their competitors are doing. *p. 298*

national income   The total income earned by the factors of production owned by a country's citizens. *p. 429*

natural experiment   Selection of a control versus experimental group in testing the outcome of an intervention is made as a result of an exogenous event outside the experiment itself and unrelated to it. *p. 446*

natural monopoly   An industry that realizes such large economies of scale that single-firm production of that good or service is most cost-efficient. *p. 273*

network externalities   The value of a product to a consumer increases with the number of that product being sold or used in the market. *p. 275*

nonexcludable   A characteristic of public goods: Once a good is produced, no one can be excluded from enjoying its benefits. *p. 340*

nonrival in consumption   A characteristic of public goods: One person's enjoyment of the benefits of a public good does not interfere with another's consumption of it. *p. 340*

normal goods   Goods for which demand goes up when income is higher and for which demand goes down when income is lower. *p. 49*

normal rate of return   A rate of return on capital that is just sufficient to keep owners and investors satisfied. For relatively risk-free firms, it should be nearly the same as the interest rate on risk-free government bonds. *p. 143*

normative economics   An approach to economics that analyzes outcomes of economic behavior, evaluates them as good or bad, and may prescribe courses of action. Also called *policy economics*. *p. 7*

North American Free Trade Agreement (NAFTA) An agreement signed by the United States, Mexico, and Canada in which the three countries agreed to establish all North America as a free-trade zone. *p. 423*

Ockham's razor The principle that irrelevant detail should be cut away. *p. 7*

official poverty line The officially established income level that distinguishes the poor from the nonpoor. It is set at three times the cost of the Department of Agriculture's minimum food budget. *p. 379*

oligopoly A form of industry (market) structure characterized by a few dominant firms. Products may be homogeneous or differentiated. *p. 288*

opportunity cost The best alternative that we forgo, or give up, when we make a choice or a decision. *p. 2*

opportunity cost The best alternative that we give up, or forgo, when we make a choice or decision. *p. 24*

optimal level of provision for public goods The level at which society's total willingness to pay per unit is equal to the marginal cost of producing the good. *p. 343*

optimal method of production The production method that minimizes cost for a given level of output. *p. 145*

optimal scale of plant The scale of plant that minimizes long-run average cost. *p. 194*

outputs Goods and services of value to households. *p. 23*

Pareto efficiency *or* Pareto optimality A condition in which no change is possible that will make some members of society better off without making some other members of society worse off. *p. 251*

partial equilibrium analysis The process of examining the equilibrium conditions in individual markets and for households and firms separately. *p. 248*

patent A barrier to entry that grants exclusive use of the patented product or process to the inventor. *p. 274*

payoff The amount that comes from a possible outcome or result. *p. 350*

perfect competition An industry structure in which there are many firms, each being small relative to the industry and producing virtually identical products, and in which no firm is large enough to have any control over prices. In perfectly competitive industries, new competitors can freely enter the market and old firms can exit. *pp. 111, 175*

perfect knowledge The assumption that households possess a knowledge of the qualities and prices of everything available in the market and that firms have all available information concerning wage rates, capital costs, technology, and output prices. *p. 111*

perfect price discrimination Occurs when a firm charges the maximum amount that buyers are willing to pay for each unit. *p. 278*

perfect substitutes Identical products. *p. 49*

perfectly elastic demand Demand in which quantity drops to zero at the slightest increase in price. *p. 91*

perfectly inelastic demand Demand in which quantity demanded does not respond at all to a change in price. *p. 91*

physical, *or* tangible, capital Material things used as inputs in the production of future goods and services. The major categories of physical capital are nonresidential structures, durable equipment, residential structures, and inventories. *p. 226*

point elasticity A measure of elasticity that uses the slope measurement. *p. 94*

positive economics An approach to economics that seeks to understand behavior and the operation of systems without making judgments. It describes what exists and how it works. *p. 7*

post hoc, ergo propter hoc Literally, "after this (in time), therefore because of this." A common error made in thinking about causation: If Event A happens before Event B, it is not necessarily true that A caused B. *p. 8*

price ceiling A maximum price that sellers may charge for a good, usually set by government. *p. 75*

price discrimination Charging different prices to different buyers for identical products, where these price differences are not an inflection of cost differences. *p. 278*

price elasticity of demand The ratio of the percentage change in quantity demanded to the percentage change in price; measures the responsiveness of quantity demanded to changes in price. *p. 90*

price floor A minimum price below which exchange is not permitted. *p. 79*

price leadership A form of oligopoly in which one dominant firm sets prices and all the smaller firms in the industry follow its pricing policy. *p. 292*

price rationing The process by which the market system allocates goods and services to consumers when quantity demanded exceeds quantity supplied. *p. 73*

principle of neutrality All else equal, taxes that are neutral with respect to economic decisions (that is, taxes that do not distort economic decisions) are generally preferable to taxes that distort economic decisions. Taxes that are not neutral impose excess burdens. *p. 397*

principle of second best The fact that a tax distorts an economic decision does not always imply that such a tax imposes an excess burden. If there are previously existing distortions, such a tax may actually improve efficiency. *p. 399*

prisoners' dilemma A game in which the players are prevented from cooperating and in which each has a dominant strategy that leaves them both worse off than if they could cooperate. *p. 297*

producer surplus The difference between the current market price and the cost of production for the firm. *p. 83*

product differentiation A strategy that firms use to achieve market power. Accomplished by producing goods that differ from others in the market. *p. 312*

product or output markets The markets in which goods and services are exchanged. *p. 44*

production function *or* total product function A numerical or mathematical expression of a relationship between inputs and outputs. It shows units of total product as a function of units of inputs. *p. 144*

production possibility frontier (ppf) A graph that shows all the combinations of goods and services that can be produced if all of society's resources are used efficiently. *p. 29*

production The process by which inputs are combined, transformed, and turned into outputs. *pp. 23, 141*

production technology The quantitative relationship between inputs and outputs. *p. 146*

productivity of an input The amount of output produced per unit of that input. *p. 210*

profit The difference between total revenue and total cost. *pp. 56, 142*

progressive tax A tax whose burden, expressed as a percentage of income, increases as income increases. *p. 390*

property income Income from the ownership of real property and financial holdings. It takes the form of profits, interest, dividends, and rents. *p. 365*

proportional tax A tax whose burden is the same proportion of income for all households. *p. 390*

protection The practice of shielding a sector of the economy from foreign competition. *p. 420*

public goods, *or* social goods Goods and services that bestow collective benefits on members of society. Generally, no one can be excluded from enjoying their benefits. The classic example is national defense.

Goods that are nonrival in consumption and their benefits are nonexcludable; sometimes known as collective goods. *pp. 257, 339*

purchasing-power-parity theory A theory of international exchange holding that exchange rates are set so that the price of similar goods in different countries is the same. *p. 688*

pure monopoly An industry with a single firm that produces a product for which there are no close substitutes and in which significant barriers to entry prevent other firms from entering the industry to compete for profits. *p. 264*

pure rent The return to any factor of production that is in fixed supply. *p. 215*

p-value The probability of obtaining the result that you find in the sample data if the null hypothesis of no relationship is true. *p. 460*

quantity demanded The amount (number of units) of a product that a household would buy in a given period if it could buy all it wanted at the current market price. *p. 45*

quantity supplied The amount of a particular product that a firm would be willing and able to offer for sale at a particular price during a given time period. *p. 56*

queuing Waiting in line as a means of distributing goods and services: a nonprice rationing mechanism. *p. 75*

quota A limit on the quantity of imports. *p. 421*

random experiment (Sometimes referred to as a randomized experiment.) A technique in which outcomes of specific interventions are determined by using the intervention in a randomly selected subset of a sample and then comparing outcomes from the exposed and control group. *p. 446*

ration coupons Tickets or coupons that entitle individuals to purchase a certain amount of a given product per month. *p. 76*

Rawlsian justice A theory of distributional justice that concludes that

the social contract emerging from the "original position" would call for an income distribution that would maximize the well-being of the worst-off member of society. *p. 374*

real income The set of opportunities to purchase real goods and services available to a household as determined by prices and money income. *p. 116*

regression discontinuity Identifies the causal effects of a policy or factor by looking at two samples that lie on either side of a threshold or cutoff. *p. 457*

regressive tax A tax whose burden, expressed as a percentage of income, falls as income increases. *p. 390*

rent-seeking behavior Actions taken by households or firms to preserve economic profits. *p. 277*

risk-averse Refers to a person's preference of a certain payoff over an uncertain one with the same expected value. *p. 352*

risk-loving Refers to a person's willingness to take bets with negative expected values. *p. 352*

risk-neutral Refers to a person's willingness to take a bet with an expected value of zero. *p. 352*

rule of reason The criterion introduced by the Supreme Court in 1911 to determine whether a particular action was illegal ("unreasonable") or legal ("reasonable") within the terms of the Sherman Act. *p. 281*

scarce Limited. *p. 2*

selection bias Selection bias is when the sample used is not random. *p. 452*

services The things we buy that do not involve the production of physical things, such as legal and medical services and education. *p. 426*

shift of a demand curve The change that takes place in a demand curve corresponding to a new relationship between quantity demanded of a good and price of that good. The shift is brought about by a change in the original conditions. *p. 53*

shift of a supply curve The change that takes place in a supply curve corresponding to a new relationship between quantity supplied of a good and the price of that good. The shift is brought about by a change in the original conditions. *p. 58*

short run The period of time for which two conditions hold: The firm is operating under a fixed scale (fixed factor) of production, and firms can neither enter nor exit an industry. *p. 144*

short-run industry supply curve The sum of the marginal cost curves (above *AVC*) of all the firms in an industry. *p. 190*

shutdown point The lowest point on the average variable cost curve. When price falls below the minimum point on *AVC*, total revenue is insufficient to cover variable costs and the firm will shut down and bear losses equal to fixed costs. *p. 189*

Smoot-Hawley tariff The U.S. tariff law of the 1930s, which set the highest tariffs in U.S. history (60 percent). It set off an international trade war and caused the decline in trade that is often considered one of the causes of the worldwide depression of the 1930s. *p. 421*

social capital, *or* **infrastructure** Capital that provides services to the public. Most social capital takes the form of public works (roads and bridges) and public services (police and fire protection). *p. 226*

social choice The problem of deciding what society wants. The process of adding up individual preferences to make a choice for society as a whole. *p. 403*

social overhead capital Basic infrastructure projects such as roads, power generation, and irrigation systems. *p. 440*

Social Security system The federal system of social insurance programs. It includes three separate programs that are financed through separate funds: the Old Age and Survivors Insurance (OASI) program, the Disability Insurance (DI) program, and the Health Insurance (HI), or Medicare program. *p. 376*

spreading overhead The process of dividing total fixed costs by more units of output. Average fixed cost declines as quantity rises. *p. 167*

stability A condition in which national output is growing steadily, with low inflation and full employment of resources. *p. 10*

statistical significance A result is said to be statistically significant if the computed p-value is less than some presubscribed number, usually 0.05. *p. 460*

substitutes Goods that can serve as replacements for one another; when the price of one increases, demand for the other increases. *p. 49*

supply curve A graph illustrating how much of a product a firm will sell at different prices. *p. 56*

supply schedule Shows how much of a product firms will sell at alternative prices. *p. 56*

surplus of government enterprises Income of government enterprises. *p. 430*

survivor bias Survivor bias exists when a sample includes only observations that have remained in the sample over time making that sample unrepresentative of the broader population. *p. 452*

tacit collusion Collusion occurs when price- and quantity-fixing agreements among producers are explicit. *Tacit collusion* occurs when such agreements are implicit. *p. 292*

tariff A tax on imports. *p. 420*

tax base The measure or value upon which a tax is levied. *p. 389*

tax incidence The ultimate distribution of a tax burden. *p. 392*

tax rate structure The percentage of a tax base that must be paid in taxes—25 percent of income, for example. *p. 389*

tax shifting Occurs when households can alter their behavior and do something to avoid paying a tax. *p. 392*

technological change The introduction of new methods of production or new products intended to increase the productivity of existing inputs or to raise marginal products. *p. 219*

terms of trade The ratio at which a country can trade domestic products for imported products. *p. 416*

theory of comparative advantage Ricardo's theory that specialization and free trade will benefit all trading parties (real wages will rise), even those that may be "absolutely" more efficient producers. *pp. 24, 411*

Tiebout hypothesis An efficient mix of public goods is produced when local land/housing prices and taxes come to reflect consumer preferences just as they do in the market for private goods. *p. 344*

tit-for-tat strategy A repeated game strategy in which a player responds in kind to an opponent's play. *p. 300*

total cost The total of (1) out-of-pocket costs and (2) opportunity cost of all factors of production. *p. 142*

total cost (*TC*) Total fixed costs plus total variable costs. *p. 165*

total fixed costs (*TFC*) *or* overhead The total of all costs that do not change with output even if output is zero. *p. 166*

total revenue The amount received from the sale of the product ($q \times P$). *p. 142*

total revenue (*TR*) The total amount that a firm takes in from the sale of its product: the price per unit times the quantity of output the firm decides to produce ($P \times q$). *p. 176*

total utility The total satisfaction a product yields. *p. 118*

total variable cost (TVC) The total of all costs that vary with output in the short run. *p. 167*

total variable cost curve A graph that shows the relationship between total variable cost and the level of a firm's output. *p. 167*

trade deficit Occurs when a country's exports of goods and services are less than its imports of goods and services. *p. 416*

trade surplus The situation when a country exports more than it imports. *p. 411*

transfer payments Cash payments made by the government to people who do not supply goods, services, or labor in exchange for these payments. They include Social Security benefits, veterans' benefits, and welfare payments. *pp. 365, 414*

unemployment compensation A state government transfer program that pays cash benefits for a certain period of time to laid-off workers who have worked for a specified period of time for a covered employer. *p. 377*

unitary elasticity A demand relationship in which the percentage change in quantity of a product demanded is the same as the percentage change in price in absolute value (a demand elasticity with an absolute value of 1). *p. 92*

utilitarian justice The idea that "a dollar in the hand of a rich person is worth less than a dollar in the hand of a poor person." If the marginal utility of income declines with income, transferring income from the rich to the poor will increase total utility. *p. 373*

utility The satisfaction a product yields. *p. 117*

utility-maximizing rule Equating the ratio of the marginal utility of a good to its price for all goods. *p. 120*

variable A measure that can change from time to time or from observation to observation. *p. 7*

variable cost A cost that depends on the level of production chosen. *p. 165*

vertical differentiation A product difference that, from everyone's perspective, makes a product better than rival products. *p. 314*

vicious-circle-of-poverty Suggests that poverty is self-perpetuating because poor nations are unable to save and invest enough to accumulate the capital stock that would help them grow. *p. 437*

voting paradox A simple demonstration of how majority-rule voting can lead to seemingly contradictory and inconsistent results. A commonly cited illustration of the kind of inconsistency described in the impossibility theorem. *p. 404*

wealth *or* net worth The total value of what a household owns minus what it owes. It is a stock measure. *p. 49*

World Trade Organization (WTO) A negotiating forum dealing with rules of trade across nations. *p. 664*

Index

Notes: Key terms and the page on which they are defined appear in **boldface.** Page numbers followed by *n* refer to information in footnotes.

Labor supply curve, **126**
in perfect competition, 393
Lagakos, David, 441n
Laissez-faire economy, **36**
Landais, Camille, 102n
Land market, **44**
Laos's Wat SisKent, 280
La Porta, Rafael, 441n
Law, economics and, 6
Laws
Corn, 411, 420
Least squares estimates, **462**, 463
Leisure, price of, 126
Lepper, Mark R., 315n
Levitt, Steve, 330
Lexus, 419
Li, Robin, 438
Liability rules, **334**
Licensing, 274n
Linden, Greg, 5
Lipton, 316
List, John, 9
Liu, Feng, 121n
Locke, John, 372n
Logrolling, **404**
Lojack, 330
Long run, **145**
decisions in, 145–146
elasticities at delicatessen in, 99
monopoly in the, 272–275
price/output determination in the, 320–321
Lopez-de-Silanes, Florencio, 441n
Lorenz curve, **366**–367
Loss
consumer, 275–277
deadweight, 84–85, 276, 397, 424
welfare, 276
Lotteries, government rules on, 274–275
Lufthansa, 299–300
Luxuries versus necessities, 99–100

M
Macroeconomics, **4**–5, 6, 8, 315
Majority-rule voting, 404
Maltenbroch, Ulrike, 315n
Malthus, Thomas, 3, 45n
Marginal cost curves, shape of, in the short un, 169
Marginal cost pricing, marginal social cost and, 327–330
Marginal costs (MC), 2, **168**–169, 175
graphing average variable costs and, 171–172
graphing total variable costs and, 170–171
relationship between average total costs and, 173–174
Marginalism, **2**
Marginal product, **147**–148
versus average product, 148
Marginal rate of substitution, **134**

Marginal rate of technical substitution, **158**
Marginal rate of transformation (MRT), **30**
Marginal revenue (MR), **177**
market demand and, 266–268
Marginal social benefit of pollution, **330**–331
Marginal social cost (MSC), **327**
marginal cost pricing and, 327–330
Marginal tax rate, **390**
Marginal utility (MU), **118**
diminishing, 48, 117–118, 122, 129, 350–351
Market(s), **36**
black, 77
capital, 44, 129
competitive, 84
constraints on, 75–79
contestable, 291
efficient, 3
financial capital, 129
healthcare, 356
input, 124–129
input/factor, 44–45
input or factor, 44
labor, 44, 360–361
land, 44
oil, 97
output, 112–117, 129
product, 65
product/output, 44–60
Market baskets, substitution and, 125
Market boundaries, 264
Market demand, **53**–54
marginal revenue and, 266–268
for private goods, 341–342
Market economy, 326, 364
decision making in, 111
Market efficiency, supply and demand and, 82–83
Market equilibrium, 60–64, 73
Market income, **365**
arguments for and against reducing inequality in, 371–374
causes of inequality in, 367–370
distribution of, 365–367
Marketing, scale economies and, 273
Market outcomes, green advertising and, 318
Market power, **264**, 283
Market signaling, **356**–358
Market structure, in an oligopoly, 289–291
Market supply, **59**
Marshall, Alfred, 45n, 47, 117, 129n
Marx, Karl, 3
Mattel, 5
Maximin strategy, **299**
McDonald's, 89, 94, 101
Measurement, importance of actual, 89
Mechanism design, **359**
Medicaid, 355, **377**
Medicare, 355, **377**
Melitz, Marc, 421n

Photo Credits

492